Applied Java™ Patterns

Stephen Stelting
Olav Maassen

Sun Microsystems Press
A Prentice Hall Title

The publisher offers discounts on this book when order in bulk quantities. For more information, contact: Corporate Sales Department, Phone: 800-382-3419; Fax 201-236-7141; E-mail: corpsales@prenhall.com; or write: Prentice Hall PTR, Corp. Sales Dept., One Lake Street, Upper Saddle River, NJ 07458.

Development/ Composition: Solveig Haugland
Cover design director: Jerry Votta
Cover designer: Nina Scuderi
Manufacturing manager: Alexis R. Heydt-Long
Marketing manager: Debby vanDijk
Acquisitions editor: Gregory G. Doench

Sun Microsystems Press Publisher: Michael Llwyd Alread

10 9 8 7 6 5 4 3 2 1

ISBN 0-13-093538-7

Sun Microsystems Press
A Prentice Hall Title

To my parents, family and friends:
Thank you all. You make life wonderful.
—SS

To the memory of Joeri Hutters
"The significance of someone's life is measured by the effect he has had on others."
—OM

Table of Contents

Preface

Why We Wrote This Book

During the many Java™ programming language courses we teach, we have found that only a few programmers know what design patterns are when asked. About one in ten is able to name a few patterns off the top of his or her head. Of course, the concepts behind the patterns are familiar to many programmers. When we demonstrate patterns in the classroom, developers know and recognize them.

We decided to create a pattern catalog for the Java programming language developers who understand at a basic level why patterns are a good idea, and are interested in applying them, but want a practical, hands-on guide to just how and why to use each individual pattern. We've kept the book casual and frank in tone, and included full working Java code examples for each.

We will have succeeded when you complete this book having not only learned about design patterns and the Java programming language, but having had fun reading it, as well.

What This Book Is About

This book will teach you the essential design patterns and how you can use them in your Java application. Furthermore, this book will show you where patterns are used in Java technology APIs and why they were used.

Who Should Read This Book

This book is intended for experienced Java programmers who want to build better applications. You should be comfortable with the Java programming language and be familiar with most of the basic Java APIs. Some knowledge of UML is useful, but not required. We recommend *UML Distilled* by Martin Fowler as a UML reference.

Conventions Used

Within this book, code examples are presented in `monospaced font`. The same font is used in the text when talking about specific classes, interfaces, methods or variables. `methodName` is just to indicate all methods that have that name, where `methodName()` refers to a method with that name that takes no parameters.

Abstract classes have a name that starts with `Abstract`, whereas classes that either implement an interface or subclass another class have a name that starts with `Concrete` (unless they are abstract). This naming convention is shown in Figure 1.

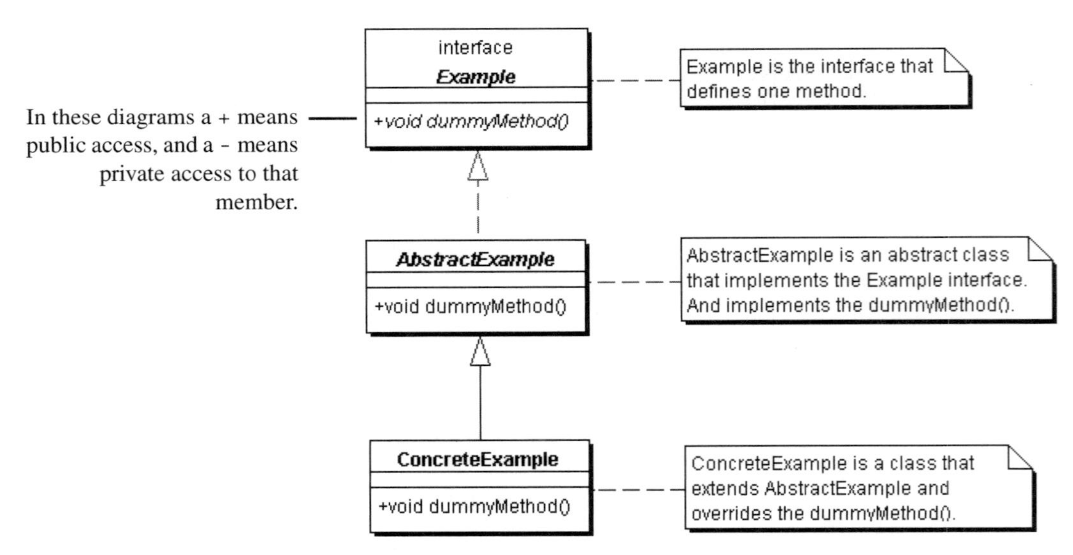

Figure 1 *Example class diagram*

A *client* is the general term used for a class that uses the classes of the design pattern, which is different from a user. A *user* is a human being interacting with the application.

The notation "[CJ2EEP]" in the *Related Patterns* section for a pattern refers to J2EE patterns, listed in the bibliography.

How This Book Is Organized

This book is divided into two parts. Part I, "Commonly Used Patterns," is organized like a pattern catalogue, reference-style.

Chapter 1: "Creational Patterns" on page 3 discusses patterns that create objects: Abstract Factory, Builder, Factory Method, Prototype, and Singleton.

Chapter 2: "Behavioral Patterns" on page 39 is focussed on the patterns that can determine the behavior of your object model: Chain of Responsibility, Command, Interpreter, Iterator, Mediator, Memento, Observer, State, Strategy, Template Method, and Visitor.

Chapter 3: "Structural Patterns" on page 139 describes patterns that can bring structure to your application and has the following patterns: Adapter, Bridge, Composite, Decorator, Facade, Flyweight, HOPP, and Proxy.

Chapter 4: "System Patterns" on page 205 describes the patterns that help you build better architectures: Callback, Router, MVC, Session, Successive Update, Transaction, and Worker Thread.

Part II, "Patterns in the Java Programming Language," presents many of the Java APIs and shows the use of patterns in those API and their benefit.

Chapter 6: "Java Core APIs" on page 279 provides an overview in the familiar core APIs like Event Handling, JavaBeans™, AWT and Swing, Collections, Input/Output, and Reflection.

Chapter 7: "Distributed Technologies" on page 303 describes selected distributed APIs and how patterns are used: JNDI, JDBC, RMI, and CORBA.

Chapter 8: "Jini and J2EE Architectures" on page 317 focuses on the two complementary frameworks Jini and J2EE. J2EE is further divided into Servlets, JSP and EJB technologies.

How to Use This Book

There are several ways to read this book. You could start at page one and read from cover to cover. However, we recommend you start with some of the easier patterns: Factory Method, Singleton, Observer, and Composite. Work your way through the book using those as starting points for your exploration. Alternatively, you might want to turn to sections in Part II first. Find an API you are familiar with and start looking for patterns there.

You can read the patterns in any order you feel most comfortable with. Later, you can use this book as a reference to refresh your memory when you want to put your knowledge of patterns into practice.

Companion Web Site

This book has a companion Web site to provide you with updates and other material: it is located at `http://www.phptr.com/appliedjavapatterns`.

Acknowledgments

A book is, above all else, a team effort. We'd like to thank all the people who made this a reality. We've worked with an exceptionally fine group. This page is dedicated to them, to let them know that their efforts are appreciated.

For Greg Doench, Prentice Hall visionary: Thank you for being the Great Unifier for this project. When we started this work, we discovered Greg was a marathon runner. When Steve mentioned that he would like to try his hand (feet?) at the sport, Greg said, "After the book is done." Now we understand why: writing a book is itself a marathon. For your ongoing help and support, and for your belief in this book, our most sincere thanks.

For Rachel Borden, Sun Press luminary: Thank you for your guidance along the path to publication. If not for your help, we'd still be scrawling ideas across massive expanses of sticky notes. Thank you for your ongoing support and dedication, and for having patience when explaining to techies how publishing works. Our thanks for getting up far too early on far too many mornings for conference calls with people on the other side of the world. Most of all, thanks for being a continuing champion of our work.

For Solveig Haugland, content editor extraordinaire: Thank you for believing in the dream, and for helping to make it a reality. Thank you for working your mambo (mojo?) and turning a jumble of unconnected ideas into something far greater—one big rambling idea, perhaps. And thank you for showing us that it *is* possible to put a bit of humor into a technical book, after all.

For our talented technical reviewers: Thanks for making us think hard about what we actually wanted to say. Our most sincere thanks go to Jennie Yip for spending long hours writing up every detail she could find, Bryan Basham, Bert Bates, John Crupi, Jim Gallentine, Werner van Mook, Nanno Schering, Juergen Schimbera, Robert Schrijvers and Fred Zuijdendorp.

Many thanks to the production team at Prentice Hall. We're genuinely sorry that we didn't get a chance to meet you, but we know that you're out there turning ideas into reality. Yours is truly inspiring work—helping to bring dreams and ideas out into the world. For your commitment and hard work on this book, and the other books you have made (many of which have a place in our hearts and on our shelves) we thank you.

Stephen Stelting would like to thank: Steve Bradshaw, Annette Baldenegro, Cindy Lewis, and the rest of the management team of Sun Educational Services: Thank you for the support you've shown and for the faith you've had in me during this past year. I appreciate your help and understanding more than I can say.

I promise to try and get a life now.

Olav Maassen wishes to thank: Harry Pallandt and Andre Arnoldus, my managers, for letting me work late many times, and for their support over the years.

Ingrid, Niels – The two biggest stars of my universe for providing all the support, encouragement and motivation for me to finish this project.

Britt – The third star of my universe for waiting long enough to be born to allow me to finish the book first before moving on to my next big project—my family.

Introduction

Why Patterns?

"If builders built houses the way programmers wrote code, the first woodpecker that came along would destroy civilization."

If you wanted to build a house, how would you do it?

Well, you ***could*** do what some people do to build a treehouse:

1. Find a sturdy tree.
2. Get a bunch of wood, a hammer, and some nails.
3. Apply the products from step 2 to step 1.
4. Hope for the best.

Of course, anyone who has tried this approach knows the results can be disappointing—in some cases, leading to the loss of the tree along with the treehouse. A better plan would be to find an architect and get his or her help in developing blueprints.

But how does the architect, the expert in building houses, make decisions? How is it possible to take the lessons from years of experience and apply them to creating a brand new home? There's a certain something, a base of knowledge, experience and perhaps a little intuition, that seems to make the architect successful.

The questions about building and designing houses are really not all that different from the ones we face in the software development world. How can we effectively design good software? How can we apply experience gained in the past to projects in the future? How can we make decisions during design that will produce software that has good characteristics, like flexibility, extensibility and efficiency?

As in our building project, we need experienced guidance. We need some equivalent of our building architect, someone who has a balance of knowledge, experience and good common sense in software design. We need a software development guru.

There aren't a lot of gurus in the world. And until cloning technology is a lot more advanced, we frequently have to fend for ourselves. In our projects, in our companies, we have to make our own software experts.

So we're back to square one. We want to design good software, but we don't know how to make the right decisions, decisions that will ultimately lead us to produce a quality product. We want to grow experienced software developers, but short of a brain transplant, we don't even know how to get the knowledge of effective design from the current generation of software experts.

What if there ***were*** a way to collect that knowledge? What if we could get experience from the gurus, and it didn't even involve painful surgery? What if we could record and summarize key concepts of software design, building a foundation for our next generation of software developers?

There is such a way—it's called design patterns.

It's well-documented that experts often solve new problems by applying solutions that have worked in the past. They identify parts of their problem that are like problems that they have encountered before. Next, they recall the solution to their earlier problems and generalize it. Finally, they adapt the general solution to the context of their current problem.

The idea behind design patterns is to develop a standardized way to represent general solutions to commonly encountered problems in software development. There are a few benefits to doing this:

- Over time, we can build up catalogs of patterns. This enables newcomers to software development to more effectively benefit from experience gained over the years.
- There is formal documentation about the tradeoffs involved in software design decisions; about the pluses and minuses of development choices. Standardizing patterns makes it easier for all development professionals—beginners and experts alike—to explicitly understand the implications of their decisions.
- The design patterns provide a common vocabulary. This makes communicating decisions to developers easier. Rather than describing a design in detail, we can use a pattern name to explain our plans.
- We can relate patterns to each other, so that a developer can easily see which patterns might belong together in a project.

Design patterns give us an effective way to share experience throughout the object-oriented programming community. Whether we've gained the knowledge in C++, Smalltalk, or the Java programming language, whether the expertise has been built up from Web projects, legacy integration or custom work, we can collect our lessons and share them with other developers. In the long run, we can improve software development across the industry.

History of the Patterns Movement

It Came From Outer Space... via U.C. Berkeley

The inspiration for design patterns in software development is usually attributed to Christopher Alexander, a professor of architecture at U.C. Berkeley. In the late '70s, he published several books that introduced the concept of patterns and provided a catalog of patterns for architectural design.

Alexander's work sparked interest in the object-oriented (OO) community, and within the next decade, a number of pioneers had developed patterns for software design. Kent Beck and Ward Cunningham were among the first, discussing a set of Smalltalk design patterns in a presentation at the 1987 OOPSLA conference. James Coplien was another who actively promoted the tenets of patterns, writing a book about C++ idioms, or patterns for C++ development, in the early '90s.

OOPSLA was an excellent venue for the growing patterns community, since it offered an environment for them to share their ideas. Another important forum for the evolution of the patterns movement was the Hillside Group, established by Kent Beck and Grady Booch.

Probably the best-known contribution to the popularity of design patterns was the 1995 book *Design Patterns: Elements of Reusable Object-Oriented Software.* The authors—Erich Gamma, Richard Helm, Ralph Johnson, and John Vlissides—are also commonly known as the "Gang of Four" or *GoF.* The book introduced a comprehensive pattern language, and gave C++ examples for the patterns discussed. Another important work that gave momentum to patterns was the book *Pattern-Oriented Software Architecture, A System of Patterns*, by Buschmann, Meunier, Rohnert, Sommerlad and Stal.

Since the publication of these two books, design patterns have enjoyed substantial interest in the software community. Java ("Java technology") grew up at the same time as patterns were gaining widespread popularity, so it was inevitable that Java developers would take an interest in applying design patterns in their projects. The growing popularity of design patterns in Java has been manifested in presentations at conferences like JavaOne, as well as patterns columns in the Java trade journals.

Basic Concepts in Patterns

"Talking the Talk"

Central to the idea of patterns is the concept of standardizing the information about a common problem and its solution. One of the most useful results of Alexander's work was the development of a template for representing patterns—what is now called a *form* or *format*. The Alexandrian Form uses five topic areas to formalize the discussion of a pattern and its solution.

Fundamentally, it's important that a pattern provide a descriptive name for the pattern and the answer to the question "What will this pattern do for you?" In addition, it should include a discussion of the problem, an explanation of how the pattern solves the problem, and an indication of the benefits, drawbacks and tradeoffs associated with the pattern's use.

Naturally, when patterns were adopted by the OO community, variations on the Alexandrian form were developed to meet the needs of software development. Most of the forms in use today are derived from one of two forms—the Canonical or "Gang of Four" forms. This book is based on a variation of the Gang of Four form, with the following topics forming our template:

- *Name* – A descriptive name for the pattern.
- *Also Known As* – Alternate names, if any.
- *Pattern Properties* – The pattern's classification. We define a pattern in terms of two major topics.

  Type:

  - *Creational* patterns for object creation
  - *Behavioral* patterns that coordinate functional interaction between objects
  - *Structural* patterns that manage static, structural relationships between objects
  - *System* patterns used to manage system-level interaction

  Level:

  - Single Class – The pattern applies to a single class
  - Component – The pattern involves a group of classes
  - Architectural – The pattern is used to coordinate the actions of systems and subsystems
- *Purpose* – A short explanation of what the pattern involves.
- *Introduction* – A brief description of a problem you might be facing where this pattern may be useful, using an example to illustrate.

- *Applicability* – When and why you might want to use this design pattern.
- *Description* – A more detailed discussion of the pattern, what it does and how it behaves.
- *Implementation* – A discussion of what must be done to implement the pattern. If you know you want to use this pattern, this section tells you how to implement it.
- *Benefits and Drawbacks* – The consequences of using the pattern and tradeoffs associated with use of the pattern.
- *Pattern Variants* – Possible implementation alternatives and variations on the pattern.
- *Related Patterns* – Other patterns that are either associated with or closely related to the pattern.
- *Example* – A Java code example.

Software Abstraction and Reuse

or "Run that by me one more time..."

Design patterns represent an important evolutionary step in software *abstraction* and *reuse*. These two concepts are central to the idea of programming—some would say they are *the* two most important ones.

Abstraction represents a way for developers to solve complex problems by breaking them up into progressively simpler ones. The solutions to simpler problems, when "tagged" with a label or name, can then be used as building blocks to solve the more complicated projects that we as developers encounter each day.

Reuse is equally vital to software development. In a sense, the history of software development is marked by a constant search to find progressively more sophisticated ways to reuse code. Why all the interest? What's the motivation? Actually, reuse is a perfectly understandable goal given the nature of software development. After all, given a complicated software project complete with a tight deadline schedule, which would you rather do? (Select the best answer.)

- Write all the code from scratch, subjecting yourself and those around you to a slow and painful process of testing and validating everything that you write.
- Use proven and tested code as the foundation for your work.

Don't get me wrong—coding is a blast. It's the testing, debugging, documentation, and post-release support that we developers don't generally like all that much. Over the years, we've come up with quite a few ways to reuse code and development concepts.

- The earliest kind of reuse was snippet reuse (a.k.a. CaP – Cut and Paste). The less said about this as a method for *effective* software reuse, the better. Likewise, this approach does not offer any real qualitative benefits in terms of code abstraction.
- Algorithmic reuse provided a more general way to manage reuse. You can reuse an algorithm, like searching and sorting, to abstract an approach (usually mathematical) to solving a particular kind of computing problem.
- Functional reuse, and its counterpart, data structure reuse, allow you to reuse a coding abstraction more directly. For example, any developer who wants to model something like an address could define a structure with all the necessary fields, then reuse the structure in any project which required an address. Likewise, an operation like `computeTax` could be defined as a function (or procedure or subroutine or method, depending on the programming language), and subsequently copied as a whole to new projects.

Two extensions of these reuse concepts are the function library and the API. They represent ways to package functionality and make functionality available to future applications without actually having to copy code.

The development of object-oriented languages represents a tremendous evolutionary leap forward in terms of abstraction and reuse. With this technology, an entire generation of more sophisticated ways to get more mileage out of code was born.

The concept of the class as blueprint for objects provided a major advancement by combining two earlier mechanisms: functional and data abstraction. By packaging an entity's structure (data) with functionality that applies to the entity (behavior), you gain a way to effectively reuse a software element.

Beyond the core concept of the class, object-oriented languages gives us a variety of other ways to leverage existing code. The concepts of subclasses and interfaces, for instance, opened new possibilities for reuse in software development. Finally, groups of classes can be associated with each other and effectively be treated as a logical software component, providing a very powerful model for reuse at the system level.

In the table below, the Reusability heading indicates the repeatability of the approach.

Comparing approaches for reuse and abstraction

Type of reuse	*Reusability*	*Abstraction*	*Genericity*
Snippet	Very poor	Nothing	Very poor
Data structures	Good	Data type	Moderate – good
Functional	Good	Method	Moderate – good
Template	Good	Operation to type	Good
Algorithmic	Good	Formula	Good
Class Interface Polymorphism Abstract class Interface	Good	Data + method	Good
Code library	Good	Functions	Good – very good
API	Good	Utility classes	Good – very good
Component	Good	Group of classes	Good – very good
Design pattern	Excellent	Problem solution	Very good

Abstraction is an indication of what has been abstracted. Genericity shows how easy it is to apply this method without rewriting or modifying code. Note that the reusability of these approaches heavily depends on how effectively the techniques are applied. Clearly, any capability can be used or misused.

Perhaps the most exciting possibility of a design pattern is that it enables us as developers to more effectively apply the other reuse techniques. A pattern can, for example, provide us with guidelines to effectively manage inheritance in a certain situation, or to effectively designate class relationships to solve a specific problem.

Summary

Design patterns are a valuable tool in software development; every developer is able to code more effectively using them. This book presents some of the best known design patterns; there are many, many more. Welcome to the world of patterns.

Part One

Commonly Used Patterns

Chapter One

Creational Patterns

Introduction to Creational Patterns

These patterns support one of the most common tasks in object-oriented programming—the creation of objects in a system. Most OO systems of any complexity require many objects to be instantiated over time, and these patterns support the creation process by helping to provide the following capabilities:

- Generic instantiation – This allows objects to be created in a system without having to identify a specific class type in code.
- Simplicity – Some of the patterns make object creation easier, so callers will not have to write large, complex code to instantiate an object.
- Creation constraints – Some patterns enforce constraints on the type or number of objects that can be created within a system.

The following patterns are discussed in this chapter:

- Abstract Factory – To provide a contract for creating families of related or dependent objects without having to specify their concrete classes.
- Builder – To simplify complex object creation by defining a class whose purpose is to build instances of another class. The Builder produces one main product, such that there might be more than one class in the product, but there is always one main class.
- Factory Method – To define a standard method to create an object, apart from a constructor, but the decision of what kind of an object to create is left to subclasses.
- Prototype – To make dynamic creation easier by defining classes whose objects can create duplicates of themselves.
- Singleton – To have only one instance of this class in the system, while allowing other classes to get access to this instance.

Of these patterns, the Abstract Factory and Factory Method are explicitly based on the concept of defining flexible object creation; they assume that the classes or interfaces to be created will be extended in an implementing system. As a result, these two patterns are frequently combined with other creational patterns.

Abstract Factory

Also known as Kit, Toolkit

Pattern Properties

Type: Creational, Object
Level: Component

Purpose

To provide a contract for creating families of related or dependent objects without having to specify their concrete classes.

Introduction

Suppose you plan to manage address and telephone information as part of a personal information manager (PIM) application. The PIM will act as a combination address book, personal planner, and appointment and contact manager, and will use the address and phone number data extensively.

You can initially produce classes to represent your address and telephone number data. Code these classes so that they store the relevant information and enforce business rules about their format. For example, all phone numbers in North America are limited to ten digits and the postal code must be in a particular format.

Shortly after coding your classes, you realize that you have to manage address and phone information for another country, such as the Netherlands. The Netherlands has different rules governing what constitutes a valid phone number and address, so you modify your logic in the `Address` and `PhoneNumber` classes to take the new country into account.

Now, as your personal network expands, you need to manage information from another foreign country... and another... and another. With each additional set of business rules, the base `Address` and `PhoneNumber` classes become even more bloated with code and even more difficult to manage. What's more, this code is brittle—with every new country added, you need to modify and recompile the classes to manage contact information.

It's better to flexibly add these paired classes to the system; to take the general rules that apply to address and phone number data, and allow any number of possible foreign variations to be "loaded" into a system.

The Abstract Factory solves this problem. Using this pattern, you define an *AddressFactory*—a generic framework for producing objects that follow the general pattern for an `Address` and `PhoneNumber`. At runtime, this factory is paired with any number of concrete factories for different countries, and each country has its own version of `Address` and `PhoneNumber` classes.

Instead of going through the nightmare of adding functional logic to the classes, extend the `Address` to a `DutchAddress` and the `PhoneNumber` to a `DutchPhoneNumber`. Instances of both classes are created by a `DutchAddressFactory`. This gives greater freedom to extend your code without having to make major structural modifications in the rest of the system.

Applicability

Use the Abstract Factory pattern when:

- The client should be independent of how the products are created.
- The application should be configured with one of multiple families of products.
- Objects need to be created as a set, in order to be compatible.
- You want to provide a collection of classes and you want to reveal just their contracts and their relationships, not their implementations.

Description

Sometimes an application needs to use a variety of different resources or operating environments. Some common examples include:

- Windowing (an application's GUI)
- A file system
- Communication with other applications or systems

In this sort of application you want to make the application flexible enough to use a variety of these resources without having to recode the application each time a new resource is introduced.

An effective way to solve this problem is to define a generic resource creator, the Abstract Factory. The factory has one or more create methods, which can be called to produce generic resources or abstract products.

Java ("Java technology") runs on many platforms, each with many different implementations of a file system or windowing. The solution Java has taken is to abstract the concepts of files and windowing and not show the concrete implementation. You can develop the application using the generic capabilities of the resources as though they represented real functionality.

During runtime, `ConcreteFactories` and `ConcreteProducts` are created and used by the application. The concrete classes conform to the contract defined by the `AbstractFactory` and `AbstractProducts`, so the concrete classes can be directly used, without being recoded or recompiled.

Implementation

The Abstract Factory class diagram is shown in Figure 1.1.

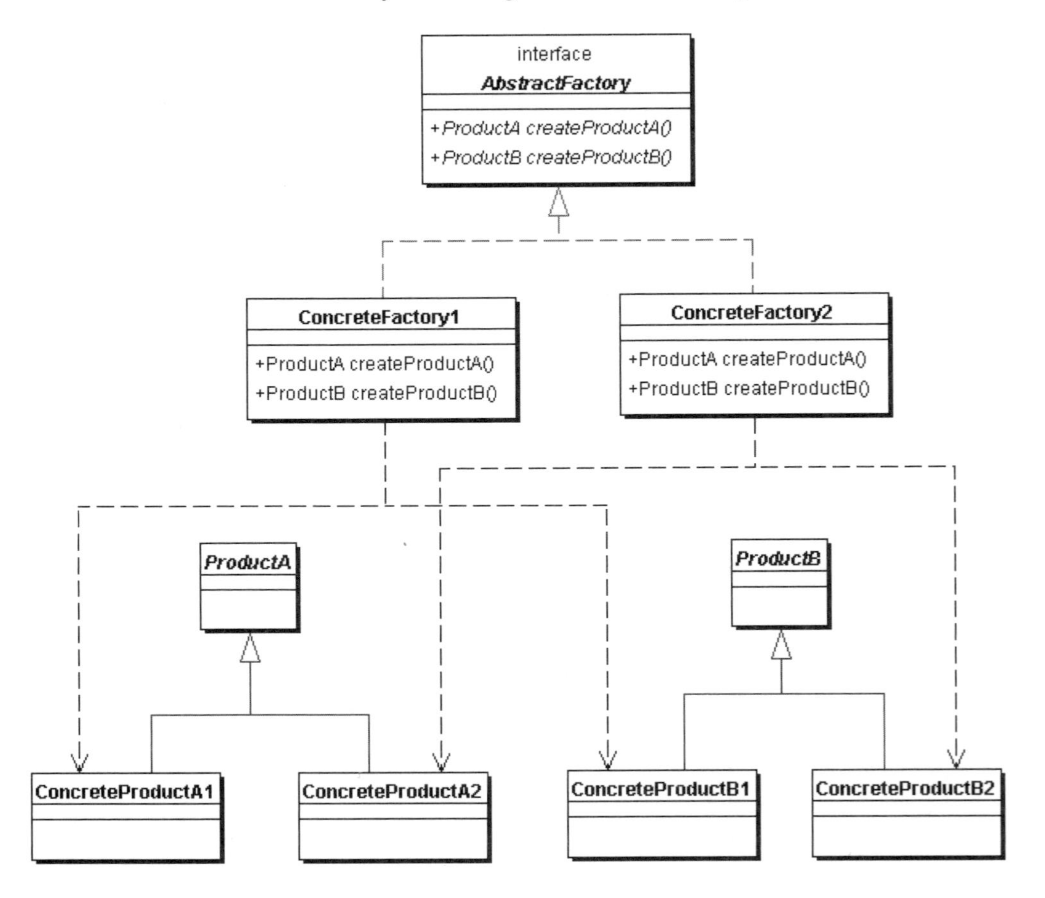

Figure 1.1 *Abstract Factory class diagram*

You typically use the following to implement the Abstract Factory pattern:

- `AbstractFactory` – An abstract class or interface that defines the create methods for abstract products.
- `AbstractProduct` – An abstract class or interface describing the general behavior of the resource that will be used by the application.
- `ConcreteFactory` – A class derived from the abstract factory. It implements create methods for one or more concrete products.
- `ConcreteProduct` – A class derived from the abstract product, providing an implementation for a specific resource or operating environment.

Benefits and Drawbacks

An Abstract Factory helps to increase the overall flexibility of an application. This flexibility manifests itself both during design time and runtime. During design, you do not have to predict all future uses for an application. Instead, you create the generic framework and then develop implementations independently from the rest of the application. At runtime, the application can easily integrate new features and resources.

A further benefit of this pattern is that it can simplify testing the rest of the application. Implementing a `TestConcreteFactory` and `TestConcreteProduct` is simple; it can simulate the expected resource behavior.

To realize the benefits of this pattern, carefully consider how to define a suitably generic interface for the abstract product. If the abstract product is improperly defined, producing some of the desired concrete products can be difficult or impossible.

Pattern Variants

As mentioned earlier, you can define the `AbstractFactory` and `AbstractProduct` as an interface or an abstract class, depending on the needs of the application and your preference.

Depending on how the factory is to be used, some variations of this pattern allow multiple `ConcreteFactory` objects to be produced, resulting in an application that can simultaneously use multiple families of `ConcreteProducts`.

Related Patterns

Related patterns include the following:

- Factory Method (page 21) – Used to implement the Abstract Factory.
- Singleton (page 34) – Often used in the Concrete Factory.
- Data Access Object [CJ2EEP] – The Data Access Object pattern can use the Abstract Factory pattern to add flexibility in creating Database-specific factories.

Note – "[CJ2EEP]" refers to J2EE patterns, listed in the bibliography (see page 559).

Example

The following code shows how international addresses and phone numbers can be supported in the Personal Information Manager with the Abstract Factory pattern. The `AddressFactory` interface represents the factory itself:

Example 1.1 `AddressFactory.java`

```
1.    public interface AddressFactory{
2.        public Address createAddress();
3.        public PhoneNumber createPhoneNumber();
4.    }
```

Note that the `AddressFactory` defines two factory methods, `createAddress` and `createPhoneNumber`. The methods produce the abstract products `Address` and `PhoneNumber`, which define methods that these products support.

Example 1.2 `Address.java`

```
1.    public abstract class Address{
2.        private String street;
3.        private String city;
4.        private String region;
5.        private String postalCode;
6.
7.        public static final String EOL_STRING =
8.            System.getProperty("line.separator");
9.        public static final String SPACE = " ";
10.
11.       public String getStreet(){ return street; }
12.       public String getCity(){ return city; }
13.       public String getPostalCode(){ return postalCode; }
14.       public String getRegion(){ return region; }
15.       public abstract String getCountry();
16.
17.       public String getFullAddress(){
18.           return street + EOL_STRING +
19.               city + SPACE + postalCode + EOL_STRING;
20.       }
21.
22.       public void setStreet(String newStreet){ street = newStreet; }
23.       public void setCity(String newCity){ city = newCity; }
24.       public void setRegion(String newRegion){ region = newRegion; }
25.       public void setPostalCode(String newPostalCode){ postalCode = newPostalCode; }
26.   }
```

Example 1.3 `PhoneNumber.java`

```
1.    public abstract class PhoneNumber{
2.        private String phoneNumber;
3.        public abstract String getCountryCode();
4.
5.        public String getPhoneNumber(){ return phoneNumber; }
6.
7.        public void setPhoneNumber(String newNumber){
8.            try{
9.                Long.parseLong(newNumber);
10.               phoneNumber = newNumber;
```

```
11.             }
12.             catch (NumberFormatException exc){
13.             }
14.         }
15.     }
```

Address and PhoneNumber are abstract classes in this example, but could easily be defined as interfaces if you did not need to define code to be used for all concrete products.

To provide concrete functionality for the system, you need to create Concrete Factory and Concrete Product classes. In this case, you define a class that implements AddressFactory, and subclass the Address and PhoneNumber classes. The three following classes show how to do this for U.S. address information.

Example 1.4 USAddressFactory.java

```
1.  public class USAddressFactory implements AddressFactory{
2.      public Address createAddress(){
3.          return new USAddress();
4.      }
5.
6.      public PhoneNumber createPhoneNumber(){
7.          return new USPhoneNumber();
8.      }
9.  }
```

Example 1.5 USAddress.java

```
1.  public class USAddress extends Address{
2.      private static final String COUNTRY = "UNITED STATES";
3.      private static final String COMMA = ",";
4.
5.      public String getCountry(){ return COUNTRY; }
6.
7.      public String getFullAddress(){
8.          return getStreet() + EOL_STRING +
9.              getCity() + COMMA + SPACE + getRegion() +
10.             SPACE + getPostalCode() + EOL_STRING +
11.             COUNTRY + EOL_STRING;
12.     }
13. }
```

Example 1.6 USPhoneNumber.java

```
1.  public class USPhoneNumber extends PhoneNumber{
2.      private static final String COUNTRY_CODE = "01";
3.      private static final int NUMBER_LENGTH = 10;
4.
5.      public String getCountryCode(){ return COUNTRY_CODE; }
6.
```

```
7.        public void setPhoneNumber(String newNumber){
8.            if (newNumber.length() == NUMBER_LENGTH){
9.                super.setPhoneNumber(newNumber);
10.           }
11.       }
12.   }
```

The generic framework from AddressFactory, Address, and PhoneNumber makes it easy to extend the system to support additional countries. With each additional country, define an additional Concrete Factory class and a matching Concrete Product class. These are files for French address information.

Example 1.7 FrenchAddressFactory.java

```
1.    public class FrenchAddressFactory implements AddressFactory{
2.        public Address createAddress(){
3.            return new FrenchAddress();
4.        }
5.
6.        public PhoneNumber createPhoneNumber(){
7.            return new FrenchPhoneNumber();
8.        }
9.    }
```

Example 1.8 FrenchAddress.java

```
1.    public class FrenchAddress extends Address{
2.        private static final String COUNTRY = "FRANCE";
3.
4.        public String getCountry(){ return COUNTRY; }
5.
6.        public String getFullAddress(){
7.            return getStreet() + EOL_STRING +
8.                getPostalCode() + SPACE + getCity() +
9.                EOL_STRING + COUNTRY + EOL_STRING;
10.       }
11.   }
```

Example 1.9 FrenchPhoneNumber.java

```
1.    public class FrenchPhoneNumber extends PhoneNumber{
2.        private static final String COUNTRY_CODE = "33";
3.        private static final int NUMBER_LENGTH = 9;
4.
5.        public String getCountryCode(){ return COUNTRY_CODE; }
6.
7.        public void setPhoneNumber(String newNumber){
8.            if (newNumber.length() == NUMBER_LENGTH){
9.                super.setPhoneNumber(newNumber);
10.           }
11.       }
12.   }
```

Builder

Pattern Properties

Type: Creational, Object
Level: Component

Purpose

To simplify complex object creation by defining a class whose purpose is to build instances of another class. The Builder produces one main product, such that there might be more than one class in the product, but there is always one main class.

Introduction

In a Personal Information Manager, users might want to manage a social calendar. To do this, you might define a class called `Appointment` to the information for a single event, and track information like the following:

- Starting and ending dates
- A description of the appointment
- A location for the appointment
- Attendees for the appointment

Naturally, this information is passed in by a user when he or she is setting up the appointment, so you define a constructor that allows you to set the state of a new `Appointment` object.

What exactly is needed to create an appointment, though? Different kinds of information are required depending on the specific type of the appointment. Some appointments might require a list of attendees (the monthly Monty Python film club meeting). Some might have start and end dates (JavaOne conference) and some might only have a single date—a plan to visit the art gallery for the M.C. Escher exhibit. When you consider these options, the task of creating an `Appointment` object is not trivial.

There are two possibilities for managing object creation, neither of them particularly attractive. You create constructors for every type of appointment you want to create, or you write an enormous constructor with a lot of functional logic. Each approach has its drawbacks—with multiple constructors, calling logic becomes more complex; with more functional logic built into the constructor, the code becomes more complex and harder to debug. Worse still, both approaches have the potential to cause problems if you later need to subclass `Appointment`.

Instead, delegate the responsibility of `Appointment` creation to a special `AppointmentBuilder` class, greatly simplifying the code for the `Appointment` itself. The `AppointmentBuilder` contains methods to create the parts of the `Appointment`, and you call the `AppointmentBuilder` methods that are relevant for the appointment type. Additionally, the `AppointmentBuilder` can ensure that the information passed in when creating the `Appointment` is valid, helping to enforce business rules. If you need to subclass `Appointment`, you either create a new builder or subclass the existing one. In either case, the task is easier than the alternative of managing object initialization through constructors.

Applicability

Use the Builder pattern when a class:

- Has complex internal structure (especially one with a variable set of related objects).
- Has attributes that depend on each other. One of the things a Builder can do is enforce staged construction of a complex object. This would be required when the Product attributes depend on one another. For instance, suppose you're building an order. You might need to ensure that you have a state set before you move on to "building" the shipping method, because the state would impact the sales tax applied to the Order itself.
- Uses other objects in the system that might be difficult or inconvenient to obtain during creation.

Description

Because this pattern is concerned with building a complex object from possibly multiple different sources, it is called the Builder. As object creation increases in complexity, managing object creation from within the constructor method can become difficult. This is especially true if the object does not depend exclusively on resources that are under its own control.

Business objects often fall into this category. They frequently require data from a database for initialization and might need to associate with a number of other business objects to accurately represent the business model. Another example is that of composite objects in a system, such as an object representing a drawing in a visual editing program. Such an object might need to be related to an arbitrary number of other objects as soon as it's created.

In cases like this, it is convenient to define another class (the Builder) that is responsible for the construction. The Builder coordinates the assembly of the product object: creating resources, storing intermediate results, and providing functional structure for the creation. Additionally, the Builder can acquire system resources required for construction of the product object.

Implementation

The Builder class diagram is shown in Figure 1.2.

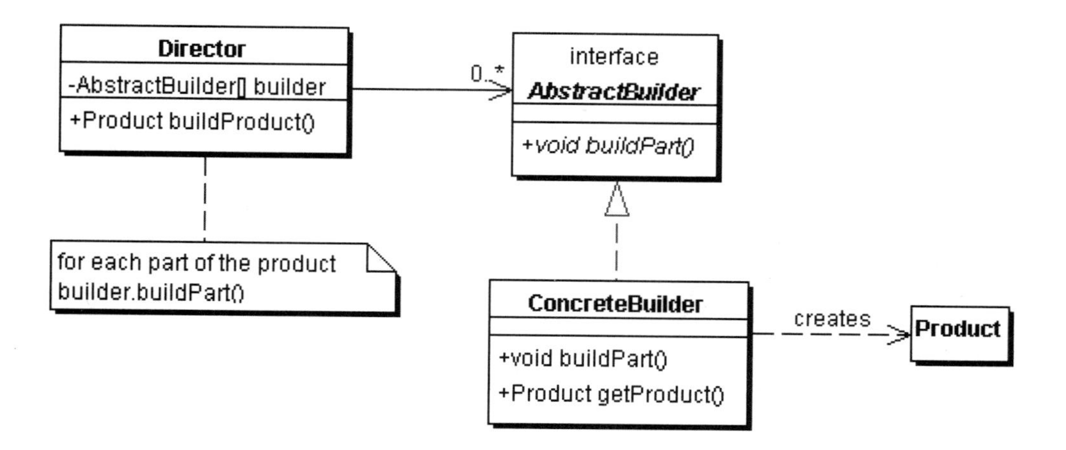

Figure 1.2 *Builder class diagram*

To implement the Builder pattern, you need:

- `Director` – Has a reference to an `AbstractBuilder` instance. The `Director` calls the creational methods on its builder instance to have the different parts and the Builder build.
- `AbstractBuilder` – The interface that defines the available methods to create the separate parts of the product.
- `ConcreteBuilder` – Implements the `AbstractBuilder` interface. The `ConcreteBuilder` implements all the methods required to create a real `Product`. The implementation of the methods knows how to process information from the `Director` and build the respective parts of a `Product`. The `ConcreteBuilder` also has either a `getProduct` method or a creational method to return the `Product` instance.
- `Product` – The resulting object. You can define the product as either an interface (preferable) or class.

Benefits and Drawbacks

The Builder pattern makes it easier to manage the overall flow during the creation of complex objects. This manifests itself in two ways:

- For objects that require phased creation (a sequence of steps to make the object fully active), the Builder acts as a higher-level object to oversee the process. It can coordinate and validate the creation of all resources and if necessary provide a fallback strategy if errors occur.
- For objects that need existing system resources during creation, such as database connections or existing business objects, the Builder provides a convenient central point to manage these resources. The Builder also provides a single point of creational control for its product, which other objects within the system can use. Like other creational patterns, this makes things easier for clients in the software system, since they need only access the Builder object to produce a resource.

The main drawback of this pattern is that there is tight coupling among the Builder, its product, and any other creational delegates used during object construction. Changes that occur for the product created by the Builder often result in modifications for both the Builder and its delegates.

Pattern Variants

At the most fundamental level, it is possible to implement a bare-bones Builder pattern around a single `Builder` class with a creational method and its product. For greater flexibility, designers often extend this base pattern with one or more of the following approaches:

- Create an abstract `Builder`. By defining an abstract class or interface that specifies the creational methods, you can produce a more generic system that can potentially host many different kinds of builders.
- Define multiple create methods for the `Builder`. Some Builders define multiple methods (essentially, they overload their creational method) to provide a variety of ways to initialize the constructed resource.
- Develop creational delegates. With this variant, a `Director` object holds the overall `Product` create method and calls a series of more granular create methods on the `Builder` object. In this case, the `Director` acts as the manager for the Builder's creation process.

Related Patterns

Related patterns include Composite (page 157). The Builder pattern is often used to produce Composite objects, since they have a very complex structure.

Example

Note: For a full working example of this code example, with additional supporting classes and/or a `RunPattern` class, see "Builder" on page 343 of the "Full Code Examples" appendix.

This code example shows how to use the Builder pattern to create an appointment for the PIM. The following list summarizes each class's purpose:

- `AppointmentBuilder`, `MeetingBuilder` – Builder classes
- `Scheduler` – Director class
- `Appointment` – Product
- `Address`, `Contact` – Support classes, used to hold information relevant to the `Appointment`
- `InformationRequiredException` – An Exception class produced when more data is required

For the base pattern, the `AppointmentBuilder` manages the creation of a complex product, an `Appointment` here. The `AppointmentBuilder` uses a series of build methods—`buildAppointment`, `buildLocation`, `buildDates`, and `buildAttendees`—to create an `Appointment` and populate it with data.

Example 1.10 `AppointmentBuilder.java`

```
1.     import java.util.Date;
2.     import java.util.ArrayList;
3.
4.     public class AppointmentBuilder{
5.
6.         public static final int START_DATE_REQUIRED = 1;
7.         public static final int END_DATE_REQUIRED = 2;
8.         public static final int DESCRIPTION_REQUIRED = 4;
9.         public static final int ATTENDEE_REQUIRED = 8;
10.        public static final int LOCATION_REQUIRED = 16;
11.
12.        protected Appointment appointment;
13.
14.        protected int requiredElements;
15.
16.        public void buildAppointment(){
17.            appointment = new Appointment();
18.        }
19.
20.        public void buildDates(Date startDate, Date endDate){
21.            Date currentDate = new Date();
22.            if ((startDate != null) && (startDate.after(currentDate))){
23.                appointment.setStartDate(startDate);
24.            }
25.            if ((endDate != null) && (endDate.after(startDate))){
26.                appointment.setEndDate(endDate);
```

```
27.             }
28.         }
29.
30.         public void buildDescription(String newDescription){
31.             appointment.setDescription(newDescription);
32.         }
33.
34.         public void buildAttendees(ArrayList attendees){
35.             if ((attendees != null) && (!attendees.isEmpty())){
36.                 appointment.setAttendees(attendees);
37.             }
38.         }
39.
40.         public void buildLocation(Location newLocation){
41.             if (newLocation != null){
42.                 appointment.setLocation(newLocation);
43.             }
44.         }
45.
46.         public Appointment getAppointment() throws InformationRequiredException{
47.             requiredElements = 0;
48.
49.             if (appointment.getStartDate() == null){
50.                 requiredElements += START_DATE_REQUIRED;
51.             }
52.
53.             if (appointment.getLocation() == null){
54.                 requiredElements += LOCATION_REQUIRED;
55.             }
56.
57.             if (appointment.getAttendees().isEmpty()){
58.                 requiredElements += ATTENDEE_REQUIRED;
59.             }
60.
61.             if (requiredElements > 0){
62.                 throw new InformationRequiredException(requiredElements);
63.             }
64.             return appointment;
65.         }
66.
67.         public int getRequiredElements(){ return requiredElements; }
68.     }
```

Example 1.11 Appointment.java

```
1.     import java.util.ArrayList;
2.     import java.util.Date;
3.     public class Appointment{
4.         private Date startDate;
5.         private Date endDate;
6.         private String description;
7.         private ArrayList attendees = new ArrayList();
8.         private Location location;
```

```
9.         public static final String EOL_STRING =
10.            System.getProperty("line.separator");
11.
12.        public Date getStartDate(){ return startDate; }
13.        public Date getEndDate(){ return endDate; }
14.        public String getDescription(){ return description; }
15.        public ArrayList getAttendees(){ return attendees; }
16.        public Location getLocation(){ return location; }
17.
18.        public void setDescription(String newDescription){ description = newDescrip-
       tion; }
19.        public void setLocation(Location newLocation){ location = newLocation; }
20.        public void setStartDate(Date newStartDate){ startDate = newStartDate; }
21.        public void setEndDate(Date newEndDate){ endDate = newEndDate; }
22.        public void setAttendees(ArrayList newAttendees){
23.            if (newAttendees != null){
24.                attendees = newAttendees;
25.            }
26.        }
27.
28.        public void addAttendee(Contact attendee){
29.            if (!attendees.contains(attendee)){
30.                attendees.add(attendee);
31.            }
32.        }
33.
34.        public void removeAttendee(Contact attendee){
35.            attendees.remove(attendee);
36.        }
37.
38.        public String toString(){
39.            return "  Description: " + description + EOL_STRING +
40.                "  Start Date: " + startDate + EOL_STRING +
41.                "  End Date: " + endDate + EOL_STRING +
42.                "  Location: " + location + EOL_STRING +
43.                "  Attendees: " + attendees;
44.        }
45.    }
```

The Scheduler class makes calls to the AppointmentBuilder, managing the creation process through the method createAppointment.

Example 1.12 Scheduler.java

```
1.     import java.util.Date;
2.     import java.util.ArrayList;
3.     public class Scheduler{
4.         public Appointment createAppointment(AppointmentBuilder builder,
5.             Date startDate, Date endDate, String description,
6.             Location location, ArrayList attendees) throws InformationRequiredExcep-
       tion{
7.                 if (builder == null){
8.                     builder = new AppointmentBuilder();
```

```
9.              }
10.             builder.buildAppointment();
11.             builder.buildDates(startDate, endDate);
12.             builder.buildDescription(description);
13.             builder.buildAttendees(attendees);
14.             builder.buildLocation(location);
15.             return builder.getAppointment();
16.         }
17.     }
```

The responsibilities of each class are summarized here:

- `Scheduler` – Calls the appropriate build methods on `AppointmentBuilder`; returns a complete `Appointment` object to its caller.
- `AppointmentBuilder` – Contains build methods and enforces business rules; creates the actual `Appointment` object.
- `Appointment` – Holds information about an appointment.

The `MeetingBuilder` class in Example 1.13 demonstrates one of the benefits of the Builder pattern. To add additional rules for the `Appointment`, extend the existing builder. In this case, the `MeetingBuilder` enforces an additional constraint: for a meeting `Appointment`, start and end dates must be specified.

Example 1.13 `MeetingBuilder.java`

```
1.  import java.util.Date;
2.  import java.util.Vector;
3.
4.  public class MeetingBuilder extends AppointmentBuilder{
5.      public Appointment getAppointment() throws InformationRequiredException{
6.          try{
7.              super.getAppointment();
8.          }
9.          finally{
10.             if (appointment.getEndDate() == null){
11.                 requiredElements += END_DATE_REQUIRED;
12.             }
13.
14.             if (requiredElements > 0){
15.                 throw new InformationRequiredException(requiredElements);
16.             }
17.         }
18.         return appointment;
19.     }
20. }
```

Factory Method

Also known as Virtual Constructor

Pattern Properties

Type: Creational
Level: Class

Purpose

To define a standard method to create an object, apart from a constructor, but the decision of what kind of an object to create is left to subclasses.

Introduction

Imagine that you're working on a Personal Information Manager (PIM) application. It will contain many pieces of information essential to your daily life: addresses, appointments, dates, books read, and so on. This information is not static; for instance, you want to be able to change an address when a contact moves, or change the details of an appointment if your lunch date needs to meet an hour later.

The PIM is responsible for changing each field. It therefore has to worry about editing (and therefore the User Interface) and validation for each field. The big disadvantage, however, is that the PIM has to be aware of all the different types of appointments and tasks that can be performed on them. Each item has different fields and the user needs to see an input screen appropriate to those fields. It will be very difficult to introduce new types of task information, because you will have to add a new editing capability to the PIM every time, suitable to update the new item type. Furthermore, every change in a specific type of task, such as adding a new field to an appointment, means you also have to update the PIM so that it is aware of this new field. You end up with a very bloated PIM that is difficult to maintain.

The solution is to let items, like appointments, be responsible for providing their own editors to manage additions and changes. The PIM only needs to know how to request an editor using the method `getEditor`, which is in every editable item. The method returns an object that implements the `ItemEditor` interface, and the PIM uses that object to request a `JComponent` as the GUI editor. Users can modify information for the item they want to edit, and the editor ensures that the changes are properly applied.

All the information on how to edit a specific item is contained in the editor, which is provided by the item itself. The graphical representation of the editor is also created by the editor itself. Now you can introduce new types of items without having to change PIM.

Applicability

Use Factory Method pattern when:

- You want to create an extensible framework. This means allowing flexibility by leaving some decisions, like the specific kind of object to create, until later.
- You want a subclass, rather than its superclass, to decide what kind of an object to create.
- You know when to create an object, but not what kind of an object.
- You need several overloaded constructors with the same parameter list, which is not allowed in Java. Instead, use several Factory Methods with different names.

Description

This pattern is called Factory Method because it creates (manufactures) objects when you want it to.

When you start writing an application, it's often not clear yet what kind of components you will be using. Normally you will have a general idea of the operations certain components should have, but the implementation is done at some other time and will not be of consequence at that moment.

This flexibility can be achieved by using interfaces for these components. But the problem with programming to interfaces is that you cannot create an object from an interface. You need an implementing class to get an object. Instead of coding a specific implementing class in your application, you extract the functionality of the constructor and put it in a method. That method is the factory method.

To create these objects, instead of coding a specific implementing class in your application, you extract the functionality of the constructor and put it in a method. This produces a `ConcreteCreator` whose responsibility it is to create the proper objects. That `ConcreteCreator` creates instances of an implementation (`ConcreteProduct`) of an interface (`Product`).

Implementation

The class diagram is shown in Figure 1.3.

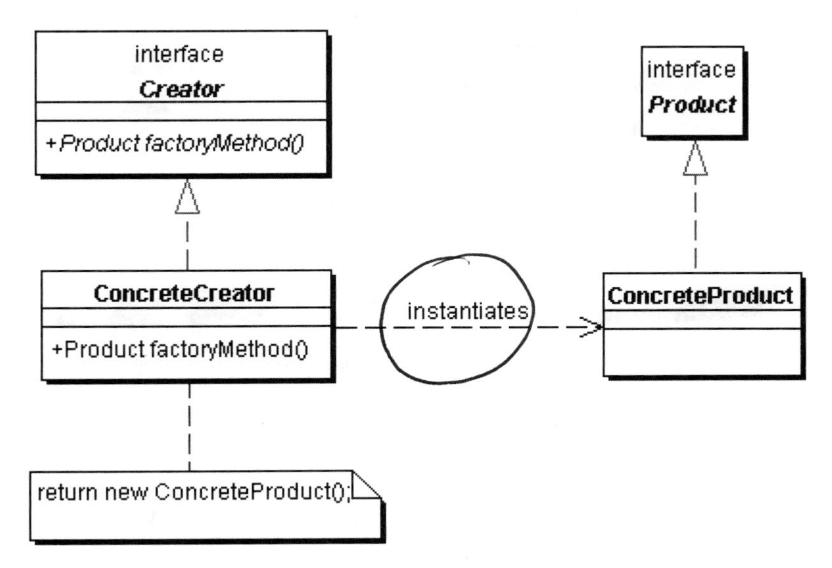

Figure 1.3 *Factory Method class diagram*

To implement the Factory Method you need:

- `Product` – The interface of objects created by the factory.
- `ConcreteProduct` – The implementing class of `Product`. Objects of this class are created by the `ConcreteCreator`.
- `Creator` – The interface that defines the factory method(s) (`factoryMethod`).
- `ConcreteCreator` – The class that extends `Creator` and that provides an implementation for the `factoryMethod`. This can return any object that implements the `Product` interface.

Benefits and Drawbacks

A major benefit to this solution is that the PIM can be very generic. It only needs to know how to request an editor for an item. The information about how to edit a specific item is contained in the editor. The editor can also create the graphical user interface (GUI) for editing. This makes the PIM more modular, making it easier to add new types of information to be managed without changing the core program itself.

JDBC (Java database connectivity) uses the Factory Method pattern in many of its interfaces. You can use another JDBC driver as long as the correct driver is loaded. The rest of your application remains the same. (For more information on patterns in JDBC, see "JDBC" on page 308.)

The drawback to this pattern is the fact that to add a new type of product, you must add another new implementing class, and you must either change an existing `ConcreteCreator` or create a new class that implements `Product`.

Pattern Variants

There are several variations for this pattern:

- `Creator` can provide a standard implementation for the factory method. That way `Creator` doesn't have to be an abstract class or interface, but can be a full-blown class. The benefit is that you aren't required to subclass the `Creator`.
- `Product` can be implemented as an abstract class. Because the `Product` is a class, you can add implementations for other methods.
- The factory method can take a parameter. It can then create more than one type of `Product` based on the given parameter. This decreases the number of factory methods needed.

Related Patterns

Related patterns include the following:

- Abstract Factory (page 6) – Might use one or more factory methods.
- Prototype (page 28) – Prevents subclassing of `Creator`.
- Template Method (page 131) – Template methods usually call factory methods.
- Data Access Object [CJ2EEP] – The Data Access Object pattern uses the Factory Method pattern to be able to create specific instances of Data Access Objects without requiring knowledge of the specific underlying database.

Example

Note: For a full working example of this code example, with additional supporting classes and/or a `RunPattern` class, see "Factory Method" on page 352 of the "Full Code Examples" appendix.

The following example uses the Factory Method pattern to produce an editor for the PIM. The PIM tracks a lot of information, and there are many cases where users need an editor to create or modify data. The example uses interfaces to improve the overall flexibility of the system.

The `Editable` interface defines a builder method, `getEditor`, which returns an `ItemEditor` interface. The benefit is that any item can provide an editor for itself, producing an object that knows what parts of a business object can change and how they can be changed. The only thing the user interface needs to do is use the `Editable` interface to get an editor.

Example 1.14 `Editable.java`

```
1.    public interface Editable {
2.        public ItemEditor getEditor();
3.    }
```

The `ItemEditor` interface provides two methods: `getGUI` and `commitChanges`. The `getGUI` method is another Factory Method—it returns a `JComponent` that provides a Swing GUI to edit the current item. This makes a very flexible system; to add a new type of item, the user interface can remain the same, because it only uses the `Editable` and the `ItemEditor` interfaces.

The `JComponent` returned by `getGUI` can have anything in it required to edit the item in the PIM. The user interface can simply the acquired `JComponent` in its editor window and use the `JComponent` functionality to edit the item. Since not everything in an application needs to be graphical, it could also be a good idea to include a `getUI` method that would return an `Object` or some other non-graphical interface.

The second method, `commitChanges`, allows the UI to tell the editor that the user wants to finalize the changes he or she has made.

Example 1.15 `ItemEditor.java`

```
1.    import javax.swing.JComponent;
2.    public interface ItemEditor {
3.        public JComponent getGUI();
4.        public void commitChanges();
5.    }
```

The following code shows the implementation for one of the PIM items, `Contact`. The `Contact` class defines two attributes: the name of the person and their relationship with the user. These attributes provide a sample of some of the information, which could be included in an entry in the PIM.

Example 1.16 `Contact.java`

```
1.    import java.awt.GridLayout;
2.    import java.io.Serializable;
3.    import javax.swing.JComponent;
4.    import javax.swing.JLabel;
```

```
5.    import javax.swing.JPanel;
6.    import javax.swing.JTextField;
7.
8.    public class Contact implements Editable, Serializable {
9.        private String name;
10.       private String relationship;
11.
12.       public ItemEditor getEditor() {
13.           return new ContactEditor();
14.       }
15.
16.       private class ContactEditor implements ItemEditor, Serializable {
17.           private transient JPanel panel;
18.           private transient JTextField nameField;
19.           private transient JTextField relationField;
20.
21.           public JComponent getGUI() {
22.               if (panel == null) {
23.                   panel = new JPanel();
24.                   nameField = new JTextField(name);
25.                   relationField = new JTextField(relationship);
26.                   panel.setLayout(new GridLayout(2,2));
27.                   panel.add(new JLabel("Name:"));
28.                   panel.add(nameField);
29.                   panel.add(new JLabel("Relationship:"));
30.                   panel.add(relationField);
31.               } else {
32.                   nameField.setText(name);
33.                   relationField.setText(relationship);
34.               }
35.               return panel;
36.           }
37.
38.           public void commitChanges() {
39.               if (panel != null) {
40.                   name = nameField.getText();
41.                   relationship = relationField.getText();
42.               }
43.           }
44.
45.           public String toString(){
46.               return "\nContact:\n" +
47.                   "    Name: " + name + "\n" +
48.                   "    Relationship: " + relationship;
49.           }
50.       }
51.   }
```

Contact implements the Editable interface, and provides its own editor. That editor only applies to the Contact class, and needs to change certain attributes of the Contact, it is best to use an inner class. The inner class has direct access to the attributes of the outer class. If you used another (non-inner) class, `Contact` would need to provide accessor and mutator methods, making it harder to restrict access to the object's private data.

Note that the editor itself is not a Swing component, but only an object that can serve as a factory for such a component. The greatest benefit is that you can serialize and send this object across a stream. To implement this feature, declare all Swing component attributes in `ContactEditor` transient—they're constructed when and where they're needed.

Prototype

Pattern Properties

Type: Creational, Object
Level: Single Class

Purpose

To make dynamic creation easier by defining classes whose objects can create duplicates of themselves.

Introduction

In the PIM, you want to be able to copy an address entry so that the user doesn't have to manually enter all the information when creating a new contact. One way to solve this is to perform the following steps:

1. Create a new `Address` object.
2. Copy the appropriate values from the existing `Address`.

While this approach solves the problem, it has one serious drawback—it violates the object-oriented principle of encapsulation. To achieve the solution mentioned above, you have to put method calls to copy the `Address` information, outside of the `Address` class. This means that it becomes harder and harder to maintain the `Address` code, since it exists throughout the code for the project. It is also difficult to reuse the `Address` class in some new project in the future.

The copy code really belongs in the `Address` class itself, so why not instead define a "copy" method in the class? This method produces a duplicate of the `Address` object with the same data as the original object—the prototype. Calling the method on an existing `Address` object solves the problem in a much more maintainable way, much truer to good object-oriented coding practices.

Applicability

Use the Prototype pattern when you want to create an object that is a copy of an existing object.

Description

The Prototype pattern is well named; as with other prototypes, it has an object that is used as the basis to create a new instance with the same values. Providing a "create based on existing state" behavior allows programs to perform operations like user-driven copy, and to initialize objects to a state that has been established through use of the system. This is often preferable to initializing the object to some generic set of values.

Classic examples for this pattern exist in graphic and text editors, where copy-paste features can greatly improve user productivity. Some business systems use this approach as well, producing an initial model from an existing business object. The copy can then be modified to its desired new state.

Implementation

The Prototype class diagram is shown in Figure 1.4.

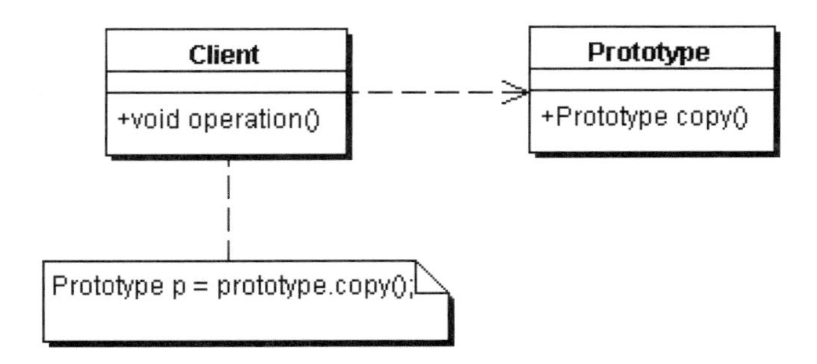

Figure 1.4 *Prototype class diagram*

To implement Prototype, you need:

- `Prototype` – Provides a copy method. That method returns an instance of the same class with the same values as the original `Prototype` instance. The new instance can be a deep or shallow copy of the original (see the *Benefits and Drawbacks* section of this pattern).

Benefits and Drawbacks

The Prototype is helpful because it allows systems to produce a copy of a usable object, with variables already set to a (presumably) meaningful value, rather than depending on some base state defined in the constructor. An example of Prototype use is shown in Figure 1.5.

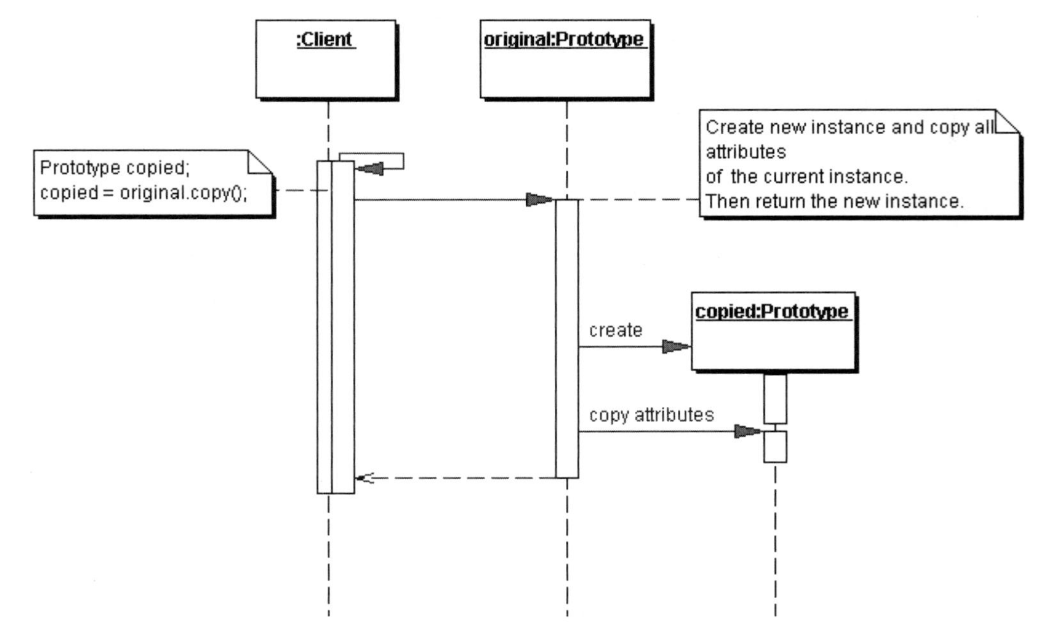

Figure 1.5 *Example of Prototype use*

A key consideration for this pattern is copy depth.

- A shallow copy duplicates only the top-level elements of a class; this provides a faster copy, but isn't suitable for all needs. Since references are copied from the original to the copy, they still refer to the same objects. The lower-level objects are shared among copies of the object, so changing one of these objects affects all of the copies.
- Deep copy operations replicate not only the top-level attributes, but also the lower-level objects. This typically takes longer than shallow copy operations, and can be very costly for objects with an arbitrarily complex structure. This makes sure that changes in one copy are isolated from other copies.

By its nature, the clone method in `Object` supports only one form of copy. For cases where you must support multiple methods of post-creation initialization.

Pattern Variants

Pattern variants include the following:

- Copy constructor – One variant of the prototype is a copy constructor. A copy constructor takes an instance of the same class as an argument and returns a new copy with the same values as the argument.

Example 1.17 `Copy constructor`

```
public class Prototype {
  private int someData;
  // some more data
  public Prototype(Prototype original) {
    super();
    this.someData = original.someData;
    //copy the rest of the data
  }
  // rest of code
}
```

  An example is the `String` class, where you can create a new String instance by calling for instance: `new String("text");`

  The benefit of this variant is that the intention of creating a new instance is very clear, but only one type of copy (deep or shallow) can be executed. It is possible to have a constructor that can use both. The constructor would take two arguments: the object to be copied and a boolean to mark whether it should apply a deep or shallow copy.

  A drawback is that the copy constructor must check the incoming reference to see if it is not null. With the normal Prototype implementation, the method is certain to be called on a valid object.

- `clone` method – The Java programming language already defines a clone method in the `java.lang.Object` class—the superclass of all Java classes. For the method to be usable on an instance, the class of that object has to implement the `java.lang.Clonable` interface to indicate that an instance of this class may be copied. Because the `clone` method is declared protected in `Object`, it has to be overridden to make it publicly available.

  According to Bloch, "`clone`() should be used judiciously" [Bloch01]. As mentioned, a class has to implement `Clonable`, but that interface does not provide a guarantee that the object can be cloned. The `Clonable` interface does not defined the `clone` method, so it is possible that the `clone` method is not available when it is not overridden. Another drawback of the `clone` method is that it has a return type of `Object`, requiring you to cast it to the appropriate type before using it.

Related Patterns

Related patterns include the following:

- Abstract Factory (page 6) – Abstract Factories can use the Prototype to create new objects based on the current use of the Factory.
- Factory Method (page 21) – Factory Methods can use a Prototype to act as a template for new objects.

Example

Note: For a full working example of this code example, with additional supporting classes and/or a `RunPattern` class, see "Prototype" on page 357 of the "Full Code Examples" appendix.

The `Address` class in this example uses the Prototype pattern to create an address based on an existing entry. The core functionality for the pattern is defined in the interface `Copyable`.

Example 1.18 `Copyable.java`

```
1.    public interface Copyable{
2.        public Object copy();
3.    }
```

The `Copyable` interface defines a copy method and guarantees that any classes that implement the interface will define a copy operation. This example produces a shallow copy—that is, it copies the object references from the original address to the duplicate.

The code also demonstrates an important feature of the copy operation: not all fields must necessarily be duplicated. In this case, the address type is not copied to the new object. A user would manually specify a new address type from the PIM user interface.

Example 1.19 `Address.java`

```
1.    public class Address implements Copyable{
2.        private String type;
3.        private String street;
4.        private String city;
5.        private String state;
6.        private String zipCode;
7.        public static final String EOL_STRING =
8.            System.getProperty("line.separator");
9.        public static final String COMMA = ",";
10.       public static final String HOME = "home";
11.       public static final String WORK = "work";
12.
```

```
13.     public Address(String initType, String initStreet,
14.         String initCity, String initState, String initZip){
15.             type = initType;
16.             street = initStreet;
17.             city = initCity;
18.             state = initState;
19.             zipCode = initZip;
20.     }
21.
22.     public Address(String initStreet, String initCity,
23.         String initState, String initZip){
24.             this(WORK, initStreet, initCity, initState, initZip);
25.     }
26.     public Address(String initType){
27.         type = initType;
28.     }
29.     public Address(){ }
30.
31.     public String getType(){ return type; }
32.     public String getStreet(){ return street; }
33.     public String getCity(){ return city; }
34.     public String getState(){ return state; }
35.     public String getZipCode(){ return zipCode; }
36.
37.     public void setType(String newType){ type = newType; }
38.     public void setStreet(String newStreet){ street = newStreet; }
39.     public void setCity(String newCity){ city = newCity; }
40.     public void setState(String newState){ state = newState; }
41.     public void setZipCode(String newZip){ zipCode = newZip; }
42.
43.     public Object copy(){
44.         return new Address(street, city, state, zipCode);
45.     }
46.
47.     public String toString(){
48.         return "\t" + street + COMMA + " " + EOL_STRING +
49.             "\t" + city + COMMA + " " + state + " " + zipCode;
50.     }
51. }
```

Singleton

Pattern Properties

Type: Creational
Level: Object

Purpose

To have only one instance of this class in the system, while allowing other classes to get access to this instance.

Introduction

Once in a while, you need a global object: one that's accessible from anywhere but which should be created only once. You want all parts of the application to be able to use the object, but they all should use the same instance.

An example is a history list—a list of actions a user has taken while using the application. Multiple parts of the application use the same `HistoryList` object to either add actions a user has taken or to undo previous actions.

One way to achieve this is to have the main application create a global object, then pass its reference to every object that might ever need it. However, it can be very difficult to determine how you want to pass the reference, and to know up front which parts of the application need to use the object. Another drawback to this solution is that it doesn't prevent another object from creating another instance of the global object—in this case, `HistoryList`.

Another way to create global values is by using static variables. The application has several static objects inside of a class and accesses them directly.

This approach has several drawbacks.

- A static object will not suffice because a static object will be created at the time the class loads and thus gives you no opportunity to supply any data before it instantiates.
- You have no control over who accesses the object. Anybody can access a publicly available static instance.
- If you realize that the singleton should be, say, a trinity, you're faced with modifying every piece of client code.

This is where the Singleton pattern comes in handy. It provides easy access for the whole application to the global object.

Applicability

Use the Singleton when you want only one instance of a class, but it should be available everywhere.

Description

The Singleton ensures a maximum of one instance is created by the JVM (not surprisingly, that's why it's called a singleton). To ensure you have control over the instantiation, make the constructor private.

This poses a problem: it's impossible to create an instance, so an accessor method is provided by a static method (`getInstance()`). That method creates the single instance, if it doesn't already exist, and returns the reference of the singleton to the caller of the method. The reference to the singleton is also stored as a static private attribute of the singleton class for future calls.

Although the accessor method can create the singleton, most of the times it is created as the class is loaded. Postponing the construction is only necessary if some form of initialization has to be done before the singleton is instantiated.

An example of a singleton is the president of the United States of America. At any given time there should only be one president. When the president of Russia picks up the red phone, he expects to get a handle to the current United States president.

Implementation

The Singleton class diagram is shown in Figure 1.6.

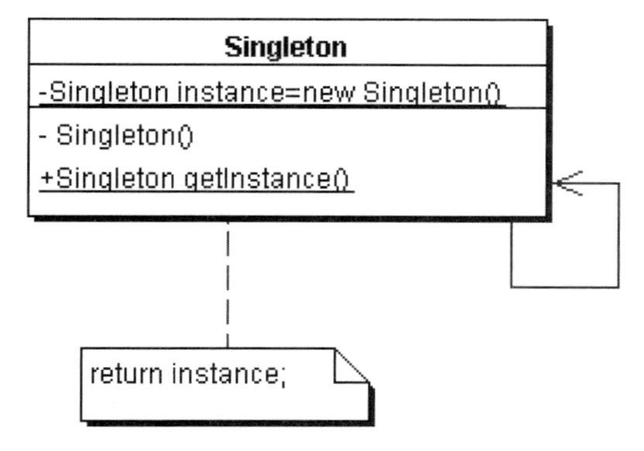

Figure 1.6 *Singleton class diagram*

To implement the Singleton pattern, you need:

- `Singleton` – Provides a private constructor, maintains a private static reference to the single instance of this class, and provides a static accessor method to return a reference to the single instance.

The rest of the implementation of the Singleton class is normal. The static accessor method can make decisions about what kind of an instance to create, based on system properties or parameters passed into the accessor method (see the *Pattern Variants* section for this pattern).

Benefits and Drawbacks

Benefits and drawbacks include the following:

- The Singleton is the only class that can create an instance of itself. You can't create one without using the static method provided.
- You don't need to pass the reference to all objects needing this Singleton.
- However, the Singleton pattern can present threading problems, depending upon the implementation. You must take care regarding control of the singleton initialization in a multithreaded application. Without the proper control, your application will get into "thread wars."

Pattern Variants

Pattern variants include the following:

- One of the Singleton's often-overlooked options is having more than one instance inside the class. The benefit is that the rest of the application can remain the same, while those that are aware of these multiple instances can use other methods to get other instances.
- The Singleton's accessor method can be the entry point to a whole set of instances, all of a different subtype. The accessor method can determine at runtime what specific subtype instance to return. This might seem odd, but it's very useful when you're using dynamic class loading. The system using the Singleton can remain unchanged, while the specific implementation of the Singleton can be different.

Related Patterns

Related patterns include the following:

- Abstract Factory (page 6)
- Builder (page 13)
- Prototype (page 28)

Example

Application users want the option of undoing previous commands. To support that functionality, a history list is needed. That history list has to be accessible from everywhere in the PIM and only one instance of it is needed. Therfore, it's a perfect candidate for the Singleton pattern.

Example 1.20 `HistoryList.java`

```
1.     import java.util.ArrayList;
2.     import java.util.Collections;
3.     import java.util.List;
4.     public class HistoryList{
5.         private List history = Collections.synchronizedList(new ArrayList());
6.         private static HistoryList instance = new HistoryList();
7.
8.         private HistoryList(){ }
9.
10.        public static HistoryList getInstance(){
11.            return instance;
12.        }
13.
14.        public void addCommand(String command){
15.            history.add(command);
16.        }
17.
18.        public Object undoCommand(){
19.            return history.remove(history.size() - 1);
20.        }
21.
22.        public String toString(){
23.            StringBuffer result = new StringBuffer();
24.            for (int i = 0; i < history.size(); i++){
25.                result.append("  ");
26.                result.append(history.get(i));
27.                result.append("\n");
28.            }
29.            return result.toString();
30.        }
31.    }
```

The `HistoryList` maintains a static reference to an instance of itself, has a private constructor, and uses a static method `getInstance` to provide a single history list object to all parts of the PIM. The additional variable in `HistoryList`, `history`, is a `List` object used to track the command strings. The `HistoryList` provides two methods, `addCommand` and `undoCommand` to support adding and removing commands from the list.

Chapter Two

Behavioral Patterns

Introduction to Behavioral Patterns

Behavioral patterns are concerned with the flow of control through a system. Some ways of organizing control within a system can yield great benefits in both efficiency and maintainability of that system. Behavioral patterns distill the essence of proven practices into readily understood, well known, and easy-to-apply heuristics.

Behavioral patterns covered in this chapter are as follows:

- Chain of Responsibility – To establish a chain within a system, so that a message can either be handled at the level where it is first received, or be directed to an object that can handle it.
- Command – To wrap a command in an object so that it can be stored, passed into methods, and returned like any other object.
- Interpreter – To define an interpreter for a language.
- Iterator – To provide a consistent way to sequentially access items in a collection that is independent of and separate from the underlying collection.
- Mediator – To simplify communication among objects in a system by introducing a single object that manages message distribution among the others.
- Memento – To preserve a "snapshot" of an object's state, so that the object can return to its original state without having to reveal its content to the rest of the world.
- Observer – To provide a way for a component to flexibly broadcast messages to interested receivers.
- State – To easily change an object's behavior at runtime.
- Strategy – To define a group of classes that represent a set of possible behaviors. These behaviors can then be flexibly plugged into an application, changing the functionality on the fly.
- Visitor – To provide a maintainable, easy way to perform actions for a family of classes. Visitor centralizes the behaviors and allows them to be modified or extended without changing the classes they operate on.
- Template Method – To provide a method that allows subclasses to override parts of the method without rewriting it.

Note: MVC, or Model-View-Controller, can be considered a behavioral pattern. However, because of its wide-ranging implications for entire systems, particular in view of the J2EE specification recommendations for servlets and JSPs, we included it in the "System Patterns" chapter on page 208.

Chain of Responsibility

Pattern Properties

Type: Behavioral
Level: Component

Purpose

To establish a chain within a system, so that a message can either be handled at the level where it is first received, or be directed to an object that can handle it.

Introduction

The Personal Information manager might be used to manage projects as well as contacts. Think of this as a tree structure of task objects. One task is the "root" of the tree, representing the project itself. The base task has a set of subtasks, each subtask has its own set of subtasks, and so on. In this way, you divide a project up into an increasingly detailed set of related objectives. This gives users the ability to group and organize actions relating to their objectives, as in the following example:

- Project (base task): Own a country
    - Subtask: Acquire a small fortune
        - Subtask: Use psychic hotlines to predict winning lottery numbers
    - Subtask: Research whether the climate is better in the Atlantic or Pacific
    - Subtask: Locate an island for sale
        - Subtask: See whether there are any islands for auction on E-Bay
    - Subtask: Research the U.N. rules for incorporation as a country
    - Subtask: Decide what to name the country

How do you manage information in a structure like this? For example, it would be helpful to be able to see who is responsible for a certain set of tasks or deliverables. How do you delegate groups of tasks to someone, or assign the tasks to someone else?

One option is to define an attribute for each task to represent the owner. When the owner for a task changes, all tasks and subtasks are updated with the new owner's name. However, this seems like an inefficient way to store a task owner, requiring much more information to be stored and maintained than you would prefer.

An alternative is to reference one or more central objects that store the task owners. While this approach more effectively manages memory, it requires a lot of work to manage the links between the tasks and the central objects used to maintain data.

What happens if you use the task tree itself to manage owners? Define a method for the `Task` class called `getOwner`, associated with an `owner` attribute. When called, the method checks whether the owner was specified (not null). If an owner was specified, the name is returned; if not, the task calls the `getOwner` method for its parent. This solution requires less work than either of the previous solutions and is still efficient in memory use. You only need to specify the owner at a single location in the tree. The `Task` objects themselves do the rest of the work, delegating the `getOwner` call to their parent tasks until one is found with the information. This is an example of the Chain of Responsibility design pattern.

Applicability

Use Chain of Responsibility when:

- There is a group of objects in a system that can all potentially respond to the same kind of message.
- Messages must be handled by one of several objects within the system.
- Messages follow the "handle or forward" model—that is, some events can be handled at the level where they are received or produced, while others must be forwarded to some other object.

Description

When some action takes place in an object-oriented system, it is often represented by an event or a message. Such a message may take the form of a method that will be called, or it may be an object within the system. Typically, the message will be directed to another object that can respond to or handle the message.

In the simplest cases, the same object that produces a message also responds to it. For instance, a text field might produce events in response to user action (such as typing on a keyboard), and also respond to those events (displaying text in the field).

In more complex cases, responding to messages can be more involved. A message requesting a change in the appearance or layout of a GUI component might be dealt with at different levels. If the request is to change the alignment of text within a field, the component itself might respond. A request to change the alignment of the entire text field would probably have to be directed to some higher-level organizing object; perhaps a panel or frame containing the text field. This kind of model is appropriate for the Chain of Responsibility pattern.

The Chain of Responsibility is a referral chain for messages. If an object cannot handle a given message, it passes the message on to some other object. Frequently, the Chain of Responsibility is implemented with a parent-child or container-contained model. With this approach, messages not handled by a child object are sent to the parent, and potentially the parent's parent, until a suitable handler object is reached.

The Chain of Responsibility is well-suited for a variety of object-oriented GUI activities. GUI help functions, component layout, formatting, and positioning all might use this pattern. In business models, the pattern is sometimes used with whole-part models. For example, a line item on an order might send a message to the order it's on—the order composite—for action.

For a real-world example of Chain of Responsibility, consider a travel request within a company. Typically, such a request will be propagated upward to the appropriate manager. Therefore, a request to travel to the grocery store for more coffee might only require approval from your manager, whereas a request to travel to Kansas could rise through an organizational hierarchy until it finally reached an individual with approval authority (perhaps the great and powerful Oz).

The Chain of Responsibility sequence diagram is shown in Figure 2.1.

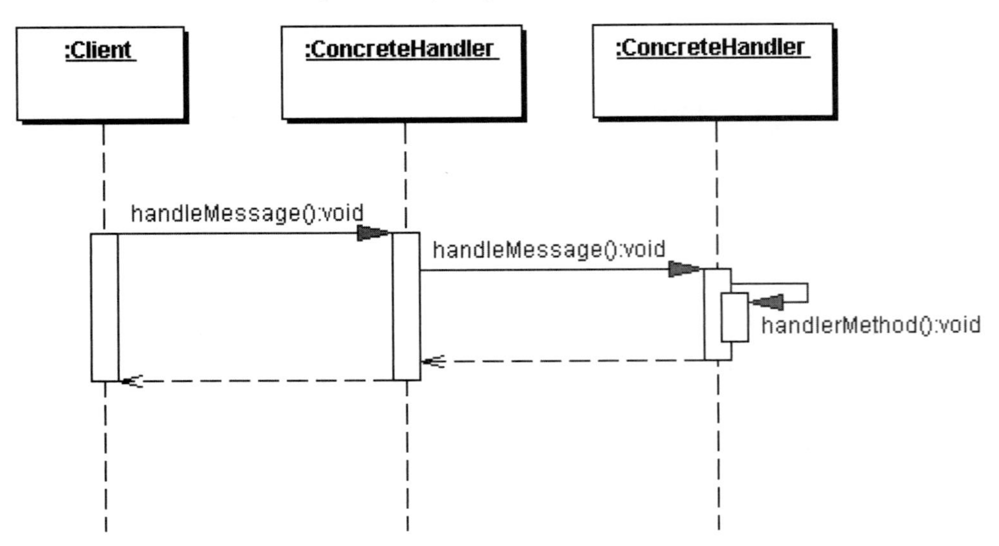

Figure 2.1 *Chain of Responsibility sequence diagram*

Implementation

The class diagram for Chain of Responsibility is shown in Figure 2.2

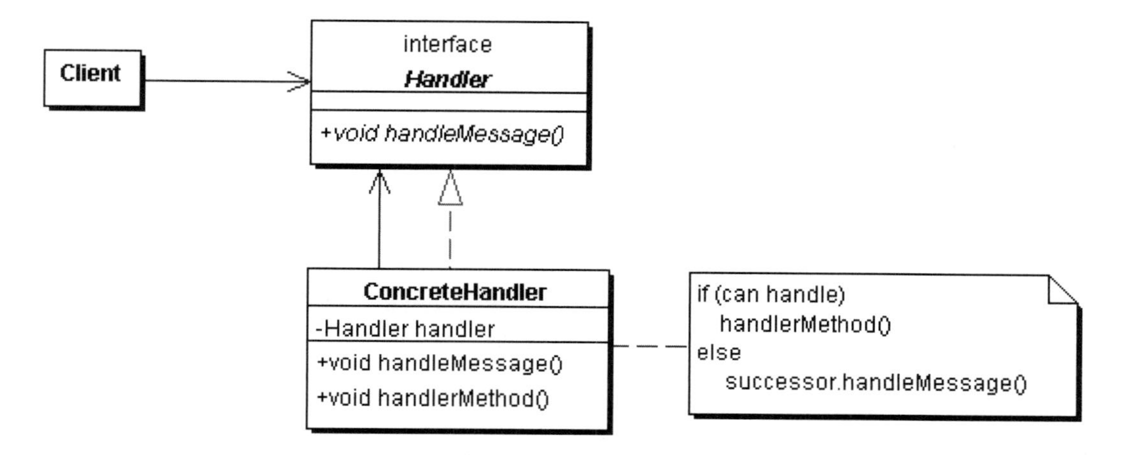

Figure 2.2 *Chain of Responsibility class diagram*

To implement the Chain of Responsibility, you need:

- `Handler` – The interface that defines the method used to pass a message to the next handler. That message is normally just the method call, but if more data needs to be encapsulated, an object can be passed as well.
- `ConcreteHandler` – A class that implements the `Handler` interface. It keeps a reference to the next `Handler` instance inline. This reference is either set in the constructor of the class or through a setter method. The implementation of the `handleMessage` method can determine how to handle the method and call a `handleMethod`, forward the message to the next `Handler` or a combination of both.

Benefits and Drawbacks

Chain of Responsibility offers great flexibility in event processing for an application, since it manages complex event handling by dividing the responsibilities among a number of simpler elements. It allows a set of classes to behave as a whole, since events produced in one class can be sent on to other handler classes within the composite.

Of course, the flexibility that this pattern provides comes with a price; the Chain of Responsibility becomes difficult to develop, test and debug. As the forwarding chain becomes more complex, you have to carefully monitor whether events are being properly forwarded.

Failure to plan for the different forwarding possibilities can result in dropped messages (messages that have no handler and so never have a response) or communication "chatter." Chatter refers to a high volume of messages and multiple forwarding stages in the chain. If many messages are produced during a short period of time and they are passed along several times before they are handled, the system might slow down.

Pattern Variants

There are many ways to adapt Chain of Responsibility to suit application requirements. The two considerations are handling strategies and forwarding strategies.

Handling strategies focus on exactly how handler behavior is implemented. Some of the possible variants include:

- Default handler – Some implementations set up a base handler, which becomes the default for the chain. It is normally used only when there is no explicitly defined forwarding class. A default handler is especially helpful in avoiding the problem of dropped messages previously mentioned in the *Benefits and Drawbacks* section for this pattern.
- Handle and extend – In this variant, event handling involves adding to a base behavior as the event is propagated along the chain. This is often helpful for activities such as logging.
- Dynamic handlers – Some Chain of Responsibility implementations allow the message forwarding structure to be changed at runtime. By defining a setter method for each class of the chain, you can define and modify the chain as it is used in the application (with all of the resulting complexity that involves).

Forwarding strategies define various approaches to handle or forward messages produced by a component:

- Handle by default – Handle any message that is not specifically forwarded.
- Propagate by default – Forward any message that is not explicitly handled.
- Forward to default handler – More complex than the base pattern, this approach uses a default event handler. Any message not explicitly handled at the component level, or forwarded to some other handler, will be sent to the default handler.

- Ignore by default – Any message that is not explicitly handled or forwarded is discarded. If the classes in the chain produce events that are not used in the application, this can be an acceptable way to reduce chatter. However, you must be careful in this approach to avoid inadvertently discarding messages that the system should handle.

Related Patterns

Related patterns include the Composite (page 157). Chain of Responsibility is often used with the Composite pattern. When both are used together, the Composite pattern provides support for a tree-based structure and basic message propagation, and the Chain of Responsibility provides rules for how some of the messages are propagated.

In addition, Composite tends to send messages "down" the tree (from the root to the branches) while Chain of Responsibility usually sends messages "up" the tree (from branches to the root).

Example

Note: For a full working example of this code example, with additional supporting classes and/or a `RunPattern` class, see "Chain of Responsibility" on page 366 of the "Full Code Examples" appendix.

The PIM can act as a project manager as well as a contact manager. This code example shows how to use the Chain of Responsibility pattern to retrieve information from within a project hierarchy.

The `ProjectItem` interface defines common methods for anything that can be part of a project.

Example 2.1 `ProjectItem.java`

```
1.    import java.io.Serializable;
2.    import java.util.ArrayList;
3.    public interface ProjectItem extends Serializable{
4.        public static final String EOL_STRING = System.getProperty("line.separator");
5.        public ProjectItem getParent();
6.        public Contact getOwner();
7.        public String getDetails();
8.        public ArrayList getProjectItems();
9.    }
```

The interface defines the methods `getParent`, `getOwner`, `getDetails`, and `getProjectItems`. Two classes implement `ProjectItem` in this example — `Project` and `Task`. The `Project` class is the base of a project, so its `getParent` method returns null. The `getOwner` and `getDetails` methods return the overall owner and details for the project, and the `getProjectItems` method returns all of the project's immediate children.

Example 2.2 `Project.java`

```
1.   import java.util.ArrayList;
2.   public class Project implements ProjectItem{
3.       private String name;
4.       private Contact owner;
5.       private String details;
6.       private ArrayList projectItems = new ArrayList();
7.
8.       public Project(){ }
9.       public Project(String newName, String newDetails, Contact newOwner){
10.          name = newName;
11.          owner = newOwner;
12.          details = newDetails;
13.      }
14.
15.      public String getName(){ return name; }
16.      public String getDetails(){ return details; }
17.      public Contact getOwner(){ return owner; }
18.      public ProjectItem getParent(){ return null; }
19.      public ArrayList getProjectItems(){ return projectItems; }
20.
21.      public void setName(String newName){ name = newName; }
22.      public void setOwner(Contact newOwner){ owner = newOwner; }
23.      public void setDetails(String newDetails){ details = newDetails; }
24.
25.      public void addProjectItem(ProjectItem element){
26.          if (!projectItems.contains(element)){
27.              projectItems.add(element);
28.          }
29.      }
30.
31.      public void removeProjectItem(ProjectItem element){
32.          projectItems.remove(element);
33.      }
34.
35.      public String toString(){
36.          return name;
37.      }
38.  }
```

The `Task` class represents some job associated with the project. Like `Project`, `Task` can keep a collection of subtasks, and its `getProjectItems` method will return these objects. For `Task`, the `getParent` method returns the parent, which will be another `Task` for the `Project`.

Example 2.3 `Task.java`

```
1.  import java.util.ArrayList;
2.  import java.util.ListIterator;
3.  public class Task implements ProjectItem{
4.      private String name;
5.      private ArrayList projectItems = new ArrayList();
6.      private Contact owner;
7.      private String details;
8.      private ProjectItem parent;
9.      private boolean primaryTask;
10.
11.     public Task(ProjectItem newParent){
12.         this(newParent, "", "", null, false);
13.     }
14.     public Task(ProjectItem newParent, String newName,
15.         String newDetails, Contact newOwner, boolean newPrimaryTask){
16.             parent = newParent;
17.             name = newName;
18.             owner = newOwner;
19.             details = newDetails;
20.             primaryTask = newPrimaryTask;
21.     }
22.
23.     public Contact getOwner(){
24.         if (owner == null){
25.             return parent.getOwner();
26.         }
27.         else{
28.             return owner;
29.         }
30.     }
31.
32.     public String getDetails(){
33.         if (primaryTask){
34.             return details;
35.         }
36.         else{
37.             return parent.getDetails() + EOL_STRING + "\t" + details;
38.         }
39.     }
40.
41.     public String getName(){ return name; }
42.     public ArrayList getProjectItems(){ return projectItems; }
43.     public ProjectItem getParent(){ return parent; }
44.     public boolean isPrimaryTask(){ return primaryTask; }
45.
46.     public void setName(String newName){ name = newName; }
47.     public void setOwner(Contact newOwner){ owner = newOwner; }
48.     public void setParent(ProjectItem newParent){ parent = newParent; }
49.     public void setPrimaryTask(boolean newPrimaryTask){ primaryTask = newPrima-
    ryTask; }
50.     public void setDetails(String newDetails){ details = newDetails; }
```

```
51.
52.         public void addProjectItem(ProjectItem element){
53.             if (!projectItems.contains(element)){
54.                 projectItems.add(element);
55.             }
56.         }
57.
58.         public void removeProjectItem(ProjectItem element){
59.             projectItems.remove(element);
60.         }
61.
62.         public String toString(){
63.             return name;
64.         }
65.     }
```

The Chain of Responsibility behavior is manifested in the `getOwner` and `getDetails` methods of `Task`. For `getOwner`, a `Task` will either return its internally referenced owner (if non-null), or that of its parent. If the parent was a `Task` and its owner was null as well, the method call is passed on to the next parent until it eventually encounters a non-null owner or it reaches the `Project` itself. This makes it easy to set up a group of `Tasks` where the same individual is the designated owner, responsible for the completion of a `Task` and all sub-`Tasks`.

The `getDetails` method is another example of Chain of Responsibility behavior, but it behaves somewhat differently. It calls the `getDetails` method of each parent until it reaches a `Task` or `Project` that is identified as a terminal node. This means that `getDetails` returns a series of `Strings` representing all the details for a particular `Task` chain.

Command

Also known as Action, Transaction

Pattern Properties

Type: Behavioral
Level: Object

Purpose

To wrap a command in an object so that it can be stored, passed into methods, and returned like any other object.

Introduction

When a user selects an action to be performed, the application needs to know where to get the relevant data and behavior. Normally, the application knows the number of options a user has and will keep the logic in a central place (hardcoded). When an option is selected, the application looks up what to do, assembles the data required, and invokes the necessary methods.

Of course, *you* are perfect (most programmers are), but your application is intended for normal users and they sometimes make mistakes. That's why many current applications allow users to undo every task back up to a certain checkpoint, such as the last time the user saved.

Imagine doing that in your application with its current design. It means creating a history list—a list of all the actions the user has performed, all the data that was required for the action, and the previous state. After about three or four actions, the history list will be bigger than the entire application, because of all the redundant data.

It makes more sense to combine the user's action into one object: the Command object. This contains the behavior and the data required for one specific action. Now an application just invokes the `execute` method on the `Command` object to execute the command. The application no longer needs to know all the available options and can be easily changed to include more user actions.

Applicability

Use the Command pattern to:

- Support undo, logging, and/or transactions.
- Queue and execute commands at different times.

- Decouple the source of the request from the object that fulfills the request.

Description

An application that doesn't use the Command pattern would have to provide a method in its handler class for each appropriate event that may occur. That means the handler needs to have all the information to be able to execute the action. Introducing new actions would require adding new methods to the handler class.

The Command pattern encapsulates both the data and functionality required to fulfill a specific action or request. It provides a separation between *when* an action needs to be taken and *how* it needs to be executed.

An application that uses the Command pattern creates a source (for instance, a GUI), a receiver (the object that carries out part of the request), and the command (`Listener`). The command receives the reference to the receiver and the source receives a reference to the command. In this example, when the user clicks the button in the GUI, the execute or listener method on a command object is created (see Figure 2.3).

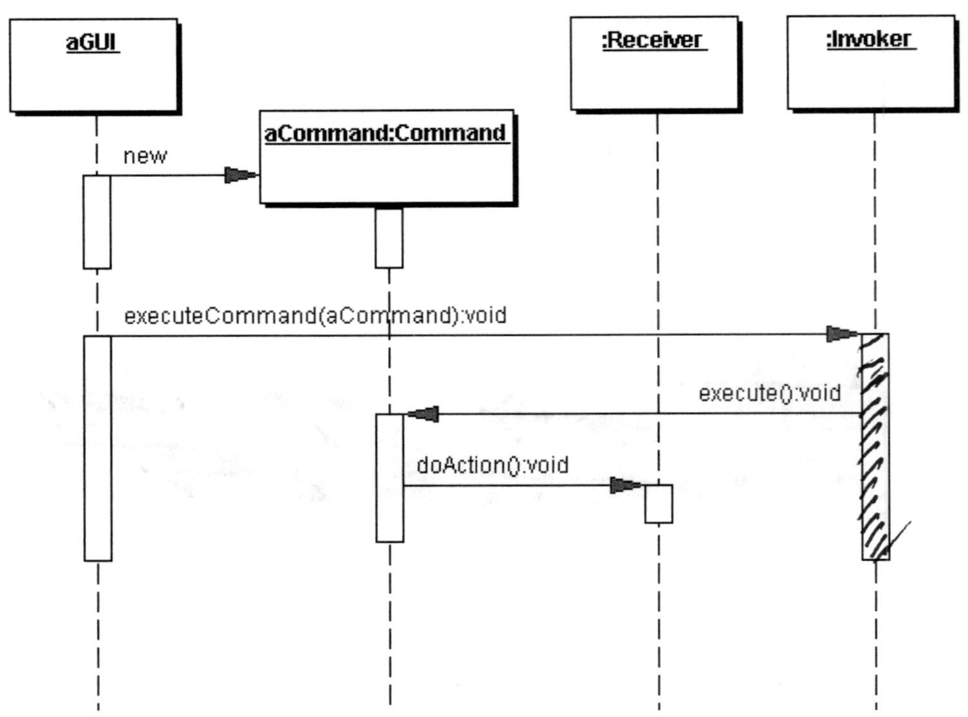

Figure 2.3 *Sequence diagram for invocation of Command*

The command object is sent to the invoker, which implements the Command interface. In its simplest form, the interface has an execute method. The implementing classes store the receiver as an instance variable. When the execute method is called, the Command calls the doAction method on the Receiver. The Command can call several methods on the Receiver.

Implementation

The Command class diagram is shown in Figure 2.4.

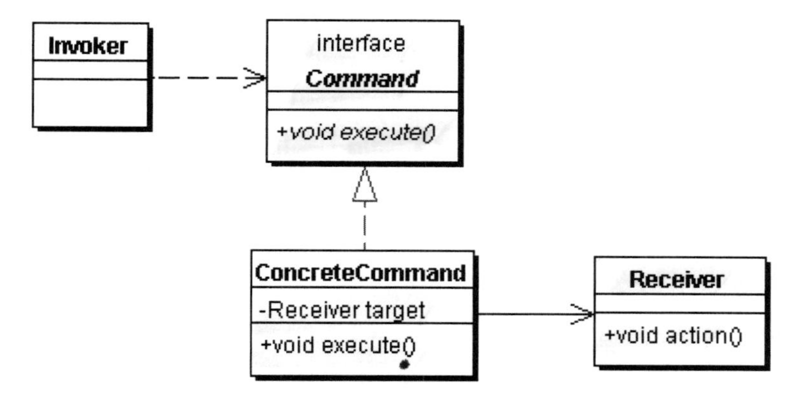

Figure 2.4 *Command class diagram*

To implement the Command pattern, you need the following:

- Command – The interface that defines the methods for the Invoker to use.
- Invoker – The invoker of the execute method of the Command object.
- Receiver – The target of the Command and the object that fulfills the request; it has all the information needed.
- ConcreteCommand – Implementation of the Command interface. It keeps a reference to the intended Receiver. When the execute method is called, ConcreteCommand will call one or more methods on the Receiver.

When implementing the Command pattern, you need to make some choices concerning the handling of calls. Do one of the following:

- The class that implements the Command interface can just be a coupling between the invoker and the receiver, and forward all the calls directly. This makes the ConcreteCommand lightweight.
- The ConcreteCommand can be the receiver and handle all the requests itself. This is most appropriate when there is no specific receiver for that request.

Of course, you can combine these two approaches and choose to handle part of the request in the `ConcreteCommand` and forward other parts.

Benefits and Drawbacks

The Command pattern offers flexibility in several ways:

- Decoupling the source or trigger of the event from the object that has the knowledge to perform the task.
- Sharing `Command` instances between several objects.
- Allowing the replacement of `Commands` and/or `Receivers` at runtime.
- Making `Commands` regular objects, thus allowing for all the normal properties.
- Easy addition of new `Commands`; just write another implementation of the interface and add it to the application.

Pattern Variants

Pattern variants include the following:

- Undo – The Command pattern lends itself to providing undo functions. When you extend the `Command` interface with an undo method, the burden of reversing the last command is placed on the implementing class.

  To support an undo for only the last command, the application needs to keep a reference only to the last command. When the client does an undo, the application has to call the `undo` method of just the last command.

  However, users might be dissatisfied with undoing only the last command. To support multi-level undo, the application must keep track of all the commands in a history list. This history list also simplifies the repetitive execution of the same command.

  To be able to undo a command, the Command needs to install some damage control. The command needs to save all the information required to repair the changed object. This information includes, but is not limited to, the receiver and any arguments and old values. The receiver has to be changed so that the command can restore the original values.

  Remember that you can use these Commands several times in different contexts. You might therefore need to copy the Command before placing it in the history list. You can do that by implementing the Prototype pattern (see “Prototype” on page 28).

Copying the `Command` helps prevent the errors that arise from repeatedly undoing and redoing several `Commands`. Going back and forth in the history list should be no problem, but if implemented incorrectly, any errors will add up. To prevent this, the command should store as much information as necessary to reverse the action. If some of the information is stored in the receiver, the Memento pattern (see "Memento" on page 88) would be most appropriate to store the state of the receiver. The receiver can provide that `Memento` object to the `Command` object as its previous state. When the command needs to be undone, the `Command` object hands the `Memento` object back to the receiver.

- `MacroCommand` – A `MacroCommand` is a collection of other `Commands`. You can create `MacroCommands` by using the Composite pattern. Figure 2.5 shows a class diagram for the undo and `MacroCommand` variant. (For more information, see "Composite" on page 157.)

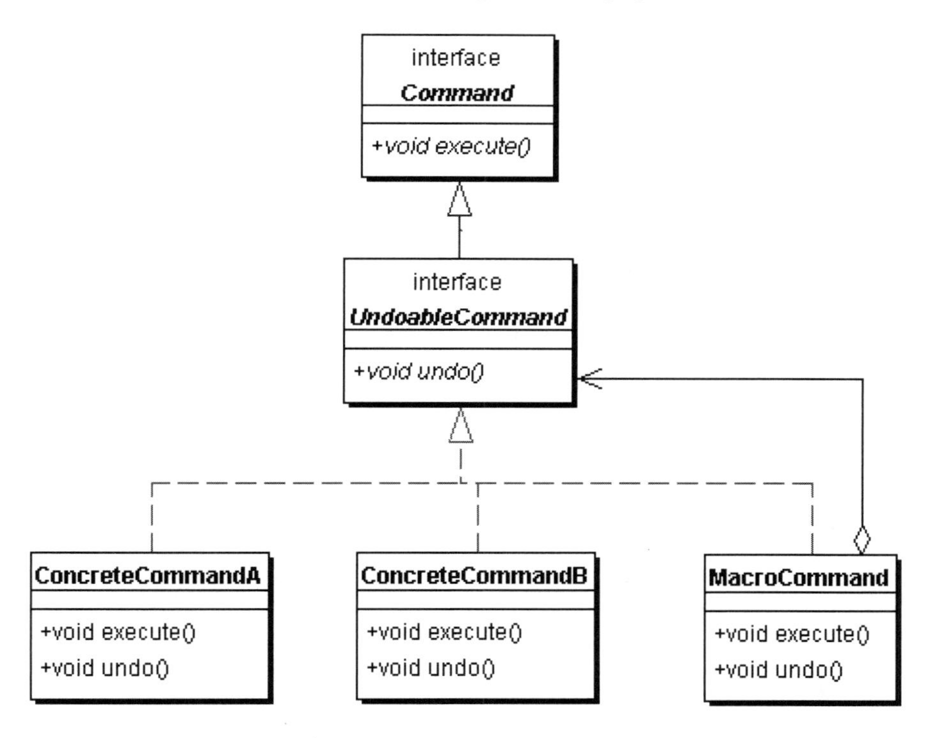

Figure 2.5 *Class diagram showing both the undo and* `MacroCommand` *variant*

A `MacroCommand` contains a list of subcommands. When the execute method is called, the `MacroCommand` forwards subcommands.

If the MacroCommand supports undo, all internal commands must support it as well. When undo is called, this call must be forwarded to the children in the reverse order of the execute method.

Related Patterns

Related patterns include the following:

- Composite (page 157) – Use the Composite pattern to implement MacroCommands.
- Memento (page 88) – Keeps the state of the receiver within the command to support undoing a Command.
- Prototype (page 28) – The Prototype pattern can be used to copy the command before placing it in the history list.
- Singleton (page 34) – In most applications, the history list is implemented as a Singleton.

Example

Note: For a full working example of this code example, with additional supporting classes and/or a RunPattern class, see "Command" on page 374 of the "Full Code Examples" appendix.

In the Personal Information Manager, users might want to update or modify information in their system. This code demonstrates how the Command pattern can provide update and undo behavior for a location.

In this example, a pair of interfaces model the generic command behavior. The basic command action is defined by the execute method in Command, while UndoableCommand extends this interface by adding undo and redo methods.

Example 2.4 Command.java

```
1.    public interface Command{
2.        public void execute();
3.    }
```

Example 2.5 UndoableCommand.java

```
1.    public interface UndoableCommand extends Command{
2.        public void undo();
3.        public void redo();
4.    }
```

In the PIM, the location of an appointment will be used to implement an undoable command. An appointment stores a description of an event, the people involved, the location, and the start and end time(s).

Example 2.6 `Appointment.java`

```
1.    import java.util.Date;
2.    public class Appointment{
3.        private String reason;
4.        private Contact[] contacts;
5.        private Location location;
6.        private Date startDate;
7.        private Date endDate;
8.
9.        public Appointment(String reason, Contact[] contacts, Location location, Date
      startDate, Date endDate){
10.           this.reason = reason;
11.           this.contacts = contacts;
12.           this.location = location;
13.           this.startDate = startDate;
14.           this.endDate = endDate;
15.       }
16.
17.       public String getReason(){ return reason; }
18.       public Contact[] getContacts(){ return contacts; }
19.       public Location getLocation(){ return location; }
20.       public Date getStartDate(){ return startDate; }
21.       public Date getEndDate(){ return endDate; }
22.
23.       public void setLocation(Location location){ this.location = location; }
24.
25.       public String toString(){
26.           return "Appointment:" + "\n    Reason: " + reason +
27.   "\n    Location: " + location + "\n    Start: " +
28.               startDate + "\n    End: " + endDate + "\n";
29.       }
30.   }
```

The class `ChangeLocationCommand` implements the `UndoableCommand` interface and provides the behavior required to change the location for an appointment.

Example 2.7 `ChangeLocationCommand.java`

```
1.    public class ChangeLocationCommand implements UndoableCommand{
2.        private Appointment appointment;
3.        private Location oldLocation;
4.        private Location newLocation;
5.        private LocationEditor editor;
6.
7.        public Appointment getAppointment(){ return appointment; }
```

```
8.
9.         public void setAppointment(Appointment appointment){ this.appointment =
         appointment; }
10.        public void setLocationEditor(LocationEditor locationEditor){ editor = loca-
         tionEditor; }
11.
12.        public void execute(){
13.            oldLocation = appointment.getLocation();
14.            newLocation = editor.getNewLocation();
15.            appointment.setLocation(newLocation);
16.        }
17.        public void undo(){
18.            appointment.setLocation(oldLocation);
19.        }
20.        public void redo(){
21.            appointment.setLocation(newLocation);
22.        }
23.    }
```

The class provides the ability to change a location using the execute method. It provides undo behavior by storing the previous value of the location and allowing a user to restore that value by calling the undo method. Finally, it supports a redo method that enables users to restore the new location, if they happen to be very indecisive.

Interpreter

Pattern Properties

Type: Behavioral
Level: Class

Purpose

To define an interpreter for a language.

Introduction

How do you solve a jigsaw puzzle? An incredibly gifted person might look through all 5,000 pieces and, after some calculations, know where all the pieces belong.

Members of another school of puzzle-solving thought use a different approach. They sort all the pieces that belong together in one part of the puzzle, then try to solve that smaller part first. You would try pieces until two of them match, repeating the process until a small part is finished. Then combine that part with other small pieces, and on and on until you complete the puzzle and discover you're missing a dozen pieces.

Solving a problem is often done this way; by splitting the problem up into subproblems, recursively. Not only that, but you have to solve the subproblems as well. When the problems are interdependent, solving them is very difficult.

The best solution is to create a simple language that describes relationships. Model a complex problem with a language and solve the sentence that describes the problem. With this approach, you should be able to greatly simplify the task of obtaining the solution. Like the puzzle, you divide the problem into progressively smaller parts. You solve the smaller parts, then you combine the solutions to obtain an overall solution. And hope that when you're done, you won't have any pieces missing.

Applicability

Use Interpreter when:

- There is a simple language to interpret.
- Recurring problems can be expressed in that language.
- Efficiency is not the main issue.

Description

The Interpreter dissects a problem by dividing it into small pieces, then puts these pieces back together as a sentence in a simple language. The other part of the interpreter uses that sentence to interpret and solve the problem step by step. This is done by creating an abstract syntax tree.

A well-known example of this approach is a regular expression. Regular expressions are used to describe patterns for which to search and modify strings, and the language used to describe these patterns is very concise.

Here's some terminology based on a mathematical example. On many occasions you might use certain formulas, like the Pythagorean Theorem:

- $(A^2 + B^2) = C^2$

So here's a simple mathematical formula:

- Result = (a + b)/c

`result`'s value depends on the values for a, b, and c.

Suppose the values are 4, 2 and 3 respectively—`result` is 2. Now, how do you know that? First, you mentally associated a with 4, b with 2, and c with 3. Next you added a and b, resulting in the value 6, which you then divided by c (3).

Solving the problem using Interpreter pattern involves a very similar set of steps. Each of the variables (a, b, and c) is an operand, as is each intermediate value (the value that is the result of some calculation).

The grammar rules (like + for adding and / for dividing) are *operations* or *operators*. Each grammar rule is implemented as a separate class, and each value to the right of that rule (the values are also called *operands*) becomes an instance variable.

Implementation

Figure 2.6 shows the Interpreter pattern class diagram.

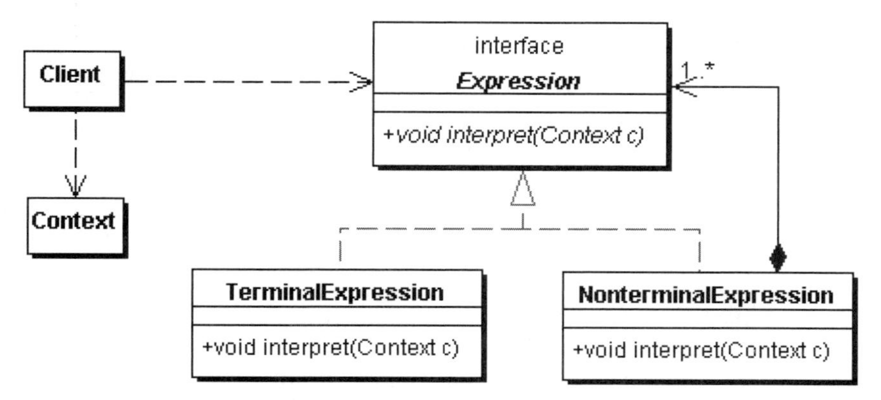

Figure 2.6 *Interpreter class diagram*

The Interpreter pattern needs:

- `Expression` – The interface through which the client interacts with the expressions.
- `TerminalExpression` – Implementation of the `Expression` interface intended for terminal nodes in the grammar and the syntax tree.
- `NonterminalExpression` – The other implementation of the `Expression` interface, intended for the nonterminal nodes in the grammar and syntax tree. It keeps a reference to the next `Expression`(s) and invokes the interpret method on each of its children.
- `Context` – Container for the information that is needed in several places in the interpreter. It can serve as a communication channel among several `Expression` instances.
- `Client` – Either builds or receives an instance of an abstract syntax tree. This syntax tree is composed of instances of `TerminalExpressions` and `NonterminalExpressions` to model a specific sentence. The client invokes the interpret method with the appropriate context where necessary.

Benefits and Drawbacks

Benefits and drawbacks include the following:

- The interpreter can be very easily changed to reflect changes in the grammar. To add a rule, create another class that implements the `Expression` interface. This class implements the new rule in the interpret method.

  You can easily change a rule by extending the old class and overriding the interpret method.

- The Interpreter pattern is inappropriate when the grammar is large. (Does this means that the Interpreter will start yelling loudly and breaking things and eventually have to be escorted out of your program? It's even worse.) The Interpreter can result in a large number of classes being produced if there are many rules in your language. Every rule you add to your language requires one or more classes in the interpreter. As the grammar gets larger, the number of classes used increases. This can eventually result in testing and maintenance problems.

- The expressions are reusable for other purposes. You can add methods to the `Expression` to increase the functionality of the expressions. To add more flexibility, use the Visitor pattern, which lets you dynamically change the interpret method. (See "Visitor" on page 121.)

- It might be difficult to create the abstract syntax tree—it isn't defined by the Interpreter pattern. The Interpreter assumes the syntax tree has been created somewhere, somehow.

Pattern Variants

The original pattern as described in the GoF *Design Patterns* book uses an abstract class instead of an interface. As stated before, we recommend that you use interfaces wherever possible, unless a partial implementation should be supplied.

Related Patterns

Related patterns include the following:

- Composite (page 157) – The structure for interpreted expressions is based on the composite pattern, using terminal expressions (leaf nodes) and nonterminal expressions (branch nodes).

- Flyweight (page 183) – To reduce the number of redundant or similar objects, you can apply the Flyweight pattern to some of the `Expressions`.

- Iterator (page 69) – Iterator is used to iterate through the abstract syntax tree and its nodes.
- Visitor (page 121) – When a Visitor pattern is used, the Interpreter gains flexibility.

Example

Note: For a full working example of this code example, with additional supporting classes and/or a `RunPattern` class, see “Interpreter” on page 381 of the “Full Code Examples” appendix.

The Expression hierarchy is at the heart of the Interpreter pattern. It defines the grammar that can be used to create and evaluate expressions. The `Expression` interface is the foundation for all expressions, and defines the interpret method that performs an evaluation.

Table 2-1 lists the interface and corresponding information.

Table 2-1 *Purpose of the Expression interface and its implementers*

Expression	Common interface for all expressions
ConstantExpression	Represents a constant value
VariableExpression	Represents a variable value, obtained by calling a method on some class
CompoundExpression	A pair of comparison expressions that evaluate to a boolean result
AndExpression	The logical “and” of two expressions
OrExpression	The logical “or” of two expressions
ComparisonExpression	A pair of expressions that evaluate to a boolean result
EqualsExpression	Performs an equals method comparison between the two expressions
ContainsExpression	Checks to see if the first `String` expression contains the second one

Example 2.8 `Expression.java`

```
1.    public interface Expression{
2.        void interpret(Context c);
3.    }
```

Example 2.9 `ConstantExpression.java`

```
1.    import java.lang.reflect.Method;
```

```
2.   import java.lang.reflect.InvocationTargetException;
3.   public class ConstantExpression implements Expression{
4.       private Object value;
5.
6.       public ConstantExpression(Object newValue){
7.           value = newValue;
8.       }
9.
10.      public void interpret(Context c){
11.          c.addVariable(this, value);
12.      }
13.  }
```

Example 2.10 `VariableExpression.java`

```
1.   import java.lang.reflect.Method;
2.   import java.lang.reflect.InvocationTargetException;
3.   public class VariableExpression implements Expression{
4.       private Object lookup;
5.       private String methodName;
6.
7.       public VariableExpression(Object newLookup, String newMethodName){
8.           lookup = newLookup;
9.           methodName = newMethodName;
10.      }
11.
12.      public void interpret(Context c){
13.          try{
14.              Object source = c.get(lookup);
15.              if (source != null){
16.                  Method method = source.getClass().getMethod(methodName, null);
17.                  Object result = method.invoke(source, null);
18.                  c.addVariable(this, result);
19.              }
20.          }
21.          catch (NoSuchMethodException exc){ }
22.          catch (IllegalAccessException exc){ }
23.          catch (InvocationTargetException exc){ }
24.      }
25.  }
```

Example 2.11 `CompoundExpression.java`

```
1.   public abstract class CompoundExpression implements Expression{
2.       protected ComparisonExpression expressionA;
3.       protected ComparisonExpression expressionB;
4.
5.      public CompoundExpression(ComparisonExpression expressionA, ComparisonExpres-
      sion expressionB){
6.           this.expressionA = expressionA;
7.           this.expressionB = expressionB;
8.       }
9.   }
```

Example 2.12 `AndExpression.java`

```
1.  public class AndExpression extends CompoundExpression{
2.      public AndExpression(ComparisonExpression expressionA, ComparisonExpression
    expressionB){
3.          super(expressionA, expressionB);
4.      }
5.
6.      public void interpret(Context c){
7.          expressionA.interpret(c);
8.          expressionB.interpret(c);
9.          Boolean result = new Boolean(((Boolean)c.get(expressionA)).booleanValue()
    && ((Boolean)c.get(expressionB)).booleanValue());
10.         c.addVariable(this, result);
11.     }
12. }
```

Example 2.13 `OrExpression.java`

```
1.  public class OrExpression  extends CompoundExpression{
2.      public OrExpression(ComparisonExpression expressionA, ComparisonExpression
    expressionB){
3.          super(expressionA, expressionB);
4.      }
5.
6.      public void interpret(Context c){
7.          expressionA.interpret(c);
8.          expressionB.interpret(c);
9.          Boolean result = new Boolean(((Boolean)c.get(expressionA)).booleanValue()
    || ((Boolean)c.get(expressionB)).booleanValue());
10.         c.addVariable(this, result);
11.     }
12. }
```

Example 2.14 `ComparisonExpression.java`

```
1.  public abstract class ComparisonExpression implements Expression{
2.      protected Expression expressionA;
3.      protected Expression expressionB;
4.
5.      public ComparisonExpression(Expression expressionA, Expression expressionB){
6.          this.expressionA = expressionA;
7.          this.expressionB = expressionB;
8.      }
9.  }
```

Example 2.15 `EqualsExpression.java`

```
1.  public class EqualsExpression extends ComparisonExpression{
2.      public EqualsExpression(Expression expressionA, Expression expressionB){
3.          super(expressionA, expressionB);
4.      }
5.
```

```
6.      public void interpret(Context c){
7.          expressionA.interpret(c);
8.          expressionB.interpret(c);
9.          Boolean result = new Boolean(c.get(expressionA).equals(c.get(expres-
    sionB)));
10.         c.addVariable(this, result);
11.     }
12. }
```

Example 2.16 `ContainsExpression.java`

```
1.  public class ContainsExpression extends ComparisonExpression{
2.      public ContainsExpression(Expression expressionA, Expression expressionB){
3.          super(expressionA, expressionB);
4.      }
5.  
6.      public void interpret(Context c){
7.          expressionA.interpret(c);
8.          expressionB.interpret(c);
9.          Object exprAResult = c.get(expressionA);
10.         Object exprBResult = c.get(expressionB);
11.         if ((exprAResult instanceof String) && (exprBResult instanceof String)){
12.             if (((String)exprAResult).indexOf((String)exprBResult) != -1){
13.                 c.addVariable(this, Boolean.TRUE);
14.                 return;
15.             }
16.         }
17.         c.addVariable(this, Boolean.FALSE);
18.         return;
19.     }
20. }
```

The `Context` class represents shared memory for expressions during evaluation. `Context` is a wrapper around a `HashMap`. In this example, the `Expression` objects provide the keys for the `HashMap`, and the results of calling the interpret method are stored as its values.

Example 2.17 `Context.java`

```
1.  import java.util.HashMap;
2.  public class Context{
3.      private HashMap map = new HashMap();
4.  
5.      public Object get(Object name){
6.          return map.get(name);
7.      }
8.  
9.      public void addVariable(Object name, Object value){
10.         map.put(name, value);
11.     }
12. }
```

With this series of expressions, it is possible to perform fairly sophisticated comparisons. ContactList holds a series of contacts in this example. It defines a method called getContactsMatchingExpression, which evaluates the Expression for every Contact and returns an ArrayList.

Example 2.18 ContactList.java

```
1.  import java.io.Serializable;
2.  import java.util.ArrayList;
3.  import java.util.Iterator;
4.  public class ContactList implements Serializable{
5.      private ArrayList contacts = new ArrayList();
6.
7.      public ArrayList getContacts(){ return contacts; }
8.      public Contact [] getContactsAsArray(){ return (Contact [])(contacts.toAr-
    ray(new Contact [1])); }
9.
10.     public ArrayList getContactsMatchingExpression(Expression expr, Context ctx,
    Object key){
11.         ArrayList results = new ArrayList();
12.         Iterator elements = contacts.iterator();
13.         while (elements.hasNext()){
14.             Object currentElement = elements.next();
15.             ctx.addVariable(key, currentElement);
16.             expr.interpret(ctx);
17.             Object interpretResult = ctx.get(expr);
18.             if ((interpretResult != null) && (interpretResult.equals(Bool-
    ean.TRUE))){
19.                 results.add(currentElement);
20.             }
21.         }
22.         return results;
23.     }
24.
25.     public void setContacts(ArrayList newContacts){ contacts = newContacts; }
26.
27.     public void addContact(Contact element){
28.         if (!contacts.contains(element)){
29.             contacts.add(element);
30.         }
31.     }
32.     public void removeContact(Contact element){
33.         contacts.remove(element);
34.     }
35.
36.     public String toString(){
37.         return contacts.toString();
38.     }
39. }
```

With the Expression hierarchy and the ContactList, it is possible to perform database-like queries for the Contacts in a ContactList. For example, you could search for all those `Contacts` with a title containing the characters "Java" by doing the following:

1. Create a `ConstantExpression` with the string "Java".
2. Create a `VariableExpression` with the target object and the string "`getTitle`".
3. Create a `ContainsExpression` with the `VariableExpression` as the first argument and the `ConstantExpression` as the second.
4. Pass the `ContainsExpression` into a `ContactList` object's `getContactsMatchingExpression` method.

Iterator

Also known as Cursor

Pattern Properties

Type: Behavioral, Object
Level: Component

Purpose

To provide a consistent way to sequentially access items in a collection that is independent of and separate from the underlying collection.

Introduction

The Personal Information Manager uses many collections, since it keeps track of large amounts of user data. Addresses, contacts, projects, appointments, notes, to-do lists—all require the ability to store groups of related objects.

To meet the storage needs of all these kinds of information, you might create classes to hold each group of items used by the information manager. In this way, you could develop collections to meet the specific needs of each group of objects.

This presents a problem, however, when you want to traverse each of the collections. If you create collection classes that are specifically intended to meet the needs of the stored objects, there is no guarantee that the elements will be retrieved and used in a uniform way. Appointments might be organized in subgroups according to date, while contacts might be stored alphabetically, and notes might be sequentially ordered.

This means that you might have to write collection-specific code to move through items in each group, and copy that code to any part of the system where you would need to use a group. Potentially, this could result in very complicated, hard-to-maintain code. Furthermore, you need know in detail the different collection types used to hold business objects of the PIM.

The Iterator pattern solves these problems by defining a uniform interface for traversing a collection—any collection. When you use iterators in a system, you can use the same method calls when navigating through a list of contacts as when you printed out a to-do list.

Applicability

Use the Iterator pattern:

- To provide a uniform, consistent way to move through the elements in collections which is not tied to the collection's implementation.
- To allow multiple collection traversal, enabling several clients to simultaneously navigate within the same underlying collection.

Description

At its foundation, the Iterator pattern allows you to standardize and simplify the code you write to move through collections in your code. Collection classes tend to be created based on storage rather than traversal requirements. The advantage of the Iterator pattern is that it provides a consistent way to handle navigation within collections regardless of the underlying structure.

An Iterator in the Java programming language ("Java") typically uses an interface to define its core operations, then provides one or more implementations which link to the underlying aggregate. The Iterator described in *Design Patterns* provides the following fundamental operations:

- First
- Next
- IsDone
- CurrentItem

These operations define the basic services that an Iterator must provide in order to do its job. In more general terms, an Iterator should provide the following core capabilities:

- Navigation – Moving forward or backward within the collection
- Retrieval – Getting the currently referenced element
- Validation – Determining if there are still elements in the collection, based on the Iterator's current position

Iterators may also provide extended operations. Some Iterators provide methods to move to the first or last element in the Iterator, for example.

Implementation

The Iterator class diagram is shown in Figure 2.7.

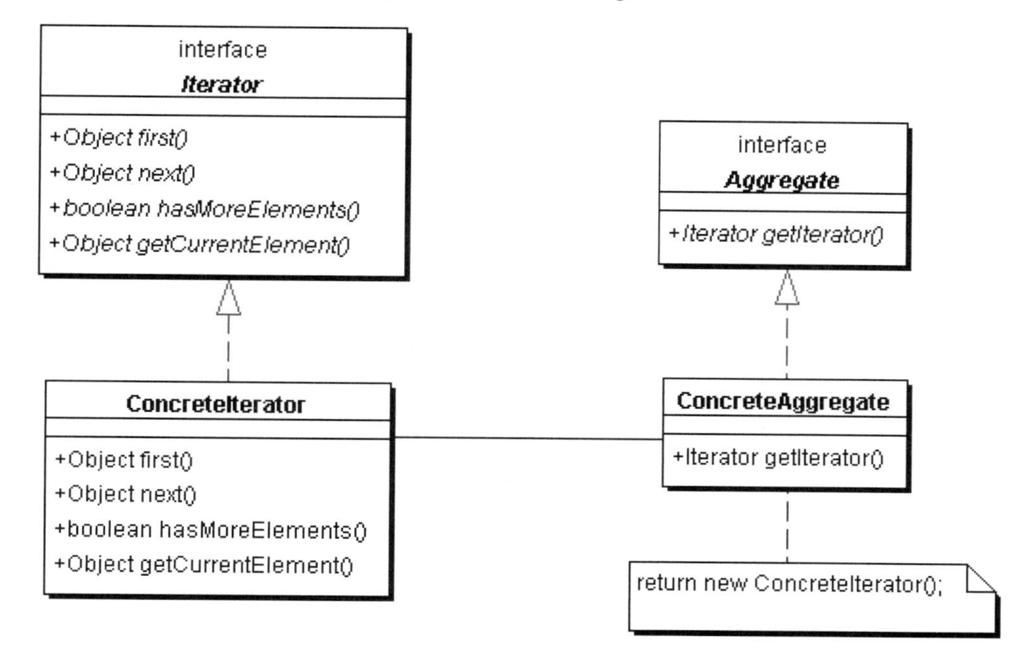

Figure 2.7 *Iterator class diagram*

To implement the Iterator pattern, you need:

- `Iterator` – This interface defines the standard iteration methods. At a minimum, the interface defines methods for navigation, retrieval and validation (`first`, `next`, `hasMoreElements` and `getCurrentItem`)
- `ConcreteIterator` – Classes that implement the `Iterator`. These classes reference the underlying collection. Normally, instances are created by the `ConcreteAggregate`. Because of the tight coupling with the `ConcreteAggregate`, the `ConcreteIterator` often is an inner class of the `ConcreteAggregate`.
- `Aggregate` – This interface defines a factory method to produce the `Iterator`.
- `ConcreteAggregate` – This class implements the `Aggregate`, building a `ConcreteIterator` on demand. The `ConcreteAggregate` performs this task in addition to its fundamental responsibility of representing a collection of objects in a system. `ConcreteAggregate` creates the `ConcreteIterator` instance.

Benefits and Drawbacks

Many of the Iterator pattern's benefits stem from the advantages of defining a uniform interface for collection traversal. This greatly simplifies the use of collections, and allows you to use polymorphism when working with collections. To print the elements in any collection, for instance, you could obtain an `Iterator`, then call the `toString` method on any object, regardless of its underlying collection.

Additionally, Iterators allow clients to keep multiple navigation points to the same collection. You can think of an Iterator as a cursor or pointer into the collection; with each call to the `Aggregate's` factory method, you can get another pointer into the collection.

A drawback of iterators is that they give the illusion of order to unordered structures. For example, a set does not support ordering, and its Iterator would likely provide the elements in an arbitrary sequence that could change over time. If you don't realize this, you could write code that assumed consistency in the underlying structure, which would result in problems later on.

Pattern Variants

The Iterator pattern has a number of implementation options.

- A `ConcreteIterator` may be internal or external. External `Iterators` provide specific methods to the clients to navigate within the collection, while internal Iterators cycle through the elements, performing some action requested by the client. The external iterator is the more flexible option, but requires more coding on the client to use the iterator.
- `ConcreteIterators` can be dynamic or static. A dynamic `ConcreteIterator` directly references its underlying collection for elements, so is always guaranteed to reflect its state. A static `ConcreteIterator`, on the other hand, creates a snapshot of the collection when it is created, and refers to the copy during client use.
- Null iterators can be defined to make traversal of complex structures, such as trees, more straightforward. Using an iterator that represents an "end node," it is possible to write simple recursive code to visit all the nodes in the tree.
- Iterators can support a variety of different ways to move through a collection. This is particularly useful in complex structures, such as the Composite pattern, where there might be a rationale to move through the elements in a variety of different ways.

- From a structural perspective, a `ConcreteIterator` can be defined as an inner class of the `ConcreteAggregate`, or it can be defined in a separate class. The `ConcreteIterator` can hold the code to move through the collection, or it might only represent the position within the collection.

Related Patterns

Related patterns include the following:

- Factory Method (page 21) – Collection classes often define a factory method to produce the Iterator.
- Visitor (page 121) – When the Visitor pattern is used on a group of objects, an Iterator is frequently used to cycle through the elements.
- Value List Handler [CJ2EEP] – The Value List Handler is based on the Iterator pattern in that it allows the client to step through a collection.

Example

Note: For a full working example of this code example, with additional supporting classes and/or a `RunPattern` class, see "Iterator" on page 389 of the "Full Code Examples" appendix.

This example uses the Java Collections Framework to provide iterating behavior for a pair of business aggregates. The `java.util.Iterator` interface defines methods for the basic navigation methods required—`hasNext` and `next`. Note that the `Iterator` interface requires one-time-only traversal, since the only way to return to the beginning is to get another `Iterator` from the collection.

The `Iterating` interface defines a single method, `getIterator`. This interface is used to identify any class in the PIM that is capable of producing an Iterator for collection traversal.

Example 2.19 `Iterating.java`

```
1.    import java.util.Iterator;
2.    import java.io.Serializable;
3.    public interface Iterating extends Serializable{
4.        public Iterator getIterator();
5.    }
```

The `ToDoList` and `ToDoListCollection` interfaces, which extend the `Iterating` interface, define the two collections in the example. `ToDoList` defines a sequential list of tasks or items, while `ToDoListCollection` represents a collection of `ToDoLists` stored in the PIM.

Example 2.20 ToDoList.java

```
1.    public interface ToDoList extends Iterating{
2.        public void add(String item);
3.        public void add(String item, int position);
4.        public void remove(String item);
5.        public int getNumberOfItems();
6.        public String getListName();
7.        public void setListName(String newListName);
8.    }
```

Example 2.21 ToDoListCollection.java

```
1.    public interface ToDoListCollection extends Iterating{
2.        public void add(ToDoList list);
3.        public void remove(ToDoList list);
4.        public int getNumberOfItems();
5.    }
```

The classes `ToDoListImpl` and `ToDoListCollectionImpl` implement the previous interfaces. `ToDoListImpl` uses an `ArrayList` to hold its elements, which provides absolute ordering and allows duplicate entries. `ToDoListCollectionImpl` uses a `HashTable`, which does not support ordering and stores its entries as key-value pairs. Although the collections behave very differently, both can provide Iterators for their stored elements.

Example 2.22 ToDoListCollectionImpl.java

```
1.    import java.util.Iterator;
2.    import java.util.HashMap;
3.    public class ToDoListCollectionImpl implements ToDoListCollection{
4.        private HashMap lists = new HashMap();
5.
6.        public void add(ToDoList list){
7.            if (!lists.containsKey(list.getListName())){
8.                lists.put(list.getListName(), list);
9.            }
10.       }
11.       public void remove(ToDoList list){
12.           if (lists.containsKey(list.getListName())){
13.               lists.remove(list.getListName());
14.           }
15.       }
16.       public int getNumberOfItems(){ return lists.size(); }
17.       public Iterator getIterator(){ return lists.values().iterator(); }
18.       public String toString(){ return getClass().toString(); }
19.   }
```

Example 2.23 `ToDoListImpl.java`

```
1.    import java.util.Iterator;
2.    import java.util.ArrayList;
3.    public class ToDoListImpl implements ToDoList{
4.        private String listName;
5.        private ArrayList items = new ArrayList();
6.
7.        public void add(String item){
8.            if (!items.contains(item)){
9.                items.add(item);
10.           }
11.       }
12.       public void add(String item, int position){
13.           if (!items.contains(item)){
14.               items.add(position, item);
15.           }
16.       }
17.       public void remove(String item){
18.           if (items.contains(item)){
19.               items.remove(items.indexOf(item));
20.           }
21.       }
22.
23.       public int getNumberOfItems(){ return items.size(); }
24.       public Iterator getIterator(){ return items.iterator(); }
25.       public String getListName(){ return listName; }
26.       public void setListName(String newListName){ listName = newListName; }
27.
28.       public String toString(){ return listName; }
29.   }
```

Both classes can provide an Iterator, so it's straightforward to write code to move through their elements. `ListPrinter` shows how the Iterators could be used to print the contents of collections out in their `String` form. The class has three methods: `printToDoList`, `printToDoListCollection` and `printIteratingElement`. In all three methods, the iteration process is based around a very simple `while` loop.

Example 2.24 `ListPrinter.java`

```
1.    import java.util.Iterator;
2.    import java.io.PrintStream;
3.    public class ListPrinter{
4.        public static void printToDoList(ToDoList list, PrintStream output){
5.            Iterator elements = list.getIterator();
6.            output.println("  List - " + list + ":");
7.            while (elements.hasNext()){
8.                output.println("\t" + elements.next());
9.            }
10.       }
```

```
11.
12.     public static void printToDoListCollection(ToDoListCollection lotsOfLists,
      PrintStream output){
13.         Iterator elements = lotsOfLists.getIterator();
14.         output.println("\"To Do\" List Collection:");
15.         while (elements.hasNext()){
16.             printToDoList((ToDoList)elements.next(), output);
17.         }
18.     }
19.
20.     public static void printIteratingElement(Iterating element, PrintStream out-
      put){
21.         output.println("Printing the element " + element);
22.         Iterator elements = element.getIterator();
23.         while (elements.hasNext()){
24.             Object currentElement = elements.next();
25.             if (currentElement instanceof Iterating){
26.                 printIteratingElement((Iterating)currentElement, output);
27.                 output.println();
28.             }
29.             else{
30.                 output.println(currentElement);
31.             }
32.         }
33.     }
34. }
```

The method `printIteratingElement` best demonstrates the power of combining the Iterator pattern with polymorphism. Here, any class that implements `Iterating` can be printed in `String` form. The method makes no assumptions about the underlying collection structure except that it can produce an `Iterator`.

Mediator

Pattern Properties

Type: Behavioral
Level: Component

Purpose

To simplify communication among objects in a system by introducing a single object that manages message distribution among the others.

Introduction

A useful feature in the PIM would be sharing information among several users, so that one user could set up a meeting that other PIM users would attend. With a shared set of data, all the participants would be up-to-date on the meeting plans.

How should you manage the appointments, assuming multiple PIMs are running? One way is to give each PIM a copy of the `Appointment` object, ensuring that they have local access to the data. This presents a problem: how do you ensure that information is consistent among all users? For example, if the user creates a meeting and later changes the date, how do the other meeting participants find out?

You can make the user's application responsible for managing the update. However, if any of the meeting participants are allowed to make updates, that means that each PIM has to keep track of all of the other PIMs. Managing communication for a large number of participants becomes very difficult. In the best case, it is inefficient and costly in terms of network bandwidth; in the worst case, the planning for a meeting degenerates into chaos. And generally, you'd prefer to leave the chaos to the meetings themselves.

Given the potential complexity of the system, it's better to delegate the task of sending and receiving specific requests to a central object, which then makes decisions about what methods to call. This is the essence of the Mediator pattern. Instead of making the `Appointment` itself responsible for sending updates, create an `AppointmentMediator`. Each time `Appointment` changes, call a method in the `Mediator` object, which might decide to call methods on the Location object to confirm. Depending on the result, the `AppointmentManager` broadcasts the original message, a revised version of the message such as a meeting time change, or a cancellation.

Applicability

Use Mediator when:

- There are complex rules for communication among objects in a system (often as a result of the business model).
- You want to keep the objects simple and manageable.
- You want the classes for these objects to be redeployable, not dependent on the business model of the system.

Description

As communication among objects in an application becomes more complex, managing communication becomes more and more difficult. Handling event processing for a simple spreadsheet control might involve writing code for the grid component. However, if the GUI is expanded to include a grid, graph, and record-display fields, it becomes much more difficult to manage the code. A change in one of the components might trigger changes in some or all of the others.

The Mediator pattern helps solve this problem, since it defines a class that has overall communications responsibility. This greatly simplifies the other classes in the system, since they no longer need to manage communication themselves, and that can help you keep much of your hair and your sanity. The mediator object—the central object to manage communication—has the role of a router for the system, centralizing the logic to send and receive messages. Components send messages to the mediator rather than to other components of the system; likewise, they rely on the mediator to send change notifications to them.

Consider implementing Mediator whenever a set of GUI components should behave as a whole. The main factor in deciding whether to implement the pattern is the overall complexity of the GUI model. Two other possible scenarios for Mediator implementation are:

- Whole-part business models, such as a product composed of a number of component parts
- Models that represent business workflow, such as an order invoice being processed by accounting, manufacturing, and shipping services

For a real-world illustration of the Mediator pattern, consider conference calls. Many telephone companies offer teleconferencing, and you could consider the switchboard as a sort of mediator. It contains logic (presumably) to route messages between the individuals involved in the conference call. The participants send messages (talk), and the switchboard responds, directing messages to specific participants. Some callers are routed to Burma or Antwerp, while messages that start with "manager" are routed only to the manager of the conference call.

Implementation

The Mediator class diagram is shown in Figure 2.8.

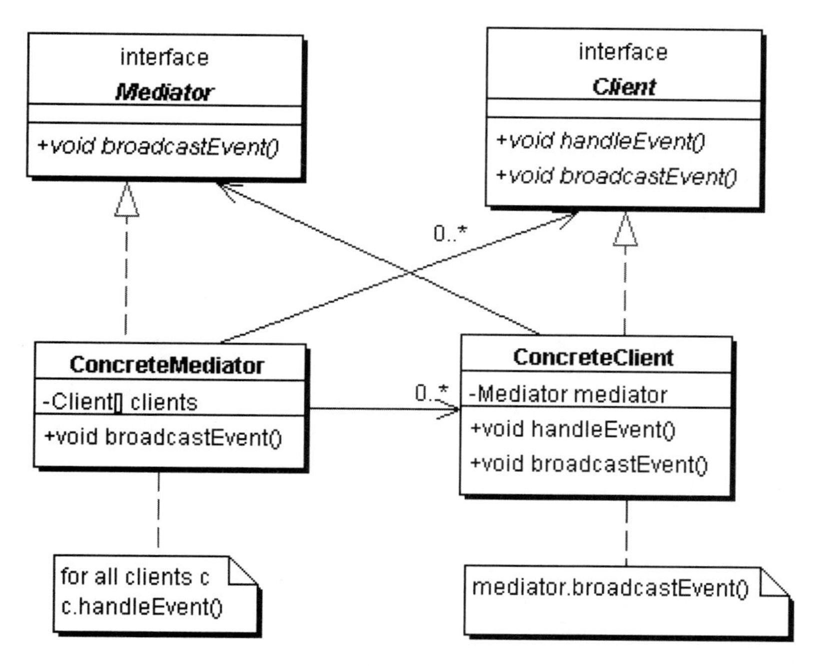

Figure 2.8 *Mediator class diagram*

The Mediator pattern requires:

- `Mediator` – The interface that defines the methods clients can call on a `Mediator`.
- `ConcreteMediator` – The class that implements the `Mediator` interface. This class mediates among several client classes. It contains application-specific information about processes, and the `ConcreteMediator` might have some hardcoded references to its clients. Based on the information the `Mediator` receives, it can either invoke specific methods on the clients, or invoke a generic method to inform clients of a change or a combination of both.
- `Client` – The interface that defines the general methods a `Mediator` can use to inform client instances.

- `ConcreteClient` – A class that implements the `Client` interface and provides an implementation to each of the client methods. The `ConcreteClient` can keep a reference to a `Mediator` instance to inform colleague clients of a change (through the `Mediator`).

Benefits and Drawbacks

The Mediator has three advantages:

- The individual components become simpler and easier to deal with, since they no longer need to directly pass messages to each other. Components are more generic, since they no longer need to contain logic to deal with their communication with other components. This application-specific information is contained in the Mediator.
- The overall communications strategy becomes easier to maintain as well, since it is now the exclusive responsibility of the mediator.
- The Mediator is often application specific and difficult to redeploy. This is hardly surprising, since the Mediator is created to encapsulate application-specific behavior so the other classes in the system remain generic. Centralizing application-specific behavior in the Mediator improves maintainability. You can reuse all other classes for other applications; you only need to rewrite the Mediator class for the new application.

Testing and debugging complex Mediator implementations can be challenging, since you must accurately test a component that consists of the Mediator and its associated objects.

The Mediator's code can become hard to manage as the number and complexity of participants increases. A possible solution is to make the mediator a composite structure, based on a number of highly focused individual mediators. (For more information about the composite pattern, see "Composite" on page 157.) In this case, the Mediator consists of a central managing object associated with a number of individual service classes, each providing a specific piece of functionality.

Pattern Variants

The Mediator pattern has a number of behavioral variations:

- Unidirectional communication – Some implementations allow send-only and receive-only clients for the system.

- Threading – Like many behavioral patterns, the Mediator is a candidate for multithreading. If multithreaded, the Mediator object can maintain a message queue, and perform tasks like managing communications with message priority.
- Configurable roles – In this variant, clients define a role (which could possibly be changed as the system runs) that would define messaging requirements. Although complex to implement, defining participants in terms of roles can lead to a more generic Mediator, and one that can be redeployed to other systems.
- Client pull – A Mediator can store detailed messages and send only a general notification to clients. Clients can then request detailed information about an event if required.

Related Patterns

Related patterns include the following:

- Observer (page 94) – This pattern is often used to manage communication between the Client and Mediator when the communication is local. There is frequently only one Mediator per system, so they are sometimes coded as Singletons or as class-level resources by making their methods static.
- HOPP (page 189) – Mediator patterns that run across a network can use the Half-Object Plus Protocol (HOPP) pattern to provide communication support.

Example

Note: For a full working example of this code example, with additional supporting classes and/or a `RunPattern` class, see "Mediator" on page 395 of the "Full Code Examples" appendix.

In this example, a Mediator manages communication among the panels of a graphical user interface. The basic design of this GUI uses one panel to select a Contact from a list, another panel to allow editing, and a third panel to show the current state of the Contact. The Mediator interacts with each panel, calling the appropriate methods to keep each part of the GUI up to date.

The class `MediatorGui` creates the main window and the three panels for the application. It also creates a mediator and matches it with the three child panels.

Example 2.25 `MediatorGui.java`

```
1.     import java.awt.Container;
2.     import java.awt.event.WindowEvent;
```

```
3.    import java.awt.event.WindowAdapter;
4.    import javax.swing.BoxLayout;
5.    import javax.swing.JButton;
6.    import javax.swing.JFrame;
7.    import javax.swing.JPanel;
8.    public class MediatorGui{
9.        private ContactMediator mediator;
10.
11.       public void setContactMediator(ContactMediator newMediator){ mediator = newMe-
      diator; }
12.
13.       public void createGui(){
14.           JFrame mainFrame = new JFrame("Mediator example");
15.           Container content = mainFrame.getContentPane();
16.           content.setLayout(new BoxLayout(content, BoxLayout.Y_AXIS));
17.           ContactSelectorPanel select = new ContactSelectorPanel(mediator);
18.           ContactDisplayPanel display = new ContactDisplayPanel(mediator);
19.           ContactEditorPanel edit = new ContactEditorPanel(mediator);
20.           content.add(select);
21.           content.add(display);
22.           content.add(edit);
23.           mediator.setContactSelectorPanel(select);
24.           mediator.setContactDisplayPanel(display);
25.           mediator.setContactEditorPanel(edit);
26.           mainFrame.addWindowListener(new WindowCloseManager());
27.           mainFrame.pack();
28.           mainFrame.setVisible(true);
29.       }
30.       private class WindowCloseManager extends WindowAdapter{
31.           public void windowClosing(WindowEvent evt){
32.               System.exit(0);
33.           }
34.       }
35.   }
36.
37.
```

The simplest of the GUI panels is the `ContactDisplayPanel`. It has a method called `contactChanged` that updates its display region with the values of the `Contact` argument.

Example 2.26 ContactDisplayPanel.java

```
1.    import java.awt.BorderLayout;
2.    import javax.swing.JPanel;
3.    import javax.swing.JScrollPane;
4.    import javax.swing.JTextArea;
5.    public class ContactDisplayPanel extends JPanel{
6.        private ContactMediator mediator;
7.        private JTextArea displayRegion;
8.
9.        public ContactDisplayPanel(){
10.           createGui();
11.       }
```

```
12.        public ContactDisplayPanel(ContactMediator newMediator){
13.            setContactMediator(newMediator);
14.            createGui();
15.        }
16.        public void createGui(){
17.            setLayout(new BorderLayout());
18.            displayRegion = new JTextArea(10, 40);
19.            displayRegion.setEditable(false);
20.            add(new JScrollPane(displayRegion));
21.        }
22.        public void contactChanged(Contact contact){
23.            displayRegion.setText(
24.                "Contact\n\tName: " + contact.getFirstName() +
25.                " " + contact.getLastName() + "\n\tTitle: " +
26.                contact.getTitle() + "\n\tOrganization: " +
27.                contact.getOrganization());
28.        }
29.        public void setContactMediator(ContactMediator newMediator){
30.            mediator = newMediator;
31.        }
32.    }
```

`ContactSelectorPanel` allows the user to choose a `Contact` for display and edit in the `MediatorGui`.

Example 2.27 `ContactSelectorPanel.java`

```
1.     import java.awt.event.ActionEvent;
2.     import java.awt.event.ActionListener;
3.     import javax.swing.JComboBox;
4.     import javax.swing.JPanel;
5.
6.     public class ContactSelectorPanel extends JPanel implements ActionListener{
7.         private ContactMediator mediator;
8.         private JComboBox selector;
9.
10.        public ContactSelectorPanel(){
11.            createGui();
12.        }
13.        public ContactSelectorPanel(ContactMediator newMediator){
14.            setContactMediator(newMediator);
15.            createGui();
16.        }
17.
18.        public void createGui(){
19.            selector = new JComboBox(mediator.getAllContacts());
20.            selector.addActionListener(this);
21.            add(selector);
22.        }
23.
24.        public void actionPerformed(ActionEvent evt){
25.            mediator.selectContact((Contact)selector.getSelectedItem());
26.        }
```

```
27.        public void addContact(Contact contact){
28.            selector.addItem(contact);
29.            selector.setSelectedItem(contact);
30.        }
31.        public void setContactMediator(ContactMediator newMediator){
32.            mediator = newMediator;
33.        }
34.    }
```

The ContactEditorPanel provides an editing interface for the currently selected Contact. It has buttons that allow a user to add or update a Contact.

Example 2.28 ContactEditorPanel.java

```
1.     import java.awt.BorderLayout;
2.     import java.awt.GridLayout;
3.     import java.awt.event.ActionEvent;
4.     import java.awt.event.ActionListener;
5.     import javax.swing.JButton;
6.     import javax.swing.JLabel;
7.     import javax.swing.JPanel;
8.     import javax.swing.JTextField;
9.     public class ContactEditorPanel extends JPanel implements ActionListener{
10.        private ContactMediator mediator;
11.        private JTextField firstName, lastName, title, organization;
12.        private JButton create, update;
13.
14.        public ContactEditorPanel(){
15.            createGui();
16.        }
17.        public ContactEditorPanel(ContactMediator newMediator){
18.            setContactMediator(newMediator);
19.            createGui();
20.        }
21.        public void createGui(){
22.            setLayout(new BorderLayout());
23.
24.            JPanel editor = new JPanel();
25.            editor.setLayout(new GridLayout(4, 2));
26.            editor.add(new JLabel("First Name:"));
27.            firstName = new JTextField(20);
28.            editor.add(firstName);
29.            editor.add(new JLabel("Last Name:"));
30.            lastName = new JTextField(20);
31.            editor.add(lastName);
32.            editor.add(new JLabel("Title:"));
33.            title = new JTextField(20);
34.            editor.add(title);
35.            editor.add(new JLabel("Organization:"));
36.            organization = new JTextField(20);
37.            editor.add(organization);
38.            add(editor, BorderLayout.CENTER);
39.
```

```
40.            JPanel control = new JPanel();
41.            create = new JButton("Create Contact");
42.            update = new JButton("Update Contact");
43.            create.addActionListener(this);
44.            update.addActionListener(this);
45.            control.add(create);
46.            control.add(update);
47.            add(control, BorderLayout.SOUTH);
48.        }
49.        public void actionPerformed(ActionEvent evt){
50.            Object source = evt.getSource();
51.            if (source == create){
52.                createContact();
53.            }
54.            else if (source == update){
55.                updateContact();
56.            }
57.        }
58.
59.        public void createContact(){
60.            mediator.createContact(firstName.getText(), lastName.getText(),
61.                title.getText(), organization.getText());
62.        }
63.        public void updateContact(){
64.            mediator.updateContact(firstName.getText(), lastName.getText(),
65.                title.getText(), organization.getText());
66.        }
67.
68.        public void setContactFields(Contact contact){
69.            firstName.setText(contact.getFirstName());
70.            lastName.setText(contact.getLastName());
71.            title.setText(contact.getTitle());
72.            organization.setText(contact.getOrganization());
73.        }
74.        public void setContactMediator(ContactMediator newMediator){
75.            mediator = newMediator;
76.        }
77.    }
```

The `ContactMediator` interface defines set methods for each of the GUI components, and for the business methods `createContact`, `updateContact`, `selectContact` and `getAllContacts`.

Example 2.29 `ContactMediator.java`

```
1.    public interface ContactMediator{
2.        public void setContactDisplayPanel(ContactDisplayPanel displayPanel);
3.        public void setContactEditorPanel(ContactEditorPanel editorPanel);
4.        public void setContactSelectorPanel(ContactSelectorPanel selectorPanel);
5.        public void createContact(String firstName, String lastName, String title,
      String organization);
6.        public void updateContact(String firstName, String lastName, String title,
      String organization);
```

```
7.        public Contact [] getAllContacts();
8.        public void selectContact(Contact contact);
9.    }
```

ContactMediatorImpl is the implementer of ContactMediator. It maintains a collection of Contacts, and methods that notify the panels of changes within the GUI.

Example 2.30 ContactMediatorImpl.java

```
1.    import java.util.ArrayList;
2.    public class ContactMediatorImpl implements ContactMediator{
3.        private ContactDisplayPanel display;
4.        private ContactEditorPanel editor;
5.        private ContactSelectorPanel selector;
6.        private ArrayList contacts = new ArrayList();
7.        private int contactIndex;
8.
9.        public void setContactDisplayPanel(ContactDisplayPanel displayPanel){
10.           display = displayPanel;
11.       }
12.       public void setContactEditorPanel(ContactEditorPanel editorPanel){
13.           editor = editorPanel;
14.       }
15.       public void setContactSelectorPanel(ContactSelectorPanel selectorPanel){
16.           selector = selectorPanel;
17.       }
18.
19.       public void createContact(String firstName, String lastName, String title,
      String organization){
20.           Contact newContact = new ContactImpl(firstName, lastName, title, organiza-
      tion);
21.           addContact(newContact);
22.           selector.addContact(newContact);
23.           display.contactChanged(newContact);
24.       }
25.       public void updateContact(String firstName, String lastName, String title,
      String organization){
26.           Contact updateContact = (Contact)contacts.get(contactIndex);
27.           if (updateContact != null){
28.               updateContact.setFirstName(firstName);
29.               updateContact.setLastName(lastName);
30.               updateContact.setTitle(title);
31.               updateContact.setOrganization(organization);
32.               display.contactChanged(updateContact);
33.           }
34.       }
35.       public void selectContact(Contact contact){
36.           if (contacts.contains(contact)){
37.               contactIndex = contacts.indexOf(contact);
38.               display.contactChanged(contact);
39.               editor.setContactFields(contact);
40.           }
```

```
41.         }
42.         public Contact [] getAllContacts(){
43.             return (Contact [])contacts.toArray(new Contact[1]);
44.         }
45.         public void addContact(Contact contact){
46.             if (!contacts.contains(contact)){
47.                 contacts.add(contact);
48.             }
49.         }
50.     }
```

The `ContactMediatorImpl` interacts with each of the panels differently. For the `ContactDisplayPanel`, the mediator calls its `contactChanged` method for the create, update and select operations. For the `ContactSelectorPanel`, the mediator provides the list of `Contacts` with the `getAllContacts` method, receives select notifications, and adds a new `Contact` object to the panel when one is created. The mediator receives create and update method calls from the `ContactEditorPanel`, and notifies the panel of select actions from the `ContactSelectorPanel`.

Memento

Also known as Token, Snapshot

Pattern Properties

Type: Behavioral
Level: Object

Purpose

To preserve a "snapshot" of an object's state, so that the object can return to its original state without having to reveal its content to the rest of the world.

Introduction

Every application has objects that need to preserve information beyond their lifespan. Often, this relates to shared data, but what if the private data of an object needs to be preserved? Sending the data to another object is a bad idea, since it goes against the rules of encapsulation. If you sent data to other objects, they would be able to read or, even worse, modify the data.

It's like going to a national park where they preserve the moose. The object whose data is being saved is that moose. You're not allowed to take a moose home with you, but postcards and moose t-shirts are available at the national park gift shop.

A better approach is to use an object to contain the data to be stored. You would send this object that could be used to recreate the original, instead of sending raw data. Other objects would not be able to read or modify the data, since the data to be stored would be encapsulated.

This is the Memento pattern, where an object is used as a "souvenir" that only has value to the original holder and helps it remember a previous state.

Applicability

Use Memento when *all* of the following apply:

- A snapshot of the state of an object should be taken.
- That snapshot is used to recreate the original state.
- A direct interface to the object to read its internal state would violate its encapsulation, because this would also reveal the internal workings.

Description

If you have implemented encapsulation correctly, all objects have private states, and will allow access to the attributes only through methods. But it might be necessary to pass the current state to another object: for instance, when the object's state must be restorable at a later point in time (undo).

One way to do this is by handing the state directly to the interested party. This has the potential for some huge drawbacks:

- It exposes the internal structure of your object.
- It enables the other object to arbitrarily change the state of your object.

The solution is to wrap the state that you wish to preserve in an object, using Memento. A Memento is an object that contains the current internal state of the Originator object. Only the Originator can store and retrieve information from the Memento. To the outside world the Memento is just an arbitrary object.

The Memento pattern is like a credit card. Although you don't know what is actually really on the card, you know what it provides (lots of buying power to buy lots of toys). In the Memento's case, it allows you to preserve and restore the state.

Implementation

The Memento class diagram is shown in Figure 2.9.

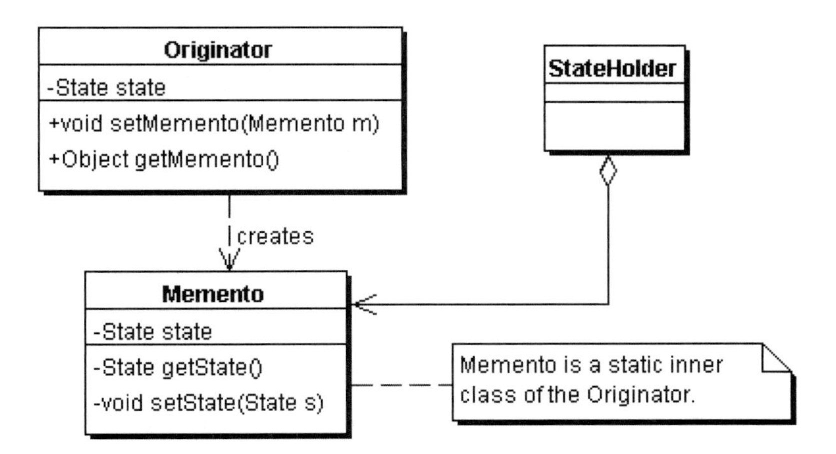

Figure 2.9 *Memento class diagram*

Implementing the Memento requires:

- `Originator` – Creates `Memento` and uses this `Memento` to later restore its state.

- `Memento` – Static inner class of the `Originator` and holder of the `Originator's` state. The `Originator` determines how much is stored in the `Memento` and only the `Originator` should be able to read the `Memento`.

  State within the `Memento` should be inaccessible to everybody except the `Originator`.

- `StateHolder` – The object that wishes to preserve the state. It never needs to know what is within a `Memento`; it only needs to know that the object it receives enables it to restore the state of the `Originator`.

Because the `Memento` should be accessible only to the `Originator`, it is best to make the `Memento` a public inner class in the `Originator`. All the methods are declared private so they are only available to the `Memento` and its enclosing class, thus providing the appropriate encapsulation.

Instances of an inner class are always associated with an instance of the outer class. This is necessary because an inner class always has access to instance variables of the outer class. That causes a problem in this situation; the `Memento` should be independent of a specific instance of an `Originator`. Therefore the `Memento` class needs to be a static inner class.

Memento objects can become very large, especially if the `Originator` keeps all its state in the `Memento` and `Mementos` are created frequently. To compensate for this, you can change `Mementos` so that they record only changes in state since the previous creation of a `Memento`. The state holder has to keep track of the order of the `Mementos`. Job promotions are an example of when you might apply this. After every promotion your employee benefits and salary are changed based on the previous salary, and you may get a new boss, new department or a bigger car. Now every `Memento` of your employee benefits only needs to record the increase or decrease in conditions/salaries since the last `Memento`.

Benefits and Drawbacks

Using the Memento pattern has the following consequences.

- Preserves encapsulation – Even when the state of the `Originator` needs to be stored outside of the `Originator` object in a client, the state is inaccessible to the client. It has a reference only to the `Memento` object, and no way to access the information that's inside. It also makes the client simpler because it no longer needs to know anything about the internal workings of the `Originator`, except how to get a `Memento` and how to use it.

- Simpler `Originator` – Suppose the `Originator` has to keep track of all the different states. The `Originator` would soon become very bloated and very difficult to handle. It is much easier to give that responsibility to the requesting party, the client. The Originator now only needs to be able to create and use Mementos instead of keeping track of multiple states.

- Expensive Mementos – Mementos are very expensive to create if every piece of the Originator's state has to be stored in the Memento. This increases dramatically as the Originator increases in size. This is where the incremental changes are important. If the Originator is large, Memento might not be a suitable pattern.
- Expensive Memento storage – The state holder is responsible for the lifecycle management after it receives the Memento from the Originator. However, it does not know how large the Memento actually is. If Mementos are not kept as small as possible, the StateHolder will pay the price.

Pattern Variants

Pattern variants include the following:

- If the Memento must be a standalone class, and not an inner class, you must define two interfaces: WideMemento and NarrowMemento. The wide interface is for the Originator of the Memento so that it can access the Memento to get its state. The state in the Memento is best set at construction time. Because you're defining an interface, you'll need to add a FactoryMethod.

  The narrow interface is intended for the StateHolder and other clients to use. If that interface doesn't have any methods, the NarrowMemento becomes obsolete and the interested parties only refer to the Memento as an Object.
- To be able to extend the Originator but not need to change the Memento code, the methods can have package access instead of being private. This allows subclasses of the Originator to use the same Memento class.

Related Patterns

Related patterns include the following:

- Command (page 51) – Command can use Mementos to keep track of state for undoable actions.
- State (page 104) – Most States use Memento.

Example

Note: For a full working example of this code example, with additional supporting classes and/or a RunPattern class, see “Memento” on page 403 of the “Full Code Examples” appendix.

Almost all parts of the Personal Information Manager keep some kind of state. These states can be saved by applying the Memento pattern, as this example with an address book will demonstrate. The AddressBook class represents a collection of addresses, a natural candidate for keeping a record of state.

Example 2.31 AddressBook.java

```
1.   import java.util.ArrayList;
2.   public class AddressBook{
3.       private ArrayList contacts = new ArrayList();
4.
5.       public Object getMemento(){
6.           return new AddressBookMemento(contacts);
7.       }
8.       public void setMemento(Object object){
9.           if (object instanceof AddressBookMemento){
10.              AddressBookMemento memento = (AddressBookMemento)object;
11.              contacts = memento.state;
12.          }
13.      }
14.
15.      private class AddressBookMemento{
16.          private ArrayList state;
17.
18.          private AddressBookMemento(ArrayList contacts){
19.              this.state = contacts;
20.          }
21.      }
22.
23.      public AddressBook(){ }
24.      public AddressBook(ArrayList newContacts){
25.          contacts = newContacts;
26.      }
27.
28.      public void addContact(Contact contact){
29.          if (!contacts.contains(contact)){
30.              contacts.add(contact);
31.          }
32.      }
33.      public void removeContact(Contact contact){
34.          contacts.remove(contact);
35.      }
36.      public void removeAllContacts(){
37.          contacts = new ArrayList();
38.      }
39.      public ArrayList getContacts(){
40.          return contacts;
```

```
41.         }
42.         public String toString(){
43.             return contacts.toString();
44.         }
45.     }
```

The inner class of AddressBook, AddressBookMemento, is used to save the state of an AddressBook, which in this case is represented by the internal ArrayList of Address objects. The memento object can be accessed by using the AddressBook methods getMemento and setMemento. Note that Address-BookMemento is a private inner class and that it has only a private constructor. This ensures that, even if the memento object is saved somewhere outside of an AddressBook object, no other object will be able to use the object or modify its state. This is consistent with the role of the Memento pattern: producing an object to maintain a snapshot of state that cannot be modified by other objects in a system.

Observer

Also known as Publisher-Subcriber

Pattern Properties

Type: Behavioral
Level: Component

Purpose

To provide a way for a component to flexibly broadcast messages to interested receivers.

Introduction

What if an object changed in the forest and nobody noticed?

Suppose you want to let Personal Information Manager users share information. This would be useful, for instance, for coordinating a regular club meeting (Organized Organization for Zebra Encoders). You could use an `Appointment` object to provide club members with current information about the meeting location, date and time. However, how do you ensure that, if the meeting time changes, a change to the appointment information is sent to everyone who's interested? (What if you held a meeting and nobody came?)

You could maintain a list of all club members and send every member the updated information. This would be appropriate if attending each meeting were required, but this isn't the case, and it seems wasteful to update everyone when some members might not choose to attend. From a technical viewpoint, such a solution could also be inefficient—for a large club, this could involve a great deal of communication overhead.

It's better to allow individual users to decide whether to receive information for a particular meeting. An `Appointment` object is stored on a central server. If club members want to receive updates for the meeting, they register with the server. Anytime the `Appointment` is updated, the server sends the new information to the currently registered attendees.

This solution, known as the Observer pattern because the central object is being observed by the interested objects, provides great flexibility in sending update information. By making listeners responsible for registering with the object, you reduce the communication overhead to only those participants who actually want to receive the updated information.

Applicability

The Observer is generally appropriate when a system has:

- At least one message sender.
- One or more message receivers that might vary within an application or among applications.

This pattern is frequently implemented in situations where the message sender does not need or want to know how receivers act upon the information it provides; it is simply concerned with broadcasting information.

Description

Some message senders, also known as *message producers*, follow a simple point-to-point communication model, creating messages that are intended for single, specific *message receivers*, or consumers. In these cases, event handling is fairly straightforward. For other kinds of message producers, however, the behavior is not so clear cut. An action can trigger a variable series of reactions, and might involve the producer and one or more consumers.

Consider a customer address. In a business model, a change of address can trigger a wide-ranging set of responses within a system. Customer information might have to be changed, customer subscriptions would have to be updated, orders might have to be modified. Potentially, even information such as shipping cost and sales tax might be affected. The Observable pattern is appropriate for this kind of problem.

In the Observer pattern, the message producers (observable components) send messages that generate events. One or more message receivers (observers) receive and act upon the events. The observable component's responsibility is to transmit events to any interested observers; that is, any observers that are registered with the observable component. A listener interface allows the observable component to indicate what events have occurred and possibly to provide details to observers.

You can think of the Observer pattern as a server-push solution. The server (in this case, the observable object or event producer) contacts the interested listeners when there is a new event of some kind.

The Observer pattern is useful for a variety of applications. Notifications are only broadcast to elements who identify themselves as interested receivers. This allows the receivers to respond in whatever way is meaningful to them. This is well-suited for any model where changes in one component might result in changes to others, and where the behavior might be configurable during runtime.

In business models, Observer can be helpful when a model exhibits complex update, delete, or refresh behavior. The flexible nature of the pattern makes it possible for a change in a business element to be broadcast to some or all other elements in the model.

Activity in the Observer pattern is comparable to what happens during dating. A single person (the observable) has one or more friends (observers) who have said they are interested in knowing how the dates go, and so they become registered listeners. As new events (dates of varying quality and success) take place in the single's life, he or she broadcasts messages to friends, providing them with details about dating experiences. The friends respond to the messages, with suggestions, congratulations, sympathy, or shock as appropriate.

Implementation

The Observable class diagram is shown in Figure 2.10.

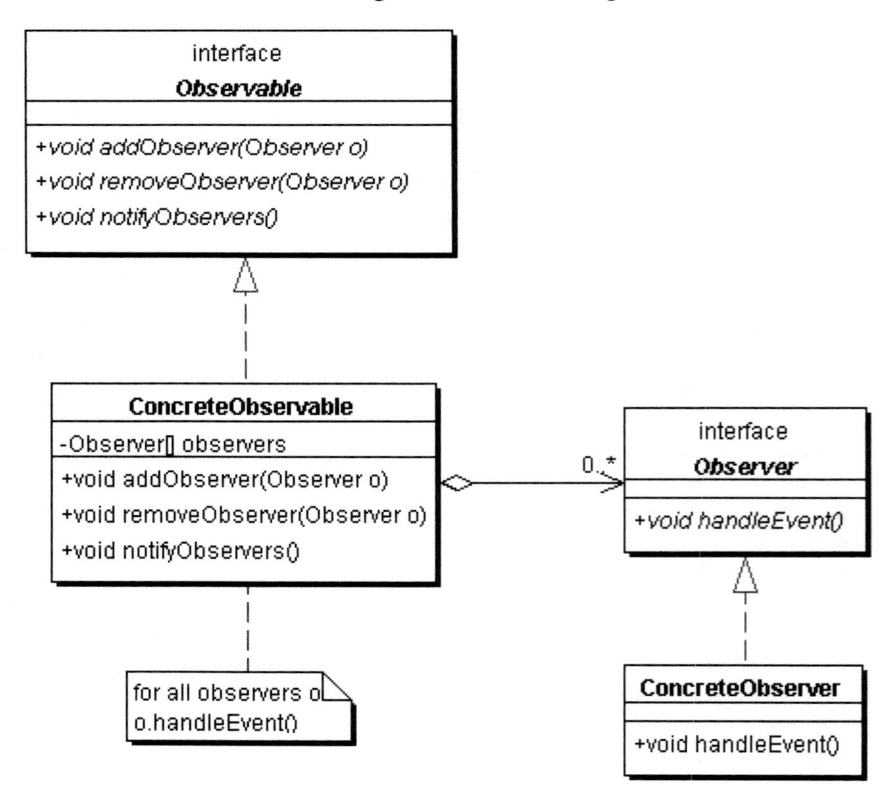

Figure 2.10 *Observable class diagram*

The Observable pattern includes the following:

- `Observable` – The interface that defines how the observers/clients can interact with an `Observable`. These methods include adding and removing observers, and one or more notification methods to send information through the `Observable` to its clients.
- `ConcreteObservable` – A class that provides implementations for each of the methods in the Observable interface. It needs to maintain a collection of `Observers`.

  The notification methods copy (or clone) the `Observer` list and iterate through the list, and call the specific listener methods on each `Observer`.
- `Observer` – The interface the `Observer` uses to communicate with the clients.
- `ConcreteObserver` – Implements the `Observable` interface and determines in each implemented method how to respond to the message received from the `Observable`.

Normally the application framework registers the specific observers to the `Observable`.

Benefits and Drawbacks

The Observer pattern's flexibility carries with it the added benefit that the observable object can be relatively simple. There is not a substantial amount of coding overhead. In addition, the pattern is useful for:

- Testing – You can code an echo observer that can display the observable's behavior.
- Incremental development – It's very easy to add additional observers as you code them.

The principal challenge for this pattern comes from implementation of the messaging model: you can use a specific or generic message broadcast strategy. Each approach has potential disadvantages.

- Generic messaging – As messaging becomes more generic, it can become more difficult to determine what is going on for an observable component. Generic messaging can result in unnecessary message traffic; some events could be broadcast to observers that would otherwise not care about them. Generic messaging also can result in additional coding overhead for observers, because they have to decode messages.
- Specific messaging – More-specific messages place greater coding requirements on the observable component, since they must produce a series of notifications under specific conditions. They might also make observers more complex, because observers must handle a variety of message types.

Pattern Variants

The Observer pattern has several variants that can be used in defining the relationship between observable and observer:

- Single observer versus multiple observers – Depending on the role of the observable component, it might support only a single observer.
- Multithreaded observable components – If an observable object is multithreaded, it can provide support for a message queue, and can provide services such as message priority and override behavior.
- Client pull – Although the pattern is oriented toward server push, you can modify it to support a limited form of client pull. In this variant, the observable typically provides the observers with notification that an event has taken place. If observers require more detail, they contact the observable, calling a method that requests additional information about the event.

Related Patterns

Related patterns include Proxy (page 197). For distributed communication, the Remote Proxy pattern is often used to manage communication between the `Observer` and `Observable`.

Example

Note: For a full working example of this code example, with additional supporting classes and/or a `RunPattern` class, see "Observer" on page 408 of the "Full Code Examples" appendix.

In the Observer example, an observer sends updates about the state of a `Task` to all registered listeners in a GUI.

It's important to recognize that any Java GUI code normally uses the Observer pattern for event handling. When you write a class that implements a listener interface like `ActionListener`, you are creating an observer. Registering that listener with a component through the method `addActionListener` associates the observer with an observable element, the Java GUI component.

In this example, the observable element is represented by the `Task` being modified in the GUI. The class `TaskChangeObservable` keeps track of the listeners for changes to the `Task` through the methods `addTaskChangeObserver` and `removeTaskChangeObserver`.

Example 2.32 `TaskChangeObservable.java`

```
1.     import java.util.ArrayList;
2.     import java.util.Iterator;
3.     public class TaskChangeObservable{
4.         private ArrayList observers = new ArrayList();
5.
6.         public void addTaskChangeObserver(TaskChangeObserver observer){
7.             if (!observers.contains(observer)){
8.                 observers.add(observer);
9.             }
10.        }
11.        public void removeTaskChangeObserver(TaskChangeObserver observer){
12.            observers.remove(observer);
13.        }
14.
15.        public void selectTask(Task task){
16.            Iterator elements = observers.iterator();
17.            while (elements.hasNext()){
18.                ((TaskChangeObserver)elements.next()).taskSelected(task);
19.            }
20.        }
21.        public void addTask(Task task){
22.            Iterator elements = observers.iterator();
23.            while (elements.hasNext()){
24.                ((TaskChangeObserver)elements.next()).taskAdded(task);
25.            }
26.        }
27.        public void updateTask(Task task){
28.            Iterator elements = observers.iterator();
29.            while (elements.hasNext()){
30.                ((TaskChangeObserver)elements.next()).taskChanged(task);
31.            }
32.        }
33.    }
```

`TaskChangeObservable` has the business methods `selectTask`, `updateTask`, and `addTask`. These methods send notifications of any changes to a `Task`.

Every observer must implement the `TaskChangeObserver` interface, allowing the `TaskChangeObservable` to call the appropriate method on each observer. If a client were to call the method `addTask` on the `TaskChangeObservable`, for instance, the observable object would iterate through its observers and call the `taskAdded` method on each.

Example 2.33 `TaskChangeObserver.java`

```
1.     public interface TaskChangeObserver{
2.         public void taskAdded(Task task);
3.         public void taskChanged(Task task);
4.         public void taskSelected(Task task);
5.     }
```

The class `ObserverGui` provides a GUI in this demonstration, and creates a `TaskChangeObservable` object. In addition, it creates three panels that implement the `TaskChangeObserver` interface, and matches them with the `TaskChangeObservable` object. By doing this, the `TaskChangeObservable` is able to effectively send updates among the three panels of the GUI.

Example 2.34 `ObserverGui.java`

```
1.   import java.awt.Container;
2.   import java.awt.event.WindowAdapter;
3.   import java.awt.event.WindowEvent;
4.   import javax.swing.BoxLayout;
5.   import javax.swing.JFrame;
6.   public class ObserverGui{
7.       public void createGui(){
8.           JFrame mainFrame = new JFrame("Observer Pattern Example");
9.           Container content = mainFrame.getContentPane();
10.          content.setLayout(new BoxLayout(content, BoxLayout.Y_AXIS));
11.          TaskChangeObservable observable = new TaskChangeObservable();
12.          TaskSelectorPanel select = new TaskSelectorPanel(observable);
13.          TaskHistoryPanel history = new TaskHistoryPanel();
14.          TaskEditorPanel edit = new TaskEditorPanel(observable);
15.          observable.addTaskChangeObserver(select);
16.          observable.addTaskChangeObserver(history);
17.          observable.addTaskChangeObserver(edit);
18.          observable.addTask(new Task());
19.          content.add(select);
20.          content.add(history);
21.          content.add(edit);
22.          mainFrame.addWindowListener(new WindowCloseManager());
23.          mainFrame.pack();
24.          mainFrame.setVisible(true);
25.      }
26.
27.      private class WindowCloseManager extends WindowAdapter{
28.          public void windowClosing(WindowEvent evt){
29.              System.exit(0);
30.          }
31.      }
32.  }
```

Example 2.35 `TaskEditorPanel.java`

```
1.   import java.awt.BorderLayout;
2.   import javax.swing.JPanel;
3.   import javax.swing.JLabel;
4.   import javax.swing.JTextField;
5.   import javax.swing.JButton;
6.   import java.awt.event.ActionEvent;
7.   import java.awt.event.ActionListener;
8.   import java.awt.GridLayout;
```

```
9.     public class TaskEditorPanel extends JPanel implements ActionListener,
         TaskChangeObserver{
10.        private JPanel controlPanel, editPanel;
11.        private JButton add, update, exit;
12.        private JTextField taskName, taskNotes, taskTime;
13.        private TaskChangeObservable notifier;
14.        private Task editTask;
15.
16.        public TaskEditorPanel(TaskChangeObservable newNotifier){
17.            notifier = newNotifier;
18.            createGui();
19.        }
20.        public void createGui(){
21.            setLayout(new BorderLayout());
22.            editPanel = new JPanel();
23.            editPanel.setLayout(new GridLayout(3, 2));
24.            taskName = new JTextField(20);
25.            taskNotes = new JTextField(20);
26.            taskTime = new JTextField(20);
27.            editPanel.add(new JLabel("Task Name"));
28.            editPanel.add(taskName);
29.            editPanel.add(new JLabel("Task Notes"));
30.            editPanel.add(taskNotes);
31.            editPanel.add(new JLabel("Time Required"));
32.            editPanel.add(taskTime);
33.
34.            controlPanel = new JPanel();
35.            add = new JButton("Add Task");
36.            update = new JButton("Update Task");
37.            exit = new JButton("Exit");
38.            controlPanel.add(add);
39.            controlPanel.add(update);
40.            controlPanel.add(exit);
41.            add.addActionListener(this);
42.            update.addActionListener(this);
43.            exit.addActionListener(this);
44.            add(controlPanel, BorderLayout.SOUTH);
45.            add(editPanel, BorderLayout.CENTER);
46.        }
47.        public void setTaskChangeObservable(TaskChangeObservable newNotifier){
48.            notifier = newNotifier;
49.        }
50.        public void actionPerformed(ActionEvent event){
51.            Object source = event.getSource();
52.            if (source == add){
53.                double timeRequired = 0.0;
54.                try{
55.                    timeRequired = Double.parseDouble(taskTime.getText());
56.                }
57.                catch (NumberFormatException exc){}
58.                notifier.addTask(new Task(taskName.getText(), taskNotes.getText(), tim-
       eRequired));
59.            }
60.            else if (source == update){
```

```
61.                 editTask.setName(taskName.getText());
62.                 editTask.setNotes(taskNotes.getText());
63.                 try{
64.                     editTask.setTimeRequired(Double.parseDouble(taskTime.getText()));
65.                 }
66.                 catch (NumberFormatException exc){}
67.                 notifier.updateTask(editTask);
68.             }
69.             else if (source == exit){
70.                 System.exit(0);
71.             }
72.
73.         }
74.         public void taskAdded(Task task){ }
75.         public void taskChanged(Task task){ }
76.         public void taskSelected(Task task){
77.             editTask = task;
78.             taskName.setText(task.getName());
79.             taskNotes.setText(task.getNotes());
80.             taskTime.setText("" + task.getTimeRequired());
81.         }
82.     }
```

Example 2.36 `TaskHistoryPanel.java`

```
1.  import java.awt.BorderLayout;
2.  import javax.swing.JPanel;
3.  import javax.swing.JScrollPane;
4.  import javax.swing.JTextArea;
5.  public class TaskHistoryPanel extends JPanel implements TaskChangeObserver{
6.      private JTextArea displayRegion;
7.
8.      public TaskHistoryPanel(){
9.          createGui();
10.     }
11.     public void createGui(){
12.         setLayout(new BorderLayout());
13.         displayRegion = new JTextArea(10, 40);
14.         displayRegion.setEditable(false);
15.         add(new JScrollPane(displayRegion));
16.     }
17.     public void taskAdded(Task task){
18.         displayRegion.append("Created task " + task + "\n");
19.     }
20.     public void taskChanged(Task task){
21.         displayRegion.append("Updated task " + task + "\n");
22.     }
23.     public void taskSelected(Task task){
24.         displayRegion.append("Selected task " + task + "\n");
25.     }
26. }
```

Example 2.37 `TaskSelectorPanel.java`

```
1.    import java.awt.event.ActionEvent;
2.    import java.awt.event.ActionListener;
3.    import javax.swing.JPanel;
4.    import javax.swing.JComboBox;
5.    public class TaskSelectorPanel extends JPanel implements ActionListener,
        TaskChangeObserver{
6.        private JComboBox selector = new JComboBox();
7.        private TaskChangeObservable notifier;
8.        public TaskSelectorPanel(TaskChangeObservable newNotifier){
9.            notifier = newNotifier;
10.           createGui();
11.       }
12.       public void createGui(){
13.           selector = new JComboBox();
14.           selector.addActionListener(this);
15.           add(selector);
16.       }
17.       public void actionPerformed(ActionEvent evt){
18.           notifier.selectTask((Task)selector.getSelectedItem());
19.       }
20.       public void setTaskChangeObservable(TaskChangeObservable newNotifier){
21.           notifier = newNotifier;
22.       }
23.
24.       public void taskAdded(Task task){
25.           selector.addItem(task);
26.       }
27.       public void taskChanged(Task task){ }
28.       public void taskSelected(Task task){ }
29.   }
```

A feature of the Observer pattern is that the `Observable` uses a standard interface for its `Observers`—in this case, `TaskChangeObserver`. This means that the Observer pattern is more generic than the Mediator pattern, but also that the observers may receive some unwanted message traffic. For instance, the `TaskEditorPanel` takes no action when its `taskAdded` and `taskChanged` methods are called.

State

Also known as Objects for States

Pattern Properties

Type: Behavioral
Level: Object

Purpose

To easily change an object's behavior at runtime.

Introduction

An application often behaves differently depending on the values of its internal variables. For instance, when you're working on a text file, you need to periodically save your work. Most current text editors allow you to save a document only when something has changed in the text. As soon as you save the content the text is considered to be "clean;" the file content is the same as the content currently on display. At this point the Save option is not available as it serves no purpose.

Implementing this decision-making in the individual methods makes the code hard to maintain and read. The result is that these methods contain long if/else statements. A common tactic is to store the state of an object in a single variable using constants for a value. With this approach the methods normally contain large switch/case statements that are very similar in each method.

Objects are state and behavior; state is kept in its attributes and the behavior is defined in methods. The State pattern allows you to change the behavior of an object dynamically. This dynamic behavior is achieved by delegating all method calls that rely on certain values to a State object. Such a State object is state and behavior as well, so that when you change State objects, you also receive a different behavior. The methods in the specific State classes no longer have to use if/else or switch statements; the State object defines the behavior for one state.

Applicability

Use the State pattern when:

- The object's behavior depends on its state and the state changes frequently.

- Methods have large conditional statements that depend on the state of the object.

Description

Objects that have different behavior based on their current state might be difficult to implement without the State pattern. As mentioned before, implementation without using the State pattern often results in using constants as a way of keeping track of the current state, and in lengthy switch statements within methods. Most of those methods in the same class have a similar structure (determining the current state).

Consider a door. What are the normal operations you can do with a simple door? You can open and close a door, leaving the door in one of its two states: Closed or Open. Calling the close method on a Closed door accomplishes nothing, but calling the close method on an Open door changes the state of the door to Closed.

The State transition diagram is shown in Figure 2.11.

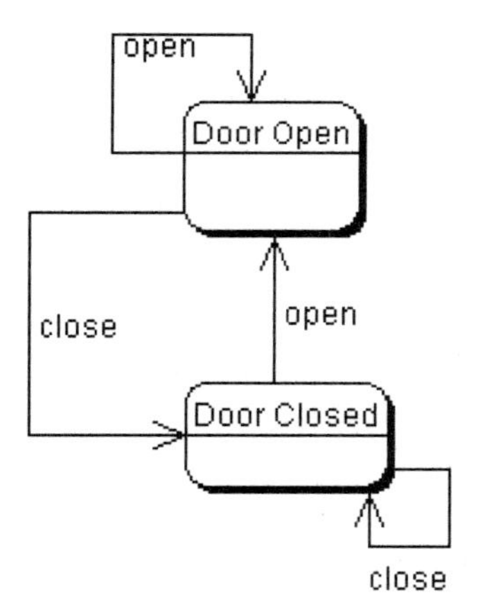

Figure 2.11 *State transition diagram for a door*

The current state of the door makes it behave differently in response to the same command.

Implementation

The class diagram for the State pattern is shown in Figure 2.12.

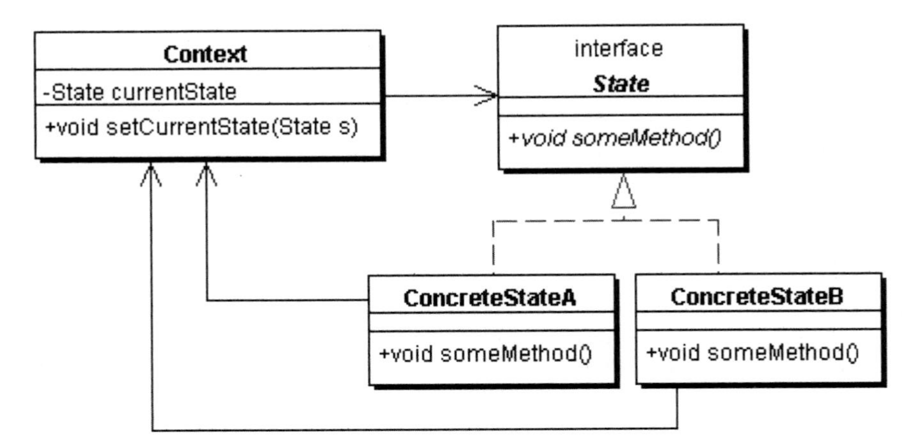

Figure 2.12 *State class diagram*

Implementing the State pattern requires:

- `Context` – Keeps a reference to the current state, and is the interface for other clients to use. It delegates all state-specific method calls to the current `State` object.
- `State` – Defines all the methods that depend on the state of the object.
- `ConcreteState` – Implements the `State` interface, and implements specific behavior for one state.

The `Context` or the `ConcreteState` can determine the transition between states. This is not specified by the State pattern. When the number of states is fixed, the most appropriate place to put the transition logic is in the `Context`.

However, you gain more flexibility by placing the transition logic in the `State` subclasses. In that case, each `State` determines the transition—which is the next State, under what circumstances the transition occurs, and when it occurs. This makes it much easier to change part of the `State` transitions and add new `States` to the system. The drawback is that each class that implements `State` is dependent on other classes—each `State` implementation must know at least one other `State`. If the `State` implementations determine the transition, the `Context` must provide a way for the `State` to set the new current `State` in the `Context`.

You can create state objects two using two methods: lazy instantiation or up-front creation.

- Lazy instantiation creates the `State` objects at the time they are needed. This is useful only if the state rarely changes. It is required if the different states are unknown at the start of the application. Lazy instantiation prevents large, costly states from being created if they will never be used.
- Up-front creation is the most common choice. All the state objects are created at startup. You reuse a state object instead of destroying and creating one each time, meaning that instantiation costs are paid only once. This makes sense if the state transitions are frequent—if a state is likely to be needed again soon.

Benefits and Drawbacks

Benefits and drawbacks include the following:

- State partitions behavior based on state – This gives you a much clearer view of the behavior. When the object is in a specific state, look at the corresponding `State` subclass. All the possible behavior from that state is included there.
- State offers structure and makes its intent clearer – The commonly used alternative to the State pattern is to use constants, and to use a switch statement to determine the appropriate actions. This is a poor solution because it creates duplication. A number of methods use almost exactly the same switch statement structure. If you want to add a new state in such a system you have to change all the methods in the `Context` class by adding a new element to each switch statement. This is both tedious and error-prone. By contrast, the same change in a system that uses the State pattern is implemented simply by creating one new state implementation.
- State transitions are explicit – When using constants for state, it is easy to confuse a state change with a variable assignment because they are syntactically the same. `States` are now compartmentalized in objects, making it much easier to recognize a state change.
- State can be shared – If `State` subclasses contain only behavior and no instance variables, they have effectively become Flyweights. (See "Flyweight" on page 183.) Any state they need can be passed to them by the `Context`. This reduces the number of objects in the system.
- The State pattern uses a large number of classes – The increased number of classes might be considered a disadvantage. The State pattern creates at least one class for every possible state. But when you consider the

alternative (long switch statements in methods), it's clear that the large number of classes is an advantage, because they present a much clearer view.

Pattern Variants

One of the challenges of the State pattern is determining who governs the state transitions. The choice between the `Context` and the `State` subclasses was discussed previously. A third option is to look up the transitions in a table structure, with a table for each state, which maps every possible input to a succeeding state [Car92]. This converts the transition code into a table lookup operation.

The benefit is the regularity. To change the transition criteria, only the data in the table has to be changed instead of the actual code. But the disadvantages are numerous:

- Table lookups are often less efficient than a method call.
- Putting the transition logic in a table makes the logic harder to understand quickly.

The main difference is that the State pattern is focused on modeling the behavior based on the state, whereas the table approach focuses on the transitions between the different states.

A combination of these two approaches combines the dynamics of the table-driven model with the State pattern. Store the transitions in a `HashMap`, but instead of having a table for each state, create a `HashMap` for every method in the `State` interface. That's because the next state is most likely different for each method.

In the `HashMap`, use the old state as the key and the new state as the value. Adding a new `State` is very easy; add the class and have the class change the appropriate `HashMaps`. This variant is also demonstrated in the *Example* section for this pattern.

Related Patterns

Related patterns include the following:

- Flyweight (page 183) – States can be shared using the Flyweight pattern.
- Singleton (page 34) – Most States are Singletons, especially when they are Flyweights.

Example

Note: For a full working example of this code example, with additional supporting classes and/or a `RunPattern` class, see "State" on page 414 of the "Full Code Examples" appendix.

Inner classes are most appropriate for States. They are very closely coupled with their enclosing class and have direct access to its attributes. The following example shows how this works in practice.

A standard feature of applications is that they only save files when necessary: when changes have been made. When changes have been made but a file has not been saved, its state is referred to as *dirty*. The content might be different from the persistent, saved version. When the file has been saved and no further changes have been made, the content is considered *clean*. For a clean state, the content and the file will be identical if no one else edits the file.

This example shows the State pattern being used to update `Appointments` for the PIM, saving them to a file as necessary. The State transition diagram for a file is shown in Figure 2.13.

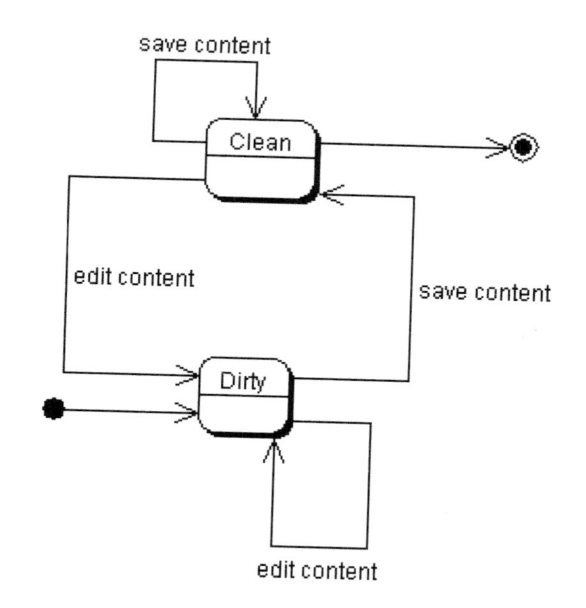

Figure 2.13 *State transition diagram for a file*

Two states (`CleanState` and `DirtyState`) implement the `State` interface. The states are responsible for determining the next state, which in this case is reasonably easy, as there are only two.

The `State` interface defines two methods, `save` and `edit`. These methods are called by the `CalendarEditor` when appropriate.

Example 2.38 `State.java`

```
1.    public interface State{
2.        public void save();
3.        public void edit();
4.    }
```

The `CalendarEditor` class manages a collection of `Appointment` objects.

Example 2.39 `CalendarEditor.java`

```
1.    import java.io.File;
2.    import java.util.ArrayList;
3.    public class CalendarEditor{
4.        private State currentState;
5.        private File appointmentFile;
6.        private ArrayList appointments = new ArrayList();
7.        private static final String DEFAULT_APPOINTMENT_FILE = "appointments.ser";
8.
9.        public CalendarEditor(){
10.           this(DEFAULT_APPOINTMENT_FILE);
11.       }
12.       public CalendarEditor(String appointmentFileName){
13.           appointmentFile = new File(appointmentFileName);
14.           try{
15.               appointments = (ArrayList)FileLoader.loadData(appointmentFile);
16.           }
17.           catch (ClassCastException exc){
18.             System.err.println("Unable to load information. The file does not con-
      tain a list of appointments.");
19.           }
20.           currentState = new CleanState();
21.       }
22.
23.       public void save(){
24.           currentState.save();
25.       }
26.
27.       public void edit(){
28.           currentState.edit();
29.       }
30.
31.       private class DirtyState implements State{
32.           private State nextState;
33.
34.           public DirtyState(State nextState){
35.               this.nextState = nextState;
36.           }
37.
38.           public void save(){
39.               FileLoader.storeData(appointmentFile, appointments);
40.               currentState = nextState;
41.           }
```

```
42.            public void edit(){ }
43.        }
44.
45.        private class CleanState implements State{
46.            private State nextState = new DirtyState(this);
47.
48.            public void save(){ }
49.            public void edit(){ currentState = nextState; }
50.        }
51.
52.        public ArrayList getAppointments(){
53.            return appointments;
54.        }
55.
56.        public void addAppointment(Appointment appointment){
57.            if (!appointments.contains(appointment)){
58.                appointments.add(appointment);
59.            }
60.        }
61.        public void removeAppointment(Appointment appointment){
62.            appointments.remove(appointment);
63.        }
64.    }
```

The class `StateGui` provides an editing interface for the `CalendarEditor`'s appointments. Notice that the GUI has a reference to the `CalendarEditor`, and that it delegates edit or save actions to the editor. This allows the editor to perform the required actions and to update its state as appropriate.

Example 2.40 `StateGui.java`

```
1.    import java.awt.Container;
2.    import java.awt.BorderLayout;
3.    import java.awt.event.ActionListener;
4.    import java.awt.event.WindowAdapter;
5.    import java.awt.event.ActionEvent;
6.    import java.awt.event.WindowEvent;
7.    import javax.swing.BoxLayout;
8.    import javax.swing.JButton;
9.    import javax.swing.JComponent;
10.   import javax.swing.JFrame;
11.   import javax.swing.JPanel;
12.   import javax.swing.JScrollPane;
13.   import javax.swing.JTable;
14.   import javax.swing.table.AbstractTableModel;
15.   import java.util.Date;
16.   public class StateGui implements ActionListener{
17.       private JFrame mainFrame;
18.       private JPanel controlPanel, editPanel;
19.       private CalendarEditor editor;
20.       private JButton save, exit;
21.
```

```
22.        public StateGui(CalendarEditor edit){
23.            editor = edit;
24.        }
25.
26.        public void createGui(){
27.            mainFrame = new JFrame("State Pattern Example");
28.            Container content = mainFrame.getContentPane();
29.            content.setLayout(new BoxLayout(content, BoxLayout.Y_AXIS));
30.
31.            editPanel = new JPanel();
32.            editPanel.setLayout(new BorderLayout());
33.            JTable appointmentTable = new JTable(new StateTableModel((Appointment
       [])editor.getAppointments().toArray(new Appointment[1])));
34.            editPanel.add(new JScrollPane(appointmentTable));
35.            content.add(editPanel);
36.
37.            controlPanel = new JPanel();
38.            save = new JButton("Save Appointments");
39.            exit = new JButton("Exit");
40.            controlPanel.add(save);
41.            controlPanel.add(exit);
42.            content.add(controlPanel);
43.
44.            save.addActionListener(this);
45.            exit.addActionListener(this);
46.
47.            mainFrame.addWindowListener(new WindowCloseManager());
48.            mainFrame.pack();
49.            mainFrame.setVisible(true);
50.        }
51.
52.
53.        public void actionPerformed(ActionEvent evt){
54.            Object originator = evt.getSource();
55.            if (originator == save){
56.                saveAppointments();
57.            }
58.            else if (originator == exit){
59.                exitApplication();
60.            }
61.        }
62.
63.        private class WindowCloseManager extends WindowAdapter{
64.            public void windowClosing(WindowEvent evt){
65.                exitApplication();
66.            }
67.        }
68.
69.        private void saveAppointments(){
70.            editor.save();
71.        }
72.
73.        private void exitApplication(){
74.            System.exit(0);
```

```
75.         }
76.
77.         private class StateTableModel extends AbstractTableModel{
78.             private final String [] columnNames = {
79.                 "Appointment", "Contacts", "Location", "Start Date", "End Date" };
80.             private Appointment [] data;
81.
82.             public StateTableModel(Appointment [] appointments){
83.                 data = appointments;
84.             }
85.
86.             public String getColumnName(int column){
87.                 return columnNames[column];
88.             }
89.             public int getRowCount(){ return data.length; }
90.             public int getColumnCount(){ return columnNames.length; }
91.             public Object getValueAt(int row, int column){
92.                 Object value = null;
93.                 switch(column){
94.                     case 0: value = data[row].getReason();
95.                         break;
96.                     case 1: value = data[row].getContacts();
97.                         break;
98.                     case 2: value = data[row].getLocation();
99.                         break;
100.                    case 3: value = data[row].getStartDate();
101.                        break;
102.                    case 4: value = data[row].getEndDate();
103.                        break;
104.                }
105.                return value;
106.            }
107.            public boolean isCellEditable(int row, int column){
108.                return ((column == 0) || (column == 2)) ? true : false;
109.            }
110.            public void setValueAt(Object value, int row, int column){
111.                switch(column){
112.                    case 0: data[row].setReason((String)value);
113.                        editor.edit();
114.                        break;
115.                    case 1:
116.                        break;
117.                    case 2: data[row].setLocation(new LocationImpl((String)value));
118.                        editor.edit();
119.                        break;
120.                    case 3:
121.                        break;
122.                    case 4:
123.                        break;
124.                }
125.            }
126.        }
127.    }
```

Strategy

Also known as Policy

Pattern Properties

Type: Behavioral
Level: Component

Purpose

To define a group of classes that represent a set of possible behaviors. These behaviors can then be flexibly plugged into an application, changing the functionality on the fly.

Introduction

Suppose the PIM contains a list of contacts. As the number of contacts grows, you might want to provide a way to sort entries and summarize the contact information.

To do this, you could make a collection class to store contacts in memory, sort the objects, and summarize their information. While this would provide a solution in the short term, a number of problems could surface (that is, rear their hideous, slime-drenched heads) over time. The most serious drawback is that the solution cannot be easily modified or extended. Any time you want to add a new variation of sorting or summarizing functionality, you would need to change the collection class itself. What's more, as the number of sorting or summarizing options increases, the size and complexity of the code in the collection grows, making it harder to debug and maintain.

What if you developed a *series* of classes instead, in which each class handles a specific way to sort or summarize the contact data? The collection class delegates the tasks to one of these classes, and so has different approaches or strategies to perform its task without the complex code of the other approach.

The Strategy pattern relies on objects having state and behavior. By replacing one object with another you can change behavior. And although this produces more classes, each class is easy to maintain and the overall solution is very extensible.

Applicability

Use the Strategy pattern when:

- You have a variety of ways to perform an action.

- You might not know which approach to use until runtime.
- You want to easily add to the possible ways to perform an action.
- You want to keep the code maintainable as you add behaviors.

Description

There are often many ways to perform the same task. Sorting, for example, can be performed with a number of well-documented algorithms such as quicksort and bubble sort, or by using multiple fields, or according to different criteria. When an object has a number of possible ways to accomplish its goals, it becomes complex and difficult to manage. Imagine the coding overhead required to produce a class to represent a document and save it in a variety of formats: a plain text file, a StarOffice document, and a Postscript file, for instance. As the number and complexity of the formats increase, the effort of managing the code in a single class becomes prohibitive.

In such cases, you can use the Strategy pattern to maintain a balance between flexibility and complexity. The pattern separates behaviors from an object, representing them in a separate class hierarchy. The object then uses the behavior that satisfies its requirements at a given time. For the document example, you could develop a class to save the document in each format, and their behavior could be collectively defined by a superclass or interface.

The Strategy pattern manages sets of basic algorithms, such as searching and sorting. You can also use it effectively with database queries, defining different approaches to perform queries, organize results, or manage data caching strategies. In the business arena, the Strategy pattern is sometimes used to represent different possible approaches to performing business actions. Placing an order for a workstation, for example, might be implemented as a Strategy if processing an order that had to be custom built was significantly different from processing one that was based on a standard product model.

Like the State pattern (see "State" on page 104), Strategy decouples part of a component into a separate group of classes. Part of a component's behavior is delegated to a set of handlers.

Benefits and Drawbacks

Each behavior is defined in its own class, so the Strategy leads to more easily maintainable behaviors. It also becomes easier to extend a model to incorporate new behaviors without extensive recoding of the application.

The primary challenge in the Strategy pattern lies in deciding exactly how to represent the callable behavior. Each Strategy must have the same interface for the calling object. You must identify one that is generic enough to apply to a number of implementations, but at the same time specific enough for the various concrete `Strategies` to use.

Implementation

The Strategy class diagram is shown in Figure 2.14.

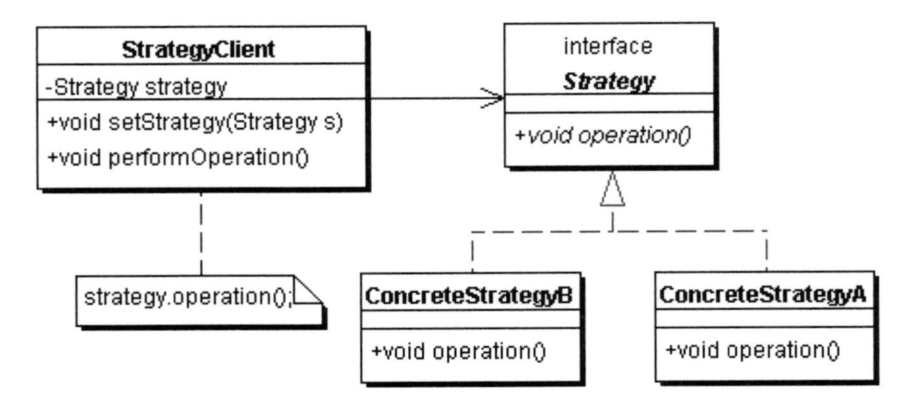

Figure 2.14 *Strategy class diagram*

To implement the Strategy pattern, use the following:

- `StrategyClient` – This is the class that uses the different strategies for certain tasks. It keeps a reference to the `Strategy` instance that it uses and has a method to replace the current `Strategy` instance with another `Strategy` implementation.
- `Strategy` – The interface that defines all the methods available for the `StrategyClient` to use.
- `ConcreteStrategy` – A class that implements the `Strategy` interface using a specific set of rules for each of the methods in the interface.

Pattern Variants

None.

Related Patterns

Related patterns include the following:

- Singleton (page 34) – Strategy implementations are sometimes represented as Singletons or static resources.
- Flyweight (page 183) – Sometimes Strategy objects are designed as Flyweights to make them less expensive to create.

- Factory Method (page 21) – The Strategy pattern is sometimes defined as a Factory so that the using class can use new Strategy implementations without having to recode other parts of the application.

Example

Note: For a full working example of this code example, with additional supporting classes and/or a RunPattern class, see "Strategy" on page 424 of the "Full Code Examples" appendix.

For many of the collections in the Personal Information Manager, it would be useful to be able to organize and summarize individual entries. This demonstration uses the Strategy pattern to summarize entries in a ContactList, a collection used to store Contact objects.

Example 2.41 ContactList.java

```
1.  import java.io.Serializable;
2.  import java.util.ArrayList;
3.  public class ContactList implements Serializable{
4.      private ArrayList contacts = new ArrayList();
5.      private SummarizingStrategy summarizer;
6.
7.      public ArrayList getContacts(){ return contacts; }
8.      public Contact [] getContactsAsArray(){ return (Contact [])(contacts.toAr-
      ray(new Contact [1])); }
9.
10.     public void setSummarizer(SummarizingStrategy newSummarizer){ summarizer =
      newSummarizer; }
11.     public void setContacts(ArrayList newContacts){ contacts = newContacts; }
12.
13.     public void addContact(Contact element){
14.         if (!contacts.contains(element)){
15.             contacts.add(element);
16.         }
17.     }
18.     public void removeContact(Contact element){
19.         contacts.remove(element);
20.     }
21.
22.     public String summarize(){
23.         return summarizer.summarize(getContactsAsArray());
24.     }
25.
26.     public String [] makeSummarizedList(){
27.         return summarizer.makeSummarizedList(getContactsAsArray());
28.     }
29. }
```

The ContactList has two methods, which can be used to provide summary information for the Contact objects in the collection—summarize and make-

SummarizedList. Both methods delegate to a SummarizingStrategy, which can be set for the ContactList with the setSummarizer method.

Example 2.42 SummarizingStrategy.java

```
1.  public interface SummarizingStrategy{
2.      public static final String EOL_STRING = System.getProperty("line.separator");
3.      public static final String DELIMITER = ":";
4.      public static final String COMMA = ",";
5.      public static final String SPACE = " ";
6.  
7.      public String summarize(Contact [] contactList);
8.      public String [] makeSummarizedList(Contact [] contactList);
9.  }
```

SummarizingStrategy is an interface that defines the two delegate methods summarize and makeSummarizedList. The interface represents the Strategy in the design pattern. In this example, two classes represent ConcreteStrategy objects: NameSummarizer and OrganizationSummarizer. Both classes summarize the list of contacts; however, each provides a different set of information and groups the data differently.

The NameSummarizer class returns only the names of the contacts with the last name first. The class uses an inner class as a comparator (NameComparator) to ensure that all of the Contact entries are grouped in ascending order by both last and first name.

Example 2.43 NameSummarizer.java

```
1.  import java.text.Collator;
2.  import java.util.Arrays;
3.  import java.util.Comparator;
4.  public class NameSummarizer implements SummarizingStrategy{
5.      private Comparator comparator = new NameComparator();
6.  
7.      public String summarize(Contact [] contactList){
8.          StringBuffer product = new StringBuffer();
9.          Arrays.sort(contactList, comparator);
10.         for (int i = 0; i < contactList.length; i++){
11.             product.append(contactList[i].getLastName());
12.             product.append(COMMA);
13.             product.append(SPACE);
14.             product.append(contactList[i].getFirstName());
15.             product.append(EOL_STRING);
16.         }
17.         return product.toString();
18.     }
19. 
20.     public String [] makeSummarizedList(Contact [] contactList){
21.         Arrays.sort(contactList, comparator);
22.         String [] product = new String[contactList.length];
```

```
23.            for (int i = 0; i < contactList.length; i++){
24.                product[i] = contactList[i].getLastName() + COMMA + SPACE +
25.                             contactList[i].getFirstName() + EOL_STRING;
26.            }
27.            return product;
28.        }
29.
30.        private class NameComparator implements Comparator{
31.            private Collator textComparator = Collator.getInstance();
32.
33.            public int compare(Object o1, Object o2){
34.                Contact c1, c2;
35.                if ((o1 instanceof Contact) && (o2 instanceof Contact)){
36.                    c1 = (Contact)o1;
37.                    c2 = (Contact)o2;
38.                    int compareResult = textComparator.compare(c1.getLastName(),
      c2.getLastName());
39.                    if (compareResult == 0){
40.                        compareResult = textComparator.compare(c1.getFirstName(),
      c2.getFirstName());
41.                    }
42.                    return compareResult;
43.                }
44.                else return textComparator.compare(o1, o2);
45.            }
46.
47.            public boolean equals(Object o){
48.                return textComparator.equals(o);
49.            }
50.        }
51.    }
```

`OrganizationSummarizer` returns a summary with a `Contact`'s organization, followed by their first and last name. The comparator used to order the `Contact` objects returns entries with ascending organization, then ascending last name.

Example 2.44 `OrganizationSummarizer.java`

```
1.     import java.text.Collator;
2.     import java.util.Arrays;
3.     import java.util.Comparator;
4.     public class OrganizationSummarizer implements SummarizingStrategy{
5.         private Comparator comparator = new OrganizationComparator();
6.
7.         public String summarize(Contact [] contactList){
8.             StringBuffer product = new StringBuffer();
9.             Arrays.sort(contactList, comparator);
10.            for (int i = 0; i < contactList.length; i++){
11.                product.append(contactList[i].getOrganization());
12.                product.append(DELIMITER);
13.                product.append(SPACE);
14.                product.append(contactList[i].getFirstName());
15.                product.append(SPACE);
```

```
16.                 product.append(contactList[i].getLastName());
17.                 product.append(EOL_STRING);
18.             }
19.             return product.toString();
20.         }
21.
22.         public String [] makeSummarizedList(Contact [] contactList){
23.             Arrays.sort(contactList, comparator);
24.             String [] product = new String[contactList.length];
25.             for (int i = 0; i < contactList.length; i++){
26.                 product[i] = contactList[i].getOrganization() + DELIMITER + SPACE +
27.                              contactList[i].getFirstName() + SPACE +
28.                              contactList[i].getLastName() + EOL_STRING;
29.             }
30.             return product;
31.         }
32.
33.         private class OrganizationComparator implements Comparator{
34.             private Collator textComparator = Collator.getInstance();
35.
36.             public int compare(Object o1, Object o2){
37.                 Contact c1, c2;
38.                 if ((o1 instanceof Contact) && (o2 instanceof Contact)){
39.                     c1 = (Contact)o1;
40.                     c2 = (Contact)o2;
41.                    int compareResult = textComparator.compare(c1.getOrganization(),
       c2.getOrganization());
42.                     if (compareResult == 0){
43.                     compareResult = textComparator.compare(c1.getLastName(), c2.get-
       LastName());
44.                     }
45.                     return compareResult;
46.                 }
47.                 else return textComparator.compare(o1, o2);
48.             }
49.
50.             public boolean equals(Object o){
51.                 return textComparator.equals(o);
52.             }
53.         }
54.     }
```

Visitor

Pattern Properties

Type: Behavioral, Object
Level: Component to System

Purpose

To provide a maintainable, easy way to perform actions for a family of classes. Visitor centralizes the behaviors and allows them to be modified or extended without changing the classes they operate on.

Introduction

Imagine you want the Personal Information Manager to have project planning capability, and the project planner is used for things like bidding, risk analysis, and time estimation. The following classes represent a complex project:

- `Project` – The root of the project hierarchy, representing the project itself
- `Task` – A work step in the project
- `DependentTask` – A work step that depends on other tasks for its own completion
- `Deliverable`: An item or document to be produced as a result of the project

To clearly identify these classes as part of a common model, they're organized around an interface called `ProjectItem`.

So far so good. Now, how do you code the ability to estimate the total cost for the project? The calculation will probably depend on the specific type of `ProjectItem`. In that interface you define a method `getCost` that should calculate the costs for that specific part of the project. This would allow you to compute the cost for every item in the project structure.

You might decide on an approach like this:

- Project – No operation, since the cost is equal to the cost of all other project items.
- Simple task – Cost is based on estimated hours of effort.
- Dependent task – Same as simple task, but adds an additional factor to represent coordination based on the task dependencies.
- Deliverable – Cost is a basic estimate of materials plus production cost.

However, how should you calculate the time required for the project, and project risk? Using the same approach as for the cost makes the code harder to maintain. With every new capability, you have to write a bunch of new methods that are spread throughout the project classes. With every new operation, the classes become larger, more complex, and harder to understand.

It is also difficult to keep track of information with this kind of approach. If you try to estimate cost, time, or risk using localized methods, you have to figure out how to maintain the intermediate results, since each method belongs to a specific project object. You will likely wind up passing the information through the entire project tree, then crossing your fingers and hoping that you'll never have to debug it.

The Visitor pattern offers an alternative. You define a single class, with a name like `CostProjectVisitor`, that performs all cost-related calculations. Instead of computing cost in the `ProjectItems` themselves, you pass them to the `Visitor` class, which keeps a running tally of the total cost.

`ProjectItems` no longer has a `getCost` method. Instead, it has a more generic `acceptVisitor` method that uses a `ProjectVisitor` to call a specific method on the `ProjectVisitor`. For instance, the `acceptVisitor` method for a `Task` object calls the method `visitTask` on the `Visitor`. If the `Visitor` is a `CostProjectVisitor`, the `visitTask` method computes the cost associated with the `Task`.

This design offers substantial benefits. Most importantly, it is very easy to add new operations to this design. To add a computation for time, you only have to write a new `TimeProjectVisitor` class with all of the necessary methods to compute project time. The code for the project objects remains unchanged, since it already supports calling the generic methods defined in the `ProjectVisitor`.

Better still, the `Visitor` provides a place to centralize state. For the `CostProjectVisitor`, you can store the intermediate result in the `Visitor` itself while you compute the cost estimate. The centralized estimation code also makes it easier to adjust the basic calculations. Using the Visitor pattern lets you easily add features such as an additional weighting factor, making it easy to calculate a project discounts or, preferably, a markup.

Applicability

Use the Visitor pattern when the following conditions are met:

- A system contains a group of related classes.
- Several non-trivial operations need to be carried out on some or all of the related classes.
- The operations must be performed differently for different classes.

Description

The Visitor pattern involves taking related operations out of a group of classes and placing them together in a single class. The motivation is code maintainability—in some situations, it simply becomes too complicated to maintain operations in the classes themselves. Visitor is useful for these situations, since it provides a very generic framework to support operations on a group of classes.

The pattern requires that all classes having operations performed on them, or *Elements*, support some form of accept method, called when the Visitor should perform an operation on the Element. The argument for that accept method is an instance of Visitor. Each Element implementation implements the accept method to call the visit method in the Visitor for its own class type. Every Visitor implementation implements the specific visit method for Element subtype.

Products that might benefit from use of the Visitor pattern include those that use complex rules for configuration. As a practical example, consider a vehicle as a purchasable product. There are dozens of decisions to make when buying a car, and many of the choices can have an impact on things like price, financing or insurance rates.

Implementation

The Visitor class diagram is shown in Figure 2.15.

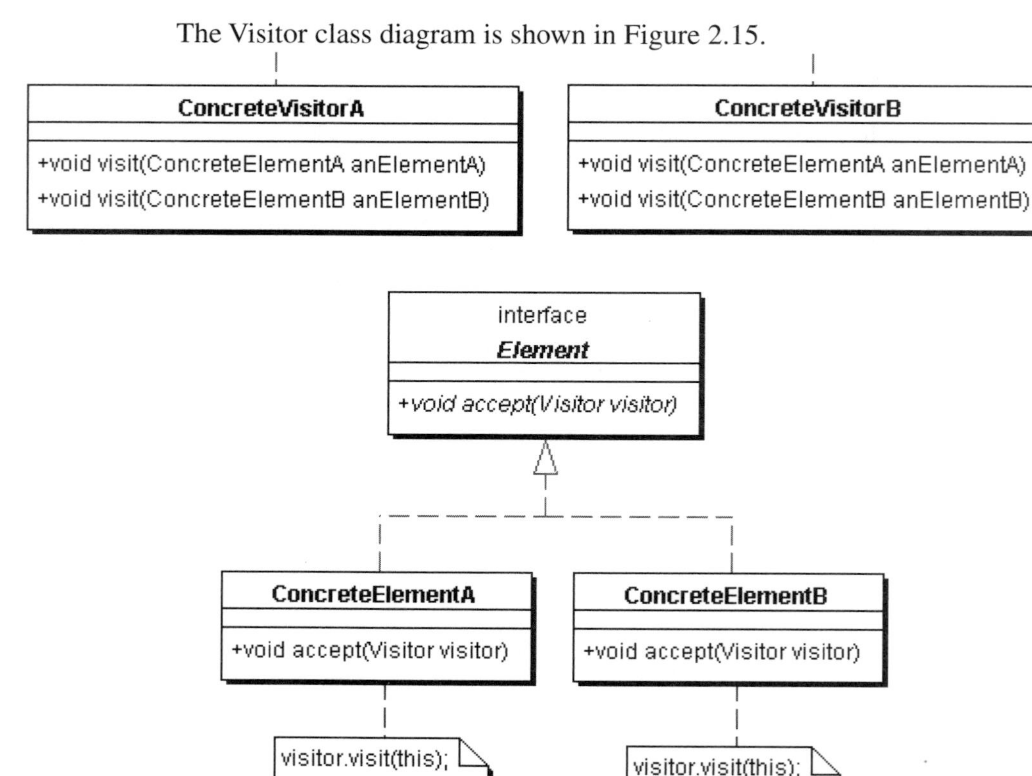

Figure 2.15 *Visitor class diagram*

To implement the Visitor pattern, use the following:

- `Visitor` – The abstract class or interface that defines a `visit` method for each of the `ConcreteElement` classes.
- `ConcreteVisitor` – Each concrete visitor class represents a specific operation to be performed for the system. It implements all the methods defined in `Visitor` for a specific operation or algorithm.
- `Element` – An abstract class or interface that represents the objects upon which the `Visitor` operates. At a minimum, it defines an `accept` method that receives a `Visitor` as an argument.
- `ConcreteElement` – A concrete element is a specific entity in the system. It implements the `accept` method defined in `Element`, calling the appropriate `visit` method defined in `Visitor`.

One issue to watch for when implementing the Visitor pattern involves overloaded methods. The pattern uses overloaded methods for the `visit` method. Figure 2.15 shows that the `Visitor` interface has two `visit` methods, each taking a different argument. These are two completely different methods from the language point of view.

Although the implementation of the accept method in each `ConcreteElement` class is very similar (even completely the same), you cannot put that operation in a superclass. Doing so results in the `visit` method being called with the supertype as argument, even though the actual type of the instance may be a specific `ConcreteElement`.

Benefits and Drawbacks

Because of its structure, the Visitor pattern makes adding behavior to a system very easy. When you initially implement the pattern, you develop a support framework for any other `Visitor` action you might want to perform in the future. To add new functionality, simply create a new class that implements the `Visitor` interface and write new functional code.

Visitors are useful because they allow you to centralize functional code for an operation. Apart from making the code easier to extend or modify in the long term, this approach makes maintaining state straightforward. The same `Visitor` object is normally used to visit every `Element` in a structure, so it provides a central location to hold data being collected, or to store intermediate results.

The downside of the pattern is that there is very little flexibility in the `Element` class chain. Any addition or modification to the `Element` class hierarchy has a good chance of triggering a rewrite of the `Visitor` code structure. Any additional class requires a new method to be defined in the `Visitor` interface and each `ConcreteVisitor` has to provide an implementation for that method.

In addition, the pattern breaks, or at least severely bends, the object-oriented principle of code encapsulation. The Visitor pattern takes code that applies to an object out of the object's class and moving it to another location.

The `Element` classes do not have to know the details of specific `Visitors`, but a `ConcreteVisitor` generally *does* have to know the details of the `Element` classes. To perform a given function or calculation, the `Visitor` frequently must use the methods of the `Element` classes in order to accomplish its task.

Pattern Variants

As with many patterns, you can represent the `Element` and `Visitor` as either abstract classes or interfaces in Java.

Another decision you need to make is how to apply the Visitor to a collection of `Elements`. It's important to stress that the Visitor pattern makes no assumptions about the structure of the `Elements` it operates on. You can use a `Con-`

creteVisitor equally effectively to traverse a simple collection, a chain structure, a list, or a tree.

Although some implementations of the Visitor place the traversal code within the ConcreteVisitor itself, the pattern doesn't require this. It is equally valid to use an external class, like an Iterator, to move through a collection. You can then pair the Visitor with the Iterator as required.

Related Patterns

Related patterns include the following. You also can use a number of patterns in conjunction with the Visitor to traverse various kinds of collections of Elements:

- Interpreter (page 59) – You can use the Visitor pattern to centralize the interpretation operation.
- Iterator (page 69) – You can use the Iterator pattern to traverse a generic collection.
- Composite (page 157) – You can combine the Composite with Visitor to walk a tree structure.

Example

Note: For a full working example of this code example, with additional supporting classes and/or a RunPattern class, see "Visitor" on page 432 of the "Full Code Examples" appendix.

The Visitor pattern is often useful when operations must be performed over a large structure, and composite results must be calculated. In this demonstration, the Visitor pattern is used to calculate the total cost for a project.

Four classes are used to represent project elements, and all of the classes implement a common interface, ProjectItem. In this example, ProjectItem defines the accept method required to host a Visitor.

Example 2.45 ProjectItem.java

```
1.    import java.io.Serializable;
2.    import java.util.ArrayList;
3.    public interface ProjectItem extends Serializable{
4.        public void accept(ProjectVisitor v);
5.        public ArrayList getProjectItems();
6.    }
```

The Project class represents the project itself, the Deliverable class a concrete product, the Task: a job of some sort. In addition, there is a subclass of

Task called DependentTask. This class holds a set of other Tasks upon which it depends for its own completion.

Example 2.46 Deliverable.java

```
1.    import java.util.ArrayList;
2.    public class Deliverable implements ProjectItem{
3.        private String name;
4.        private String description;
5.        private Contact owner;
6.        private double materialsCost;
7.        private double productionCost;
8.
9.        public Deliverable(){ }
10.       public Deliverable(String newName, String newDescription,
11.           Contact newOwner, double newMaterialsCost, double newProductionCost){
12.           name = newName;
13.           description = newDescription;
14.           owner = newOwner;
15.           materialsCost = newMaterialsCost;
16.           productionCost = newProductionCost;
17.       }
18.
19.       public String getName(){ return name; }
20.       public String getDescription(){ return description; }
21.       public Contact getOwner(){ return owner; }
22.       public double getMaterialsCost(){ return materialsCost; }
23.       public double getProductionCost(){ return productionCost; }
24.
25.       public void setMaterialsCost(double newCost){ materialsCost = newCost; }
26.       public void setProductionCost(double newCost){ productionCost = newCost; }
27.       public void setName(String newName){ name = newName; }
28.       public void setDescription(String newDescription){ description = newDescrip-
      tion; }
29.       public void setOwner(Contact newOwner){ owner = newOwner; }
30.
31.       public void accept(ProjectVisitor v){
32.           v.visitDeliverable(this);
33.       }
34.
35.       public ArrayList getProjectItems(){
36.           return null;
37.       }
38.   }
```

Example 2.47 DependentTask.java

```
1.    import java.util.ArrayList;
2.    public class DependentTask extends Task{
3.        private ArrayList dependentTasks = new ArrayList();
4.        private double dependencyWeightingFactor;
5.
```

```
6.        public DependentTask(){ }
7.        public DependentTask(String newName, Contact newOwner,
8.            double newTimeRequired, double newWeightingFactor){
9.            super(newName, newOwner, newTimeRequired);
10.           dependencyWeightingFactor = newWeightingFactor;
11.       }
12.
13.       public ArrayList getDependentTasks(){ return dependentTasks; }
14.       public double getDependencyWeightingFactor(){ return dependencyWeightingFac-
        tor; }
15.
16.       public void setDependencyWeightingFactor(double newFactor){ dependencyWeight-
        ingFactor = newFactor; }
17.
18.       public void addDependentTask(Task element){
19.           if (!dependentTasks.contains(element)){
20.               dependentTasks.add(element);
21.           }
22.       }
23.
24.       public void removeDependentTask(Task element){
25.           dependentTasks.remove(element);
26.       }
27.
28.       public void accept(ProjectVisitor v){
29.           v.visitDependentTask(this);
30.       }
31.   }
```

Example 2.48 `Project.java`

```
1.    import java.util.ArrayList;
2.    public class Project implements ProjectItem{
3.        private String name;
4.        private String description;
5.        private ArrayList projectItems = new ArrayList();
6.
7.        public Project(){ }
8.        public Project(String newName, String newDescription){
9.            name = newName;
10.           description = newDescription;
11.       }
12.
13.       public String getName(){ return name; }
14.       public String getDescription(){ return description; }
15.       public ArrayList getProjectItems(){ return projectItems; }
16.
17.       public void setName(String newName){ name = newName; }
18.       public void setDescription(String newDescription){ description = newDescrip-
        tion; }
19.
20.       public void addProjectItem(ProjectItem element){
21.           if (!projectItems.contains(element)){
22.               projectItems.add(element);
```

```
23.            }
24.        }
25.
26.        public void removeProjectItem(ProjectItem element){
27.            projectItems.remove(element);
28.        }
29.
30.        public void accept(ProjectVisitor v){
31.            v.visitProject(this);
32.        }
33.    }
```

Example 2.49 `Task.java`

```
1.     import java.util.ArrayList;
2.     public class Task implements ProjectItem{
3.         private String name;
4.         private ArrayList projectItems = new ArrayList();
5.         private Contact owner;
6.         private double timeRequired;
7.
8.         public Task(){ }
9.         public Task(String newName, Contact newOwner,
10.            double newTimeRequired){
11.            name = newName;
12.            owner = newOwner;
13.            timeRequired = newTimeRequired;
14.        }
15.
16.        public String getName(){ return name; }
17.        public ArrayList getProjectItems(){ return projectItems; }
18.        public Contact getOwner(){ return owner; }
19.        public double getTimeRequired(){ return timeRequired; }
20.
21.        public void setName(String newName){ name = newName; }
22.        public void setOwner(Contact newOwner){ owner = newOwner; }
23.        public void setTimeRequired(double newTimeRequired){ timeRequired = newTimeRe-
       quired; }
24.
25.        public void addProjectItem(ProjectItem element){
26.            if (!projectItems.contains(element)){
27.                projectItems.add(element);
28.            }
29.        }
30.
31.        public void removeProjectItem(ProjectItem element){
32.            projectItems.remove(element);
33.        }
34.
35.        public void accept(ProjectVisitor v){
36.            v.visitTask(this);
37.        }
38.    }
```

The basic interface that defines the `Visitor` behavior is the `ProjectVisitor`. It defines a `visit` method for each of the project classes.

Example 2.50 `ProjectVisitor.java`

```
1.   public interface ProjectVisitor{
2.       public void visitDependentTask(DependentTask p);
3.       public void visitDeliverable(Deliverable p);
4.       public void visitTask(Task p);
5.       public void visitProject(Project p);
6.   }
```

With this framework in place, you can define classes that implement the `ProjectVisitor` interface and perform some computation on project items. The class `ProjectCostVisitor` shows how project cost calculations could be managed.

Example 2.51 `ProjectCostVisitor.java`

```
1.   public class ProjectCostVisitor implements ProjectVisitor{
2.       private double totalCost;
3.       private double hourlyRate;
4.
5.       public double getHourlyRate(){ return hourlyRate; }
6.       public double getTotalCost(){ return totalCost; }
7.
8.       public void setHourlyRate(double rate){ hourlyRate = rate; }
9.
10.      public void resetTotalCost(){ totalCost = 0.0; }
11.
12.      public void visitDependentTask(DependentTask p){
13.          double taskCost = p.getTimeRequired() * hourlyRate;
14.          taskCost *= p.getDependencyWeightingFactor();
15.          totalCost += taskCost;
16.      }
17.      public void visitDeliverable(Deliverable p){
18.          totalCost += p.getMaterialsCost() + p.getProductionCost();
19.      }
20.      public void visitTask(Task p){
21.          totalCost += p.getTimeRequired() * hourlyRate;
22.      }
23.      public void visitProject(Project p){ }
24.  }
```

All behavior for the calculation, as well as variable storage, is centralized in the `Visitor` class. To add a new behavior, you would create a new class that implements `ProjectVisitor` and redefine the four `visit` methods.

Template Method

Pattern Properties

Type: Behavioral
Level: Object

Purpose

To provide a method that allows subclasses to override parts of the method without rewriting it.

Introduction

When working with projects, you frequently need to estimate the expense involved in performing a certain task or producing a deliverable. The Personal Information Manager uses a number of classes to represent its projects. At a minimum, the `Task` and `Deliverable` classes would be used to represent project elements. As a project grew more complex, you might create additional classes like `Project` or `DependentTask` to satisfy more sophisticated modeling needs.

While it is possible to create a `getCostEstimate` method for each of the classes, such an approach involves a lot of code duplication. As the number of classes increases, it becomes more and more difficult to maintain the code in all of the project classes.

A better approach is to group all of the project-related classes under a superclass, and define the method `getCostEstimate` there. But what would you do if parts of the `getCostEstimate` method depended on information that was specific to each of the `Project` classes? What if the `Task` had a different way of calculating hours from the `Deliverable`?

In that case, define `getCostEstimate` so that it calls an abstract method, `getTimeRequired`, and allows the `Task` and `Deliverable` classes to define the method as appropriate. This approach, called the Template Method, provides the benefits of code reusability, while still allowing classes to modify certain parts of the behavior to meet their needs.

Applicability

Use the Template Method pattern:

- To provide a skeleton structure for a method, allowing subclasses to redefine specific parts of the method.

- To centralize pieces of a method that are defined in all subtypes of a class, but which always have a small difference in each subclass.
- To control which operations subclasses are required to override.

Description

When you are building complex class hierarchies for your application, code is often duplicated at several places. This is undesirable, since you want to reuse as much code as you can. Refactoring your code so that the common methods are in a superclass is a step in the right direction. The problem is that sometimes an operation that has been refactored relies on specific information that is only available in a subclass. Because of this, developers often decide not to refactor and accept the duplicate code in multiple subclasses.

When many methods in related classes have a similar structure, the Template Method can help. First, determine which parts of the method are similar. These parts should be centralized in the superclass, while the other operations should remain in the subclasses.

The newly defined template method contains the structure of the operation. For each part of the operation that can vary, an abstract method is defined in the superclass. Subclasses override these methods to provide their own implementation. When the template method is called on a subclass, the code in the superclass is executed.

When you make the template method in the superclass `final`, subclasses are limited in what parts of their superclass they can override.

This pattern is called Template Method because it provides a method that contains the structure of the operation, but leaves some of the steps open by calling abstract methods. It is like a template, since the subclasses fill in the blanks by providing implementations for the abstract methods.

Implementation

Figure 2.16 shows the class diagram for the Template Method pattern.

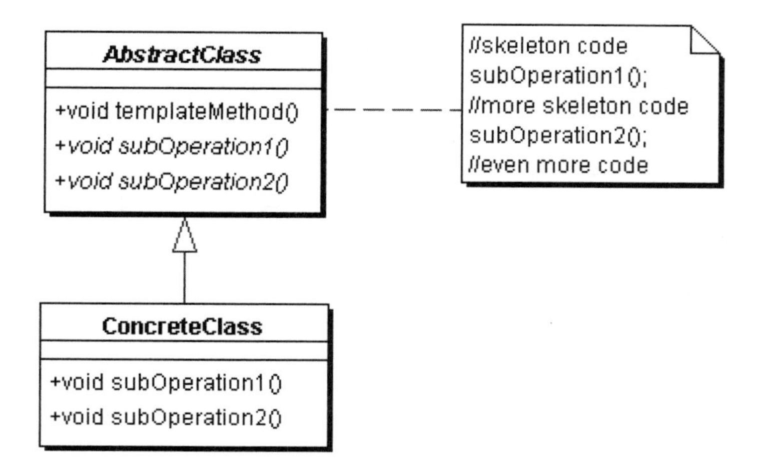

Figure 2.16 *Template Method class diagram*

Implementing the Template Method requires:

- `AbstractClass` – The `AbstractClass` is (perhaps not surprisingly) an abstract class that contains the template method and defines one or more abstract methods. The template method contains the skeletal code and calls one or more of the abstract methods. To prevent subclasses from overriding the template method it should be declared final.
- `ConcreteClass` – The `ConcreteClass` extends the `AbstractClass` and implements the abstract methods of the `AbstractClass`. It relies on the `AbstractClass` to provide the structure of the operation contained in the template method.

Benefits and Drawbacks

The main benefit of the Template Method pattern is that it promotes code reuse. Without the Template Method, code is duplicated in many subclasses. This benefit makes the Template Method essential for frameworks. A framework contains many methods that only minimally rely on specific implementations in the subclass. Using the Template Method pattern means the entire structure can be provided by the framework. If you use this framework, you only have to override a few methods to be able to use it.

If the template method calls too many abstract methods, you'll soon get tired of using the `AbstractClass` as a superclass. It is better to have the template method call a limited number of abstract methods.

Pattern Variants

One variant is to have the Template Method call concrete methods instead of abstract methods. The `AbstractClass` provides a default implementation for each of the methods called by the Template Method. These methods are called *hook methods*.

The rationale is that when you use the `AbstractClass`, you don't have to override all the methods to be able to use the Template Method. The `AbstractClass` might not even need to be abstract.

One responsibility the provider of the Template Method has is to document which methods are used in other template methods. In the normal Template Method pattern, it is clear which methods need to be overridden, because all these methods are abstract. If the hook methods are not mentioned in the documentation, they cannot be identified as such.

Related Patterns

Related patterns include the following:

- Factory Method (page 21) – Template methods often call Factory Methods to create new instances without knowing the exact class being created.
- Strategy (page 114) – The Strategy pattern uses composition to completely replace behavior, while the Template Method pattern uses inheritance to replace parts of the behavior.
- Intercepting Filter [CJ2EEP] – The Intercepting Filter uses the Template Method pattern to implement its Template Filter Strategy.

Example

Note: For a full working example of this code example, with additional supporting classes and/or a `RunPattern` class, see "Template Method" on page 440 of the "Full Code Examples" appendix.

This example uses project classes from the Personal Information Manager to illustrate the Template Method.

`ProjectItem` is the abstract class that defines the Template Method in this demonstration. Its method `getCostEstimate` returns a total value for the project item that is calculated using the following equation:

```
time estimate * hourly rate + materials cost
```

The hourly rate is defined in the `ProjectItem` class (using the rate variable, getter and setter methods in the class), but the methods `getTimeRequired` and getMaterialsCost are abstract. This requires the subclasses to override them, providing their own way to calculate the values.

Example 2.52 ProjectItem.java

```
1.   import java.io.Serializable;
2.   public abstract class ProjectItem implements Serializable{
3.       private String name;
4.       private String description;
5.       private double rate;
6.
7.       public ProjectItem(){}
8.       public ProjectItem(String newName, String newDescription, double newRate){
9.           name = newName;
10.          description = newDescription;
11.          rate = newRate;
12.      }
13.
14.      public void setName(String newName){ name = newName; }
15.      public void setDescription(String newDescription){ description = newDescrip-
       tion; }
16.      public void setRate(double newRate){ rate = newRate; }
17.
18.      public String getName(){ return name; }
19.      public String getDescription(){ return description; }
20.      public final double getCostEstimate(){
21.          return getTimeRequired() * getRate() + getMaterialsCost();
22.      }
23.      public double getRate(){ return rate; }
24.
25.      public String toString(){ return getName(); }
26.
27.      public abstract double getTimeRequired();
28.      public abstract double getMaterialsCost();
29.  }
```

The Deliverable class represents a concrete product of some kind. Because it represents a physical item, the value returned by its getTimeRequired method is a fixed amount. Similarly, the getMaterialsCost method returns a fixed value.

Example 2.53 Deliverable.java

```
1.   public class Deliverable extends ProjectItem{
2.       private double materialsCost;
3.       private double productionTime;
4.
5.       public Deliverable(){ }
6.       public Deliverable(String newName, String newDescription,
7.           double newMaterialsCost, double newProductionTime,
8.           double newRate){
```

```
9.              super(newName, newDescription, newRate);
10.             materialsCost = newMaterialsCost;
11.             productionTime = newProductionTime;
12.         }
13.
14.         public void setMaterialsCost(double newCost){ materialsCost = newCost; }
15.         public void setProductionTime(double newTime){ productionTime = newTime; }
16.
17.         public double getMaterialsCost(){ return materialsCost; }
18.         public double getTimeRequired(){ return productionTime; }
19.     }
```

The `Task` class represents a job that can consist of any number of subtasks or deliverables. For this reason, `getTimeRequired` calculates the total time for the `Task` and all its children by iterating through its list of project items and calling the `getTimeRequired` method. The method `getMaterialsCost` follows a similar strategy, working through the list of project items and calling each child's `getMaterialsCost` method.

Example 2.54 `Task.java`

```
1.      import java.util.ArrayList;
2.      import java.util.Iterator;
3.      public class Task extends ProjectItem{
4.          private ArrayList projectItems = new ArrayList();
5.          private double taskTimeRequired;
6.
7.          public Task(){ }
8.          public Task(String newName, String newDescription,
9.              double newTaskTimeRequired, double newRate){
10.             super(newName, newDescription, newRate);
11.             taskTimeRequired = newTaskTimeRequired;
12.         }
13.
14.         public void setTaskTimeRequired(double newTaskTimeRequired){ taskTimeRequired
        = newTaskTimeRequired; }
15.         public void addProjectItem(ProjectItem element){
16.             if (!projectItems.contains(element)){
17.                 projectItems.add(element);
18.             }
19.         }
20.         public void removeProjectItem(ProjectItem element){
21.             projectItems.remove(element);
22.         }
23.
24.         public double getTaskTimeRequired(){ return taskTimeRequired; }
25.         public Iterator getProjectItemIterator(){ return projectItems.iterator(); }
26.         public double getMaterialsCost(){
27.             double totalCost = 0;
28.             Iterator items = getProjectItemIterator();
29.             while (items.hasNext()){
30.                 totalCost += ((ProjectItem)items.next()).getMaterialsCost();
```

```
31.            }
32.            return totalCost;
33.        }
34.        public double getTimeRequired(){
35.            double totalTime = taskTimeRequired;
36.            Iterator items = getProjectItemIterator();
37.            while (items.hasNext()){
38.                totalTime += ((ProjectItem)items.next()).getTimeRequired();
39.            }
40.            return totalTime;
41.        }
42.    }
```

Chapter Three

Structural Patterns

Introduction to Structural Patterns

Structural patterns describe effective ways both to partition and to combine the elements of an application. The ways structural patterns affect applications varies widely: for instance, the Adapter pattern can let two incompatible systems communicate, while Facade lets you present a simplified interface to a user without removing all the options available in the system.

- Adapter – To act as an intermediary between two classes, converting the interface of one class so that it can be used with the other.
- Bridge – To divide a complex component into two separate but related inheritance hierarchies: the functional abstraction and the internal implementation. This makes it easier to change either aspect of the component.
- Composite – To develop a flexible way to create hierarchical tree structures of arbitrary complexity, while enabling every element in the structure to operate with a uniform interface.
- Decorator – To provide a way to flexibly add or remove component functionality without changing its external appearance or function.
- Facade – To provide a simplified interface to a group of subsystems or a complex subsystem.
- Flyweight – To reduce the number of very low-level, detailed objects objects within a system by sharing objects.
- Half-Object Plus Protocol (HOPP) – To provide a single entity that lives in two or more address spaces.
- Proxy – To provide a representative of another object, for reasons such as access, speed, or security.

Adapter

Also known as Wrapper

Pattern Properties

Type: Structural, Object
Level: Component

Purpose

To act as an intermediary between two classes, converting the interface of one class so that it can be used with the other.

Introduction

One of the frequently cited advantages of object-oriented programming is that it enables code reuse. Since data and behavior are centralized in a class, you can (at least in principle) move the class from one project to another and reuse the functionality with very little effort.

Unfortunately, we developers are somewhat limited in our ability to predict the future. Since we cannot know in advance what the coding requirements will be for a project in the future, we cannot always know how to design a class for optimum reusability.

Imagine that, in order to speed up the development of your Personal Information Manager application, you decide to cooperate with one of your foreign friends. He has been working on a similar project and he can provide you with a commercial implementation of an address system. But when you receive the files, the interface doesn't match the interfaces you have been using. To make matters worse, the code is not in English, but in your friend's native language.

You see yourself faced with two equally unattractive solutions.

- Your first option is to rewrite the new component so that it implements all the required interfaces. Rewriting the new component is a bad idea because you will have to do the same rewrite every time you receive the newest version from your friend.
- The second option is to rewrite your own application and start using the new (foreign) interfaces. Here the downside is that you have to go through your whole code to change every occurrence of the old interfaces, and your code becomes harder to understand because you don't speak your friend's native language. What might be meaningful names to your friend don't mean anything to you.

What you need here is a translator—a component that translates the calls to one interface into calls on another interface. This is what the Adapter pattern does. It behaves similarly to a power adapter, converting one type into another otherwise-incompatible type. By using the Adapter pattern your application can keep on using your interfaces while allowing use of the new components. And when a new version arrives, the only thing you have to change is the Adapter.

Applicability

Use Adapter when:

- You want to use an object in an environment that expects an interface that is different from the object's interface.
- Interface translation among multiple sources must occur.
- An object should act as an intermediary for one of a group of classes, and it is not possible to know which class will be used until runtime.

Description

Sometimes you'd like to use a class in a new framework without recoding it to match the new environment. In such cases, you can design an `Adaptee` class to act as a translator. This class receives calls from the environment and modifies the calls to be compatible with the `Adaptee` class.

Typical environments where an Adapter can be useful include applications that support plug-in behavior like graphics, text, or media editors. Web browsers are another environment where the Adapter can be useful. Applications involving internationalization (language conversion, for example) might benefit from Adapters, as well as those that use components (such as JavaBeans™) that are added on the fly.

A real-world example of the Adapter is a foreign language phrase book. The phrase book translates common expressions (messages) from one language to another, enabling two otherwise incompatible individuals to communicate with each other. This assumes, of course, that the phrase book translates the messages properly based on the context: "I need to buy some matches," for example, might not map correctly to "My hovercraft is full of eels" in all circumstances.

Implementation

The Adapter class diagram interface is shown in Figure 3.1.

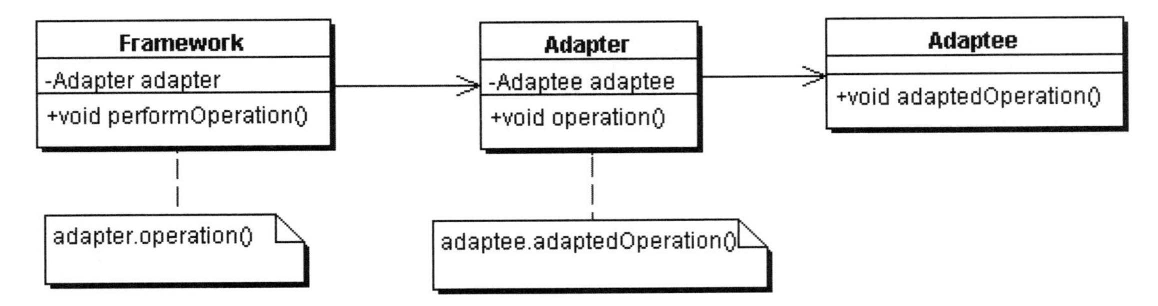

Figure 3.1 *Adapter class diagram interface*

Implementing the Adapter pattern requires the following:

- `Framework` – The `Framework` uses the `Adapter`. It either constructs the `ConcreteAdapter` or it gets set somewhere.
- `Adapter` – The interface that defines the methods the `Framework` uses.
- `ConcreteAdapter` – An implementation of the `Adapter` interface. It keeps a reference to the `Adaptee` and translates the method calls from the `Framework` into method calls on the `Adaptee`. This translation also possibly involves wrapping or modifying parameters and return types.
- `Adaptee` – The interface that defines the methods of the type that will be adapted. This interface allows the specific `Adaptee` to be dynamically loaded at runtime.
- `ConcreteAdaptee` – An implementation of the `Adaptee` interface. The class that needs to be adapted so that the `Framework` can use this class.

For more complex communication, it can be useful to establish an action map to better understand how to manage the communication. An action map is a table showing how the Adapter maps methods and call parameters between the caller and adaptee. Table 3-1 shows the mapping for a single method.

Table 3-1 Example action map

Framework	Adapter Action	Adaptee
method1	None	method2
argument1	None	argument1
argument2	wrapper	argument2
	create	argument3

The Unified Modeling Language (UML) can effectively represent this; typically, the sequence diagram is a useful tool for action mapping. The Adapter sequence diagram for action mapping is shown in Figure 3.2.

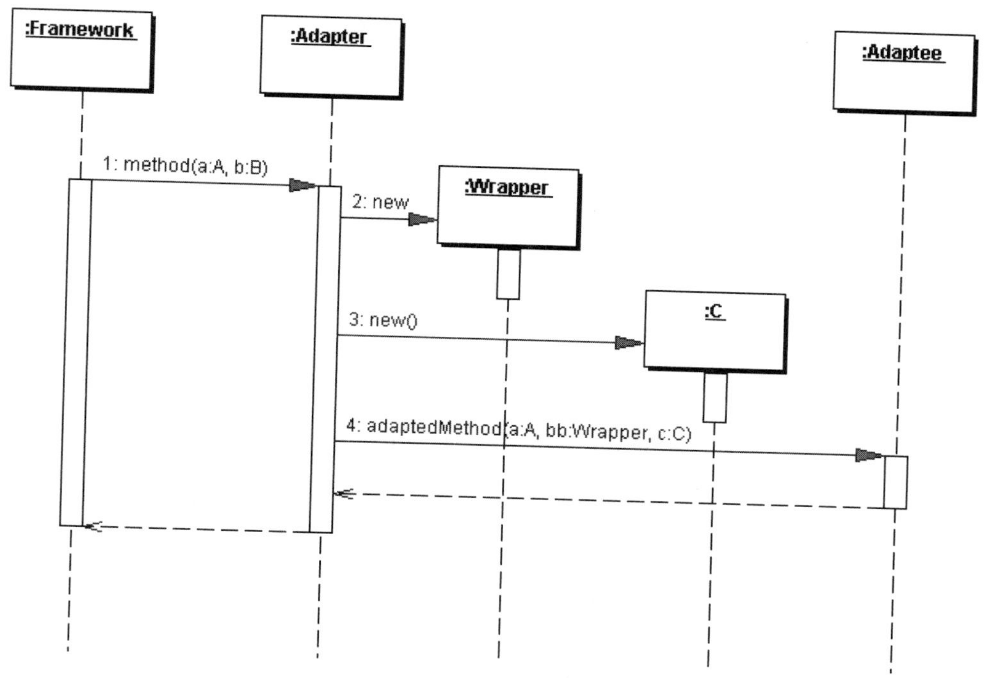

Figure 3.2 *Sequence diagram for action mapping*

Benefits and Drawbacks

The Adapter offers greatly improved reuse, allowing two or more objects to interact that would otherwise be incompatible. However, some planning and forethought are required in order to develop a framework flexible enough to be conveniently adaptable. This problem has two aspects: functional call structure and parameter translation.

If there is a functional mismatch between the call framework and the Adaptee, the Adapter needs to manage the call requirements of the Adaptee, invoking any required setup methods before the framework's call can be satisfied.

Another challenge for the Adapter is the transfer of parameters, since passed parameters are not always compatible between the framework and the Adaptee. In these cases, the Adapter usually either creates appropriate objects when there is no direct equivalent between the two environments, or wraps an object to make it usable by the Adaptee.

The most generic of environments for the Adapter are typically built around the Command pattern, using some form of messaging or introspection/reflection. In its most generic form, the Command pattern might eliminate the need for an Adapter. (See “Command” on page 51.)

Pattern Variants

Adapters are, by their very nature, dynamic and it’s rare to see two that are exactly alike. Nevertheless, there are some common variations. Three of these common variations are listed here:

- Multi-Adaptee Adapters – Depending on the system design, it can be advantageous to make an Adapter part of the calling framework. Such an Adapter often acts as an intermediary between the system and multiple Adaptees.
- Non-Interface-based Adapters – Use of the interface in the Java programming language makes it possible to develop even more flexible Adapters. But it may not always be possible to use interfaces. For instance, it’s not possible when you're given complete components that do not implement any interface. In those situations you will see the Adapter pattern used without using interfaces. It goes without saying that these implementations are less flexible.
- An interface layer between the caller and Adapter, and another between the Adapter and Adaptee – An interface layer between caller and Adapter allows new Adapters to be more easily added to the system during runtime. An interface between Adapter and Adaptee allows the Adaptees to be dynamically loaded during runtime. In combination, these interface layers make it possible to develop a truly pluggable Adapter design, where the Adaptees can be changed as needed in a running system.

Related Patterns

Related patterns include the following:

- Bridge (page 150) – Although the Adapter and the Bridge pattern are very similar, their intent is different. The Bridge pattern separates the abstraction and the implementation of a component and allows each to be changed independently. The Adapter pattern allows using an otherwise incompatible existing object.
- Decorator (page 166) – The Adapter pattern is intended to change the interface of an object, but keep the same functionality. The Decorator leaves the interface of the object the same but enhances its functionality.

- Proxy (page 197) – Both the Adapter pattern and the Proxy pattern provide a front interface to an object. The difference is that the Adapter pattern provides a different interface and the Proxy pattern provides the same interface as the object.
- Business Delegate [CJ2EEP] – The Business Delegate pattern can be used as a Proxy. The Business Delegate can be a local representative of the business tier.

  The Business Delegate can also operate as an Adapter for otherwise incompatible systems.

Example

In this example, the PIM uses an API provided by a foreign source. Two files represent the interface into a purchased set of classes intended to represent contacts. The basic operations are defined in the interface called `Chovnatlh`.

Example 3.1 `Chovnatlh.java`

```
1.    public interface Chovnatlh{
2.        public String tlhapWa$DIchPong();
3.        public String tlhapQavPong();
4.        public String tlhapPatlh();
5.        public String tlhapGhom();
6.
7.        public void cherWa$DIchPong(String chu$wa$DIchPong);
8.        public void cherQavPong(String chu$QavPong);
9.        public void cherPatlh(String chu$patlh);
10.       public void cherGhom(String chu$ghom);
11.   }
```

The implementation for these methods is provided in the associated class, `ChovnatlhImpl`.

Example 3.2 `ChovnatlhImpl.java`

```
1.    // pong = name
2.    // wa'DIch = first
3.    // Qav = last
4.    // patlh = rank (title)
5.    // ghom = group (organization)
6.    // tlhap = take (get)
7.    // cher = set up (set)
8.    // chu' = new
9.    // chovnatlh = specimen (contact)
10.
11.   public class ChovnatlhImpl implements Chovnatlh{
12.       private String wa$DIchPong;
13.       private String QavPong;
14.       private String patlh;
15.       private String ghom;
16.
```

```
17.        public ChovnatlhImpl(){ }
18.        public ChovnatlhImpl(String chu$wa$DIchPong, String chu$QavPong,
19.            String chu$patlh, String chu$ghom){
20.                wa$DIchPong = chu$wa$DIchPong;
21.                QavPong = chu$QavPong;
22.                patlh = chu$patlh;
23.                ghom = chu$ghom;
24.        }
25.
26.        public String tlhapWa$DIchPong(){ return wa$DIchPong; }
27.        public String tlhapQavPong(){ return QavPong; }
28.        public String tlhapPatlh(){ return patlh; }
29.        public String tlhapGhom(){ return ghom; }
30.
31.        public void cherWa$DIchPong(String chu$wa$DIchPong){ wa$DIchPong =
      chu$wa$DIchPong; }
32.        public void cherQavPong(String chu$QavPong){ QavPong = chu$QavPong; }
33.        public void cherPatlh(String chu$patlh){ patlh = chu$patlh; }
34.        public void cherGhom(String chu$ghom){ ghom = chu$ghom; }
35.
36.        public String toString(){
37.            return wa$DIchPong + " " + QavPong + ": " + patlh + ", " + ghom;
38.        }
39.    }
```

With help from a translator, it is possible to match the methods to those found in the `Contact` interface. The `ContactAdapter` class performs this task by using a variable to hold an internal `ChovnatlhImpl` object. This object manages the information required to hold the `Contact` information: name, title, and organization.

Example 3.3 `Contact.java`

```
1.     import java.io.Serializable;
2.     public interface Contact extends Serializable{
3.         public static final String SPACE = " ";
4.         public String getFirstName();
5.         public String getLastName();
6.         public String getTitle();
7.         public String getOrganization();
8.
9.         public void setFirstName(String newFirstName);
10.        public void setLastName(String newLastName);
11.        public void setTitle(String newTitle);
12.        public void setOrganization(String newOrganization);
13.    }
```

Example 3.4 `ContactAdapter.java`

```
1.     public class ContactAdapter implements Contact{
2.         private Chovnatlh contact;
3.
4.         public ContactAdapter(){
5.             contact = new ChovnatlhImpl();
6.         }
```

```
7.        public ContactAdapter(Chovnatlh newContact){
8.            contact = newContact;
9.        }
10.
11.       public String getFirstName(){
12.           return contact.tlhapWa$DIchPong();
13.       }
14.       public String getLastName(){
15.           return contact.tlhapQavPong();
16.       }
17.       public String getTitle(){
18.           return contact.tlhapPatlh();
19.       }
20.       public String getOrganization(){
21.           return contact.tlhapGhom();
22.       }
23.
24.       public void setContact(Chovnatlh newContact){
25.           contact = newContact;
26.       }
27.       public void setFirstName(String newFirstName){
28.           contact.cherWa$DIchPong(newFirstName);
29.       }
30.       public void setLastName(String newLastName){
31.           contact.cherQavPong(newLastName);
32.       }
33.       public void setTitle(String newTitle){
34.           contact.cherPatlh(newTitle);
35.       }
36.       public void setOrganization(String newOrganization){
37.           contact.cherGhom(newOrganization);
38.       }
39.
40.       public String toString(){
41.           return contact.toString();
42.       }
43.   }
```

Bridge

Also known as Handle/Body

Pattern Properties

Type: Structural, Object
Level: Component

Purpose

To divide a complex component into two separate but related inheritance hierarchies: the functional abstraction and the internal implementation. This makes it easier to change either aspect of the component.

Introduction

If you want to develop a To Do list for the Personal Information Manager, you might want to have flexibility in how it's represented to the user—listed items like tasks or contacts with bullets, numbers, maybe hieroglyphs. Additionally, you might want to have some way to modify the basic list functionality, giving users the ability to choose between an unordered list, a sequential list or a prioritized list.

To support this feature in the software, develop a group of list classes, each of which would provide a specific way to display the list and organize its information. This solution quickly becomes impractical, however, since there are many combinations of ways to display a list, and ways to store the list information.

It is be better to separate the To Do list's representation from its underlying implementation. The Bridge pattern accomplishes this by defining two classes or interfaces that work together. For the PIM, these are `List` and `ListImpl`. The `List` represents display functionality, but delegates the actual storage of list items to its underlying implementation, the `ListImpl` class.

The benefit of this approach is apparent when you add capabilities to the basic behavior. To add characters or numbering, subclass `List`. To support features like grouping items sequentially, extend `ListImpl`. The beauty of this solution is that you can "mix and match" the classes, producing a much greater range of total functionality.

Applicability

Use Bridge when:

- You want flexibility between the component's abstraction and implementation, avoiding a static relationship between the two.
- Any changes of the implementation should be invisible to clients.
- You identify multiple component abstractions and implementations.
- Subclassing is appropriate, but you want to manage the two aspects of the system separately.

Description

Complex elements in a system can sometimes vary in both their external functionality and their underlying implementation. In such cases, inheritance is an undesirable solution, since the number of classes you must create increases as a function of both these aspects. Two representations and implementations yield four classes to develop, while three representations and implementations result in nine classes (see Table 3-2).

In addition, inheritance ties a component into a static model, making it difficult to change in the future. Changing a component is particularly challenging since they tend to vary as a system is being developed and used. It would be preferable to create a dynamic way to vary both aspects of the component on an as-needed basis.

Enter the Bridge pattern. The Bridge solves the problem by decoupling the two aspects of the component. With two separate inheritance chains—one devoted to functionality, the other to implementation—it's much easier to mix and match elements from each side. This provides greater overall flexibility at a lower coding cost.

In addition, the coding requirements for the Bridge give you an overall savings in the number of classes written as you increase the number of variations. Table 3-2 shows the number of terminal classes required using strict inheritance compared with the Bridge pattern.

Table 3-2 *Class coding requirements*

External representations	Implementations	Classes required with inheritance	Classes required with Bridge
2	2	4	4
3	2	6	5
4	4	16	8
5	4	20	9

Comparison of Inheritance Pattern and Bridge Pattern

The Bridge design allows you to *multiplex* the external representation and internal implementation choices for the component. Multiplexing simply means associating any combination of external and internal elements, to get a greater range of options.

Dividing the component according to its two differentiating concepts also tends to produce a component that is easier to understand and maintain. This is because each inheritance chain revolves around a single concept, abstraction or implementation.

The Bridge is a useful pattern for any system that should display localized flexibility during runtime. An example is GUI systems that must be portable among platforms, requiring that an underlying implementation be applied when the application is started in a different operating system. Systems that change their representation of data depending on locale (for example, altering date, language, or monetary representation) are often good candidates for the Bridge, as well. Similarly, the Bridge is often effective for business entities that can potentially map back to a number of different database sources.

A conceptual example for the Bridge is a technical support switchboard. A number of pre-established phone lines connect a user with a variety of technical support personnel. Naturally, the response will be markedly different depending on the experience of the technical support representative who is on the line. The response probably varies according to the question as well; there will be a somewhat different response to users complaining about broken cup-holders on their PCs.

Implementation

The Bridge class diagram is shown in Figure 3.3.

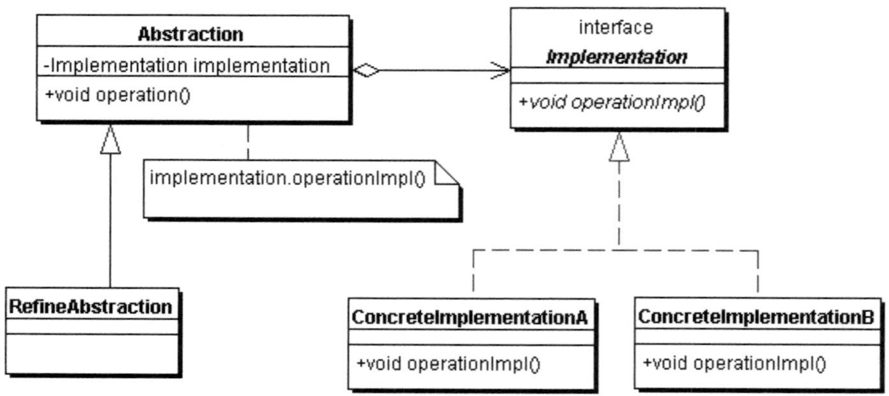

Figure 3.3 *Bridge class diagram*

Implementing the Bridge pattern requires the following classes:

- `Abstraction` – The `Abstraction` class defines the functional abstraction for the `Bridge`, providing standard behavior and structure. It contains a reference to an `Implementation` instance. This `Implementation` instance is usually set with either a setter method (to allow modification at run-time) or through the constructor.
- `RefineAbstraction` – The `RefineAbstraction` class extends the `Abstraction` class and provides additional or modified behavior.
- `Implementation` – The `Implementation` interface represents the underlying functionality used by the `Abstraction` instances.
- `ConcreteImplementation` – `ConcreteImplementation` implements the `Implementation` interface. It provides the behavior and structure for `Implementation` classes.

Benefits and Drawbacks

The Bridge offers the potential to share underlying implementation objects among multiple abstraction objects. It provides greater flexibility when changing implementations, and the changes can occur without any action required on the part of the client.

When designing an application that uses the Bridge pattern, it is important to properly define which responsibilities belong to the functional abstraction and which belong to the internal implementation class. Likewise, you must carefully consider what represents the true base model for your implementation of the Bridge pattern. A common problem you might experience when using the Bridge stems from developing the pattern implementation around one or two possible variations. The danger is that future development of the pattern will reveal that some of the assumed elements of core behavior actually represented specific variations based on the abstraction and/or implementation.

Like many of the distributed object patterns, you might also need to consider what the concept of equality really means for the Bridge. Does the abstraction or the implementation, or both, represent the important object for comparison?

Pattern Variants

Pattern variants include the following:

- Automatic Bridges – Some Bridge pattern implementations are made to vary their implementation without any action by the end user, relying instead on information provided from the application or operating platform to customize themselves.

- Shared implementations – Some implementation classes, especially stateless ones (classes that do not maintain an internal state), can be shared among multiple application objects. Depending on how widely they can be shared, such classes can potentially be implemented as an interface.
- Single implementation – Sometimes there is only a single implementation class, which services multiple abstraction classes. If there is only a single implementation, it is probably not necessary to define a base class for the implementation part of a Bridge.

Related Patterns

Related patterns include the following:

- Adapter (page 142) – The Bridge and the Adapter pattern are very similar in structure but differ in their intent. The Bridge pattern separates the abstraction and the implementation to allow both to change independently, and is an upfront design choice. The Adapter pattern enables use of an object whose interface would otherwise be incompatible.
- Singleton (page 34) – As mentioned in the variants section the Singleton pattern can be used when "implementation" classes can be shared.
- Flyweight (page 183) – When the tree structure becomes large, applying the Flyweight pattern can help reduce the number of objects managed by the tree.

Example

Note: For a full working example of this code example, with additional supporting classes and/or a `RunPattern` class, see "Bridge" on page 448 of the "Full Code Examples" appendix.

This example shows how to use the Bridge pattern to extend the functionality of a To Do list for the PIM. The To Do list is fairly straightforward—simply a list with the ability to add and remove `Strings`.

For the Bridge pattern, an element is defined in two parts: an abstraction and an implementation. The implementation is the class that does all the real work—in this case, it stores and retrieves list entries. The general behavior for the PIM list is defined in the `ListImpl` interface.

Example 3.5 `ListImpl.java`

```
1.    public interface ListImpl{
2.        public void addItem(String item);
3.        public void addItem(String item, int position);
4.        public void removeItem(String item);
```

```
5.         public int getNumberOfItems();
6.         public String getItem(int index);
7.         public boolean supportsOrdering();
8.     }
```

The `OrderedListImpl` class implements `ListImpl`, and stores list entries in an internal `ArrayList` object.

Example 3.6 `OrderedListImpl.java`

```
1.     import java.util.ArrayList;
2.     public class OrderedListImpl implements ListImpl{
3.         private ArrayList items = new ArrayList();
4.
5.         public void addItem(String item){
6.             if (!items.contains(item)){
7.                 items.add(item);
8.             }
9.         }
10.        public void addItem(String item, int position){
11.            if (!items.contains(item)){
12.                items.add(position, item);
13.            }
14.        }
15.
16.        public void removeItem(String item){
17.            if (items.contains(item)){
18.                items.remove(items.indexOf(item));
19.            }
20.        }
21.
22.        public boolean supportsOrdering(){
23.            return true;
24.        }
25.
26.        public int getNumberOfItems(){
27.            return items.size();
28.        }
29.
30.        public String getItem(int index){
31.            if (index < items.size()){
32.                return (String)items.get(index);
33.            }
34.            return null;
35.        }
36.    }
```

The abstraction represents the operations on the list that are available to the outside world. The `BaseList` class provides general list capabilities.

Example 3.7 `BaseList.java`

```
1.    public class BaseList{
2.        protected ListImpl implementor;
3.
4.        public void setImplementor(ListImpl impl){
5.            implementor = impl;
6.        }
7.
8.        public void add(String item){
9.            implementor.addItem(item);
10.       }
11.       public void add(String item, int position){
12.           if (implementor.supportsOrdering()){
13.               implementor.addItem(item, position);
14.           }
15.       }
16.
17.       public void remove(String item){
18.           implementor.removeItem(item);
19.       }
20.
21.       public String get(int index){
22.           return implementor.getItem(index);
23.       }
24.
25.       public int count(){
26.           return implementor.getNumberOfItems();
27.       }
28.   }
```

Note that all the operations are delegated to the implementer variable, which represents the list implementation. Whenever operations are requested of the `List`, they are actually delegated "across the bridge" to the associated `ListImpl` object.

It's easy to extend the features provided by the `BaseList`—you subclass the `BaseList` and add additional functionality. The `NumberedList` class demonstrates the power of the Bridge; by overriding the get method, the class is able to provide numbering of the items on the list.

Example 3.8 `NumberedList.java`

```
1.    public class NumberedList extends BaseList{
2.        public String get(int index){
3.            return (index + 1) + ". " + super.get(index);
4.        }
5.    }
```

Composite

Pattern Properties

Type: Structural, Object
Level: Component

Purpose

To develop a flexible way to create hierarchical tree structures of arbitrary complexity, while enabling every element in the structure to operate with a uniform interface.

Introduction

You've decided to enhance the Personal Information Manager to let users manage a complex project. Features of this enhancement include defining the project as a group of tasks and related subtasks, and associating deliverables with tasks. A natural way to accomplish this from a programming perspective is to define a tree structure, where the root task (which represents the project itself) branches out to subprojects, subsubprojects, and so on. Therefore, you define a `Task` class that holds a collection of other `Task` and `Deliverable` objects. Since both the `Task` and `Deliverable` relate to the project, you define a common parent for them—the `ProjectItem` class.

However, what happens if users need to perform an action that depends on the whole tree? For example, a project manager wants a time estimate for tasks and deliverables for one project. To accommodate this, you write code to traverse the tree and call the appropriate methods at each branch. That's a lot of work, however, involving separate code to walk the tree, call the methods, and collect the results. And with different classes (`Task` and `Deliverable`) at each branch of the tree, you might need to handle them differently when getting time estimates. For a large number of classes or a complex tree, the code quickly becomes difficult to manage.

There's a better way to solve this problem. With the Composite pattern, you can use polymorphism and recursion to provide an efficient, simple, easy-to-maintain solution.

Begin by defining a standard method for all classes that provides the time estimate, called `getTimeRequired`. Define this method for the `ProjectItem` interface, and implement that behavior in all classes that are types of `Project-Item`. For `Deliverable`, define `getTimeRequired` to return 0, because a deliverable does not have time associated directly with it. For the `Task` class, return a time consisting of the time for the task plus the sum of the `getTimeRequired` calls for all of the `Task` children.

Using this pattern, you define `getTimeRequired` so that it automatically calculates the project time estimates for any part of the tree. Just call the `getTimeRequired` method for the part of the `Task` needed, and the code in the method takes care of the job of traversing the tree and calculating results.

Applicability

Use the Composite pattern when:

- There is a component model with a branch-leaf structure (whole-part or container-contained).
- The structure can have any level of complexity, and is dynamic.
- You want to treat the component structure uniformly, using common operations throughout the hierarchy.

Description

Object-oriented developers are often interested in developing components that follow a whole-part model. Whole-part model is a model that allows you to treat a collection of identical objects (the parts) as one entity (the whole).Typically, these structures should be flexible and easy to use. Users should be able to modify the structure as an application runs, adding or removing parts to suit their needs. At the same time, it's desirable to keep the complexity of the structure hidden behind the scenes, so that users perceive only a seamless, unified product.

The Composite pattern supports these characteristics by defining a class structure that supports extensibility. This structure is composed of a component, leaf, and Composite class.

- The base component provides the core model, defining standard methods or variables to be used by all the objects in the Composite.
- Leaf classes support terminal behavior. That is, they represent parts of the Composite, but they cannot contain other components.
- Composite or branch classes can have other components added to them, permitting extensibility of the Composite structure.

A drawing created using graphical editing tools is a common example of the Composite pattern in action. With a drawing, a number of elementary shapes can be associated and treated as a whole; you also can define drawings so that they contain other drawings, or a mixture of drawings and shapes.

Additional possibilities for Composite pattern use include applications with organizational charts, task breakdowns, schedules, and outlining features. Applications that support grouping are also good candidates for the Composite pattern, provided that the grouping action can be performed recursively and that the final product, as well as its component elements, have the same functional behavior.

Implementation

The basic Composite class diagram is shown in Figure 3.4.

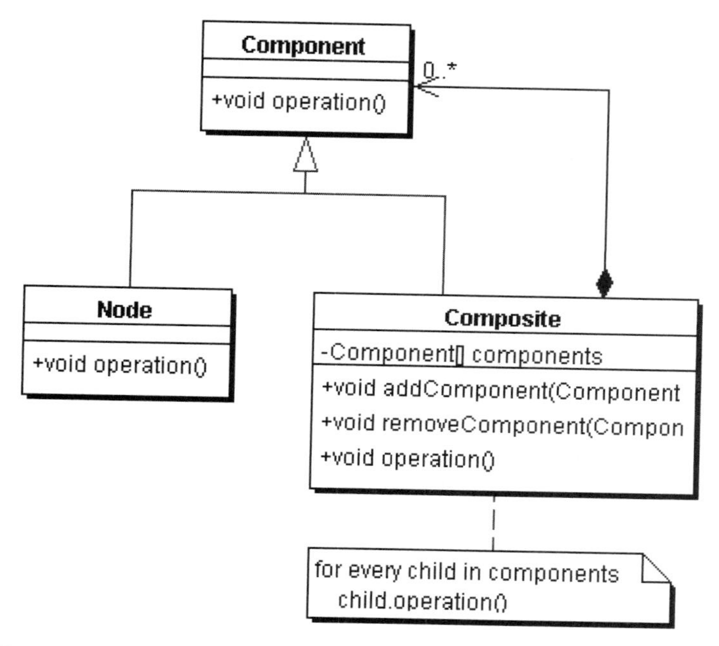

Figure 3.4 *Composite class diagram*

The Composite has three elements:

- `Component` – The `Component` interface defines methods available for all parts of the tree structure. `Component` may be implemented as abstract class when you need to provide standard behavior to all of the sub-types. Normally, the component is not instantiable; its subclasses or implementing classes, also called nodes, are instantiable and are used to create a collection or tree structure.
- `Composite` – This class is defined by the components it contains; it is composed by its components. The `Composite` supports a dynamic group of `Components` so it has methods to add and remove `Component` instances from its collection. The methods defined in the `Component` are

implemented to execute the behavior specific for this type of `Composite` and to call the same method on each of its nodes. These `Composite` classes are also called branch or container classes.

- `Leaf` – The class that implements the `Component` interface and that provides an implementation for each of the `Component`'s methods. The distinction between a `Leaf` class and a `Composite` class is that the `Leaf` contains no references to other `Components`. The `Leaf` classes represent the lowest levels of the containment structure.

A general consideration when implementing this pattern is whether each component should have a reference to its container (composite). The benefit of such a reference is that it eases the traversal of the tree, but it also decreases your flexibility.

Benefits and Drawbacks

The Composite pattern provides a powerful combination: considerable flexibility of structure and an extremely manageable interface.

The structure can be changed at any time by calling the appropriate methods on a Composite to add or remove Components. Changing a Composite's Components means you're able to change the behavior of the Composites.

No matter where you are in the tree structure, you can call the same method on each of the individual components.

The use of interfaces further increases the flexibility. Interfaces allow the construction of frameworks using the Composite pattern and they enable the introduction of new types at runtime.

At the same time, use of interfaces can be a drawback when you want to define attributes and provide default implementations in order to let each of the nodes inherit behavior. In that case, the Component needs to be an abstract class.

Another drawback of the pattern arises from its flexibility—because it is so dynamic, the Composite pattern is often difficult to test and debug. It normally requires a more sophisticated test/validation strategy that is designed around the concept of the whole-part object hierarchy. If testing becomes a problem, the best approach is to build the testing into the Composite class implementation.

Additionally, the Composite normally requires full advance knowledge of the structure being modeled (in other words, a full class design for the Composite), or a more sophisticated class-loading mechanism. The interface form of this pattern (discussed in the *Pattern Variants* section) can be a useful alternative for providing dynamic behavior during runtime.

Pattern Variants

Some variations on the base Composite pattern include:

- The root node – To improve manageability in systems, some Composite implementers define a distinct object that acts as the base for the entire Composite object hierarchy. If the root object is represented as a separate class, it can be implemented as a Singleton, or the access to the root node can be granted through a Singleton, without the class itself being a Singleton.
- Rule-based branching – For more complex Composite structures, typically those with multiple types of nodes and branches, you might need to enforce rules about how and when certain kinds of nodes can be joined to certain branch types.

Related Patterns

Related patterns include the following:

- Chain of Responsibility (page 42) – Used with the Composite pattern when methods need to be propagated "up" the tree, from leaves to branch nodes.
- Flyweight (page 183) – When the tree structure becomes large, applying the Flyweight pattern can help reduce the number of objects managed by the tree.
- Iterator (page 69) – The Iterator pattern can be used with the Composite pattern to encapsulate the traversal of the tree, which otherwise could become complicated. Iterator is sometimes used to traverse a Composite.
- Visitor (page 121) – Used with Composite to centralize behavior that would otherwise have to be split among the leaf and branch classes.
- Composite View [CJ2EEP] – The Composite View pattern describes how a view can be composed of several other views (which in turn can be composed of views), similar to the Composite pattern.

Example

Note: For a full working example of this code example, with additional supporting classes and/or a `RunPattern` class, see "Composite" on page 453 of the "Full Code Examples" appendix.

The Composite class diagram for the code example is shown in Figure 3.5.

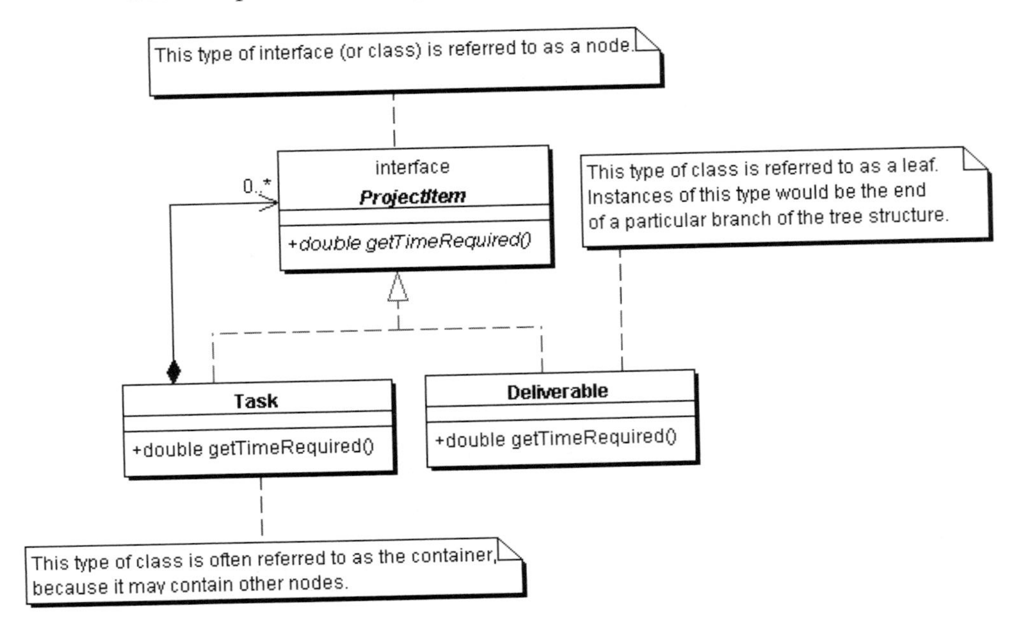

Figure 3.5 *Composite class diagram for the code example*

The example demonstrates how to use the Composite pattern to calculate the time required to complete a project or some part of a project. The example has four principal parts:

- `Deliverable` – A class that represents an end product of a completed `Task`.
- `Project` – The class used as the root of the composite, representing the entire project.
- `ProjectItem` – This interface describes functionality common to all items that can be part of a project. The `getTimeRequired` method is defined in this interface.
- `Task` – A class that represents a collection of actions to perform. The task has a collection of `ProjectItem` objects.

The general functionality available to every object that can be part of a project is defined in the `ProjectItem` interface. In this example, there is only a single method defined: `getTimeRequired`.

Example 3.9 `ProjectItem.java`

```
1.    import java.io.Serializable;
```

```
2.    public interface ProjectItem extends Serializable{
3.        public double getTimeRequired();
4.    }
```

Since the project items can be organized into a tree structure, two kinds of classes are ProjectItems. The Deliverable class represents a terminal node, which cannot reference other project items.

Example 3.10 Deliverable.java

```
1.    import java.io.Serializable;
2.    public interface ProjectItem extends Serializable{
3.        public double getTimeRequired();
4.    }
```

The Project and Task classes are nonterminal or branch nodes. Both classes keep a collection of ProjectItems that represent children: associated tasks or deliverables.

Example 3.11 Project.java

```
1.    import java.util.ArrayList;
2.    import java.util.Iterator;
3.    public class Project implements ProjectItem{
4.        private String name;
5.        private String description;
6.        private ArrayList projectItems = new ArrayList();
7.
8.        public Project(){ }
9.        public Project(String newName, String newDescription){
10.           name = newName;
11.           description = newDescription;
12.       }
13.
14.       public String getName(){ return name; }
15.       public String getDescription(){ return description; }
16.       public ArrayList getProjectItems(){ return projectItems; }
17.       public double getTimeRequired(){
18.           double totalTime = 0;
19.           Iterator items = projectItems.iterator();
20.           while(items.hasNext()){
21.               ProjectItem item = (ProjectItem)items.next();
22.               totalTime += item.getTimeRequired();
23.           }
24.           return totalTime;
25.       }
26.
27.       public void setName(String newName){ name = newName; }
28.       public void setDescription(String newDescription){ description = newDescrip-
      tion; }
29.
30.       public void addProjectItem(ProjectItem element){
31.           if (!projectItems.contains(element)){
```

```
32.                 projectItems.add(element);
33.             }
34.         }
35.         public void removeProjectItem(ProjectItem element){
36.             projectItems.remove(element);
37.         }
38.     }
```

Example 3.12 `Project.java`

```
1.      import java.util.ArrayList;
2.      import java.util.Iterator;
3.      public class Project implements ProjectItem{
4.          private String name;
5.          private String description;
6.          private ArrayList projectItems = new ArrayList();
7.
8.          public Project(){ }
9.          public Project(String newName, String newDescription){
10.             name = newName;
11.             description = newDescription;
12.         }
13.
14.         public String getName(){ return name; }
15.         public String getDescription(){ return description; }
16.         public ArrayList getProjectItems(){ return projectItems; }
17.         public double getTimeRequired(){
18.             double totalTime = 0;
19.             Iterator items = projectItems.iterator();
20.             while(items.hasNext()){
21.                 ProjectItem item = (ProjectItem)items.next();
22.                 totalTime += item.getTimeRequired();
23.             }
24.             return totalTime;
25.         }
26.
27.         public void setName(String newName){ name = newName; }
28.         public void setDescription(String newDescription){ description = newDescrip-
        tion; }
29.
30.         public void addProjectItem(ProjectItem element){
31.             if (!projectItems.contains(element)){
32.                 projectItems.add(element);
33.             }
34.         }
35.         public void removeProjectItem(ProjectItem element){
36.             projectItems.remove(element);
37.         }
38.     }
```

Example 3.13 `Task.java`

```
1.      import java.util.ArrayList;
2.      import java.util.Iterator;
3.      public class Task implements ProjectItem{
4.          private String name;
5.          private String details;
```

```
6.          private ArrayList projectItems = new ArrayList();
7.          private Contact owner;
8.          private double timeRequired;
9.
10.         public Task(){ }
11.         public Task(String newName, String newDetails,
12.             Contact newOwner, double newTimeRequired){
13.             name = newName;
14.             details = newDetails;
15.             owner = newOwner;
16.             timeRequired = newTimeRequired;
17.         }
18.
19.         public String getName(){ return name; }
20.         public String getDetails(){ return details; }
21.         public ArrayList getProjectItems(){ return projectItems; }
22.         public Contact getOwner(){ return owner; }
23.         public double getTimeRequired(){
24.             double totalTime = timeRequired;
25.             Iterator items = projectItems.iterator();
26.             while(items.hasNext()){
27.                 ProjectItem item = (ProjectItem)items.next();
28.                 totalTime += item.getTimeRequired();
29.             }
30.             return totalTime;
31.         }
32.
33.         public void setName(String newName){ name = newName; }
34.         public void setDetails(String newDetails){ details = newDetails; }
35.         public void setOwner(Contact newOwner){ owner = newOwner; }
36.         public void setTimeRequired(double newTimeRequired){ timeRequired = newTimeRe-
        quired; }
37.
38.         public void addProjectItem(ProjectItem element){
39.             if (!projectItems.contains(element)){
40.                 projectItems.add(element);
41.             }
42.         }
43.         public void removeProjectItem(ProjectItem element){
44.             projectItems.remove(element);
45.         }
46.     }
```

The `getTimeRequired` method shows how the Composite pattern runs. To get the time estimate for any part of the project, you simply call the method `getTimeRequired` for a `Project` or `Task` object. This method behaves differently depending on the method implementer:

- `Deliverable`: Return 0.
- `Project` or `Task`: Return the sum of the time required for the object plus the results of calling the `getTimeRequired` method for all `ProjectItems` associated with this node.

Decorator

Also known as Wrapper

Pattern Properties

Type: Structural, Object
Level: Component

Purpose

To provide a way to flexibly add or remove component functionality without changing its external appearance or function.

Introduction

The Composite pattern example in the previous section added project functionality to the Personal Information Manager, with a `Project` composed of a hierarchy of `Task` and `Deliverable` objects. All classes implemented the `ProjectItem` interface, which identified them as classes that belonged to a project.

What if you wanted to extend the basic capabilities of the `Task` and `Deliverable` classes, adding extra features like the following?

- Dependent items – A `ProjectItem` that depends on another `Task` or `Deliverable` for completion.
- Supporting documents – A `Task` or `Deliverable` that can reference additional reference documentation.

If you added these capabilities by subclassing, you would have to code a lot of classes. For instance, to make only `Deliverable` support these features, you would have to write four classes: `Deliverable`, `DependentDeliverable`, `SupportedDeliverable`, and `SupportedDependentDeliverable`.

Faced with this drawback, you might consider object composition as a way to add the new functionality. Coding optional support into `Deliverable` and `Task` for both new features, however, can mean maintaining duplicate code in multiple locations. At the very least, you increase the amount and complexity of the code.

What if, instead, you produce classes that have "plugin" capabilities? Instead of trying to add features to `Task` and `Deliverable` directly, you create dependent classes that can be attached to any `ProjectItem` to extend the basic functionality. You could say it's the coding equivalent of adding a 3D sound set to your standard stereo. Your basic audio capabilities remain the same, only now you have some extra feature to play with. For example, define a `DependentProjectItem` and a `SupportedProjectItem`. Each class has only the code needed to support its optional capability, and a reference to the real `ProjectItem` that it extends. This means you have less code to maintain, and the freedom to use any combination of these `Decorator` classes to add groups of capabilities to `ProjectItems`.

Applicability

Use the Decorator pattern when:

- You want to make dynamic changes that are transparent to users, without the restrictions of subclassing.
- Component capabilities can be added or withdrawn as the system runs.
- There are a number of independently varying features that you should apply dynamically, and which you can use in any combination on a component.

Description

Some objects have complex functionality and/or structure that can be added or removed in an accurate component model. In the same way that overlays can be added to a map, showing additional features such as cities or elevation, you might want the flexibility to add and remove certain features for an object.

The Decorator pattern works by allowing layers to be added to and removed from a base object. Each layer can provide behavior (methods) and state (variables) to augment the base object. The layers can be chained and freely associated with this pattern, allowing you to create advanced object behavior from a set of fairly simple building blocks.

The Decorator pattern is naturally suited for applications involving overlays and views that can be dynamically built. Groupware products, which allow networked teams to combine edit work on a single base document, are one example. Some image editors are well-suited to the Decorator, as well as most applications involving text, paragraph or document formatting. At a lower level, the Decorator allows functionality to be built up as a combination of filters applied to a base model. Stream-based I/O or communication endpoints (sockets) offer a few examples, like the `BufferedReader`, which allows you to read line by line from a `Reader` object.

The Decorator pattern can be compared to the various optional extras available for an automobile. Working with a base model, the factory can add additional features such as rust-proofing, cruise control, upgraded sound systems, remote entry, and so on. With each "layer" added to the vehicle, the vehicle acquires new characteristics, and the price increases accordingly. (Of course, unlike the Decorator pattern, customers cannot change these features once they drive the vehicle off the lot.)

Implementation

The Decorator class diagram is shown in Figure 3.6.

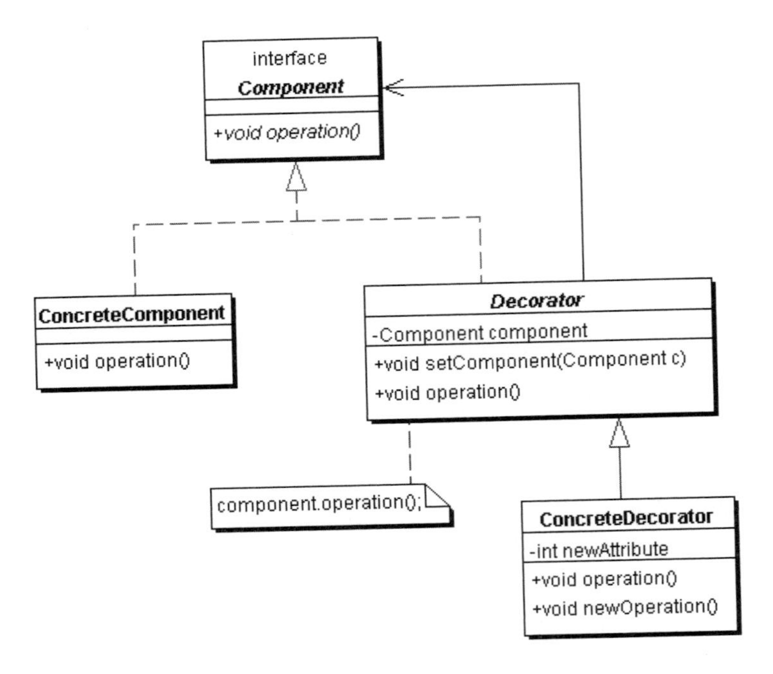

Figure 3.6 *Decorator class diagram*

For the Decorator pattern, implement the following:

- `Component` – Represents the component containing generic behavior. It can be an abstract class or an interface.
- `Decorator` – `Decorator` defines the standard behaviors expected of all Decorators. `Decorator` can be an abstract class or an interface. The `Decorator` provides support for containment; that is, it holds a reference to a `Component`, which can be a `ConcreteComponent` or another `Decorator`. By defining the `Decorator` class hierarchy as a subclass of the component(s) they extend, the same reference can be used for either purpose.
- One or more `ConcreteDecorators` – Each `Decorator` subclass needs to support chaining (reference to a component, plus the ability to add and remove that reference). Beyond the base requirement, each `Decorator` can define additional methods and/or variables to extend the component.

Benefits and Drawbacks

The Decorator offers the opportunity to easily adjust and augment the behavior of an object during runtime. In addition, coding can become substantially easier, since you need to write a series of classes, each targeted at a specific bit of functionality, rather than coding all behavior into the component itself. This also tends to make the component more easily extensible in the future, since changes can be introduced by coding new classes.

Depending on their behavior, some Decorator layers may be shared among multiple component objects (normally, layers that have stateless behavior, i.e. no state is maintained or used). This can reduce memory consumption in the system.

When taken to an extreme, the Decorator pattern usually produces a large number of layers: this means lots of little objects between a user and the real object. This can have a number of consequences. Debugging and testing code becomes more difficult, and the operating speed of a system can be reduced if the Decorator is improperly designed.

You must ensure that object equality is treated properly; this is especially important for the Decorator pattern, since object layers sit "in front" of each other. Typically, if equality testing is required in an application, you must code an equality operation that identifies the underlying object, or the combination of the base object and the order and "values" of each of the layers, rather than just the top layer.

Finally, it might require some work to properly handle removing layers from a system, since they could exist anywhere within the Decorator chain. To simplify matters, some Decorators define both a forward and a backward reference to make them easier to remove.

Pattern Variants

Pattern variants include the following:

- As mentioned in "Benefits and Drawbacks," it is sometimes desirable to develop `Decorator` classes with a forward and a backward reference to make them easier to remove as a system runs.
- Some Decorator implementations don't use an abstract `Decorator`. Normally, this variation is used when there is only a single variation possible for the component.
- You can create overriding `Decorators`, which will redefine some parts of a component's behavior. Take care when using such a `Decorator`, however, since components based on this pattern can exhibit unpredictable behavior unless there are strict rules in the code governing when and how behavior can be overridden.

Related Patterns

Related patterns include the following:

- Adapter (page 142) – The Adapter pattern is intended to change the interface on the same functionality, whereas the Decorator leaves the interface the same but changes the functionality.
- Composite (page 157) – The Decorator may be viewed as a simpler version of the Composite pattern; instead of having a collection of Components, the Decorator keeps a maximum of one reference to another Component. The other difference is that the Decorator enhances the functionality instead of just passing on the method calls.
- Strategy (page 114) – The Decorator pattern is used to modify or extend an object's external functionality, while the Strategy pattern is used to modify an object's internal behavior.
- Intercepting Filter [CJ2EEP] – The Intercepting Filter pattern uses the Decorator pattern to decorate a service request without having to change the request.

Example

Note: For a full working example of this code example, with additional supporting classes and/or a `RunPattern` class, see "Decorator" on page 462 of the "Full Code Examples" appendix.

This example demonstrates how to use the Decorator pattern to extend the capability of the elements in a project. The foundation of the project is the `ProjectItem` interface. It is implemented by any class that can be used within a project. In this case, `ProjectItem` defines a single method, `getTimeRequired`.

Example 3.14 `ProjectItem.java`

```
1.   import java.io.Serializable;
2.   public interface ProjectItem extends Serializable{
3.       public static final String EOL_STRING = System.getProperty("line.separator");
4.       public double getTimeRequired();
5.   }
```

`Task` and `Deliverable` implement `ProjectItem` and provide the basic project functionality. As in previous demonstrations, `Task` represents some job in a project and `Deliverable` represents some concrete product.

Example 3.15 `Deliverable.java`

```
1.   public class Deliverable implements ProjectItem{
2.       private String name;
3.       private String description;
4.       private Contact owner;
5.
6.       public Deliverable(){ }
7.       public Deliverable(String newName, String newDescription,
8.           Contact newOwner){
9.           name = newName;
10.          description = newDescription;
11.          owner = newOwner;
12.      }
13.
14.      public String getName(){ return name; }
15.      public String getDescription(){ return description; }
16.      public Contact getOwner(){ return owner; }
17.      public double getTimeRequired(){ return 0; }
18.
19.      public void setName(String newName){ name = newName; }
20.      public void setDescription(String newDescription){ description = newDescrip-
     tion; }
21.      public void setOwner(Contact newOwner){ owner = newOwner; }
22.
23.      public String toString(){
24.          return "Deliverable: " + name;
25.      }
26.  }
```

Example 3.16 `Task.java`

```
1.   import java.util.ArrayList;
2.   import java.util.Iterator;
3.   public class Task implements ProjectItem{
4.       private String name;
5.       private ArrayList projectItems = new ArrayList();
6.       private Contact owner;
7.       private double timeRequired;
8.
9.       public Task(){ }
10.      public Task(String newName, Contact newOwner,
11.          double newTimeRequired){
12.          name = newName;
13.          owner = newOwner;
14.          timeRequired = newTimeRequired;
15.      }
16.
17.      public String getName(){ return name; }
18.      public ArrayList getProjectItems(){ return projectItems; }
19.      public Contact getOwner(){ return owner; }
20.      public double getTimeRequired(){
21.          double totalTime = timeRequired;
22.          Iterator items = projectItems.iterator();
23.          while(items.hasNext()){
24.              ProjectItem item = (ProjectItem)items.next();
25.              totalTime += item.getTimeRequired();
26.          }
```

```
27.            return totalTime;
28.        }
29.
30.        public void setName(String newName){ name = newName; }
31.        public void setOwner(Contact newOwner){ owner = newOwner; }
32.       public void setTimeRequired(double newTimeRequired){ timeRequired = newTimeRe-
      quired; }
33.
34.        public void addProjectItem(ProjectItem element){
35.            if (!projectItems.contains(element)){
36.                projectItems.add(element);
37.            }
38.        }
39.        public void removeProjectItem(ProjectItem element){
40.            projectItems.remove(element);
41.        }
42.
43.        public String toString(){
44.            return "Task: " + name;
45.        }
46.    }
```

It's time to introduce a decorator to extend the basic capabilities of these classes. The class `ProjectDecorator` will provide the central ability to augment `Task` and `Deliverable`.

Example 3.17 `ProjectDecorator.java`

```
1.     public abstract class ProjectDecorator implements ProjectItem{
2.         private ProjectItem projectItem;
3.
4.         protected ProjectItem getProjectItem(){ return projectItem; }
5.         public void setProjectItem(ProjectItem newProjectItem){ projectItem = new-
      ProjectItem; }
6.
7.         public double getTimeRequired(){
8.             return projectItem.getTimeRequired();
9.         }
10.    }
```

The `ProjectDecorator` implements the `ProjectItem` interface and maintains a variable for another `ProjectItem`, which represents the "decorated" element. Note that `ProjectDecorator` delegates the `getTimeRequired` method to its internal element. This would be done for any method that would depend on the functionality of the underlying component. If a `Task` with a required time of five days were decorated, you would still expect it to return a value of five days, regardless of any other capabilities it might have.

There are two subclasses of `ProjectDecorator` in this example. Both demonstrate a way to add some extra feature to project elements. The `DependentProjectItem` class is used to show that a `Task` or `Deliverable` depends on another `ProjectItem` for completion.

Example 3.18 `DependentProjectItem.java`

```
1.    public class DependentProjectItem extends ProjectDecorator{
2.        private ProjectItem dependentItem;
3.
4.        public DependentProjectItem(){ }
5.        public DependentProjectItem(ProjectItem newDependentItem){
6.            dependentItem = newDependentItem;
7.        }
8.
9.        public ProjectItem getDependentItem(){ return dependentItem; }
10.
11.       public void setDependentItem(ProjectItem newDependentItem){ dependentItem =
      newDependentItem; }
12.
13.       public String toString(){
14.           return getProjectItem().toString() + EOL_STRING
15.               + "\tProjectItem dependent on: " + dependentItem;
16.       }
17.   }
```

`SupportedProjectItem` decorates a `ProjectItem`, and keeps an `ArrayList` of supporting documents—file objects that represent additional information or resources.

Example 3.19 `SupportedProjectItem.java`

```
1.    import java.util.ArrayList;
2.    import java.io.File;
3.    public class SupportedProjectItem extends ProjectDecorator{
4.        private ArrayList supportingDocuments = new ArrayList();
5.
6.        public SupportedProjectItem(){ }
7.        public SupportedProjectItem(File newSupportingDocument){
8.            addSupportingDocument(newSupportingDocument);
9.        }
10.
11.       public ArrayList getSupportingDocuments(){
12.           return supportingDocuments;
13.       }
14.
15.       public void addSupportingDocument(File document){
16.           if (!supportingDocuments.contains(document)){
17.               supportingDocuments.add(document);
18.           }
19.       }
20.
21.       public void removeSupportingDocument(File document){
22.           supportingDocuments.remove(document);
23.       }
24.
25.       public String toString(){
26.           return getProjectItem().toString() + EOL_STRING
27.               + "\tSupporting Documents: " + supportingDocuments;
28.       }
29.   }
```

The benefit of defining additional capabilities in this way is that it is easy to create project items that have a combination of capabilities. Using these classes, you can make a simple task that depends on another project item, or a task with supporting documents. You can even chain Decorators together and create a task that depends on another task and has supporting documents. This flexibility is a key strength of the Decorator pattern.

Facade

Pattern Properties

Type: Structural
Level: Component

Purpose

To provide a simplified interface to a group of subsystems or a complex subsystem.

Introduction

Users like to be able to modify a GUI to make it more visually appealing or usable. For example, some users might have a visual impairment and have trouble reading a small font, so they need to increase the font size. Forcing the user to step through all the setup screens, (in the current small font size), wading through the modem and printer and scanner settings until reaching the setup options needed, wouldn't be very user friendly. A wizard, which would be designed for helping the visually impaired do setup, would be much better.

This kind of help should not limit the options to use and customize the application. Instead, you want to provide a specialized view of the system, and at the same time keep all the other features. This kind of a Facade pattern is a front end, or wizard, for the system.

Applicability

Use Facade to:

- Make complex systems easier to use by providing a simpler interface without removing the advanced options.
- Reduce coupling between clients and subsystems.
- Layer subsystems by providing Facades for sets of subsystems.

Description

Most modern software systems are fairly complex. Design patterns help you structure applications and better deal with the complexity. They often accomplish this by dividing functionality among a series of smaller classes. Additional classes can also be produced as a result of system partitioning. Dividing a system into several subsystems helps you deal with complex systems and provides the opportunity to partition the work.

Dividing a system into a number of specialized classes is a good object-oriented design practice. However, having a large number of classes in a system can be a drawback as well.

Clients using that system have to deal with more objects. Users tend to become confused when presented with hundreds of configuration options. Car manufacturers, among others, recognize this and adapt their products accordingly; for instance, when was the last time you had to set the air/gas ratio inside your car engine? Doing that every time you start your car is not practical. What you want is that you would only have to insert the car key and turn it to start the car (or actually the car engine). The rest should be handled for you. A client benefits from having only a few basic options. A Facade can provide these options and can then determine which subsystems to call.

Normally the Facade will delegate most of the work to the subsystems, but it can do some work itself.

Note that it is not the intent of a Facade to *hide* the subsystems. The intention is to provide a *simpler interface* to a set of subsystems, but clients who need the more elaborate options can still interact with the subsystems.

A setup wizard is one example of a Facade.

Implementation

The Facade object diagram is shown in Figure 3.7.

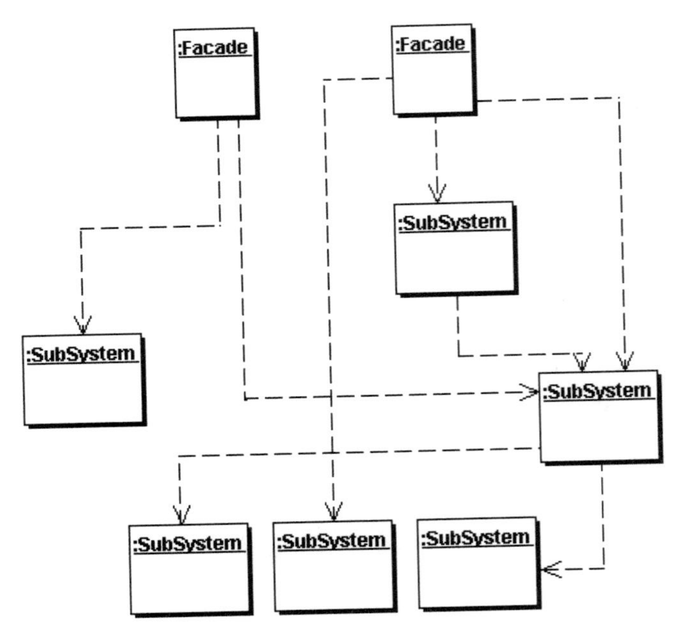

Figure 3.7 *Facade object diagram*

Implement the following for Facade:

- `Facade` – The class for clients to use. It knows about the subsystems it uses and their respective responsibilities. Normally all client requests will be delegated to the appropriate subsystems.
- `Subsystem` – This is a set of classes. They can be used by clients directly or will do work assigned to them by the `Facade`. It does not have knowledge of the `Facade`; for the subsystem the `Facade` will be just another client.

Benefits and Drawbacks

The benefit of the Facade pattern is that it provides a simple interface to a complex system without reducing the options provided by the total system. This interface protects the client from an overabundance of options.

The Facade translates the client requests to the subsystems that can fulfill those requests. Most of the time, one request will be delegated to more than one subsystem. Because the client interacts only with the Facade, the internal working of the system can change, while the client to the Facade can remain unchanged.

The Facade promotes low coupling between client and subsystems. It can also be used to reduce coupling between subsystems. Every subsystem can have its own Facade and other parts of the system use the Facade to communicate with the subsystem.

Pattern Variants

Pattern variants include the following:

- You can implement the Facade as an interface or an abstract class. This leaves the implementation details to a later time. It also reduces coupling.
- Several Facades can provide different interfaces to the same set of subsystems.
- The Facade pattern is sometimes varied in order to hide the subsystems. When the Facade pattern is used at the boundary between systems in an architecture, one of its goals is to reduce the complexity of system-system interaction. For instance, a system where calls pass through a central facade is more maintainable than one with a large number of cross-coupled classes).

Related Patterns

Related patterns include the following:

- Abstract Factory (page 6) – The Abstract Factory creates families of related objects. To simplify access to the different objects the factory has created, the factory can also create a Facade object.
- Mediator (page 77) – The Mediator pattern and the Facade pattern seem very similar. The difference is in the intent and in the implementation. The Mediator helps ease the communication between components and it adds behavior. The Facade is only an abstraction of the interface of one or more subsystems.
- Singleton (page 34) – The Facade uses the Singleton pattern to guarantee a single, globally accessible point of access for a subsystem.
- Session Facade [CJ2EEP] – The Session Facade pattern is a Facade that encapsulates the complexities of Enterprise JavaBeans™, to simplify the interface for its clients.

Example

Note: For a full working example of this code example, with additional supporting classes and/or a `RunPattern` class, see "Facade" on page 468 of the "Full Code Examples" appendix.

To make the PIM more functional for users, you want to give them the opportunity to customize the application. Some examples of items to customize include font type, font size, colors, which services to start when, default currency, etc. This example tracks a set of nationality-based settings.

In this example, the Facade class is the `InternationalizationWizard`. This class coordinates between a client and a number of objects associated with a selected nationality.

Example 3.20 `InternationalizationWizard.java`

```
1.    import java.util.HashMap;
2.    import java.text.NumberFormat;
3.    import java.util.Locale;
4.    public class InternationalizationWizard{
5.        private HashMap map;
6.        private Currency currency = new Currency();
7.        private InternationalizedText propertyFile = new InternationalizedText();
8.
9.        public InternationalizationWizard() {
10.           map = new HashMap();
11.           Nation[] nations = {
12.               new Nation("US", '$', "+1", "us.properties", NumberFormat.getIn-
      stance(Locale.US)),
```

```
13.            new Nation("The Netherlands", 'f', "+31", "dutch.properties", Number-
     Format.getInstance(Locale.GERMANY)),
14.            new Nation("France", 'f', "+33", "french.properties", NumberFormat.get-
     Instance(Locale.FRANCE))
15.        };
16.        for (int i = 0; i < nations.length; i++) {
17.            map.put(nations[i].getName(), nations[i]);
18.        }
19.    }
20.
21.    public void setNation(String name) {
22.        Nation nation = (Nation)map.get(name);
23.        if (nation != null) {
24.            currency.setCurrencySymbol(nation.getSymbol());
25.            currency.setNumberFormat(nation.getNumberFormat());
26.            PhoneNumber.setSelectedInterPrefix(nation.getDialingPrefix());
27.            propertyFile.setFileName(nation.getPropertyFileName());
28.        }
29.    }
30.
31.    public Object[] getNations(){
32.        return map.values().toArray();
33.    }
34.    public Nation getNation(String name){
35.        return (Nation)map.get(name);
36.    }
37.    public char getCurrencySymbol(){
38.        return currency.getCurrencySymbol();
39.    }
40.    public NumberFormat getNumberFormat(){
41.        return currency.getNumberFormat();
42.    }
43.    public String getPhonePrefix(){
44.        return PhoneNumber.getSelectedInterPrefix();
45.    }
46.    public String getProperty(String key){
47.        return propertyFile.getProperty(key);
48.    }
49.    public String getProperty(String key, String defaultValue){
50.        return propertyFile.getProperty(key, defaultValue);
51.    }
52. }
```

Note that the `InternationalizationWizard` has a number of get methods, which it delegates to its associated objects. It also has a method `setNation`, used to change the nation used by the client.

Although the Facade manages the internationalized settings for a number of objects in this example, it is still possible to manage each object individually. This is one of the benefits of this pattern—it allows a group of objects to be managed collectively in some situations, but still provides the freedom to individually manage the components as well.

Calling the `setNation` method in this class sets the current nation. That makes the wizard alter the `Currency` setting, the `PhoneNumber`, and a set of localized language strings, `InternationalizedText`.

Example 3.21 `Currency.java`

```
1.     import java.text.NumberFormat;
2.     public class Currency{
3.         private char currencySymbol;
4.         private NumberFormat numberFormat;
5.
6.         public void setCurrencySymbol(char newCurrencySymbol){ currencySymbol =
         newCurrencySymbol; }
7.         public void setNumberFormat(NumberFormat newNumberFormat){ numberFormat =
         newNumberFormat; }
8.
9.         public char getCurrencySymbol(){ return currencySymbol; }
10.        public NumberFormat getNumberFormat(){ return numberFormat; }
11.    }
```

Example 3.22 `InternationalizedText.java`

```
1.     import java.util.Properties;
2.     import java.io.File;
3.     import java.io.IOException;
4.     import java.io.FileInputStream;
5.     public class InternationalizedText{
6.         private static final String DEFAULT_FILE_NAME = "";
7.         private Properties textProperties = new Properties();
8.
9.         public InternationalizedText(){
10.            this(DEFAULT_FILE_NAME);
11.        }
12.        public InternationalizedText(String fileName){
13.            loadProperties(fileName);
14.        }
15.
16.        public void setFileName(String newFileName){
17.            if (newFileName != null){
18.                loadProperties(newFileName);
19.            }
20.        }
21.        public String getProperty(String key){
22.            return getProperty(key, "");
23.        }
24.        public String getProperty(String key, String defaultValue){
25.            return textProperties.getProperty(key, defaultValue);
26.        }
27.
28.        private void loadProperties(String fileName){
29.            try{
30.                FileInputStream input = new FileInputStream(fileName);
31.                textProperties.load(input);
32.            }
33.            catch (IOException exc){
34.                textProperties = new Properties();
35.            }
```

```
36.         }
37.     }
```

Example 3.23 `PhoneNumber.java`

```
1.      public class PhoneNumber {
2.          private static String selectedInterPrefix;
3.          private String internationalPrefix;
4.          private String areaNumber;
5.          private String netNumber;
6.
7.          public PhoneNumber(String intPrefix, String areaNumber, String netNumber) {
8.              this.internationalPrefix = intPrefix;
9.              this.areaNumber = areaNumber;
10.             this.netNumber = netNumber;
11.         }
12.
13.         public String getInternationalPrefix(){ return internationalPrefix; }
14.         public String getAreaNumber(){ return areaNumber; }
15.         public String getNetNumber(){ return netNumber; }
16.         public static String getSelectedInterPrefix(){ return selectedInterPrefix; }
17.
18.         public void setInternationalPrefix(String newPrefix){ internationalPrefix =
        newPrefix; }
19.         public void setAreaNumber(String newAreaNumber){ areaNumber = newAreaNumber; }
20.         public void setNetNumber(String newNetNumber){ netNumber = newNetNumber; }
21.         public static void setSelectedInterPrefix(String prefix) { selectedInterPrefix
        = prefix; }
22.
23.         public String toString(){
24.             return internationalPrefix + areaNumber + netNumber;
25.         }
26.     }
```

General country data is stored in a helper class, `Nation`. The `InternationalizationWizard` creates a collection of nations when it is first instantiated.

Example 3.24 `Nation.java`

```
1.      import java.text.NumberFormat;
2.      public class Nation {
3.          private char symbol;
4.          private String name;
5.          private String dialingPrefix;
6.          private String propertyFileName;
7.          private NumberFormat numberFormat;
8.
9.          public Nation(String newName, char newSymbol, String newDialingPrefix,
10.             String newPropertyFileName, NumberFormat newNumberFormat) {
11.             name = newName;
12.             symbol = newSymbol;
13.             dialingPrefix = newDialingPrefix;
14.             propertyFileName = newPropertyFileName;
15.             numberFormat = newNumberFormat;
16.         }
17.
18.         public String getName(){ return name; }
```

```
19.        public char getSymbol(){ return symbol; }
20.        public String getDialingPrefix(){ return dialingPrefix; }
21.        public String getPropertyFileName(){ return propertyFileName; }
22.        public NumberFormat getNumberFormat(){ return numberFormat; }
23.
24.        public String toString(){ return name; }
25.    }
```

Flyweight

Pattern Properties

Type: Structural
Level: Component

Purpose

To reduce the number of very low-level, detailed objects within a system by sharing objects.

Introduction

Object-oriented programming causes many objects to exist during execution, especially if there are several low-level objects. This places a big load on the Java Virtual Machine's (JVMs) memory.

Many objects in the Personal Information Manager can be edited, so they use the State pattern (see "State" on page 104) to determine whether to save the items' content. Each of these items can have its own collection of State objects.

One way to alleviate the problem of having many objects is to share objects. Many of these low-level objects only differ slightly, while most of their state and behavior is identical. Sharing instances reduces the number dramatically, without losing any functionality.

For a set of objects, the Flyweight pattern separates those parts of the objects that are the same from the parts that are different. The data that distinguishes the different instances (also called the externalized data) is provided to the single generic instance when needed.

Applicability

Use Flyweight when all of the following are true:

- The application uses many identical, or nearly identical, objects.
- For each nearly identical object, the non-identical parts can be separated from the identical part allowing that identical part to be shared.
- Groups of nearly identical objects can be replaced by one shared object once the non-identical parts of the state have been removed.
- If the application needs to distinguish among the nearly identical objects in their original state.

Description

The Flyweight pattern is intended to reduce the number of objects within an application, and does so by sharing objects. The objects contain some internal data, but all the data concerning the context within which they operate is supplied by an external source. Each shared object should be as generic as possible and independent of context.

By sharing objects, Flyweight significantly reduces the number of objects. The shared object is used by several clients and is indistinguishable from an object that is not shared.

An example of a Flyweight is a layout manager. When building a GUI you use several components and containers. To determine the layout, you use layout managers. In general, each layout manager is nearly identical; they differ only in the specific components they manage and some set attributes. If you would remove these components and attributes, each instance of that specific layout manager type is identical. When the layout manager functionality is required, the components and attributes are passed to the single shared instance. Having a shared object for each layout manager type and feeding it the specific context reduces the number of objects.

The clients using the shared object are responsible for providing and/or calculating the context information. That information is passed into the shared object when needed.

The Flyweight is shared, so a client should not create a Flyweight directly, but always obtain one through a factory (see "Abstract Factory" on page 6). Such a factory ensures the proper sharing of the Flyweights.

Not all Flyweights have to be shared, nor do the implementing classes need to be shared. This pattern allows object sharing, but does not require it.

Use Flyweight only when it's easy to identify and extract the external data from the objects, and when the number of different states is limited.

Implementation

The Flyweight class diagram is shown in Figure 3.8.

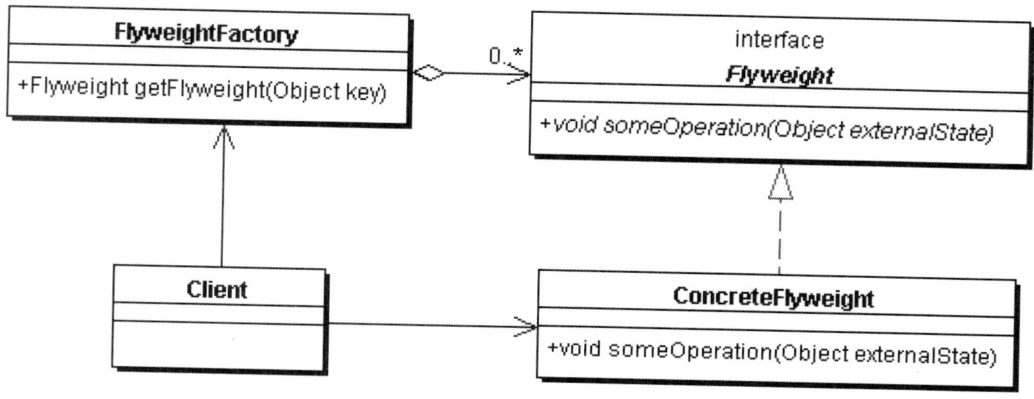

Figure 3.8 *Flyweight class diagram*

To implement the Flyweight you need:

- `Flyweight` – The interface defines the methods clients can use to pass external state into the flyweight objects.
- `ConcreteFlyweight` – This implements the `Flyweight` interface, and implements the ability to store internal data. The internal data has to be representative for all the instances where you need the `Flyweight`.
- `FlyweightFactory` (see "Abstract Factory" on page 6) – This factory is responsible for creating and managing the `Flyweights`. Providing access to `Flyweight` creation through the factory ensures proper sharing. The factory can create all the flyweights at the start of the application, or wait until they are needed.
- `Client` (page 183) – The client is responsible for creating and providing the context for the flyweights. The only way to get a reference to a flyweight is through `FlyweightFactory`.

Benefits and Drawbacks

The obvious benefit of this pattern is the reduced number of objects to handle. This can save a lot of space, both in memory and on storage devices, if the objects are persisted.

The most space will be saved when the context information for the flyweight is computed instead of stored. However, this also leads to the drawback of this pattern: runtime costs.

Instead of storing many objects, clients now have to calculate the context and provide this to the flyweight. The flyweight then uses this information to compute/provide functions. Handling fewer objects should increase runtime performance if implemented correctly. Note that if the context information is small, and the flyweight is large, the savings will be significant.

Pattern Variants

None.

Related Patterns

Related patterns include the following:

- Abstract Factory (page 6) – The Abstract Factory pattern is used to provide access to flyweights so that these factories ensure proper sharing of the Flyweight instances.
- Composite (page 157) – The Composite is often used to provide structure.
- State (page 104) – The State pattern is often implemented using the Flyweight pattern.
- Strategy (page 114) – The Strategy pattern is another pattern that can benefit from being implemented as a Flyweight.

Example

Note: For a full working example of this code example, with additional supporting classes and/or a `RunPattern` class, see "Flyweight" on page 477 of the "Full Code Examples" appendix.

This example uses the Flyweight pattern to share common `State` objects within the PIM. The State pattern example used state objects to edit and store information for a set of `Appointments`. In this example, the `States` will be used to manage edits and save for multiple collections of objects.

The `State` interface provides standard behavior for all application states. It defines two basic methods, `edit` and `save`.

Example 3.25 `State.java`

```
1.    package flyweight.example;
2.
3.    import java.io.File;
4.    import java.io.IOException;
5.    import java.io.Serializable;
```

```
6.
7.    public interface State {
8.        public void save(File f, Serializable s) throws IOException;
9.        public void edit();
10.   }
```

State is implemented by two classes—CleanState and DirtyState. This example uses these classes to track the state of multiple objects, so the classes have additional support to track which items need to be refreshed.

Example 3.26 `CleanState.java`

```
1.    import java.io.File;
2.    import java.io.FileOutputStream;
3.    import java.io.IOException;
4.    import java.io.ObjectOutputStream;
5.    import java.io.Serializable;
6.
7.    public class CleanState implements State{
8.        public void save(File file, Serializable s, int type) throws IOException{ }
9.
10.       public void edit(int type){
11.           StateFactory.setCurrentState(StateFactory.DIRTY);
12.           ((DirtyState)StateFactory.DIRTY).incrementStateValue(type);
13.       }
14.   }
```

Example 3.27 `DirtyState.java`

```
1.    package flyweight.example;
2.
3.    import java.io.File;
4.    import java.io.FileOutputStream;
5.    import java.io.IOException;
6.    import java.io.ObjectOutputStream;
7.    import java.io.Serializable;
8.
9.    public class DirtyState implements State {
10.       public void save(File file, Serializable s) throws IOException {
11.           //serialize s to f
12.           FileOutputStream fos = new FileOutputStream(file);
13.           ObjectOutputStream out = new ObjectOutputStream(fos);
14.           out.writeObject(s);
15.       }
16.
17.       public void edit() {
18.           //ignored
19.       }
20.   }
```

Since these two classes are used to track the overall state of the application, they are managed by a `StateFactory` class that creates both objects and provides them on demand.

Example 3.28 StateFactory.java

```
1.    public class StateFactory {
2.        public static final State CLEAN = new CleanState();
3.        public static final State DIRTY = new DirtyState();
4.        private static State currentState = CLEAN;
5.
6.        public static State getCurrentState(){
7.            return currentState;
8.        }
9.
10.       public static void setCurrentState(State state){
11.           currentState = state;
12.       }
13.   }
14.
```

Half-Object Plus Protocol (HOPP)

Pattern Properties

Type: Structural
Level: Component

Purpose

To provide a single entity that lives in two or more address spaces.

Introduction

A distributed Java application spreads objects over different address spaces—multiple Java Virtual Machines. For some technologies like RMI, remote objects can invoke methods on objects that actually reside on another JVM, allowing you to distribute state and behavior. Regardless of the technology used, objects in different JVMs need to communicate with each other in order for a distributed application to function. If they can't, what we have is a failure to communicate.

Suppose you have machine A and machine B, each with a JVM running. An object in JVM A needs object B's *stub* (see "Proxy" on page 197) to call methods on an object in JVM B. It can get it through several means. Once A has the stub, A can call methods on the stub and those method calls will be forwarded to B.

The downside is that *all* method calls on the stub will be forwarded across the network, which isn't always desirable. Sometimes you want the stub to execute some of the invoked methods locally, without going to the remote object.

This is an example of an object that exists in two or more address spaces. The *proxy* (the local representation of a remote object) is considered to be part of the remote object. By executing methods locally and in the remote JVM, an object executes behavior in multiple address spaces. This is what the HOPP pattern accomplishes for you.

Applicability

Use the HOPP pattern when:

- An object has to be in two different address spaces and cannot be split.
- Part of the functionality should execute remotely but some methods need to be invoked locally.

- Optimizations, such as caching, or the combining of multiple requests into a single network transaction, need to be applied in a way that is transparent to the caller.

Description

Distributed applications are hard to write. One of the problems encountered is that a single entity (object) needs to be in several address spaces. This might be because the object needs to access multiple physical devices on different machines or simply because the object cannot be split in a logical way.

To split an object in half and have the two halves communicate remotely can be accomplished by executing `rmic` with the `-keep` or `-keepgenerated` option. This saves the source code of the stub. Next, edit the source so that certain methods are handled by the stub and not forwarded to the remote object. When you compile the changed source you have your own customized version of the stub.

Unfortunately, this limits your further use of `rmic` because each time you use `rmic` on the remote object, you will have to do the manual editing again. And again. And again.

The solution is to split the object in half and provide communication between the two halves. Implement each half so that it can interact with the objects in its address space. The protocol is responsible for synchronizing the two halves and sending information back and forth.

This is the approach of the HOPP pattern—create an object that implements the required remote interfaces and which contains a reference to the original stub of the remote object. The methods that should behave normally (send to the remote object) are forwarded to the stub. Methods that should execute locally are handled by the new class.

The name HOPP comes from the fact that the client to the split object receives one half of the object. That one half also contains the protocol how to communicate with the other half, hence Half-Object Plus Protocol.

Implementation

The HOPP class diagram is shown in Figure 3.9.

To implement the HOPP pattern, you need:

- `HOPP` – This interface defines the methods that are available to the client of the HOPP. Both halves of the HOPP object implement this interface.
- `LocalHOPP` – This class implements the `HOPP` interface. Some of the methods are executed locally; others are forwarded to the `RemoteObjectProxy`.
- `RemoteObjectProxy` – This class is a Remote Proxy and forwards all the requests to the other half of the object in the other address space. This proxy encapsulates the protocol that links the two half objects.

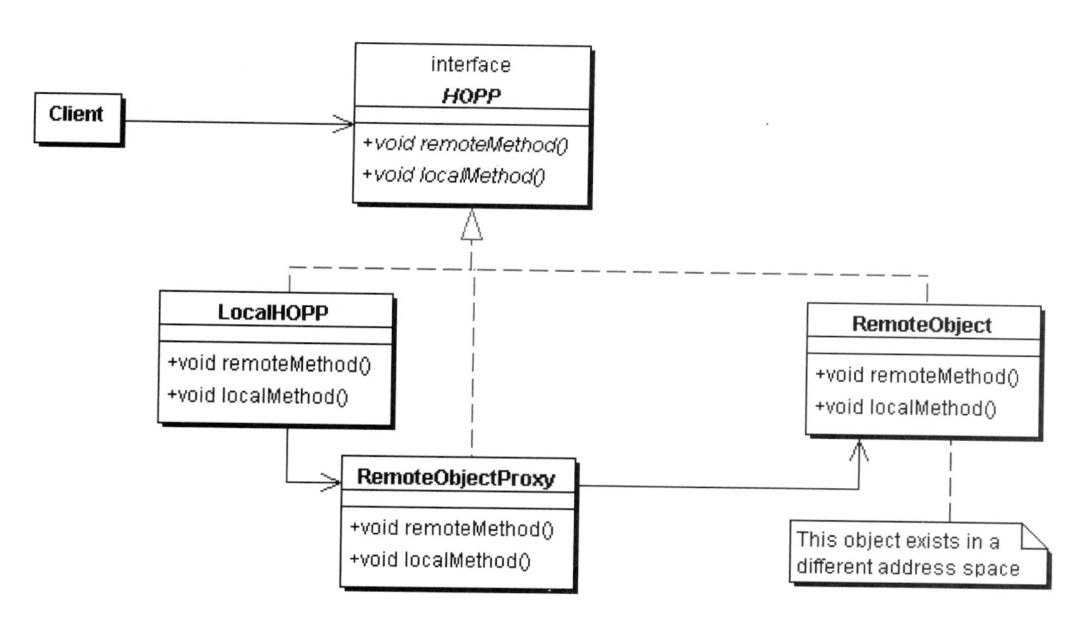

Figure 3.9 *HOPP class diagram*

- `RemoteObject` – This half of the HOPP contains all the methods to execute remotely.
- `Client` – `Client` calls methods on the HOPP interface. These method calls are transparent to the client, regardless of whether it is using a Remote Proxy (see "Proxy" on page 197), a HOPP, or a local object.

Benefits and Drawbacks

The benefit of this pattern is having one object that resides in two address spaces, without too much overhead. For the clients using one part of the HOPP, it is transparent. The clients do not care whether the object lives in one or more address spaces.

It is even possible to hide the difference completely, so that the client thinks it is using a local object while parts of it are not. You can implement the opposite so that a client thinks it is using a Remote Proxy, while in fact it is using a HOPP that contains a Remote Proxy. This has the benefit that some of the methods that were intended to be invoked remotely are now executed locally.

A very powerful advantage is that this pattern allows tailor-made optimizations. Each half of the HOPP can determine when and how it wishes to communicate with the other half. These communication strategies can improve performance by decreasing the number of calls across a network without the client code on either end being affected.

The drawback to this pattern is that some of the functionality needs to be duplicated. This is necessary because each half should have enough functionality to handle local objects.

Pattern Variants

Pattern variants include the following:

- Both halves keep a reference to each other and send messages back and forth. In the classic form only the HOPP on the client side has a reference to the other half. This carries the consequence that communication can only be initiated by the client side HOPP by calling a method on the remote half. The remote half is able to respond only once to each call through the value it returns. When it's necessary that both halves can initiate communication, they both need a reference to the other half.
- Smart HOPP (SHOPP). In this implementation, the local part of the HOPP can choose its counterpart from several connection strategies. This is helpful when, for instance, the application is distributed across a flexible network where machines come and go.

- Asymmetric HOPP. In this version of the HOPP, pattern both halves don't need to implement exactly the same interface. The remote part of the HOPP may provide a new proxy for the other half to use. That new proxy can contain new optimizations, or may even be a proxy to a different remote object.

Related Patterns

Related patterns include the following:

- Mediator (page 77) – The objects that need to be mediated are distributed on multiple address spaces. The Mediator can use the HOPP to simplify communication.
- Proxy, specifically Remote Proxy (page 197) – The HOPP pattern uses the Proxy pattern for transparent communication between the two halves.

Example

Note: For a full working example of this code example, with additional supporting classes and/or a `RunPattern` class, see "Half-Object Plus Protocol (HOPP)" on page 483 of the "Full Code Examples" appendix.

A Personal Information Manager should be available everywhere, but its data should only be stored in one place. This example uses RMI and the HOPP pattern to hold a personal calendar on a server, while making its information available to remote callers.

The `Calendar` interface defines all methods that will be available remotely. This interface extends `java.rmi.Remote` and all its methods throw `java.rmi.RemoteException`. In this case, `Calendar` defines three methods: `getHost`, `getAppointments`, and `addAppointment`.

Example 3.29 `Calendar.java`

```
1.     import java.rmi.Remote;
2.     import java.rmi.RemoteException;
3.     import java.util.Date;
4.     import java.util.ArrayList;
5.     public interface Calendar extends Remote{
6.         public String getHost() throws RemoteException;
7.         public ArrayList getAppointments(Date date) throws RemoteException;
8.         public void addAppointment(Appointment appointment, Date date) throws Remote-
         Exception;
9.     }
```

`Calendar` is implemented by two classes—the RMI remote object and its stub, or proxy. (See "Proxy" on page 197.) The remote object class, `CalendarImpl`, provides method implementations, while the stub manages communication to the remote object. The Java RMI compiler (`rmic`) needs to be run on the `CalendarImpl` to generate a stub and a skeleton class. The skeleton class is provided for backward compatibility, but, as of Java 1.2, is no longer necessary.

Example 3.30 `CalendarImpl.java`

```
1.     import java.rmi.Naming;
2.     import java.rmi.server.UnicastRemoteObject;
3.     import java.io.File;
4.     import java.util.Date;
5.     import java.util.ArrayList;
6.     import java.util.HashMap;
7.     public class CalendarImpl implements Calendar{
8.         private static final String REMOTE_SERVICE = "calendarimpl";
9.         private static final String DEFAULT_FILE_NAME = "calendar.ser";
10.        private HashMap appointmentCalendar = new HashMap();
11.
12.        public CalendarImpl(){
13.            this(DEFAULT_FILE_NAME);
14.        }
15.        public CalendarImpl(String filename){
16.            File inputFile = new File(filename);
17.            appointmentCalendar = (HashMap)FileLoader.loadData(inputFile);
18.            if (appointmentCalendar == null){
19.                appointmentCalendar = new HashMap();
20.            }
21.            try {
22.                UnicastRemoteObject.exportObject(this);
23.                Naming.rebind(REMOTE_SERVICE, this);
24.            }
25.            catch (Exception exc){
26.               System.err.println("Error using RMI to register the CalendarImpl " +
      exc);
27.            }
28.        }
29.
30.        public String getHost(){ return ""; }
31.        public ArrayList getAppointments(Date date){
32.            ArrayList returnValue = null;
33.            Long appointmentKey = new Long(date.getTime());
34.            if (appointmentCalendar.containsKey(appointmentKey)){
35.                returnValue = (ArrayList)appointmentCalendar.get(appointmentKey);
36.            }
37.            return returnValue;
38.        }
39.
40.        public void addAppointment(Appointment appointment, Date date){
41.            Long appointmentKey = new Long(date.getTime());
42.            if (appointmentCalendar.containsKey(appointmentKey)){
43.                ArrayList appointments = (ArrayList)appointmentCalendar.get(appoint-
      mentKey);
44.                appointments.add(appointment);
45.            }
46.            else {
```

```
47.                 ArrayList appointments = new ArrayList();
48.                 appointments.add(appointment);
49.                 appointmentCalendar.put(appointmentKey, appointments);
50.             }
51.         }
52.     }
```

The CalendarImpl object must use the RMI support class UnicastRemoteObject so that it can handle incoming communication requests. In this case, the CalendarImpl constructor exports itself using the static method UnicastRemoteObject.exportObject.

CalendarImpl also needs to have some way of publishing itself to the outside world. In RMI, the naming service is called the rmiregistry. It must be running before the CalendarImpl object is created. The rmiregistry is like a telephone book, providing a connection between a name and an object. When the CalendarImpl object registers itself with the rmiregistry through the rebind method it binds the name “calendarimp” to the stub of this remote object.

For a client to use the remote object it has to do a lookup in the rmiregistry of the host machine and receive the stub to the remote object. You can compare the stub to a telephone number. You can use that number from anywhere, on any phone, and you get connected to someone answering the number you’re calling. In this example, the CalendarHOPP class acts as the client for the CalendarImpl object.

Example 3.31 CalendarHOPP.java

```
1.    import java.rmi.Naming;
2.    import java.rmi.RemoteException;
3.    import java.util.Date;
4.    import java.util.ArrayList;
5.    public class CalendarHOPP implements Calendar, java.io.Serializable{
6.        private static final String PROTOCOL = "rmi://";
7.        private static final String REMOTE_SERVICE = "/calendarimpl";
8.        private static final String HOPP_SERVICE = "calendar";
9.        private static final String DEFAULT_HOST = "localhost";
10.       private Calendar calendar;
11.       private String host;
12.
13.       public CalendarHOPP(){
14.           this(DEFAULT_HOST);
15.       }
16.       public CalendarHOPP(String host){
17.           try {
18.               this.host = host;
19.               String url = PROTOCOL + host + REMOTE_SERVICE;
20.               calendar = (Calendar)Naming.lookup(url);
21.               Naming.rebind(HOPP_SERVICE, this);
22.           }
23.           catch (Exception exc){
24.             System.err.println("Error using RMI to look up the CalendarImpl or reg-
    ister the CalendarHOPP " + exc);
25.           }
```

```
26.     }
27.
28.     public String getHost(){ return host; }
29.     public ArrayList getAppointments(Date date) throws RemoteException{ return
      calendar.getAppointments(date); }
30.
31.     public void addAppointment(Appointment appointment, Date date) throws Remote-
      Exception { calendar.addAppointment(appointment, date); }
32. }
```

The `CalendarHOPP` provides a key benefit over a conventional RMI client – it can locally run what would normally be remote methods. This can provide a substantial benefit in terms of communication overhead. The HOPP implements the same remote interface, but it will not export itself. It keeps a reference to the stub and forwards all the method calls to the stub that it does not (or cannot) handle. Now it can implement the methods that it wants to execute locally—in this example, the `getHost` method. The HOPP can be registered with the `rmiregistry` like a normal stub, but it now has the ability to execute methods locally.

Proxy

Also known as Surrogate

Pattern Properties

Type: Structural
Level: Component

Purpose

To provide a representative of another object, for reasons such as access, speed, or security.

Introduction

Your career is taking off and your social life is humming, so your Personal Information Manager has to manage many appointments and dates. Your address book contains all the addresses of all the people you've ever socialized with or had professional contact with, including information on their families, hobbies, and other potentially valuable data. The number of contacts started out small but is now in the thousands.

However, you often pull out your PIM just to change a meeting time, make a note to buy beer, or something equally simple. Being presented with the whole address book object every time you use the PIM would be unnecessary and annoying. Just opening the book is a very expensive operation, unnecessarily delaying activities that don't require its use.

As a user, you don't care about any of that—you just want the address book to be available when you need to use it. (Ideally, the address book should be there even before you know you need to use it.) And when you use it, you don't always need all of it. For example, you just want to know how many contacts you have in your address book, or you want to add a new contact to your addressbook, without seeing and being able to edit the whole thing. You just need a small part of the address book.

The solution is a placeholder object that provides the an interface to the address book, or a part of it. The placeholder looks like the address book, but doesn't involve the overhead of running it. However, when you do need the whole address book to perform a task like updating a colleague's address, the placeholder object creates the real address book, to perform address book tasks assigned to it. That placeholder object is a Proxy.

Applicability

Use the Proxy pattern when you need a more elaborate reference to an object instead of just a regular one:

- Remote proxy – When you need a local representative for an object in another address space (JVM).
- Virtual proxy – Acts as a placeholder and delays creating expensive objects. (This is the version described in the Introduction section.)
- Protection proxy – Determines access rights to the real object.

Description

A proxy (or *stub*) is a representative for another object. To enable the proxy to represent the real object, the proxy has to implement the exact same interface as the real object. Furthermore, the proxy keeps a reference to the real object. The proxy needs the reference to the real object so that it can call methods on the real object if necessary. The clients will be interacting with the proxy, but the proxy can delegate the execution to the real object. The proxy implements the same interface as the real object, but can perform tasks that the real object does not, such as remote communication or security.

The proxy is a sort of stand-in for the real object. You can compare the Proxy pattern to the system of filming dangerous stunts for movies. The proxy is the body double for the real object, the movie star. During the dangerous stunts the proxy jumps out of the plane instead of the real object. Because the proxy implements the same interface as the real object, audiences cannot tell the difference, and think that real object jumped. But when the camera switches to close-up (when the real object is needed for a full complement of movie star tasks), the proxy calls the real object to perform the acting work.

Several rules govern the different kinds of proxies.

- Remote – The remote proxy is responsible for all the network hassle. It has to marshall (pack) and unmarshall (unpack) all the arguments sent and received.
- Virtual – The real object is very expensive to create, so postpone the creation as long as possible, or perform the creation a piece at a time, rather than all at once. If the proxy keeps a lot of information for the real subject, you don't need to instantiate the real object for access to these variables.
- Protection – You can use the protection proxy to control who accesses which method, and to give permission on a method based on the individual caller.

Implementation

The Proxy class diagram is shown in Figure 3.10.

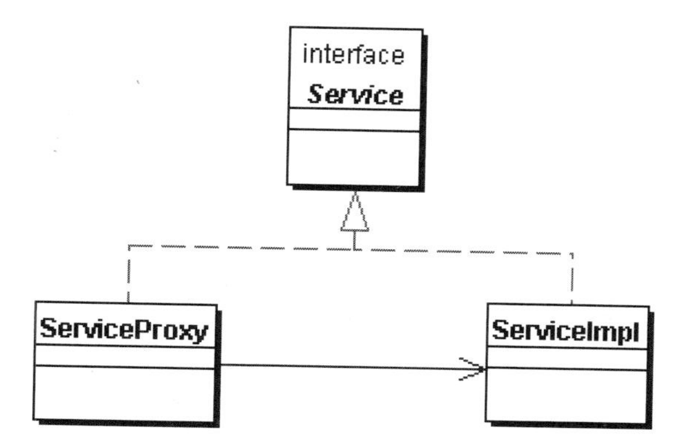

Figure 3.10 *Proxy class diagram*

For Proxy, implement the following:

- `Service` – The interface that both the proxy and the real object will implement.
- `ServiceProxy` – `ServiceProxy` implements `Service` and forwards method calls to the real object (`ServiceImpl`) when appropriate.
- `ServiceImpl` – The real, full implementation of the interface. This object will be represented by the `Proxy` object.

Benefits and Drawbacks

The consequences of this pattern vary considerably depending on the specific type of proxy.

- Remote proxy – The remote proxy benefit is that you can hide the network from the client. The client will think it has a local object that performs the work. In fact it has a local object that sends a request over the network to get the work done. Don't forget that a potential downside to this is that because you don't realize you're invoking network behavior, you might not be prepared for the time penalties that result.
- Virtual proxy – The great benefit of this proxy is that you have a placeholder to interact with and you don't have to create the real product until you really need it. Furthermore, it can perform some optimization as to when and how to create the real object.

- Protection proxy – This proxy's benefit is that it will allow access control to be determined.

Pattern Variants

One variant of this pattern is when the proxy does not know the real object other than by its interface. It allows for greater flexibility, but this works only if the proxy is not responsible for creating and/or destroying the real object.

Related Patterns

Related patterns include the following:

- Adapter (page 142) – An Adapter provides a front interface to a specific object, as does the Proxy pattern. However, the Proxy provides the same interface as the object, and the Adapter provides a different interface.
- HOPP (page 189) – The HOPP pattern can use the Proxy pattern for the communication between the two distributed halves of the HOPP.
- Business Delegate [CJ2EEP] – The Business Delegate pattern can be used as a Proxy. The Business Delegate can be a local representative of the Business tier.

Example

Note: For a full working example of this code example, with additional supporting classes and/or a `RunPattern` class, see "Proxy" on page 492 of the "Full Code Examples" appendix.

An address book grows tremendously over a period of time, since it stores all professional and social contacts. In addition, users don't need the address book every time they use the PIM. They do need some kind of address book placeholder to act as a starting point for them to use for graphical purposes, however. This example uses the Proxy pattern to represent the address book.

`AddressBook` defines the interface for accessing the PIM address book. At the very least, it needs to have the ability to add new contacts and to retrieve and store addresses.

Example 3.32 `AddressBook.java`

```
1.  import java.io.IOException;
2.  import java.util.ArrayList;
3.  public interface AddressBook {
4.      public void add(Address address);
5.      public ArrayList getAllAddresses();
6.      public Address getAddress(String description);
```

```
7.
8.        public void open();
9.        public void save();
10.   }
```

Retrieving the data for the address book might be very time-consuming, given the incredible popularity of the users. Therefore, the proxy should delay creation of the real address book for as long as possible. The proxy, represented by AddressBookProxy, has the responsibility for creating the address book—but only when absolutely necessary.

Example 3.33 AddressBookProxy.java

```
1.    import java.io.File;
2.    import java.io.IOException;
3.    import java.util.ArrayList;
4.    import java.util.Iterator;
5.    public class AddressBookProxy implements AddressBook{
6.        private File file;
7.        private AddressBookImpl addressBook;
8.        private ArrayList localAddresses = new ArrayList();
9.
10.       public AddressBookProxy(String filename){
11.           file = new File(filename);
12.       }
13.
14.       public void open(){
15.           addressBook = new AddressBookImpl(file);
16.           Iterator addressIterator = localAddresses.iterator();
17.           while (addressIterator.hasNext()){
18.               addressBook.add((Address)addressIterator.next());
19.           }
20.       }
21.
22.       public void save(){
23.           if (addressBook != null){
24.               addressBook.save();
25.           } else if (!localAddresses.isEmpty()){
26.               open();
27.               addressBook.save();
28.           }
29.       }
30.
31.       public ArrayList getAllAddresses(){
32.           if (addressBook == null) {
33.               open();
34.           }
35.           return addressBook.getAllAddresses();
36.       }
37.
38.       public Address getAddress(String description){
39.           if (!localAddresses.isEmpty()){
40.               Iterator addressIterator = localAddresses.iterator();
41.               while (addressIterator.hasNext()){
42.                   AddressImpl address = (AddressImpl)addressIterator.next();
43.                   if (address.getDescription().equalsIgnoreCase(description)){
44.                       return address;
```

```
45.                 }
46.             }
47.         }
48.         if (addressBook == null){
49.             open();
50.         }
51.         return addressBook.getAddress(description);
52.     }
53.
54.     public void add(Address address){
55.         if (addressBook != null){
56.             addressBook.add(address);
57.         } else if (!localAddresses.contains(address)){
58.             localAddresses.add(address);
59.         }
60.     }
61. }
```

Note that the `AddressBookProxy` has its own `ArrayList` for addresses. If the user adds an address by calling the add method, the proxy can use its internal address book without using the real address book.

The `AddressBookImpl` class represents the real address book for a user. It is associated with a file that stores an `ArrayList` with all the user's addresses. `AddressBookProxy` would create an `AddressBookImpl` object only when it is needed—when a user called the method `getAllAddresses`, for example.

Example 3.34 `AddressBookImpl.java`

```
1.  import java.io.File;
2.  import java.io.IOException;
3.  import java.util.ArrayList;
4.  import java.util.Iterator;
5.  public class AddressBookImpl implements AddressBook {
6.      private File file;
7.      private ArrayList addresses = new ArrayList();
8.
9.      public AddressBookImpl(File newFile) {
10.         file = newFile;
11.         open();
12.     }
13.
14.     public ArrayList getAllAddresses(){ return addresses; }
15.
16.     public Address getAddress(String description){
17.         Iterator addressIterator = addresses.iterator();
18.         while (addressIterator.hasNext()){
19.             AddressImpl address = (AddressImpl)addressIterator.next();
20.             if (address.getDescription().equalsIgnoreCase(description)){
21.                 return address;
22.             }
23.         }
24.         return null;
25.     }
26.
27.     public void add(Address address) {
28.         if (!addresses.contains(address)){
```

```
29.                 addresses.add(address);
30.             }
31.         }
32.
33.         public void open(){
34.             addresses = (ArrayList)FileLoader.loadData(file);
35.         }
36.
37.         public void save(){
38.             FileLoader.storeData(file, addresses);
39.         }
40.     }
```

Chapter Four

System Patterns

Introduction to System Patterns

System patterns are the most diverse of the four pattern types. They embrace your application at its most abstract, architectural level. System patterns can apply to major processes within an application, or even between applications.

System patterns include the following:

- Model-View-Controller (MVC) – To divide a component or subsystem into three logical parts—model, view, and controller—making it easier to modify or customize each part.
- Session – To provide a way for servers in distributed systems to distinguish among clients, allowing applications to associate state with the client-server communication.
- Worker Thread – To improve throughput and minimize average latency.
- Callback – To allow a client to register with a server for extended operations. This enables the server to notify the client when the operation has been completed.
- Successive Update – To provide a way for clients to receive updates from a server on an ongoing basis. The updates generally reflect a change in server data, a new or updated resource, or a change in the state of the business model.
- Router – To decouple multiple sources of information from the targets of that information.
- Transaction – To group a collection of methods so that they either all succeed or they all fail collectively.

Model-View-Controller (MVC)

Pattern Properties

Type: Behavioral
Level: Component / Architecture

Purpose

To divide a component or subsystem into three logical parts—model, view, and controller—making it easier to modify or customize each part.

Introduction

Assume that you want to represent a contact in the Personal Information Manager, such as a professional acquaintance (or even an unprofessional acquaintance; you could make the PIM very versatile). You create a single class to represent contact information such as name, organization, position, and so on. Next, you need be able to represent the contact visually so you add code for that to the class; perhaps as a series of data fields in a panel. Finally, you add a series of methods so that any change in the GUI would trigger calls to update the business information.

There are a few problems with this solution:

1. Although you could say that all these parts represent the contact and should be together, using a single class tends to make the code more complex and harder to maintain.
2. The code is not easily extensible. What happens if you want different visual representations for the contact? You can't do this effectively with a single class.

To manage complexity and plan for change, a better approach is to break out the three functional parts into separate classes. One class represents the business information, one the visual representation, and one the control mapping between the GUI and the business information.

In this way, the three parts of the Contact business entity are associated together and work as a whole. Later, to modify the Contact, you potentially limit changes to a single class. For instance, to update the Contact view for a Web browser, you only need to create an "HTML Contact" view.

This pattern, called Model-View-Controller (or simply MVC), is very useful when you want to create components that are both flexible and maintainable.

It is normally used for cases where change and reuse is expected in the component, since dividing a complex component into three classes or subsystems requires some design effort.

Applicability

MVC is useful when there is a component or subsystem that has some of the following characteristics:

- It is possible to view the component or subsystem in different ways. The internal representation for the system may be completely different from the representation on a screen.
- There are different possible types of behavior, meaning that multiple sources are allowed to invoke behavior on the same component but the behavior may be different.
- Behavior or representation that changes as the component is used.
- You often want the ability to adapt or reuse such a component under a variety of circumstances with a minimum amount of recoding.

Description

A problem that has always faced object-oriented developers is how to code suitably generic components. The problem is especially challenging when a component is complex or flexible in its use.

Consider a table. The concept of a table could be applied many ways depending on the needs of an application. You can approach a table as a way to store data as a logical structure consisting of cells, rows and columns. However, there are many ways to manage what is stored and how to represent that storage.

For storage decisions, a table might only allow some forms of data (decimal numbers) or it might permit special operations (such as summing). It might behave like a database table, where rows represent records (groups of data elements representing a single entity) and columns represent fields (a data type with consistent identity and storage among all records). Alternatively, a table might have no restrictions on data storage and no special significance attached to its rows and columns.

A table could also be presented in a number of ways in an application. It could be visually displayed as a grid, graph, or chart. Or it might have no graphical presence at all. It could even use the same underlying storage to supply information to more than one form of display, such as a grid that updates a chart when a user entered values.

When there are so many possible ways to use a control like a table, you're presented with a dilemma. Clearly it would be nice to be able to have some form of reuse, so you would not have to code every new table from scratch. At the same time, it's hard to imagine just how to code a single component like this to be reusable. An implementation that was too generic would require a great deal of work to modify each time it was used, eliminating many of the benefits of reuse.

MVC offers an elegant alternative. It defines a complex element in terms of three logical subunits:

- Model – The element's state, and means for changing the state
- View – The representation of the element (visual or non-visual)
- Controller – The element's control functionality, mapping actions on the view to their impact on the model

Many businesses today are based on the MVC pattern. Corporate management provides the model, establishing the company purpose and setting up rules that govern how the business grows and functions. The sales and marketing departments provide the view, representing the company and its products to the outside world. Finally, product development and manufacturing represent the controller, taking information from the view and translating it to actions that have impact on the model.

By breaking the element down in this way, each part can be treated independently of the others—or, at least, almost independently. For the element to behave as a whole, each part must properly interface with the other two. The view must be able to send messages to the controller and get information from the model in order to meet its responsibilities. However, MVC offers a substantial benefit: it is possible to easily change parts of the component, making a system using MVC extremely versatile. A table implemented this way can be converted from a grid to a graph representation by changing the view.

The table example focused on a component, but you can apply the MVC pattern at the architectural level as well. In an MVC component the model handles the component's state, the view represents the component's UI, and the controller performs the component's event handling (or action mapping) functions. At the architectural level, you can translate these features to a subsystem: the model actually represents the business model, the view is the presentation of the model (the face of the data), and the controller defines business actions or operations.

MVC is a pattern that encourages good encapsulation. The principles of good object-oriented programming recommend that you define elements in terms of their interface (how they interact with the outside world, other objects, components or systems) and implementation (how they maintain state and function internally). MVC supports this, since it explicitly breaks an element's responsibilities into:

- Model – The implementation (state: attributes and internal behavior)
- View – The outbound/outgoing interface (behavior: defines the services that can be used to represent the model)
- Controller – The inbound/incoming interface (behavior: accepts request for updates on the model)

Implementation

The MVC component diagram is shown in Figure 4.1.

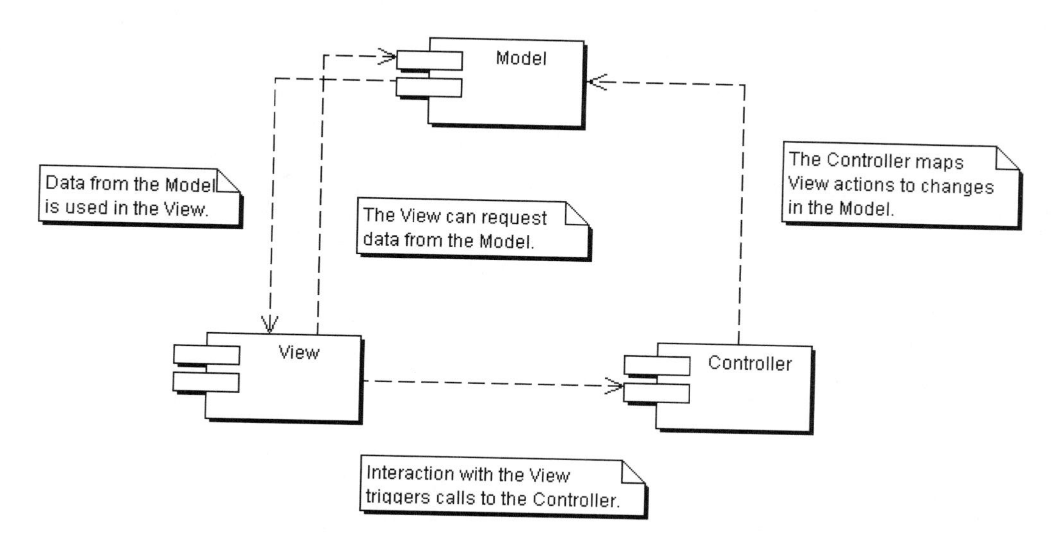

Figure 4.1 *MVC component diagram*

A component diagram has been used to describe this pattern. Each of the three parts of the MVC pattern is a component, that can contain many classes and interfaces.

Implementing the MVC pattern requires the following components:

- `Model` – This component contains one or more classes and interfaces that are responsible for maintaining the data model. The state of the model is kept in attributes and the implementation of methods. To be able to notify view components of any change in the model, the model keeps a reference to each registered view (there can be more than one at the same time). When a change occurs, every view component that has registered should be notified.
- `View` – The classes and interfaces of the view provide a representation of the data in the model component. The view may consist of visual GUI components, but is not required to. A view must be registered with the model to be notified of changes to the model data. When a notification of such a change is received, the view component is responsible for determining if and how to represent this change.

  The view component also keeps a reference to the model to retrieve data from the model, but it can only retrieve information, not change it. The view can also be used to render the controller, but requests for change are always forwarded to a controller component; so the view needs to keep a reference to one or more controllers.
- `Controller` – This component manages changes to the model. It keeps a reference to the model component who is responsible for carrying out the change, whereas the controller calls one or more update methods. The requests for change may come from a view component.

Benefits and Drawbacks

MVC provides an excellent way to make an element that is flexible and adaptable to a variety of new situations. The flexibility can be used both statically and dynamically. New view or controller classes can be added to the application (static), and view or controller objects can be changed in the application at runtime.

Usually, the greatest challenge for MVC is to determine the true base representation; to define a suitable set of interfaces among model, view, and controller. An MVC element is often developed to satisfy a specific set of needs, like most software, so vision and careful analysis are required in order to implement the element so that you don't impose application-specific restrictions on it.

Pattern Variants

MVC variants often revolve around different implementation choices for the view.

- Model push versus view pull – You can implement MVC in one of two ways the model can send updates to its view (or views), or a view can retrieve information as needed from the model. The choice affects how the relationship is implemented in the system.
- Multiple view targets – A model can provide information to more than one view. This is particularly useful for some GUI implementations, since the same data must sometimes drive multiple representations.
- "Look but don't touch" views – Not all views require a controller. Some provide only a visual representation of model data, but don't support any changes to the model from that view.

Related Patterns

Related patterns include the following:

- Observer (page 94) – The MVC pattern often uses the Observable pattern to manage communication. This is usually done for the following parts of the system:
  - Between the view and controller, so that a change in the view triggers a response in the controller
  - Between the model and view, so the view is notified of a change in the model.
- Strategy (page 114) – The controller is often implemented with the Strategy pattern to simplify changing controllers.

Example

Note: For a full working example of this code example, with additional supporting classes and/or a `RunPattern` class, see "Model-View-Controller (MVC)" on page 501 of the "Full Code Examples" appendix.

This code example provides a component-level MVC pattern to manage a contact in the Personal Information Manager. The `ContactModel` class provides the model for this demonstration, in this case storing the contact's first name, last name, title and organization.

Example 4.1 ContactModel.java

```
1.  import java.util.ArrayList;
2.  import java.util.Iterator;
3.  public class ContactModel{
4.      private String firstName;
5.      private String lastName;
6.      private String title;
7.      private String organization;
8.      private ArrayList contactViews = new ArrayList();
9.
10.     public ContactModel(){
11.         this(null);
12.     }
13.     public ContactModel(ContactView view){
14.         firstName = "";
15.         lastName = "";
16.         title = "";
17.         organization = "";
18.         if (view != null){
19.             contactViews.add(view);
20.         }
21.     }
22.
23.     public void addContactView(ContactView view){
24.         if (!contactViews.contains(view)){
25.             contactViews.add(view);
26.         }
27.     }
28.
29.     public void removeContactView(ContactView view){
30.         contactViews.remove(view);
31.     }
32.
33.     public String getFirstName(){ return firstName; }
34.     public String getLastName(){ return lastName; }
35.     public String getTitle(){ return title; }
36.     public String getOrganization(){ return organization; }
37.
38.     public void setFirstName(String newFirstName){ firstName = newFirstName; }
39.     public void setLastName(String newLastName){ lastName = newLastName; }
40.     public void setTitle(String newTitle){ title = newTitle; }
41.    public void setOrganization(String newOrganization){ organization = newOrgani-
   zation; }
42.
43.     public void updateModel(String newFirstName, String newLastName,
44.         String newTitle, String newOrganization){
45.         if (!isEmptyString(newFirstName)){
46.             setFirstName(newFirstName);
47.         }
48.         if (!isEmptyString(newLastName)){
49.             setLastName(newLastName);
50.         }
```

```
51.            if (!isEmptyString(newTitle)){
52.                setTitle(newTitle);
53.            }
54.            if (!isEmptyString(newOrganization)){
55.                setOrganization(newOrganization);
56.            }
57.            updateView();
58.        }
59.
60.        private boolean isEmptyString(String input){
61.            return ((input == null) || input.equals(""));
62.        }
63.
64.        private void updateView(){
65.            Iterator notifyViews = contactViews.iterator();
66.            while (notifyViews.hasNext()){
67.                ((ContactView)notifyViews.next()).refreshContactView(firstName, last-
    Name, title, organization);
68.            }
69.        }
70.    }
```

The `ContactModel` maintains an `ArrayList` of `ContactView` objects, updating them whenever the model data changes. The standard behavior for all views is defined by the `ContactView` interface method `refreshContact-View`.

Example 4.2 `ContactView.java`

```
1.    public interface ContactView{
2.        public void refreshContactView(String firstName,
3.            String lastName, String title, String organization);
4.    }
```

Two views are used in this example. The first, `ContactDisplayView`, displays the updated model information but does not support a controller, an example of “view-only” behavior.

Example 4.3 `ContactDisplayView.java`

```
1.    import javax.swing.JPanel;
2.    import javax.swing.JScrollPane;
3.    import javax.swing.JTextArea;
4.    import java.awt.BorderLayout;
5.    public class ContactDisplayView extends JPanel implements ContactView{
6.        private JTextArea display;
7.
8.        public ContactDisplayView(){
9.            createGui();
10.       }
11.
```

```
12.     public void createGui(){
13.         setLayout(new BorderLayout());
14.         display = new JTextArea(10, 40);
15.         display.setEditable(false);
16.         JScrollPane scrollDisplay = new JScrollPane(display);
17.         this.add(scrollDisplay, BorderLayout.CENTER);
18.     }
19.
20.     public void refreshContactView(String newFirstName,
21.         String newLastName, String newTitle, String newOrganization){
22.         display.setText("UPDATED CONTACT:\nNEW VALUES:\n" +
23.             "\tName: " + newFirstName + " " + newLastName +
24.              "\n" + "\tTitle: " + newTitle + "\n" +
25.             "\tOrganization: " + newOrganization);
26.     }
27. }
```

The second view is ContactEditView, which allows a user to update the contact defined by the model.

Example 4.4 ContactEditView.java

```
1.  import javax.swing.BoxLayout;
2.  import javax.swing.JButton;
3.  import javax.swing.JLabel;
4.  import javax.swing.JTextField;
5.  import javax.swing.JPanel;
6.  import java.awt.GridLayout;
7.  import java.awt.BorderLayout;
8.  import java.awt.event.ActionListener;
9.  import java.awt.event.ActionEvent;
10. public class ContactEditView extends JPanel implements ContactView{
11.     private static final String UPDATE_BUTTON = "Update";
12.     private static final String EXIT_BUTTON = "Exit";
13.     private static final String CONTACT_FIRST_NAME = "First Name  ";
14.     private static final String CONTACT_LAST_NAME = "Last Name  ";
15.     private static final String CONTACT_TITLE = "Title  ";
16.     private static final String CONTACT_ORG = "Organization  ";
17.     private static final int FNAME_COL_WIDTH = 25;
18.     private static final int LNAME_COL_WIDTH = 40;
19.     private static final int TITLE_COL_WIDTH = 25;
20.     private static final int ORG_COL_WIDTH = 40;
21.     private ContactEditController controller;
22.     private JLabel firstNameLabel, lastNameLabel, titleLabel, organizationLabel;
23.     private JTextField firstName, lastName, title, organization;
24.     private JButton update, exit;
25.
26.     public ContactEditView(ContactModel model){
27.         controller = new ContactEditController(model, this);
28.         createGui();
29.     }
30.     public ContactEditView(ContactModel model, ContactEditController newControl-
    ler){
```

```
31.             controller = newController;
32.             createGui();
33.         }
34. 
35.         public void createGui(){
36.             update = new JButton(UPDATE_BUTTON);
37.             exit = new JButton(EXIT_BUTTON);
38. 
39.             firstNameLabel = new JLabel(CONTACT_FIRST_NAME);
40.             lastNameLabel = new JLabel(CONTACT_LAST_NAME);
41.             titleLabel = new JLabel(CONTACT_TITLE);
42.             organizationLabel = new JLabel(CONTACT_ORG);
43. 
44.             firstName = new JTextField(FNAME_COL_WIDTH);
45.             lastName = new JTextField(LNAME_COL_WIDTH);
46.             title = new JTextField(TITLE_COL_WIDTH);
47.             organization = new JTextField(ORG_COL_WIDTH);
48. 
49.             JPanel editPanel = new JPanel();
50.             editPanel.setLayout(new BoxLayout(editPanel, BoxLayout.X_AXIS));
51. 
52.             JPanel labelPanel = new JPanel();
53.             labelPanel.setLayout(new GridLayout(0, 1));
54. 
55.             labelPanel.add(firstNameLabel);
56.             labelPanel.add(lastNameLabel);
57.             labelPanel.add(titleLabel);
58.             labelPanel.add(organizationLabel);
59. 
60.             editPanel.add(labelPanel);
61. 
62.             JPanel fieldPanel = new JPanel();
63.             fieldPanel.setLayout(new GridLayout(0, 1));
64. 
65.             fieldPanel.add(firstName);
66.             fieldPanel.add(lastName);
67.             fieldPanel.add(title);
68.             fieldPanel.add(organization);
69. 
70.             editPanel.add(fieldPanel);
71. 
72.             JPanel controlPanel = new JPanel();
73.             controlPanel.add(update);
74.             controlPanel.add(exit);
75.             update.addActionListener(controller);
76.             exit.addActionListener(new ExitHandler());
77. 
78.             setLayout(new BorderLayout());
79.             add(editPanel, BorderLayout.CENTER);
80.             add(controlPanel, BorderLayout.SOUTH);
81.         }
82. 
83.         public Object getUpdateRef(){ return update; }
84.         public String getFirstName(){ return firstName.getText(); }
```

```
85.        public String getLastName(){ return lastName.getText(); }
86.        public String getTitle(){ return title.getText(); }
87.        public String getOrganization(){ return organization.getText(); }
88.
89.        public void refreshContactView(String newFirstName,
90.            String newLastName, String newTitle,
91.            String newOrganization){
92.            firstName.setText(newFirstName);
93.            lastName.setText(newLastName);
94.            title.setText(newTitle);
95.            organization.setText(newOrganization);
96.        }
97.
98.        private class ExitHandler implements ActionListener{
99.            public void actionPerformed(ActionEvent event){
100.               System.exit(0);
101.           }
102.       }
103.   }
```

The updates to the model are possible due to the controller associated with the ContactEditView. In this example, Java event-handling features (and by extension the Observer pattern) manage communication between the ContactEditView and its associated Controller. ContactEditController updates the ContactModel when the update behavior is triggered by the ContactEditView, calling the method updateModel with new data provided by the editable fields of its associated view.

Example 4.5 ContactEditController.java

```
1.     import java.awt.event.*;
2.
3.     public class ContactEditController implements ActionListener{
4.         private ContactModel model;
5.         private ContactEditView view;
6.
7.         public ContactEditController(ContactModel m, ContactEditView v){
8.             model = m;
9.             view = v;
10.        }
11.
12.        public void actionPerformed(ActionEvent evt){
13.            Object source = evt.getSource();
14.            if (source == view.getUpdateRef()){
15.                updateModel();
16.            }
17.        }
18.
19.        private void updateModel(){
20.            String firstName = null;
21.            String lastName = null;
22.            if (isAlphabetic(view.getFirstName())){
```

```
23.                 firstName = view.getFirstName();
24.             }
25.             if (isAlphabetic(view.getLastName())){
26.                 lastName = view.getLastName();
27.             }
28.             model.updateModel( firstName, lastName,
29.                 view.getTitle(), view.getOrganization());
30.         }
31.
32.         private boolean isAlphabetic(String input){
33.             char [] testChars = {'1', '2', '3', '4', '5', '6', '7', '8', '9', '0'};
34.             for (int i = 0; i < testChars.length; i++){
35.                 if (input.indexOf(testChars[i]) != -1){
36.                     return false;
37.                 }
38.             }
39.             return true;
40.         }
41.     }
```

Session

Pattern Properties

Type: Processing
Level: Architectural

Purpose

To provide a way for servers in distributed systems to distinguish among clients, allowing applications to associate state with the client-server communication.

Introduction

In a networked Personal Information Manager, it's likely that you want to centralize some of the information, like a company's customers.

Clients would need to routinely update contact information on the server, and the updates might occur over several stages. Users might modify information about the contact's position and company, then modify contact addresses. Since there can be any number of address updates, and users can potentially be entering the information in real time, you decide to allow the client to submit the changes over multiple interactions with the server.

This brings up a problem—how do you track a user's changes that relate to a specific contact, when these changes take place in stages? Multiple clients will be making updates at the same time, and the server will need to know which updates come from which clients. Otherwise, one client might update the wrong customer record.

The most efficient approach is to associate a temporary identity with each user, so that the server can keep better track of workflow. When a user begins to edit information on the server, the server starts a *session*, issuing it a *session ID*. Each time the user performs an edit, such as adding or removing an address, the user's application sends the session's ID to the server. When the contact information has been updated, the application the user is using sends a *finalize* message to the server to indicate that the client is done updating that contact information. The server then ends the session.

This solution, also known as the Session pattern, provides a number of benefits to the server. It provides the server with a way to differentiate among clients, and to keep track of a particular client's progress in workflow. Finally, it allows the server to store information that is in flux, instead of storing the information on the client. With a session, the server can cache the user's information in memory until the user has completed the edits.

Applicability

The Session pattern is appropriate for client-server or peer-to-peer systems with the following requirement:

- Client identity – You need some way to distinguish among callers in a multiuser system.

Additionally, Session is normally used for systems with one or both of the following characteristics:

- Operation continuity – You want to be able to associate specified operations with each other in the system. Operations might follow a transactional or a workflow model.
- Data persistence – You need to associate data with the client over the time that the client interacts with the server.

Description

Information about the Session pattern is divided into the following sections.

Stateful and Stateless Communication

Communication between distributed systems can be *stateful* or *stateless*.

- An example of stateful communication is sockets. Requests from the client to the server can be made sequential and the server is aware of the previous calls.
- Stateless communication is when the server does not take into account what has happened before. The server does not distinguish one call from the other and each call is self-contained—all information needed is provided by the call. This model is usually straightforward to implement, and can greatly simplify both client and server code.

  The Internet is an example of this stateless model. In the Web, Hypertext Transfer Protocol (HTTP) is a stateless communication mechanism between a Web browser and a server. With a core set of simple operations, it is well-suited for its original purpose: the transfer of documents across the Web.

Applications Often Require Stateful Communication

Applications sometimes have more complex communication needs, and stateless communication isn't appropriate. In particular, business applications often require support for some or all of the following:

- Workflow – A connected sequence of business operations

- Transactions – An associated set of operations that succeed or fail as a unit
- Application data – Information associated with client-server interaction

Consider a classic e-commerce application. While a customer shops for products, the system must store data that represent the contents of the shopping cart. Online shopping also uses workflow to define the series of actions required to check out, pay for items, and ship an order. Such applications clearly need a way to represent the ongoing interaction between client and server over the duration of the shopping trip.

Session Pattern and Stateful Communication

The Session pattern is useful for these more-complex applications. The Session allows you to establish the identity of multiple clients, and might also provide one or more objects to represent the conversational state between a client and a server. It provides continuity between a client and server over an extended period of time, potentially spanning many requests over the application lifetime.

The Session pattern is quite useful when you want to support workflow between multiple client-server interactions—associating multiple actions as a whole. Without the concept of a session, a server has no way to effectively keep track of which operations belong to which client.

In Web applications, you can frequently see sessions being introduced for just this purpose. Under normal circumstances, the Web operates with a stateless model. If you want to support e-commerce, however, you need a way to manage a session. As users shop in a Web site, they can potentially add (and remove) many items from their shopping cart before they purchase items. If you don't use a session to track their activities and to store the items that they might purchase, your e-commerce Web site is reduced to a simple online purchase form.

Real-World Stateful Communication

Any situation in the real world with the concept of identity and transactional state provides an example of a Session. A delicatessen, for instance, uses face recognition to establish client (customer) identity and enable the use of its services. This enables the server (deli worker) to distinguish among the requests of different customers, and manage multiple requests. Perhaps customer 42 takes a long time to make up his mind, asking first for a pound of anchovies and pastrami, then cancelling the pastrami and switching to corned beef, and adding a ham on rye to the order.

Even though the customer may make many requests, the server knows that the final order belongs to the same customer, and no other customer will end up with 42's pastrami. The only danger in this system is the possibility that other deli customers may lose patience with customer 42. Of course, that might motivate the owner to hire more help and make the delicatessen multithreaded.

Implementation

The Session has two fundamental requirements:

- Session identification – A server must be able to maintain the client's identity over the lifetime of the application.
- Session representation – Depending on the needs of the application, one or more session objects might be used to represent state.

Benefits and Drawbacks

The central benefits of the Session pattern are evident from its characteristics: identifying service requesters and maintaining state-based resources. Secondary advantages might exist, as well, depending on the model chosen for implementing the pattern. For instance, if client identity is established as a result of a login, the Session can manage accountability and prioritization when accessing server-side resources. If Session information is stored in a database, the server can maintain information about a client's state over a series of business transactions.

A drawback of the Session is its increased workload on the server, and the increased complexity required of server software. Beyond its normal requirements, a Session-based server must have some way to establish client identity, store and retrieve associated information, and validate client identity on a number of occasions during the application.

Pattern Variants

The principal variations of the Session center around the key issues of identity and state.

- *Managing session identity* – You can use three approaches:
    - Security-based identification – A login provides a session ID for the client.
    - Implicit identification – A long-term connection between client and server automatically validates identity.
    - Arbitrary identification – The server assigns a unique session ID to each client. The ID is arbitrary and is used only to track a client during a single use of the server.
- *Managing session state* – In Sessions where state is required, you can maintain information in the following ways, on the client or the server:

- Object-based storage, client side –The client takes responsibility for data storage and sends what is required to the server. This reduces overall application security; data is present on a client, potentially a less secure machine. However, it is easy to associate the data with a client, since the client stores the information and sends it to the server. Another benefit of this approach is that it reduces the load on the server, requiring a client application to store its own data.

  How this is implemented varies depending on your technology; in HTTP, this approach is implemented using cookies.

- Object-based storage, server side – The server stores any data for its clients, and uses what is required during client requests. The server maintains all the application data, so there is a heavier load on the server. However, overall system security tends to be higher since data is maintained on the server. System efficiency is usually higher as well, since there is no redundant transfer of data. The challenge that you might face with server-side storage lies in establishing client identity, since the client and its data are decoupled in the application.

  In HTTP and Java, this approach means using `HttpSession`.

Related Patterns

None.

Example

Note: For a full working example of this code example, with additional supporting classes and/or a `RunPattern` class, see "Session" on page 507 of the "Full Code Examples" appendix.

A Session component diagram for a client-matching session is shown in Figure 4.2.

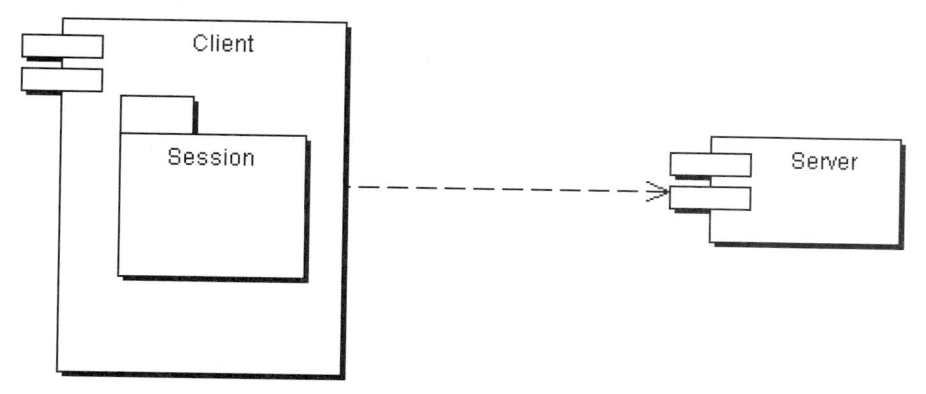

Figure 4.2 *Session component for a client-matching session*

A second Session component diagram, this time for server-maintained sessions, is shown in Figure 4.3.

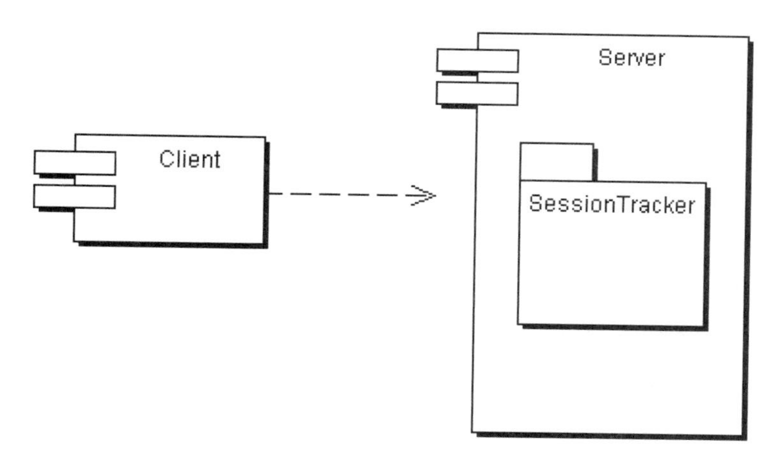

Figure 4.3 *Session component for server-maintained sessions*

A Session tracker diagram is shown in Figure 4.4.

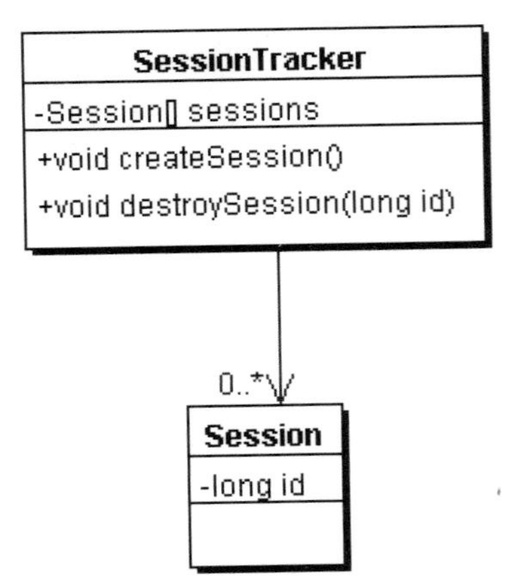

Figure 4.4 *Session tracker*

In this example, the client requester uses the server to perform a series of operations for updating contact information in a shared address book. A user can perform four operations:

- Add a contact
- Add an address (associated with the current contact)
- Remove an address (associated with the current contact)
- Save the contact and address changes

These operations are defined in the class `SessionClient`.

Example 4.6 `SessionClient.java`

```
1.     import java.net.MalformedURLException;
2.     import java.rmi.Naming;
3.     import java.rmi.NotBoundException;
4.     import java.rmi.RemoteException;
5.     public class SessionClient{
6.         private static final String SESSION_SERVER_SERVICE_NAME = "sessionServer";
7.         private static final String SESSION_SERVER_MACHINE_NAME = "localhost";
8.         private long sessionID;
9.         private SessionServer sessionServer;
10.
11.        public SessionClient(){
12.            try{
13.                String url = "//" + SESSION_SERVER_MACHINE_NAME + "/" +
       SESSION_SERVER_SERVICE_NAME;
14.                sessionServer = (SessionServer)Naming.lookup(url);
15.            }
16.            catch (RemoteException exc){}
17.            catch (NotBoundException exc){}
18.            catch (MalformedURLException exc){}
```

```
19.             catch (ClassCastException exc){}
20.         }
21.
22.         public void addContact(Contact contact) throws SessionException{
23.             try{
24.                 sessionID = sessionServer.addContact(contact, 0);
25.             }
26.             catch (RemoteException exc){}
27.         }
28.
29.         public void addAddress(Address address) throws SessionException{
30.             try{
31.                 sessionServer.addAddress(address, sessionID);
32.             }
33.             catch (RemoteException exc){}
34.         }
35.
36.         public void removeAddress(Address address) throws SessionException{
37.             try{
38.                 sessionServer.removeAddress(address, sessionID);
39.             }
40.             catch (RemoteException exc){}
41.         }
42.
43.         public void commitChanges() throws SessionException{
44.             try{
45.                 sessionID = sessionServer.finalizeContact(sessionID);
46.             }
47.             catch (RemoteException exc){}
48.         }
49.     }
```

Each client method calls a corresponding method on the remote server. `SessionServer` defines the four methods available to the clients through RMI.

Example 4.7 `SessionServer.java`

```
1.     import java.rmi.Remote;
2.     import java.rmi.RemoteException;
3.     public interface SessionServer extends Remote{
4.         public long addContact(Contact contact, long sessionID) throws RemoteExcep-
       tion, SessionException;
5.         public long addAddress(Address address, long sessionID) throws RemoteExcep-
       tion, SessionException;
6.         public long removeAddress(Address address, long sessionID) throws RemoteExcep-
       tion, SessionException;
7.         public long finalizeContact(long sessionID) throws RemoteException, SessionEx-
       ception;
8.     }
```

`SessionServerImpl` implements the `SessionServer` interface, providing an RMI server. It delegates business behavior to the class `SessionServerDelegate`.

Example 4.8 `SessionServerImpl.java`

```
1.     import java.rmi.Naming;
2.     import java.rmi.server.UnicastRemoteObject;
3.     public class SessionServerImpl implements SessionServer{
4.         private static final String SESSION_SERVER_SERVICE_NAME = "sessionServer";
5.         public SessionServerImpl(){
6.             try {
7.                 UnicastRemoteObject.exportObject(this);
8.                 Naming.rebind(SESSION_SERVER_SERVICE_NAME, this);
9.             }
10.            catch (Exception exc){
11.               System.err.println("Error using RMI to register the SessionServerImpl
        " + exc);
12.            }
13.        }
14.
15.        public long addContact(Contact contact, long sessionID) throws SessionExcep-
        tion{
16.            return SessionServerDelegate.addContact(contact, sessionID);
17.        }
18.
19.        public long addAddress(Address address, long sessionID) throws SessionExcep-
        tion{
20.            return SessionServerDelegate.addAddress(address, sessionID);
21.        }
22.
23.        public long removeAddress(Address address, long sessionID) throws SessionEx-
        ception{
24.            return SessionServerDelegate.removeAddress(address, sessionID);
25.        }
26.
27.        public long finalizeContact(long sessionID) throws SessionException{
28.            return SessionServerDelegate.finalizeContact(sessionID);
29.        }
30.    }
```

Example 4.9 `SessionServerDelegate.java`

```
1.     import java.util.ArrayList;
2.     import java.util.HashMap;
3.     public class SessionServerDelegate{
4.         private static final long NO_SESSION_ID = 0;
5.         private static long nextSessionID = 1;
6.         private static ArrayList contacts = new ArrayList();
7.         private static ArrayList addresses = new ArrayList();
8.         private static HashMap editContacts = new HashMap();
9.
10.        public static long addContact(Contact contact, long sessionID) throws Session-
        Exception{
11.            if (sessionID <= NO_SESSION_ID){
12.                sessionID = getSessionID();
13.            }
14.            if (contacts.indexOf(contact) != -1){
15.                if (!editContacts.containsValue(contact)){
16.                    editContacts.put(new Long(sessionID), contact);
```

```
17.                 }
18.                 else{
19.                   throw new SessionException("This contact is currently being edited
    by another user.",
20.                         SessionException.CONTACT_BEING_EDITED);
21.                 }
22.             }
23.             else{
24.                 contacts.add(contact);
25.                 editContacts.put(new Long(sessionID), contact);
26.             }
27.             return sessionID;
28.         }
29.
30.         public static long addAddress(Address address, long sessionID) throws Session-
    Exception{
31.             if (sessionID  <= NO_SESSION_ID){
32.                 throw new SessionException("A valid session ID is required to add an
    address",
33.                     SessionException.SESSION_ID_REQUIRED);
34.             }
35.             Contact contact = (Contact)editContacts.get(new Long(sessionID));
36.             if (contact == null){
37.               throw new SessionException("You must select a contact before adding an
    address",
38.                     SessionException.CONTACT_SELECT_REQUIRED);
39.             }
40.             if (addresses.indexOf(address) == -1){
41.                 addresses.add(address);
42.             }
43.             contact.addAddress(address);
44.             return sessionID;
45.         }
46.
47.         public static long removeAddress(Address address, long sessionID) throws Ses-
    sionException{
48.             if (sessionID  <= NO_SESSION_ID){
49.               throw new SessionException("A valid session ID is required to remove an
    address",
50.                     SessionException.SESSION_ID_REQUIRED);
51.             }
52.             Contact contact = (Contact)editContacts.get(new Long(sessionID));
53.             if (contact == null){
54.               throw new SessionException("You must select a contact before removing
    an address",
55.                     SessionException.CONTACT_SELECT_REQUIRED);
56.             }
57.             if (addresses.indexOf(address) == -1){
58.                 throw new SessionException("There is no record of this address",
59.                     SessionException.ADDRESS_DOES_NOT_EXIST);
60.             }
61.             contact.removeAddress(address);
62.             return sessionID;
63.         }
```

```
64.
65.     public static long finalizeContact(long sessionID) throws SessionException{
66.         if (sessionID  <= NO_SESSION_ID){
67.           throw new SessionException("A valid session ID is required to finalize
   a contact",
68.                 SessionException.SESSION_ID_REQUIRED);
69.         }
70.         Contact contact = (Contact)editContacts.get(new Long(sessionID));
71.         if (contact == null){
72.           throw new SessionException("You must select and edit a contact before
   committing changes",
73.                 SessionException.CONTACT_SELECT_REQUIRED);
74.         }
75.         editContacts.remove(new Long(sessionID));
76.         return NO_SESSION_ID;
77.     }
78.
79.     private static long getSessionID(){
80.         return nextSessionID++;
81.     }
82.
83.     public static ArrayList getContacts(){ return contacts; }
84.     public static ArrayList getAddresses(){ return addresses; }
85.     public static ArrayList getEditContacts(){ return new ArrayList(editCon-
   tacts.values()); }
86. }
```

SessionServerDelegate generates a session ID for clients when they perform their first operation, adding a Contact. Subsequent operations on the Contact's addresses require the session ID, since the ID is used to associate the addresses with a specific Contact within the SessionServerDelegate.

Worker Thread

Also known as Background Thread, Thread Pool

Pattern Properties

Type: Processing
Level: Architectural

Purpose

To improve throughput and minimize average latency.

Introduction

When you introduce threading to an application, your main goal is to use threads to eliminate bottlenecks. However, it requires skill to implement correctly. One way to maximize efficiency in a multithreaded application is to take advantage of the fact that not all threaded tasks have the same priority. For some of the tasks that need to be performed, timing is crucial. For others, they just need to be executed; exactly when isn't important.

To save yourself some long nights, you can separate these tasks from the rest of your application and use the Worker Thread pattern. The worker thread picks up a task from a queue and executes it; when it's finished, it just picks up the next task from the queue.

Threading is easier with Worker Thread because when you want something done, but not specifically now, you put it in the queue. And your code will become easier to read because all the thread object issues are in the worker thread and the queue.

Applicability

Use Worker Thread when:

- You want to improve throughput
- You want to introduce concurrency

Description

One approach to implementing threads is as follows: when you start a new task, create a new `Thread` object and start it. The thread performs its designated task, then dies. That's simple enough. However, creating the thread instance is very expensive in terms of performance, it takes a lot of time, and you only get one task out of it. A more efficient approach is to create a longer-lived "worker thread" that performs many tasks for you, one after the other.

That's the essence of the Worker Thread pattern. The worker thread executes many unrelated tasks, one after the other. Instead of creating a new thread whenever you have a new task, you give the task to the existing worker thread, which handles the task for you.

The Worker Thread might still be handling the first task when you're ready to hand it the next task. Solutions include the following:

- Your application waits until the Worker Thread becomes available again, but that kills a lot of the benefit you gain from multithreading.
- Your application creates a new instance of the worker thread each time the other worker thread is unavailable, but then you're back at square one—creating a new thread each time you have a new task.

The solution to this problem of the temporarily unavailable thread is to store the tasks until the worker thread is available again. The new task is stored in a queue and when the worker thread has finished with a task, it checks the queue and takes the next task. The task doesn't get performed any sooner, but at least your application isn't standing around waiting to hand off the task. If there are no tasks, it waits for the next task to arrive. Putting a task on the queue is less expensive than creating a new thread.

Implementation

A Worker Thread class diagram is shown in Figure 4.5

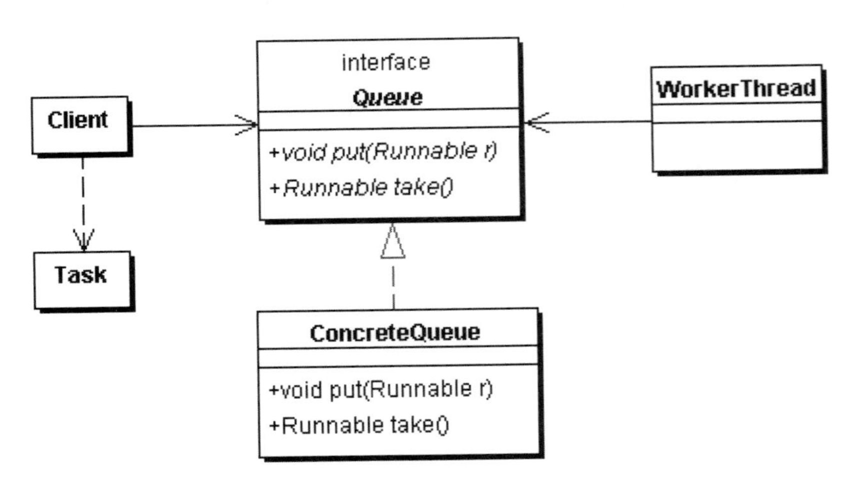

Figure 4.5 *Worker Thread class diagram*

For the Worker Thread pattern, implement the following:

- `Client` – The client is responsible for creating the `Task` instances and putting the `Tasks` on the `Queue`.
- `Task` – The `Task` is the class that contains the work that needs to be executed. It implements the `java.lang.Runnable` interface.
- `Queue` – The `Queue` interface defines the methods by which the `Client` is able to hand off the `Tasks` and the `WorkerThread` to retrieve the `Tasks`.
- `ConcreteQueue` – The `ConcreteQueue` class implements the `Queue` interface and is responsible for storing and retrieving the `Tasks`. It determines the order in which `Tasks` are provided to the `WorkerThread`.
- `WorkerThread` – The `WorkerThread` takes `Tasks` from the `Queue` and executes them. If there are no `Tasks` on the `Queue` it waits. Because the `Queue` and the `WorkerThread` are tightly coupled, often the `WorkerThread` class is an inner class of the `ConcreteQueue` class.

Benefits and Drawbacks

The `WorkerThread` influences performance in several ways.

1. The client no longer needs to create thread objects in order to run several tasks. It only needs to put the task on the queue, which in performance is less expensive than creating a thread object.
2. A Thread that is not running is taking up performance because the scheduler still schedules the thread to be run, if the thread is in a runnable state. Creating and starting a thread per task means that the scheduler has to schedule each of these threads individually, which takes more time than when the scheduler has to schedule only one worker thread. More threads means more scheduling. A task that is sitting in the queue and isn't running takes up no time whatsoever.
3. The drawback of this design can occur when tasks are dependent on each other. Because the queue can be sequential, the system can get into a deadlock. That's disastrous from a threading and from a performance point of view.

   There are a couple of possible solutions for this dilemma:

   - Make sure that there are as many worker threads as there are tasks that need to be run concurrently. That means that you need to implement an expandable thread pool. The thread pool is discussed in the "Pattern Variants" section.

- Only allow tasks on the queue that do not depend on other tasks. Sometimes such behavior cannot be guaranteed. In that case, the client cannot put the task on the queue, but has to instantiate its own thread or start another queue with worker threads.
- Create a smart queue that understands how the tasks work together and knows when to give which task to a worker thread. This should be considered a last resort as this smart queue will be tightly bound to the application and may become a maintenance nightmare.

Pattern Variants

Thread pool is a variant in which there is not just one instance of the worker thread, but several instances in a pool. (Hence the name thread pool.) This pool manages the `WorkerThread` class instances. The pool creates the worker threads, determines when they are not needed for a while, and might ultimately destroy some worker thread instances.

The pool decides how many workers to create at startup and what the maximum will be. The pool can either choose to create some threads when it starts, so that it always has some threads available, or it can wait until the first request is made (lazy instantiation).

When there are too many tasks for the current number of threads, however, the system (like a drain) gets clogged. Several solutions exist:

- Increase the number of workers – This works for a limited time only; as this fixes the symptom, not the problem. Generally, you should choose a better solution.
- Don’t limit the number of tasks in the queue – Just let the queue grow until the system runs out of memory. This solution is better than increasing the number of workers, but still will fail due to a shortage of resources.
- Limit the size of the queue – When the backlog gets too big, clients no longer make calls to add tasks to the queue. The queue can then focus on processing the backlog of tasks.
- Ask clients to stop sending tasks – Clients can then choose to send either no requests, or fewer requests.
- Drop requests that are stored in the queue – If the pool can be certain that the client will retry, it's safe to drop new requests. Dropping old requests is the right choice when it's likely that the clients posting the request have gone away.
- Let the client run the task itself – The client becomes single-threaded while running the task, and can’t create new tasks until the first task is completed.

Related Patterns

None.

Example

Note: For a full working example of this code example, with additional supporting classes and/or a RunPattern class, see "Worker Thread" on page 517 of the "Full Code Examples" appendix.

In a typical application, certain jobs have to be done. It's not always important that they happen now, just that they do happen. You can compare this to cleaning a house. It's not important that it happen at a particular time, as long as somebody does it sometime this week—or month, or year, depending on your standards.

This example uses a Queue to hold tasks. The Queue interface defines two basic methods, put and take. These methods are used to add and remove tasks, represented by the RunnableTask interface, on the Queue.

Example 4.10 Queue.java

```
1.  public interface Queue{
2.      void put(RunnableTask r);
3.      RunnableTask take();
4.  }
```

Example 4.11 RunnableTask.java

```
1.  public interface RunnableTask{
2.      public void execute();
3.  }
```

The ConcreteQueue class implements the Queue and provides a worker thread to operate on the RunnableTask objects. The inner class defined for ConcreteQueue, Worker, has a run method that continually searches the queue for new tasks to perform. When a task becomes available, the worker thread pops the RunnableTask off the queue and runs its execute method.

Example 4.12 ConcreteQueue.java

```
1.  import java.util.Vector;
2.  public class ConcreteQueue implements Queue{
3.      private Vector tasks = new Vector();
4.      private boolean waiting;
5.      private boolean shutdown;
6.
7.      public void setShutdown(boolean isShutdown){ shutdown = isShutdown; }
8.
9.      public ConcreteQueue(){
10.         tasks = new Vector();
```

```
11.             waiting = false;
12.             new Thread(new Worker()).start();
13.         }
14.
15.         public void put(RunnableTask r){
16.             tasks.add(r);
17.             if (waiting){
18.                 synchronized (this){
19.                     notifyAll();
20.                 }
21.             }
22.         }
23.
24.         public RunnableTask take(){
25.             if (tasks.isEmpty()){
26.                 synchronized (this){
27.                     waiting = true;
28.                     try{
29.                         wait();
30.                     } catch (InterruptedException ie){
31.                         waiting = false;
32.                     }
33.                 }
34.             }
35.             return (RunnableTask)tasks.remove(0);
36.         }
37.
38.         private class Worker implements Runnable{
39.             public void run(){
40.                 while (!shutdown){
41.                     RunnableTask r = take();
42.                     r.execute();
43.                 }
44.             }
45.         }
46.     }
```

Two classes, `AddressRetriever` and `ContactRetriever`, implement the `RunnableTask` interface in this example. The classes are very similar; both use RMI to request that a business object be retrieved from a server. As their names suggest, each class retrieves a specific kind of business object, making `Address` and `Contact` objects from the server available to clients.

Example 4.13 `AddressRetriever.java`

```
1.     import java.rmi.Naming;
2.     import java.rmi.RemoteException;
3.     public class AddressRetriever implements RunnableTask{
4.         private Address address;
5.         private long addressID;
6.         private String url;
7.
8.         public AddressRetriever(long newAddressID, String newUrl){
9.             addressID = newAddressID;
10.            url = newUrl;
11.        }
12.
```

```
13.     public void execute(){
14.         try{
15.             ServerDataStore dataStore = (ServerDataStore)Naming.lookup(url);
16.             address = dataStore.retrieveAddress(addressID);
17.         }
18.         catch (Exception exc){
19.         }
20.     }
21. 
22.     public Address getAddress(){ return address; }
23.     public boolean isAddressAvailable(){ return (address == null) ? false : true; }
24. }
```

Example 4.14 `ContractRetriever.java`

```
1.  import java.rmi.Naming;
2.  import java.rmi.RemoteException;
3.  public class ContactRetriever implements RunnableTask{
4.      private Contact contact;
5.      private long contactID;
6.      private String url;
7. 
8.      public ContactRetriever(long newContactID, String newUrl){
9.          contactID = newContactID;
10.         url = newUrl;
11.     }
12. 
13.     public void execute(){
14.         try{
15.             ServerDataStore dataStore = (ServerDataStore)Naming.lookup(url);
16.             contact = dataStore.retrieveContact(contactID);
17.         }
18.         catch (Exception exc){
19.         }
20.     }
21. 
22.     public Contact getContact(){ return contact; }
23.     public boolean isContactAvailable(){ return (contact == null) ? false : true; }
24. }
```

Callback

Pattern Properties

Type: Processing (Behavioral)
Level: Architectural

Purpose

To allow a client to register with a server for extended operations. This enables the server to notify the client when the operation has been completed.

Introduction

A networked Personal Information Manager will periodically make expensive requests of a server. For example, the time required to retrieve an entire project stored on a server is very unpredictable—the project might have thousands of tasks and deliverables.

A networked Personal Information Manager will periodically make expensive requests of a server. If a client wants to retrieve an entire project—potentially hundreds or thousands of individual tasks with corresponding budgets, timelines, and so on—it might take a lot of time to retrieve that information. At best, the time to retrieve the project would be unpredictable.

In this situation, it would be limiting for the server to keep an open network connection. Although one open connection might actually improve the server's efficiency, having an open connection for each client severely limits the number of client requests it can process concurrently.

Rather than requiring that the client and server remain connected, it would be better to enable the server to contact the client when it finishes the client's request. The Callback pattern uses this approach.

- The client sends a request for a project to the server, providing its callback information along with the request.
- The client then disconnects from the server and allows the server to spend time on retrieving the project.
- When the server completes the task, it contacts the client and sends the requested project information.

The benefits include conserving bandwidth and allowing the server to more effectively use its processing time. This solution also gives the server freedom to perform tasks like request queuing and using task priority, to more effectively manage its workload and available resources.

Applicability

Use the Callback pattern for a client-server system with time-consuming client operations, and when one or both of the following are true:

- You want to conserve server resources for active communication.
- The client can and should continue work until the information becomes available. This can be accomplished with simple threading in the client.

Description

For some distributed systems, a server must perform longer-term processing to satisfy client requests. In these systems, synchronous communication is probably not the best option. If the server maintains contact with the client during processing, it uses resources that could be better applied to other tasks, such as communicating with another client. Imagine a system where a user wanted to perform a complex query on a moderately large database table; for instance, a table of customer information with more than 10,000 records. In a synchronous client-server system, the client process has to wait, possibly for a long time, for the server to finish. The server performs the query and handles any necessary tasks to organize, format, and package the data, until it finally returns the data to the client.

The alternative is to create a system that allows a client to register for server notification. When the server has completed the requested operation, it actively notifies the client. In the meantime, both the client and server are free to use their resources for more productive purposes than maintaining this specific communication link.

The Callback pattern provides this capability, allowing for asynchronous client-server communication. The process consists of three simple steps:

1. Client registration – The client makes a request, providing contact information to the server.

   For instance, the client contacts the server and makes a request. Normally, the client requests information, such as all the sales figures for the 2001 fiscal year, or action, like entering the user in the Frito-lay trip to Elbonia sweepstakes. Since the client doesn't expect an immediate response, it provides contact information to the server.

2. Server processing – The server processes the client's request and formats a response if required. During this time, the client can be involved in other tasks, and the server can handle communication requests for other clients.

3. Server callback – When the server has completed the client's request, it sends a notification message to the client. The notification generally takes one of two forms:

- The information requested by the client. This approach is generally used when the client definitely needs all the data or when the data is relatively low-bandwidth to send.
- A message informing the client that the data or parts of the data is available. This is generally done for larger amounts of information, so that the client may retrieve parts of the data, either as the parts become available or if not all the data is needed by the client and the client just requests the data it needs.

For an example of the Callback pattern, consider a father and his three sons on a shopping trip. Number 1 son wants a new Robot Laser Geek action figure; Number 2 son wants a laptop, and Number 3 son wants the latest *Soft Core Java* book. However:

- These things can take a long time to find, especially since they're not sold in the same stores.
- The sons have 5-minute attention spans and get cranky if they have to go shopping for a long time.
- The father can only shop for one or two things at a time; if he has to do more, his performance plummets.

Luckily, the father can drop his sons at the mall's arcade to play games or fight amongst themselves, or do whatever else they want. The father then goes shopping for one of the items, buys it, drops it off, sets off to find another item, and so on.

You can use Callback in a number of applications.

- Agent software, now popular on the Web, can use Callback to notify a client when the request is complete. For instance, consider a job search agent on Monster.com. A user can enter search criteria for a desired job; for example, they might be looking for jobs; one requiring a good nose for a good lager, for example. Subsequently, the server notifies the user when a tasting position at the local microbrewery becomes available.
- Applications requiring costly database operations, such as data mining, frequently use Callback to increase the number of clients that they can service effectively.
- You can use the Callback pattern for applications that have a detailed server-side workflow. For example, a server involved in order processing often performs a variety of operations once a client has submitted an order. The server often checks inventory, validates payment and shipping information, and coordinates with other information systems, such as warehouse, manufacturing, invoicing, and shipping. The Callback pattern allows the server to notify the client about the status of the order after these steps have been performed. Since these operations can take hours or days, most customers prefer a Callback solution as well.

Implementation

The Callback component diagram is shown in Figure 4.6.

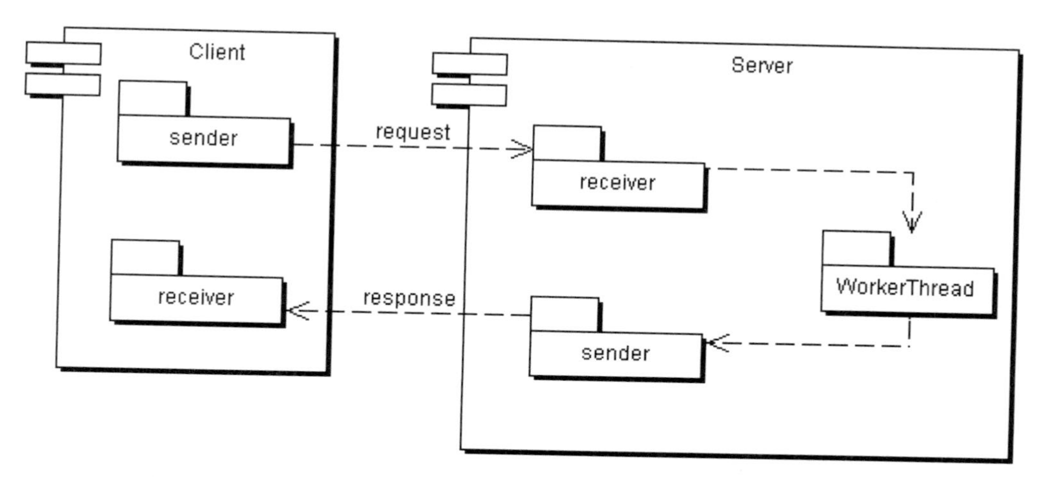

Figure 4.6 *Callback component diagram*

The Callback sequence diagram is shown in Figure 4.7.

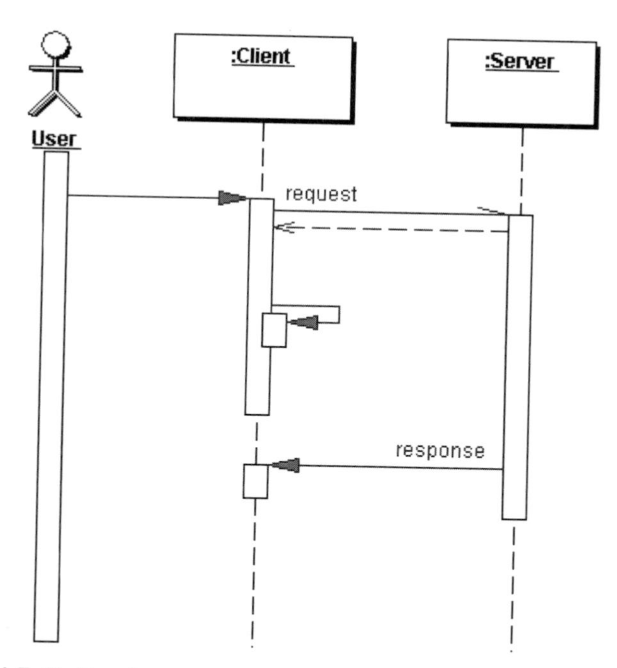

Figure 4.7 *Callback sequence diagram*

Callback imposes some basic requirements on both client and server:

- Client – The client must provide a callback interface for the server, so the server can contact the client when its request is done.
- Server – Beyond the traditional calling interface for the client, the server needs some way to notify clients when processing is complete. In addition, the server must be able to process and possibly store client requests.

Benefits and Drawbacks

The Callback pattern's major advantage is its improvement of a system's operating efficiency, especially server performance. You can see most of the improvement in two areas:

- Server-side processing – The server does not have to maintain communication threads to service waiting clients, so it can channel those resources into processing client requests or servicing other callers. Furthermore the processing can be performed when the server sees fit. It doesn't have to process the request immediately.
- Server communication – The server does not have to maintain an open connection while the client waits for its results. This means that a server can support a greater number of callers with its limited communication resources, such as sockets.

  This is a major motivation for some to choose the Callback pattern for their systems. In cases where server load is large or unpredictable (such as on the Web), this capability offers substantial advantages to designers. In the most extreme cases, it can mean the difference between running a group of servers in parallel and using a single machine to service client requests.

  Another benefit is that the client does not have to wait for the full processing by the server and it can continue with other tasks. The client can go about its business while it's waiting for the server response. When results are available, they can be displayed immediately.

Depending on the implementation of the pattern, Callback can queue client requests, allowing the server to organize and prioritize its workload. It also potentially allows the server to notify clients of changes beyond the typical lifetime of a client. Web agents are a good example of this, since they allow a client to enter a query in one Web session, and be notified of the results in another.

One challenge of the Callback is that it requires a client to listen for the callback from the server. This often makes client code more complex, and increases the load on client systems. An additional drawback stems from the fact that Callback decouples the request from the client. This often makes it difficult to cancel or modify a request once it has been sent to the server.

Pattern Variants

Variations of the Callback pattern generally center on server processing strategies and approaches to client notification. Two major approaches are common in server-side processing:

- Direct processing – With this approach, the server creates a worker thread to fulfill each client's request. This is straightforward to implement, but is sometimes difficult to scale to large numbers of service requesters.
- Request queue – The server maintains a queue of client requests and a pool of worker threads. The worker threads (see "Worker Thread" on page 231) are assigned to perform client processing on an ongoing basis.

A few options are available for client notification, depending on the application requirements:

- Active callback – A client uses server-like process to listen for incoming communications. This allows the client to directly receive server notification.
- Client polling – Also known as client pull, this requires a client to periodically check on the status of its request. When the request or parts of the request are complete, the client will request that information from the server.
- Explicit acknowledgment – A server may retransmit a message until it receives client confirmation. This is sometimes used for cases where the server processing can take longer than the client application's lifetime. Although this is not relevant in TCP since the socket won't open unless the client is there to do its part, it is meaningful when using unreliable communication technologies like UDP.

Related Patterns

Related patterns include Worker Thread (page 231). The Worker Thread pattern is used to help schedule client requests. The requests are put in a queue and the worker threads process them.

Example

Note: For a full working example of this code example, with additional supporting classes and/or a `RunPattern` class, see "Callback" on page 525 of the "Full Code Examples" appendix.

In the Personal Information Manager, one of the items that can vary most in size is a project. A project might consist of only a few tasks, or it could be made up of hundreds or even thousands of individual work steps. This example demonstrates how the Callback pattern could be used to retrieve a project object stored on a server machine.

The interface `CallbackServer` defines a single server-side method, `getProject`. Note that the method requires callback information—the client machine name and the name of the RMI client object—in addition to the project ID. The class `CallbackServerImpl` implements this interface.

Example 4.15 `CallbackServer.java`

```
1.     import java.rmi.Remote;
2.     import java.rmi.RemoteException;
3.     public interface CallbackServer extends Remote{
4.         public void getProject(String projectID, String callbackMachine,
5.           String callbackObjectName) throws RemoteException;
6.     }
```

Example 4.16 `CallbackServerImpl.java`

```
1.     import java.rmi.Naming;
2.     import java.rmi.server.UnicastRemoteObject;
3.     public class CallbackServerImpl implements CallbackServer{
4.         private static final String CALLBACK_SERVER_SERVICE_NAME = "callbackServer";
5.         public CallbackServerImpl(){
6.             try {
7.                 UnicastRemoteObject.exportObject(this);
8.                 Naming.rebind(CALLBACK_SERVER_SERVICE_NAME, this);
9.             }
10.            catch (Exception exc){
11.              System.err.println("Error using RMI to register the CallbackServerImpl
    " + exc);
12.            }
13.        }
14.
15.        public void getProject(String projectID, String callbackMachine,
16.          String callbackObjectName){
17.            new CallbackServerWorkThread(projectID, callbackMachine, callbackObject-
   Name);
18.        }
19.
20.    }
```

In the `getProject` method, `CallbackServerImpl` delegates the task of retrieving the project to a worker object, `CallbackServerDelegate`. This object runs on its own thread and does the work of retrieving a project and sending it to a client.

Example 4.17 `CallbackServerDelegate.java`

```
1.  import java.net.MalformedURLException;
2.  import java.rmi.Naming;
3.  import java.rmi.NotBoundException;
4.  import java.rmi.RemoteException;
5.  public class CallbackServerDelegate implements Runnable{
6.      private Thread processingThread;
7.      private String projectID;
8.      private String callbackMachine;
9.      private String callbackObjectName;
10.
11.     public CallbackServerDelegate(String newProjectID, String newCallbackMachine,
12.       String newCallbackObjectName){
13.         projectID = newProjectID;
14.         callbackMachine = newCallbackMachine;
15.         callbackObjectName = newCallbackObjectName;
16.         processingThread = new Thread(this);
17.         processingThread.start();
18.     }
19.
20.     public void run(){
21.         Project result = getProject();
22.         sendProjectToClient(result);
23.     }
24.
25.     private Project getProject(){
26.         return new Project(projectID, "Test project");
27.     }
28.
29.     private void sendProjectToClient(Project project){
30.         try{
31.             String url = "//" + callbackMachine + "/" + callbackObjectName;
32.             Object remoteClient = Naming.lookup(url);
33.             if (remoteClient instanceof CallbackClient){
34.                 ((CallbackClient)remoteClient).receiveProject(project);
35.             }
36.         }
37.         catch (RemoteException exc){}
38.         catch (NotBoundException exc){}
39.         catch (MalformedURLException exc){}
40.     }
41. }
```

In the `CallbackServerDelegate` `run` method, the object retrieves a project by calling the `getProject` method, then sends it to a client with the `sendProjectToClient` method. The latter method represents the callback to the client; the `CallbackServerDelegate` makes a call to an RMI object of type

CallbackClient on the client machine. The interface CallbackClient also defines a single RMI method, receiveProject.

Example 4.18 CallbackClient.java

```
1.    import java.rmi.Remote;
2.    import java.rmi.RemoteException;
3.    public interface CallbackClient extends Remote{
4.        public void receiveProject(Project project) throws RemoteException;
5.    }
```

The implementer of CallbackClient, CallbackClientImpl, is both a client and a server. Its method requestProject looks up the CallbackServer and calls the remote method getProject. The class also defines the remote method receiveProject, which is called by the server work thread when the project is ready for the client. CallbackClientImpl has a boolean variable, projectAvailable, to allow a client program to determine when the project is ready for display.

Example 4.19 CallbackClientImpl.java

```
1.    import java.net.InetAddress;
2.    import java.net.MalformedURLException;
3.    import java.net.UnknownHostException;
4.    import java.rmi.Naming;
5.    import java.rmi.server.UnicastRemoteObject;
6.    import java.rmi.NotBoundException;
7.    import java.rmi.RemoteException;
8.    public class CallbackClientImpl implements CallbackClient{
9.        private static final String CALLBACK_CLIENT_SERVICE_NAME = "callbackClient";
10.       private static final String CALLBACK_SERVER_SERVICE_NAME = "callbackServer";
11.       private static final String CALLBACK_SERVER_MACHINE_NAME = "localhost";
12.
13.       private Project requestedProject;
14.       private boolean projectAvailable;
15.
16.       public CallbackClientImpl(){
17.           try {
18.               UnicastRemoteObject.exportObject(this);
19.               Naming.rebind(CALLBACK_CLIENT_SERVICE_NAME, this);
20.           }
21.           catch (Exception exc){
22.             System.err.println("Error using RMI to register the CallbackClientImpl
      " + exc);
23.           }
24.       }
25.
26.       public void receiveProject(Project project){
27.           requestedProject = project;
28.           projectAvailable = true;
29.       }
30.
31.       public void requestProject(String projectName){
32.           try{
```

```
33.             String url = "//" + CALLBACK_SERVER_MACHINE_NAME + "/" +
        CALLBACK_SERVER_SERVICE_NAME;
34.             Object remoteServer = Naming.lookup(url);
35.             if (remoteServer instanceof CallbackServer){
36.                 ((CallbackServer)remoteServer).getProject(projectName,
37.                     InetAddress.getLocalHost().getHostName(),
38.                     CALLBACK_CLIENT_SERVICE_NAME);
39.             }
40.             projectAvailable = false;
41.         }
42.         catch (RemoteException exc){}
43.         catch (NotBoundException exc){}
44.         catch (MalformedURLException exc){}
45.         catch (UnknownHostException exc){}
46.     }
47.
48.     public Project getProject(){ return requestedProject; }
49.     public boolean isProjectAvailable(){ return projectAvailable; }
50. }
```

The basic sequence of action is as follows. When a client requires a project, the `CallbackClientImpl` object calls the method `getProject` on the `CallbackServerImpl` object. The `CallbackServerImpl` creates a `CallbackServerWorkThread` object to retrieve the project. When the `CallbackServerWorkThread` completes its task, it calls the client method `receiveProject`, sending the `Project` instance to the requester, the `CallbackClientImpl` object.

Successive Update

Also known as Client Pull / Server Push

Pattern Properties

Type: Processing (Behavioral)
Level: Architectural

Purpose

To provide a way for clients to receive updates from a server on an ongoing basis. The updates generally reflect a change in server data, a new or updated resource, or a change in the state of the business model.

Introduction

Suppose you wanted to use the Personal Information Manager as a way to coordinate work between multiple users. For example, you could enable multiple users to share information about the part of the project that they were currently working on. If you subdivided a project into `Task` and `Deliverable` objects, you might want to allow interested users (such as the project manager) to get updates on the progress of one or more `Tasks`.

If you create a server, it is straightforward to centralize the project information—you would simply store the `Project`, `Task` and `Deliverable` objects on the server. But how should you manage the task of keeping the clients up to date?

You can follow two strategies, each of which is a form of the Successive Update pattern. Make the client responsible for regularly querying the server, requesting updates on a `Task`; or alternatively, make the server responsible for sending `Task` updates out to clients.

In both cases, you expand the role of server and enable a groupware-style solution. You can send periodic updates to clients and ensure that they are coordinated in the work that they do.

Applicability

Use Successive Update for client-server systems when:

- Server-side resources or data are in flux, changing due to interactions with multiple clients or external updates.
- You want a client to receive updates without forcing the user to do a manual refresh.

Description

Successive Update is used for applications that require an ongoing refresh of the client's state. While it is possible to manually update the data, it is tedious and frustrating for an end user who must frequently refresh information—imagine having to manually send a request to your server every minute that you used an application. Although such a system might gives its users strong, muscular fingers, overall it would probably not be popular in conventional IT businesses.

To provide an acceptable alternative, Successive Update automates what users would otherwise have to do manually. The client and server establish an automatic update strategy, eliminating the need for the user to become directly involved. You can implement Successive Update using a variety of approaches, but it is frequently associated with two techniques at two ends of a spectrum—client pull and server push.

Client Pull

Client pull schedules a periodic refresh of information that is managed on the client side. The server performs its normal task, providing information when requested by its clients. Client pull is essentially a regular series of requests for server information.

A Successive Update sequence diagram for client pull is shown in Figure 4.8.

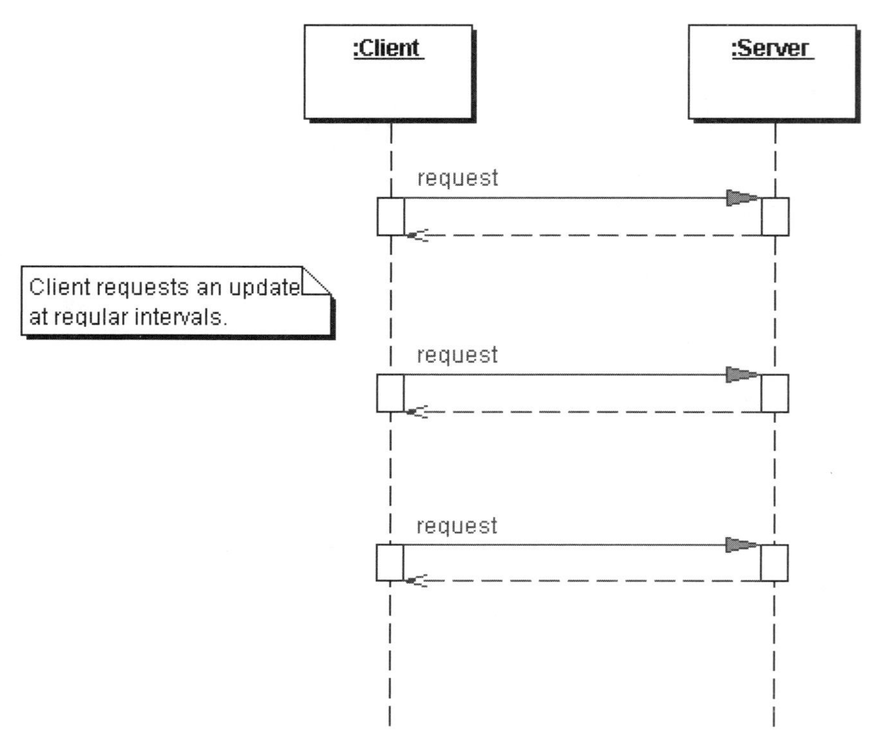

Figure 4.8 *Successive Update sequence diagram (client pull)*

Client pull is best suited to situations where some or all of the following are true:

- The amount of information to transfer is small
- Application data is in constant flux
- Information update does not have to be instantaneous

Examples of client pull are common on the Web. Stock tickers, sports tickers, and news tickers (pretty much anything with a ticker) are often managed using client pull. Applications that allow users to examine resources that are updated over time, such as browsing a remote directory structure, offer another possible use for client pull.

Anyone who has gone on an automobile trip with children has seen a direct example of client pull technology. The clients (ages 3-12) periodically poll the servers for status updates. Client queries usually take the form of "Are we there yet?" or "Can we stop? I want a drink." Requests generally occur with a polling rate between 30 seconds and a minute.

Server Push

Solutions using server push require the server process to send change notifications to all interested clients. This permits timely notification when changes have occurred in system data.

A Successive Update sequence diagram for server push is shown in Figure 4.9.

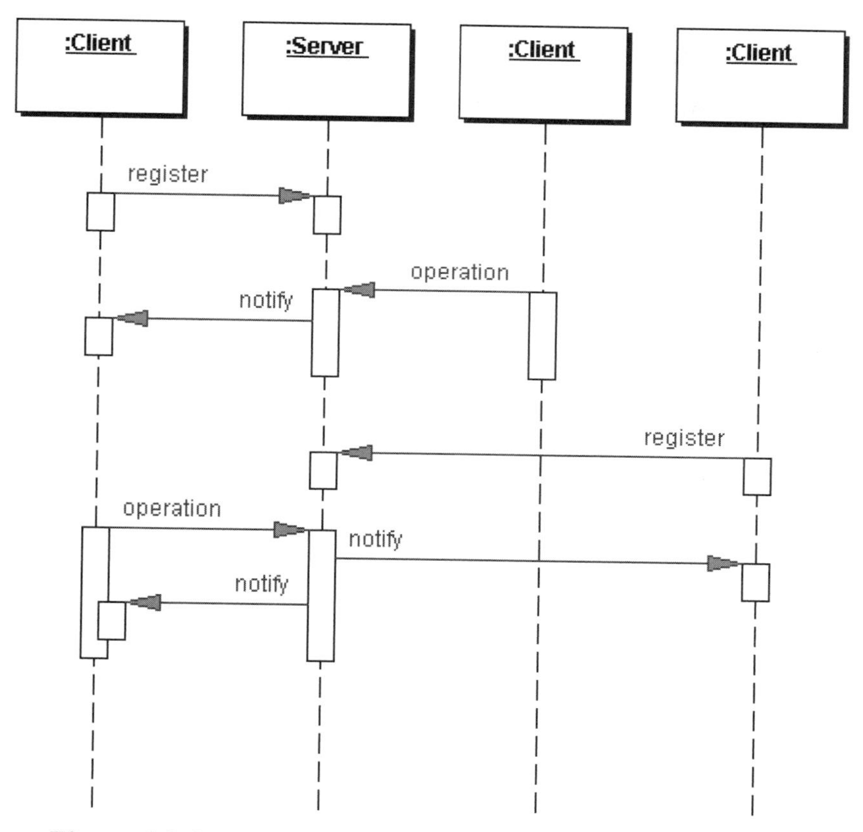

Figure 4.9 *Successive Update sequence diagram (server push)*

Server push is most appropriate for cases where:

- Real-time (or near real-time) updates are required by the client
- Data changes on an infrequent, unpredictable basis

Server push is frequently used on the Web for interactive applications such as gaming or chat rooms. Business applications sometimes use it to provide updates for collaborative resources, such as documents that are managed by groupware.

Mailing lists offer an excellent example of server push. After requesting to be put on a company's mailing list, the client (customer) receives a series of messages from the server (company) notifying her or him about a variety of products that are (or presumably will be) for sale. The client can then respond to these notifications by buying a year's subscription to Horse and Hound magazine, or frantically trying to find the Web site that lets you get off mailing lists.

Implementation

Successive Update has different client and server requirements based on the strategy followed. For client pull solutions, the client must have some way to establish a polling interval for the server. Frequently, this is managed by a thread in the client to periodically query the server and provide the client with results. The server has no special requirements in this implementation. Server push requires the server to keep track of the interested clients in some way. The server must send a notification each time events occur on the server that warrant a client update.

Benefits and Drawbacks

The benefits and drawbacks of the Successive Update pattern vary depending on whether the implementation uses a client pull or server push solution.

Depending on the rate at which the data changes, either strategy may put less load on the server. If the rate of change is high, client pull puts less load on the server; if the changes are less frequent, server push puts a lower demand on the server. Server push provides the most responsive update of information and might be a more efficient communication overall.

Disadvantages for client pull include the lack of timely updates of information and the risk of redundant data transfer. The client always asks for an update even when nothing has changed on the server, so the same data will be resent. Both drawbacks stem from the fact that a client cannot truly determine when there has been a change on the server. For server push, drawbacks may include increased server workload, or possible irrelevant traffic for clients. A server usually sends information about all its changes to clients, and the client has to be able to be contacted by the server, which might not be an easy task because of the client application or a firewall.

Pattern Variants

The most common variation in implementing a Successive Update strategy involves choosing an update approach that is a combination of both client pull and server push. Depending on an application's requirements, an application can rely on client pull for routine events, but use server push for time-critical notifications. Applications that mix the two update strategies typically define time-critical notifications:

- Notifications that could potentially cause an application error, such as deleting a customer record.
- Normal events, such as those that cannot result in an error or loss of data, like creating a new customer.

For server push, the server module can transmit its notifications to explicitly defined clients, provided that the list of clients is relatively short and the information is not large. As the number of supported clients grows, the server can quickly become overwhelmed with such an approach, although not as quickly as when being polled by all the clients. For notification of many clients, broadcasting information is often preferable. In this case, the server sends its message to one or more servers, which retransmit to clients that have registered themselves as interested participants. This approach is used in the Web and multicasting technologies, and reduces the load on the originating server.

Related Patterns

Related patterns include the following:

- Observer (page 94) – Clients often use the Observer pattern to register with the server for a server push solution.
- Callback (page 238) – Successive update might use the Callback pattern for server push.
- Mediator (page 77) – In server push solutions, the server often acts as a Mediator, sending updates to interested clients as the updates are received.

Example

Note: For a full working example of this code example, with additional supporting classes and/or a `RunPattern` class, see “Successive Update” on page 532 of the “Full Code Examples” appendix.

The example code shows a simple client pull solution for the Personal Information Manager. Clients use the server to centralize information about tasks they are working on. Each client stays up-to-date by periodically requesting updates from the server.

In the sample code, the `PullClient` class retrieves a task for a client. Its responsibility is to locate the RMI server so that it can request tasks on a regular basis.

Example 4.20 `PullClient.java`

```
1.    import java.net.MalformedURLException;
2.    import java.rmi.Naming;
3.    import java.rmi.NotBoundException;
4.    import java.rmi.RemoteException;
5.    import java.util.Date;
6.    public class PullClient{
7.        private static final String UPDATE_SERVER_SERVICE_NAME = "updateServer";
8.        private static final String UPDATE_SERVER_MACHINE_NAME = "localhost";
9.        private ClientPullServer updateServer;
10.       private ClientPullRequester requester;
11.       private Task updatedTask;
12.       private String clientName;
13.
14.       public PullClient(String newClientName){
15.           clientName = newClientName;
16.           try{
17.               String url = "//" + UPDATE_SERVER_MACHINE_NAME + "/" +
      UPDATE_SERVER_SERVICE_NAME;
18.               updateServer = (ClientPullServer)Naming.lookup(url);
19.           }
20.           catch (RemoteException exc){}
21.           catch (NotBoundException exc){}
22.           catch (MalformedURLException exc){}
23.           catch (ClassCastException exc){}
24.       }
25.
26.       public void requestTask(String taskID){
27.           requester = new ClientPullRequester(this, updateServer, taskID);
28.       }
29.
30.       public void updateTask(Task task){
31.           requester.updateTask(task);
32.       }
33.
34.       public Task getUpdatedTask(){
35.           return updatedTask;
36.       }
37.
38.       public void setUpdatedTask(Task task){
39.           updatedTask = task;
40.           System.out.println(clientName + ": received updated task: " + task);
41.       }
42.
43.       public String toString(){
44.           return clientName;
45.       }
46.   }
```

When the client wants to receive updates on a task, it calls the method `requestTask` on the `PullClient`. The `PullClient` object creates a worker thread (see “Worker Thread” on page 231), which is the `ClientPullRequester` object. This object resides on the client, and regularly issues a request to the server for updated task information.

Example 4.21 `ClientPullRequester.java`

```
1.    import java.rmi.RemoteException;
2.    public class ClientPullRequester implements Runnable{
3.        private static final int DEFAULT_POLLING_INTERVAL = 10000;
4.        private Thread processingThread;
5.        private PullClient parent;
6.        private ClientPullServer updateServer;
7.        private String taskID;
8.        private boolean shutdown;
9.        private Task currentTask = new TaskImpl();
10.       private int pollingInterval = DEFAULT_POLLING_INTERVAL;
11.
12.       public ClientPullRequester(PullClient newParent, ClientPullServer newUpdate-
      Server,
13.         String newTaskID){
14.           parent = newParent;
15.           taskID = newTaskID;
16.           updateServer = newUpdateServer;
17.           processingThread = new Thread(this);
18.           processingThread.start();
19.       }
20.
21.       public void run(){
22.           while (!isShutdown()){
23.               try{
24.                 currentTask = updateServer.getTask(taskID, currentTask.getLastEdit-
      Date());
25.                   parent.setUpdatedTask(currentTask);
26.               }
27.               catch (RemoteException exc){ }
28.               catch (UpdateException exc){
29.                   System.out.println("  " + parent + ": " + exc.getMessage());
30.               }
31.               try{
32.                   Thread.sleep(pollingInterval);
33.               }
34.               catch (InterruptedException exc){ }
35.           }
36.       }
37.
38.       public void updateTask(Task changedTask){
39.           try{
40.               updateServer.updateTask(taskID, changedTask);
41.           }
42.           catch (RemoteException exc){ }
43.           catch (UpdateException exc){
44.               System.out.println("  " + parent + ": " + exc.getMessage());
45.           }
46.       }
47.
48.       public int getPollingInterval(){ return pollingInterval; }
49.       public boolean isShutdown(){ return shutdown; }
50.
51.       public void setPollingInterval(int newPollingInterval){ pollingInterval = new-
      PollingInterval; }
52.       public void setShutdown(boolean isShutdown){ shutdown = isShutdown; }
53.   }
```

The RMI server's behavior is defined by the `ClientPullServer` interface and managed by the `ClientPullServerImpl` class. Two methods allow clients to interact with a server, `getTask` and `updateTask`.

Example 4.22 `ClientPullServer.java`

```
1.    import java.rmi.Remote;
2.    import java.rmi.RemoteException;
3.    import java.util.Date;
4.    public interface ClientPullServer extends Remote{
5.        public Task getTask(String taskID, Date lastUpdate) throws RemoteException,
        UpdateException;
6.        public void updateTask(String taskID, Task updatedTask) throws RemoteExcep-
        tion, UpdateException;
7.    }
```

Example 4.23 `ClientPullServerImpl.java`

```
1.    import java.util.Date;
2.    import java.rmi.Naming;
3.    import java.rmi.server.UnicastRemoteObject;
4.    public class ClientPullServerImpl implements ClientPullServer{
5.        private static final String UPDATE_SERVER_SERVICE_NAME = "updateServer";
6.        public ClientPullServerImpl(){
7.            try {
8.                UnicastRemoteObject.exportObject(this);
9.                Naming.rebind(UPDATE_SERVER_SERVICE_NAME, this);
10.           }
11.           catch (Exception exc){
12.               System.err.println("Error using RMI to register the ClientPullServer-
        Impl " + exc);
13.           }
14.       }
15.
16.       public Task getTask(String taskID, Date lastUpdate) throws UpdateException{
17.           return UpdateServerDelegate.getTask(taskID, lastUpdate);
18.       }
19.
20.       public void updateTask(String taskID, Task updatedTask) throws UpdateExcep-
        tion{
21.           UpdateServerDelegate.updateTask(taskID, updatedTask);
22.       }
23.   }
```

The class `UpdateServerDelegate` performs the server-side behavior for `ClientPullServerImpl`. Specifically, it retrieves `Task` objects, and ensures that up-to-date copies of `Tasks` are provided to clients by comparing the last update `Date`.

Example 4.24 `UpdateServerDelegate.java`

```
1.    import java.util.Date;
2.    import java.util.HashMap;
3.    public class UpdateServerDelegate{
```

```
4.      private static HashMap tasks = new HashMap();
5.
6.      public static Task getTask(String taskID, Date lastUpdate) throws UpdateExcep-
     tion{
7.          if (tasks.containsKey(taskID)){
8.              Task storedTask = (Task)tasks.get(taskID);
9.              if (storedTask.getLastEditDate().after(lastUpdate)){
10.                 return storedTask;
11.             }
12.             else{
13.                 throw new UpdateException("Task " + taskID + " does not need to be
     updated", UpdateException.TASK_UNCHANGED);
14.             }
15.         }
16.         else{
17.             return loadNewTask(taskID);
18.         }
19.     }
20.
21.     public static void updateTask(String taskID, Task task) throws UpdateExcep-
     tion{
22.         if (tasks.containsKey(taskID)){
23.             if (task.getLastEditDate().equals(((Task)tasks.get(taskID)).getLastE-
     ditDate())){
24.                 ((TaskImpl)task).setLastEditDate(new Date());
25.                 tasks.put(taskID, task);
26.             }
27.             else{
28.                 throw new UpdateException("Task " + taskID + " data must be
     refreshed before editing", UpdateException.TASK_OUT_OF_DATE);
29.             }
30.         }
31.     }
32.
33.     private static Task loadNewTask(String taskID){
34.         Task newTask = new TaskImpl(taskID, "", new Date(), null);
35.         tasks.put(taskID, newTask);
36.         return newTask;
37.     }
38. }
```

Router

Also known as Request Router, Multiplexer

Pattern Properties

Type: Concurrency
Level: Architectural

Purpose

To decouple multiple sources of information from the targets of that information.

Introduction

As a socially and professionally sought-after PIM user who exchanges information frequently with other PIM users, you put a significant strain on the application. There is, as a result, a lot going on in the PIM application, and many parts of the same application might need to respond to or be informed of the same event. This is not necessarily a GUI event, but might be just anything that is going on. Your boss might want to know if your 2:00 to 3:00 appointment clears up so you can go to another meeting in her place. You might want to know if a certain stock price plunges, so you can buy another 100 shares cheap.

In a complex system like the PIM, there can certainly be multiple sources of information. There can also be multiple destinations for information—multiple parties who want to receive information from the same event source. To make things easier on an event source and to save it the effort of notifying all listeners, it's a good idea to separate the distribution of the event into a distinct entity. The Router pattern follows this practice, since it combines multiple event source and multiple listeners.

Without a way to identify individual clients, the server will be limited to operations that could be performed in a single operation. This would force you to make one of two choices. You could develop a huge operation—we're talking an operation that would show up on satellite photos—that would hold all data. You could redesign the application model so it could handle stateless operations, perhaps designing it around a checkout system for the data. Of course, that would mean that you would also have to plan for error recovery, and security for the check-out system. When you get right down to it, neither choice is very appealing. Each solution would require a radical redesign of the application and the way the user interacts with the system.

Applicability

Use Router when:

- There are multiple sources of information
- There are multiple destinations receiving that information

Description

In the PIM, information is central and is shared between the many parts of the application and the different applications. The distribution of the information could be handled by each source.

Then every destination has to be registered with the source and that source has to maintain a list of all destinations and notify them when a change has occurred. Suppose you wanted to enhance your application by using multithreading when sending messages; you would have to implement that for each source. It would be much easier to manage the distribution of information separately, which is what the Router pattern does.

The Router pattern works like a router in network traffic. It receives information from a source and determines, based on where the information is coming from, to which destination(s) it should send the message. To be able to do that the router keeps a mapping between the various input channels (sources) and their destinations. The management of the each of the routes from a source to its destinations is captured in the mapping. Destinations can be added and removed by calling the appropriate methods on the router instead of on the source.

Because of the amount of information that is passed, the throughput of information should be done as fast as possible, or the system slows down dramatically. If the throughput fails or is disruptive for some reason, that specific target is dropped. By implementing this kind of control, the quality of service can be guaranteed for the other destinations.

Implementation

A Router class diagram is shown in Figure 4.10

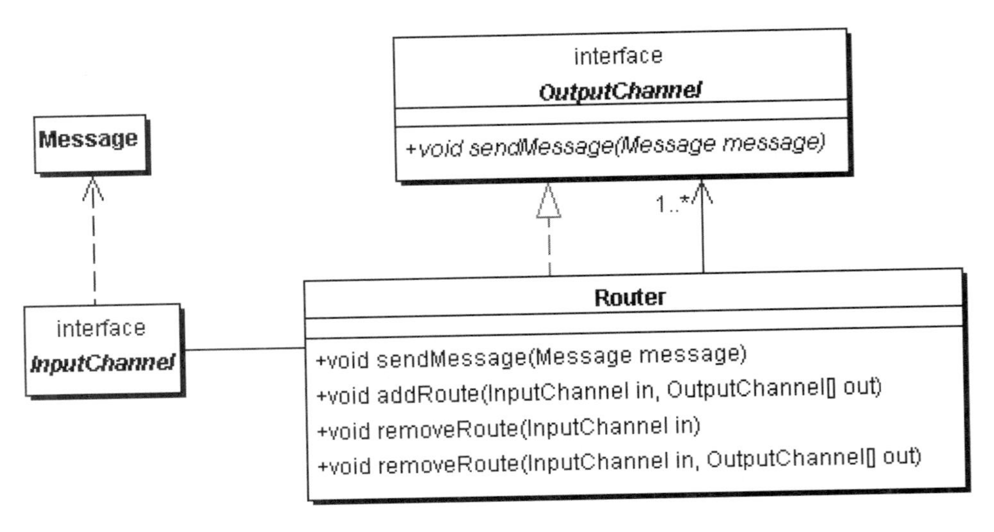

Figure 4.10 *Router class diagram*

The Router pattern needs the following:

- `InputChannel` – Can be of any type. It is used for mapping `Input` and `Output` in the `Router`; also known as the source.
- `OutputChannel` – An interface that defines the method for sending the message.
- `Message` – This class contains the information that needed to be distributed. To allow the `Router` to map this message to a specific route, the message also contains a reference to the source.
- `Router` – The `Router` maintains the map between `InputChannel` and specific `OutputChannels`, and implements the `OutputChannel` interface. When it receives messages, it forwards them to the specified `Output-Channels`.

Benefits and Drawbacks

Benefits and drawbacks include the following:

1. Decouples the source from the destination. The input doesn't need to know the destination; it only needs to know the router. The router knows the mapping between the source and destination.

2. When trouble occurs on one specific channel, it doesn't need to affect the other channels. One channel does not have the ability to block the `Router`, it continues doing its work of routing messages from an input to outputs.
3. Different strategies for `InputChannels` and `OutputChannels`. The Router can have each `Channel` in its own `Thread` or combine all the `InputChannels` in one `Thread`.
4. Simplifies the `Clients`, because the `Router` takes over the task of message distribution.
5. Enhances reliability. One channel can no longer block the system. If it's not working, the `Channel` can be ignored or other measures can be taken like dropping the problem channel. However, the `Router` still does its job.

Pattern Variants

A variation to this pattern is to have the `Router` keep a mapping between an arbitrary key and the destinations. A source might have different destinations based on certain conditions. For instance, if it has two separate methods each with its own `OutputChannels`. In the normal implementation of the Router pattern there is only one route per `InputSource`. The trick here is to create a key and let that key be registered with the Router as the `InputChannel`, instead of the "real" `InputChannel`.

The source calls the send method on the `Router` with two parameters: the key and the actual message. The `Router` looks up the key and sends the message to the `OutputChannels` that it has just looked up.

Related Patterns

Related patterns include the following:

- Mediator (page 77) – The Router is similar to the Mediator pattern. The difference is that the Mediator makes decisions based on the content of the message and can therefore be application specific. The Router makes decisions based on the source of the message.
- Observer (page 94) – The Router pattern can be made more flexible by using the Observer pattern to allow listeners to be registered.
- WorkerThread (page 231) – The Worker Thread can be applied to the Router to increase the efficiency.

Example

Note: For a full working example of this code example, with additional supporting classes and/or a `RunPattern` class, see "Router" on page 540 of the "Full Code Examples" appendix.

The Router can be useful at various places in the example application. In almost every situation where there is more than one interested party in any event, you can use the Router. The Router is essentially an implementation of a listener structure; you will see some similarities.

The code for the `Message` class is shown here. It is a container for the source (an `InputChannel`) and the actual message—in this case, some `String`.

Example 4.25 `Message.java`

```
1.    import java.io.Serializable;
2.    public class Message implements Serializable{
3.        private InputChannel source;
4.        private String message;
5.
6.        public Message(InputChannel source, String message){
7.            this.source = source;
8.            this.message = message;
9.        }
10.
11.       public InputChannel getSource(){ return source; }
12.       public String getMessage(){ return message; }
13.   }
```

Example 4.26 `InputChannel.java`

```
1.    import java.io.Serializable;
2.    public interface InputChannel extends Serializable{}
```

The `OutputChannel` is the interface that defines the method for sending the message to the target. Since the `OutputChannel` can be used to communicate between machines, it is defined as a remote interface.

Example 4.27 `OutputChannel.java`

```
1.    import java.rmi.Remote;
2.    import java.rmi.RemoteException;
3.    public interface OutputChannel extends Remote{
4.        public void sendMessage(Message message) throws RemoteException;
5.    }
```

The `Router` uses a hashmap to store links between the specific `InputChannel` and various `OutputChannels`. When it receives a message, it looks up the destinations in its map.

It loops through the collection and sends the message to each of the destinations. In this example, the `Router` creates a worker thread (see "Worker Thread" on page 231) to send a message to each of its `OutputChannel` objects. Thread pools are often used to improve performance in applications such as these.

Example 4.28 `Router.java`

```
1.  import java.rmi.Naming;
2.  import java.rmi.RemoteException;
3.  import java.rmi.server.UnicastRemoteObject;
4.  import java.util.HashMap;
5.  public class Router implements OutputChannel{
6.      private static final String ROUTER_SERVICE_NAME = "router";
7.      private HashMap links = new HashMap();
8.
9.      public Router(){
10.         try {
11.             UnicastRemoteObject.exportObject(this);
12.             Naming.rebind(ROUTER_SERVICE_NAME, this);
13.         }
14.         catch (Exception exc){
15.             System.err.println("Error using RMI to register the Router " + exc);
16.         }
17.     }
18.
19.     public synchronized void sendMessage(Message message) {
20.         Object key = message.getSource();
21.         OutputChannel[] destinations = (OutputChannel[])links.get(key);
22.         new RouterWorkThread(message, destinations);
23.     }
24.
25.     public void addRoute(InputChannel source, OutputChannel[] destinations) {
26.         links.put(source, destinations);
27.     }
28.
29.     private class RouterWorkThread implements Runnable{
30.         private OutputChannel [] destinations;
31.         private Message message;
32.         private Thread runner;
33.
34.         private RouterWorkThread(Message newMessage, OutputChannel[] newDestina-
    tions){
35.             message = newMessage;
36.             destinations = newDestinations;
37.             runner = new Thread(this);
38.             runner.start();
39.         }
40.
41.         public void run() {
42.             for (int i = 0; i < destinations.length; i++){
43.                 try{
44.                     destinations[i].sendMessage(message);
45.                 }
46.                 catch(RemoteException exc){
47.                     System.err.println("Unable to send message to " + destina-
    tions[i]);
48.                 }
49.             }
50.         }
51.     }
52. }
```

When using the Router pattern, be careful about the size of message to be delivered. Generally, the message should be as small as possible. It is easy to be fooled by some Java objects, though. An object might have references to other objects, which refer to other objects, and so on—and what seemed like a small object might turn out to be very large indeed. For instance, sending a `java.awt.Button` is not a good idea, because the whole GUI will be serialized and sent.

It's a lot like buying your child a toy in a store. The purchase of a single Outlaw Robot Laser Geek might not seem expensive at first, but by the time you get all the accessories (extra pocket protector, laser-spitting hornrimmed glasses), you might wonder if it would just be cheaper to buy him or her a sweater.

Transaction

Pattern Properties

Type: Concurrency
Level: Architectural

Purpose

To group a collection of methods so that they either all succeed or they all fail collectively.

Introduction

In object-oriented programming, you are usually dealing with multiple instances of multiple classes. Sometimes, however, you must treat multiple objects as though they were a single object—at least, you must ensure that state remains consistent among objects as an operation is performed.

One example is transferring funds from one account to another. The tasks of removing money from one account and adding it to another account should both be performed, or neither should be performed. The end results should always be in balance: the amount deducted from the first must be added to the second and vice versa. If the deduction from the first account fails (the first account is already over its limit) the second account should not be increased.

If you simply trust that every operation is successful, transferring funds would be very easy and very risky. If the transfer fails, you might see funds magically disappear from one of your accounts—a Bad Thing from your perspective. You might also see funds magically appear on another account—a Good Thing for you, but the banks consider this a Very Bad Thing. Invoking a series of methods in a situation like this should either completely succeed or completely fail.

This is where the Transaction is needed. It makes sure that all participants fail or succeed collectively. How the participants deal with success or failure is up to the individual implementation.

Applicability

Transaction should be used when:

- Several methods need to fully synchronized
- A recovery option should be available

Description

For some tasks, multiple parts of an application must cooperate. When a single part of that task fails, all of its parts should fail. The combined methods inside the task need to fail or succeed unanimously. If any one participant fails to do its part, all participants should fail, and all participants should return to the state they had before that task started.

The solution to this situation is the Transaction pattern. Every participant in the transaction tries to accomplish its task. The transaction manager is informed when one of the tasks fails. The manager then informs all the participants to revert back to their original state. The transaction manager can be just any object as long as it knows all the participants (directly or indirectly).

After all participants have reported to the transaction manager success in updating, the transaction manager tells all the participants to commit their changes. Commit means that the temporary state they have kept is now the permanent state.

If any participant fails, the manager cancels the transaction and calls the cancel method on each participant. The participants revert back to their previous state they had before the transaction started. This roll-back, as it is also known, can also occur when the transaction manager decides to cancel the transaction even without a failing participant. The result is the same—the transaction is called and rolled back.

To identify a transaction, a transaction ID may be used, either some arbitrary long or object. The benefit to using an object as ID over a long is that an object can contain information and behavior, the long doesn't contain behavior but it is smaller. And sending a long over a network is very much less expensive than sending an object.

The normal sequence to use a transaction is:

- Create a transaction ID (either as object or long)
- Invoke join on all participants and abort the transaction if the joining fails for any of the participants.
- Try the action, invoke the necessary business methods and call cancel as soon as any participant fails.
- When the action is completed, call commit on all participants.

Implementation

A Transaction class diagram is shown in Figure 4.11

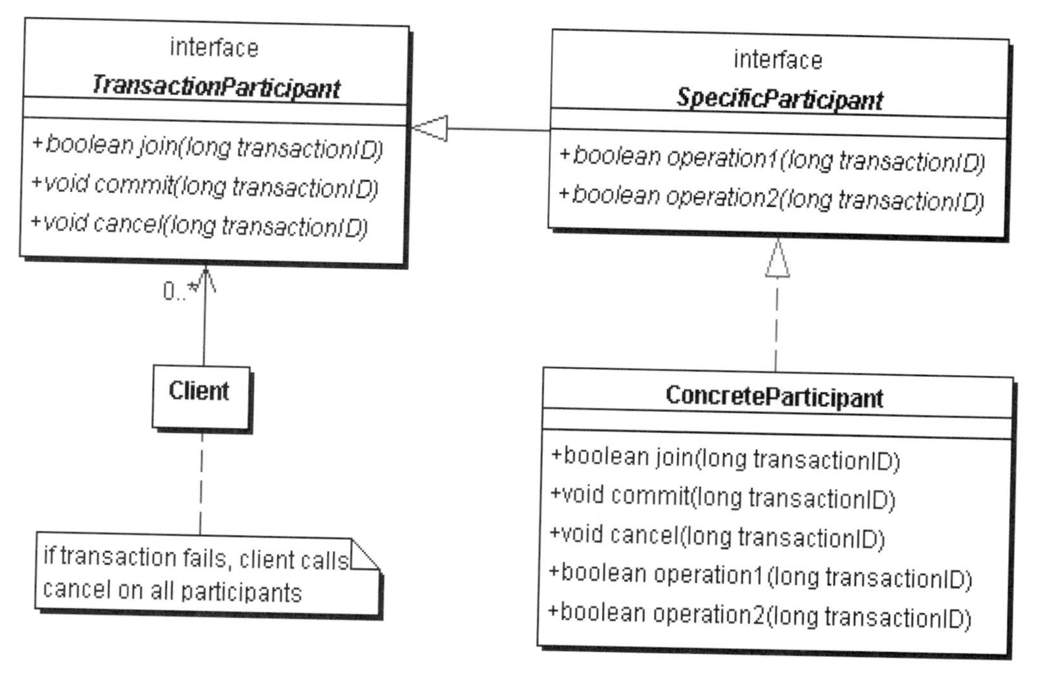

Figure 4.11 *Transaction class diagram*

The Transaction pattern needs:

- `TransactionParticipant` – The interface that defines the methods to control every participant.
- `SpecificParticipant` – As an extension to the generic interface, this interface contains the business methods. All methods involved in the transaction take an ID as parameter. Methods involved in transaction can throw `Exceptions` as a signal of failure.
- `ConcreteParticipant` – Implements `SpecificParticipant` interface. It defines what happens if the transaction manager (in this case, client) decides to roll-back or commit. It has to keep a reference to the original state to be able to restore it when cancel is invoked.
- `Client` – Acts as transaction manager. The client calls the join method on the participants to start the transaction and ultimately calls either cancel or commit on the participants.

Benefits and Drawbacks

The obvious benefit of this pattern is that several methods can be combined to act as one atomic operation. The result is that the application will always have a consistent state. The new state will not be persisted until all participants have succeeded in their actions.

The drawback is that this setup will decrease performance. When an object is already involved in a transaction and the join method is called again to start another transaction, the object has to decide what to do. The most common choice is to throw an exception at the caller of the join method, which states that it is currently involved. The transaction manager can either roll-back the second transaction or wait until the participant becomes available.

Pattern Variants

1. Two-phase commit – The transaction manager wants to be sure that all participants can commit before it calls commit on them. So before calling commit, it first performs a voting round where each participant tells the manager if it can commit (first phase). If one of the participants fails to be able to commit, the transaction will be cancelled and cancel will be called on all the participants (roll-back is performed). When all participants agree, commit will be called (second phase).

   The difference is the pre-commit phase, which checks if everybody can commit and which signals all the participants that the next signal will either be a cancel or a commit.

2. Optimistic versus conservative transactions – There are two approaches to implementing transactions: optimistic and conservative. This choice has to be made at almost every point in the implementation. Pure forms only rarely exist.

   The basic difference is that in the optimistic approach, the participants can always join, but may not always be able to commit. While in the conservative approach, the join may fail, but when joined, the participant can always commit.

   One of the other differences is in the way these approaches join transactions. In the conservative approach, the client first has to call join on the participant to join in a specific transaction before any sensitive methods can be called. In the optimistic way the participant will do the join for the client if this has not been done yet.

Related Patterns

None.

Example

Note: For a full working example of this code example, with additional supporting classes and/or a `RunPattern` class, see "Transaction" on page 548 of the "Full Code Examples" appendix.

The Personal Information Manager stores appointments based on their date. Naturally, since users lead active lives, appointments change all the time. A user's appointment book is constantly being updated with new or changing appointments.

If a number of users need to agree on a date for an appointment, it would be helpful if their appointment books could coordinate, arriving at a date that would work for everybody. That's what this example demonstrates—how the Transaction pattern can be used to allow address books to reschedule a date for an appointment.

The basic interface that supports transactions is `AppointmentTransactionParticipant`. It defines three methods to manage transactions (`join`, `commit`, and `cancel`) and the business method `changeDate`. This class is a `Remote` class, since it is used to communicate between transaction participants that might reside on different Java Virtual Machines.

Example 4.29 `AppointmentTransactionParticipant.java`

```
1.   import java.util.Date;
2.   import java.rmi.Remote;
3.   import java.rmi.RemoteException;
4.   public interface AppointmentTransactionParticipant extends Remote{
5.       public boolean join(long transactionID) throws RemoteException;
6.       public void commit(long transactionID) throws TransactionException, RemoteEx-
     ception;
7.       public void cancel(long transactionID) throws RemoteException;
8.       public boolean changeDate(long transactionID, Appointment appointment,
9.           Date newStartDate) throws TransactionException, RemoteException;
10.  }
```

The class `AppointmentBook` represents a user's calendar, and implements the `AppointmentTransactionParticipant` interface. In addition to providing support to change an `Appointment` date, the `AppointmentBook` can initiate a change of an `Appointment`. Its method `changeAppointment` accepts a transaction ID, an `Appointment` object, an array of other `AppointmentBooks` that should be transaction participants, and an array of possible alternate dates for the appointment. The `changeAppointment` method allows one of the `AppointmentBook` objects to communicate with the others using RMI, calling the `changeDate` method on every one of the participants until all agree on an alternate date for the `Appointment`.

Example 4.30 `AppointmentBook.java`

```
1.   import java.util.ArrayList;
```

```
2.     import java.util.HashMap;
3.     import java.util.Date;
4.     import java.rmi.Naming;
5.     import java.rmi.server.UnicastRemoteObject;
6.     import java.rmi.RemoteException;
7.     public class AppointmentBook implements AppointmentTransactionParticipant{
8.         private static final String TRANSACTION_SERVICE_PREFIX = "transactionPartici-
       pant";
9.         private static final String TRANSACTION_HOSTNAME = "localhost";
10.        private static int index = 1;
11.        private String serviceName = TRANSACTION_SERVICE_PREFIX + index++;
12.        private HashMap appointments = new HashMap();
13.        private long currentTransaction;
14.        private Appointment currentAppointment;
15.        private Date updateStartDate;
16.
17.        public AppointmentBook(){
18.            try {
19.                UnicastRemoteObject.exportObject(this);
20.                Naming.rebind(serviceName, this);
21.            }
22.            catch (Exception exc){
23.              System.err.println("Error using RMI to register the AppointmentBook "
       + exc);
24.            }
25.        }
26.
27.        public String getUrl(){
28.            return "//" + TRANSACTION_HOSTNAME + "/" + serviceName;
29.        }
30.
31.        public void addAppointment(Appointment appointment){
32.            if (!appointments.containsValue(appointment)){
33.                if (!appointments.containsKey(appointment.getStartDate())){
34.                    appointments.put(appointment.getStartDate(), appointment);
35.                }
36.            }
37.        }
38.        public void removeAppointment(Appointment appointment){
39.            if (appointments.containsValue(appointment)){
40.                appointments.remove(appointment.getStartDate());
41.            }
42.        }
43.
44.        public boolean join(long transactionID){
45.            if (currentTransaction != 0){
46.                return false;
47.            } else {
48.                currentTransaction = transactionID;
49.                return true;
50.            }
51.        }
52.        public void commit(long transactionID) throws TransactionException{
53.            if (currentTransaction != transactionID){
54.                throw new TransactionException("Invalid TransactionID");
55.            } else {
56.                removeAppointment(currentAppointment);
57.                currentAppointment.setStartDate(updateStartDate);
58.                appointments.put(updateStartDate, currentAppointment);
59.            }
```

```
60.         }
61.         public void cancel(long transactionID){
62.             if (currentTransaction == transactionID){
63.                 currentTransaction = 0;
64.                 appointments.remove(updateStartDate);
65.             }
66.         }
67.         public boolean changeDate(long transactionID, Appointment appointment,
68.           Date newStartDate) throws TransactionException{
69.             if ((appointments.containsValue(appointment)) && (!appointments.contains-
      Key(newStartDate))){
70.                 appointments.put(newStartDate, null);
71.                 updateStartDate = newStartDate;
72.                 currentAppointment = appointment;
73.                 return true;
74.             }
75.             return false;
76.         }
77.
78.         public boolean changeAppointment(Appointment appointment, Date[] possible-
      Dates,
79.           AppointmentTransactionParticipant[] participants, long transactionID){
80.             try{
81.                 for (int i = 0; i < participants.length; i++){
82.                     if (!participants[i].join(transactionID)){
83.                         return false;
84.                     }
85.                 }
86.                 for (int i = 0; i < possibleDates.length; i++){
87.                     if (isDateAvailable(transactionID, appointment, possibleDates[i],
      participants)){
88.                         try{
89.                             commitAll(transactionID, participants);
90.                             return true;
91.                         }
92.                         catch(TransactionException exc){ }
93.                     }
94.                 }
95.             }
96.             catch (RemoteException exc){ }
97.             try{
98.                 cancelAll(transactionID, participants);
99.             }
100.            catch (RemoteException exc){}
101.            return false;
102.        }
103.
104.        private boolean isDateAvailable(long transactionID, Appointment appointment,
105.          Date date, AppointmentTransactionParticipant[] participants){
106.            try{
107.                for (int i = 0; i < participants.length; i++){
108.                    try{
109.                        if (!participants[i].changeDate(transactionID, appointment,
      date)){
110.                            return false;
111.                        }
112.                    }
113.                    catch (TransactionException exc){
114.                        return false;
115.                    }
```

```
116.                }
117.            }
118.            catch (RemoteException exc){
119.                return false;
120.            }
121.            return true;
122.        }
123.        private void commitAll(long transactionID, AppointmentTransactionParticipant[]
        participants)
124.            throws TransactionException, RemoteException{
125.            for (int i = 0; i < participants.length; i++){
126.                participants[i].commit(transactionID);
127.            }
128.        }
129.        private void cancelAll(long transactionID, AppointmentTransactionParticipant[]
        participants)
130.            throws RemoteException{
131.            for (int i = 0; i < participants.length; i++){
132.                participants[i].cancel(transactionID);
133.            }
134.        }
135.        public String toString(){
136.            return serviceName + " " + appointments.values().toString();
137.        }
138.    }
```

Part Two

Patterns in the Java Programming Language

Chapter Five

Introduction to Java Programming Language Patterns

In the first part of this book, a common set of patterns is discussed. The patterns are listed with descriptions of their characteristics, the benefits and drawbacks associated with them, examples of their use and code samples demonstrating the patterns in action.

The basic patterns discussed are platform and language-neutral. While it's true that Java is especially well-suited to some of these patterns, they can be implemented in languages that support the core object-oriented properties of inheritance, encapsulation, polymorphism, and abstract classes.

Now it's time to shift gears and look at pattern use in the Java APIs. Since the Java programming language and the Design Patterns movement grew up together, the developers used a number of design patterns when they created the Java APIs. The goal is to gain an understanding of how Java is put together, and to answer questions like:

- How does Java as a language make use of patterns?
- How does it use patterns to make its APIs more effective?

The Java APIs provide additional demonstrations of pattern use. Like the Personal Information Manager examples in Part 1, these real-world patterns provide useful insight into how patterns can be effectively applied to solve problems.

At this point, it's worth explaining what exactly is meant by "API." It's become a somewhat vague term in recent years. These days, API is used to refer to a single class, a group of classes, a single package or a set or related packages. The important quality that defines an API is the fact that it provides a programming framework for a set of related functional capabilities.

A number of the APIs in the following chapters are actually designed as a set of related classes. To appreciate the way that an API functions as a whole, it makes sense to spend some time discussing its basic structure. This provides a perspective on how patterns support the API – how they help a specific API to better do its job. This means that this section of the book is effectively part architectural evaluation, part pattern study. This provides a few practical benefits:

1. It can help you appreciate some of the ways that patterns are actually used within the API. Studying the Java APIs demonstrates how patterns can be applied to achieve practical goals.
2. It shows how you can use patterns with the APIs. Examining a set of APIs can help you see how to effectively use a pattern to interact with an API or framework.

In the pages that follow, you'll take a look at a number of Java APIs and see what makes them tick. This should give you new insight into their use and usefulness – perhaps even on why they're designed the way they are. With these thoughts in mind, let's begin our exploration.

Note – The APIs discussed in the following chapters are divided into several sections. First, the Packages section describes which packages contain the classes and interfaces that make up the API. Next, the Overview section provides a brief review of each API. The Overview section is not meant to teach an entire API. It is a reminder to those who know the API, and a list of highlights for those of you who plan to learn more about it as you continue to program. The final section is called Pattern Use; it presents design patterns used in the APIs, and describes how they are used.

Chapter Six

Java Core APIs

Event Handling

Packages

java.awt.event, javax.swing.event, java.util (some classes)
Use: J2SE (delegation model since JDK1.1)

Overview

Event handling allows two or more objects to communicate about a change of state within a system. In an event-based system, one object acts as the event producer, and creates an event object to represent some change in its state. It then passes the event to one or more registered receivers by calling some method on each receiver object.

Event handling has been part of Java since the beginning. It is part of the AWT and, since J2SE v1.2, has also been part of Swing. Event handling plays an important role in many of the Java APIs, including AWT, Swing, and JavaBeans. Therefore, support for event-handling is available in the java.util package.

As of JDK 1.1, the current event handling model was introduced, the delegation model. It was designed to be simple, flexible, and allow for a more robust system. Application code and GUI code can now be easily separated and can be changed independently of each other. The introduction of specialized event types and listeners made compile-time type-checking available.

Event handling happens this way. Each event type has its own Event class. The Event source, which is where an event might occur, such as a Component, keeps a list of listeners that have registered with the source, stating they are interested in any event that occurs at that source. When an event occurs, the Event source instantiates an Event object and sends it to the listeners for that event-specific interface. To do this, it invokes a listener method on each of the listeners passing the Event object as an argument.

All events extend from java.util.EventObject, which keeps a reference to the source of the event. Specific types of events add functionality; for instance, the ActionEvent contains the ActionCommand, which can be set on the source.

The event listeners are interfaces that define the methods the source can call when a certain condition occurs; for instance, when a button is clicked or a mouse is moved. These interfaces all extend the interface java.util.EventListener.

The event sources don't need to implement an interface or extend some class to be a source. However, they must keep a list of event listeners who have registered for events from this source. The listeners are registered with the source by calling add*XXX*Listener(*XXX*Listener). To remove them from the list, call removeXXXListener(XXXListener). XXX is replaced by the name of the event type.

Generally speaking, event sources can be unicast (only one listener allowed) or multicast (multiple listeners allowed). Within AWT and Swing, all event sources are multicast. To make things easier, a specialized Multicaster exists, java.awt.AWTEventMulticaster. The AWTEventMulticaster provides an efficient and thread-safe multicast event dispatching for the AWT events defined in the java.awt.event package [JLS].

The AWTEventMulticaster implements all AWT event listener interfaces so it can be used for any of the AWT events. The AWTEventMulticaster constructor takes two event listeners. When a new listener is added, a new AWTEventMulticaster is created passing the current AWTEventMulticaster and the new listener as arguments. This mechanism chains AWTEventMulticasters together. To propagate an event, each multicaster calls the listener method on its two children: one is an event handler with a listener method, the other is the next AWTEventMulticaster in the chain). This is how event multicasting is achieved.

Swing uses a different class, instead of AWTEventMulticaster. The class javax.swing.event.EventListenerList can even be used for keeping a list of listeners of an unknown type. When one event source has listeners of different types, EventListenerList is responsible for maintaining the entire list of listeners.

A package outside of the GUI APIs that uses event handling is org.xml.sax, one of the newcomers in Java 1.4. SAX is used to parse an XML document where event handling is used to notify the different handlers. However, this API doesn't use the java.util.EventListener and java.util.EventObject.

Pattern Use

Observer (see page 94)**:** This is the most obvious pattern in the event handling. There are many listener interfaces, event types, and event sources. Each is a variation on the Observer pattern, whose objective is to decouple the event source from the listener. The event source defines the type of event and the moment at which the event occurred. The listener provides the information about what to do when the event occurs.

Adapter (see page 142)**:** The java.awt.event package contains many classes that end with the word Adapter, so you might expect that the Adapter pattern would be implemented there. However, the event adapters do not perform the same function as a true Adapter pattern implementation. They exist to convert event handling interfaces into classes, For example, the MouseListener interface has a corresponding MouseAdapter, which implements the interface and defines a series of empty methods. Since the event adapter classes do not actually execute functional behavior or convert between two different interfaces, they cannot be considered as true Adapters.

Factory Method (see page 21)**:** The `AWTEventMulticaster` provides static factory methods to create a chain of event listeners of the appropriate type. It has overloaded methods for registering (`add`) and de-registering (`remove`) each type of event listener in the `java.awt.event` package. For example, `public static ActionListener add(ActionListener a, ActionListener b)`. The return type of the method is a listener of the type just registered. The implementation of the method is such that the returned object can simply be the listener that was registered, but most of the time it is a new `AWTEventMulticaster` instance that has a reference to the old `AWTEventMulticaster` and the new listener instance.

Composite (see page 157)**:** The `AWTEventMulticaster` creates its own chain or tree of listeners. Every time a new listener is added to the `AWTEventMulticaster`, a new multicaster instance is created. That new instance receives a reference to the new registered listener and the old tree, represented by the current `AWTEventMulticaster`.

When a listener method is called, the `AWTEventMulticaster` propagates the method call to the two listeners to which it has a reference: one is an AWT event listener (true listener) and an `AWTEventMulticaster` instance, which does the same for its own two references. With this approach, the entire tree is called recursively.

Chain of Responsibility (see page 42)**:** The `AWTEventMulticaster` forwards all of the calls to the methods that are defined in the listener interfaces, to the listeners `AWTEventMulticaster` has a reference to. `AWTEventMulticaster` doesn't have to do much itself. It simply calls the method on each of its children. If a child is an AWT event listener, it executes the event handling behavior. If it is an `AWTEventMulticaster`, it forwards the method call to its own children.

Command (see page 51)**:** `AWTEventMulticaster` is structured much like the Macro Command. It contains a collection, in this case a collection of two, of other Command objects. One object is terminal (the actual listener), and the other is another Macro Command (another `AWTEventMulticaster`). The different event listener methods are used instead of the execute method in the Command pattern.

The caller of the method (the source of the event) is unaware of the structure, and doesn't need to know anything about it. The event source only needs to call the `execute` method once on the event listener, and that listener behaves like a Macro Command executing the proper methods.

JavaBeans

Packages

java.beans, java.beans.beancontext
Use: J2SE (since JDK1.1)

Overview

JavaBeans™ provides a standardized model for the Java programming language that enables classes to be developed as components. Components have a standard way of representing data and behavior, so they're more easily shared between developers. A component model such as JavaBeans potentially enables a developer to reuse another developer's code even if they work in different companies in different parts of the world. In the component model, technical roles are divided into component programmers, component assemblers, and application assemblers. The programmers are the only ones who actually have to code; the component and application assemblers use development tools that allowed them to visually manipulate and combine beans. This enables them to build new beans, or entire applications. JavaBeans can be visual, but they don't have to be.

That a component model is a good idea is demonstrated by the fact that components also underlie Java 2 Enterprise Edition, but the visual use of JavaBeans was only moderately successful.

However, that isn't to say that JavaBeans are insignificant. When JavaBeans were conceived they required quite a change in Java. The old event model (hierarchical) had to be replaced with a more flexible event model so responsibilities could properly be distributed. The new event model became known as the delegation model. (See "Event Handling" on page 281.) This event model is core to the Java Beans architecture.

At the same time, emphasis was also placed on code conventions, because naming is an essential part of the introspection of JavaBeans. All of the AWT components became JavaBeans.

JavaBeans are generally supposed to support events, properties, introspection, customization, and persistence. The current event model allows decoupling event sources and event listeners. Every JavaBean can be a source of events and/or a listener to events. The JavaBean identifies itself as a listener by implementing the appropriate listener interfaces and methods defined in those interfaces. To identify itself as an event source, the bean has to provide `add` `XXXListener` and `remove` *`XXX`*`Listener` methods.

For other tools and applications to find the properties of a JavaBean, the bean has to stick to specific method naming. If the bean has what we now know as getters and setters with a particular name, like `String getName()` and `void setName(String n)`, then other applications can safely assume the bean has a property called `name` of a type `String`, even though the internal representation may be different. This property can then be used in property sheets of a visual editor or in other applications. JSPs, JavaServer Pages, make use of JavaBeans in this way. Values returned from an HTML form are set as properties, which can later be retrieved for some processing.

Normally, all public methods are exported. If bean providers want to limit the number of properties, events, and methods exported, they can supply a class that implements the `BeanInfo` interface. The `BeanInfo` interface defines methods for other objects to easily query what members and events are available. The code that determines which methods are exported is in the implementation of `BeanInfo`.

A bean can provide its own `PropertyEditor` for new data types, allowing the bean to be included in a visual component environment. Such an editor can either support `Strings` as values, or it may even use its own `java.awt.Component` to do the editing.

When the bean can provide its own customizer for more complex customization, that type of editor should extend from `java.awt.Component` and implement `java.beans.Customizer` so that a graphical editor can integrate the editor in the GUI.

A JavaBean needs to support some way of persisting itself, so it has to either implement `java.io.Serializable` or `java.io.Externalizable`. When the bean is persisted, its internal state should be saved so that the bean may later be restored with the same data. This serialized version of a bean can even be treated as its own type. The `java.beans.Beans.instantiate` method takes several arguments, one of which is the name of a Bean as a `String`. The instantiate method first tries to locate a file with the specified name with a trailing `.ser`; if that fails, it tries to locate a class with the bean name and, if found, instantiate that.

Pattern Use

Factory Method (see page 21)**:** In JavaBeans, the Factory Method is used to instantiate beans through the `Beans.instantiate` method and to abstract the real creation of the object. The caller of the method sees no difference between whether the bean has been restored from serialization or that a new object has been created—making it easier to reuse beans. A customizer only has to change some properties to let the bean appear as a different type, serialize the bean, and give it a name with the `.ser` extension.

Singleton (see page 34)**:** Applications use the `Introspector` to find information about a Bean. The `Introspector` provides information about what methods, events, and properties a bean instance supports. It traverses the inheritance tree and looks for implicit and explicit information to use in building a `BeanInfo` object. Only one Introspector is needed to provide this functionality.

To prevent redundancy, only a single instance is used so it can cache information for other requests.

Adapter (see page 142)**:** The Adapter is specifically mentioned in the JavaBeans Specification ([JBS] although there it is called Adaptor). The task of the Adapter is to decouple the event source from the actual listeners and perform one or more of the following tasks:

- Implement a queue for the incoming events so that events may be searched in the situation where a specific event in a series of events is missed.
- Provide a filter to prevent all events from arriving at the actual target, letting only those events pass that fulfill certain criteria. You could set up an Adapter between a temperature bean and a warning bean and only forward the change events if the temperature changes more that 0.1 degrees Celsius instead of just every minuscule change.
- Demultiplexing. A class can implement a specific method from an interface only once. If the same object is going to listen to multiple sources of the same event, but the reaction should be different based on the source, the implementation of the listener method has to change for every new source and the method will become bloated with large `switch` statements. Here the Adapter pattern is used to demultiplex. That means an `Adapter` instance is created for every event source and that instance is registered with the source. When the listener method gets called, the Adapter invokes another method on the actual listener, a different method for each different source. Now the actual listener no longer needs to determine where the event came from. That is the responsibility of the adapter.
- Connect a source and a listener. This is useful when the event source and actual listener are of different event types. Its functionality is essentially that of the "true" Adapter, as described in the Adapter pattern.

Observer (see page 94)**:** JavaBeans provides support for *bound* and *constrained* properties in beans.

- Bound properties mean that beans can be connected together, and when a bound property changes, all interested beans are notified. These properties are called bound because they allow other classes and objects to bind behavior to the changes of the property.

  The bound property acts as the Observable and the beans interested in the changes are the Observers to that property. They are registered through the method `addPropertyChangeListener(PropertyChangeListener listener)` and must implement the `PropertyChangeListener` interface.

  When the property change occurs a `PropertyChangeEvent` is created with, among others, the old and new values and the `propertyChange` method is called on the listeners passing the `PropertyChangeEvent` as the argument.

- Constrained properties are a variation on this principle, the difference is that the listeners may throw a `PropertyVetoException` if the listener objects to the change from the old to the new value. The listeners are registered through the method `addVetoableChangeListener(VetoableChangeListener listener)` and they must implement the `VetoableChangeListener` interface. The bean where the property change occurs calls the `vetoableChange` method on the registered listeners passing a `PropertyChangeEvent` as the argument. If a `PropertyVetoException` occurs, the same bean will undo the change and call the same listeners but with a `PropertyChangeEvent` that has reversed the new and old values, effectively rolling back the previous change.

AWT and Swing – The Graphical User Interface APIs

Packages

Primary AWT packages are `java.awt` and `java.awt.event`
Other packages include `java.awt.color`, `java.awt.datatransfer`, `java.awt.dnd`, `java.awt.font`, `java.awt.geom`, `java.awt.im`, `java.awt.im.spi`, `java.awt.image`, `java.awt.image.renderable`, `java.awt.print`
Use: J2SE (JDK1.0, greatly expanded in JDK1.2 and 1.3)

Primary Swing package is `javax.swing`
Other packages include `javax.swing.border`, `javax.swing.colorchooser`, `javax.swing.event`, `javax.swing.filechooser`, `javax.swing.plaf`, `javax.swing.plaf.basic`, `javax.swing.plaf.metal`, `javax.swing.plaf.multi`, `javax.swing.table`, `javax.swing.text`, `javax.swing.text.html`, `javax.swing.text.html.parser`, `javax.swing.text.rtf`, `javax.swing.tree`, `javax.swing.undo`.
Use: J2SE (since JDK1.2, expanded for JDK1.3)

Common Features

Central to both AWT and Swing are the concepts of the *component*, *container*, and *layout manager*. A component is a graphical element of some kind like a button, label or text box. A container is also a kind of graphical element, but is distinguished by its ability to hold other elements. Containers are the organizers of the Java graphics APIs, enabling developers to group graphical elements within the GUI space. Windows are containers, holding components such as buttons and checkboxes inside themselves.

Layout managers are not graphical. They're worker objects, specialists that can determine size and position for components inside a container. A container delegates the task of managing its space to its associated layout manager, relying on it for advice about how and where it should place elements.

Another important feature of AWT and Swing is the event-handling model. In Java graphical applications, user interaction is represented by event objects that are produced by components. For example, if a user were to click on a big red button in a Java GUI labeled “History Eraser”, that button would produce an `ActionEvent`.

So would this act irrevocably erase our existence? Luckily, not in this universe. Unless there is an associated event handler, the event produced will not trigger any program response. In this example, there has to be a class implementing the `ActionListener` interface which has been registered with the button through a call to `addActionListener`. In that case, the `ActionEvent` is passed to the associated `ActionListener` through a call to its `actionPer-`

formed method. To date, no one has written an event handler for the History Eraser button, so we're all still safe.

The AWT Architectural Model

The Abstract Window Toolkit (AWT) has been around as long as the language itself. It is built around a simple set of components that allow you to create basic GUIs. When you create an AWT application, its components are guaranteed to have the same look and feel as the platform where JVM runs. In other words, the same code produces a Solaris GUI when run on Solaris, a Macintosh GUI on MacOS and a Windows GUI on a Wintel platform.

There's a very straightforward explanation for this—an AWT application looks like its elements are native to a platform because they really are. AWT bases its functionality on the concept of the *peer*. Every AWT component has a peer class associated with the operating system, which does most of the real work. The classes that developers use to create graphical components in AWT provide a programming wrapper around the peers. For instance, in AWT a programmer uses the `java.awt.Button` class to create a button. Associated with that button is an implementor of the `java.awt.peer.ButtonPeer` interface, which performs most of the real tasks associated with painting the component on-screen.

It follows that there must be some way to keep track of the platform-specific peers within AWT. The `Toolkit` class provides that capability. Inside `Toolkit` is the code used to link to the underlying operating system. Developers rarely use this class directly, but it is important to AWT, since it ultimately loads graphical libraries, creates peer objects, and manages other platform-dependent resources such as cursors.

Because the basic AWT components are directly linked to the underlying operating system through their peers, they are also referred to as *heavyweight components* since they rely directly on the operating system to do things like draw them on-screen. The decision to base the AWT architecture around peers had some important consequences, and development efforts must usually take these into account:

Benefits

- There is less code to write in the API, since the underlying platform does most of the work.
- GUIs look and behave as they would on the operating system on which they are run.

Drawbacks

- If you want to support true platform independence, you must consider the least common denominator when providing components. This means that AWT GUIs are not as feature-rich as they could have been with other approaches.
- If there are any quirks in the graphical components of an operating system, the AWT application inherits those along with the functionality.
- Since peers have to be used for many operations of the GUI components, they can potentially slow down an application and present scaling issues.

Because of the drawbacks of the peer components, it might be better for developers to directly extend one of the two base classes of the model: `Component` or `Container`. Since neither of these classes has native platform peers, any direct subclass of them would inherit the core functionality of AWT without suffering from the limitations of the peer architecture. Naturally, this comes at a price—developers have to write the code to draw components from scratch.

The Swing Architectural Model

The entire Swing architecture is based on the concept of extending functionality from the AWT Container class. This includes the vast majority of graphical components in Swing subclass `JComponent`, which is itself a subclass of the `Container` class in AWT. This basic architectural decision has a number of consequences:

- Swing is built on the core classes of AWT, so it inherits the basic AWT model. This means that Swing applications use the same approach for arranging space (the layout managers, containers, and components) and handling events. It also means that developers can use similar coding techniques for both Swing and AWT applications.
- Since most Swing components are mostly Java code, there's a lot more flexibility. It's possible to create a much larger set of graphical components and make them much more customizable since they're basically smart pixels on-screen.
- Swing components are subclassed from Container, so they can all hold other components. This is a big change from the AWT model, where only a few selected graphical elements were able to hold other items.

Building an entire architecture on another one is not without drawbacks of course. The inheritance hierarchy for the Swing classes can get fairly complex, and can sometimes make it difficult to see exactly where behavior is being performed. The `JButton` class is a typical example; its inheritance hierarchy is shown as follows:

`Object > Component > Container > JComponent > AbstractButton > JButton`

There are still a few heavyweight classes that remain in Swing. They must be heavyweight in order to interact with the underlying operating system. The four top-level windowing classes are heavyweights, subclassed from their counterparts in AWT, and are shown in Table 6-1:

Table 6-1 *AWT and Swing classes*

AWT Class	**Swing Equivalent**
`Applet`	`JApplet`
`Dialog`	`JDialog`
`Frame`	`JFrame`
`Window`	`JWindow`

These four classes retain the look and feel of their underlying operating system. For all other graphical elements, however, even their appearance can be changed. Swing components delegate the task of representing themselves onscreen to an associated UI class, which can be changed. The upshot of this is that a Swing application can look like a Solaris GUI even if it is run on a Windows platform. This capability is called pluggable look and feel, or PLaF for short.

General Pattern Use

Observer (see page 94): As complex architectures, AWT and Swing both use their share of design patterns. The most often used pattern is Observer, of course. The Observer pattern allows for a flexible way of communicating between objects. Both architectures use the Observer pattern to manage event handling. In both cases, the graphical components represent the `Observable` class, and programmers write the `Observer`.

Composite and Chain of Responsibility (see page 157 and page 42): Since both AWT and Swing graphical elements are based on the AWT `Container` and `Component` classes, the APIs allow for GUI tree structures to be created. This suggests Composite and Chain of Responsibility patterns in the API.

- The Composite pattern is found in several `Container-Component` methods, although it occurs less frequently than you might think. The list methods, used to print out the graphical components to a stream, use the Composite pattern, as does the method `readObject` (used to serialize object state to a stream). Several methods fall short of true Composite behavior because they call different methods for `Containers` and `Components` rather than using a single method defined in the `Component` class and overridden in the other classes.

- Chain of Responsibility is demonstrated in a number of methods. Recall that Chain of Responsibility involves delegation of behavior, often to the parent in a tree structure. Most `Component` methods that involve getting standard component properties use this pattern. Examples are `getForeground`, `getBackground`, `getCursor`, and `getLocale`.

Pattern Use in AWT

Singleton (see page 34): The `Toolkit` class provides an interesting example of the Singleton design pattern. `Toolkit` uses Singleton to produce what is called a default `Toolkit` and to ensure that this single default `Toolkit` is globally available. This `Toolkit` is obtained by a call to the static `getDefaultToolkit` method, and is normally used by developers to obtain a `Toolkit` if they need to do things like create a print job. Since `Toolkit` is an abstract class, redefined for a specific operating system, it is entirely possible that concrete implementations of `Toolkit` have constructors and allow other instances of `Toolkit` to be created within the system—in fact, Sun's implementation for Windows does. The "default" toolkit, however, remains the same.

Bridge (see page 150): You could potentially say that the AWT peer architecture is similar to the Bridge pattern, which separates a component into two hierarchies: an abstraction and an implementation hierarchy. The AWT components represent the Abstraction for the Bridge, the peers are their Implementor counterparts, and a specific peer for an operating system is a ConcreteImplementor. There are two slight deviations from the classic Bridge pattern:

- Many of the component classes actually perform *some* behavior, rather than delegating to their Implementor, the peer.
- The component classes are not refined. This means that there is not really a distinction between `Abstraction` and `RefinedAbstraction` as there is in the classic Bridge pattern.

Prototype (see page 28): AWT also has a number of Prototype implementors that have some way of making a copy of an instance. Predictably, these classes represent potentially reusable resources in the AWT architecture: `Insets`, `GridBagConstraints`, `Area`, and `PageFormat`.

Pattern Use in Swing

MVC (see page 208): Probably the best-documented design pattern in the Swing API is the Model-View-Controller (MVC).

Almost all of the complex GUI elements in Swing use the component-level form of the MVC pattern. There are a number of excellent reasons for using the pattern, including the following:

- It's possible to use a single underlying model to drive multiple view-controller pairs.
- It's much easier to customize a component using this pattern, since programmers frequently only have to modify select parts of the component functionality.

Swing implements the MVC pattern very consistently in the API. Model functionality is represented by interfaces, as is controller behavior. The View elements are managed through a UI class hierarchy, which has its foundation in the `javax.swing.plaf` package. The basic view behavior is set out as a series of abstract classes, which can subsequently be refined to provide a different look and feel.

As an example, consider the `JButton`, the class which is used to represent a simple push button. It is associated with a `ButtonModel` implementor for the model, a `ButtonUI` for its view, and possibly one or more event handlers for its controller.

Prototype (see page 28): Like AWT, Swing also has a number of utility classes that can be cloned, and which therefore implement the Prototype design pattern: `AbstractAction`, `SimpleAttributeSet`, `HTMLEditorKit`, `DefaultTreeSelectionModel`.

Collections Framework

Packages

`java.util`
Use: J2SE (1.0; organized as an explicit API since JDK1.2)

Description

The Collections Framework allows developers to use features, such as dynamic resizing without writing all the code themselves. The Collections API has changed since collections were first introduced in Java. The Collections Framework aims to provide a more sophisticated way for programmers to deal with collections of objects.

It's important to recognize that there's really only one way to store a group of items in the Java language—an array. Arrays are a pretty basic kind of object storage. They provide a fixed set of references to objects. The data type of all the references is set during array creation, and the size remains fixed throughout the array's existence.

The classes and interfaces used for the original collection capability in JDK1.0 were pretty basic. The JDK provided just three concrete classes based on two kinds of collections:

- `Vector` and `Stack` – Collections sorted with an integer index that provides absolute position with the collection.
- `Hashtable` – A collection organized around key-value pairs. The key must be a unique Object, which is used to locate the value. The value can be any Object, and is the element intended for storage in the `Hashtable`. For any hash structure, the test for uniqueness is based on the return value of the `hashCode()` method. If two objects return the same value for `hashCode`, they are assumed to be equal for the purposes of comparison for their keys.

We've come a long way since then. The modern Collections Framework consists of a set of ten concrete classes that are built on top of an entire coordinating layer of interfaces and abstract classes. What's more, the framework gives programmers a way to modify the functionality of the individual collections. Programmers can use the `java.util.Collections` class to enhance an existing collection, for instance to synchronize an unsynchronized collection.

When the development team created the Collections Framework for the JDK 1.2, they completely retrofitted the earlier collections so that these "older"collections are part of the new model. It's fairly impressive that they managed to shoehorn the original classes into the new framework, especially with so little change to the API. The team was able to update the model with little functional modification and no deprecation.

Of course, there are a few differences between the original classes and the ones from the new model. The older collection classes were designed to be thread safe from the start. So, if you look in the documentation for the `Hashtable`, `Stack`, or `Vector` classes, you will see a lot of synchronized methods.

Are there synchronized methods in any of the modern collection classes? Nope. The new model uses collection classes to provide basic storage functionality, and that's all. The `Collections` class provides methods to create threadsafe versions of the collections. The example below shows how it's done:

Example 6.1 `Collections class and threadsafe versions of collections`

```
List internalList = new LinkedList();
List threadSafeList =
      Collections.synchronizedList(internalList);
```

The `LinkedList` provides storage, and the `synchronizedList` method makes it into a synchronized collection. Making synchronization available as an option is a real advantage for programmers. Basically, it means they don't have to use synchronized collection code (with the associated performance hit) unless they really need the capability.

As stated earlier, the Collections Framework is based on a set of interfaces. The API has two basic behavioral chains. The first one is based on the `Collection` interface, which represents collections that perform simple storage used to cross-reference the elements. The second is based on the `Map` interface, and describes collections which are organized around key-value pairs.

Collection is the parent to three subinterfaces:

- `Set` – This interface defines methods available to any collection without any defined sequence or ordering of the contained elements.
- `List` – This interfaces defines behavior for collections which use a numeric index to define an element's position.
- `SortedSet` – This interface is used to describe collections that use 'natural ordering" to organize elements. The elements of a `SortedSet` must implement the interface `Comparable`, which defines a `compareTo` method. The `compareTo` method returns a numeric result used to organize the objects within the `SortedSet`.

`Map` has a subinterface, as well—the `SortedMap`. Like `SortedSet`, this interface is used for maps with natural ordering. The collections that implement this interface must have a way to compare keys of the elements that will indicate whether one is greater than, equal to or less than the other. The keys must implement the `Comparable` interface.

Pattern Use

A number of patterns figure heavily in the Collections Framework. In the general framework, there is strong use of the Prototype and Iterator patterns. The Collections class also has a pattern associated with it—the Decorator.

Prototype (see page 28): The Prototype pattern uses one object as a template or basis for the creation of a new object. Given the purpose of the collection classes, it's not surprising that they all support a copy operation *clone*. That copy operation returns a new copy of the current collections. All of the collection classes implement the `Cloneable` interface and provide a shallow copy when their `clone` method is called. In this case, a *shallow copy* means that a new collection instance is returned, but all of the internally stored elements are the same objects as those stored in the original collection.

Iterator (see page 69): All Collection implementors give you the ability to retrieve an object to easily (and generically) cycle through the elements of the collection. The Iterator pattern, too, enables simpler cycling through the elements of a collection. The `Collection` interface defines a method called `iterator`, and the `List` interface has a `listIterator` method. These methods return interface implementors that allow users to move through a collection. The `Iterator` interface is for forward-only navigation, and the `ListIterator` provides both forward and backward movement within a collection.

The names are a not-so-subtle giveaway. Actually, both interfaces fall a bit short of the classic Iterator pattern, since they don't define all of the core methods—specifically, neither interface provides an explicit `first` method. The goal is to abstract navigational functionality from the underlying collection implementation, though. So, the central intent of these interfaces is the same as for the Iterator pattern.

Collection classes use inner classes to provide concrete Iterators. When you call `iterator` or `listIterator`, the collection creates an inner class object and returns it to the caller.

Decorator (see page 166): The `Collections` class uses the Decorator pattern to extend the functionality of collections by providing objects that modify the behavior of the collections without changing the collections. The class has three groups of methods that generate classes with additional capabilities. Table 6-2 shows the groups of methods and what they produce:

Table 6-2 *Method names and functionality*

Begins with	*Resulting functionality*
`singleton`	Produces an immutable, one-element collection
`synchronized`	Produces a collection with synchronized methods
`unmodifiable`	Produces an immutable collection

Calling any of the methods from these groups produces an object that enhances the capabilities of the collection that you pass in and adds to what it can do.

The `Collections` class actually has a set of inner classes that it uses to provide these added capabilities. So, calling `synchronizedCollection` will generate a wrapper object around the inner collection which will ensure that methods belonging to the `Collection` interface will be synchronized.

Note: There's one exception to that rule. Creating a synchronized collection will **not** give you a synchronized iterator method—you have to manually synchronize the `Iterator` and `ListIterator`.

It's tempting to think that the methods prefixed with the word singleton represent the Singleton design pattern. However, the intent of the methods is quite different. These methods do **not** ensure that you can have only one instance of the collection object—they ensure that the collection can only contain a single element. Any attempt to add or remove elements from the resulting collection will result in an `UnsupportedOperationException`.

Input-Output (I/O)

Packages

`java.io`
Use: J2SE (since version 1.0)

Description

The main goal of the Java I/O API is to allow developers to use streams. Streams provide basic input-output capabilities in Java. If you want to write to a file, use a stream; if you want to read from standard input, use a stream. If you want to write across a network—well, you get the idea.

The `java.io` package contains four general types of stream, which are based on four abstract classes. These classes provide functionality based on stream direction (input or output) and level whether the stream information is based on bytes or characters.

Table 6-3 *Stream types in the* `java.io` *package*

Low-level (bytes)		*High-level (characters)*	
Input	Output	Input	Output
InputStream	OutputStream	Reader	Writer

All other streams in Java subclass one of these four classes, and extend the functionality of the class by adding a specific capability. For example, the `FileWriter` is a type of `Writer` (output, writes characters) and it adds the ability to write characters to a file on disk. The `DataInputStream` is a kind of `InputStream` (input, reads bytes) and it also allows developers to read different data types, such as an `int`, `float`, or `boolean` value.

How do you create a stream with combinations of abilities in Java? You "chain" them together, using the concept of a filter stream. You can attach filter streams to other streams by passing the target stream into the filter's constructor. The filter can then add its own functionality to the associated stream. For example, you could read lines of text from the standard input stream by using these lines of code:

Example 6.2 `Streams in Java`

```
BufferedReader readIn =
      new BufferedReader(new InputStreamReader(System.in));
    String textLine = readIn.readLine();
```

In this example, input ultimately comes from `System.in` (keyboard input) in the form of bytes. By adding an `InputStreamReader`, you can use the passed bytes to make Java language characters. Finally, the `BufferedReader` places the characters from the `InputStreamReader` into a buffer. The `BufferedReader` can detect when the end of line is reached, and release the buffered characters as a `String`.

There aren't a lot of stream classes in the `java.io` package. However, since you can mix and match filter streams, you ultimately have much more functionality available than you might think. You can think of Java I/O as a pipeline. When you write code, you attach different I/O objects, or "pipes," to each other. With each section of pipe added, you modify the flow through the pipeline.

Pattern Use

It's evident that a lot of I/O programming involves stream chaining. To support this capability, the API relies heavily on a variation of the structural pattern, the Decorator (see page 166).

Each of the four abstract classes—`InputStream`, `OutputStream`, `Reader` and `Writer`—acts as the base for a decorator chain. The I/O classes that support decorator behavior have one or more constructors that accept an argument of another I/O class to chain. `java.io` contains the following categories of I/O classes:

1. Base I/O classes (also called node streams) – These classes provide endpoints of communication; they are actually attached to some end location. For example, a `FileReader` is not a decorator because it is directly connected to a file.

2. Paired streams – At first glance, these streams might appear to be Decorators, since they have the ability to be attached to another stream. However, the classes are actually designed to work in complementary pairs—the output of one feeds the input of another. You can think of these classes as base I/O classes; they can be decorated themselves, but their true function is to establish a communication channel to another stream.

3. `PipedWriterFilter` streams – The filter streams use the Decorator pattern to support chaining. The filter classes use the following rules to manage decorator behavior:

    - A filter decorates a class using a constructor that accepts one of the four base I/O classes: `InputStream`, `OutputStream`, `Reader`, or `Writer`.

    - The filter class usually decorates classes of the same type. This means that an `InputStream` that is also a filter will decorate another `InputStream`, for example. The important exceptions to this rule are the `InputStreamReader` and `OutputStreamWriter`, which translate between bytes and characters.

Reflection

Packages

`java.lang.reflect`
Use: J2SE (since JDK 1.1)

Overview

The reflection API allows you to discover information about classes and objects at runtime. This capability is called introspection, and is useful when you want to dynamically include new classes in your programs while they are running. Using reflection, you can load a class dynamically using only its name.

Although most of the API is in `java.lang.reflect`, you should also regard `java.lang.Class` as part of this API. The class `Class` acts as a gateway to the reflection functionalities. The reflection API defines several classes that encapsulate the different types of information, classes like `Method`, `Field`, `Constructor`, and `Modifier`. These classes are final and, except for the `Modifier`, only the JVM can create instances of these types.

Thanks to this API, you can dynamically use instances of previously unknown origin; for instance, when the class of an object is unknown at the time of development. You can invoke methods, call constructors, modify fields, create new arrays, and access and modify their elements.

Example 6.3 `Using instances of unknown origin`

```
Class class = Class.forName("some class name");
Object o = class.newInstance();
```

The code demonstrates how you can create an object from only having the name of the class. The method `forName` takes a String as argument and tries to locate a class file matching that name and loads that class in the class loader. The method returns an instance of Class which describes the class. When `newInstance` is called on the Class object it creates an instance using the constructor with no arguments. The String could be read from a file, property or other source.

When you receive an object from somewhere and you want to find out the specific type of the instance, use code similar to the following code. The method `getClass` returns the Class instance describing the class of the object. The method `getName` returns the name of the Class.

It can be useful sometimes during debugging, when you don't know the type of a received object:

```
Object unknownTypeObject = //received somehow
```

```
System.out.println(unknownTypeObject.getClass().getName());
```

An addition to the Reflection API was made when J2SE v1.3 was released. As of 1.3, you can use the dynamic proxy class. The class is created at runtime and implements a number of interfaces specified at runtime. The `Proxy` class, which is responsible for creating this class, also acts as the superclass to every proxy.

The method to create an instance of the dynamic proxy takes three arguments: a `ClassLoader`, an array of interfaces, and an `InvocationHandler`. The proxy instance created delegates all method calls to the `InvocationHandler`, which is responsible for carrying them out. To keep the invocation as generic as possible, the `InvocationHandler` implements a single method, `invoke`.

The Reflection API provides many advanced features, many of which the average developer will never use. The flexibility that reflection offers through these advanced features comes at a price, which is performance. According to *Effective Java* [Bloch01], interfaces should be preferred to reflection.

However, this doesn't mean that reflection is obsolete. Certain applications can receive great benefits from reflection, particularly those based on JavaBeans, object inspectors, interpreters, and services like object serialization, which need to get information on an object at runtime.

Pattern Use

Factory Method (see page 21)**:** The Factory Method pattern is used to create instances without having to call a constructor directly. It also enables you to gain the option of returning different types instead of just the class of the constructor called. Given the dynamic nature of the dynamic proxy, using a regular constructor wouldn't work, because you need to know the name of the class/constructor before you can invoke it. When using a constructor is out of the question, the next best thing is a static method to create an instance. The class `Proxy` has two factory methods; one (`getProxyClass`) gets the `Class` object that describes the dynamic proxy with the specified interfaces. The other factory method (`newProxyInstance`) is more of a convenience method. It uses the `getProxyClass` method to get the class, then uses that `Class` to get the constructor and invoke the constructor.

The `Array` class, which is the wrapper class for arrays implements the Factory Method for a different reason. Creating an array requires knowing the exact type of the elements, and the resulting object is an array of elements of that particular type, which cannot be changed later. This is like the normal array where you declare the type when the array is created and cannot be changed. The object created by the factory method is not an instance of `Array`, which eliminates the possibility of using a constructor, because the constructor of `Array` returns an `Array` instance. So instead of a constructor, a Factory Method is used.

Facade (see page 175)**:** In this API the class Class acts as a front to the whole reflection of a real class. The most-used options are available through the Class. The other reflection classes are still available for more specialized modification, invocation, or reflection.

Proxy (see page 197)**:** The classes Field, Method and Constructor encapsulate the whole concept of a specific field, method, or constructor respectively. You can request all information through the reflection classes. For example, using a Method object, which is tied to a specific method in a class, you can request the declared modifiers, a list of parameter types required to invoke the method, and the return type. You can even use the Method object to invoke the method.

The Method class acts as a proxy to the specific method. Instead of being a proxy to another object, here the Field, Method, Constructor, and Modifier are proxies to parts of an object.

Another implementation of the Proxy pattern is the Proxy class. The factory method in the Proxy class creates the required class for the needed functionality. The resulting subclass of Proxy implements all specified interfaces and methods. The implementation of the methods are such that all calls are forwarded to the single handler method inside of the InvocationHandler.

To the outside world, an instance of the dynamic proxy behaves as expected. All of its interfaces and all defined methods can be invoked on the proxy instance. The real implementation of the methods is in the InvocationHandler.

Chapter Seven

Distributed Technologies

Java Naming and Directory Interface (JNDI)

Packages

`javax.naming`, `javax.naming.directory`, `javax.naming.event`, `javax.naming.ldap`, `javax.naming.spi`
Use: J2SE (JDK 1.3), J2EE (J2EE1.2)

Description

The Java Naming and Directory Interface API was developed to provide a standardized way to access lookup services from within Java code.

It's a vague definition, but it's that way on purpose. JNDI allows you to standardize access across a whole range of naming and directory services. It's like having all the phonebooks in the world at your fingertips, without actually having to carry them around with you. Which actually makes it more like having 24-hour access to a telephone operator who has the complete set of phonebooks.

In the pre-JNDI days, developers had to use individual APIs to access different services. For instance, to communicate using RMI, an IT group would potentially have to set up and maintain an RMI registry implementation so that applications could find out which servers hosted which remote objects. To manage JDBC communication, the group would have to set up some way to store lookup information for a remote database. To manage directory services, they would have to maintain some scheme to manage navigation within their directory schema.

That's three different lookup services, with three different technologies, potentially handled three entirely different ways. Some IT departments might welcome the challenge, but the frustration of development and maintenance would quickly drive most developers bananas.

JNDI consolidated the task of managing lookup services, so that an application could use the single technology for all its needs. What's more, JNDI made it easy to separate the configuration of the resources from their lookup characteristics, so that you need to put almost no environment-specific information in your code.

JNDI is also fairly easy to use. To access a resource, just create a helper object called a `Context`, use it to retrieve a resource by its logical name, then convert it to the expected object type, as shown in Example 7.1:

Example 7.1 `Using JNDI`

```
javax.naming.InitialContext jndiCtx = new InitialContext();
  Object resource = jndiCtx.lookup("datasource");
  javax.sql.DataSource hal = (javax.sql.DataSource)resource;
```

Once JNDI returns the resource, you just use it as you normally would. In this case, the `DataSource` could be used to connect to a database.

Java applications use the JNDI API to access a JNDI Naming Manager. The Naming Manager in turn uses one or more JNDI service provider interface (SPI) implementations to access underlying managed services. These services might be associated with directory structure and file storage, such as LDAP, NDS or NIS or they might equally well be associated with distributed object communications, such as RMI or CosNaming for CORBA.

Two major types of JNDI services are available. Naming services provide a way to associate an object with a name. You can subsequently use The name to locate a specific object. Directory services offer a way to group lookup information in a logical hierarchy, like a directory structure. In the hierarchy, names are associated with directories, which can in turn maintain sets of attributes and values. For both naming and directory services, the JNDI name is simply shorthand used to identify an object in a computing environment. In the same way that names are shorthand for representing people, the JNDI names represent complex objects.

In JNDI, a context represents the starting point that developers use to look up a resource. A context holds a set of associations between names and objects called bindings. A context also enforces a naming convention, which is a set of rules used to establish what constitutes an acceptable name.

JNDI consists of five packages, which do an admirable job of partitioning related capabilities. Table 7-1 shows the functional breakdown:

Table 7-1 *Packages and corresponding use*

Package	**Use**
`javax.naming`	Provides the basic JNDI framework.
`javax.naming.directory`	Provides extensions for directory services.
`javax.naming.event`	Provides extensions for event handling.
`javax.naming.ldap`	Provides extensions to support LDAP v.3.
`javax.naming.spi`	Service-provider interface. It's the core model that is extended to provide an underlying service that JNDI uses.

Pattern Use

The following patterns are features of certain kinds of JNDI resources:

Factory Method (see page 21): The Factory Method pattern provides a standard method to create some product, so this pattern is typically encountered for any JNDI resource that is capable of producing a connection. This pattern is typically encountered for any JNDI resource capable of producing a connection. One of the best illustrations is the JDBC `DataSource`, often stored in JNDI as part of a J2EE solution. The `DataSource` class is actually a Factory for `Connection` objects enabling clients to communicate with a RDBMS.

Factory patterns are very much in evidence in the service provider interface. Underlying service implementations that are paired with JNDI require factories so that API calls can be paired to implementations that map to the underlying service structure. The `DirObjectFactory`, `DirStateFactory`, `InitialContextFactory`, `ObjectFactory`, and `StateFactory` all provide Factory Method implementations that subsequently produce concrete products which are associated with specific kinds of services.

HOPP (see page 189): Many distributed communication technologies can support division of functionality between local and remote objects, so it's no surprise that RMI, CORBA and EJB technologies are all capable of supporting a HOPP implementation. Of course, JNDI itself does not directly support or implement the pattern, but since it provides a channel for these remote objects, it aids in the distribution.

Prototype (see page 28): The JNDI architecture provides a few Prototype implementations to support the duplication of objects. In JNDI, this pattern mostly applies to lookup resources, the objects used to keep track of resource names or directory attributes:

- `javax.naming`: `Reference`, `Name`, `CompoundName`, `CompositeName`
- `javax.naming.directory`: `BasicAttribute`, `Attributes`, `Attribute`, `BasicAttributes`

JDBC

Packages

java.sql JDBC 2.1 Core API
javax.sql JDBC 2.0 Optional package
Use: J2SE (1.0; restructured to JDBC 2.1 in 1.2)

Overview

Databases are everywhere; it's hard to imagine a big enterprise application without some kind of persistence. To access the data in those databases from Java, you can use Java Database Connectivity (JDBC). JDBC is a generic SQL database access framework that provides a uniform interface on top of a variety of different database connectivity modules. JDBC provides a way to manipulate the data in a database independent from any particular DBMS.

One of the challenges with this kind of framework is that each database can have its own SQL version, with minor but important differences. The framework had to be flexible as well as simple. This results in an API with only a few interfaces, and only a few methods in each interface. The consequence is that JDBC is reasonably easy of use.

To communicate with the database, you need a driver that understands and speaks the databases' protocol. You can get this drive with the database from the vendor, or from some third party. The driver contains implementations for the interfaces specific for this protocol.

Every driver has a class that implements the `Driver` interface. When the class is loaded, it creates an instance of itself and registers with the `DriverManager`. The `DriverManager` keeps a list of drivers it can use. When a connection is requested the `DriverManager` tries to locate a suitable driver. `DriverManager` checks its list of drivers and starts with the first driver specified at creation time (reading from the `jdbc.drivers` property) and continues until a suitable driver has been located. Drivers that were loaded during execution are added to the end of the list, so they are tried as well, but later. After a suitable driver is found, the `getConnection` method returns a `Connection` instance. The `Connection` object represents the session with the database. When a client calls the `createStatement` method on a Connection object, the `Connection` object creates a `Statement` objects for executing SQL queries on the database. Other types of Statements for more specfialized purposes are available, as well.

The `Statement` object is the object that receives a SQL statement as a String from the client and executes the query on the database to change or retrieve information. Depending on the type of query, either executeUpdate or exceuteQuery is called. The `Statement` returns a ResultSet when information is requested (SELECT).

The ResultSet object is a representation of a table of data that encapsulates the result of the executed SELECT. Every time you call the next method on the result set, to iterate through the data table, the cursor is set to the next line in the results. When the cursor is moved to the next line, you can retrieve the values in the columns of that specific line. To read other lines, you call the next method multiple times.

Databases tend to grow fairly large so the results could be big, as well. To prevent memory problems from occurring, the ResultSet fetches only a limited number of rows in batches. When the end of the current batch is reached, the ResultSet requests a new batch from the database. This is transparent for the user.Typical use could be as shown in Example 7.2:

Example 7.2 Obtaining results from a database

```
Connection con = DriverManager.getConnection("some url");
Statement stmt = con.createStatement();
String query = "SELECT * FROM students WHERE " +
        " iq GREATER THAN 140 AND sociallife='non-existent'";
ResultSet nerds = stmt.executeQuery(query);
while (nerds.next()) {
    String name = nerds.getString(1);
    int iq = nerds.getInt(2);
    //read entries from the resultset and process them
}
```

JDBC originally only supported going to the next row in the result set, because this is the most basic functionality that all supported datbaases provide. Currently many databases have a more advanced control structure, so more advanced features are implemented in JDBC 2.1. ResultSets now support moving forward and backward through the results, as well as relative and absolute positioning of the cursor. Also they have the option of being updatable. This means that if you execute a query and then the underlying database changes, the result set changes to reflect it.

The more advanced features like support for JNDI naming, Java Transaction Service (JTS) API, connection pooling, and rowsets are in the optional package (javax.sql).

Pattern Use

The JDBC framework consists of many related objects that are only defined by their interfaces. This requires static methods so that you can create instances of the implementing classes without knowing their actual class.

Abstract Factory (see page 6)**:** Classes that implement the Connection interface use the Abstract Factory pattern. The Abstract Factory provides flexibility. You can write an application without knowing what database has been or will be chosen. You know the `Connection` interface, and you therefore know how to create statements.

This benefit of flexibility also extends to runtime. The implementing class is determined at runtime, so the application doesn't need to be changed just because another database or another driver has been chosen.

Factory Method (see page 21)**:** It's easy to see that JDBC uses Factory Methods quite heavily. JDBC was designed to be flexible so that developers could use the framework without knowing the implementing classes. Therefore most of the JDBC API consists of interfaces. Because you can not call the constructor on an interface, Factory Methods are used to create instances of the required type. This is the case with the `getConnection` method in `DriverManager`. It instantiates an object that implements `Connection` and returns that object.

The Factory Methods provide a flexible way of creating objects without having to know their actual type.

Bridge (see page 150)**:** The Bridge pattern underlies the whole JDBC API. JDBC provides a uniform interface to multiple databases. It is this collection of interfaces that provides the decoupling of the implementation from the client, the purpose of the Bridge pattern. The interfaces are the functional abstraction that separates out the implementation.

The application that uses JDBC can change without affecting the implementation of a JDBC driver. The driver—that is, the implementation of the JDBC interfaces—can change its internal workings, and the application that uses the driver can remain unchanged.

RMI

Packages

`java.rmi`, `java.rmi.dgc`, `java.rmi.registry`, `java.rmi.server`, `java.rmi.activation`
Use: J2SE

Overview

RMI enables you to communicate by making remote method calls. Basically, it allows an application to run methods on objects that are not in the same address space. This enables Java to use the same approach for distributed communication as it does for local communications—the Java client can make a series of simple method calls to a object. Neither the client nor the server needs to write large amounts of code to manage remote communication in RMI—the task is handled behind the scenes by the RMI communications infrastructure.

RMI uses an interface to define the methods which can be called on the RMI server by the client. This interface must extend `java.rmi.Remote`, which indentifies any class that uses the interface as an RMI participant. The interface is used by both the RMI client and server. The server implements the interface, providing the actual functionality. The client uses the interface to identify which methods it can run remotely.

To call methods on an RMI server, a client must get a reference to the remote server object during runtime. The client must obtain an object called a stub which enables it to locate and communicate with a specific remote object running in some other address space. There are two ways to get a stub so that you can make remote method calls. The most common way is to use a naming service, such as JNDI or the rmiregistry. Naming services allow clients to perform lookup operations for remote objects, and to obtain stubs for remote communication. Another way to obtain a stub is to make a remote method call on an object which itself returns a stub.

The stub on the client is responsible for communicating with the remote object on the server. It greatly simplifies the task of remote communication for the client. In client code, a remote method call looks exactly like an ordinary method call. When a client application makes a remote method call, the stub receives the call, communicates with the server, and returns the result to the client.

The stub marshalls arguments used in methods, and the stub unmarshalls the return value before returning it to the client. Marshalling is a specialized form of serialization, where the object is wrapped in a `java.rmi.MarshalledObject`. The `MarshalledObject` contains the serialized object URI where the class file of the send object can be located, plus codebase, annotated with a codebase property. The codebase is a String representation of the URL where the object's class file is located.

Creating an RMI application is not complicated. The first thing to do is define the remote interface; that is, the interface that determines what methods are available remotely. It has to extend java.rmi.Remote and all methods have to declare throwing at least a java.rmi.RemoteException.

The remote object implements the remote interface however it sees fit. When a remote object is send across its address space, not the remote object is send, but the stub is. To accomplish this the remote object has to "export" itself, which means that the JVM has to be notified that this is a remote object and it should behave accordingly. An unexported remote object sent across the wire behaves like any other regular (non-remote) object and gets copied across the network. This can lead to unexpected behaviour. There are two ways to export a remote object. The first is to extend java.rmi.server.UnicastRemoteObject. In the constructor of this class, the object is exported. The other way to export the remote object is to explicitly call the exportObject method in UnicastRemoteObject. Then the remote object is not required to extend UnicastRemoteObject.

To make the remote object available to other objects, the remote object can register itself with a name service.

The client looks up a remote object through a name service. It gets an object back, which it can cast to the expected type (remote interface) tied to the name used in the request. From there on, the client uses that object to invoke methods on. The stub forwards the calls to the remote object and waits for the return value. The stub may throw java.rmi.RemoteException to signal that there was a problem in communicating with the remote object.

The stub can be automatically generated by the rmic tool.

Pattern Use

Abstract Factory (see page 6)**:** The Abstract Factory pattern is used to create families of related products. In RMI, the `RMISocketFactory` implements this pattern by defining methods to create the sockets used in RMI communications. The `RMISocketFactory` defines abstract methods to create the client and server sockets used for RMI communications. On a specific JVM, a concrete subclass of `RMISocketFactory` will provide the functionality to create the RMI sockets.

Factory Method (see page 21): An Abstract Factory will often use one or more Factory Methods to create its individual products. The two interfaces implemented by `RMISocketFactory`, `RMIClientSocketFactory` and `RMIServerSocketFactory`, define factory methods for the creation of client and server sockets, respectively. These interfaces are implemented in `RMISocketFactory` as abstract methods, and a subclass supplies concrete implementations of these methods for RMI during runtime.

Decorator (see page 166)**:** The Decorator pattern lets you extend an object's functionality by creating another object. This object has the same interface as the original and references the original object for most operations, but adds some additional features.

RMI uses the Decorator pattern during object serialization. When RMI sends objects to another address space, the objects are marshalled; the `java.rmi.MarshalledObject` class handles the task of sending and receiving copies of the objects. To do this, the `MarshalledObject` class uses a sub-class of the `java.io.ObjectOutputStream` and the `java.io.ObjectInputStream` during communication. These special subclasses extend the basic functionality of their underlying `java.io.InputStream` and `java.io.OutputStream` by allowing two MarshalledObjects to be compared for equality even if they reside on different JVMs.

Proxy (see page 197)**:** The RMI stub, which is used by a client to communicate with a server object, is an implementation of the Proxy pattern. The stub implements the same remote interface as the remote object on the server, so it acts as the remote object for the RMI client. When a client makes a remote call, the stub forwards the method call to the real remote object on the server. The benefit here is that the network communication is hidden from the client. It frees the client from setting up connections, managing a communication session and participating in distributed garbage collection.

CORBA

Packages

JavaIDL: org.omg.CORBA, org.omg.CORBA_2_3, org.omg.CORBA_2_3.portable, org.omg.CORBA.DynAnyPackage, org.omg.CORBAORBPackage, org.omg.CORBA.portable, org.omg.CORBATypeCodePackage
CosNaming: org.omg.CosNaming, org.omg.CosNaming.NamingContextPackage, org.omg.SendingContext
RMI-IIOP: javax.rmi.CORBA, org.omg.stub.java.rmi
Use: J2SE (JDK 1.2)

Overview

The Common Object Request Broker Architecture, or CORBA, is a distributed object communication architecture. In simplest terms, it's a way for an application to request services from another application by calling remote methods.

CORBA pretty much provides the ultimate in interoperability. Many programming languages support the CORBA standard, and the architecture is defined so that a client and server written in different CORBA-compliant languages can interact without knowing or caring about remote implementation details.

Central to the architecture is the Object Request Broker, or ORB. The ORB functions as the router for all distributed communication. Every client and server in a system depends on an ORB for messaging.

To interact with the ORB, CORBA participants map their code to IDL, the Interface Definition Language. IDL is a platform-neutral language used to define calling interfaces for CORBA participants. This is key to the magic behind client-server communication. IDL provides a description of the contract between a client and server. In this way, a client knows what methods it can invoke, but does *not* know what language the methods will be written in.

The CORBA framework uses the Internet Inter-ORB Protocol (IIOP) to manage its distributed communication. This lower-level protocol was introduced in recent revisions of the CORBA specification to enable distributed communications across the most pervasive of networks—the Internet.

Java and CORBA

The Java API was created to allow Java programs to interoperate with the CORBA model at several levels. Three CORBA-related technologies are represented in Java APIs: JavaIDL, CosNaming, and RMI-IIOP.

- JavaIDL – JavaIDL represents direct CORBA capabilities in the Java programming language. The API, with its associated compiler tool, provides a way to map between Java code and the Interface Definition Language. Practically speaking, this means that Java code can use the API to function as a CORBA client or server module. In broader terms, the API allows a Java program to interact with an ORB, effectively allowing Java programs to leverage the power of CORBA.

- CosNaming – The CosNaming service provides a way for Java programs to use a CORBA naming service. CORBA's naming service pretty much does what you'd expect it to do—it keeps track of an object with a string representing the object's name.

  A Java server using CosNaming will register its remote objects with the service; a client will look them up and use them. This is sort of like the services provided by the Java Naming and Directory Interface—well, actually, it's identical. CosNaming was introduced before JNDI to accommodate Java CORBA applications. JNDI has subsequently integrated CosNaming as one of its possible services. This means that you can write CORBA programs that use the original API to implement CosNaming, or you can use JNDI to access the CosNaming services.

- RMI-IIOP – RMI-IIOP was a recent addition to the batch of CORBA technologies. It allows RMI programs to communicate using CORBA's underlying protocol. Originally, RMI used a protocol called the Java Remote Method Protocol (JRMP) to provide transport capabilities. This protocol was developed by Java and for Java; there are no other technologies that use or support it. IIOP, on the other hand, which is CORBA's communication protocol, is very widely supported. It makes sense, given Java's goals of universality, to use a protocol like IIOP for inter-application communication.

It's a tribute to the RMI architecture team that they were able to transparently swap out JRMP for CORBA's IIOP. There are no changes to developer code at all; it's all done behind the scenes. You can convert an existing RMI application to IIOP without changing a line of code.

Together, these three technologies compose the CORBA functionality in Java. Actually, Java developers use very few of the classes in the packages when writing code. For JavaIDL, the ORB class is the one that is used in the majority of applications. For CosNaming, there are about half a dozen classes and interfaces which are commonly used. And RMI-IIOP solutions rarely use any of the classes defined in the packages.

So what about all the CORBA classes and interfaces? What happens to them? The CORBA APIs have a total of 143 classes that provide support services. That is, the classes are used by code that is generated by associated CORBA utilities, such as `idl2java`.

Pattern Use

The CORBA APIs in Java implement a few basic design patterns.

Singleton (see page 34): The ORB is supposed to provide a single point of contact for CORBA communication in a JVM. This means that there can only be one instance of an ORB in any running Java application. To satisfy this requirement, the API uses the Singleton pattern. The ORB class in the `org.omg.CORBA` package provides an implementation of the Singleton pattern. Its `init` method provides a single-instance ORB resource for use in Java applications.

Factory Method (see page 21): The ORB class provides many create methods, since it is the main resource provider for CORBA solutions. A number of these methods satisfy the requirements for the Factory pattern, producing objects that can be flexibly specified during the creation process.

Chapter Eight

Jini and J2EE Architectures

Jini

Packages

Core packages: `net.jini.core.discovery`, `net.jini.core.entry`, `net.jini.core.event`, `net.jini.core.lease`, `net.jini.core.lookup`, `net.jini.core.transaction`, `net.jini.core.transaction.server`
Utilities and helper packages: `net.jini.admin`, `net.jini.discovery`, `net.jini.entry`, `net.jini.event`, `net.jini.lease`, `net.jini.lookup`, `net.jini.lookup.entry`, `net.jini.space`, `com.sun.jini.admin`, `com.sun.jini.discovery`, `com.sun.jini.fiddler`, `com.sun.jini.lease`, `com.sun.jini.lease.landlord`, `com.sun.jini.lookup`, `com.sun.jini.lookup.entry`, `com.sun.jini.mahout`, `com.sun.jini.mahout.binder`, `com.sun.jini.mercury`, `com.sun.jini.norm`, `com.sun.jini.outrigger`, `com.sun.jini.reggie`, `com.sun.jini.start` (And you thought the Swing list was long.)
Use: Jini 1.0

Description

Although many applications claim to use a service-based architecture, Jini truly promotes a service-based architecture. This is done by creating clear and simple interfaces.

The main assumption in Jini is that the network is an entity to be aware of, and that is unreliable. How often have you tried to download a file and it failed, or connect to some server and the server was not available. Not to mention the incredible speed that all users get on the Internet. The network is not just a line in your UML diagram; it is a very real part of your system. A disconnection can occur (user trips over a wire), the bandwidth can be very slim, and a multitude of errors can occur on any type of network. The same unreliability holds true for every network.

Jini forces you to at least acknowledge that the network exists and things might go wrong. And that forced acknowledgement provides you with the opportunity to handle the errors, before the application blows up in your face or the user's.

The Jini architecture was designed with the following goals:

- Enable network plug-and-work
- Erase software/hardware distinction
- Enable spontaneous networking
- Promote service-based architecture
- Promote simplicity

Lookup Service

If you want others to use your service in a service-based architecture, you provide them with your interface as they know how to use your service. Because of this, interfaces are essential to Jini services. Service users are unaware of the particular implementing class, so they want to be able to search for any implementing class for a specified interface. This is somewhat similar to RMI.

RMI uses a naming service to bind a name to a particular object. However, using a name is very limiting. If you don't know the exact name, you're stuck. It makes much more sense to be able to look up something the same way as in the yellow pages section of the phone book; by capability. And in Java, capability is specified in an interface. For this purpose, looking up services by interface, Jini introduced *lookup services*. The lookup service interface is defined in `net.jini.lookup.ServiceRegistrar`.

This `ServiceRegistrar` is the repository for Jini services. Services register themselves with the `serviceRegistrar` and service consumers (users of the service) look up services in it. It supports the lookup services based on a template (`net.jini.core.lookup.ServiceTemplate`) to retrieve any arbitrary service that fulfills the template or a collection of services that comply to the template.

Another way Jini provides flexibility and ease of use is in how the lookup services are discovered. Although it is possible to specify on what machine(s) a lookup service is running, lookup services can be located dynamically at runtime. So neither the Jini service nor the service consumer need to know where the lookup service is running.

Within Jini the part of a Jini service that is transported across the network is called the Service proxy even though that object may be the full Jini service.

Leases

One of Jini's most distinguishing features is *leases*. Every resource a service consumer uses, or is interested in, is leased. A lease is an acknowledgement from the user of the service to the service (holder of the resource) that it is still interested in that particular resource. The lease has a duration after which the lease expires and the resource can be reclaimed. If the service wants to continue to use the resource it has to renew the lease. If the service consumer fails to renew the lease (no longer interested, network failure, and so on), the resource can be reclaimed and re-used.

The lease is not a guarantee. A service consumer can faithfully maintain the lease, but the lease can still fail. The service can cancel leases and free resources whenever it sees fit. The recommendation here is of course that the service should only do that when necessary. It can even happen while the service consumer is using the service. However, lease failure is not as devastating as it may seem. You have already recognized that the network is unreliable, so the service consumer has to be prepared to deal with the unavailability.

Suppose the leased resource is a telephone line service and the service has 10 phone lines available. Normally when those 10 lines are in use and a new line is requested, it will be unavailable. But suppose a fire has broken out, the need for a phone line is top priority. The phone line service cancels the lease on one of the phone lines, claims the resource (the phone line) and makes it available for the call to the fire department.

The lease concept is almost everywhere. When a service registers with the lookup service, one of the things the service receives back is a `net.jini.core.lease.Lease` instance. The service uses that object to cancel or renew the lease it has on the lookup service. When the service fails to renew the lease (or cancels it), it will be removed from the lookup service. This practice keeps the lookup service up to date.

Distributed Events

The traditional Java event handling is not suitable for distributed events. One reason is that not a single method in a listener interface throws a `RemoteException`, which is required for the listener to be in another address space. Furthermore, the event objects keep a reference to the source. If that source is a GUI component, that component has to be serialized to be sent across the network. The trouble is that this results in the *entire* graphical user interface being serialized and sent, because all components keep a reference to their parent. In distributed programming the objects have to be as small as possible. The last reason is that the current event handling system does not support leases.

The Jini event handling system has to keep the uncertainty of the network in mind. Instead of having many different listener interfaces, Jini only provides one, `net.jini.core.event.EventListener`, with only one listener method `notify(net.jini.core.event.RemoteEvent re)`. And the `notify` method throws two exceptions: `UnknownEventException` and `RemoteException`.

The `RemoteEvent` is intended to be as small as possible, while still carrying the information required by the listener. It extends from `java.util.EventObject`, so it contains a source (the remote service), an event ID, a handback object, and a sequence number. The event ID serves as an identifier to the specific events the listener has registered to. The handback object is, as the name suggests, the object that the listener provides when registering and that the event source hands back to listener when the event occurs (see "Pattern Use" in this section). Finally the sequence number is provided for the uncertainty in the network. Events could arrive out of order or some may just disappear. It is up to the listener what action to take if events arrive out of order.

The event ID and the sequence number are unknown to the listener before registering. When the listener registers, the event source returns an instance of `net.jini.core.event.EventRegistration`, which contains the eventID, the current sequence number, a `Lease` object, and a reference to the source.

Pattern Use

HOPP (see page 189)**:** When a Jini client (either a service wanting to register or a service consumer wanting to look a service up) wants to use lookup service, it first locates one or more instances through the discovery protocols. It can use a `LookupLocator`, a `LookupDiscovery`, or a `LookupLocatorDiscovery` to discover a lookup service.

When the client has discovered a lookup service it receives an instance of a `ServiceRegistrar`. The `ServiceRegistrar` is very likely to be a remote object and the instance received is a proxy to that remote object.

Every service in Jini has a unique ID. A lookup service is a Jini service, so it has an unique ID. That ID should be received by the service once and afterwards remembered whenever it restarts. Although the `ServiceRegistrar` proxy forwards most calls to the remote object it doesn't make sense to make an expensive remote call when the result doesn't change. Therefore the service proxy keeps an attribute with the value of the service ID of the lookup service.

Proxy (see page 197)**:** The meaning of a proxy in Jini is broader than the Proxy design pattern. In the Proxy design pattern, a proxy is a placeholder to another object. In Jini the part of the service that is downloaded to the service consumer is called the *service proxy*. But that service proxy might very well be the full service, completely transparent to the consumer.

Observer (see page 94)**:** When a service consumer is looking for a specific type of service, the service might not be available at the time of the request. It would be inefficient to repeat the lookup until a service is found. It is much better to do the lookup once and be notified when a change has occurred. To do that the client uses the `notify` method on the `ServiceRegistrar` object. Because this involves remote event handling the consumer supplies the template for the service it is looking for, the handback object, the remote listener instance to be notified of the change, a requested lease duration and the type of transitions.

Java 2, Enterprise Edition (J2EE)

Overview

The advent of J2EE marked an important evolutionary shift in Java, a shift from treating the language as a series of APIs to representing it as a development framework. Conceptually, that's exactly what J2EE is—an architectural framework used to create enterprise applications.

Since the release of JDK 1.1, distributed programming technologies have been a special strength for Java. Sockets, JDBC, RMI, CORBA—all have offered programmers ways to develop multitier distributed applications.

With the introduction of J2EE, however, the application of these technologies underwent a dramatic metamorphosis. J2EE went beyond providing APIs for a single form of distributed communication; it defined an entire model intended to support distributed architectures.

As its name implies, J2EE is substantially more than a single technology. As an "edition," J2EE represents a collection of Java technologies that can be used together to implement an architectural model. In this case, the model is intended to support the development and deployment of large-scale distributed applications.

Core J2EE Concepts

This section covers the core J2EE concepts, after which specific J2EE technologies will be covered.

J2EE Tiers

Fundamentally, the J2EE model is based on four logical units, or *tiers*, for an enterprise application:

- Client tier – Provides a user interface. The client tier can be written in Java, or it can be designed using some other programming language. In J2EE, the client tier usually communicates with the Web tier using HTTP. In some J2EE applications, the client tier interacts directly with the EJB or database tiers.
- Web tier – Represented by a Web browser or standalone client application, provides enterprise functionality to an end user. The web tier hosts the Web application, which provides application functionality to clients in the form of a related set of HTTP-transported content. This is typically scripted documents using technologies like HTML or XML.
- EJB tier (or application server tier) – Acts as host to the object-oriented business model, representing the application in terms of a related set of objects relating to the problem domain.
- The database, or persistence, tier (also known as the Enterprise Information Service tier) – Represents all enterprise resources for the application, such as databases, legacy applications, or collaborating enterprise systems.

Of the four tiers, the ones most strongly associated with Java technology are the web tier and application server tier. Although the other two tiers of the system can potentially leverage Java technology, there is an implicit assumption that the web server and application server use Java technology if they're part of a J2EE solution.

Core Technical Concepts

Central to the J2EE model are three related technical concepts: components, containers, and connectors. The component is the basic program unit in J2EE.

J2EE advocates the creation of enterprise architectures as a set of collaborating Java components. There are a few motivations for this:

- Components tend to make enterprise systems more flexible and extensible – All other things being equal, it is much easier to modify a system composed of a set of components than to modify a monolithic architecture.
- Components can be standardized – It is easier to enforce a standard coding convention for a specific kind of component than for a monolithic application, code library, or framework. Doing this makes it easier to develop components that can plug into other systems, frameworks, and application models. This opens the door for reuse of parts of an enterprise architecture.
- Components can be service-based – We tend to describe applications in terms of what they can do for us. Moving to object-oriented development, it is natural to refine behavioral characteristics into a set of services to be provided. It is much easier to develop an application when its basic building blocks naturally support the concept of a service.

Core Component Technologies

J2EE is based around three central component technologies:

- Enterprise JavaBeans (EJBs), which are used for the Application Server tier.
- JavaServer Pages (JSPs) and servlets, which are Web tier technologies.

The Java components, by definition, require something to act as a host for them, something to control when they're created and how their methods are called—something to regulate their life within a system. This is the task of the *container.*

A container provides the services that a J2EE component requires in order to do its job. Naturally, these services are different depending on what kind of component technology we're talking about. For the Web tier, for instance, a fundamental task of the container is translating between Web communications (HTTP requests) and methods calls on the Java components. For the Application Server, on the other hand, the container manages communication with EJBs through some protocol layer on top of RMI-IIOP.

Containers provide required services to enterprise components, but they also provide necessary services for the enterprise application itself. One of the main motivations to develop enterprise systems based on existing software products like Web servers, application server and databases is to leverage hard-to-code capabilities like persistence management, security and transaction support. In today's world, there usually isn't enough time to code these services—by the time a development wrote them, the system would already be obsolete.

J2EE-compliant products provide these services to a J2EE application in a configurable way. Better still, they separate the services and their use from the components themselves—ultimately improving the reusability of components in a wider range of application environments. J2EE manages the configuration of the container-based services through XML documents. The documents provide a way to specify how the containers should handle security, or persistence on a component-by-component basis.

Communication and the Connector Technologies

Enterprise systems, especially those designed in recent years, tend to bring groups of dissimilar technologies together. Doing this often means managing communication between very different kinds of applications. It's not unusual, for instance, to have an enterprise application which needs to communicate with a database, messaging system, e-mail system and legacy system.

Of course, each technology tends to have its own communication standard, its own way of interacting with the world. For a given kind of technology, there are often different standard communication methods, in fact. Within the database arena, for example, nearly every RDBMS tends to have its own API. Historically, this has caused major integration problems for enterprise systems —a large amount of effort has to be spent just getting everything to talk together.

The way that J2EE solved the problem was to create generic communication technologies: the connector technologies. Conceptually, connectors are Java APIs that buffer J2EE applications from the differences between specific communication models. Java developers write their code to the API specification, which in turn is used to link to some underlying communication layer. Often, this means that the APIs connect to an adaptor module which in turn communicates with another application, system or service.

At a minimum, this approach can standardize communication within a technology category – JavaMail for e-mail services or JDBC for relational database communication. Using this approach, J2EE developers can use the same Java coding techniques when they write database code, developing implementation-neutral JDBC code. The exact way that JDBC communicates with an associated RDBMS is handled by the JDBC driver; the API will be the same for developer regardless of what lies beneath.

Main J2EE Resources

When we work with J2EE as developers, we naturally tend to think about it in terms of its Java technologies—as a set of APIs that play well together. In addition to the APIs, Sun has developed a number of other standard resources that comprise what you think of as J2EE:

- The specifications – Associated with the main J2EE technologies are documents that describe how the technologies can be expected to work in an enterprise environment and how developers can use them in this context.

- The reference implementation – Like many Java technologies, J2EE has a sample implementation available to both developers and vendors so that it's possible to work with a baseline implementation of the technology. It implements the core J2EE APIs and provides a Web container, EJB container, relational database and various tools for testing and deploying J2EE applications.
- Blueprints for J2EE – Guidelines for creating enterprise applications, and best practices for J2EE development.
- The sample application – The Java Pet Store provides an open-source sample J2EE application to demonstrate how the architecture can be used in practice.
- Compatibility testing – Vendors who want to develop J2EE-compliant servers can use a Compatibility Test Suite to validate that their applications fully support the specification.

Component Patterns

The three major component technologies for J2EE are EJBs, JSPs, and servlets. Although there is potentially a fourth technology in Applets, a potential technology for Client-tier Web applications, it is less central to the core J2EE model. In the sections that follow, we'll discuss the three component APIs and present the design patterns that they implement.

Servlets and JSPs

Packages

javax.servlet, javax.servlet.http, javax.servlet.jsp, javax.servlet.jsp.taglib
Use: J2EE (J2EE1.2)

Overview

The servlet API provides one of the two Web component technologies for J2EE. The general model for the servlet API is quite straightforward, based on two packages which hold all of the core functionality:

- javax.servlet – Provides the generic servlet model
- javax.servlet.http – Adapts the servlet model to HTTP and HTTPS

The base architectural model for servlets makes no assumptions for the request-response protocol apart from the fact that it runs on a TCP/IP backbone. Predictably, the resources which are available to a servlet built on this model are a bit basic, consisting of only those things that would be available from a bare-bones set of assumptions about the communication channel.

For all practical purposes, the majority of servlet work is based on the functionality from the javax.servlet.http package. This adapts the core servlet architecture to the Web world, providing a model which assumes either HTTP or HTTPS as the underlying protocol.

Main API Elements

Three API elements provide the structural foundation for servlets: the Servlet interface, the GenericServlet class and the HttpServlet class.

- The Servlet interface defines, among other things, the methods of a servlet's lifecycle: init, destroy and service.
- The GenericServlet is an abstract class that provides a basic implementation of the interface, with the exception of the service method. Since any servlet will at least have to specify some behavior in response to a client request, this method is left unimplemented for the GenericServlet.
- The HttpServlet is also an abstract class, but all of its methods are implemented. This class provides a service method that branches into seven doXxx methods, which correspond to most of the modern HTTP requests: doGet, doPost, doPut, doHead, doOptions, doTrace and doDelete.

Life Cycle

As a component, the servlet's lifecycle depends on management by a Web container. The container orchestrates calls to a number of methods in the servlet API. The following list shows the major servlet lifecycle methods and the order in which they're called:

- Create one or more servlet objects
- Initialize the servlet through calls to `init`
- Process client requests by using worker threads to run a servlet's service methods, which branch to a series of `doXxx` methods that match basic HTTP commands (`doGet`, `doPut`, `doPost`, and so on)
- Call the `destroy` method
- Destroy the servlet objects

JavaServer Pages

JavaServer Pages are a way for HTML specialists and scripting specialists to write dynamic HTML pages. These pages use HTML-like *JSP tags* that can contain or call Java code. The JSP-specific elements of the HTML page are converted to Java servlets.

The first time a JSP is called in a Web server, it is run through an interpreter. The interpreter converts the file into a Java source file, translating the JSP tags into Java code. The Java file is then compiled and is structurally equivalent to a servlet. In fact, when a JSP subsequently runs, its lifecycle is exactly the same as the servlet and can basically be managed in the same way by the Web container.

JSPs and servlets share an architectural model as well as many of the same classes. The few modifications to the JSP model, as well as the support classes for the technology, are located in the `javax.servlet.jsp` package. For JSPs, the interfaces `JspPage` and `HttpJspPage` define the core functional model. However, although there are different interfaces that specify JSP structure, the type of methods are the same—`jspInit`, `jspDestroy` and `_jspService` are the analogs of the servlet `init`, `destroy`, and `service` methods.

The JSP API also defines a set of classes that allow the creation of custom tag libraries. This technology allows you to extend JSPs with Java code. You only need to write three components: a Java class containing the Java functionality to implement, and an XML file that functions as a deployment descriptor, stating basic information about it, such as attributes that it can use. The third component is the use in the JSP itself, where the JSP scripter specifies the Java class file, the XML file, and any other information for implementation, such as attributes.

Pattern Use

Template Method (see page 131): The servlet API comes close to providing an example of the Template Method design pattern in a couple of places, falling short in only one key area; it actually provides a default implementation for the methods. The methods in the `HttpServlet` that come close to this pattern implementation are provided in the following list:

- The `service` method branches to the doXxx methods. Developers usually override one or more of the `doXxx` methods to implement servlet behavior.
- The `init(ServletConfig)` method calls the `init` method. Developers are supposed to override the `init` method if there is any required initialization behavior.

Session (see page 220): The servlet API provides two mechanisms in support of the Session pattern—the `Cookie` class and the `HttpSession` interface. As its name suggests, the Cookie class represents HTTP cookies, which allow the servlet API to use session information stored on a Web client. The `HttpSession` interface is used for server-side storage of session information.

Observer (see page 94): Like many Java APIs, Servlets use the event handling model. By extension, this means they use the Observer pattern. For Servlets, the Observer is used to notify listeners of changes to HttpSession and ServletContext objects. Table 8-1 shows the Servlet listener interfaces which can be used to create observers in a Web application::

Table 8-1 *Interfaces and corresponding purpose*

Interface	**Purpose**
HttpSessionActivationListener	Session activation or passivation
HttpSessionAttributesListener	Change in attributes for a session
HttpSessionBindingListener	Notifies an object that it is being bound to or unbound from a session
HttpSessionListener	Session creation or destruction
ServletContextAttributesListener	Change in attributes for the servlet context
ServletContextListener	Servlet creation and destruction

Enterprise JavaBeans

Packages

`javax.ejb`, `javax.ejb.spi`
Use: J2EE (J2EE1.2)

Description

In a sense, Enterprise JavaBeans are the heart and soul of the J2EE architecture. They represent the core business model, defined in terms of a collaborating set of components. EJBs are used to enforce business rules, to encapsulate business logic, and to encompass the business model within an enterprise application.

There are three fundamental categories of EJBs:

- **Session Beans** – EJBs that directly support business logic. Session Beans can be either *Stateful* or *Stateless*. A Stateful Session Bean is associated with a specific client session, while a Stateless Session Bean represents a generic business resource, not dependent on any specific client caller.
- **Entity Beans** – Designed to be directly associated with a DBMS or other persistent data store, providing an "objectized" form for the data
- **Message-driven Beans** – Designed to be asynchronous receivers of message notifications from JMS technology. These beans can receive and react to messages using the JMS API as a J2EE application runs.

To create an EJB, you need to write three Java code elements:

- A Home interface, used to manage the EJBs lifecycle (contains create, locate and remove methods)
- A Remote interface, used to define business methods
- The Enterprise Bean implementation

In addition, you write an XML document called a deployment descriptor that specifies details about how the Enterprise Bean should be managed: it contains configuration, administration, and resource management information.

EJBs, even more than the other J2EE component technologies, depend strongly on their containers. In a very real way, EJBs need their underlying container to create them, call them—really, to regulate every aspect of their life.

It's interesting to observe that the entire EJB architecture is interface-based. The only real classes that are defined for the model are the exceptions. This illustrates even more dramatically the dependence of an EJB on its container, since part of the task of the container is to generate the support code that implements the Home and Remote interfaces and ties both of them to the underlying Enterprise Bean.

Deploying an Enterprise Bean involves producing the classes which implement the Home and Remote interfaces. It involves providing code to map between method calls on the interfaces and actual method invocations on the underlying Bean. In some cases, it involves producing additional management code based on information supplied in the deployment descriptor.

It's often a big adjustment to former middleware programmers to "let go" and accept that the container takes care of the additional services required by the EJBs. It can be difficult to get used to the concept of large amounts of support code being automatically produced.

General Pattern Use

Enterprise JavaBeans have a number of patterns, but many of them are supplied by the container, implemented by the underlying framework as part of the task of producing a functional, integrated EJB.

HOPP (see page 189): Clients never interact with an Enterprise Bean directly. They always pass method calls to either the Home or Remote interface, which then trigger calls to an EJB. You could say that clients don't even talk directly to the Home or Remote implementers, but to the stubs that then communicate with matching server-side implementers. This demonstrates the application of the HOPP pattern, and it is used for all EJB communication.

Factory Method (see page 21): EJBs use the Home interface as the first point of contact for an EJB resource. Clients, whether servlets, JSPs or other EJBs, call a create or locate method on the Home in order to obtain a reference to the Remote stub, which can then be used to call business methods. The fact that the create method triggers the creation of Enterprise Bean resources suggests that a Builder pattern is present for EJBs. Technically, the pattern goes a bit beyond the simple Factory Method, since it generally involves creating a support framework for the Enterprise Bean as well. For instance, calling create on a Stateful Session Bean triggers creation of both the Bean itself and the Bean's remote implementer.

Proxy (see page 197): Conceptually, you could say that Enterprise JavaBeans provides Proxy-like pattern behavior, because method calls to both the Home and Remote interfaces are ultimately translated to calls on the underlying Enterprise Bean. Of course, there is processing which occurs and a change in the method name being called, so the structure does not represent a classic Proxy implementation.

Session (see page 220): EJBs support the Session pattern through the Stateful Session Bean. It's important to recognize that this pattern only applies to Session Beans that are explicitly designed to be Stateful. The Stateless Session Bean does not maintain the concept of consistent caller identity, so even if it does persist data over time, the data cannot be associated with a specific client.

Connector Pattern Use: Factory Method

J2EE offers a great many APIs to bridge between different enterprise technologies. This is only natural, since the express purpose of the J2EE architecture has more or less always been to allow integration with as many enterprise systems as possible. The basic model for connector technologies is tried and proven—it represents the refinement of a model that was pioneered in JDK1.1 with JDBC.

For connector technologies, the API defines a programming abstraction, a layer of code between the Java application and some underlying implementation. The implementation may be the system or service itself, but more frequently it tends to be a translator, an adaptor module between the API and the actual end resource.

By defining a code model in this way, it's possible to make a fairly generic API, something that can be used for generic capability programming, then applied to any one of a number of implementations within a family of technologies.

The J2EE APIs that represent connector technologies are shown in the following list

- Java Messaging Service (JMS) – Connector API to asynchronous messaging services. Examples include JMQueue and JMX.
- JavaMail – Connector to e-mail technologies such as POP3.
- Connector Architecture – A generic connector API, supporting a variety of Enterprise Information System (EIS) resources, such as nonrelational databases and ERP systems.

Two other J2EE connector technologies already discussed in this section are:

- Java Database Connectivity API (JDBC)
- Java Naming and Directory Interface (JNDI)

Regardless of the specific technology being used, certain design patterns tend to naturally occur because of the general architecture and distributed model behind the connector model. Since most of the connector technologies rely on JNDI to supply initial connection capabilities to callers on any of the tiers, the connectors typically provide a connection factory, which implements the Factory Method design pattern. Conceptually, most of the connectors also provide adaptor capabilities, at least at an architectural level

Architectural Pattern Use

A few patterns within J2EE are more accurately associated with the architecture as a whole than with any single technology. Because J2EE operates as a federated enterprise model, many of these patterns can be leveraged at a number of points, or even multiple points, within a J2EE system. Since J2EE is a flexible architectural model which consists of a number of tiers which can be used together, the APIs that support these patterns can be used at a number of points, or even multiple points, within a J2EE system.

Transaction (see page 265): Frequently, the connectors link a J2EE application to some other system which supports transaction management. The Java Transaction API (JTA) provides support for distributed transaction coordination—what is commonly called a *two-phase commit*. For technologies that support this API, they must be general transactional services. This in turn means that they must support the Commit/Rollback pattern.

Session (see page 220): J2EE also provides support for the Session pattern. The incentive for using this pattern within a J2EE model is clear: mid-term data persistence is usually important in an enterprise application. Most non-trivial business operations require some form of intermediate storage, to maintain state between operational phases or to ensure that the data will not be lost or corrupted while in flux.

In a typical enterprise application, short-term data is stored on the clients and long-term data is stored in a database or other EIS resource. Somewhere between these two extremes is data that is related to business process; that is, to work that is being done and requires several actions to complete. Mid-term persistence is what the Session pattern is all about: the storage of information that is in flux due to a client's interaction with the system. J2EE is an n-tier system, so there are a few options for where to store Session data:

- On the client tier – J2EE Web clients can use cookies to store session-based information.
- On the web tier – The servlet API defines an `HttpSession` interface to address client storage requirements.
- On the EJB tier – Stateful session beans serve this purpose, as defined in the EJB specification.

Appendix A

Full Code Examples

System Requirements

This appendix includes full, runnable code examples for each pattern. Most of the patterns in the main part of this book included only the code that is crucial for your understanding of the pattern. This appendix includes all required class files, and a `RunPattern` class, which shows you how the code runs, and includes print statements specifying what occurs in the code.

The following patterns use Remote Method Invocation (RMI) in their code examples: Callback, HOPP, Router, Session, Successive Update, Transaction, and Worker Thread.

To run these examples, your computer must be network-enabled. Specifically, your system must be able to use TCP/IP sockets for networking and recognize "`localhost`" as a valid loopback IP address.

The rmiregistry is started from the `RunPattern` file in each of these examples. Because rmiregistry is a server process, these examples will appear to block when they are finished. You must manually terminate the Java process to exit the rmiregistry.

Creational Pattern Code Examples

Abstract Factory

The following code samples show how international addresses and phone numbers can be supported in the Personal Information Manager with the Abstract Factory pattern. The AddressFactory interface represents the factory itself:

Example A.1 AddressFactory.java

```
1.    public interface AddressFactory{
2.        public Address createAddress();
3.        public PhoneNumber createPhoneNumber();
4.    }
```

Note that the AddressFactory defines two factory methods, createAddress and createPhoneNumber. The methods produce the abstract products Address and PhoneNumber, which define methods that these products support.

Example A.2 Address.java

```
1.    public abstract class Address{
2.        private String street;
3.        private String city;
4.        private String region;
5.        private String postalCode;
6.
7.        public static final String EOL_STRING =
8.            System.getProperty("line.separator");
9.        public static final String SPACE = " ";
10.
11.       public String getStreet(){ return street; }
12.       public String getCity(){ return city; }
13.       public String getPostalCode(){ return postalCode; }
14.       public String getRegion(){ return region; }
15.       public abstract String getCountry();
16.
17.       public String getFullAddress(){
18.           return street + EOL_STRING +
19.               city + SPACE + postalCode + EOL_STRING;
20.       }
21.
22.       public void setStreet(String newStreet){ street = newStreet; }
23.       public void setCity(String newCity){ city = newCity; }
24.       public void setRegion(String newRegion){ region = newRegion; }
25.       public void setPostalCode(String newPostalCode){ postalCode = newPostalCode; }
26.   }
```

Example A.3 PhoneNumber.java

```
1.   public abstract class PhoneNumber{
2.       private String phoneNumber;
3.       public abstract String getCountryCode();
4.
5.       public String getPhoneNumber(){ return phoneNumber; }
6.
7.       public void setPhoneNumber(String newNumber){
8.           try{
9.               Long.parseLong(newNumber);
10.              phoneNumber = newNumber;
11.          }
12.          catch (NumberFormatException exc){
13.          }
14.      }
15.  }
```

Address and PhoneNumber are abstract classes in this example, but could easily be defined as interfaces if you did not need to define code to be used for all concrete products.

To provide concrete functionality for the system, you need to create Concrete Factory and Concrete Product classes. In this case, you define a class that implements AddressFactory, and subclass the Address and PhoneNumber classes. The three following classes show how to do this for U.S. address information.

Example A.4 USAddressFactory.java

```
1.   public class USAddressFactory implements AddressFactory{
2.       public Address createAddress(){
3.           return new USAddress();
4.       }
5.
6.       public PhoneNumber createPhoneNumber(){
7.           return new USPhoneNumber();
8.       }
9.   }
```

Example A.5 USAddress.java

```
1.   public class USAddress extends Address{
2.       private static final String COUNTRY = "UNITED STATES";
3.       private static final String COMMA = ",";
4.
5.       public String getCountry(){ return COUNTRY; }
6.
7.       public String getFullAddress(){
8.           return getStreet() + EOL_STRING +
9.               getCity() + COMMA + SPACE + getRegion() +
10.              SPACE + getPostalCode() + EOL_STRING +
```

```
11.                 COUNTRY + EOL_STRING;
12.         }
13. }
```

Example A.6 USPhoneNumber.java

```
1.  public class USPhoneNumber extends PhoneNumber{
2.      private static final String COUNTRY_CODE = "01";
3.      private static final int NUMBER_LENGTH = 10;
4.  
5.      public String getCountryCode(){ return COUNTRY_CODE; }
6.  
7.      public void setPhoneNumber(String newNumber){
8.          if (newNumber.length() == NUMBER_LENGTH){
9.              super.setPhoneNumber(newNumber);
10.         }
11.     }
12. }
```

The generic framework from AddressFactory, Address, and PhoneNumber makes it easy to extend the system to support additional countries. With each additional country, define an additional Concrete Factory class and a matching Concrete Product class. These are files for French address information.

Example A.7 FrenchAddressFactory.java

```
1.  public class FrenchAddressFactory implements AddressFactory{
2.      public Address createAddress(){
3.          return new FrenchAddress();
4.      }
5.  
6.      public PhoneNumber createPhoneNumber(){
7.          return new FrenchPhoneNumber();
8.      }
9.  }
```

Example A.8 FrenchAddress.java

```
1.  public class FrenchAddress extends Address{
2.      private static final String COUNTRY = "FRANCE";
3.  
4.      public String getCountry(){ return COUNTRY; }
5.  
6.      public String getFullAddress(){
7.          return getStreet() + EOL_STRING +
8.              getPostalCode() + SPACE + getCity() +
9.              EOL_STRING + COUNTRY + EOL_STRING;
10.     }
11. }
```

Example A.9 FrenchPhoneNumber.java

```
1.     public class FrenchPhoneNumber extends PhoneNumber{
2.         private static final String COUNTRY_CODE = "33";
3.         private static final int NUMBER_LENGTH = 9;
4.
5.         public String getCountryCode(){ return COUNTRY_CODE; }
6.
7.         public void setPhoneNumber(String newNumber){
8.             if (newNumber.length() == NUMBER_LENGTH){
9.                 super.setPhoneNumber(newNumber);
10.            }
11.        }
12.    }
```

The RunPattern class provides an example of the AbstractFactory in use. It uses the USAddressFactory and the FrenchAddressFactory to create two different sets of address/phone number combinations. It is significant that once the factory objects have been loaded, we can deal with their products by using the Address and PhoneNumber interfaces. There are no method calls which depend on the distinction between a USAddress and a FrenchAddress.

Example A.10 RunPattern.java

```
1.     public class RunPattern{
2.         public static void main(String [] arguments){
3.             System.out.println("Example for the AbstractFactory pattern");
4.             System.out.println();
5.             System.out.println(" (take a look in the RunPattern code. Notice that you
           can");
6.             System.out.println("  use the Address and PhoneNumber classes when writ-
           ing");
7.             System.out.println("  almost all of the code. This allows you to write a
           very");
8.             System.out.println("  generic framework, and plug in Concrete Factories");
9.             System.out.println("  and Products to specialize the behavior of your
           code)");
10.            System.out.println();
11.
12.            System.out.println("Creating U.S. Address and Phone Number:");
13.            AddressFactory usAddressFactory = new USAddressFactory();
14.            Address usAddress = usAddressFactory.createAddress();
15.            PhoneNumber usPhone = usAddressFactory.createPhoneNumber();
16.
17.            usAddress.setStreet("142 Lois Lane");
18.            usAddress.setCity("Metropolis");
19.            usAddress.setRegion("WY");
20.            usAddress.setPostalCode("54321");
21.            usPhone.setPhoneNumber("7039214722");
22.
23.            System.out.println("U.S. address:");
24.            System.out.println(usAddress.getFullAddress());
```

```
25.             System.out.println("U.S. phone number:");
26.             System.out.println(usPhone.getPhoneNumber());
27.             System.out.println();
28.             System.out.println();
29.
30.             System.out.println("Creating French Address and Phone Number:");
31.             AddressFactory frenchAddressFactory = new FrenchAddressFactory();
32.             Address frenchAddress = frenchAddressFactory.createAddress();
33.             PhoneNumber frenchPhone = frenchAddressFactory.createPhoneNumber();
34.
35.             frenchAddress.setStreet("21 Rue Victor Hugo");
36.             frenchAddress.setCity("Courbevoie");
37.             frenchAddress.setPostalCode("40792");
38.             frenchPhone.setPhoneNumber("011324290");
39.
40.             System.out.println("French address:");
41.             System.out.println(frenchAddress.getFullAddress());
42.             System.out.println("French phone number:");
43.             System.out.println(frenchPhone.getPhoneNumber());
44.         }
45.     }
```

Builder

This code example shows how to use the Builder pattern to create an appointment for the PIM. The following list summarizes each class's purpose:

- AppointmentBuilder, MeetingBuilder – Builder classes
- Scheduler – Director class
- Appointment – Product
- Address, Contact – Support classes, used to hold information relevant to the Appointment
- InformationRequiredException – An Exception class produced when more data is required

For the base pattern, the AppointmentBuilder manages the creation of a complex product, which is an Appointment in this example. The Appointment-Builder uses a series of build methods—buildAppointment, buildLocation, buildDates, and buildAttendees—to create an Appointment and populate it.

Example A.11 AppointmentBuilder.java

```
1.     import java.util.Date;
2.     import java.util.ArrayList;
3.
4.     public class AppointmentBuilder{
5.
6.         public static final int START_DATE_REQUIRED = 1;
7.         public static final int END_DATE_REQUIRED = 2;
8.         public static final int DESCRIPTION_REQUIRED = 4;
9.         public static final int ATTENDEE_REQUIRED = 8;
10.        public static final int LOCATION_REQUIRED = 16;
11.
12.        protected Appointment appointment;
13.
14.        protected int requiredElements;
15.
16.        public void buildAppointment(){
17.            appointment = new Appointment();
18.        }
19.
20.        public void buildDates(Date startDate, Date endDate){
21.            Date currentDate = new Date();
22.            if ((startDate != null) && (startDate.after(currentDate))){
23.                appointment.setStartDate(startDate);
24.            }
25.            if ((endDate != null) && (endDate.after(startDate))){
26.                appointment.setEndDate(endDate);
27.            }
28.        }
29.
30.        public void buildDescription(String newDescription){
```

```
31.             appointment.setDescription(newDescription);
32.         }
33.
34.         public void buildAttendees(ArrayList attendees){
35.             if ((attendees != null) && (!attendees.isEmpty())){
36.                 appointment.setAttendees(attendees);
37.             }
38.         }
39.
40.         public void buildLocation(Location newLocation){
41.             if (newLocation != null){
42.                 appointment.setLocation(newLocation);
43.             }
44.         }
45.
46.         public Appointment getAppointment() throws InformationRequiredException{
47.             requiredElements = 0;
48.
49.             if (appointment.getStartDate() == null){
50.                 requiredElements += START_DATE_REQUIRED;
51.             }
52.
53.             if (appointment.getLocation() == null){
54.                 requiredElements += LOCATION_REQUIRED;
55.             }
56.
57.             if (appointment.getAttendees().isEmpty()){
58.                 requiredElements += ATTENDEE_REQUIRED;
59.             }
60.
61.             if (requiredElements > 0){
62.                 throw new InformationRequiredException(requiredElements);
63.             }
64.             return appointment;
65.         }
66.
67.         public int getRequiredElements(){ return requiredElements; }
68.     }
```

Example A.12 `Appointment.java`

```
1.      import java.util.ArrayList;
2.      import java.util.Date;
3.      public class Appointment{
4.          private Date startDate;
5.          private Date endDate;
6.          private String description;
7.          private ArrayList attendees = new ArrayList();
8.          private Location location;
9.          public static final String EOL_STRING =
10.             System.getProperty("line.separator");
11.
12.         public Date getStartDate(){ return startDate; }
13.         public Date getEndDate(){ return endDate; }
14.         public String getDescription(){ return description; }
```

```
15.        public ArrayList getAttendees(){ return attendees; }
16.        public Location getLocation(){ return location; }
17.
18.        public void setDescription(String newDescription){ description = newDescrip-
         tion; }
19.        public void setLocation(Location newLocation){ location = newLocation; }
20.        public void setStartDate(Date newStartDate){ startDate = newStartDate; }
21.        public void setEndDate(Date newEndDate){ endDate = newEndDate; }
22.        public void setAttendees(ArrayList newAttendees){
23.            if (newAttendees != null){
24.                attendees = newAttendees;
25.            }
26.        }
27.
28.        public void addAttendee(Contact attendee){
29.            if (!attendees.contains(attendee)){
30.                attendees.add(attendee);
31.            }
32.        }
33.
34.        public void removeAttendee(Contact attendee){
35.            attendees.remove(attendee);
36.        }
37.
38.        public String toString(){
39.            return "  Description: " + description + EOL_STRING +
40.                "  Start Date: " + startDate + EOL_STRING +
41.                "  End Date: " + endDate + EOL_STRING +
42.                "  Location: " + location + EOL_STRING +
43.                "  Attendees: " + attendees;
44.        }
45.    }
```

The `Scheduler` class makes calls to the `AppointmentBuilder`, managing the creation process through the method `createAppointment`.

Example A.13 `Scheduler.java`

```
1.     import java.util.Date;
2.     import java.util.ArrayList;
3.     public class Scheduler{
4.         public Appointment createAppointment(AppointmentBuilder builder,
5.             Date startDate, Date endDate, String description,
6.             Location location, ArrayList attendees) throws InformationRequiredExcep-
         tion{
7.                 if (builder == null){
8.                     builder = new AppointmentBuilder();
9.                 }
10.            builder.buildAppointment();
11.            builder.buildDates(startDate, endDate);
12.            builder.buildDescription(description);
13.            builder.buildAttendees(attendees);
14.            builder.buildLocation(location);
```

```
15.             return builder.getAppointment();
16.         }
17.     }
```

The responsibilities of each class are summarized here:

- `Scheduler` – Calls the appropriate build methods on `AppointmentBuilder`; returns a complete `Appointment` object to its caller.
- `AppointmentBuilder` – Contains build methods and enforces business rules; creates the actual `Appointment` object.
- `Appointment` – Holds information about an appointment.

The `MeetingBuilder` class in Example A.14 demonstrates one of the benefits of using the Builder pattern. To add additional rules for the `Appointment`, extend the existing builder. In this case, the `MeetingBuilder` enforces an additional constraint: for an `Appointment` that is a meeting, both start and end dates must be specified.

Example A.14 `MeetingBuilder.java`

```
1.  import java.util.Date;
2.  import java.util.Vector;
3.
4.  public class MeetingBuilder extends AppointmentBuilder{
5.      public Appointment getAppointment() throws InformationRequiredException{
6.          try{
7.              super.getAppointment();
8.          }
9.          finally{
10.             if (appointment.getEndDate() == null){
11.                 requiredElements += END_DATE_REQUIRED;
12.             }
13.
14.             if (requiredElements > 0){
15.                 throw new InformationRequiredException(requiredElements);
16.             }
17.         }
18.         return appointment;
19.     }
20. }
```

Support classes used for this example include the class `InformationRequiredException` and the interfaces `Location` and `Contact`. The `Address` and `Contact` interfaces are marker interfaces used to represent supporting information for the `Appointment` in this example; their implementation is represented by the `LocationImpl` and `ContactImpl` classes.

Example A.15 `InformationRequiredException.java`

```
1.  public class InformationRequiredException extends Exception{
```

```
2.      private static final String MESSAGE = "Appointment cannot be created because
       further information is required";
3.      public static final int START_DATE_REQUIRED = 1;
4.      public static final int END_DATE_REQUIRED = 2;
5.      public static final int DESCRIPTION_REQUIRED = 4;
6.      public static final int ATTENDEE_REQUIRED = 8;
7.      public static final int LOCATION_REQUIRED = 16;
8.      private int informationRequired;
9.
10.     public InformationRequiredException(int itemsRequired){
11.         super(MESSAGE);
12.         informationRequired = itemsRequired;
13.     }
14.
15.     public int getInformationRequired(){ return informationRequired; }
16. }
```

Example A.16 `Location.java`

```
1. import java.io.Serializable;
2. public interface Location extends Serializable{
3.     public String getLocation();
4.     public void setLocation(String newLocation);
5. }
```

Example A.17 `LocationImpl.java`

```
1. public class LocationImpl implements Location{
2.     private String location;
3.
4.     public LocationImpl(){ }
5.     public LocationImpl(String newLocation){
6.         location = newLocation;
7.     }
8.
9.     public String getLocation(){ return location; }
10.
11.    public void setLocation(String newLocation){ location = newLocation; }
12.
13.    public String toString(){ return location; }
14. }
```

Example A.18 `Contact.java`

```
1. import java.io.Serializable;
2. public interface Contact extends Serializable{
3.     public static final String SPACE = " ";
4.     public String getFirstName();
5.     public String getLastName();
6.     public String getTitle();
7.     public String getOrganization();
8.
9.     public void setFirstName(String newFirstName);
```

```
10.        public void setLastName(String newLastName);
11.        public void setTitle(String newTitle);
12.        public void setOrganization(String newOrganization);
13.    }
```

Example A.19 `ContactImpl.java`

```
1.     public class ContactImpl implements Contact{
2.         private String firstName;
3.         private String lastName;
4.         private String title;
5.         private String organization;
6.
7.         public ContactImpl(String newFirstName, String newLastName,
8.             String newTitle, String newOrganization){
9.                 firstName = newFirstName;
10.                lastName = newLastName;
11.                title = newTitle;
12.                organization = newOrganization;
13.        }
14.
15.        public String getFirstName(){ return firstName; }
16.        public String getLastName(){ return lastName; }
17.        public String getTitle(){ return title; }
18.        public String getOrganization(){ return organization; }
19.
20.        public void setFirstName(String newFirstName){ firstName = newFirstName; }
21.        public void setLastName(String newLastName){ lastName = newLastName; }
22.        public void setTitle(String newTitle){ title = newTitle; }
23.        public void setOrganization(String newOrganization){ organization = newOrgani-
       zation; }
24.
25.        public String toString(){
26.            return firstName + SPACE + lastName;
27.        }
28.    }
```

The `RunPattern` file executes this example. It demonstrates the use of the `Builder` pattern by creating three separate `Appointment` objects using the `AppointmentBuilder` and `MeetingBuilder`.

Example A.20 `RunPattern.java`

```
1.     import java.util.Calendar;
2.     import java.util.Date;
3.     import java.util.ArrayList;
4.     public class RunPattern{
5.         private static Calendar dateCreator = Calendar.getInstance();
6.
7.         public static void main(String [] arguments){
8.             Appointment appt = null;
9.
```

```
10.         System.out.println("Example for the Builder pattern");
11.         System.out.println();
12.         System.out.println("This example demonstrates the use of the Builder");
13.         System.out.println("pattern to create Appointment objects for the PIM.");
14.         System.out.println();
15.
16.         System.out.println("Creating a Scheduler for the example.");
17.         Scheduler pimScheduler = new Scheduler();
18.
19.         System.out.println("Creating an AppointmentBuilder for the example.");
20.         System.out.println();
21.         AppointmentBuilder apptBuilder = new AppointmentBuilder();
22.         try{
23.             System.out.println("Creating a new Appointment with an Appointment-
    Builder");
24.             appt = pimScheduler.createAppointment(
25.                 apptBuilder, createDate(2066, 9, 22, 12, 30),
26.                 null, "Trek convention", new LocationImpl("Fargo, ND"),
27.                 createAttendees(4));
28.             System.out.println("Successfully created an Appointment.");
29.             System.out.println("Appointment information:");
30.             System.out.println(appt);
31.             System.out.println();
32.         }
33.         catch (InformationRequiredException exc){
34.             printExceptions(exc);
35.         }
36.
37.         System.out.println("Creating a MeetingBuilder for the example.");
38.         MeetingBuilder mtgBuilder = new MeetingBuilder();
39.         try{
40.           System.out.println("Creating a new Appointment with a MeetingBuilder");
41.             System.out.println("(notice that the same create arguments will pro-
    duce");
42.             System.out.println(" an exception, since the MeetingBuilder enforces
    a");
43.             System.out.println(" mandatory end date)");
44.             appt = pimScheduler.createAppointment(
45.                 mtgBuilder, createDate(2066, 9, 22, 12, 30),
46.                 null, "Trek convention", new LocationImpl("Fargo, ND"),
47.                 createAttendees(4));
48.             System.out.println("Successfully created an Appointment.");
49.             System.out.println("Appointment information:");
50.             System.out.println(appt);
51.             System.out.println();
52.         }
53.         catch (InformationRequiredException exc){
54.             printExceptions(exc);
55.         }
56.
57.         System.out.println("Creating a new Appointment with a MeetingBuilder");
58.         System.out.println("(This time, the MeetingBuilder will provide an end
    date)");
59.         try{
```

```
60.             appt = pimScheduler.createAppointment(
61.                 mtgBuilder,
62.                 createDate(2002, 4, 1, 10, 00),
63.                 createDate(2002, 4, 1, 11, 30),
64.                 "OOO Meeting",
65.                 new LocationImpl("Butte, MT"),
66.                 createAttendees(2));
67.             System.out.println("Successfully created an Appointment.");
68.             System.out.println("Appointment information:");
69.             System.out.println(appt);
70.             System.out.println();
71.         }
72.         catch (InformationRequiredException exc){
73.             printExceptions(exc);
74.         }
75.     }
76.
77.     public static Date createDate(int year, int month, int day, int hour, int
    minute){
78.         dateCreator.set(year, month, day, hour, minute);
79.         return dateCreator.getTime();
80.     }
81.
82.     public static ArrayList createAttendees(int numberToCreate){
83.         ArrayList group = new ArrayList();
84.         for (int i = 0; i < numberToCreate; i++){
85.             group.add(new ContactImpl("John", getLastName(i), "Employee (non-
    exempt)", "Yoyodyne Corporation"));
86.         }
87.         return group;
88.     }
89.
90.     public static String getLastName(int index){
91.         String name = "";
92.         switch (index % 6){
93.             case 0: name = "Worfin";
94.                 break;
95.             case 1: name = "Smallberries";
96.                 break;
97.             case 2: name = "Bigbootee";
98.                 break;
99.             case 3: name = "Haugland";
100.                break;
101.            case 4: name = "Maassen";
102.                break;
103.            case 5: name = "Sterling";
104.                break;
105.        }
106.        return name;
107.    }
108.
109.    public static void printExceptions(InformationRequiredException exc){
110.        int statusCode = exc.getInformationRequired();
111.
```

```
112.         System.out.println("Unable to create Appointment: additional information is
        required");
113.           if ((statusCode & InformationRequiredException.START_DATE_REQUIRED) > 0){
114.              System.out.println("  A start date is required for this appointment to
        be complete.");
115.           }
116.           if ((statusCode & InformationRequiredException.END_DATE_REQUIRED) > 0){
117.              System.out.println("  An end date is required for this appointment to
        be complete.");
118.           }
119.          if ((statusCode & InformationRequiredException.DESCRIPTION_REQUIRED) > 0){
120.             System.out.println("  A description is required for this appointment to
        be complete.");
121.           }
122.           if ((statusCode & InformationRequiredException.ATTENDEE_REQUIRED) > 0){
123.              System.out.println("  At least one attendee is required for this
        appointment to be complete.");
124.           }
125.           if ((statusCode & InformationRequiredException.LOCATION_REQUIRED) > 0){
126.             System.out.println("  A location is required for this appointment to be
        complete.");
127.           }
128.           System.out.println();
129.       }
130.   }
```

Factory Method

The following example uses the Factory Method pattern to produce an editor for the PIM. The PIM tracks a lot of information, and there are many cases where users need an editor to create or modify data. The example uses interfaces to improve the overall flexibility of the system.

The `Editable` interface defines a builder method, `getEditor`, which returns an `ItemEditor` interface. The benefit is that any item can provide an editor for itself, producing an object that knows what parts of a business object can change and how they can be changed. The only thing the user interface needs to do is use the `Editable` interface to get an editor.

Example A.21 `Editable.java`

```
1.     public interface Editable {
2.         public ItemEditor getEditor();
3.     }
```

The `ItemEditor` interface provides two methods: `getGUI` and `commitChanges`. The `getGUI` method is another Factory Method—it returns a `JComponent` that provides a Swing GUI to edit the current item. This makes a very flexible system; to add a new type of item, the user interface can remain the same, because it only uses the `Editable` and the `ItemEditor` interfaces.

The `JComponent` returned by `getGUI` can have anything in it required to edit the item in the PIM. The user interface can simply the acquired `JComponent` in its editor window and use the `JComponent` functionality to edit the item. Since not everything in an application needs to be graphical, it could also be a good idea to include a `getUI` method that would return an `Object` or some other non-graphical interface.

The second method, `commitChanges`, allows the UI to tell the editor that the user wants to finalize the changes he or she has made.

Example A.22 `ItemEditor.java`

```
1.     import javax.swing.JComponent;
2.     public interface ItemEditor {
3.         public JComponent getGUI();
4.         public void commitChanges();
5.     }
```

The following code shows the implementation for one of the PIM items, `Contact`. The `Contact` class defines two attributes: the name of the person and their relationship with the user. These attributes provide a sample of some of the information, which could be included in an entry in the PIM.

Example A.23 Contact.java

```
1.   import java.awt.GridLayout;
2.   import java.io.Serializable;
3.   import javax.swing.JComponent;
4.   import javax.swing.JLabel;
5.   import javax.swing.JPanel;
6.   import javax.swing.JTextField;
7.
8.   public class Contact implements Editable, Serializable {
9.       private String name;
10.      private String relationship;
11.
12.      public ItemEditor getEditor() {
13.          return new ContactEditor();
14.      }
15.
16.      private class ContactEditor implements ItemEditor, Serializable {
17.          private transient JPanel panel;
18.          private transient JTextField nameField;
19.          private transient JTextField relationField;
20.
21.          public JComponent getGUI() {
22.              if (panel == null) {
23.                  panel = new JPanel();
24.                  nameField = new JTextField(name);
25.                  relationField = new JTextField(relationship);
26.                  panel.setLayout(new GridLayout(2,2));
27.                  panel.add(new JLabel("Name:"));
28.                  panel.add(nameField);
29.                  panel.add(new JLabel("Relationship:"));
30.                  panel.add(relationField);
31.              } else {
32.                  nameField.setText(name);
33.                  relationField.setText(relationship);
34.              }
35.              return panel;
36.          }
37.
38.          public void commitChanges() {
39.              if (panel != null) {
40.                  name = nameField.getText();
41.                  relationship = relationField.getText();
42.              }
43.          }
44.
45.          public String toString(){
46.              return "\nContact:\n" +
47.                  "    Name: " + name + "\n" +
48.                  "    Relationship: " + relationship;
49.          }
50.      }
51.  }
```

Contact implements the Editable interface, and provides its own editor. That editor only applies to the Contact class, and needs to change certain attributes of the Contact, it is best to use an inner class. The inner class has direct access to the attributes of the outer class. If you used another (non-inner) class, Contact would need to provide accessor and mutator methods, making it harder to restrict access to the object's private data.

Note that the editor itself is not a Swing component, but only an object that can serve as a factory for such a component. The greatest benefit is that you can serialize and send this object across a stream. To implement this feature, declare all Swing component attributes in ContactEditor transient—they're constructed when and where they're needed.

The EditorGui represents a generic editor you might use in the PIM. Note that the class uses the ItemEditor interface to entirely manage its edit window. It constructs a JPanel for its edit window, and places the JComponent obtained by the call to getGUI inside. The Swing component provides all the edit capabilities for the Contact, while the EditorGui provides control buttons and a JTextArea to display the state of the Contact object.

Example A.24 EditorGui.java

```
1.     import java.awt.Container;
2.     import java.awt.event.ActionListener;
3.     import java.awt.event.WindowAdapter;
4.     import java.awt.event.ActionEvent;
5.     import java.awt.event.WindowEvent;
6.     import javax.swing.BoxLayout;
7.     import javax.swing.JButton;
8.     import javax.swing.JComponent;
9.     import javax.swing.JFrame;
10.    import javax.swing.JPanel;
11.    import javax.swing.JTextArea;
12.    public class EditorGui implements ActionListener{
13.        private JFrame mainFrame;
14.        private JTextArea display;
15.        private JButton update, exit;
16.        private JPanel controlPanel, displayPanel, editorPanel;
17.        private ItemEditor editor;
18.
19.        public EditorGui(ItemEditor edit){
20.            editor = edit;
21.        }
22.
23.        public void createGui(){
24.            mainFrame = new JFrame("Factory Pattern Example");
25.            Container content = mainFrame.getContentPane();
26.            content.setLayout(new BoxLayout(content, BoxLayout.Y_AXIS));
27.
28.            editorPanel = new JPanel();
29.            editorPanel.add(editor.getGUI());
```

```
30.             content.add(editorPanel);
31.
32.             displayPanel = new JPanel();
33.             display = new JTextArea(10, 40);
34.             display.setEditable(false);
35.             displayPanel.add(display);
36.             content.add(displayPanel);
37.
38.             controlPanel = new JPanel();
39.             update = new JButton("Update Item");
40.             exit = new JButton("Exit");
41.             controlPanel.add(update);
42.             controlPanel.add(exit);
43.             content.add(controlPanel);
44.
45.             update.addActionListener(this);
46.             exit.addActionListener(this);
47.
48.             mainFrame.addWindowListener(new WindowCloseManager());
49.             mainFrame.pack();
50.             mainFrame.setVisible(true);
51.         }
52.
53.
54.         public void actionPerformed(ActionEvent evt){
55.             Object originator = evt.getSource();
56.             if (originator == update){
57.                 updateItem();
58.             }
59.             else if (originator == exit){
60.                 exitApplication();
61.             }
62.         }
63.
64.         private class WindowCloseManager extends WindowAdapter{
65.             public void windowClosing(WindowEvent evt){
66.                 exitApplication();
67.             }
68.         }
69.
70.         private void updateItem(){
71.             editor.commitChanges();
72.             display.setText(editor.toString());
73.         }
74.
75.         private void exitApplication(){
76.             System.exit(0);
77.         }
78.     }
79.
```

Note that the Update Item button makes a call to the `ItemEditor`'s `commitChanges` method.

The RunPattern class runs this pattern by creating a Contact and an EditorGui object. The EditorGui constructor sets the ItemEditor for the example.

Example A.25 RunPattern.java

```
1.  import javax.swing.JComponent;
2.  import javax.swing.JFrame;
3.  import java.awt.event.WindowAdapter;
4.  import java.awt.event.WindowEvent;
5.
6.
7.  public class RunPattern{
8.      public static void main(String [] arguments){
9.          System.out.println("Example for the FactoryMethod pattern");
10.         System.out.println();
11.
12.         System.out.println("Creating a Contact object");
13.         System.out.println();
14.         Contact someone = new Contact();
15.
16.         System.out.println("Creating a GUI editor for the Contact");
17.         System.out.println();
18.         System.out.println("The GUI defined in the EditorGui class is a truly
    generic editor.");
19.         System.out.println("It accepts an argument of type ItemEditor, and dele-
    gates");
20.         System.out.println(" all editing tasks to its ItemEditor and the associated
    GUI.");
21.         System.out.println(" The getEditor() Factory Method is used to obtain the
    ItemEditor");
22.         System.out.println(" for the example.");
23.         System.out.println();
24.         System.out.println("Notice that the editor in the top portion of the GUI
    is,");
25.         System.out.println(" in fact, returned by the ItemEditor belonging to
    the");
26.         System.out.println(" Contact class, and has appropriate fields for that
    class.");
27.
28.         EditorGui runner = new EditorGui(someone.getEditor());
29.         runner.createGui();
30.     }
31. }
32.
```

Prototype

The `Address` class in this example uses the Prototype pattern to create an address based on an existing entry. The core functionality for the pattern is defined in the interface `Copyable`.

Example A.26 `Copyable.java`

```
1.   public interface Copyable{
2.       public Object copy();
3.   }
```

The `Copyable` interface defines a copy method and guarantees that any classes that implement the interface will define a copy operation. This example produces a shallow copy—that is, it copies the object references from the original address to the duplicate.

The code also demonstrates an important feature of the copy operation: not all fields must necessarily be duplicated. In this case, the address type is not copied to the new object. A user would manually specify a new address type from the PIM user interface.

Example A.27 `Address.java`

```
1.   public class Address implements Copyable{
2.       private String type;
3.       private String street;
4.       private String city;
5.       private String state;
6.       private String zipCode;
7.       public static final String EOL_STRING =
8.           System.getProperty("line.separator");
9.       public static final String COMMA = ",";
10.      public static final String HOME = "home";
11.      public static final String WORK = "work";
12.
13.      public Address(String initType, String initStreet,
14.          String initCity, String initState, String initZip){
15.              type = initType;
16.              street = initStreet;
17.              city = initCity;
18.              state = initState;
19.              zipCode = initZip;
20.      }
21.
22.      public Address(String initStreet, String initCity,
23.          String initState, String initZip){
24.              this(WORK, initStreet, initCity, initState, initZip);
25.      }
26.      public Address(String initType){
27.          type = initType;
```

```
28.         }
29.         public Address(){ }
30.
31.         public String getType(){ return type; }
32.         public String getStreet(){ return street; }
33.         public String getCity(){ return city; }
34.         public String getState(){ return state; }
35.         public String getZipCode(){ return zipCode; }
36.
37.         public void setType(String newType){ type = newType; }
38.         public void setStreet(String newStreet){ street = newStreet; }
39.         public void setCity(String newCity){ city = newCity; }
40.         public void setState(String newState){ state = newState; }
41.         public void setZipCode(String newZip){ zipCode = newZip; }
42.
43.         public Object copy(){
44.             return new Address(street, city, state, zipCode);
45.         }
46.
47.         public String toString(){
48.             return "\t" + street + COMMA + " " + EOL_STRING +
49.                 "\t" + city + COMMA + " " + state + " " + zipCode;
50.         }
51.     }
```

The RunPattern class demonstrates the use of this pattern by creating an Address object, then duplicating that object by calling its copy method. The fact that the Address objects return two different hash code values (numeric values that represent unique object identity) further confirms that the copy operation has produced a different object from the first.

Example A.28 RunPattern.java

```
1.  public class RunPattern{
2.      public static void main(String [] arguments){
3.          System.out.println("Example for Prototype pattern");
4.          System.out.println();
5.          System.out.println("This example will create an Address object,");
6.          System.out.println(" which it will then duplicate by calling the");
7.          System.out.println(" object's clone method.");
8.          System.out.println();
9.
10.         System.out.println("Creating first address.");
11.         Address address1 = new Address("8445 Silverado Trail", "Rutherford", "CA",
    "91734");
12.         System.out.println("First address created.");
13.         System.out.println("    Hash code = " + address1.hashCode());
14.         System.out.println(address1);
15.         System.out.println();
16.
17.         System.out.println("Creating second address using the clone() method.");
18.         Address address2 = (Address)address1.copy();
```

```
19.            System.out.println("Second address created.");
20.            System.out.println("     Hash code = " + address2.hashCode());
21.            System.out.println(address2);
22.            System.out.println();
23.
24.
25.        }
26.    }
```

Singleton

Application users want the option of undoing previous commands. To support that functionality, a history list is needed. That history list has to be accessible from everywhere in the PIM and only one instance of it is needed. Therefore, it's a perfect candidate for the implementation of the Singleton pattern.

Example A.29 `HistoryList.java`

```
1.  import java.util.ArrayList;
2.  import java.util.Collections;
3.  import java.util.List;
4.  public class HistoryList{
5.      private List history = Collections.synchronizedList(new ArrayList());
6.      private static HistoryList instance = new HistoryList();
7.  
8.      private HistoryList(){ }
9.  
10.     public static HistoryList getInstance(){
11.         return instance;
12.     }
13. 
14.     public void addCommand(String command){
15.         history.add(command);
16.     }
17. 
18.     public Object undoCommand(){
19.         return history.remove(history.size() - 1);
20.     }
21. 
22.     public String toString(){
23.         StringBuffer result = new StringBuffer();
24.         for (int i = 0; i < history.size(); i++){
25.             result.append("  ");
26.             result.append(history.get(i));
27.             result.append("\n");
28.         }
29.         return result.toString();
30.     }
31. }
```

The `HistoryList` maintains a static reference to an instance of itself, has a private constructor, and uses a static method `getInstance` to provide a single history list object to all parts of the PIM. The additional variable in `HistoryList`, `history`, is a `List` object used to track the command strings. The `HistoryList` provides two methods, `addCommand` and `undoCommand` to support adding and removing commands from the list.

The `SingletonGui` class provides a basic Swing GUI that demonstrates how the `HistoryList` might be used in a PIM editor. This GUI provides a basic set of commands: create contact, create appointment, undo, refresh and exit. For the create commands, you retrieve the `HistoryList` with a call to its static getInstance method, then call the `addCommand` method. For the undo command, you call `getInstance` followed by the `undoCommand` method. The `refresh` method calls the `toString` method in the `HistoryList` to retrieve the current set of history list entries for display.

Example A.30 `SingletonGUI.java`

```
1.  import java.awt.Container;
2.  import javax.swing.BoxLayout;
3.  import javax.swing.JButton;
4.  import javax.swing.JFrame;
5.  import javax.swing.JPanel;
6.  import javax.swing.JTextArea;
7.  import java.awt.event.ActionEvent;
8.  import java.awt.event.ActionListener;
9.  import java.awt.event.WindowAdapter;
10. import java.awt.event.WindowEvent;
11. public class SingletonGui implements ActionListener{
12.     private JFrame mainFrame;
13.     private JTextArea display;
14.     private JButton newContact, newAppointment, undo, refresh, exit;
15.     private JPanel controlPanel, displayPanel;
16.     private static int historyCount;
17.
18.     public void createGui(){
19.         mainFrame = new JFrame("Singleton Pattern Example");
20.         Container content = mainFrame.getContentPane();
21.         content.setLayout(new BoxLayout(content, BoxLayout.Y_AXIS));
22.
23.         displayPanel = new JPanel();
24.         display = new JTextArea(20, 60);
25.         display.setEditable(false);
26.         displayPanel.add(display);
27.         content.add(displayPanel);
28.
29.         controlPanel = new JPanel();
30.         newContact = new JButton("Create contact");
31.         newAppointment = new JButton("Create appointment");
32.         undo = new JButton("Undo");
33.         refresh = new JButton("Refresh");
34.         exit = new JButton("Exit");
35.         controlPanel.add(newContact);
36.         controlPanel.add(newAppointment);
37.         controlPanel.add(undo);
38.         controlPanel.add(refresh);
39.         controlPanel.add(exit);
40.         content.add(controlPanel);
41.
42.         newContact.addActionListener(this);
43.         newAppointment.addActionListener(this);
```

```
44.            undo.addActionListener(this);
45.            refresh.addActionListener(this);
46.            exit.addActionListener(this);
47.
48.            mainFrame.addWindowListener(new WindowCloseManager());
49.            mainFrame.pack();
50.            mainFrame.setVisible(true);
51.        }
52.
53.        public void refreshDisplay(String actionMessage){
54.            display.setText(actionMessage + "\nCOMMAND HISTORY:\n" +
55.                HistoryList.getInstance().toString());
56.        }
57.
58.        public void actionPerformed(ActionEvent evt){
59.            Object originator = evt.getSource();
60.            if (originator == newContact){
61.                addCommand(" New Contact");
62.            }
63.            else if (originator == newAppointment){
64.                addCommand(" New Appointment");
65.            }
66.            else if (originator == undo){
67.                undoCommand();
68.            }
69.            else if (originator == refresh){
70.                refreshDisplay("");
71.            }
72.            else if (originator == exit){
73.                exitApplication();
74.            }
75.        }
76.
77.        private class WindowCloseManager extends WindowAdapter{
78.            public void windowClosing(WindowEvent evt){
79.                exitApplication();
80.            }
81.        }
82.
83.        private void addCommand(String message){
84.            HistoryList.getInstance().addCommand((++historyCount) + message);
85.            refreshDisplay("Add Command: " + message);
86.        }
87.
88.        private void undoCommand(){
89.            Object result = HistoryList.getInstance().undoCommand();
90.            historyCount--;
91.            refreshDisplay("Undo Command: " + result);
92.        }
93.
94.        private void exitApplication(){
95.            System.exit(0);
96.        }
97.    }
```

Example A.31 RunPattern.java

```
1.   import java.awt.Container;
2.   import javax.swing.BoxLayout;
3.   import javax.swing.JButton;
4.   import javax.swing.JFrame;
5.   import javax.swing.JPanel;
6.   import javax.swing.JTextArea;
7.   import java.awt.event.ActionEvent;
8.   import java.awt.event.ActionListener;
9.   import java.awt.event.WindowAdapter;
10.  import java.awt.event.WindowEvent;
11.  public class SingletonGui implements ActionListener{
12.      private JFrame mainFrame;
13.      private JTextArea display;
14.      private JButton newContact, newAppointment, undo, refresh, exit;
15.      private JPanel controlPanel, displayPanel;
16.      private static int historyCount;
17.
18.      public void createGui(){
19.          mainFrame = new JFrame("Singleton Pattern Example");
20.          Container content = mainFrame.getContentPane();
21.          content.setLayout(new BoxLayout(content, BoxLayout.Y_AXIS));
22.
23.          displayPanel = new JPanel();
24.          display = new JTextArea(20, 60);
25.          display.setEditable(false);
26.          displayPanel.add(display);
27.          content.add(displayPanel);
28.
29.          controlPanel = new JPanel();
30.          newContact = new JButton("Create contact");
31.          newAppointment = new JButton("Create appointment");
32.          undo = new JButton("Undo");
33.          refresh = new JButton("Refresh");
34.          exit = new JButton("Exit");
35.          controlPanel.add(newContact);
36.          controlPanel.add(newAppointment);
37.          controlPanel.add(undo);
38.          controlPanel.add(refresh);
39.          controlPanel.add(exit);
40.          content.add(controlPanel);
41.
42.          newContact.addActionListener(this);
43.          newAppointment.addActionListener(this);
44.          undo.addActionListener(this);
45.          refresh.addActionListener(this);
46.          exit.addActionListener(this);
47.
48.          mainFrame.addWindowListener(new WindowCloseManager());
49.          mainFrame.pack();
50.          mainFrame.setVisible(true);
51.      }
```

```
52.
53.         public void refreshDisplay(String actionMessage){
54.             display.setText(actionMessage + "\nCOMMAND HISTORY:\n" +
55.                 HistoryList.getInstance().toString());
56.         }
57.
58.         public void actionPerformed(ActionEvent evt){
59.             Object originator = evt.getSource();
60.             if (originator == newContact){
61.                 addCommand(" New Contact");
62.             }
63.             else if (originator == newAppointment){
64.                 addCommand(" New Appointment");
65.             }
66.             else if (originator == undo){
67.                 undoCommand();
68.             }
69.             else if (originator == refresh){
70.                 refreshDisplay("");
71.             }
72.             else if (originator == exit){
73.                 exitApplication();
74.             }
75.         }
76.
77.         private class WindowCloseManager extends WindowAdapter{
78.             public void windowClosing(WindowEvent evt){
79.                 exitApplication();
80.             }
81.         }
82.
83.         private void addCommand(String message){
84.             HistoryList.getInstance().addCommand((++historyCount) + message);
85.             refreshDisplay("Add Command: " + message);
86.         }
87.
88.         private void undoCommand(){
89.             Object result = HistoryList.getInstance().undoCommand();
90.             historyCount--;
91.             refreshDisplay("Undo Command: " + result);
92.         }
93.
94.         private void exitApplication(){
95.             System.exit(0);
96.         }
97.     }
```

Behavioral Pattern Code Examples

Chain of Responsibility

The PIM can act as a project manager as well as a contact manager. This code example shows how to use the Chain of Responsibility pattern to retrieve information from within a project hierarchy.

The `ProjectItem` interface defines common methods for anything that can be part of a project.

Example A.32 `ProjectItem.java`

```
1.     import java.io.Serializable;
2.     import java.util.ArrayList;
3.     public interface ProjectItem extends Serializable{
4.         public static final String EOL_STRING = System.getProperty("line.separator");
5.         public ProjectItem getParent();
6.         public Contact getOwner();
7.         public String getDetails();
8.         public ArrayList getProjectItems();
9.     }
```

The interface defines the methods `getParent`, `getOwner`, `getDetails`, and `getProjectItems`. Two classes implement `ProjectItem` in this example — `Project` and `Task`. The `Project` class is the base of a project, so its `getParent` method returns null. The `getOwner` and `getDetails` method returns the overall owner and details for the project, and the `getProjectItems` method returns all of the project's immediate children.

Example A.33 `Project.java`

```
1.     import java.util.ArrayList;
2.     public class Project implements ProjectItem{
3.         private String name;
4.         private Contact owner;
5.         private String details;
6.         private ArrayList projectItems = new ArrayList();
7.
8.         public Project(){ }
9.         public Project(String newName, String newDetails, Contact newOwner){
10.            name = newName;
11.            owner = newOwner;
12.            details = newDetails;
13.        }
14.
15.        public String getName(){ return name; }
16.        public String getDetails(){ return details; }
17.        public Contact getOwner(){ return owner; }
18.        public ProjectItem getParent(){ return null; }
19.        public ArrayList getProjectItems(){ return projectItems; }
20.
21.        public void setName(String newName){ name = newName; }
```

```
22.         public void setOwner(Contact newOwner){ owner = newOwner; }
23.         public void setDetails(String newDetails){ details = newDetails; }
24.
25.         public void addProjectItem(ProjectItem element){
26.             if (!projectItems.contains(element)){
27.                 projectItems.add(element);
28.             }
29.         }
30.
31.         public void removeProjectItem(ProjectItem element){
32.             projectItems.remove(element);
33.         }
34.
35.         public String toString(){
36.             return name;
37.         }
38.     }
```

The `Task` class represents some job associated with the project. Like `Project`, `Task` can keep a collection of subtasks, and its `getProjectItems` method will return these objects. For `Task`, the `getParent` method returns the parent, which will be another `Task` or the `Project`.

Example A.34 `Task.java`

```
1.      import java.util.ArrayList;
2.      import java.util.ListIterator;
3.      public class Task implements ProjectItem{
4.          private String name;
5.          private ArrayList projectItems = new ArrayList();
6.          private Contact owner;
7.          private String details;
8.          private ProjectItem parent;
9.          private boolean primaryTask;
10.
11.         public Task(ProjectItem newParent){
12.             this(newParent, "", "", null, false);
13.         }
14.         public Task(ProjectItem newParent, String newName,
15.             String newDetails, Contact newOwner, boolean newPrimaryTask){
16.                 parent = newParent;
17.                 name = newName;
18.                 owner = newOwner;
19.                 details = newDetails;
20.                 primaryTask = newPrimaryTask;
21.         }
22.
23.         public Contact getOwner(){
24.             if (owner == null){
25.                 return parent.getOwner();
26.             }
27.             else{
```

```
28.                return owner;
29.            }
30.        }
31.
32.        public String getDetails(){
33.            if (primaryTask){
34.                return details;
35.            }
36.            else{
37.                return parent.getDetails() + EOL_STRING + "\t" + details;
38.            }
39.        }
40.
41.        public String getName(){ return name; }
42.        public ArrayList getProjectItems(){ return projectItems; }
43.        public ProjectItem getParent(){ return parent; }
44.        public boolean isPrimaryTask(){ return primaryTask; }
45.
46.        public void setName(String newName){ name = newName; }
47.        public void setOwner(Contact newOwner){ owner = newOwner; }
48.        public void setParent(ProjectItem newParent){ parent = newParent; }
49.        public void setPrimaryTask(boolean newPrimaryTask){ primaryTask = newPrima-
       ryTask; }
50.        public void setDetails(String newDetails){ details = newDetails; }
51.
52.        public void addProjectItem(ProjectItem element){
53.            if (!projectItems.contains(element)){
54.                projectItems.add(element);
55.            }
56.        }
57.
58.        public void removeProjectItem(ProjectItem element){
59.            projectItems.remove(element);
60.        }
61.
62.        public String toString(){
63.            return name;
64.        }
65.    }
```

The Chain of Responsibility behavior is manifested in the `getOwner` and `getDetails` methods of `Task`. For `getOwner`, a `Task` will either return its internally referenced owner (if non-null), or that of its parent. If the parent was a `Task` and its owner was null as well, the method call is passed on to the next parent until it eventually encountered a non-null owner or it reaches the `Project` itself. This makes it easy to set up a group of `Tasks` where the same individual is the designated owner, responsible for the completion of a `Task` and all subtasks of `Tasks`.

The `getDetails` method is another example of Chain of Responsibility behavior, but it behaves somewhat differently. It calls the `getDetails` method of each parent until it reaches a `Task` or `Project` that is identified as a terminal node. This means that `getDetails` returns a series of `Strings` representing all the details for a particular `Task` chain.

Support classes for the example include the `Contact` interface and `ContactImpl` class, which are used by `Project` and `Task` to define an owner.

Example A.35 `Contact.java`

```
1.  import java.io.Serializable;
2.  public interface Contact extends Serializable{
3.      public static final String SPACE = " ";
4.      public String getFirstName();
5.      public String getLastName();
6.      public String getTitle();
7.      public String getOrganization();
8.
9.      public void setFirstName(String newFirstName);
10.     public void setLastName(String newLastName);
11.     public void setTitle(String newTitle);
12.     public void setOrganization(String newOrganization);
13. }
```

Example A.36 `ContactImpl.java`

```
1.  public class ContactImpl implements Contact{
2.      private String firstName;
3.      private String lastName;
4.      private String title;
5.      private String organization;
6.
7.      public ContactImpl(){}
8.      public ContactImpl(String newFirstName, String newLastName,
9.          String newTitle, String newOrganization){
10.             firstName = newFirstName;
11.             lastName = newLastName;
12.             title = newTitle;
13.             organization = newOrganization;
14.     }
15.
16.     public String getFirstName(){ return firstName; }
17.     public String getLastName(){ return lastName; }
18.     public String getTitle(){ return title; }
19.     public String getOrganization(){ return organization; }
20.
21.     public void setFirstName(String newFirstName){ firstName = newFirstName; }
22.     public void setLastName(String newLastName){ lastName = newLastName; }
23.     public void setTitle(String newTitle){ title = newTitle; }
24.     public void setOrganization(String newOrganization){ organization = newOrgani-
    zation; }
25.
26.     public String toString(){
27.         return firstName + SPACE + lastName;
28.     }
29. }
```

The DataCreator class provide support classes to generate data and serialize it to a file, while the DataRetriever class retrieves the data for use in the example. The RunPattern class coordinates between the other classes in the example, getting a project, then retrieving the owner and details for each Task and for the Project itself.

Example A.37 DataCreator.java

```
1.  import java.io.Serializable;
2.  import java.io.ObjectOutputStream;
3.  import java.io.FileOutputStream;
4.  import java.io.IOException;
5.
6.  public class DataCreator{
7.      private static final String DEFAULT_FILE = "data.ser";
8.
9.      public static void main(String [] args){
10.         String fileName;
11.         if (args.length == 1){
12.             fileName = args[0];
13.         }
14.         else{
15.             fileName = DEFAULT_FILE;
16.         }
17.         serialize(fileName);
18.     }
19.
20.     public static void serialize(String fileName){
21.         try{
22.             serializeToFile(createData(), fileName);
23.         }
24.         catch (IOException exc){
25.             exc.printStackTrace();
26.         }
27.     }
28.
29.     private static Serializable createData(){
30.         Contact contact1 = new ContactImpl("Dennis", "Moore", "Managing Director",
    "Highway Man, LTD");
31.         Contact contact2 = new ContactImpl("Joseph", "Mongolfier", "High Flyer",
    "Lighter than Air Productions");
32.         Contact contact3 = new ContactImpl("Erik", "Njoll", "Nomad without Portfo-
    lio", "Nordic Trek, Inc.");
33.         Contact contact4 = new ContactImpl("Lemming", "", "Principal Investigator",
    "BDA");
34.
35.         Project project = new Project("IslandParadise", "Acquire a personal island
    paradise", contact2);
36.
37.         Task task1 = new Task(project, "Fortune", "Acquire a small fortune",
    contact4, true);
38.         Task task2 = new Task(project, "Isle", "Locate an island for sale", null,
    true);
```

```
39.         Task task3 = new Task(project, "Name", "Decide on a name for the island",
     contact3, false);
40.         project.addProjectItem(task1);
41.         project.addProjectItem(task2);
42.         project.addProjectItem(task3);
43.
44.         Task task4 = new Task(task1, "Fortune1", "Use psychic hotline to predict
     winning lottery numbers", null, false);
45.         Task task5 = new Task(task1, "Fortune2", "Invest winnings to ensure 50%
     annual interest", contact1, true);
46.         Task task6 = new Task(task2, "Isle1", "Research whether climate is better
     in the Atlantic or Pacific", contact1, true);
47.         Task task7 = new Task(task2, "Isle2", "Locate an island for auction on
     EBay", null, false);
48.         Task task8 = new Task(task2, "Isle2a", "Negotiate for sale of the island",
     null, false);
49.         Task task9 = new Task(task3, "Name1", "Research every possible name in the
     world", null, true);
50.         Task task10 = new Task(task3, "Name2", "Eliminate any choices that are not
     coffee-related", contact4, false);
51.         task1.addProjectItem(task4);
52.         task1.addProjectItem(task5);
53.         task2.addProjectItem(task6);
54.         task2.addProjectItem(task7);
55.         task2.addProjectItem(task8);
56.         task3.addProjectItem(task9);
57.         task3.addProjectItem(task10);
58.         return project;
59.     }
60.
61.     private static void serializeToFile(Serializable content, String fileName)
     throws IOException{
62.         ObjectOutputStream serOut = new ObjectOutputStream(new FileOutput-
     Stream(fileName));
63.         serOut.writeObject(content);
64.         serOut.close();
65.     }
66. }
```

Example A.38 `DataRetriever.java`

```
1.  import java.io.File;
2.  import java.io.FileInputStream;
3.  import java.io.IOException;
4.  import java.io.ObjectInputStream;
5.
6.  public class DataRetriever{
7.      public static Object deserializeData(String fileName){
8.          Object returnValue = null;
9.          try{
10.             File inputFile = new File(fileName);
11.             if (inputFile.exists() && inputFile.isFile()){
12.                 ObjectInputStream readIn = new ObjectInputStream(new FileInput-
    Stream(fileName));
13.                 returnValue = readIn.readObject();
```

```
14.                 readIn.close();
15.             }
16.             else {
17.                 System.err.println("Unable to locate the file " + fileName);
18.             }
19.         }
20.         catch (ClassNotFoundException exc){
21.             exc.printStackTrace();
22.
23.         }
24.         catch (IOException exc){
25.             exc.printStackTrace();
26.
27.         }
28.         return returnValue;
29.     }
30. }
```

Example A.39 RunPattern.java

```
1.  import java.io.File;
2.  import java.util.ArrayList;
3.  import java.util.Iterator;
4.  public class RunPattern{
5.      public static void main(String [] arguments){
6.          System.out.println("Example for the Chain of Responsibility pattern");
7.          System.out.println();
8.          System.out.println("This code uses chain of responsibility to obtain");
9.          System.out.println(" the owner for a particular ProjectItem, and to");
10.         System.out.println(" build up a list of project details. In each case,");
11.         System.out.println(" a call to the appropriate getter method, getOwner");
12.         System.out.println(" or getDetails, will pass the method call up the");
13.         System.out.println(" project tree.");
14.         System.out.println("For getOwner, the call will return the first non-
    null");
15.         System.out.println(" owner field encountered. For getDetails, the method");
16.         System.out.println(" will build a series of details, stopping when it");
17.         System.out.println(" reaches a ProjectItem that is designated as a");
18.         System.out.println(" primary task.");
19.         System.out.println();
20.
21.         System.out.println("Deserializing a test Project for Visitor pattern");
22.         System.out.println();
23.         if (!(new File("data.ser").exists())){
24.             DataCreator.serialize("data.ser");
25.         }
26.         Project project = (Project)(DataRetriever.deserializeData("data.ser"));
27.
28.         System.out.println("Retrieving Owner and details for each item in the
    Project");
29.         System.out.println();
30.         getItemInfo(project);
31.     }
```

```
32.
33.     private static void getItemInfo(ProjectItem item){
34.         System.out.println("ProjectItem: " + item);
35.         System.out.println("  Owner: " + item.getOwner());
36.         System.out.println("  Details: " + item.getDetails());
37.         System.out.println();
38.         if (item.getProjectItems() != null){
39.             Iterator subElements = item.getProjectItems().iterator();
40.             while (subElements.hasNext()){
41.                 getItemInfo((ProjectItem)subElements.next());
42.             }
43.         }
44.     }
45. }
```

Command

In the Personal Information Manager, users might want to update or modify information in their system. This code demonstrates how the Command pattern can provide update and undo behavior for a location.

In this example, a pair of interfaces model the generic command behavior. The basic command action is defined by the `execute` method in `Command`, while `UndoableCommand` extends this interface by adding undo and redo methods.

Example A.40 `Command.java`

```
1.    public interface Command{
2.        public void execute();
3.    }
```

Example A.41 `UndoableCommand.java`

```
1.    public interface UndoableCommand extends Command{
2.        public void undo();
3.        public void redo();
4.    }
```

In the PIM, the location of an appointment will be used to implement an undoable command. An appointment stores a description of an event, the people involved, the location, and the start and end time(s).

Example A.42 `Appointment.java`

```
1.    import java.util.Date;
2.    public class Appointment{
3.        private String reason;
4.        private Contact[] contacts;
5.        private Location location;
6.        private Date startDate;
7.        private Date endDate;
8.
9.        public Appointment(String reason, Contact[] contacts, Location location, Date
      startDate, Date endDate){
10.           this.reason = reason;
11.           this.contacts = contacts;
12.           this.location = location;
13.           this.startDate = startDate;
14.           this.endDate = endDate;
15.       }
16.
17.       public String getReason(){ return reason; }
18.       public Contact[] getContacts(){ return contacts; }
19.       public Location getLocation(){ return location; }
20.       public Date getStartDate(){ return startDate; }
21.       public Date getEndDate(){ return endDate; }
```

```
22.
23.     public void setLocation(Location location){ this.location = location; }
24.
25.     public String toString(){
26.         return "Appointment:" + "\n    Reason: " + reason +
27. "\n    Location: " + location + "\n    Start: " +
28.             startDate + "\n    End: " + endDate + "\n";
29.     }
30. }
```

The class ChangeLocationCommand implements the UndoableCommand interface and provides the behavior required to change the location for an appointment.

Example A.43 ChangeLocationCommand.java

```
1.  public class ChangeLocationCommand implements UndoableCommand{
2.      private Appointment appointment;
3.      private Location oldLocation;
4.      private Location newLocation;
5.      private LocationEditor editor;
6.
7.      public Appointment getAppointment(){ return appointment; }
8.
9.      public void setAppointment(Appointment appointment){ this.appointment =
    appointment; }
10.     public void setLocationEditor(LocationEditor locationEditor){ editor = loca-
    tionEditor; }
11.
12.     public void execute(){
13.         oldLocation = appointment.getLocation();
14.         newLocation = editor.getNewLocation();
15.         appointment.setLocation(newLocation);
16.     }
17.     public void undo(){
18.         appointment.setLocation(oldLocation);
19.     }
20.     public void redo(){
21.         appointment.setLocation(newLocation);
22.     }
23. }
```

The class provides the ability to change a location using the execute method. It provides undo behavior by storing the previous value of the location and allowing a user to restore that value by calling the undo method. Finally, it supports a redo method that enables users to restore the new location, if they happen to be very indecisive.

Support classes for this example include CommandGui, used to provide a user interface to edit the appointment location.

Example A.44 CommandGui.java

```
1.   import java.awt.Container;
2.   import java.awt.event.ActionListener;
3.   import java.awt.event.WindowAdapter;
4.   import java.awt.event.ActionEvent;
5.   import java.awt.event.WindowEvent;
6.   import javax.swing.BoxLayout;
7.   import javax.swing.JButton;
8.   import javax.swing.JComponent;
9.   import javax.swing.JFrame;
10.  import javax.swing.JLabel;
11.  import javax.swing.JPanel;
12.  import javax.swing.JTextArea;
13.  import javax.swing.JTextField;
14.  public class CommandGui implements ActionListener, LocationEditor{
15.      private JFrame mainFrame;
16.      private JTextArea display;
17.      private JTextField updatedLocation;
18.      private JButton update, undo, redo, exit;
19.      private JPanel controlPanel, displayPanel, editorPanel;
20.      private UndoableCommand command;
21.      private Appointment appointment;
22.
23.      public CommandGui(UndoableCommand newCommand){
24.          command = newCommand;
25.      }
26.
27.      public void setAppointment(Appointment newAppointment){
28.          appointment = newAppointment;
29.      }
30.
31.      public void createGui(){
32.          mainFrame = new JFrame("Command Pattern Example");
33.          Container content = mainFrame.getContentPane();
34.          content.setLayout(new BoxLayout(content, BoxLayout.Y_AXIS));
35.
36.          editorPanel = new JPanel();
37.          editorPanel.add(new JLabel("Location"));
38.          updatedLocation = new JTextField(20);
39.          editorPanel.add(updatedLocation);
40.          content.add(editorPanel);
41.
42.          displayPanel = new JPanel();
43.          display = new JTextArea(10, 40);
44.          display.setEditable(false);
45.          displayPanel.add(display);
46.          content.add(displayPanel);
47.
48.          controlPanel = new JPanel();
49.          update = new JButton("Update Location");
50.          undo = new JButton("Undo Location");
51.          redo = new JButton("Redo Location");
```

```
52.             exit = new JButton("Exit");
53.             controlPanel.add(update);
54.             controlPanel.add(undo);
55.             controlPanel.add(redo);
56.             controlPanel.add(exit);
57.             content.add(controlPanel);
58.
59.             update.addActionListener(this);
60.             undo.addActionListener(this);
61.             redo.addActionListener(this);
62.             exit.addActionListener(this);
63.
64.             refreshDisplay();
65.             mainFrame.addWindowListener(new WindowCloseManager());
66.             mainFrame.pack();
67.             mainFrame.setVisible(true);
68.         }
69.
70.         public void actionPerformed(ActionEvent evt){
71.             Object originator = evt.getSource();
72.             if (originator == update){
73.                 executeCommand();
74.             }
75.             if (originator == undo){
76.                 undoCommand();
77.             }
78.             if (originator == redo){
79.                 redoCommand();
80.             }
81.             else if (originator == exit){
82.                 exitApplication();
83.             }
84.         }
85.
86.         private class WindowCloseManager extends WindowAdapter{
87.             public void windowClosing(WindowEvent evt){
88.                 exitApplication();
89.             }
90.         }
91.
92.         public Location getNewLocation(){
93.             return new LocationImpl(updatedLocation.getText());
94.         }
95.
96.         private void executeCommand(){
97.             command.execute();
98.             refreshDisplay();
99.         }
100.
101.        private void undoCommand(){
102.            command.undo();
103.            refreshDisplay();
104.        }
105.
```

```
106.        private void redoCommand(){
107.            command.redo();
108.            refreshDisplay();
109.        }
110.
111.        private void refreshDisplay(){
112.            display.setText(appointment.toString());
113.        }
114.
115.        private void exitApplication(){
116.            System.exit(0);
117.        }
118.    }
```

Notice that the CommandGui class implements the interface LocationEditor. This interface defines a method getNewLocation, which provides a way for the ChangeLocationCommand to retrieve the new location from the GUI.

Example A.45 LocationEditor.java

```
1.    public interface LocationEditor{
2.        public Location getNewLocation();
3.    }
```

The interfaces Contact and Location, with their corresponding implementation classes ContactImpl and LocationImpl, provide additional business objects used by the Appointment class.

Example A.46 Contact.java

```
1.    import java.io.Serializable;
2.    public interface Contact extends Serializable{
3.        public static final String SPACE = " ";
4.        public String getFirstName();
5.        public String getLastName();
6.        public String getTitle();
7.        public String getOrganization();
8.
9.        public void setFirstName(String newFirstName);
10.       public void setLastName(String newLastName);
11.       public void setTitle(String newTitle);
12.       public void setOrganization(String newOrganization);
13.   }
```

Example A.47 ContactImpl.java

```
1.    public class ContactImpl implements Contact{
2.        private String firstName;
3.        private String lastName;
```

```
4.      private String title;
5.      private String organization;
6.      public static final String EOL_STRING =
7.          System.getProperty("line.separator");
8.
9.      public ContactImpl(){ }
10.     public ContactImpl(String newFirstName, String newLastName,
11.         String newTitle, String newOrganization){
12.             firstName = newFirstName;
13.             lastName = newLastName;
14.             title = newTitle;
15.             organization = newOrganization;
16.     }
17.
18.     public String getFirstName(){ return firstName; }
19.     public String getLastName(){ return lastName; }
20.     public String getTitle(){ return title; }
21.     public String getOrganization(){ return organization; }
22.
23.     public void setFirstName(String newFirstName){ firstName = newFirstName; }
24.     public void setLastName(String newLastName){ lastName = newLastName; }
25.     public void setTitle(String newTitle){ title = newTitle; }
26.     public void setOrganization(String newOrganization){ organization = newOrgani-
    zation; }
27.
28.     public String toString(){
29.         return firstName + " " + lastName;
30.     }
31. }
```

Example A.48 Location.java

```
1.  import java.io.Serializable;
2.  public interface Location extends Serializable{
3.      public String getLocation();
4.      public void setLocation(String newLocation);
5.  }
```

Example A.49 LocationImpl.java

```
1.  public class LocationImpl implements Location{
2.      private String location;
3.
4.      public LocationImpl(){ }
5.      public LocationImpl(String newLocation){
6.          location = newLocation;
7.      }
8.
9.      public String getLocation(){ return location; }
10.
11.     public void setLocation(String newLocation){ location = newLocation; }
12.
13.     public String toString(){ return location; }
14. }
```

RunPattern loads the data for a sample Appointment and creates an instance of CommandGui. The GUI enables you to make changes to the location of the Appointment, with update, undo and redo behavior.

Example A.50 RunPattern.java

```
1.  import java.util.Calendar;
2.  import java.util.Date;
3.
4.  public class RunPattern{
5.      private static Calendar dateCreator = Calendar.getInstance();
6.
7.      public static void main(String [] arguments){
8.          System.out.println("Example for the Command pattern");
9.          System.out.println();
10.         System.out.println("This sample will use a command class called");
11.         System.out.println(" ChangeLocationCommand to update the location");
12.         System.out.println(" of an Appointment object.");
13.         System.out.println("The ChangeLocationCommand has the additional");
14.         System.out.println(" ability to undo and redo commands, so it can");
15.         System.out.println(" set the locaition back to its original value,");
16.         System.out.println(" if desired.");
17.         System.out.println();
18.
19.         System.out.println("Creating an Appointment for use in the demo");
20.         Contact [] people = { new ContactImpl(), new ContactImpl() };
21.         Appointment appointment = new Appointment("Java Twister Semi-Finals",
22.             people, new LocationImpl(""), createDate(2001, 10, 31, 14, 30),
23.             createDate(2001, 10, 31, 14, 31));
24.
25.         System.out.println("Creating the ChangeLocationCommand");
26.         ChangeLocationCommand cmd = new ChangeLocationCommand();
27.         cmd.setAppointment(appointment);
28.
29.         System.out.println("Creating the GUI");
30.         CommandGui application = new CommandGui(cmd);
31.         application.setAppointment(appointment);
32.         cmd.setLocationEditor(application);
33.         application.createGui();
34.
35.     }
36.     public static Date createDate(int year, int month, int day, int hour, int
    minute){
37.         dateCreator.set(year, month, day, hour, minute);
38.         return dateCreator.getTime();
39.     }
40. }
```

Interpreter

The Expression hierarchy is at the heart of the Interpreter pattern. It defines the grammar that can be used to create and evaluate expressions. The `Expression` interface is the foundation for all expressions, and defines the interpret method that performs an evaluation.

Table A-1 lists the interface and corresponding information.

Table A-1 *Purpose of the Expression interface and its implementers*

Expression	Common interface for all expressions
ConstantExpression	Represents a constant value
VariableExpression	Represents a variable value, obtained by calling a method on some class
CompoundExpression	A pair of comparison expressions that evaluate to a boolean result
AndExpression	The logical "and" of two expressions
OrExpression	The logical "or" of two expressions
ComparisonExpression	A pair of expressions that evaluate to a boolean result
EqualsExpression	Performs an equals method comparison between the two expressions
ContainsExpression	Checks to see if the first `String` expression contains the second one

Example A.51 `Expression.java`

```
1.     public interface Expression{
2.         void interpret(Context c);
3.     }
```

Example A.52 `ConstantExpression.java`

```
1.     import java.lang.reflect.Method;
2.     import java.lang.reflect.InvocationTargetException;
3.     public class ConstantExpression implements Expression{
4.         private Object value;
5.
6.         public ConstantExpression(Object newValue){
7.             value = newValue;
8.         }
9.
10.        public void interpret(Context c){
11.            c.addVariable(this, value);
12.        }
13.    }
```

Example A.53 VariableExpression.java

```
1.    import java.lang.reflect.Method;
2.    import java.lang.reflect.InvocationTargetException;
3.    public class VariableExpression implements Expression{
4.        private Object lookup;
5.        private String methodName;
6.
7.        public VariableExpression(Object newLookup, String newMethodName){
8.            lookup = newLookup;
9.            methodName = newMethodName;
10.       }
11.
12.       public void interpret(Context c){
13.           try{
14.               Object source = c.get(lookup);
15.               if (source != null){
16.                   Method method = source.getClass().getMethod(methodName, null);
17.                   Object result = method.invoke(source, null);
18.                   c.addVariable(this, result);
19.               }
20.           }
21.           catch (NoSuchMethodException exc){ }
22.           catch (IllegalAccessException exc){ }
23.           catch (InvocationTargetException exc){ }
24.       }
25.   }
```

Example A.54 CompoundExpression.java

```
1.    public abstract class CompoundExpression implements Expression{
2.        protected ComparisonExpression expressionA;
3.        protected ComparisonExpression expressionB;
4.
5.        public CompoundExpression(ComparisonExpression expressionA, ComparisonExpres-
      sion expressionB){
6.            this.expressionA = expressionA;
7.            this.expressionB = expressionB;
8.        }
9.    }
```

Example A.55 AndExpression.java

```
1.    public class AndExpression extends CompoundExpression{
2.        public AndExpression(ComparisonExpression expressionA, ComparisonExpression
      expressionB){
3.            super(expressionA, expressionB);
4.        }
5.
6.        public void interpret(Context c){
7.            expressionA.interpret(c);
8.            expressionB.interpret(c);
```

```
9.          Boolean result = new Boolean(((Boolean)c.get(expressionA)).booleanValue()
        && ((Boolean)c.get(expressionB)).booleanValue());
10.         c.addVariable(this, result);
11.     }
12. }
```

Example A.56 `OrExpression.java`

```
1.  public class OrExpression  extends CompoundExpression{
2.      public OrExpression(ComparisonExpression expressionA, ComparisonExpression
        expressionB){
3.          super(expressionA, expressionB);
4.      }
5.
6.      public void interpret(Context c){
7.          expressionA.interpret(c);
8.          expressionB.interpret(c);
9.          Boolean result = new Boolean(((Boolean)c.get(expressionA)).booleanValue()
        || ((Boolean)c.get(expressionB)).booleanValue());
10.         c.addVariable(this, result);
11.     }
12. }
```

Example A.57 `ComparisonExpression.java`

```
1.  public abstract class ComparisonExpression implements Expression{
2.      protected Expression expressionA;
3.      protected Expression expressionB;
4.
5.      public ComparisonExpression(Expression expressionA, Expression expressionB){
6.          this.expressionA = expressionA;
7.          this.expressionB = expressionB;
8.      }
9.  }
```

Example A.58 `EqualsExpression.java`

```
1.  public class EqualsExpression extends ComparisonExpression{
2.      public EqualsExpression(Expression expressionA, Expression expressionB){
3.          super(expressionA, expressionB);
4.      }
5.
6.      public void interpret(Context c){
7.          expressionA.interpret(c);
8.          expressionB.interpret(c);
9.          Boolean result = new Boolean(c.get(expressionA).equals(c.get(expres-
        sionB)));
10.         c.addVariable(this, result);
11.     }
12. }
```

Example A.59 ContainsExpression.java

```
1.   public class ContainsExpression extends ComparisonExpression{
2.       public ContainsExpression(Expression expressionA, Expression expressionB){
3.           super(expressionA, expressionB);
4.       }
5.
6.       public void interpret(Context c){
7.           expressionA.interpret(c);
8.           expressionB.interpret(c);
9.           Object exprAResult = c.get(expressionA);
10.          Object exprBResult = c.get(expressionB);
11.          if ((exprAResult instanceof String) && (exprBResult instanceof String)){
12.              if (((String)exprAResult).indexOf((String)exprBResult) != -1){
13.                  c.addVariable(this, Boolean.TRUE);
14.                  return;
15.              }
16.          }
17.          c.addVariable(this, Boolean.FALSE);
18.          return;
19.      }
20.  }
```

The Context class represents shared memory for expressions during evaluation. Context is a wrapper around a HashMap. In this example, the Expression objects provide the keys for the HashMap, and the results of calling the interpret method are stored as its values.

Example A.60 Context.java

```
1.   import java.util.HashMap;
2.   public class Context{
3.       private HashMap map = new HashMap();
4.
5.       public Object get(Object name){
6.           return map.get(name);
7.       }
8.
9.       public void addVariable(Object name, Object value){
10.          map.put(name, value);
11.      }
12.  }
```

With this series of expressions, it is possible to perform fairly sophisticated comparisons. ContactList holds a series of contacts in this example. It defines a method called getContactsMatchingExpression, which evaluates the Expression for every Contact and returns an ArrayList.

Example A.61 `ContactList.java`

```
1.    import java.io.Serializable;
2.    import java.util.ArrayList;
3.    import java.util.Iterator;
4.    public class ContactList implements Serializable{
5.        private ArrayList contacts = new ArrayList();
6.
7.        public ArrayList getContacts(){ return contacts; }
8.        public Contact [] getContactsAsArray(){ return (Contact []) (contacts.toAr-
      ray(new Contact [1])); }
9.
10.       public ArrayList getContactsMatchingExpression(Expression expr, Context ctx,
      Object key){
11.           ArrayList results = new ArrayList();
12.           Iterator elements = contacts.iterator();
13.           while (elements.hasNext()){
14.               Object currentElement = elements.next();
15.               ctx.addVariable(key, currentElement);
16.               expr.interpret(ctx);
17.               Object interpretResult = ctx.get(expr);
18.               if ((interpretResult != null) && (interpretResult.equals(Bool-
      ean.TRUE))){
19.                   results.add(currentElement);
20.               }
21.           }
22.           return results;
23.       }
24.
25.       public void setContacts(ArrayList newContacts){ contacts = newContacts; }
26.
27.       public void addContact(Contact element){
28.           if (!contacts.contains(element)){
29.               contacts.add(element);
30.           }
31.       }
32.       public void removeContact(Contact element){
33.           contacts.remove(element);
34.       }
35.
36.       public String toString(){
37.           return contacts.toString();
38.       }
39.   }
```

With the `Expression` hierarchy and the `ContactList`, it is possible to perform database-like queries for the `Contacts` in a `ContactList`. For example, you could search for all those `Contacts` with a title containing the characters "Java" by doing the following:

1. Create a `ConstantExpression` with the string "Java".
2. Create a `VariableExpression` with the target object and the string

"getTitle".

3. Create a ContainsExpression with the VariableExpression as the first argument and the ConstantExpression as the second.
4. Pass the ContainsExpression into a ContactList object's getContactsMatchingExpression method.

Contact and its implementer ContactImpl represent the business objects to be evaluated in this example.

Example A.62 Contact.java

```
1.    import java.io.Serializable;
2.    public interface Contact extends Serializable{
3.        public static final String SPACE = " ";
4.        public String getFirstName();
5.        public String getLastName();
6.        public String getTitle();
7.        public String getOrganization();
8.
9.        public void setFirstName(String newFirstName);
10.       public void setLastName(String newLastName);
11.       public void setTitle(String newTitle);
12.       public void setOrganization(String newOrganization);
13.   }
```

Example A.63 ContactImpl.java

```
1.    public class ContactImpl implements Contact{
2.        private String firstName;
3.        private String lastName;
4.        private String title;
5.        private String organization;
6.
7.        public ContactImpl(){}
8.        public ContactImpl(String newFirstName, String newLastName,
9.            String newTitle, String newOrganization){
10.               firstName = newFirstName;
11.               lastName = newLastName;
12.               title = newTitle;
13.               organization = newOrganization;
14.       }
15.
16.       public String getFirstName(){ return firstName; }
17.       public String getLastName(){ return lastName; }
18.       public String getTitle(){ return title; }
19.       public String getOrganization(){ return organization; }
20.
21.       public void setFirstName(String newFirstName){ firstName = newFirstName; }
22.       public void setLastName(String newLastName){ lastName = newLastName; }
23.       public void setTitle(String newTitle){ title = newTitle; }
24.      public void setOrganization(String newOrganization){ organization = newOrgani-
```

```
    zation; }
25.
26.     public String toString(){
27.         return firstName + SPACE + lastName;
28.     }
29. }
```

This code shows how the `Interpreter` could be used to search among a set of `Contacts` in a structure like an address book. Recognize, however, that the `Expressions` could be used with any other classes, providing search functionality for any of the PIM business objects.

`RunPattern` demonstrates the Interpreter functionality by creating a `ContactList` and running a group of matching expressions on the elements in the list.

Example A.64 `RunPattern.java`

```
1.  public class RunPattern{
2.      public static void main(String [] arguments){
3.          System.out.println("Example for the Interpreter pattern");
4.          System.out.println("In this demonstration, the syntax defined");
5.          System.out.println(" by the Interpreter can be used to search");
6.          System.out.println(" among a collection of Contacts, returning");
7.          System.out.println(" the subset that match the given search criteria.");
8.
9.          ContactList candidates = makeContactList();
10.         Context ctx = new Context();
11.
12.         System.out.println("Contents of the ContactList:");
13.         System.out.println(candidates);
14.         System.out.println();
15.
16.         Contact testContact = new ContactImpl();
17.         VariableExpression varLName = new VariableExpression(testContact, "get-
    LastName");
18.         ConstantExpression constLName = new ConstantExpression("u");
19.        ContainsExpression eqLName = new ContainsExpression(varLName, constLName);
20.
21.         System.out.println("Contents of the search on ContactList:");
22.         System.out.println("(search was contains 'u' in Lase Name)");
23.         Object result = candidates.getContactsMatchingExpression(eqLName, ctx,
    testContact);
24.         System.out.println(result);
25.
26.        VariableExpression varTitle = new VariableExpression(testContact, "getTi-
    tle");
27.         ConstantExpression constTitle = new ConstantExpression("LT");
28.         EqualsExpression eqTitle = new EqualsExpression(varTitle, constTitle);
29.
30.         System.out.println("Contents of the search on ContactList:");
31.         System.out.println("(search was all LT personnel)");
32.         result = candidates.getContactsMatchingExpression(eqTitle, ctx, testCon-
```

```
        tact);
33.         System.out.println(result);
34.         System.out.println();
35.
36.         VariableExpression varLastName = new VariableExpression(testContact, "get-
        LastName");
37.         ConstantExpression constLastName = new ConstantExpression("S");
38.         ContainsExpression cLName = new ContainsExpression(varLastName, constLast-
        Name);
39.
40.         AndExpression andExpr = new AndExpression(eqTitle, cLName);
41.
42.         System.out.println("Contents of the search on ContactList:");
43.         System.out.println("(search was all LT personnel with 'S' in Last Name)");
44.         result = candidates.getContactsMatchingExpression(andExpr, ctx, testCon-
        tact);
45.         System.out.println(result);
46.     }
47.
48.     private static ContactList makeContactList(){
49.         ContactList returnList = new ContactList();
50.         returnList.addContact(new ContactImpl("James", "Kirk", "Captain", "USS
        Enterprise"));
51.         returnList.addContact(new ContactImpl("Mr.", "Spock", "Science Officer",
        "USS Enterprise"));
52.         returnList.addContact(new ContactImpl("LT", "Uhura", "LT", "USS Enter-
        prise"));
53.         returnList.addContact(new ContactImpl("LT", "Sulu", "LT", "USS Enter-
        prise"));
54.         returnList.addContact(new ContactImpl("Ensign", "Checkov", "Ensign", "USS
        Enterprise"));
55.         returnList.addContact(new ContactImpl("Dr.", "McCoy", "Ship's Doctor",
        "USS Enterprise"));
56.         returnList.addContact(new ContactImpl("Montgomery", "Scott", "LT", "USS
        Enterprise"));
57.         return returnList;
58.     }
59. }
```

Iterator

This example uses the Java Collection Framework to provide iterating behavior for a pair of business aggregates. The `java.util.Iterator` interface defines methods for the basic navigation methods required—`hasNext` and `next`. Note that the `Iterator` interface requires one-time-only traversal, since the only way to return to the beginning is to get another `Iterator` from the collection.

The `Iterating` interface defines a single method, `getIterator`. This interface is used to identify any class in the PIM that is capable of producing an Iterator for collection traversal.

Example A.65 `Iterating.java`

```
1.    import java.util.Iterator;
2.    import java.io.Serializable;
3.    public interface Iterating extends Serializable{
4.        public Iterator getIterator();
5.    }
```

The `ToDoList` and `ToDoListCollection` interfaces, which extend Iterating, define the two collections in the example. `ToDoList` defines a sequential list of tasks or items, while `ToDoListCollection` represents a collection of to-do lists stored in the PIM.

Example A.66 `ToDoList.java`

```
1.    public interface ToDoList extends Iterating{
2.        public void add(String item);
3.        public void add(String item, int position);
4.        public void remove(String item);
5.        public int getNumberOfItems();
6.        public String getListName();
7.        public void setListName(String newListName);
8.    }
```

Example A.67 `ToDoListCollection.java`

```
1.    public interface ToDoListCollection extends Iterating{
2.        public void add(ToDoList list);
3.        public void remove(ToDoList list);
4.        public int getNumberOfItems();
5.    }
```

The classes `ToDoListImpl` and `ToDoListCollectionImpl` implement the previous interfaces. `ToDoListImpl` uses an `ArrayList` to hold its elements, which provides absolute ordering and allows duplicate entries. `ToDoListCollectionImpl` uses a `HashTable`, which does not support ordering and stores its entries as key-value pairs. Although the collections behave very differently, both can provide Iterators for their stored elements.

Example A.68 `ToDoListCollectionImpl.java`

```
1.  import java.util.Iterator;
2.  import java.util.HashMap;
3.  public class ToDoListCollectionImpl implements ToDoListCollection{
4.      private HashMap lists = new HashMap();
5.
6.      public void add(ToDoList list){
7.          if (!lists.containsKey(list.getListName())){
8.              lists.put(list.getListName(), list);
9.          }
10.     }
11.     public void remove(ToDoList list){
12.         if (lists.containsKey(list.getListName())){
13.             lists.remove(list.getListName());
14.         }
15.     }
16.     public int getNumberOfItems(){ return lists.size(); }
17.     public Iterator getIterator(){ return lists.values().iterator(); }
18.     public String toString(){ return getClass().toString(); }
19. }
```

Example A.69 `ToDoListImpl.java`

```
1.  import java.util.Iterator;
2.  import java.util.ArrayList;
3.  public class ToDoListImpl implements ToDoList{
4.      private String listName;
5.      private ArrayList items = new ArrayList();
6.
7.      public void add(String item){
8.          if (!items.contains(item)){
9.              items.add(item);
10.         }
11.     }
12.     public void add(String item, int position){
13.         if (!items.contains(item)){
14.             items.add(position, item);
15.         }
16.     }
17.     public void remove(String item){
18.         if (items.contains(item)){
19.             items.remove(items.indexOf(item));
20.         }
21.     }
22.
23.     public int getNumberOfItems(){ return items.size(); }
24.     public Iterator getIterator(){ return items.iterator(); }
25.     public String getListName(){ return listName; }
```

```
26.        public void setListName(String newListName){ listName = newListName; }
27.
28.        public String toString(){ return listName; }
29.    }
```

Both classes can provide an Iterator, so it's straightforward to write code to move through their elements. `ListPrinter` shows how the Iterators could be used to print the contents of collections out in their `String` form. The class has three methods: `printToDoList`, `printToDoListCollection` and `printIteratingElement`. In all three methods, the iteration process is based around a very simple `while` loop.

Example A.70 `ListPrinter.java`

```
1.    import java.util.Iterator;
2.    import java.io.PrintStream;
3.    public class ListPrinter{
4.        public static void printToDoList(ToDoList list, PrintStream output){
5.            Iterator elements = list.getIterator();
6.            output.println("  List - " + list + ":");
7.            while (elements.hasNext()){
8.                output.println("\t" + elements.next());
9.            }
10.       }
11.
12.       public static void printToDoListCollection(ToDoListCollection lotsOfLists,
      PrintStream output){
13.           Iterator elements = lotsOfLists.getIterator();
14.           output.println("\"To Do\" List Collection:");
15.           while (elements.hasNext()){
16.               printToDoList((ToDoList)elements.next(), output);
17.           }
18.       }
19.
20.       public static void printIteratingElement(Iterating element, PrintStream out-
      put){
21.           output.println("Printing the element " + element);
22.           Iterator elements = element.getIterator();
23.           while (elements.hasNext()){
24.               Object currentElement = elements.next();
25.               if (currentElement instanceof Iterating){
26.                   printIteratingElement((Iterating)currentElement, output);
27.                   output.println();
28.               }
29.               else{
30.                   output.println(currentElement);
31.               }
32.           }
33.       }
34.   }
```

The method `printIteratingElement` best demonstrates the power of combining the Iterator pattern with polymorphism. Here, any class that implements `Iterating` can be printed in `String` form. The method makes no assumptions about the underlying collection structure except that it can produce an `Iterator`.

This example uses two support classes, `DataCreator` and `DataRetriever`, to produce a sample set of to-do lists and store them in a file.

Example A.71 `DataCreator.java`

```
1.   import java.io.Serializable;
2.   import java.io.ObjectOutputStream;
3.   import java.io.FileOutputStream;
4.   import java.io.IOException;
5.   public class DataCreator{
6.       private static final String DEFAULT_FILE = "data.ser";
7.
8.       public static void main(String [] args){
9.           String fileName;
10.          if (args.length == 1){
11.              fileName = args[0];
12.          }else{
13.              fileName = DEFAULT_FILE;
14.          }
15.          serialize(fileName);
16.      }
17.
18.      public static void serialize(String fileName){
19.          try{
20.              serializeToFile(createData(), fileName);
21.          } catch (IOException exc){
22.              exc.printStackTrace();
23.          }
24.      }
25.
26.      private static Serializable createData(){
27.          ToDoListCollection data = new ToDoListCollectionImpl();
28.          ToDoList listOne = new ToDoListImpl();
29.          ToDoList listTwo = new ToDoListImpl();
30.          ToDoList listThree = new ToDoListImpl();
31.          listOne.setListName("Daily Routine");
32.          listTwo.setListName("Programmer hair washing procedure");
33.          listThree.setListName("Reading List");
34.          listOne.add("Get up (harder some days than others)");
35.          listOne.add("Brew cuppa Java");
36.          listOne.add("Read JVM Times");
37.          listTwo.add("Lather");
38.          listTwo.add("Rinse");
39.          listTwo.add("Repeat");
40.          listTwo.add("(eventually throw a TooMuchHairConditioner exception)");
41.          listThree.add("The complete annotated aphorisms of Duke");
42.          listThree.add("How green was my Java");
```

```
43.            listThree.add("URL, sweet URL");
44.            data.add(listOne);
45.            data.add(listTwo);
46.            data.add(listThree);
47.            return data;
48.        }
49.
50.        private static void serializeToFile(Serializable data, String fileName) throws
       IOException{
51.            ObjectOutputStream serOut = new ObjectOutputStream(new FileOutput-
       Stream(fileName));
52.            serOut.writeObject(data);
53.            serOut.close();
54.        }
55.    }
```

Example A.72 `DataRetriever.java`

```
1.     import java.io.File;
2.     import java.io.FileInputStream;
3.     import java.io.IOException;
4.     import java.io.ObjectInputStream;
5.
6.     public class DataRetriever{
7.         public static Object deserializeData(String fileName){
8.             Object returnValue = null;
9.             try{
10.                File inputFile = new File(fileName);
11.                if (inputFile.exists() && inputFile.isFile()){
12.                    ObjectInputStream readIn = new ObjectInputStream(new FileInput-
       Stream(fileName));
13.                    returnValue = readIn.readObject();
14.                    readIn.close();
15.                }else{
16.                    System.err.println("Unable to locate the file " + fileName);
17.                }
18.            }catch (ClassNotFoundException exc){
19.                exc.printStackTrace();
20.            }catch (IOException exc){
21.                exc.printStackTrace();
22.            }
23.            return returnValue;
24.        }
25.    }
```

`RunPattern` coordinates this example by loading the sample data, then calling the `ListPrinter` method `printToDoListCollection` to print all lists and their elements.

Example A.73 RunPattern.java

```
1.    import java.io.File;
2.    import java.io.IOException;
3.    public class RunPattern{
4.        public static void main(String [] arguments){
5.            System.out.println("Example for the Iterator pattern");
6.            System.out.println(" This code sample demonstrates how an Iterator can
      enforce");
7.            System.out.println(" uniformity of processing for different collection
      types.");
8.            System.out.println(" In this case, there are two classes, ToDoListImpl
      and");
9.            System.out.println(" ToDoListCollectionImpl, that have different storage
      needs.");
10.           System.out.println(" ToDoListImpl uses an ArrayList to store its elements
      in");
11.           System.out.println(" ordered form. The ToDoListCollectionImpl uses a Hash-
      Map,");
12.           System.out.println(" since it must differentiate between ToDoListImpl
      objects by");
13.           System.out.println(" their String identifiers.");
14.           System.out.println();
15.           System.out.println("Although the two classes use different underlying col-
      lections,");
16.           System.out.println(" the ListPrinter class can use the Iterator produced by
      each");
17.           System.out.println(" to print out a set of list contents.");
18.           System.out.println();
19.
20.           if (!(new File("data.ser").exists())){
21.               DataCreator.serialize("data.ser");
22.           }
23.           ToDoListCollection lists = (ToDoListCollection)(DataRetriever.deserialize-
      Data("data.ser"));
24.
25.           System.out.println("Lists retrieved. Printing out contents using the Iter-
      ator");
26.           System.out.println();
27.           ListPrinter.printToDoListCollection(lists, System.out);
28.       }
29.   }
```

Mediator

In this example, a Mediator manages communication among the panels of a graphical user interface. The basic design of this GUI uses one panel to select a Contact from a list, another panel to allow editing, and a third panel to show the current state of the Contact. The Mediator interacts with each panel, calling the appropriate methods to keep each part of the GUI up to date.

The class `MediatorGui` creates the main window and the three panels for the application. It also creates a mediator and matches it with the three child panels.

Example A.74 `MediatorGui.java`

```
1.  import java.awt.Container;
2.  import java.awt.event.WindowEvent;
3.  import java.awt.event.WindowAdapter;
4.  import javax.swing.BoxLayout;
5.  import javax.swing.JButton;
6.  import javax.swing.JFrame;
7.  import javax.swing.JPanel;
8.  public class MediatorGui{
9.      private ContactMediator mediator;
10.
11.     public void setContactMediator(ContactMediator newMediator){ mediator = newMe-
    diator; }
12.
13.     public void createGui(){
14.         JFrame mainFrame = new JFrame("Mediator example");
15.         Container content = mainFrame.getContentPane();
16.         content.setLayout(new BoxLayout(content, BoxLayout.Y_AXIS));
17.         ContactSelectorPanel select = new ContactSelectorPanel(mediator);
18.         ContactDisplayPanel display = new ContactDisplayPanel(mediator);
19.         ContactEditorPanel edit = new ContactEditorPanel(mediator);
20.         content.add(select);
21.         content.add(display);
22.         content.add(edit);
23.         mediator.setContactSelectorPanel(select);
24.         mediator.setContactDisplayPanel(display);
25.         mediator.setContactEditorPanel(edit);
26.         mainFrame.addWindowListener(new WindowCloseManager());
27.         mainFrame.pack();
28.         mainFrame.setVisible(true);
29.     }
30.     private class WindowCloseManager extends WindowAdapter{
31.         public void windowClosing(WindowEvent evt){
32.             System.exit(0);
33.         }
34.     }
35. }
36.
37.
```

The simplest of the GUI panels is the ContactDisplayPanel. It has a method called contactChanged that updates its display region with the values of the Contact argument.

Example A.75 ContactDisplayPanel.java

```
1.  import java.awt.BorderLayout;
2.  import javax.swing.JPanel;
3.  import javax.swing.JScrollPane;
4.  import javax.swing.JTextArea;
5.  public class ContactDisplayPanel extends JPanel{
6.      private ContactMediator mediator;
7.      private JTextArea displayRegion;
8.  
9.      public ContactDisplayPanel(){
10.         createGui();
11.     }
12.     public ContactDisplayPanel(ContactMediator newMediator){
13.         setContactMediator(newMediator);
14.         createGui();
15.     }
16.     public void createGui(){
17.         setLayout(new BorderLayout());
18.         displayRegion = new JTextArea(10, 40);
19.         displayRegion.setEditable(false);
20.         add(new JScrollPane(displayRegion));
21.     }
22.     public void contactChanged(Contact contact){
23.         displayRegion.setText(
24.             "Contact\n\tName: " + contact.getFirstName() +
25.             " " + contact.getLastName() + "\n\tTitle: " +
26.             contact.getTitle() + "\n\tOrganization: " +
27.             contact.getOrganization());
28.     }
29.     public void setContactMediator(ContactMediator newMediator){
30.         mediator = newMediator;
31.     }
32. }
```

ContactSelectorPanel allows the user to choose a Contact for display and edit in the MediatorGui.

Example A.76 ContactSelectorPanel.java

```
1.  import java.awt.event.ActionEvent;
2.  import java.awt.event.ActionListener;
3.  import javax.swing.JComboBox;
4.  import javax.swing.JPanel;
5.  
6.  public class ContactSelectorPanel extends JPanel implements ActionListener{
7.      private ContactMediator mediator;
```

```
8.          private JComboBox selector;
9.
10.         public ContactSelectorPanel(){
11.             createGui();
12.         }
13.         public ContactSelectorPanel(ContactMediator newMediator){
14.             setContactMediator(newMediator);
15.             createGui();
16.         }
17.
18.         public void createGui(){
19.             selector = new JComboBox(mediator.getAllContacts());
20.             selector.addActionListener(this);
21.             add(selector);
22.         }
23.
24.         public void actionPerformed(ActionEvent evt){
25.             mediator.selectContact((Contact)selector.getSelectedItem());
26.         }
27.         public void addContact(Contact contact){
28.             selector.addItem(contact);
29.             selector.setSelectedItem(contact);
30.         }
31.         public void setContactMediator(ContactMediator newMediator){
32.             mediator = newMediator;
33.         }
34.     }
```

The ContactEditorPanel provides an editing interface for the currently selected Contact. It has buttons that allow a user to add or update a Contact.

Example A.77 ContactEditorPanel.java

```
1.      import java.awt.BorderLayout;
2.      import java.awt.GridLayout;
3.      import java.awt.event.ActionEvent;
4.      import java.awt.event.ActionListener;
5.      import javax.swing.JButton;
6.      import javax.swing.JLabel;
7.      import javax.swing.JPanel;
8.      import javax.swing.JTextField;
9.      public class ContactEditorPanel extends JPanel implements ActionListener{
10.         private ContactMediator mediator;
11.         private JTextField firstName, lastName, title, organization;
12.         private JButton create, update;
13.
14.         public ContactEditorPanel(){
15.             createGui();
16.         }
17.         public ContactEditorPanel(ContactMediator newMediator){
18.             setContactMediator(newMediator);
19.             createGui();
20.         }
```

```
21.     public void createGui(){
22.         setLayout(new BorderLayout());
23.
24.         JPanel editor = new JPanel();
25.         editor.setLayout(new GridLayout(4, 2));
26.         editor.add(new JLabel("First Name:"));
27.         firstName = new JTextField(20);
28.         editor.add(firstName);
29.         editor.add(new JLabel("Last Name:"));
30.         lastName = new JTextField(20);
31.         editor.add(lastName);
32.         editor.add(new JLabel("Title:"));
33.         title = new JTextField(20);
34.         editor.add(title);
35.         editor.add(new JLabel("Organization:"));
36.         organization = new JTextField(20);
37.         editor.add(organization);
38.         add(editor, BorderLayout.CENTER);
39.
40.         JPanel control = new JPanel();
41.         create = new JButton("Create Contact");
42.         update = new JButton("Update Contact");
43.         create.addActionListener(this);
44.         update.addActionListener(this);
45.         control.add(create);
46.         control.add(update);
47.         add(control, BorderLayout.SOUTH);
48.     }
49.     public void actionPerformed(ActionEvent evt){
50.         Object source = evt.getSource();
51.         if (source == create){
52.             createContact();
53.         }
54.         else if (source == update){
55.             updateContact();
56.         }
57.     }
58.
59.     public void createContact(){
60.         mediator.createContact(firstName.getText(), lastName.getText(),
61.             title.getText(), organization.getText());
62.     }
63.     public void updateContact(){
64.         mediator.updateContact(firstName.getText(), lastName.getText(),
65.             title.getText(), organization.getText());
66.     }
67.
68.     public void setContactFields(Contact contact){
69.         firstName.setText(contact.getFirstName());
70.         lastName.setText(contact.getLastName());
71.         title.setText(contact.getTitle());
72.         organization.setText(contact.getOrganization());
73.     }
74.     public void setContactMediator(ContactMediator newMediator){
```

```
75.             mediator = newMediator;
76.         }
77.     }
```

The `ContactMediator` interface defines set methods for each of the GUI components, and for the business methods `createContact`, `updateContact`, `selectContact` and `getAllContacts`.

Example A.78 `ContactMediator.java`

```
1.  public interface ContactMediator{
2.      public void setContactDisplayPanel(ContactDisplayPanel displayPanel);
3.      public void setContactEditorPanel(ContactEditorPanel editorPanel);
4.      public void setContactSelectorPanel(ContactSelectorPanel selectorPanel);
5.      public void createContact(String firstName, String lastName, String title,
    String organization);
6.      public void updateContact(String firstName, String lastName, String title,
    String organization);
7.      public Contact [] getAllContacts();
8.      public void selectContact(Contact contact);
9.  }
```

`ContactMediatorImpl` is the implementer of `ContactMediator`. It maintains a collection of Contacts, and methods that notify the panels of changes within the GUI.

Example A.79 `ContactMediatorImpl.java`

```
1.  import java.util.ArrayList;
2.  public class ContactMediatorImpl implements ContactMediator{
3.      private ContactDisplayPanel display;
4.      private ContactEditorPanel editor;
5.      private ContactSelectorPanel selector;
6.      private ArrayList contacts = new ArrayList();
7.      private int contactIndex;
8.
9.      public void setContactDisplayPanel(ContactDisplayPanel displayPanel){
10.         display = displayPanel;
11.     }
12.     public void setContactEditorPanel(ContactEditorPanel editorPanel){
13.         editor = editorPanel;
14.     }
15.     public void setContactSelectorPanel(ContactSelectorPanel selectorPanel){
16.         selector = selectorPanel;
17.     }
18.
19.     public void createContact(String firstName, String lastName, String title,
    String organization){
20.         Contact newContact = new ContactImpl(firstName, lastName, title, organiza-
    tion);
21.         addContact(newContact);
22.         selector.addContact(newContact);
```

```
23.             display.contactChanged(newContact);
24.         }
25.         public void updateContact(String firstName, String lastName, String title,
        String organization){
26.             Contact updateContact = (Contact)contacts.get(contactIndex);
27.             if (updateContact != null){
28.                 updateContact.setFirstName(firstName);
29.                 updateContact.setLastName(lastName);
30.                 updateContact.setTitle(title);
31.                 updateContact.setOrganization(organization);
32.                 display.contactChanged(updateContact);
33.             }
34.         }
35.         public void selectContact(Contact contact){
36.             if (contacts.contains(contact)){
37.                 contactIndex = contacts.indexOf(contact);
38.                 display.contactChanged(contact);
39.                 editor.setContactFields(contact);
40.             }
41.         }
42.         public Contact [] getAllContacts(){
43.             return (Contact [])contacts.toArray(new Contact[1]);
44.         }
45.         public void addContact(Contact contact){
46.             if (!contacts.contains(contact)){
47.                 contacts.add(contact);
48.             }
49.         }
50.     }
```

The ContactMediatorImpl interacts with each of the panels differently. For the ContactDisplayPanel, the mediator calls its contactChanged method for the create, update and select operations. For the ContactSelectorPanel, the mediator provides the list of Contacts with the getAllContacts method, receives select notifications, and adds a new Contact object to the panel when one is created. The mediator receives create and update method calls from the ContactEditorPanel, and notifies the panel of select actions from the ContactSelectorPanel.

Contact and ContactImpl define the business class used in this example.

Example A.80 Contact.java

```
1.  import java.io.Serializable;
2.  public interface Contact extends Serializable{
3.      public static final String SPACE = " ";
4.      public String getFirstName();
5.      public String getLastName();
6.      public String getTitle();
7.      public String getOrganization();
8.
9.      public void setFirstName(String newFirstName);
```

```
10.        public void setLastName(String newLastName);
11.        public void setTitle(String newTitle);
12.        public void setOrganization(String newOrganization);
13.    }
```

Example A.81 `ContactImpl.java`

```
1.    public class ContactImpl implements Contact{
2.        private String firstName;
3.        private String lastName;
4.        private String title;
5.        private String organization;
6.
7.        public ContactImpl(){}
8.        public ContactImpl(String newFirstName, String newLastName,
9.            String newTitle, String newOrganization){
10.               firstName = newFirstName;
11.               lastName = newLastName;
12.               title = newTitle;
13.               organization = newOrganization;
14.       }
15.
16.       public String getFirstName(){ return firstName; }
17.       public String getLastName(){ return lastName; }
18.       public String getTitle(){ return title; }
19.       public String getOrganization(){ return organization; }
20.
21.       public void setFirstName(String newFirstName){ firstName = newFirstName; }
22.       public void setLastName(String newLastName){ lastName = newLastName; }
23.       public void setTitle(String newTitle){ title = newTitle; }
24.       public void setOrganization(String newOrganization){ organization = newOrgani-
      zation; }
25.
26.       public String toString(){
27.           return firstName + SPACE + lastName;
28.       }
29.   }
```

`RunPattern` creates the GUI and its mediator, and loads a sample contact.

Example A.82 `RunPattern.java`

```
1.    public class RunPattern{
2.        public static void main(String [] arguments){
3.            System.out.println("Example for the Mediator pattern");
4.            System.out.println("In this demonstration, the ContactMediatorImpl class
      will");
5.            System.out.println(" coordinate updates between three controls in a GUI -
      the");
6.            System.out.println(" ContactDisplayPanel, the ContactEditorPanel, and
      the");
7.            System.out.println(" ContactSelectorPanel. As its name suggests, the Medi-
      ator");
```

```
8.          System.out.println(" mediates the activity between the elements of the
       GUI,");
9.          System.out.println(" translating method calls from one panel into the
       appropriate");
10.         System.out.println(" method calls on the other GUI components.");
11.
12.         Contact contact = new ContactImpl("", "", "", "");
13.         Contact contact1 = new ContactImpl("Duke", "", "Java Advocate", "The Pat-
       terns Guild");
14.         ContactMediatorImpl mediator = new ContactMediatorImpl();
15.         mediator.addContact(contact);
16.         mediator.addContact(contact1);
17.         MediatorGui gui = new MediatorGui();
18.         gui.setContactMediator(mediator);
19.         gui.createGui();
20.
21.
22.     }
23. }
24.
```

Memento

Almost all parts of the Personal Information Manager keep some kind of state. These states can be saved by applying the Memento pattern, as this example with an address book will demonstrate. The `AddressBook` class represents a collection of addresses, a natural candidate for keeping a record of state.

Example A.83 `AddressBook.java`

```
1.  import java.util.ArrayList;
2.  public class AddressBook{
3.      private ArrayList contacts = new ArrayList();
4.
5.      public Object getMemento(){
6.          return new AddressBookMemento(contacts);
7.      }
8.      public void setMemento(Object object){
9.          if (object instanceof AddressBookMemento){
10.             AddressBookMemento memento = (AddressBookMemento)object;
11.             contacts = memento.state;
12.         }
13.     }
14.
15.     private class AddressBookMemento{
16.         private ArrayList state;
17.
18.         private AddressBookMemento(ArrayList contacts){
19.             this.state = contacts;
20.         }
21.     }
22.
23.     public AddressBook(){ }
24.     public AddressBook(ArrayList newContacts){
25.         contacts = newContacts;
26.     }
27.
28.     public void addContact(Contact contact){
29.         if (!contacts.contains(contact)){
30.             contacts.add(contact);
31.         }
32.     }
33.     public void removeContact(Contact contact){
34.         contacts.remove(contact);
35.     }
36.     public void removeAllContacts(){
37.         contacts = new ArrayList();
38.     }
39.     public ArrayList getContacts(){
40.         return contacts;
41.     }
42.     public String toString(){
```

```
43.          return contacts.toString();
44.      }
45.  }
```

The inner class of AddressBook, AddressBookMemento, is used to save the state of an AddressBook, which in this case is represented by the internal ArrayList of Address objects. The memento object can be accessed by using the AddressBook methods getMemento and setMemento. Note that AddressBookMemento is a private inner class and that it has only a private constructor. This ensures that, even if the memento object is saved somewhere outside of an AddressBook object, no other object will be able to use the object or modify its state. This is consistent with the role of the Memento pattern: producing an object to maintain a snapshot of state that cannot be modified by other objects in a system.

Support classes used in this example provide business objects for the contacts stored in the AddressBook, and their associated addresses. The Address and Contact interfaces define the behavior expected of these business objects, while the AddressImpl and ContactImpl classes implement the required behavior.

Example A.84 Address.java

```
1.  import java.io.Serializable;
2.  public interface Address extends Serializable{
3.      public static final String EOL_STRING = System.getProperty("line.separator");
4.      public static final String SPACE = " ";
5.      public static final String COMMA = ",";
6.      public String getType();
7.      public String getDescription();
8.      public String getStreet();
9.      public String getCity();
10.     public String getState();
11.     public String getZipCode();
12.
13.     public void setType(String newType);
14.     public void setDescription(String newDescription);
15.     public void setStreet(String newStreet);
16.     public void setCity(String newCity);
17.     public void setState(String newState);
18.     public void setZipCode(String newZip);
19. }
```

Example A.85 AddressImpl.java

```
1.  public class AddressImpl implements Address{
2.      private String type;
3.      private String description;
4.      private String street;
5.      private String city;
6.      private String state;
```

```
7.        private String zipCode;
8.
9.        public AddressImpl(){ }
10.       public AddressImpl(String newDescription, String newStreet,
11.           String newCity, String newState, String newZipCode){
12.           description = newDescription;
13.           street = newStreet;
14.           city = newCity;
15.           state = newState;
16.           zipCode = newZipCode;
17.       }
18.
19.       public String getType(){ return type; }
20.       public String getDescription(){ return description; }
21.       public String getStreet(){ return street; }
22.       public String getCity(){ return city; }
23.       public String getState(){ return state; }
24.       public String getZipCode(){ return zipCode; }
25.
26.       public void setType(String newType){ type = newType; }
27.       public void setDescription(String newDescription){ description = newDescrip-
      tion; }
28.       public void setStreet(String newStreet){ street = newStreet; }
29.       public void setCity(String newCity){ city = newCity; }
30.       public void setState(String newState){ state = newState; }
31.       public void setZipCode(String newZip){ zipCode = newZip; }
32.
33.       public String toString(){
34.           return street + EOL_STRING + city + COMMA + SPACE +
35.               state + SPACE + zipCode + EOL_STRING;
36.       }
37.   }
```

Example A.86 `Contact.java`

```
1.    import java.io.Serializable;
2.    public interface Contact extends Serializable{
3.        public static final String SPACE = " ";
4.        public String getFirstName();
5.        public String getLastName();
6.        public String getTitle();
7.        public String getOrganization();
8.
9.        public void setFirstName(String newFirstName);
10.       public void setLastName(String newLastName);
11.       public void setTitle(String newTitle);
12.       public void setOrganization(String newOrganization);
13.   }
```

Example A.87 `ContactImpl.java`

```
1.    public class ContactImpl implements Contact{
2.        private String firstName;
```

```
3.      private String lastName;
4.      private String title;
5.      private String organization;
6.      private Address address;
7.
8.      public ContactImpl(){}
9.      public ContactImpl(String newFirstName, String newLastName,
10.         String newTitle, String newOrganization, Address newAddress){
11.             firstName = newFirstName;
12.             lastName = newLastName;
13.             title = newTitle;
14.             organization = newOrganization;
15.             address = newAddress;
16.     }
17.
18.     public String getFirstName(){ return firstName; }
19.     public String getLastName(){ return lastName; }
20.     public String getTitle(){ return title; }
21.     public String getOrganization(){ return organization; }
22.     public Address getAddress(){ return address; }
23.
24.     public void setFirstName(String newFirstName){ firstName = newFirstName; }
25.     public void setLastName(String newLastName){ lastName = newLastName; }
26.     public void setTitle(String newTitle){ title = newTitle; }
27.     public void setOrganization(String newOrganization){ organization = newOrgani-
    zation; }
28.     public void setAddress(Address newAddress){ address = newAddress; }
29.
30.     public String toString(){
31.         return firstName + " " + lastName;
32.     }
33. }
```

The RunPattern class demonstrates the use of the Memento by creating an address book with an initial set of people. Next, RunPattern saves the state of this group of contacts to an AddressBookMemento object and creates a different set of people. Finally, RunPattern restores the address book to its original state by calling its setMemento method.

Example A.88 RunPattern.java

```
1.  public class RunPattern{
2.      public static void main(String [] arguments){
3.          System.out.println("Example for the Memento pattern");
4.          System.out.println();
5.          System.out.println("This example will use the AddressBook to demonstrate");
6.          System.out.println(" how a Memento can be used to save and restore
    state.");
7.          System.out.println("The AddressBook has an inner class, AddressBookMe-
    mento,");
8.          System.out.println(" that is used to store the AddressBook state... in
    this");
9.          System.out.println(" case, its internal list of contacts.");
```

```
10.            System.out.println();
11.
12.            System.out.println("Creating the AddressBook");
13.            AddressBook book = new AddressBook();
14.
15.            System.out.println("Adding Contact entries for the AddressBook");
16.            book.addContact(new ContactImpl("Peter", "Taggart", "Commander", "NSEA
        Protector", new AddressImpl()));
17.            book.addContact(new ContactImpl("Tawny", "Madison", "Lieutenant", "NSEA
        Protector", new AddressImpl()));
18.          book.addContact(new ContactImpl("Dr.", "Lazarus", "Dr.", "NSEA Protector",
        new AddressImpl()));
19.            book.addContact(new ContactImpl("Tech Sargent", "Chen", "Tech Sargent",
        "NSEA Protector", new AddressImpl()));
20.
21.            System.out.println("Contacts added. Current Contact list:");
22.            System.out.println(book);
23.            System.out.println();
24.
25.            System.out.println("Creating a Memento for the address book");
26.            Object memento = book.getMemento();
27.          System.out.println("Now that a Memento exists, it can be used to restore");
28.          System.out.println(" the state of this AddressBook object, or to set the");
29.            System.out.println(" state of a new AddressBook.");
30.            System.out.println();
31.
32.            System.out.println("Creating new entries for the AddressBook");
33.            book.removeAllContacts();
34.           book.addContact(new ContactImpl("Jason", "Nesmith", "", "Actor's Guild",
        new AddressImpl()));
35.         book.addContact(new ContactImpl("Gwen", "DeMarco", "", "Actor's Guild", new
        AddressImpl()));
36.          book.addContact(new ContactImpl("Alexander", "Dane", "", "Actor's Guild",
        new AddressImpl()));
37.           book.addContact(new ContactImpl("Fred", "Kwan", "", "Actor's Guild", new
        AddressImpl()));
38.
39.            System.out.println("New Contacts added. Current Contact list:");
40.            System.out.println(book);
41.            System.out.println();
42.          System.out.println("Using the Memento object to restore the AddressBook");
43.            System.out.println(" to its original state.");
44.            book.setMemento(memento);
45.            System.out.println("AddressBook restored. Current Contact list:");
46.            System.out.println(book);
47.
48.      }
49.  }
```

Observer

In the Observer example, an observer sends updates about the state of a Task to all registered listeners in a GUI.

It's important to recognize that any Java GUI code normally uses the Observer pattern for event handling. When you write a class that implements a listener interface like ActionListener, you are creating an observer. Registering that listener with a component through the method addActionListener associates the observer with an observable element, the Java GUI component.

In this example, the observable element is represented by the Task being modified in the GUI. The class TaskChangeObservable keeps track of the listeners for changes to the Task through the methods addTaskChangeObserver and removeTaskChangeObserver.

Example A.89 TaskChangeObservable.java

```
1.    import java.util.ArrayList;
2.    import java.util.Iterator;
3.    public class TaskChangeObservable{
4.        private ArrayList observers = new ArrayList();
5.
6.        public void addTaskChangeObserver(TaskChangeObserver observer){
7.            if (!observers.contains(observer)){
8.                observers.add(observer);
9.            }
10.       }
11.       public void removeTaskChangeObserver(TaskChangeObserver observer){
12.           observers.remove(observer);
13.       }
14.
15.       public void selectTask(Task task){
16.           Iterator elements = observers.iterator();
17.           while (elements.hasNext()){
18.               ((TaskChangeObserver)elements.next()).taskSelected(task);
19.           }
20.       }
21.       public void addTask(Task task){
22.           Iterator elements = observers.iterator();
23.           while (elements.hasNext()){
24.               ((TaskChangeObserver)elements.next()).taskAdded(task);
25.           }
26.       }
27.       public void updateTask(Task task){
28.           Iterator elements = observers.iterator();
29.           while (elements.hasNext()){
30.               ((TaskChangeObserver)elements.next()).taskChanged(task);
31.           }
32.       }
33.   }
```

TaskChangeObservable has the business methods selectTask, updateTask, and addTask. These methods send notifications of any changes to a Task.

Every observer must implement the TaskChangeObserver interface, allowing the TaskChangeObservable to call the appropriate method on each observer. If a client were to call the method addTask on the TaskChangeObservable, for instance, the observable object would iterate through its observers and call the taskAdded method on each.

Example A.90 TaskChangeObserver.java

```
1.  public interface TaskChangeObserver{
2.      public void taskAdded(Task task);
3.      public void taskChanged(Task task);
4.      public void taskSelected(Task task);
5.  }
```

The class ObserverGui provides a GUI in this demonstration, and creates a TaskChangeObservable object. In addition, it creates three panels that implement the TaskChangeObserver interface, and matches them with the TaskChangeObservable object. By doing this, the TaskChangeObservable is able to effectively send updates among the three panels of the GUI.

Example A.91 ObserverGui.java

```
1.  import java.awt.Container;
2.  import java.awt.event.WindowAdapter;
3.  import java.awt.event.WindowEvent;
4.  import javax.swing.BoxLayout;
5.  import javax.swing.JFrame;
6.  public class ObserverGui{
7.      public void createGui(){
8.          JFrame mainFrame = new JFrame("Observer Pattern Example");
9.          Container content = mainFrame.getContentPane();
10.         content.setLayout(new BoxLayout(content, BoxLayout.Y_AXIS));
11.         TaskChangeObservable observable = new TaskChangeObservable();
12.         TaskSelectorPanel select = new TaskSelectorPanel(observable);
13.         TaskHistoryPanel history = new TaskHistoryPanel();
14.         TaskEditorPanel edit = new TaskEditorPanel(observable);
15.         observable.addTaskChangeObserver(select);
16.         observable.addTaskChangeObserver(history);
17.         observable.addTaskChangeObserver(edit);
18.         observable.addTask(new Task());
19.         content.add(select);
20.         content.add(history);
21.         content.add(edit);
22.         mainFrame.addWindowListener(new WindowCloseManager());
23.         mainFrame.pack();
24.         mainFrame.setVisible(true);
25.     }
26.
```

```
27.         private class WindowCloseManager extends WindowAdapter{
28.             public void windowClosing(WindowEvent evt){
29.                 System.exit(0);
30.             }
31.         }
32.     }
```

Example A.92 TaskEditorPanel.java

```
1.      import java.awt.BorderLayout;
2.      import javax.swing.JPanel;
3.      import javax.swing.JLabel;
4.      import javax.swing.JTextField;
5.      import javax.swing.JButton;
6.      import java.awt.event.ActionEvent;
7.      import java.awt.event.ActionListener;
8.      import java.awt.GridLayout;
9.      public class TaskEditorPanel extends JPanel implements ActionListener,
          TaskChangeObserver{
10.         private JPanel controlPanel, editPanel;
11.         private JButton add, update, exit;
12.         private JTextField taskName, taskNotes, taskTime;
13.         private TaskChangeObservable notifier;
14.         private Task editTask;
15.
16.         public TaskEditorPanel(TaskChangeObservable newNotifier){
17.             notifier = newNotifier;
18.             createGui();
19.         }
20.         public void createGui(){
21.             setLayout(new BorderLayout());
22.             editPanel = new JPanel();
23.             editPanel.setLayout(new GridLayout(3, 2));
24.             taskName = new JTextField(20);
25.             taskNotes = new JTextField(20);
26.             taskTime = new JTextField(20);
27.             editPanel.add(new JLabel("Task Name"));
28.             editPanel.add(taskName);
29.             editPanel.add(new JLabel("Task Notes"));
30.             editPanel.add(taskNotes);
31.             editPanel.add(new JLabel("Time Required"));
32.             editPanel.add(taskTime);
33.
34.             controlPanel = new JPanel();
35.             add = new JButton("Add Task");
36.             update = new JButton("Update Task");
37.             exit = new JButton("Exit");
38.             controlPanel.add(add);
39.             controlPanel.add(update);
40.             controlPanel.add(exit);
41.             add.addActionListener(this);
42.             update.addActionListener(this);
43.             exit.addActionListener(this);
```

```
44.             add(controlPanel, BorderLayout.SOUTH);
45.             add(editPanel, BorderLayout.CENTER);
46.         }
47.         public void setTaskChangeObservable(TaskChangeObservable newNotifier){
48.             notifier = newNotifier;
49.         }
50.         public void actionPerformed(ActionEvent event){
51.             Object source = event.getSource();
52.             if (source == add){
53.                 double timeRequired = 0.0;
54.                 try{
55.                     timeRequired = Double.parseDouble(taskTime.getText());
56.                 }
57.                 catch (NumberFormatException exc){}
58.              notifier.addTask(new Task(taskName.getText(), taskNotes.getText(), tim-
        eRequired));
59.             }
60.             else if (source == update){
61.                 editTask.setName(taskName.getText());
62.                 editTask.setNotes(taskNotes.getText());
63.                 try{
64.                    editTask.setTimeRequired(Double.parseDouble(taskTime.getText()));
65.                 }
66.                 catch (NumberFormatException exc){}
67.                 notifier.updateTask(editTask);
68.             }
69.             else if (source == exit){
70.                 System.exit(0);
71.             }
72.
73.         }
74.         public void taskAdded(Task task){ }
75.         public void taskChanged(Task task){ }
76.         public void taskSelected(Task task){
77.             editTask = task;
78.             taskName.setText(task.getName());
79.             taskNotes.setText(task.getNotes());
80.             taskTime.setText("" + task.getTimeRequired());
81.         }
82.     }
```

Example A.93 TaskHistoryPanel.java

```
1.     import java.awt.BorderLayout;
2.     import javax.swing.JPanel;
3.     import javax.swing.JScrollPane;
4.     import javax.swing.JTextArea;
5.     public class TaskHistoryPanel extends JPanel implements TaskChangeObserver{
6.         private JTextArea displayRegion;
7.
8.         public TaskHistoryPanel(){
9.             createGui();
10.        }
```

```
11.         public void createGui(){
12.             setLayout(new BorderLayout());
13.             displayRegion = new JTextArea(10, 40);
14.             displayRegion.setEditable(false);
15.             add(new JScrollPane(displayRegion));
16.         }
17.         public void taskAdded(Task task){
18.             displayRegion.append("Created task " + task + "\n");
19.         }
20.         public void taskChanged(Task task){
21.             displayRegion.append("Updated task " + task + "\n");
22.         }
23.         public void taskSelected(Task task){
24.             displayRegion.append("Selected task " + task + "\n");
25.         }
26.     }
```

Example A.94 `TaskSelectorPanel.java`

```
1.      import java.awt.event.ActionEvent;
2.      import java.awt.event.ActionListener;
3.      import javax.swing.JPanel;
4.      import javax.swing.JComboBox;
5.      public class TaskSelectorPanel extends JPanel implements ActionListener,
          TaskChangeObserver{
6.          private JComboBox selector = new JComboBox();
7.          private TaskChangeObservable notifier;
8.          public TaskSelectorPanel(TaskChangeObservable newNotifier){
9.              notifier = newNotifier;
10.             createGui();
11.         }
12.         public void createGui(){
13.             selector = new JComboBox();
14.             selector.addActionListener(this);
15.             add(selector);
16.         }
17.         public void actionPerformed(ActionEvent evt){
18.             notifier.selectTask((Task)selector.getSelectedItem());
19.         }
20.         public void setTaskChangeObservable(TaskChangeObservable newNotifier){
21.             notifier = newNotifier;
22.         }
23.
24.         public void taskAdded(Task task){
25.             selector.addItem(task);
26.         }
27.         public void taskChanged(Task task){ }
28.         public void taskSelected(Task task){ }
29.     }
```

A feature of the Observer pattern is that the `Observable` uses a standard interface for its `Observers`—in this case, `TaskChangeObserver`. This means that the Observer pattern is more generic than the Mediator pattern, but also that the observers may receive some unwanted message traffic. For instance, the `TaskEditorPanel` takes no action when its `taskAdded` and `taskChanged` methods are called.

The `Task` class represents the business object in the GUI, which in this demonstration is a simple job.

Example A.95 `Task.java`

```
1.    public class Task{
2.        private String name = "";
3.        private String notes = "";
4.        private double timeRequired;
5.
6.        public Task(){ }
7.        public Task(String newName, String newNotes, double newTimeRequired){
8.            name = newName;
9.            notes = newNotes;
10.           timeRequired = newTimeRequired;
11.       }
12.
13.       public String getName(){ return name; }
14.       public String getNotes(){ return notes; }
15.       public double getTimeRequired(){ return timeRequired; }
16.       public void setName(String newName){ name = newName; }
17.       public void setTimeRequired(double newTimeRequired){ timeRequired = newTimeRe-
      quired; }
18.       public void setNotes(String newNotes){ notes = newNotes; }
19.       public String toString(){ return name + " " + notes; }
20.   }
```

`RunPattern` creates the GUI for this example, creating the observable and its observers in the process.

Example A.96 `RunPattern.java`

```
1.    public class RunPattern{
2.        public static void main(String [] arguments){
3.            System.out.println("Example for the Observer pattern");
4.            System.out.println("This demonstration uses a central observable");
5.            System.out.println(" object to send change notifications to several");
6.            System.out.println(" JPanels in a GUI. Each JPanel is an Observer,");
7.            System.out.println(" receiving notifcations when there has been some");
8.            System.out.println(" change in the shared Task that is being edited.");
9.            System.out.println();
10.
11.           System.out.println("Creating the ObserverGui");
12.           ObserverGui application = new ObserverGui();
13.           application.createGui();
14.       }
15.   }
```

State

Inner classes are most appropriate for States. They are very closely coupled with their enclosing class and have direct access to its attributes. The following example shows how this works in practice.

A standard feature of applications is that they only save files when necessary: when changes have been made. When changes have been made but a file has not been saved, its state is referred to as *dirty*. The content might be different from the persistent, saved version. When the file has been saved and no further changes have been made, the content is considered *clean*. For a clean state, the content and the file will be identical if no one else edits the file.

This example shows the State pattern being used to update `Appointments` for the PIM, saving them to a file as necessary. The State transition diagram for a file is shown in Figure A.1.

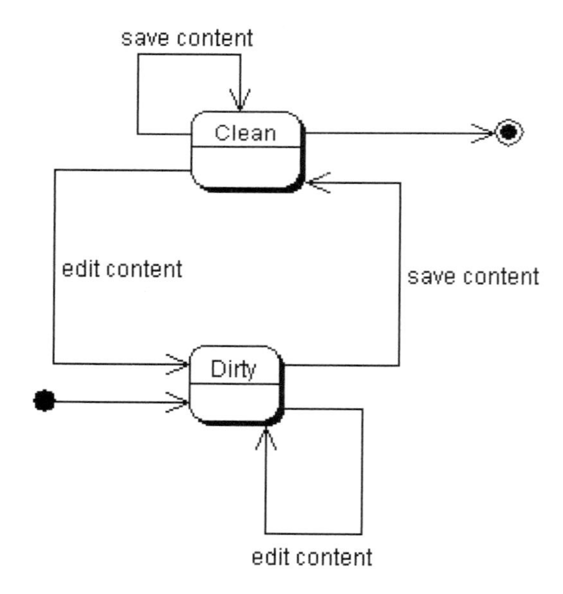

Figure A.1 *State transition diagram for a file*

Two states (`CleanState` and `DirtyState`) implement the `State` interface. The states are responsible for determining the next state, which in this case is reasonably easy, as there are only two.

The `State` interface defines two methods, `save` and `edit`. These methods are called by the `CalendarEditor` when appropriate.

Example A.97 `State.java`

```
1.    public interface State{
2.        public void save();
3.        public void edit();
4.    }
```

The `CalendarEditor` class manages a collection of `Appointment` objects.

Example A.98 `CalendarEditor.java`

```
1.    import java.io.File;
2.    import java.util.ArrayList;
3.    public class CalendarEditor{
4.        private State currentState;
5.        private File appointmentFile;
6.        private ArrayList appointments = new ArrayList();
7.        private static final String DEFAULT_APPOINTMENT_FILE = "appointments.ser";
8.
9.        public CalendarEditor(){
10.           this(DEFAULT_APPOINTMENT_FILE);
11.       }
12.       public CalendarEditor(String appointmentFileName){
13.           appointmentFile = new File(appointmentFileName);
14.           try{
15.               appointments = (ArrayList)FileLoader.loadData(appointmentFile);
16.           }
17.           catch (ClassCastException exc){
18.             System.err.println("Unable to load information. The file does not con-
    tain a list of appointments.");
19.           }
20.           currentState = new CleanState();
21.       }
22.
23.       public void save(){
24.           currentState.save();
25.       }
26.
27.       public void edit(){
28.           currentState.edit();
29.       }
30.
31.       private class DirtyState implements State{
32.           private State nextState;
33.
34.           public DirtyState(State nextState){
35.               this.nextState = nextState;
36.           }
37.
38.           public void save(){
39.               FileLoader.storeData(appointmentFile, appointments);
40.               currentState = nextState;
41.           }
```

```
42.            public void edit(){ }
43.        }
44.
45.        private class CleanState implements State{
46.            private State nextState = new DirtyState(this);
47.
48.            public void save(){ }
49.            public void edit(){ currentState = nextState; }
50.        }
51.
52.        public ArrayList getAppointments(){
53.            return appointments;
54.        }
55.
56.        public void addAppointment(Appointment appointment){
57.            if (!appointments.contains(appointment)){
58.                appointments.add(appointment);
59.            }
60.        }
61.        public void removeAppointment(Appointment appointment){
62.            appointments.remove(appointment);
63.        }
64.    }
```

The class `StateGui` provides an editing interface for the `CalendarEditor's` appointments. Notice that the GUI has a reference to the `CalendarEditor`, and that it delegates and edit or save actions to the editor. This allows the editor to perform the required actions and to update its state as appropriate.

Example A.99 `StateGui.java`

```
1.    import java.awt.Container;
2.    import java.awt.BorderLayout;
3.    import java.awt.event.ActionListener;
4.    import java.awt.event.WindowAdapter;
5.    import java.awt.event.ActionEvent;
6.    import java.awt.event.WindowEvent;
7.    import javax.swing.BoxLayout;
8.    import javax.swing.JButton;
9.    import javax.swing.JComponent;
10.   import javax.swing.JFrame;
11.   import javax.swing.JPanel;
12.   import javax.swing.JScrollPane;
13.   import javax.swing.JTable;
14.   import javax.swing.table.AbstractTableModel;
15.   import java.util.Date;
16.   public class StateGui implements ActionListener{
17.       private JFrame mainFrame;
18.       private JPanel controlPanel, editPanel;
19.       private CalendarEditor editor;
20.       private JButton save, exit;
21.
```

```
22.        public StateGui(CalendarEditor edit){
23.            editor = edit;
24.        }
25.
26.        public void createGui(){
27.            mainFrame = new JFrame("State Pattern Example");
28.            Container content = mainFrame.getContentPane();
29.            content.setLayout(new BoxLayout(content, BoxLayout.Y_AXIS));
30.
31.            editPanel = new JPanel();
32.            editPanel.setLayout(new BorderLayout());
33.            JTable appointmentTable = new JTable(new StateTableModel((Appointment
       [])editor.getAppointments().toArray(new Appointment[1])));
34.            editPanel.add(new JScrollPane(appointmentTable));
35.            content.add(editPanel);
36.
37.            controlPanel = new JPanel();
38.            save = new JButton("Save Appointments");
39.            exit = new JButton("Exit");
40.            controlPanel.add(save);
41.            controlPanel.add(exit);
42.            content.add(controlPanel);
43.
44.            save.addActionListener(this);
45.            exit.addActionListener(this);
46.
47.            mainFrame.addWindowListener(new WindowCloseManager());
48.            mainFrame.pack();
49.            mainFrame.setVisible(true);
50.        }
51.
52.
53.        public void actionPerformed(ActionEvent evt){
54.            Object originator = evt.getSource();
55.            if (originator == save){
56.                saveAppointments();
57.            }
58.            else if (originator == exit){
59.                exitApplication();
60.            }
61.        }
62.
63.        private class WindowCloseManager extends WindowAdapter{
64.            public void windowClosing(WindowEvent evt){
65.                exitApplication();
66.            }
67.        }
68.
69.        private void saveAppointments(){
70.            editor.save();
71.        }
72.
73.        private void exitApplication(){
74.            System.exit(0);
```

```
75.         }
76.
77.         private class StateTableModel extends AbstractTableModel{
78.             private final String [] columnNames = {
79.                 "Appointment", "Contacts", "Location", "Start Date", "End Date" };
80.             private Appointment [] data;
81.
82.             public StateTableModel(Appointment [] appointments){
83.                 data = appointments;
84.             }
85.
86.             public String getColumnName(int column){
87.                 return columnNames[column];
88.             }
89.             public int getRowCount(){ return data.length; }
90.             public int getColumnCount(){ return columnNames.length; }
91.             public Object getValueAt(int row, int column){
92.                 Object value = null;
93.                 switch(column){
94.                     case 0: value = data[row].getReason();
95.                         break;
96.                     case 1: value = data[row].getContacts();
97.                         break;
98.                     case 2: value = data[row].getLocation();
99.                         break;
100.                    case 3: value = data[row].getStartDate();
101.                        break;
102.                    case 4: value = data[row].getEndDate();
103.                        break;
104.                }
105.                return value;
106.            }
107.            public boolean isCellEditable(int row, int column){
108.                return ((column == 0) || (column == 2)) ? true : false;
109.            }
110.            public void setValueAt(Object value, int row, int column){
111.                switch(column){
112.                    case 0: data[row].setReason((String)value);
113.                        editor.edit();
114.                        break;
115.                    case 1:
116.                        break;
117.                    case 2: data[row].setLocation(new LocationImpl((String)value));
118.                        editor.edit();
119.                        break;
120.                    case 3:
121.                        break;
122.                    case 4:
123.                        break;
124.                }
125.            }
126.        }
127. }
```

Five business support classes and interfaces are used in this example: Appointment, Contact, ContactImpl, Location, and LocationImpl.

Example A.100 Appointment.java

```
1.  import java.io.Serializable;
2.  import java.util.Date;
3.  import java.util.ArrayList;
4.  public class Appointment implements Serializable{
5.      private String reason;
6.      private ArrayList contacts;
7.      private Location location;
8.      private Date startDate;
9.      private Date endDate;
10.
11.     public Appointment(String reason, ArrayList contacts, Location location, Date
    startDate, Date endDate){
12.         this.reason = reason;
13.         this.contacts = contacts;
14.         this.location = location;
15.         this.startDate = startDate;
16.         this.endDate = endDate;
17.     }
18.
19.     public String getReason(){ return reason; }
20.     public ArrayList getContacts(){ return contacts; }
21.     public Location getLocation(){ return location; }
22.     public Date getStartDate(){ return startDate; }
23.     public Date getEndDate(){ return endDate; }
24.
25.     public void setReason(String reason){ this.reason = reason; }
26.     public void setContacts(ArrayList contacts){ this.contacts = contacts; }
27.     public void setLocation(Location location){ this.location = location; }
28.     public void setStartDate(Date startDate){ this.startDate = startDate; }
29.     public void setEndDate(Date endDate){ this.endDate = endDate; }
30.
31.     public String toString(){
32.         return "Appointment:" + "\n    Reason: " + reason +
33. "\n    Location: " + location + "\n    Start: " +
34.             startDate + "\n    End: " + endDate + "\n";
35.     }
36. }
```

Example A.101 Contact.java

```
1.  import java.io.Serializable;
2.  public interface Contact extends Serializable{
3.      public static final String SPACE = " ";
4.      public String getFirstName();
5.      public String getLastName();
6.      public String getTitle();
```

```
7.        public String getOrganization();
8.
9.        public void setFirstName(String newFirstName);
10.       public void setLastName(String newLastName);
11.       public void setTitle(String newTitle);
12.       public void setOrganization(String newOrganization);
13.   }
```

Example A.102 `ContactImpl.java`

```
1.    public class ContactImpl implements Contact{
2.        private String firstName;
3.        private String lastName;
4.        private String title;
5.        private String organization;
6.
7.        public ContactImpl(){}
8.        public ContactImpl(String newFirstName, String newLastName,
9.            String newTitle, String newOrganization){
10.               firstName = newFirstName;
11.               lastName = newLastName;
12.               title = newTitle;
13.               organization = newOrganization;
14.       }
15.
16.       public String getFirstName(){ return firstName; }
17.       public String getLastName(){ return lastName; }
18.       public String getTitle(){ return title; }
19.       public String getOrganization(){ return organization; }
20.
21.       public void setFirstName(String newFirstName){ firstName = newFirstName; }
22.       public void setLastName(String newLastName){ lastName = newLastName; }
23.       public void setTitle(String newTitle){ title = newTitle; }
24.       public void setOrganization(String newOrganization){ organization = newOrgani-
      zation; }
25.
26.       public String toString(){
27.           return firstName + SPACE + lastName;
28.       }
29.   }
```

Example A.103 `Location.java`

```
1.    import java.io.Serializable;
2.    public interface Location extends Serializable{
3.        public String getLocation();
4.        public void setLocation(String newLocation);
5.    }
```

Example A.104 `LocationImpl.java`

```
1.    public class LocationImpl implements Location{
2.        private String location;
```

```
3.
4.        public LocationImpl(){ }
5.        public LocationImpl(String newLocation){
6.            location = newLocation;
7.        }
8.
9.        public String getLocation(){ return location; }
10.
11.       public void setLocation(String newLocation){ location = newLocation; }
12.
13.       public String toString(){ return location; }
14.   }
```

DataCreator and FileLoader are used to create a sample set of Appointment objects, and to manage their storage and retrieval from a file.

Example A.105 DataCreator.java

```
1.    import java.io.Serializable;
2.    import java.io.ObjectOutputStream;
3.    import java.io.FileOutputStream;
4.    import java.io.IOException;
5.    import java.util.Calendar;
6.    import java.util.Date;
7.    import java.util.ArrayList;
8.    public class DataCreator{
9.        private static final String DEFAULT_FILE = "data.ser";
10.       private static Calendar dateCreator = Calendar.getInstance();
11.
12.       public static void main(String [] args){
13.           String fileName;
14.           if (args.length == 1){
15.               fileName = args[0];
16.           }
17.           else{
18.               fileName = DEFAULT_FILE;
19.           }
20.           serialize(fileName);
21.       }
22.
23.       public static void serialize(String fileName){
24.           try{
25.               serializeToFile(createData(), fileName);
26.           }
27.           catch (IOException exc){
28.               exc.printStackTrace();
29.           }
30.       }
31.
32.       private static Serializable createData(){
33.           ArrayList appointments = new ArrayList();
34.           ArrayList contacts = new ArrayList();
```

```
35.         contacts.add(new ContactImpl("Test", "Subject", "Volunteer", "United Pat-
        terns Consortium"));
36.         Location location1 = new LocationImpl("Punxsutawney, PA");
37.         appointments.add(new Appointment("Slowpokes anonymous", contacts,
        location1, createDate(2001, 1, 1, 12, 01), createDate(2001, 1, 1, 12, 02)));
38.         appointments.add(new Appointment("Java focus group", contacts, location1,
        createDate(2001, 1, 1, 12, 30), createDate(2001, 1, 1, 14, 30)));
39.         appointments.add(new Appointment("Something else", contacts, location1,
        createDate(2001, 1, 1, 12, 01), createDate(2001, 1, 1, 12, 02)));
40.         appointments.add(new Appointment("Yet another thingie", contacts,
        location1, createDate(2001, 1, 1, 12, 01), createDate(2001, 1, 1, 12, 02)));
41.         return appointments;
42.     }
43.
44.     private static void serializeToFile(Serializable content, String fileName)
        throws IOException{
45.         ObjectOutputStream serOut = new ObjectOutputStream(new FileOutput-
        Stream(fileName));
46.         serOut.writeObject(content);
47.         serOut.close();
48.     }
49.
50.     public static Date createDate(int year, int month, int day, int hour, int
        minute){
51.         dateCreator.set(year, month, day, hour, minute);
52.         return dateCreator.getTime();
53.     }
54. }
```

Example A.106 `FileLoader.java`

```
1.  import java.io.File;
2.  import java.io.FileInputStream;
3.  import java.io.FileOutputStream;
4.  import java.io.IOException;
5.  import java.io.ObjectInputStream;
6.  import java.io.ObjectOutputStream;
7.  import java.io.Serializable;
8.  public class FileLoader{
9.      public static Object loadData(File inputFile){
10.         Object returnValue = null;
11.         try{
12.             if (inputFile.exists()){
13.                 if (inputFile.isFile()){
14.                  ObjectInputStream readIn = new ObjectInputStream(new FileInput-
        Stream(inputFile));
15.                     returnValue = readIn.readObject();
16.                     readIn.close();
17.                 }
18.                 else {
19.                     System.err.println(inputFile + " is a directory.");
20.                 }
21.             }
22.             else {
23.                 System.err.println("File " + inputFile + " does not exist.");
```

```
24.                }
25.            }
26.            catch (ClassNotFoundException exc){
27.                exc.printStackTrace();
28.
29.            }
30.            catch (IOException exc){
31.                exc.printStackTrace();
32.
33.            }
34.            return returnValue;
35.        }
36.        public static void storeData(File outputFile, Serializable data){
37.            try{
38.                ObjectOutputStream writeOut = new ObjectOutputStream(new FileOutput-
      Stream(outputFile));
39.                writeOut.writeObject(data);
40.                writeOut.close();
41.            }
42.            catch (IOException exc){
43.                exc.printStackTrace();
44.            }
45.        }
46.    }
```

RunPattern runs the demonstration, creating a CalendarEditor object (which retrieves its initial entries from the file with test Appointments) and matching it with a StateGui object.

Example A.107 RunPattern.java

```
1.    import java.io.File;
2.    public class RunPattern{
3.        public static void main(String [] arguments){
4.            System.out.println("Example for the State pattern");
5.            System.out.println();
6.
7.            if (!(new File("appointments.ser").exists())){
8.                DataCreator.serialize("appointments.ser");
9.            }
10.
11.           System.out.println("Creating CalendarEditor");
12.           CalendarEditor appointmentBook = new CalendarEditor();
13.           System.out.println("");
14.
15.           System.out.println("Created. Appointments:");
16.           System.out.println(appointmentBook.getAppointments());
17.
18.           System.out.println("Created. Creating GUI:");
19.           StateGui application = new StateGui(appointmentBook);
20.           application.createGui();
21.           System.out.println("");
22.       }
23.   }
```

Strategy

For many of the collections in the Personal Information Manager, it would be useful to be able to organize and summarize individual entries. This demonstration uses the Strategy pattern to summarize entries in a ContactList, a collection used to store Contact objects.

Example A.108 ContactList.java

```
1.  import java.io.Serializable;
2.  import java.util.ArrayList;
3.  public class ContactList implements Serializable{
4.      private ArrayList contacts = new ArrayList();
5.      private SummarizingStrategy summarizer;
6.
7.      public ArrayList getContacts(){ return contacts; }
8.      public Contact [] getContactsAsArray(){ return (Contact [])(contacts.toAr-
    ray(new Contact [1])); }
9.
10.     public void setSummarizer(SummarizingStrategy newSummarizer){ summarizer =
    newSummarizer; }
11.     public void setContacts(ArrayList newContacts){ contacts = newContacts; }
12.
13.     public void addContact(Contact element){
14.         if (!contacts.contains(element)){
15.             contacts.add(element);
16.         }
17.     }
18.     public void removeContact(Contact element){
19.         contacts.remove(element);
20.     }
21.
22.     public String summarize(){
23.         return summarizer.summarize(getContactsAsArray());
24.     }
25.
26.     public String [] makeSummarizedList(){
27.         return summarizer.makeSummarizedList(getContactsAsArray());
28.     }
29. }
```

The ContactList has two methods, which can be used to provide summary information for the Contact objects in the collection—summarize and makeSummarizedList. Both methods delegate to a SummarizingStrategy, which can be set for the ContactList with the setSummarizer method.

Example A.109 SummarizingStrategy.java

```
1.  public interface SummarizingStrategy{
2.      public static final String EOL_STRING = System.getProperty("line.separator");
3.      public static final String DELIMITER = ":";
```

```
4.        public static final String COMMA = ",";
5.        public static final String SPACE = " ";
6.
7.        public String summarize(Contact [] contactList);
8.        public String [] makeSummarizedList(Contact [] contactList);
9.    }
```

SummarizingStrategy is an interface that defines the two delegate methods summarize and makeSummarizedList. The interface represents the Strategy in the design pattern. In this example, two classes represent ConcreteStrategy objects: NameSummarizer and OrganizationSummarizer. Both classes summarize the list of contacts; however, each provides a different set of information and groups the data differently.

The NameSummarizer class returns only the names of the contacts with the last name first. The class uses an inner class as a comparator (NameComparator) to ensure that all of the Contact entries are grouped in ascending order by both last and first name.

Example A.110 NameSummarizer.java

```
1.    import java.text.Collator;
2.    import java.util.Arrays;
3.    import java.util.Comparator;
4.    public class NameSummarizer implements SummarizingStrategy{
5.        private Comparator comparator = new NameComparator();
6.
7.        public String summarize(Contact [] contactList){
8.            StringBuffer product = new StringBuffer();
9.            Arrays.sort(contactList, comparator);
10.           for (int i = 0; i < contactList.length; i++){
11.               product.append(contactList[i].getLastName());
12.               product.append(COMMA);
13.               product.append(SPACE);
14.               product.append(contactList[i].getFirstName());
15.               product.append(EOL_STRING);
16.           }
17.           return product.toString();
18.       }
19.
20.       public String [] makeSummarizedList(Contact [] contactList){
21.           Arrays.sort(contactList, comparator);
22.           String [] product = new String[contactList.length];
23.           for (int i = 0; i < contactList.length; i++){
24.               product[i] = contactList[i].getLastName() + COMMA + SPACE +
25.                            contactList[i].getFirstName() + EOL_STRING;
26.           }
27.           return product;
28.       }
29.
30.       private class NameComparator implements Comparator{
31.           private Collator textComparator = Collator.getInstance();
```

```
32.
33.            public int compare(Object o1, Object o2){
34.                Contact c1, c2;
35.                if ((o1 instanceof Contact) && (o2 instanceof Contact)){
36.                    c1 = (Contact)o1;
37.                    c2 = (Contact)o2;
38.                    int compareResult = textComparator.compare(c1.getLastName(),
       c2.getLastName());
39.                    if (compareResult == 0){
40.                        compareResult = textComparator.compare(c1.getFirstName(),
       c2.getFirstName());
41.                    }
42.                    return compareResult;
43.                }
44.                else return textComparator.compare(o1, o2);
45.            }
46.
47.            public boolean equals(Object o){
48.                return textComparator.equals(o);
49.            }
50.        }
51.    }
```

OrganizationSummarizer returns a summary with a Contact's organization, followed by their first and last name. The comparator used to order the Contact objects returns entries with ascending organization, then ascending last name.

Example A.111 OrganizationSummarizer.java

```
1.     import java.text.Collator;
2.     import java.util.Arrays;
3.     import java.util.Comparator;
4.     public class OrganizationSummarizer implements SummarizingStrategy{
5.         private Comparator comparator = new OrganizationComparator();
6.
7.         public String summarize(Contact [] contactList){
8.             StringBuffer product = new StringBuffer();
9.             Arrays.sort(contactList, comparator);
10.            for (int i = 0; i < contactList.length; i++){
11.                product.append(contactList[i].getOrganization());
12.                product.append(DELIMITER);
13.                product.append(SPACE);
14.                product.append(contactList[i].getFirstName());
15.                product.append(SPACE);
16.                product.append(contactList[i].getLastName());
17.                product.append(EOL_STRING);
18.            }
19.            return product.toString();
20.        }
21.
22.        public String [] makeSummarizedList(Contact [] contactList){
```

```
23.            Arrays.sort(contactList, comparator);
24.            String [] product = new String[contactList.length];
25.            for (int i = 0; i < contactList.length; i++){
26.                product[i] = contactList[i].getOrganization() + DELIMITER + SPACE +
27.                             contactList[i].getFirstName() + SPACE +
28.                             contactList[i].getLastName() + EOL_STRING;
29.            }
30.            return product;
31.        }
32.
33.        private class OrganizationComparator implements Comparator{
34.            private Collator textComparator = Collator.getInstance();
35.
36.            public int compare(Object o1, Object o2){
37.                Contact c1, c2;
38.                if ((o1 instanceof Contact) && (o2 instanceof Contact)){
39.                    c1 = (Contact)o1;
40.                    c2 = (Contact)o2;
41.                    int compareResult = textComparator.compare(c1.getOrganization(),
    c2.getOrganization());
42.                    if (compareResult == 0){
43.                        compareResult = textComparator.compare(c1.getLastName(),
    c2.getLastName());
44.                    }
45.                    return compareResult;
46.                }
47.                else return textComparator.compare(o1, o2);
48.            }
49.
50.            public boolean equals(Object o){
51.                return textComparator.equals(o);
52.            }
53.        }
54.    }
```

The ContactList uses the Contact interface and its implementer, ContactImpl, to represent individual contacts.

Example A.112 Contact.java

```
1.    import java.io.Serializable;
2.    public interface Contact extends Serializable{
3.        public static final String SPACE = " ";
4.        public String getFirstName();
5.        public String getLastName();
6.        public String getTitle();
7.        public String getOrganization();
8.
9.        public void setFirstName(String newFirstName);
10.       public void setLastName(String newLastName);
11.       public void setTitle(String newTitle);
12.       public void setOrganization(String newOrganization);
13.   }
```

Example A.113 `ContactImpl.java`

```
1.  public class ContactImpl implements Contact{
2.      private String firstName;
3.      private String lastName;
4.      private String title;
5.      private String organization;
6.
7.      public ContactImpl(){}
8.      public ContactImpl(String newFirstName, String newLastName,
9.          String newTitle, String newOrganization){
10.             firstName = newFirstName;
11.             lastName = newLastName;
12.             title = newTitle;
13.             organization = newOrganization;
14.     }
15.
16.     public String getFirstName(){ return firstName; }
17.     public String getLastName(){ return lastName; }
18.     public String getTitle(){ return title; }
19.     public String getOrganization(){ return organization; }
20.
21.     public void setFirstName(String newFirstName){ firstName = newFirstName; }
22.     public void setLastName(String newLastName){ lastName = newLastName; }
23.     public void setTitle(String newTitle){ title = newTitle; }
24.     public void setOrganization(String newOrganization){ organization = newOrgani-
    zation; }
25.
26.     public String toString(){
27.         return firstName + SPACE + lastName;
28.     }
29. }
```

The `DataCreator` and `DataRetriever` classes are used to create and retrieve a test group of contacts for use in the example.

Example A.114 `DataCreator.java`

```
1.  import java.io.Serializable;
2.  import java.io.ObjectOutputStream;
3.  import java.io.FileOutputStream;
4.  import java.io.IOException;
5.  public class DataCreator{
6.      private static final String DEFAULT_FILE = "data.ser";
7.
8.      public static void main(String [] args){
9.          String fileName;
10.         if (args.length == 1){
11.             fileName = args[0];
12.         }
13.         else{
14.             fileName = DEFAULT_FILE;
```

```
15.             }
16.             serialize(fileName);
17.         }
18.
19.         public static void serialize(String fileName){
20.             try{
21.                 serializeToFile(makeContactList(), fileName);
22.             }
23.             catch (IOException exc){
24.                 exc.printStackTrace();
25.             }
26.         }
27.
28.         private static Serializable makeContactList(){
29.             ContactList list = new ContactList();
30.             list.addContact(new ContactImpl("David", "St. Hubbins", "Lead Guitar", "The
        New Originals"));
31.             list.addContact(new ContactImpl("Mick", "Shrimpton", "Drummer", "The New
        Originals"));
32.             list.addContact(new ContactImpl("Nigel", "Tufnel", "Lead Guitar", "The New
        Originals"));
33.             list.addContact(new ContactImpl("Derek", "Smalls", "Bass", "The New Origi-
        nals"));
34.             list.addContact(new ContactImpl("Viv", "Savage", "Keyboards", "The New
        Originals"));
35.             list.addContact(new ContactImpl("Nick", "Shrimpton", "CEO", "Fishy Busi-
        ness, LTD"));
36.             list.addContact(new ContactImpl("Nickolai", "Lobachevski", "Senior
        Packer", "Fishy Business, LTD"));
37.             list.addContact(new ContactImpl("Alan", "Robertson", "Comptroller", "Uni-
        versal Exports"));
38.             list.addContact(new ContactImpl("William", "Telle", "President", "Univer-
        sal Exports"));
39.             list.addContact(new ContactImpl("Harvey", "Manfredjensenden", "Inspector",
        "Universal Imports"));
40.             list.addContact(new ContactImpl("Deirdre", "Pine", "Chief Mechanic", "The
        Universal Joint"));
41.             list.addContact(new ContactImpl("Martha", "Crump-Pinnett", "Lead Devel-
        oper", "Avatar Inc."));
42.             list.addContact(new ContactImpl("Bryan", "Basham", "CTO", "IOVA"));
43.             return list;
44.         }
45.
46.         private static void serializeToFile(Serializable content, String fileName)
        throws IOException{
47.             ObjectOutputStream serOut = new ObjectOutputStream(new FileOutput-
        Stream(fileName));
48.             serOut.writeObject(content);
49.             serOut.close();
50.         }
51.     }
```

Example A.115 `DataRetriever.java`

```
1.  import java.io.File;
2.  import java.io.FileInputStream;
3.  import java.io.IOException;
4.  import java.io.ObjectInputStream;
5.
6.  public class DataRetriever{
7.      public static Object deserializeData(String fileName){
8.          Object returnValue = null;
9.          try{
10.             File inputFile = new File(fileName);
11.             if (inputFile.exists() && inputFile.isFile()){
12.                 ObjectInputStream readIn = new ObjectInputStream(new FileInput-
    Stream(fileName));
13.                 returnValue = readIn.readObject();
14.                 readIn.close();
15.             }
16.             else {
17.                 System.err.println("Unable to locate the file " + fileName);
18.             }
19.         }
20.         catch (ClassNotFoundException exc){
21.             exc.printStackTrace();
22.
23.         }
24.         catch (IOException exc){
25.             exc.printStackTrace();
26.
27.         }
28.         return returnValue;
29.     }
30. }
```

`RunPattern` demonstrates how the Strategy works by first creating a `ContactList`, then printing out its entries with each of the two `SummarizingStrategy` objects.

Example A.116 `RunPattern.java`

```
1.  import java.io.File;
2.  public class RunPattern{
3.      public static void main(String [] arguments){
4.          System.out.println("Example for the Strategy pattern");
5.          System.out.println();
6.         System.out.println("This code uses two Strategy classes, NameSummarizer and
    OrganizationSummarizer,");
7.          System.out.println(" to provide a sorted, summarized list for a Con-
    tactList. The ContactList object");
8.         System.out.println(" maintains a collection of Contacts, and delegates the
    task of representing");
9.          System.out.println(" its information to an associated object which imple-
    ments SummarizingStrategy.");
```

```
10.             System.out.println();
11.
12.             System.out.println("Deserializing stored ContactList from the data.ser
        file");
13.             System.out.println();
14.             if (!(new File("data.ser").exists())){
15.                 DataCreator.serialize("data.ser");
16.             }
17.             ContactList list = (ContactList)(DataRetriever.deserialize-
        Data("data.ser"));
18.
19.             System.out.println("Creating NameSummarizer for the ContactList");
20.             System.out.println("(this Strategy displays only the last and first
        name,");
21.             System.out.println(" and sorts the list by last name, followed by the
        first)");
22.             list.setSummarizer(new NameSummarizer());
23.
24.             System.out.println("Name Summarizer Output for the ContactList:");
25.             System.out.println(list.summarize());
26.             System.out.println();
27.
28.             System.out.println("Creating OrganizationSummarizer for the ContactList");
29.             System.out.println("(this Strategy displays the organization, followed by
        the first");
30.             System.out.println(" and last name. It sorts by the organization, followed
        by last name)");
31.             list.setSummarizer(new OrganizationSummarizer());
32.
33.             System.out.println("Organization Summarizer Output for the ContactList:");
34.             System.out.println(list.summarize());
35.             System.out.println();
36.         }
37.     }
38.
```

Visitor

The Visitor pattern is often useful when operations must be performed over a large structure, and composite results must be calculated. In this demonstration, the Visitor pattern is used to calculate the total cost for a project.

Four classes are used to represent project elements, and all of the classes implement a common interface, `ProjectItem`. In this example, `ProjectItem` defines the `accept` method required to host a `Visitor`.

Example A.117 `ProjectItem.java`

```
1.    import java.io.Serializable;
2.    import java.util.ArrayList;
3.    public interface ProjectItem extends Serializable{
4.        public void accept(ProjectVisitor v);
5.        public ArrayList getProjectItems();
6.    }
```

The `Project` class represents the project itself, the `Deliverable` class a concrete product, the `Task`: a job of some sort. In addition, there is a subclass of `Task` called `DependentTask`. This class holds a set of other `Tasks` upon which it depends for its own completion.

Example A.118 `Deliverable.java`

```
1.    import java.util.ArrayList;
2.    public class Deliverable implements ProjectItem{
3.        private String name;
4.        private String description;
5.        private Contact owner;
6.        private double materialsCost;
7.        private double productionCost;
8.
9.        public Deliverable(){ }
10.       public Deliverable(String newName, String newDescription,
11.           Contact newOwner, double newMaterialsCost, double newProductionCost){
12.           name = newName;
13.           description = newDescription;
14.           owner = newOwner;
15.           materialsCost = newMaterialsCost;
16.           productionCost = newProductionCost;
17.       }
18.
19.       public String getName(){ return name; }
20.       public String getDescription(){ return description; }
21.       public Contact getOwner(){ return owner; }
22.       public double getMaterialsCost(){ return materialsCost; }
23.       public double getProductionCost(){ return productionCost; }
24.
25.       public void setMaterialsCost(double newCost){ materialsCost = newCost; }
```

```
26.       public void setProductionCost(double newCost){ productionCost = newCost; }
27.       public void setName(String newName){ name = newName; }
28.       public void setDescription(String newDescription){ description = newDescrip-
      tion; }
29.       public void setOwner(Contact newOwner){ owner = newOwner; }
30.
31.       public void accept(ProjectVisitor v){
32.           v.visitDeliverable(this);
33.       }
34.
35.       public ArrayList getProjectItems(){
36.           return null;
37.       }
38.   }
```

Example A.119 `DependentTask.java`

```
1.    import java.util.ArrayList;
2.    public class DependentTask extends Task{
3.        private ArrayList dependentTasks = new ArrayList();
4.        private double dependencyWeightingFactor;
5.
6.        public DependentTask(){ }
7.        public DependentTask(String newName, Contact newOwner,
8.            double newTimeRequired, double newWeightingFactor){
9.            super(newName, newOwner, newTimeRequired);
10.           dependencyWeightingFactor = newWeightingFactor;
11.       }
12.
13.       public ArrayList getDependentTasks(){ return dependentTasks; }
14.       public double getDependencyWeightingFactor(){ return dependencyWeightingFac-
      tor; }
15.
16.       public void setDependencyWeightingFactor(double newFactor){ dependencyWeight-
      ingFactor = newFactor; }
17.
18.       public void addDependentTask(Task element){
19.           if (!dependentTasks.contains(element)){
20.               dependentTasks.add(element);
21.           }
22.       }
23.
24.       public void removeDependentTask(Task element){
25.           dependentTasks.remove(element);
26.       }
27.
28.       public void accept(ProjectVisitor v){
29.           v.visitDependentTask(this);
30.       }
31.   }
```

Example A.120 Project.java

```
1.     import java.util.ArrayList;
2.     public class Project implements ProjectItem{
3.         private String name;
4.         private String description;
5.         private ArrayList projectItems = new ArrayList();
6.
7.         public Project(){ }
8.         public Project(String newName, String newDescription){
9.             name = newName;
10.            description = newDescription;
11.        }
12.
13.        public String getName(){ return name; }
14.        public String getDescription(){ return description; }
15.        public ArrayList getProjectItems(){ return projectItems; }
16.
17.        public void setName(String newName){ name = newName; }
18.        public void setDescription(String newDescription){ description = newDescrip-
       tion; }
19.
20.        public void addProjectItem(ProjectItem element){
21.            if (!projectItems.contains(element)){
22.                projectItems.add(element);
23.            }
24.        }
25.
26.        public void removeProjectItem(ProjectItem element){
27.            projectItems.remove(element);
28.        }
29.
30.        public void accept(ProjectVisitor v){
31.            v.visitProject(this);
32.        }
33.    }
```

Example A.121 Task.java

```
1.     import java.util.ArrayList;
2.     public class Task implements ProjectItem{
3.         private String name;
4.         private ArrayList projectItems = new ArrayList();
5.         private Contact owner;
6.         private double timeRequired;
7.
8.         public Task(){ }
9.         public Task(String newName, Contact newOwner,
10.            double newTimeRequired){
11.            name = newName;
12.            owner = newOwner;
13.            timeRequired = newTimeRequired;
14.        }
```

```
15.
16.        public String getName(){ return name; }
17.        public ArrayList getProjectItems(){ return projectItems; }
18.        public Contact getOwner(){ return owner; }
19.        public double getTimeRequired(){ return timeRequired; }
20.
21.        public void setName(String newName){ name = newName; }
22.        public void setOwner(Contact newOwner){ owner = newOwner; }
23.        public void setTimeRequired(double newTimeRequired){ timeRequired = newTimeRe-
       quired; }
24.
25.        public void addProjectItem(ProjectItem element){
26.            if (!projectItems.contains(element)){
27.                projectItems.add(element);
28.            }
29.        }
30.
31.        public void removeProjectItem(ProjectItem element){
32.            projectItems.remove(element);
33.        }
34.
35.        public void accept(ProjectVisitor v){
36.            v.visitTask(this);
37.        }
38.    }
```

The basic interface that defines the `Visitor` behavior is the `ProjectVisitor`. It defines a `visit` method for each of the project classes.

Example A.122 `ProjectVisitor.java`

```
1.    public interface ProjectVisitor{
2.        public void visitDependentTask(DependentTask p);
3.        public void visitDeliverable(Deliverable p);
4.        public void visitTask(Task p);
5.        public void visitProject(Project p);
6.    }
```

With this framework in place, you can define classes that implement the `ProjectVisitor` interface and perform some computation on project items. The class `ProjectCostVisitor` shows how project cost calculations could be managed.

Example A.123 `ProjectCostVisitor.java`

```
1.    public class ProjectCostVisitor implements ProjectVisitor{
2.        private double totalCost;
3.        private double hourlyRate;
4.
5.        public double getHourlyRate(){ return hourlyRate; }
6.        public double getTotalCost(){ return totalCost; }
```

```
7.
8.      public void setHourlyRate(double rate){ hourlyRate = rate; }
9.
10.     public void resetTotalCost(){ totalCost = 0.0; }
11.
12.     public void visitDependentTask(DependentTask p){
13.         double taskCost = p.getTimeRequired() * hourlyRate;
14.         taskCost *= p.getDependencyWeightingFactor();
15.         totalCost += taskCost;
16.     }
17.     public void visitDeliverable(Deliverable p){
18.         totalCost += p.getMaterialsCost() + p.getProductionCost();
19.     }
20.     public void visitTask(Task p){
21.         totalCost += p.getTimeRequired() * hourlyRate;
22.     }
23.     public void visitProject(Project p){ }
24. }
```

All behavior for the calculation, as well as variable storage, is centralized in the `Visitor` class. To add a new behavior, you would create a new class that implements `ProjectVisitor` and redefine the four `visit` methods.

The `Contact` interface and `ContactImpl` class represent the owner for a `Task` or `Deliverable`.

Example A.124 Contact.java

```
1.  import java.io.Serializable;
2.  public interface Contact extends Serializable{
3.      public static final String SPACE = " ";
4.      public String getFirstName();
5.      public String getLastName();
6.      public String getTitle();
7.      public String getOrganization();
8.
9.      public void setFirstName(String newFirstName);
10.     public void setLastName(String newLastName);
11.     public void setTitle(String newTitle);
12.     public void setOrganization(String newOrganization);
13. }
```

Example A.125 ContactImpl.java

```
1.  public class ContactImpl implements Contact{
2.      private String firstName;
3.      private String lastName;
4.      private String title;
5.      private String organization;
6.
7.      public ContactImpl(){}
8.      public ContactImpl(String newFirstName, String newLastName,
9.          String newTitle, String newOrganization){
```

```
10.             firstName = newFirstName;
11.             lastName = newLastName;
12.             title = newTitle;
13.             organization = newOrganization;
14.     }
15.
16.     public String getFirstName(){ return firstName; }
17.     public String getLastName(){ return lastName; }
18.     public String getTitle(){ return title; }
19.     public String getOrganization(){ return organization; }
20.
21.     public void setFirstName(String newFirstName){ firstName = newFirstName; }
22.     public void setLastName(String newLastName){ lastName = newLastName; }
23.     public void setTitle(String newTitle){ title = newTitle; }
24.     public void setOrganization(String newOrganization){ organization = newOrgani-
    zation; }
25.
26.     public String toString(){
27.         return firstName + SPACE + lastName;
28.     }
29. }
```

`DataCreator` is a support class which generates a sample `Project` and saves it to a file. The `DataRetriever` class loads the data from the file, restoring the saved `Project`.

Example A.126 `DataCreator.java`

```
1.  import java.io.Serializable;
2.  import java.io.ObjectOutputStream;
3.  import java.io.FileOutputStream;
4.  import java.io.IOException;
5.  public class DataCreator{
6.      private static final String DEFAULT_FILE = "data.ser";
7.
8.      public static void main(String [] args){
9.          String fileName;
10.         if (args.length == 1){
11.             fileName = args[0];
12.         }
13.         else{
14.             fileName = DEFAULT_FILE;
15.         }
16.         serialize(fileName);
17.     }
18.
19.     public static void serialize(String fileName){
20.         try{
21.             serializeToFile(createData(), fileName);
22.         }
23.         catch (IOException exc){
24.             exc.printStackTrace();
```

```
25.             }
26.         }
27.
28.         private static Serializable createData(){
29.             Contact contact = new ContactImpl("Test", "Subject", "Volunteer", "United
        Patterns Consortium");
30.
31.             Project project = new Project("Project 1", "Test Project");
32.
33.             Task task1 = new Task("Task 1", contact, 1);
34.             Task task2 = new Task("Task 2", contact, 1);
35.
36.             project.addProjectItem(new Deliverable("Deliverable 1", "Layer 1 deliver-
        able", contact, 50.0, 50.0));
37.             project.addProjectItem(task1);
38.             project.addProjectItem(task2);
39.             project.addProjectItem(new DependentTask("Dependent Task 1", contact, 1,
        1));
40.
41.             Task task3 = new Task("Task 3", contact, 1);
42.             Task task4 = new Task("Task 4", contact, 1);
43.             Task task5 = new Task("Task 5", contact, 1);
44.             Task task6 = new Task("Task 6", contact, 1);
45.
46.             DependentTask dtask2 = new DependentTask("Dependent Task 2", contact, 1,
        1);
47.
48.             task1.addProjectItem(task3);
49.             task1.addProjectItem(task4);
50.             task1.addProjectItem(task5);
51.             task1.addProjectItem(dtask2);
52.
53.             dtask2.addDependentTask(task5);
54.             dtask2.addDependentTask(task6);
55.             dtask2.addProjectItem(new Deliverable("Deliverable 2", "Layer 3 deliver-
        able", contact, 50.0, 50.0));
56.
57.             task3.addProjectItem(new Deliverable("Deliverable 3", "Layer 3 deliver-
        able", contact, 50.0, 50.0));
58.             task4.addProjectItem(new Task("Task 7", contact, 1));
59.             task4.addProjectItem(new Deliverable("Deliverable 4", "Layer 3 deliver-
        able", contact, 50.0, 50.0));
60.             return project;
61.         }
62.
63.         private static void serializeToFile(Serializable content, String fileName)
        throws IOException{
64.             ObjectOutputStream serOut = new ObjectOutputStream(new FileOutput-
        Stream(fileName));
65.             serOut.writeObject(content);
66.             serOut.close();
67.         }
68.     }
```

Example A.127 `DataRetriever.java`

```
1.   import java.io.Serializable;
2.   public interface Contact extends Serializable{
3.       public static final String SPACE = " ";
4.       public String getFirstName();
5.       public String getLastName();
6.       public String getTitle();
7.       public String getOrganization();
8.
9.       public void setFirstName(String newFirstName);
10.      public void setLastName(String newLastName);
11.      public void setTitle(String newTitle);
12.      public void setOrganization(String newOrganization);
13.  }
14.
```

`RunPattern` gives a demonstration of the `ProjectCostVisitor` in action. It retrieves a stored project, then iterates through all of the items of that project and calculates the total cost estimate.

Example A.128 `RunPattern.java`

```
1.   import java.io.Serializable;
2.   public interface Contact extends Serializable{
3.       public static final String SPACE = " ";
4.       public String getFirstName();
5.       public String getLastName();
6.       public String getTitle();
7.       public String getOrganization();
8.
9.       public void setFirstName(String newFirstName);
10.      public void setLastName(String newLastName);
11.      public void setTitle(String newTitle);
12.      public void setOrganization(String newOrganization);
13.  }
```

Template Method

This example uses project classes from the Personal Information Manager to illustrate the Template Method.

ProjectItem is the abstract class that defines the Template Method in this demonstration. Its method getCostEstimate returns a total value for the project item that is calculated using the following equation:

```
time estimate * hourly rate + materials cost
```

The hourly rate is defined in the ProjectItem class (using the rate variable, getter and setter methods in the class), but the methods getTimeRequired and getMaterialsCost are abstract. This requires the subclasses to override them, providing their own way to calculate the values.

Example A.129 ProjectItem.java

```
1.     import java.io.Serializable;
2.     public abstract class ProjectItem implements Serializable{
3.         private String name;
4.         private String description;
5.         private double rate;
6.
7.         public ProjectItem(){}
8.         public ProjectItem(String newName, String newDescription, double newRate){
9.             name = newName;
10.            description = newDescription;
11.            rate = newRate;
12.        }
13.
14.        public void setName(String newName){ name = newName; }
15.        public void setDescription(String newDescription){ description = newDescrip-
       tion; }
16.        public void setRate(double newRate){ rate = newRate; }
17.
18.        public String getName(){ return name; }
19.        public String getDescription(){ return description; }
20.        public final double getCostEstimate(){
21.            return getTimeRequired() * getRate() + getMaterialsCost();
22.        }
23.        public double getRate(){ return rate; }
24.
25.        public String toString(){ return getName(); }
26.
27.        public abstract double getTimeRequired();
28.        public abstract double getMaterialsCost();
29.    }
```

The Deliverable class represents a concrete product of some kind. Because it represents a physical item, the value returned by its getTimeRequired method is a fixed amount. Similarly, the `getMaterialsCost` method returns a fixed value.

Example A.130 `Deliverable.java`

```
1.     public class Deliverable extends ProjectItem{
2.         private double materialsCost;
3.         private double productionTime;
4.
5.         public Deliverable(){ }
6.         public Deliverable(String newName, String newDescription,
7.             double newMaterialsCost, double newProductionTime,
8.             double newRate){
9.             super(newName, newDescription, newRate);
10.            materialsCost = newMaterialsCost;
11.            productionTime = newProductionTime;
12.        }
13.
14.        public void setMaterialsCost(double newCost){ materialsCost = newCost; }
15.        public void setProductionTime(double newTime){ productionTime = newTime; }
16.
17.        public double getMaterialsCost(){ return materialsCost; }
18.        public double getTimeRequired(){ return productionTime; }
19.    }
```

The `Task` class represents a job that can consist of any number of subtasks or deliverables. For this reason, `getTimeRequired` calculates the total time for the `Task` and all its children by iterating through its list of project items and calling the `getTimeRequired` method. The method `getMaterialsCost` follows a similar strategy, working through the list of project items and calling each child's `getMaterialsCost` method.

Example A.131 `Task.java`

```
1.     import java.util.ArrayList;
2.     import java.util.Iterator;
3.     public class Task extends ProjectItem{
4.         private ArrayList projectItems = new ArrayList();
5.         private double taskTimeRequired;
6.
7.         public Task(){ }
8.         public Task(String newName, String newDescription,
9.             double newTaskTimeRequired, double newRate){
10.            super(newName, newDescription, newRate);
11.            taskTimeRequired = newTaskTimeRequired;
12.        }
13.
14.       public void setTaskTimeRequired(double newTaskTimeRequired){ taskTimeRequired
        = newTaskTimeRequired; }
15.        public void addProjectItem(ProjectItem element){
16.            if (!projectItems.contains(element)){
```

```
17.                 projectItems.add(element);
18.             }
19.         }
20.         public void removeProjectItem(ProjectItem element){
21.             projectItems.remove(element);
22.         }
23.
24.         public double getTaskTimeRequired(){ return taskTimeRequired; }
25.         public Iterator getProjectItemIterator(){ return projectItems.iterator(); }
26.         public double getMaterialsCost(){
27.             double totalCost = 0;
28.             Iterator items = getProjectItemIterator();
29.             while (items.hasNext()){
30.                 totalCost += ((ProjectItem)items.next()).getMaterialsCost();
31.             }
32.             return totalCost;
33.         }
34.         public double getTimeRequired(){
35.             double totalTime = taskTimeRequired;
36.             Iterator items = getProjectItemIterator();
37.             while (items.hasNext()){
38.                 totalTime += ((ProjectItem)items.next()).getTimeRequired();
39.             }
40.             return totalTime;
41.         }
42.     }
```

RunPattern creates a Deliverable object and a simple Task chain, then computes a cost estimate for each by calling the method getCostEstimate. Each object uses the template defined in the ProjectItem class, but applies its own methods when computing the time required and cost of materials.

Example A.132 RunPattern.java

```
1.      public class RunPattern{
2.          public static void main(String [] arguments){
3.              System.out.println("Example for the Template Method pattern");
4.              System.out.println("This code demonstrates how the template method can");
5.              System.out.println(" be used to define a variable implementation for a");
6.              System.out.println(" common operation. In this case, the ProjectItem");
7.              System.out.println(" abstract class defines the method getCostEstimate,");
8.              System.out.println(" which is a combination of the cost for time and");
9.              System.out.println(" materials. The two concrete subclasses used here,");
10.             System.out.println(" Task and Deliverable, have different methods of");
11.             System.out.println(" providing a cost estimate.");
12.             System.out.println();
13.
14.             System.out.println("Creating a demo Task and Deliverable");
15.             System.out.println();
16.             Task primaryTask = new Task("Put a JVM on the moon", "Lunar mission as part
        of the JavaSpace program ;)", 240.0, 100.0);
17.             primaryTask.addProjectItem(new Task("Establish ground control", "",
        1000.0, 10.0));
```

```
18.         primaryTask.addProjectItem(new Task("Train the Javanaughts", "", 80.0,
    30.0));
19.        Deliverable deliverableOne = new Deliverable("Lunar landing module", "Ask
    the local garage if they can make a few minor modifications to one of their
    cars", 2800, 40.0, 35.0);
20.
21.         System.out.println("Calculating the cost estimates using the Template
    Method, getCostEstimate.");
22.         System.out.println();
23.         System.out.println("Total cost estimate for: " + primaryTask);
24.         System.out.println("\t" + primaryTask.getCostEstimate());
25.         System.out.println();
26.
27.         System.out.println("Total cost estimate for: " + deliverableOne);
28.         System.out.println("\t" + deliverableOne.getCostEstimate());
29.     }
30. }
```

Structural Pattern Code Examples

Adapter

In this example, the PIM uses an API provided by a foreign source. Two files represent the interface into a purchased set of classes intended to represent contacts. The basic operations are defined in the interface called `Chovnatlh`.

Example A.133 `Chovnatlh.java`

```
1.   public interface Chovnatlh{
2.       public String tlhapWa$DIchPong();
3.       public String tlhapQavPong();
4.       public String tlhapPatlh();
5.       public String tlhapGhom();
6.
7.       public void cherWa$DIchPong(String chu$wa$DIchPong);
8.       public void cherQavPong(String chu$QavPong);
9.       public void cherPatlh(String chu$patlh);
10.      public void cherGhom(String chu$ghom);
11.  }
```

The implementation for these methods is provided in the associated class, `ChovnatlhImpl`.

Example A.134 `ChovnatlhImpl.java`

```
1.   // pong = name
2.   // wa'DIch = first
3.   // Qav = last
4.   // patlh = rank (title)
5.   // ghom = group (organization)
6.   // tlhap = take (get)
7.   // cher = set up (set)
8.   // chu' = new
9.   // chovnatlh = specimen (contact)
10.
11.  public class ChovnatlhImpl implements Chovnatlh{
12.      private String wa$DIchPong;
13.      private String QavPong;
14.      private String patlh;
15.      private String ghom;
16.
17.      public ChovnatlhImpl(){ }
18.      public ChovnatlhImpl(String chu$wa$DIchPong, String chu$QavPong,
19.          String chu$patlh, String chu$ghom){
20.              wa$DIchPong = chu$wa$DIchPong;
21.              QavPong = chu$QavPong;
22.              patlh = chu$patlh;
23.              ghom = chu$ghom;
24.      }
25.
26.      public String tlhapWa$DIchPong(){ return wa$DIchPong; }
```

```
27.        public String tlhapQavPong(){ return QavPong; }
28.        public String tlhapPatlh(){ return patlh; }
29.        public String tlhapGhom(){ return ghom; }
30.
31.        public void cherWa$DIchPong(String chu$wa$DIchPong){ wa$DIchPong =
       chu$wa$DIchPong; }
32.        public void cherQavPong(String chu$QavPong){ QavPong = chu$QavPong; }
33.        public void cherPatlh(String chu$patlh){ patlh = chu$patlh; }
34.        public void cherGhom(String chu$ghom){ ghom = chu$ghom; }
35.
36.        public String toString(){
37.            return wa$DIchPong + " " + QavPong + ": " + patlh + ", " + ghom;
38.        }
39.    }
```

With help from a translator, it is possible to match the methods to those found in the `Contact` interface. The `ContactAdapter` class performs this task by using a variable to hold an internal `ChovnatlhImpl` object. This object manages the information required to hold the `Contact` information: name, title, and organization.

Example A.135 `Contact.java`

```
1.    import java.io.Serializable;
2.    public interface Contact extends Serializable{
3.        public static final String SPACE = " ";
4.        public String getFirstName();
5.        public String getLastName();
6.        public String getTitle();
7.        public String getOrganization();
8.
9.        public void setFirstName(String newFirstName);
10.       public void setLastName(String newLastName);
11.       public void setTitle(String newTitle);
12.       public void setOrganization(String newOrganization);
13.   }
```

Example A.136 `ContactAdapter.java`

```
1.    public class ContactAdapter implements Contact{
2.        private Chovnatlh contact;
3.
4.        public ContactAdapter(){
5.            contact = new ChovnatlhImpl();
6.        }
7.        public ContactAdapter(Chovnatlh newContact){
8.            contact = newContact;
9.        }
10.
11.       public String getFirstName(){
12.           return contact.tlhapWa$DIchPong();
13.       }
```

```
14.         public String getLastName(){
15.             return contact.tlhapQavPong();
16.         }
17.         public String getTitle(){
18.             return contact.tlhapPatlh();
19.         }
20.         public String getOrganization(){
21.             return contact.tlhapGhom();
22.         }
23.
24.         public void setContact(Chovnatlh newContact){
25.             contact = newContact;
26.         }
27.         public void setFirstName(String newFirstName){
28.             contact.cherWa$DIchPong(newFirstName);
29.         }
30.         public void setLastName(String newLastName){
31.             contact.cherQavPong(newLastName);
32.         }
33.         public void setTitle(String newTitle){
34.             contact.cherPatlh(newTitle);
35.         }
36.         public void setOrganization(String newOrganization){
37.             contact.cherGhom(newOrganization);
38.         }
39.
40.         public String toString(){
41.             return contact.toString();
42.         }
43.     }
```

The RunPattern class demonstrates the use of the adapter by creating a ContactAdapter, then using it to create a sample Contact. The ChovnatlhImpl object stores the actual information and makes it available to RunPattern when the toString method is called on the ContactAdapter.

Example A.137 Contact.java

```
1.     import java.io.Serializable;
2.     public interface Contact extends Serializable{
3.         public static final String SPACE = " ";
4.         public String getFirstName();
5.         public String getLastName();
6.         public String getTitle();
7.         public String getOrganization();
8.
9.         public void setFirstName(String newFirstName);
10.        public void setLastName(String newLastName);
11.        public void setTitle(String newTitle);
12.        public void setOrganization(String newOrganization);
13.    }
```

Bridge

This example shows how to use the Bridge pattern to extend the functionality of a to-do list for the PIM. The to-do list is fairly straightforward—simply a list with the ability to add and remove Strings.

For the Bridge pattern, an element is defined in two parts: an abstraction and an implementation. The implementation is the class that does all the real work—in this case, it stores and retrieves list entries. The general behavior for the PIM list is defined in the ListImpl interface.

Example A.138 ListImpl.java

```
1.    public interface ListImpl{
2.        public void addItem(String item);
3.        public void addItem(String item, int position);
4.        public void removeItem(String item);
5.        public int getNumberOfItems();
6.        public String getItem(int index);
7.        public boolean supportsOrdering();
8.    }
```

The OrderedListImpl class implements ListImpl, and stores list entries in an internal ArrayList object.

Example A.139 OrderedListImpl.java

```
1.    import java.util.ArrayList;
2.    public class OrderedListImpl implements ListImpl{
3.        private ArrayList items = new ArrayList();
4.
5.        public void addItem(String item){
6.            if (!items.contains(item)){
7.                items.add(item);
8.            }
9.        }
10.       public void addItem(String item, int position){
11.           if (!items.contains(item)){
12.               items.add(position, item);
13.           }
14.       }
15.
16.       public void removeItem(String item){
17.           if (items.contains(item)){
18.               items.remove(items.indexOf(item));
19.           }
20.       }
21.
22.       public boolean supportsOrdering(){
23.           return true;
24.       }
```

```
25.
26.         public int getNumberOfItems(){
27.             return items.size();
28.         }
29.
30.         public String getItem(int index){
31.             if (index < items.size()){
32.                 return (String)items.get(index);
33.             }
34.             return null;
35.         }
36.     }
```

The abstraction represents the operations on the list that are available to the outside world. The `BaseList` class provides general list capabilities.

Example A.140 `BaseList.java`

```
1.      public class BaseList{
2.          protected ListImpl implementor;
3.
4.          public void setImplementor(ListImpl impl){
5.              implementor = impl;
6.          }
7.
8.          public void add(String item){
9.              implementor.addItem(item);
10.         }
11.         public void add(String item, int position){
12.             if (implementor.supportsOrdering()){
13.                 implementor.addItem(item, position);
14.             }
15.         }
16.
17.         public void remove(String item){
18.             implementor.removeItem(item);
19.         }
20.
21.         public String get(int index){
22.             return implementor.getItem(index);
23.         }
24.
25.         public int count(){
26.             return implementor.getNumberOfItems();
27.         }
28.     }
```

Note that all the operations are delegated to the implementer variable, which represents the list implementation. Whenever operations are requested of the `List`, they are actually delegated "across the bridge" to the associated `ListImpl` object.

It's easy to extend the features provided by the BaseList—you subclass the BaseList and add additional functionality. The NumberedList class demonstrates the power of the Bridge; by overriding the get method, the class is able to provide numbering of the items on the list.

Example A.141 NumberedList.java

```
1.    public class NumberedList extends BaseList{
2.        public String get(int index){
3.            return (index + 1) + ". " + super.get(index);
4.        }
5.    }
```

The OrnamentedList class shows another abstraction. In this case, the extension allows each list item to be prepended with a designated symbol, such as an asterisk or other character.

Example A.142 OrnamentedList.java

```
1.    public class OrnamentedList extends BaseList{
2.        private char itemType;
3.
4.        public char getItemType(){ return itemType; }
5.        public void setItemType(char newItemType){
6.            if (newItemType > ' '){
7.                itemType = newItemType;
8.            }
9.        }
10.
11.       public String get(int index){
12.           return itemType + " " + super.get(index);
13.       }
14.   }
```

RunPattern demonstrates this example in action. The main method creates an OrderedListImpl object and populates it with items. Next, it associates the implementation with three different abstraction objects, and prints the list contents. This illustrates two important principles: that the same implementation can be used with multiple abstractions, and that each abstraction can modify the appearance of the underlying data.

Example A.143 RunPattern.java

```
1.    public class RunPattern{
2.        public static void main(String [] arguments){
3.            System.out.println("Example for the Bridge pattern");
4.            System.out.println();
5.            System.out.println("This example divides complex behavior among two");
6.           System.out.println(" classes - the abstraction and the implementation.");
```

```
7.            System.out.println();
8.           System.out.println("In this case, there are two classes which can provide
        the");
9.            System.out.println(" abstraction - BaseList and OrnamentedList. The
        BaseList");
10.           System.out.println(" provides core funtionality, while the Ornament-
        edList");
11.           System.out.println(" expands on the model by adding a list character.");
12.           System.out.println();
13.          System.out.println("The OrderedListImpl class provides the underlying stor-
        age");
14.           System.out.println(" capability for the list, and can be flexibly paired
        with");
15.           System.out.println(" either of the classes which provide the abstrac-
        tion.");
16.
17.           System.out.println("Creating the OrderedListImpl object.");
18.           ListImpl implementation = new OrderedListImpl();
19.
20.           System.out.println("Creating the BaseList object.");
21.           BaseList listOne = new BaseList();
22.           listOne.setImplementor(implementation);
23.           System.out.println();
24.
25.           System.out.println("Adding elements to the list.");
26.           listOne.add("One");
27.           listOne.add("Two");
28.           listOne.add("Three");
29.           listOne.add("Four");
30.           System.out.println();
31.
32.           System.out.println("Creating an OrnamentedList object.");
33.           OrnamentedList listTwo = new OrnamentedList();
34.           listTwo.setImplementor(implementation);
35.           listTwo.setItemType('+');
36.           System.out.println();
37.
38.           System.out.println("Creating an NumberedList object.");
39.           NumberedList listThree = new NumberedList();
40.           listThree.setImplementor(implementation);
41.           System.out.println();
42.
43.           System.out.println("Printing out first list (BaseList)");
44.           for (int i = 0; i < listOne.count(); i++){
45.               System.out.println("\t" + listOne.get(i));
46.           }
47.           System.out.println();
48.
49.           System.out.println("Printing out second list (OrnamentedList)");
50.           for (int i = 0; i < listTwo.count(); i++){
51.               System.out.println("\t" + listTwo.get(i));
52.           }
53.           System.out.println();
54.
```

```
55.            System.out.println("Printing our third list (NumberedList)");
56.            for (int i = 0; i < listThree.count(); i++){
57.                System.out.println("\t" + listThree.get(i));
58.            }
59.        }
60.    }
```

Composite

The example demonstrates how to use the Composite pattern to calculate the time required to complete a project or some part of a project. The example has four principal parts:

- Deliverable – A class that represents an end product of a completed Task.
- Project – The class used as the root of the composite, representing the entire project.
- ProjectItem – This interface describes functionality common to all items that can be part of a project. The getTimeRequired method is defined in this interface.
- Task – A class that represents a collection of actions to perform. The task has a collection of ProjectItem objects.

The general functionality available to every object that can be part of a project is defined in the ProjectItem interface. In this example, there is only a single method defined: getTimeRequired.

Example A.144 ProjectItem.java

```
1.     import java.io.Serializable;
2.     public interface ProjectItem extends Serializable{
3.         public double getTimeRequired();
4.     }
```

Since the project items can be organized into a tree structure, two kinds of classes are ProjectItems. The Deliverable class represents a terminal node, which cannot reference other project items.

Example A.145 Deliverable.java

```
1.     import java.io.Serializable;
2.     public interface ProjectItem extends Serializable{
3.         public double getTimeRequired();
4.     }
```

The Project and Task classes are nonterminal or branch nodes. Both classes keep a collection of ProjectItems that represent children: associated tasks or deliverables.

Example A.146 Project.java

```
1.     import java.util.ArrayList;
2.     import java.util.Iterator;
```

```
3.    public class Project implements ProjectItem{
4.        private String name;
5.        private String description;
6.        private ArrayList projectItems = new ArrayList();
7.
8.        public Project(){ }
9.        public Project(String newName, String newDescription){
10.           name = newName;
11.           description = newDescription;
12.       }
13.
14.       public String getName(){ return name; }
15.       public String getDescription(){ return description; }
16.       public ArrayList getProjectItems(){ return projectItems; }
17.       public double getTimeRequired(){
18.           double totalTime = 0;
19.           Iterator items = projectItems.iterator();
20.           while(items.hasNext()){
21.               ProjectItem item = (ProjectItem)items.next();
22.               totalTime += item.getTimeRequired();
23.           }
24.           return totalTime;
25.       }
26.
27.       public void setName(String newName){ name = newName; }
28.       public void setDescription(String newDescription){ description = newDescrip-
      tion; }
29.
30.       public void addProjectItem(ProjectItem element){
31.           if (!projectItems.contains(element)){
32.               projectItems.add(element);
33.           }
34.       }
35.       public void removeProjectItem(ProjectItem element){
36.           projectItems.remove(element);
37.       }
38.   }
```

Example A.147 `Project.java`

```
1.    import java.util.ArrayList;
2.    import java.util.Iterator;
3.    public class Project implements ProjectItem{
4.        private String name;
5.        private String description;
6.        private ArrayList projectItems = new ArrayList();
7.
8.        public Project(){ }
9.        public Project(String newName, String newDescription){
10.           name = newName;
11.           description = newDescription;
12.       }
13.
```

```
14.        public String getName(){ return name; }
15.        public String getDescription(){ return description; }
16.        public ArrayList getProjectItems(){ return projectItems; }
17.        public double getTimeRequired(){
18.            double totalTime = 0;
19.            Iterator items = projectItems.iterator();
20.            while(items.hasNext()){
21.                ProjectItem item = (ProjectItem)items.next();
22.                totalTime += item.getTimeRequired();
23.            }
24.            return totalTime;
25.        }
26.
27.        public void setName(String newName){ name = newName; }
28.        public void setDescription(String newDescription){ description = newDescrip-
       tion; }
29.
30.        public void addProjectItem(ProjectItem element){
31.            if (!projectItems.contains(element)){
32.                projectItems.add(element);
33.            }
34.        }
35.        public void removeProjectItem(ProjectItem element){
36.            projectItems.remove(element);
37.        }
38.    }
```

Example A.148 `Task.java`

```
1.     import java.util.ArrayList;
2.     import java.util.Iterator;
3.     public class Task implements ProjectItem{
4.         private String name;
5.         private String details;
6.         private ArrayList projectItems = new ArrayList();
7.         private Contact owner;
8.         private double timeRequired;
9.
10.        public Task(){ }
11.        public Task(String newName, String newDetails,
12.            Contact newOwner, double newTimeRequired){
13.            name = newName;
14.            details = newDetails;
15.            owner = newOwner;
16.            timeRequired = newTimeRequired;
17.        }
18.
19.        public String getName(){ return name; }
20.        public String getDetails(){ return details; }
21.        public ArrayList getProjectItems(){ return projectItems; }
22.        public Contact getOwner(){ return owner; }
23.        public double getTimeRequired(){
24.            double totalTime = timeRequired;
```

```
25.         Iterator items = projectItems.iterator();
26.         while(items.hasNext()){
27.             ProjectItem item = (ProjectItem)items.next();
28.             totalTime += item.getTimeRequired();
29.         }
30.         return totalTime;
31.     }
32.
33.     public void setName(String newName){ name = newName; }
34.     public void setDetails(String newDetails){ details = newDetails; }
35.     public void setOwner(Contact newOwner){ owner = newOwner; }
36.     public void setTimeRequired(double newTimeRequired){ timeRequired = newTimeRe-
    quired; }
37.
38.     public void addProjectItem(ProjectItem element){
39.         if (!projectItems.contains(element)){
40.             projectItems.add(element);
41.         }
42.     }
43.     public void removeProjectItem(ProjectItem element){
44.         projectItems.remove(element);
45.     }
46. }
```

The `getTimeRequired` method shows how the Composite pattern runs. To get the time estimate for any part of the project, you simply call the method `getTimeRequired` for a `Project` or `Task` object. This method behaves differently depending on the method implementer:

- `Deliverable`: Return 0.
- `Project` or `Task`: Return the sum of the time required for the object plus the results of calling the `getTimeRequired` method for all `ProjectItems` associated with this node.

The `Contact` interface and `ContactImpl` class provide support code to represent the owner of a task or deliverable.

Example A.149 Contact.java

```
1.  import java.io.Serializable;
2.  public interface Contact extends Serializable{
3.      public static final String SPACE = " ";
4.      public String getFirstName();
5.      public String getLastName();
6.      public String getTitle();
7.      public String getOrganization();
8.
9.      public void setFirstName(String newFirstName);
10.     public void setLastName(String newLastName);
11.     public void setTitle(String newTitle);
12.     public void setOrganization(String newOrganization);
13. }
```

Example A.150 `ContactImpl.java`

```
1.  public class ContactImpl implements Contact{
2.      private String firstName;
3.      private String lastName;
4.      private String title;
5.      private String organization;
6.
7.      public ContactImpl(){}
8.      public ContactImpl(String newFirstName, String newLastName,
9.          String newTitle, String newOrganization){
10.             firstName = newFirstName;
11.             lastName = newLastName;
12.             title = newTitle;
13.             organization = newOrganization;
14.     }
15.
16.     public String getFirstName(){ return firstName; }
17.     public String getLastName(){ return lastName; }
18.     public String getTitle(){ return title; }
19.     public String getOrganization(){ return organization; }
20.
21.     public void setFirstName(String newFirstName){ firstName = newFirstName; }
22.     public void setLastName(String newLastName){ lastName = newLastName; }
23.     public void setTitle(String newTitle){ title = newTitle; }
24.     public void setOrganization(String newOrganization){ organization = newOrgani-
    zation; }
25.
26.     public String toString(){
27.         return firstName + SPACE + lastName;
28.     }
29. }
```

This example uses a small demonstration project to illustrate the Command pattern. To simplify the task of managing a stored copy of the project information, the `DataCreator` class creates a sample project and serializes it to a file.

Example A.151 `DataCreator.java`

```
1.  import java.io.Serializable;
2.  import java.io.ObjectOutputStream;
3.  import java.io.FileOutputStream;
4.  import java.io.IOException;
5.  public class DataCreator{
6.      private static final String DEFAULT_FILE = "data.ser";
7.
8.      public static void main(String [] args){
9.          String fileName;
10.         if (args.length == 1){
11.             fileName = args[0];
12.         }
13.         else{
```

```
14.                 fileName = DEFAULT_FILE;
15.             }
16.             serialize(fileName);
17.         }
18.
19.         public static void serialize(String fileName){
20.             try{
21.                 serializeToFile(createData(), fileName);
22.             }
23.             catch (IOException exc){
24.                 exc.printStackTrace();
25.             }
26.         }
27.
28.         private static Serializable createData(){
29.             Contact contact1 = new ContactImpl("Dennis", "Moore", "Managing Director",
        "Highway Man, LTD");
30.             Contact contact2 = new ContactImpl("Joseph", "Mongolfier", "High Flyer",
        "Lighter than Air Productions");
31.             Contact contact3 = new ContactImpl("Erik", "Njoll", "Nomad without Portfo-
        lio", "Nordic Trek, Inc.");
32.             Contact contact4 = new ContactImpl("Lemming", "", "Principal Investigator",
        "BDA");
33.
34.             Project project = new Project("IslandParadise", "Acquire a personal island
        paradise");
35.             Deliverable deliverable1 = new Deliverable("Island Paradise", "",
        contact1);
36.             Task task1 = new Task("Fortune", "Acquire a small fortune", contact4,
        11.0);
37.             Task task2 = new Task("Isle", "Locate an island for sale", contact2, 7.5);
38.             Task task3 = new Task("Name", "Decide on a name for the island", contact3,
        3.2);
39.             project.addProjectItem(deliverable1);
40.             project.addProjectItem(task1);
41.             project.addProjectItem(task2);
42.             project.addProjectItem(task3);
43.
44.             Deliverable deliverable11 = new Deliverable("$1,000,000", "(total net worth
        after taxes)", contact1);
45.             Task task11 = new Task("Fortune1", "Use psychic hotline to predict winning
        lottery numbers", contact4, 2.5);
46.             Task task12 = new Task("Fortune2", "Invest winnings to ensure 50% annual
        interest", contact1, 14.0);
47.             task1.addProjectItem(task11);
48.             task1.addProjectItem(task12);
49.             task1.addProjectItem(deliverable11);
50.
51.             Task task21 = new Task("Isle1", "Research whether climate is better in the
        Atlantic or Pacific", contact1, 1.8);
52.             Task task22 = new Task("Isle2", "Locate an island for auction on EBay",
        contact4, 5.0);
53.             Task task23 = new Task("Isle2a", "Negotiate for sale of the island",
        contact3, 17.5);
54.             task2.addProjectItem(task21);
```

```
55.             task2.addProjectItem(task22);
56.             task2.addProjectItem(task23);
57.
58.            Deliverable deliverable31 = new Deliverable("Island Name", "", contact1);
59.             task3.addProjectItem(deliverable31);
60.             return project;
61.         }
62.
63.         private static void serializeToFile(Serializable content, String fileName)
       throws IOException{
64.             ObjectOutputStream serOut = new ObjectOutputStream(new FileOutput-
       Stream(fileName));
65.             serOut.writeObject(content);
66.             serOut.close();
67.         }
68.     }
```

The DataRetriever class provides a resource to deserialize an object from a file with the deserializeData method.

Example A.152 DataRetriever.java

```
1.     import java.io.File;
2.     import java.io.FileInputStream;
3.     import java.io.IOException;
4.     import java.io.ObjectInputStream;
5.
6.     public class DataRetriever{
7.         public static Object deserializeData(String fileName){
8.             Object returnValue = null;
9.             try{
10.                File inputFile = new File(fileName);
11.                if (inputFile.exists() && inputFile.isFile()){
12.                    ObjectInputStream readIn = new ObjectInputStream(new FileInput-
      Stream(fileName));
13.                    returnValue = readIn.readObject();
14.                    readIn.close();
15.                }else{
16.                    System.err.println("Unable to locate the file " + fileName);
17.                }
18.            }catch (ClassNotFoundException exc){
19.                exc.printStackTrace();
20.
21.            }catch (IOException exc){
22.                exc.printStackTrace();
23.            }
24.            return returnValue;
25.        }
26.    }
```

The RunPattern class uses DataRetriever to deserialize the project, then calls the getTimeRequired method to calculate the time requirements for the entire project.

Example A.153 RunPattern.java

```
1.  import java.io.File;
2.  public class RunPattern{
3.      public static void main(String [] arguments){
4.          System.out.println("Example for the Composite pattern");
5.          System.out.println();
6.          System.out.println("This code sample will propagate a method call through-
    out");
7.          System.out.println(" a tree structure. The tree represents a project, and
    is");
8.          System.out.println(" composed of three kinds of ProjectItems - Project,
    Task,");
9.          System.out.println(" and Deliverable. Of these three classes, Project and
    Task");
10.         System.out.println(" can store an ArrayList of ProjectItems. This means
    that");
11.         System.out.println(" they can act as branch nodes for our tree. The Deliv-
    erable");
12.         System.out.println(" is a terminal node, since it cannot hold any Projec-
    tItems.");
13.         System.out.println();
14.         System.out.println("In this example, the method defined by ProjectItem,");
15.         System.out.println(" getTimeRequired, provides the method to demonstrate
    the");
16.         System.out.println(" pattern. For branch nodes, the method will be passed
    on");
17.         System.out.println(" to the children. For terminal nodes (Deliverables),
    a");
18.         System.out.println(" single value will be returned.");
19.         System.out.println();
20.         System.out.println("Note that it is possible to make this method call ANY-
    WHERE");
21.         System.out.println(" in the tree, since all classes implement the getTim-
    eRequired");
22.         System.out.println(" method. This means that you are able to calculate the
    time");
23.         System.out.println(" required to complete the whole project OR any part of
    it.");
24.         System.out.println();
25.
26.         System.out.println("Deserializing a test Project for the Composite pat-
    tern");
27.         System.out.println();
28.         if (!(new File("data.ser").exists())){
29.             DataCreator.serialize("data.ser");
30.         }
31.         Project project = (Project)(DataRetriever.deserializeData("data.ser"));
32.
33.         System.out.println("Calculating total time estimate for the project");
```

```
34.             System.out.println("\t" + project.getDescription());
35.             System.out.println("Time Required: " + project.getTimeRequired());
36.
37.         }
38.     }
```

Decorator

This example demonstrates how to use the Decorator pattern to extend the capability of the elements in a project. The foundation of the project is the ProjectItem interface. It is implemented by any class that can be used within a project. In this case, ProjectItem defines a single method, getTimeRequired.

Example A.154 ProjectItem.java

```
1.  import java.io.Serializable;
2.  public interface ProjectItem extends Serializable{
3.      public static final String EOL_STRING = System.getProperty("line.separator");
4.      public double getTimeRequired();
5.  }
```

Task and Deliverable implement ProjectItem and provide the basic project functionality. As in previous demonstrations, Task represents some job in a project and Deliverable represents some concrete product.

Example A.155 Deliverable.java

```
1.  public class Deliverable implements ProjectItem{
2.      private String name;
3.      private String description;
4.      private Contact owner;
5.  
6.      public Deliverable(){ }
7.      public Deliverable(String newName, String newDescription,
8.          Contact newOwner){
9.          name = newName;
10.         description = newDescription;
11.         owner = newOwner;
12.     }
13. 
14.     public String getName(){ return name; }
15.     public String getDescription(){ return description; }
16.     public Contact getOwner(){ return owner; }
17.     public double getTimeRequired(){ return 0; }
18. 
19.     public void setName(String newName){ name = newName; }
20.     public void setDescription(String newDescription){ description = newDescrip-
    tion; }
21.     public void setOwner(Contact newOwner){ owner = newOwner; }
22. 
23.     public String toString(){
24.         return "Deliverable: " + name;
25.     }
26. }
```

Example A.156 `Task.java`

```
1.  import java.util.ArrayList;
2.  import java.util.Iterator;
3.  public class Task implements ProjectItem{
4.      private String name;
5.      private ArrayList projectItems = new ArrayList();
6.      private Contact owner;
7.      private double timeRequired;
8.
9.      public Task(){ }
10.     public Task(String newName, Contact newOwner,
11.         double newTimeRequired){
12.         name = newName;
13.         owner = newOwner;
14.         timeRequired = newTimeRequired;
15.     }
16.
17.     public String getName(){ return name; }
18.     public ArrayList getProjectItems(){ return projectItems; }
19.     public Contact getOwner(){ return owner; }
20.     public double getTimeRequired(){
21.         double totalTime = timeRequired;
22.         Iterator items = projectItems.iterator();
23.         while(items.hasNext()){
24.             ProjectItem item = (ProjectItem)items.next();
25.             totalTime += item.getTimeRequired();
26.         }
27.         return totalTime;
28.     }
29.
30.     public void setName(String newName){ name = newName; }
31.     public void setOwner(Contact newOwner){ owner = newOwner; }
32.     public void setTimeRequired(double newTimeRequired){ timeRequired = newTimeRe-
    quired; }
33.
34.     public void addProjectItem(ProjectItem element){
35.         if (!projectItems.contains(element)){
36.             projectItems.add(element);
37.         }
38.     }
39.     public void removeProjectItem(ProjectItem element){
40.         projectItems.remove(element);
41.     }
42.
43.     public String toString(){
44.         return "Task: " + name;
45.     }
46. }
```

It's time to introduce a decorator to extend the basic capabilities of these classes. The class `ProjectDecorator` will provide the central ability to augment `Task` and `Deliverable`.

Example A.157 ProjectDecorator.java

```
1.   public abstract class ProjectDecorator implements ProjectItem{
2.       private ProjectItem projectItem;
3.
4.       protected ProjectItem getProjectItem(){ return projectItem; }
5.       public void setProjectItem(ProjectItem newProjectItem){ projectItem = new-
     ProjectItem; }
6.
7.       public double getTimeRequired(){
8.           return projectItem.getTimeRequired();
9.       }
10.  }
```

The ProjectDecorator implements the ProjectItem interface and maintains a variable for another ProjectItem, which represents the "decorated" element. Note that ProjectDecorator delegates the getTimeRequired method to its internal element. This would be done for any method that would depend on the functionality of the underlying component. If a Task with a required time of five days were decorated, you would still expect it to return a value of five days, regardless of any other capabilities it might have.

There are two subclasses of ProjectDecorator in this example. Both demonstrate a way to add some extra feature to project elements. The DependentProjectItem class is used to show that a Task or Deliverable depends on another ProjectItem for completion.

Example A.158 DependentProjectItem.java

```
1.   public class DependentProjectItem extends ProjectDecorator{
2.       private ProjectItem dependentItem;
3.
4.       public DependentProjectItem(){ }
5.       public DependentProjectItem(ProjectItem newDependentItem){
6.           dependentItem = newDependentItem;
7.       }
8.
9.       public ProjectItem getDependentItem(){ return dependentItem; }
10.
11.      public void setDependentItem(ProjectItem newDependentItem){ dependentItem =
     newDependentItem; }
12.
13.      public String toString(){
14.          return getProjectItem().toString() + EOL_STRING
15.              + "\tProjectItem dependent on: " + dependentItem;
16.      }
17.  }
```

SupportedProjectItem decorates a ProjectItem, and keeps an ArrayList of supporting documents—file objects that represent additional information or resources.

Example A.159 `SupportedProjectItem.java`

```
1.   import java.util.ArrayList;
2.   import java.io.File;
3.   public class SupportedProjectItem extends ProjectDecorator{
4.       private ArrayList supportingDocuments = new ArrayList();
5.
6.       public SupportedProjectItem(){ }
7.       public SupportedProjectItem(File newSupportingDocument){
8.           addSupportingDocument(newSupportingDocument);
9.       }
10.
11.      public ArrayList getSupportingDocuments(){
12.          return supportingDocuments;
13.      }
14.
15.      public void addSupportingDocument(File document){
16.          if (!supportingDocuments.contains(document)){
17.              supportingDocuments.add(document);
18.          }
19.      }
20.
21.      public void removeSupportingDocument(File document){
22.          supportingDocuments.remove(document);
23.      }
24.
25.      public String toString(){
26.          return getProjectItem().toString() + EOL_STRING
27.              + "\tSupporting Documents: " + supportingDocuments;
28.      }
29.  }
```

The benefit of defining additional capabilities in this way is that it is easy to create project items that have a combination of capabilities. Using these classes, you can make a simple task that depends on another project item, or a task with supporting documents. You can even chain Decorators together and create a task that depends on another task and has supporting documents. This flexibility is a key strength of the Decorator pattern.

In this example, the `Contact` interface and its implementer `ContactImpl` provide support for an owner of a `Task` or `Deliverable`.

Example A.160 `Contact.java`

```
1.   import java.io.Serializable;
2.   public interface Contact extends Serializable{
3.       public static final String SPACE = " ";
4.       public String getFirstName();
5.       public String getLastName();
6.       public String getTitle();
7.       public String getOrganization();
8.
```

```
9.      public void setFirstName(String newFirstName);
10.     public void setLastName(String newLastName);
11.     public void setTitle(String newTitle);
12.     public void setOrganization(String newOrganization);
13. }
```

Example A.161 ContactImpl.java

```
1.  public class ContactImpl implements Contact{
2.      private String firstName;
3.      private String lastName;
4.      private String title;
5.      private String organization;
6.  
7.      public ContactImpl(){}
8.      public ContactImpl(String newFirstName, String newLastName,
9.          String newTitle, String newOrganization){
10.             firstName = newFirstName;
11.             lastName = newLastName;
12.             title = newTitle;
13.             organization = newOrganization;
14.     }
15. 
16.     public String getFirstName(){ return firstName; }
17.     public String getLastName(){ return lastName; }
18.     public String getTitle(){ return title; }
19.     public String getOrganization(){ return organization; }
20. 
21.     public void setFirstName(String newFirstName){ firstName = newFirstName; }
22.     public void setLastName(String newLastName){ lastName = newLastName; }
23.     public void setTitle(String newTitle){ title = newTitle; }
24.     public void setOrganization(String newOrganization){ organization = newOrgani-
    zation; }
25. 
26.     public String toString(){
27.         return firstName + SPACE + lastName;
28.     }
29. }
```

The `RunPattern` class creates several `ProjectItems` and prints out their `String` values. Next, it creates several `Decorators`, associates them with one of the `Task` objects by calling the `setProjectItem` methods, and shows the `String` value of the newly decorated `Task`.

Example A.162 RunPattern.java

```
1.  import java.io.File;
2.  public class RunPattern{
3.      public static void main(String [] arguments){
4.          System.out.println("Example for the Decorator pattern");
5.          System.out.println();
```

```
6.          System.out.println("This demonstration will show how Decorator classes can
        be used");
7.          System.out.println(" to extend the basic functionality of ProjectItems. The
        Task and");
8.          System.out.println(" Deliverable classes provide the basic ProjectItems,
        and their");
9.          System.out.println(" functionality will be extended by adding subclasses of
        the");
10.         System.out.println(" abstract class ProjectDecorator.");
11.         System.out.println();
12.         System.out.println("Note that the toString method has been overridden for
        all ProjectItems,");
13.         System.out.println(" to more effectively show how Decorators are associated
        with their");
14.         System.out.println(" ProjectItems.");
15.         System.out.println();
16.
17.         System.out.println("Creating ProjectItems.");
18.         Contact contact1 = new ContactImpl("Simone", "Roberto", "Head Researcher
        and Chief Archivist", "Institute for Advanced (Java) Studies");
19.         Task task1 = new Task("Perform months of diligent research", contact1,
        20.0);
20.         Task task2 = new Task("Obtain grant from World Java Foundation", contact1,
        40.0);
21.         Deliverable deliverable1 = new Deliverable("Java History", "Comprehensive
        history of the design of all Java APIs", contact1);
22.         System.out.println("ProjectItem objects created. Results:");
23.         System.out.println(task1);
24.         System.out.println(task2);
25.         System.out.println(deliverable1);
26.         System.out.println();
27.
28.         System.out.println("Creating decorators");
29.         ProjectDecorator decorator1 = new SupportedProjectItem(new File("JavaHis-
        tory.txt"));
30.         ProjectDecorator decorator2 = new DependentProjectItem(task2);
31.         System.out.println("Decorators created. Adding decorators to the first
        task");
32.         decorator1.setProjectItem(task1);
33.         decorator2.setProjectItem(decorator1);
34.         System.out.println();
35.         System.out.println("Decorators added. Results");
36.         System.out.println(decorator2);
37.
38.         System.out.println("");
39.     }
40. }
```

Facade

To make the PIM more functional for users, you want to give them the opportunity to customize the application. Some examples of items to customize include font type, font size, colors, which services to start when, default currency, etc. This example tracks a set of nationality-based settings.

In this example, the Facade class is the `InternationalizationWizard`. This class coordinates between a client and a number of objects associated with a selected nationality.

Example A.163 `InternationalizationWizard.java`

```
1.  import java.util.HashMap;
2.  import java.text.NumberFormat;
3.  import java.util.Locale;
4.  public class InternationalizationWizard{
5.      private HashMap map;
6.      private Currency currency = new Currency();
7.      private InternationalizedText propertyFile = new InternationalizedText();
8.
9.      public InternationalizationWizard() {
10.         map = new HashMap();
11.         Nation[] nations = {
12.             new Nation("US", '$', "+1", "us.properties", NumberFormat.getIn-
    stance(Locale.US)),
13.             new Nation("The Netherlands", 'f', "+31", "dutch.properties", Number-
    Format.getInstance(Locale.GERMANY)),
14.             new Nation("France", 'f', "+33", "french.properties", NumberFormat.get-
    Instance(Locale.FRANCE))
15.         };
16.         for (int i = 0; i < nations.length; i++) {
17.             map.put(nations[i].getName(), nations[i]);
18.         }
19.     }
20.
21.     public void setNation(String name) {
22.         Nation nation = (Nation)map.get(name);
23.         if (nation != null) {
24.             currency.setCurrencySymbol(nation.getSymbol());
25.             currency.setNumberFormat(nation.getNumberFormat());
26.             PhoneNumber.setSelectedInterPrefix(nation.getDialingPrefix());
27.             propertyFile.setFileName(nation.getPropertyFileName());
28.         }
29.     }
30.
31.     public Object[] getNations(){
32.         return map.values().toArray();
33.     }
34.     public Nation getNation(String name){
35.         return (Nation)map.get(name);
36.     }
37.     public char getCurrencySymbol(){
```

```
38.             return currency.getCurrencySymbol();
39.         }
40.         public NumberFormat getNumberFormat(){
41.             return currency.getNumberFormat();
42.         }
43.         public String getPhonePrefix(){
44.             return PhoneNumber.getSelectedInterPrefix();
45.         }
46.         public String getProperty(String key){
47.             return propertyFile.getProperty(key);
48.         }
49.         public String getProperty(String key, String defaultValue){
50.             return propertyFile.getProperty(key, defaultValue);
51.         }
52.     }
```

Note that the `InternationalizationWizard` has a number of get methods, which it delegates to its associated objects. It also has a method `setNation`, used to change the nation used by the client.

Although the Facade manages the internationalized settings for a number of objects in this example, it is still possible to manage each object individually. This is one of the benefits of this pattern—it allows a group of objects to be managed collectively in some situations, but still provides the freedom to individually manage the components as well.

Calling the `setNation` method in this class sets the current nation. That makes the wizard alter the `Currency` setting, the `PhoneNumber`, and a set of localized language strings, `InternationalizedText`.

Example A.164 `Currency.java`

```
1.     import java.text.NumberFormat;
2.     public class Currency{
3.         private char currencySymbol;
4.         private NumberFormat numberFormat;
5.
6.         public void setCurrencySymbol(char newCurrencySymbol){ currencySymbol =
         newCurrencySymbol; }
7.         public void setNumberFormat(NumberFormat newNumberFormat){ numberFormat =
         newNumberFormat; }
8.
9.         public char getCurrencySymbol(){ return currencySymbol; }
10.        public NumberFormat getNumberFormat(){ return numberFormat; }
11.    }
```

Example A.165 `InternationalizedText.java`

```
1.     import java.util.Properties;
2.     import java.io.File;
3.     import java.io.IOException;
4.     import java.io.FileInputStream;
5.     public class InternationalizedText{
```

```
6.        private static final String DEFAULT_FILE_NAME = "";
7.        private Properties textProperties = new Properties();
8.
9.        public InternationalizedText(){
10.           this(DEFAULT_FILE_NAME);
11.       }
12.       public InternationalizedText(String fileName){
13.           loadProperties(fileName);
14.       }
15.
16.       public void setFileName(String newFileName){
17.           if (newFileName != null){
18.               loadProperties(newFileName);
19.           }
20.       }
21.       public String getProperty(String key){
22.           return getProperty(key, "");
23.       }
24.       public String getProperty(String key, String defaultValue){
25.           return textProperties.getProperty(key, defaultValue);
26.       }
27.
28.       private void loadProperties(String fileName){
29.           try{
30.               FileInputStream input = new FileInputStream(fileName);
31.               textProperties.load(input);
32.           }
33.           catch (IOException exc){
34.               textProperties = new Properties();
35.           }
36.       }
37.   }
```

Example A.166 `PhoneNumber.java`

```
1.    public class PhoneNumber {
2.        private static String selectedInterPrefix;
3.        private String internationalPrefix;
4.        private String areaNumber;
5.        private String netNumber;
6.
7.        public PhoneNumber(String intPrefix, String areaNumber, String netNumber) {
8.            this.internationalPrefix = intPrefix;
9.            this.areaNumber = areaNumber;
10.           this.netNumber = netNumber;
11.       }
12.
13.       public String getInternationalPrefix(){ return internationalPrefix; }
14.       public String getAreaNumber(){ return areaNumber; }
15.       public String getNetNumber(){ return netNumber; }
16.       public static String getSelectedInterPrefix(){ return selectedInterPrefix; }
17.
18.       public void setInternationalPrefix(String newPrefix){ internationalPrefix =
        newPrefix; }
```

```
19.     public void setAreaNumber(String newAreaNumber){ areaNumber = newAreaNumber; }
20.     public void setNetNumber(String newNetNumber){ netNumber = newNetNumber; }
21.     public static void setSelectedInterPrefix(String prefix) { selectedInterPrefix
      = prefix; }
22.
23.     public String toString(){
24.         return internationalPrefix + areaNumber + netNumber;
25.     }
26. }
```

General country data is stored in a helper class, `Nation`. The `InternationalizationWizard` creates a collection of nations when it is first instantiated.

Example A.167 `Nation.java`

```
1.  import java.text.NumberFormat;
2.  public class Nation {
3.      private char symbol;
4.      private String name;
5.      private String dialingPrefix;
6.      private String propertyFileName;
7.      private NumberFormat numberFormat;
8.
9.      public Nation(String newName, char newSymbol, String newDialingPrefix,
10.         String newPropertyFileName, NumberFormat newNumberFormat) {
11.         name = newName;
12.         symbol = newSymbol;
13.         dialingPrefix = newDialingPrefix;
14.         propertyFileName = newPropertyFileName;
15.         numberFormat = newNumberFormat;
16.     }
17.
18.     public String getName(){ return name; }
19.     public char getSymbol(){ return symbol; }
20.     public String getDialingPrefix(){ return dialingPrefix; }
21.     public String getPropertyFileName(){ return propertyFileName; }
22.     public NumberFormat getNumberFormat(){ return numberFormat; }
23.
24.     public String toString(){ return name; }
25. }
```

To better illustrate the use of the Facade in a user environment, the class `FacadeGui` creates a simple Swing GUI which demonstrates the effect of changing the country, calling the get methods for the `InternationalizationWizard` to provide language, currency and phone number information.

Example A.168 FacadeGui.java

```
1.    import java.awt.Container;
2.    import java.awt.GridLayout;
3.    import java.awt.event.ActionListener;
4.    import java.awt.event.ActionEvent;
5.    import java.awt.event.ItemListener;
6.    import java.awt.event.ItemEvent;
7.    import java.awt.event.WindowAdapter;
8.    import java.awt.event.WindowEvent;
9.    import javax.swing.BoxLayout;
10.   import javax.swing.JButton;
11.   import javax.swing.JComboBox;
12.   import javax.swing.JFrame;
13.   import javax.swing.JLabel;
14.   import javax.swing.JPanel;
15.   import javax.swing.JTextField;
16.   public class FacadeGui implements ActionListener, ItemListener{
17.       private static final String GUI_TITLE = "title";
18.       private static final String EXIT_CAPTION = "exit";
19.       private static final String COUNTRY_LABEL = "country";
20.       private static final String CURRENCY_LABEL = "currency";
21.       private static final String PHONE_LABEL = "phone";
22.
23.       private JFrame mainFrame;
24.       private JButton exit;
25.       private JComboBox countryChooser;
26.       private JPanel controlPanel, displayPanel;
27.       private JLabel countryLabel, currencyLabel, phoneLabel;
28.       private JTextField currencyTextField, phoneTextField;
29.       private InternationalizationWizard nationalityFacade;
30.
31.       public FacadeGui(InternationalizationWizard wizard){
32.           nationalityFacade = wizard;
33.       }
34.
35.       public void createGui(){
36.           mainFrame = new JFrame(nationalityFacade.getProperty(GUI_TITLE));
37.           Container content = mainFrame.getContentPane();
38.           content.setLayout(new BoxLayout(content, BoxLayout.Y_AXIS));
39.
40.           displayPanel = new JPanel();
41.           displayPanel.setLayout(new GridLayout(3, 2));
42.
43.           countryLabel = new JLabel(nationalityFacade.getProperty(COUNTRY_LABEL));
44.           countryChooser = new JComboBox(nationalityFacade.getNations());
45.          currencyLabel = new JLabel(nationalityFacade.getProperty(CURRENCY_LABEL));
46.           currencyTextField = new JTextField();
47.           phoneLabel = new JLabel(nationalityFacade.getProperty(PHONE_LABEL));
48.           phoneTextField = new JTextField();
49.
50.           currencyTextField.setEditable(false);
51.           phoneTextField.setEditable(false);
```

```
52.
53.         displayPanel.add(countryLabel);
54.         displayPanel.add(countryChooser);
55.         displayPanel.add(currencyLabel);
56.         displayPanel.add(currencyTextField);
57.         displayPanel.add(phoneLabel);
58.         displayPanel.add(phoneTextField);
59.         content.add(displayPanel);
60.
61.         controlPanel = new JPanel();
62.         exit = new JButton(nationalityFacade.getProperty(EXIT_CAPTION));
63.         controlPanel.add(exit);
64.         content.add(controlPanel);
65.
66.         exit.addActionListener(this);
67.         countryChooser.addItemListener(this);
68.
69.         mainFrame.addWindowListener(new WindowCloseManager());
70.         mainFrame.pack();
71.         mainFrame.setVisible(true);
72.     }
73.
74.     private void updateGui(){
75.        nationalityFacade.setNation(countryChooser.getSelectedItem().toString());
76.         mainFrame.setTitle(nationalityFacade.getProperty(GUI_TITLE));
77.         countryLabel.setText(nationalityFacade.getProperty(COUNTRY_LABEL));
78.         currencyLabel.setText(nationalityFacade.getProperty(CURRENCY_LABEL));
79.         phoneLabel.setText(nationalityFacade.getProperty(PHONE_LABEL));
80.         exit.setText(nationalityFacade.getProperty(EXIT_CAPTION));
81.
82.         currencyTextField.setText(nationalityFacade.getCurrencySymbol() + " " +
83.             nationalityFacade.getNumberFormat().format(5280.50));
84.         phoneTextField.setText(nationalityFacade.getPhonePrefix());
85.
86.         mainFrame.invalidate();
87.         countryLabel.invalidate();
88.         currencyLabel.invalidate();
89.         phoneLabel.invalidate();
90.         exit.invalidate();
91.         mainFrame.validate();
92.     }
93.
94.     public void actionPerformed(ActionEvent evt){
95.         Object originator = evt.getSource();
96.         if (originator == exit){
97.             exitApplication();
98.         }
99.     }
100.    public void itemStateChanged(ItemEvent evt){
101.        Object originator = evt.getSource();
102.        if (originator == countryChooser){
103.            updateGui();
104.        }
105.    }
```

```
106.
107.     public void setNation(Nation nation){
108.         countryChooser.setSelectedItem(nation);
109.     }
110.
111.     private class WindowCloseManager extends WindowAdapter{
112.         public void windowClosing(WindowEvent evt){
113.             exitApplication();
114.         }
115.     }
116.
117.     private void exitApplication(){
118.         System.exit(0);
119.     }
120. }
```

The class DataCreator produces a set of InternationalizedText objects to use in this example.

Example A.169 DataCreator.java

```
1.  import java.util.Properties;
2.  import java.io.IOException;
3.  import java.io.FileOutputStream;
4.  public class DataCreator{
5.      private static final String GUI_TITLE = "title";
6.      private static final String EXIT_CAPTION = "exit";
7.      private static final String COUNTRY_LABEL = "country";
8.      private static final String CURRENCY_LABEL = "currency";
9.      private static final String PHONE_LABEL = "phone";
10.
11.     public static void serialize(String fileName){
12.         saveFrData();
13.         saveUsData();
14.         saveNlData();
15.     }
16.
17.     private static void saveFrData(){
18.         try{
19.             Properties textSettings = new Properties();
20.           textSettings.setProperty(GUI_TITLE, "Demonstration du Pattern Facade");
21.             textSettings.setProperty(EXIT_CAPTION, "Sortir");
22.             textSettings.setProperty(COUNTRY_LABEL, "Pays");
23.             textSettings.setProperty(CURRENCY_LABEL, "Monnaie");
24.             textSettings.setProperty(PHONE_LABEL, "Numero de Telephone");
25.           textSettings.store(new FileOutputStream("french.properties"), "French
    Settings");
26.         }
27.         catch (IOException exc){
28.             System.err.println("Error storing settings to output");
29.             exc.printStackTrace();
30.         }
31.     }
```

```
32.        private static void saveUsData(){
33.            try{
34.                Properties textSettings = new Properties();
35.                textSettings.setProperty(GUI_TITLE, "Facade Pattern Demonstration");
36.                textSettings.setProperty(EXIT_CAPTION, "Exit");
37.                textSettings.setProperty(COUNTRY_LABEL, "Country");
38.                textSettings.setProperty(CURRENCY_LABEL, "Currency");
39.                textSettings.setProperty(PHONE_LABEL, "Phone Number");
40.                textSettings.store(new FileOutputStream("us.properties"), "US Set-
       tings");
41.            }
42.            catch (IOException exc){
43.                System.err.println("Error storing settings to output");
44.                exc.printStackTrace();
45.            }
46.        }
47.        private static void saveNlData(){
48.            try{
49.                Properties textSettings = new Properties();
50.                textSettings.setProperty(GUI_TITLE, "Facade Pattern voorbeeld");
51.                textSettings.setProperty(EXIT_CAPTION, "Exit");
52.                textSettings.setProperty(COUNTRY_LABEL, "Land");
53.                textSettings.setProperty(CURRENCY_LABEL, "Munt eenheid");
54.                textSettings.setProperty(PHONE_LABEL, "Telefoonnummer");
55.                textSettings.store(new FileOutputStream("dutch.properties"), "Dutch
       Settings");
56.            }
57.            catch (IOException exc){
58.                System.err.println("Error storing settings to output");
59.                exc.printStackTrace();
60.            }
61.        }
62.    }
```

The RunPattern class creates the InternationalizationWizard and associates it with the GUI; subsequently, the InternationalizationWizard (Facade) can be used to obtain information about the currently selected country.

Example A.170 RunPattern.java

```
1.     import java.io.File;
2.     public class RunPattern{
3.         public static void main(String [] arguments){
4.             System.out.println("Example for the Facade pattern");
5.             System.out.println();
6.           System.out.println("This code sample uses an InternationalizatgionWizard (a
       Facade)");
7.            System.out.println(" to manage communication between the rest of the appli-
       cation and");
8.             System.out.println(" a series of other classes.");
9.             System.out.println();
10.          System.out.println("The InternationalizatgionWizard maintains a colleciton
       of Nation");
```

```
11.         System.out.println(" objects. When the setNation method is called, the wiz-
        ard sets the");
12.         System.out.println(" default nation, updating the Currency, PhoneNumber and
        localized");
13.         System.out.println(" String resources (InternationalizedText) avail-
        able.");
14.         System.out.println();
15.         System.out.println("Calls to get Strings for the GUI, the currency symbol
        or the dialing");
16.         System.out.println(" prefix are routed through the Facade, the Internation-
        alizationWizard.");
17.         System.out.println();
18.
19.         if (!(new File("data.ser").exists())){
20.             DataCreator.serialize("data.ser");
21.         }
22.
23.         System.out.println("Creating the InternationalizationWizard and setting
        the nation to US.");
24.         System.out.println();
25.         InternationalizationWizard wizard = new InternationalizationWizard();
26.         wizard.setNation("US");
27.
28.         System.out.println("Creating the FacadeGui.");
29.         System.out.println();
30.         FacadeGui application = new FacadeGui(wizard);
31.         application.createGui();
32.         application.setNation(wizard.getNation("US"));
33.     }
34. }
```

Flyweight

This example uses the Flyweight pattern to share common State objects within the PIM. The State pattern example used state objects to edit and store information for a set of Appointments. In this example, the States will be used to manage edits and save for multiple collections of objects.

The State interface provides standard behavior for all application states. It defines two basic methods, edit and save.

Example A.171 State.java

```
1.   package flyweight.example;
2.
3.   import java.io.File;
4.   import java.io.IOException;
5.   import java.io.Serializable;
6.
7.   public interface State {
8.       public void save(File f, Serializable s) throws IOException;
9.       public void edit();
10.  }
```

State is implemented by two classes—CleanState and DirtyState. This example uses these classes to track the state of multiple objects, so the classes have additional support to track which items need to be refreshed.

Example A.172 CleanState.java

```
1.   import java.io.File;
2.   import java.io.FileOutputStream;
3.   import java.io.IOException;
4.   import java.io.ObjectOutputStream;
5.   import java.io.Serializable;
6.
7.   public class CleanState implements State{
8.       public void save(File file, Serializable s, int type) throws IOException{ }
9.
10.      public void edit(int type){
11.          StateFactory.setCurrentState(StateFactory.DIRTY);
12.          ((DirtyState)StateFactory.DIRTY).incrementStateValue(type);
13.      }
14.  }
```

Example A.173 DirtyState.java

```
1.   package flyweight.example;
2.
3.   import java.io.File;
4.   import java.io.FileOutputStream;
5.   import java.io.IOException;
```

```
6.     import java.io.ObjectOutputStream;
7.     import java.io.Serializable;
8.
9.     public class DirtyState implements State {
10.        public void save(File file, Serializable s) throws IOException {
11.            //serialize s to f
12.            FileOutputStream fos = new FileOutputStream(file);
13.            ObjectOutputStream out = new ObjectOutputStream(fos);
14.            out.writeObject(s);
15.        }
16.
17.        public void edit() {
18.            //ignored
19.        }
20.    }
```

Since these two classes are used to track the overall state of the application, they are managed by a `StateFactory` class that creates both objects and provides them on demand.

Example A.174 `StateFactory.java`

```
1.     public class StateFactory {
2.         public static final State CLEAN = new CleanState();
3.         public static final State DIRTY = new DirtyState();
4.         private static State currentState = CLEAN;
5.
6.         public static State getCurrentState(){
7.             return currentState;
8.         }
9.
10.        public static void setCurrentState(State state){
11.            currentState = state;
12.        }
13.    }
```

The example tracks collections of items which are held within the class `ManagedList`. This class makes it possible to ensure that only classes of a certain type are allowed to be stored in a specific `ManagedList`.

Example A.175 `ManagedList.java`

```
1.     import java.util.ArrayList;
2.     public class ManagedList{
3.         private ArrayList elements = new ArrayList();
4.         private Class classType;
5.
6.         public ManagedList(){ }
7.         public ManagedList(Class newClassType){
8.             classType = newClassType;
9.         }
```

```
10.
11.         public void setClassType(Class newClassType){
12.             classType = newClassType;
13.         }
14.
15.         public void addItem(Object item){
16.             if ((item != null) && (classType.isInstance(item))){
17.                 elements.add(item);
18.             } else {
19.                 elements.add(item);
20.             }
21.         }
22.
23.         public void removeItem(Object item){
24.             elements.remove(item);
25.         }
26.
27.         public ArrayList getItems(){
28.             return elements;
29.         }
30.     }
```

The `Address` and `Contact` classes (interface and implementations) provide support for the business objects used in this pattern.

Example A.176 `Address.java`

```
1.      import java.io.Serializable;
2.      public interface Address extends Serializable{
3.          public static final String EOL_STRING = System.getProperty("line.separator");
4.          public static final String SPACE = " ";
5.          public static final String COMMA = ",";
6.          public String getType();
7.          public String getDescription();
8.          public String getStreet();
9.          public String getCity();
10.         public String getState();
11.         public String getZipCode();
12.
13.         public void setType(String newType);
14.         public void setDescription(String newDescription);
15.         public void setStreet(String newStreet);
16.         public void setCity(String newCity);
17.         public void setState(String newState);
18.         public void setZipCode(String newZip);
19.     }
20.
```

Example A.177 AddressImpl.java

```
1.    public class AddressImpl implements Address{
2.        private String type;
3.        private String description;
4.        private String street;
5.        private String city;
6.        private String state;
7.        private String zipCode;
8.        public static final String HOME = "home";
9.        public static final String WORK = "work";
10.
11.       public AddressImpl(){ }
12.       public AddressImpl(String newDescription, String newStreet,
13.           String newCity, String newState, String newZipCode){
14.           description = newDescription;
15.           street = newStreet;
16.           city = newCity;
17.           state = newState;
18.           zipCode = newZipCode;
19.       }
20.
21.       public String getType(){ return type; }
22.       public String getDescription(){ return description; }
23.       public String getStreet(){ return street; }
24.       public String getCity(){ return city; }
25.       public String getState(){ return state; }
26.       public String getZipCode(){ return zipCode; }
27.
28.       public void setType(String newType){ type = newType; }
29.       public void setDescription(String newDescription){ description = newDescrip-
      tion; }
30.       public void setStreet(String newStreet){ street = newStreet; }
31.       public void setCity(String newCity){ city = newCity; }
32.       public void setState(String newState){ state = newState; }
33.       public void setZipCode(String newZip){ zipCode = newZip; }
34.
35.       public String toString(){
36.           return street + EOL_STRING + city + COMMA + SPACE +
37.               state + SPACE + zipCode + EOL_STRING;
38.       }
39.   }
```

Example A.178 Contact.java

```
1.    import java.io.Serializable;
2.    public interface Contact extends Serializable{
3.        public static final String SPACE = " ";
4.        public String getFirstName();
5.        public String getLastName();
6.        public String getTitle();
7.        public String getOrganization();
8.
```

```
9.         public void setFirstName(String newFirstName);
10.        public void setLastName(String newLastName);
11.        public void setTitle(String newTitle);
12.        public void setOrganization(String newOrganization);
13.    }
```

Example A.179 `ContactImpl.java`

```
1.     public class ContactImpl implements Contact{
2.         private String firstName;
3.         private String lastName;
4.         private String title;
5.         private String organization;
6.
7.         public ContactImpl(){}
8.         public ContactImpl(String newFirstName, String newLastName,
9.             String newTitle, String newOrganization){
10.                firstName = newFirstName;
11.                lastName = newLastName;
12.                title = newTitle;
13.                organization = newOrganization;
14.        }
15.
16.        public String getFirstName(){ return firstName; }
17.        public String getLastName(){ return lastName; }
18.        public String getTitle(){ return title; }
19.        public String getOrganization(){ return organization; }
20.
21.        public void setFirstName(String newFirstName){ firstName = newFirstName; }
22.        public void setLastName(String newLastName){ lastName = newLastName; }
23.        public void setTitle(String newTitle){ title = newTitle; }
24.        public void setOrganization(String newOrganization){ organization = newOrgani-
       zation; }
25.
26.        public String toString(){
27.            return firstName + SPACE + lastName;
28.        }
29.    }
```

RunPattern provides a way to test the Flyweight. It creates ManagedList objects for addresses and contacts, then uses common State objects to manage saving the objects to two different files.

Example A.180 `RunPattern.java`

```
1.     public class RunPattern{
2.         public static void main(String [] arguments) throws java.io.IOException{
3.             System.out.println("Example for the Flyweight pattern");
4.             System.out.println();
5.             System.out.println("In this sample, State objects are shared between mul-
       tiple");
```

```
6.            System.out.println(" parts of the PIM. Two lists, representing a Contact
        list");
7.            System.out.println(" and an Address Book, are used for the demonstra-
        tion.");
8.            System.out.println(" The State objects - CleanState and DirtyState - rep-
        resent");
9.            System.out.println(" the Flyweight objects in this example.");
10.           System.out.println();
11.
12.           System.out.println("Creating ManagedList objects to hold Contacts and
        Addresses");
13.           ManagedList contactList = new ManagedList(Contact.class);
14.           ManagedList addressList = new ManagedList(Address.class);
15.           System.out.println();
16.
17.           System.out.println("Printing the State for the application");
18.           printPIMState();
19.           System.out.println();
20.
21.           System.out.println("Editing the Address and Contact lists");
22.           StateFactory.getCurrentState().edit(State.CONTACTS);
23.           StateFactory.getCurrentState().edit(State.ADDRESSES);
24.           contactList.addItem(new ContactImpl("f", "l", "t", "o"));
25.           addressList.addItem(new AddressImpl("d", "s", "c", "st", "z"));
26.           System.out.println("Printing the State for the application");
27.           printPIMState();
28.           System.out.println();
29.
30.           System.out.println("Saving the Contact list");
31.         StateFactory.getCurrentState().save(new java.io.File("contacts.ser"), con-
        tactList.getItems(), State.CONTACTS);
32.           System.out.println("Printing the State for the application");
33.           printPIMState();
34.           System.out.println();
35.
36.           System.out.println("Saving the Address list");
37.           StateFactory.getCurrentState().save(new java.io.File("addresses.ser"),
        addressList.getItems(), State.ADDRESSES);
38.           System.out.println("Printing the State for the application");
39.           printPIMState();
40.       }
41.
42.       private static void printPIMState(){
43.           System.out.println("  Current State of the PIM: " + StateFactory.getCur-
        rentState().getClass());
44.           System.out.println("  Object ID: " + StateFactory.getCurrentState().hash-
        Code());
45.           System.out.println();
46.       }
47.   }
```

Half-Object Plus Protocol (HOPP)

A Personal Information Manager should be available everywhere, but its data should only be stored in one place. This example uses RMI and the HOPP pattern to hold a personal calendar on a server, while making its information available to remote callers.

The Calendar interface defines all methods that will be available remotely. This interface extends java.rmi.Remote and all its methods throw java.rmi.RemoteException. In this case, Calendar defines three methods: getHost, getAppointments, and addAppointment.

Example A.181 Calendar.java

```
1.     import java.rmi.Remote;
2.     import java.rmi.RemoteException;
3.     import java.util.Date;
4.     import java.util.ArrayList;
5.     public interface Calendar extends Remote{
6.         public String getHost() throws RemoteException;
7.         public ArrayList getAppointments(Date date) throws RemoteException;
8.         public void addAppointment(Appointment appointment, Date date) throws Remote-
         Exception;
9.     }
```

Calendar is implemented by two classes—the RMI remote object and its stub, or proxy. (See "Proxy" on page 492.) The remote object class, CalendarImpl, provides method implementations, while the stub manages communication to the remote object. The Java RMI compiler (rmic) needs to be run on the CalendarImpl to generate a stub and a skeleton class. The skeleton class is provided for backward compatibility, but, as of Java 1.2, is no longer necessary.

Example A.182 CalendarImpl.java

```
1.     import java.rmi.Naming;
2.     import java.rmi.server.UnicastRemoteObject;
3.     import java.io.File;
4.     import java.util.Date;
5.     import java.util.ArrayList;
6.     import java.util.HashMap;
7.     public class CalendarImpl implements Calendar{
8.         private static final String REMOTE_SERVICE = "calendarimpl";
9.         private static final String DEFAULT_FILE_NAME = "calendar.ser";
10.        private HashMap appointmentCalendar = new HashMap();
11.
12.        public CalendarImpl(){
13.            this(DEFAULT_FILE_NAME);
14.        }
15.        public CalendarImpl(String filename){
16.            File inputFile = new File(filename);
```

```
17.            appointmentCalendar = (HashMap)FileLoader.loadData(inputFile);
18.            if (appointmentCalendar == null){
19.                appointmentCalendar = new HashMap();
20.            }
21.            try {
22.                UnicastRemoteObject.exportObject(this);
23.                Naming.rebind(REMOTE_SERVICE, this);
24.            }
25.            catch (Exception exc){
26.                System.err.println("Error using RMI to register the CalendarImpl " +
    exc);
27.            }
28.        }
29.
30.        public String getHost(){ return ""; }
31.        public ArrayList getAppointments(Date date){
32.            ArrayList returnValue = null;
33.            Long appointmentKey = new Long(date.getTime());
34.            if (appointmentCalendar.containsKey(appointmentKey)){
35.                returnValue = (ArrayList)appointmentCalendar.get(appointmentKey);
36.            }
37.            return returnValue;
38.        }
39.
40.        public void addAppointment(Appointment appointment, Date date){
41.            Long appointmentKey = new Long(date.getTime());
42.            if (appointmentCalendar.containsKey(appointmentKey)){
43.                ArrayList appointments = (ArrayList)appointmentCalendar.get(appoint-
    mentKey);
44.                appointments.add(appointment);
45.            }
46.            else {
47.                ArrayList appointments = new ArrayList();
48.                appointments.add(appointment);
49.                appointmentCalendar.put(appointmentKey, appointments);
50.            }
51.        }
52.    }
```

The `CalendarImpl` object must use the RMI support class `UnicastRemoteObject` so that it can handle incoming communication requests. In this case, the `CalendarImpl` constructor exports itself using the static method `UnicastRemoteObject.exportObject`.

`CalendarImpl` also needs to have some way of publishing itself to the outside world. In RMI, the naming service is called the `rmiregistry`. It must be running before the `CalendarImpl` object is created. The `rmiregistry` is like a telephone book, providing a connection between a name and an object. When the `CalendarImpl` object registers itself with the `rmiregistry` through the `rebind` method it binds the name "calendarimpl" to the stub of this remote object.

For a client to use the remote object it has to do a lookup in the `rmiregistry` of the host machine and receive the stub to the remote object. You can compare the stub to a telephone number. You can use that number from anywhere, on any phone, and you get connected to someone answering the number you're calling. In this example, the `CalendarHOPP` class acts as the client for the `CalendarImpl` object.

Example A.183 `CalendarHOPP.java`

```
1.  import java.rmi.Naming;
2.  import java.rmi.RemoteException;
3.  import java.util.Date;
4.  import java.util.ArrayList;
5.  public class CalendarHOPP implements Calendar, java.io.Serializable{
6.      private static final String PROTOCOL = "rmi://";
7.      private static final String REMOTE_SERVICE = "/calendarimpl";
8.      private static final String HOPP_SERVICE = "calendar";
9.      private static final String DEFAULT_HOST = "localhost";
10.     private Calendar calendar;
11.     private String host;
12.
13.     public CalendarHOPP(){
14.         this(DEFAULT_HOST);
15.     }
16.     public CalendarHOPP(String host){
17.         try {
18.             this.host = host;
19.             String url = PROTOCOL + host + REMOTE_SERVICE;
20.             calendar = (Calendar)Naming.lookup(url);
21.             Naming.rebind(HOPP_SERVICE, this);
22.         }
23.         catch (Exception exc){
24.             System.err.println("Error using RMI to look up the CalendarImpl or reg-
      ister the CalendarHOPP " + exc);
25.         }
26.     }
27.
28.     public String getHost(){ return host; }
29.     public ArrayList getAppointments(Date date) throws RemoteException{ return
      calendar.getAppointments(date); }
30.
31.     public void addAppointment(Appointment appointment, Date date) throws Remote-
      Exception { calendar.addAppointment(appointment, date); }
32. }
```

The `CalendarHOPP` provides a key benefit over a conventional RMI client – it can locally run what would normally be remote methods. This can provide a substantial benefit in terms of communication overhead. The HOPP implements the same remote interface, but it will not export itself. It keeps a reference to the stub and forwards all the method calls to the stub that it does not (or cannot) handle. Now it can implement the methods that it wants to execute locally—in this example, the getHost method. The HOPP can be registered with the rmiregistry like a normal stub, but it now has the ability to execute methods locally.

Support classes for this example provide the ability to create Appointment objects to be stored by CalendarImpl.

Example A.184 Appointment.java

```
1.    import java.io.Serializable;
2.    import java.util.Date;
3.    import java.util.ArrayList;
4.    public class Appointment implements Serializable{
5.        private String description;
6.        private ArrayList contacts;
7.        private Location location;
8.        private Date startDate;
9.        private Date endDate;
10.
11.       public Appointment(String description, ArrayList contacts, Location location,
        Date startDate, Date endDate){
12.           this.description = description;
13.           this.contacts = contacts;
14.           this.location = location;
15.           this.startDate = startDate;
16.           this.endDate = endDate;
17.       }
18.
19.       public String getDescription(){ return description; }
20.       public ArrayList getContacts(){ return contacts; }
21.       public Location getLocation(){ return location; }
22.       public Date getStartDate(){ return startDate; }
23.       public Date getEndDate(){ return endDate; }
24.
25.       public void setDescription(String description){ this.description = descrip-
        tion; }
26.       public void setContacts(ArrayList contacts){ this.contacts = contacts; }
27.       public void setLocation(Location location){ this.location = location; }
28.       public void setStartDate(Date startDate){ this.startDate = startDate; }
29.       public void setEndDate(Date endDate){ this.endDate = endDate; }
30.
31.       public String toString(){
32.           return "Appointment:" + "\n    Description: " + description +
33.   "\n    Location: " + location + "\n    Start: " +
34.               startDate + "\n    End: " + endDate + "\n";
35.       }
36.   }
```

Example A.185 Contact.java

```
1.    import java.io.Serializable;
2.    public interface Contact extends Serializable{
3.        public static final String SPACE = " ";
```

```
4.       public String getFirstName();
5.       public String getLastName();
6.       public String getTitle();
7.       public String getOrganization();
8.
9.       public void setFirstName(String newFirstName);
10.      public void setLastName(String newLastName);
11.      public void setTitle(String newTitle);
12.      public void setOrganization(String newOrganization);
13.  }
```

Example A.186 `ContactImpl.java`

```
1.   public class ContactImpl implements Contact{
2.       private String firstName;
3.       private String lastName;
4.       private String title;
5.       private String organization;
6.
7.       public ContactImpl(){}
8.       public ContactImpl(String newFirstName, String newLastName,
9.           String newTitle, String newOrganization){
10.              firstName = newFirstName;
11.              lastName = newLastName;
12.              title = newTitle;
13.              organization = newOrganization;
14.      }
15.
16.      public String getFirstName(){ return firstName; }
17.      public String getLastName(){ return lastName; }
18.      public String getTitle(){ return title; }
19.      public String getOrganization(){ return organization; }
20.
21.      public void setFirstName(String newFirstName){ firstName = newFirstName; }
22.      public void setLastName(String newLastName){ lastName = newLastName; }
23.      public void setTitle(String newTitle){ title = newTitle; }
24.     public void setOrganization(String newOrganization){ organization = newOrgani-
    zation; }
25.
26.      public String toString(){
27.          return firstName + SPACE + lastName;
28.      }
29.  }
```

Example A.187 `Location.java`

```
1.   import java.io.Serializable;
2.   public interface Location extends Serializable{
3.       public String getLocation();
4.       public void setLocation(String newLocation);
5.   }
```

Example A.188 LocationImpl.java

```
1.    public class LocationImpl implements Location{
2.        private String location;
3.
4.        public LocationImpl(){ }
5.        public LocationImpl(String newLocation){
6.            location = newLocation;
7.        }
8.
9.        public String getLocation(){ return location; }
10.
11.       public void setLocation(String newLocation){ location = newLocation; }
12.
13.       public String toString(){ return location; }
14.   }
```

FileLoader class provides methods to load the Appointment collection from a file and save it to a file when required.

Example A.189 FileLoader.java

```
1.    import java.io.File;
2.    import java.io.FileInputStream;
3.    import java.io.FileOutputStream;
4.    import java.io.IOException;
5.    import java.io.ObjectInputStream;
6.    import java.io.ObjectOutputStream;
7.    import java.io.Serializable;
8.    public class FileLoader{
9.        public static Object loadData(File inputFile){
10.           Object returnValue = null;
11.           try{
12.               if (inputFile.exists()){
13.                   if (inputFile.isFile()){
14.                    ObjectInputStream readIn = new ObjectInputStream(new FileInput-
      Stream(inputFile));
15.                       returnValue = readIn.readObject();
16.                       readIn.close();
17.                   }
18.                   else {
19.                       System.err.println(inputFile + " is a directory.");
20.                   }
21.               }
22.               else {
23.                   System.err.println("File " + inputFile + " does not exist.");
24.               }
25.           }
26.           catch (ClassNotFoundException exc){
27.               exc.printStackTrace();
28.
29.           }
30.           catch (IOException exc){
```

```
31.                 exc.printStackTrace();
32.
33.             }
34.             return returnValue;
35.         }
36.         public static void storeData(File outputFile, Serializable data){
37.             try{
38.                 ObjectOutputStream writeOut = new ObjectOutputStream(new FileOutput-
        Stream(outputFile));
39.                 writeOut.writeObject(data);
40.                 writeOut.close();
41.             }
42.             catch (IOException exc){
43.                 exc.printStackTrace();
44.             }
45.         }
46.     }
```

The RunPattern class demonstrates this pattern by creating CalendarHOPP and CalendarImpl objects. It uses the CalendarHOPP to perform a local call (getHost), then as a way to access the remote resources—the stored collection of appointments managed by the CalendarImpl object.

Example A.190 RunPattern.java

```
1.      import java.util.Calendar;
2.      import java.util.Date;
3.      import java.util.ArrayList;
4.      import java.io.IOException;
5.      import java.rmi.RemoteException;
6.      public class RunPattern{
7.          private static Calendar dateCreator = Calendar.getInstance();
8.          public static void main(String [] arguments) throws RemoteException{
9.              System.out.println("Example for the HOPP pattern");
10.             System.out.println();
11.             System.out.println("This example will use RMI to demonstrate the HOPP pat-
        tern.");
12.             System.out.println(" In the sample, there will be two objects created, Cal-
        endarImpl");
13.             System.out.println(" and CalendarHOPP. The CalendarImpl object provides the
        true");
14.             System.out.println(" server-side implementation, while the CalendarHOPP
        would be");
15.             System.out.println(" a client or middle-tier representative. The Calendar-
        HOPP will");
16.             System.out.println(" provide some functionality, in this case supplying the
        hostname");
17.             System.out.println(" in response to the getHost method.");
18.             System.out.println();
19.             System.out.println("Note: This example runs the rmiregistry, CalendarHOPP
        and CalendarImpl");
20.             System.out.println(" on the same machine.");
21.             System.out.println();
```

```
22.
23.         try{
24.             Process p1 = Runtime.getRuntime().exec("rmic CalendarImpl");
25.             Process p2 = Runtime.getRuntime().exec("rmic CalendarHOPP");
26.             p1.waitFor();
27.             p2.waitFor();
28.         }
29.         catch (IOException exc){
30.           System.err.println("Unable to run rmic utility. Exiting application.");
31.             System.exit(1);
32.         }
33.         catch (InterruptedException exc){
34.           System.err.println("Threading problems encountered while using the rmic
    utility.");
35.         }
36.
37.         System.out.println("Starting the rmiregistry");
38.         System.out.println();
39.         Process rmiProcess = null;
40.         try{
41.             rmiProcess = Runtime.getRuntime().exec("rmiregistry");
42.             Thread.sleep(15000);
43.         }
44.         catch (IOException exc){
45.             System.err.println("Unable to start the rmiregistry. Exiting applica-
    tion.");
46.             System.exit(1);
47.         }
48.         catch (InterruptedException exc){
49.             System.err.println("Threading problems encountered when starting the
    rmiregistry.");
50.         }
51.
52.        System.out.println("Creating the CalendarImpl object, which provides the
    server-side implementation.");
53.        System.out.println("(Note: If the CalendarImpl object does not have a file
    containing Appointments,");
54.        System.out.println("  this call will produce an error message. This will
    not affect the example.)");
55.         CalendarImpl remoteObject = new CalendarImpl();
56.
57.         System.out.println();
58.        System.out.println("Creating the CalendarHOPP object, which provides cli-
    ent-side functionality.");
59.         CalendarHOPP localObject = new CalendarHOPP();
60.
61.         System.out.println();
62.       System.out.println("Getting the hostname. The CalendarHOPP will handle this
    method locally.");
63.         System.out.println("Hostname is " + localObject.getHost());
64.         System.out.println();
65.
66.       System.out.println("Creating and adding appointments. The CalendarHOPP will
    forward");
67.         System.out.println(" these calls to the CalendarImpl object.");
```

```
68.            Contact attendee = new ContactImpl("Jenny", "Yip", "Chief Java Expert",
        "MuchoJava LTD");
69.            ArrayList contacts = new ArrayList();
70.            contacts.add(attendee);
71.            Location place = new LocationImpl("Albuquerque, NM");
72.            localObject.addAppointment(new Appointment("Opening speeches at annual
        Java Guru's dinner",
73.                contacts, place, createDate(2001, 4, 1, 16, 0),
74.                createDate(2001, 4, 1, 18, 0)), createDate(2001, 4, 1, 0, 0));
75.            localObject.addAppointment(new Appointment("Java Guru post-dinner Cafe
        time",
76.                contacts, place, createDate(2001, 4, 1, 19, 30),
77.                createDate(2001, 4, 1, 21, 45)), createDate(2001, 4, 1, 0, 0));
78.            System.out.println("Appointments added.");
79.            System.out.println();
80.
81.            System.out.println("Getting the Appointments for a date. The CalendarHOPP
        will forward");
82.            System.out.println(" this call to the CalendarImpl object.");
83.            System.out.println(localObject.getAppointments(createDate(2001, 4, 1, 0,
        0)));
84.        }
85.
86.        public static Date createDate(int year, int month, int day, int hour, int
        minute){
87.            dateCreator.set(year, month, day, hour, minute);
88.            return dateCreator.getTime();
89.        }
90.    }
```

Proxy

An address book grows tremendously over a period of time, since it stores all professional and social contacts. In addition, users don't need the address book every time they use the PIM. They do need some kind of address book placeholder to act as a starting point for them to use for graphical purposes, however. This example uses the Proxy pattern to represent the address book.

`AddressBook` defines the interface for accessing the PIM address book. At the very least, it needs to have the ability to add new contacts and to retrieve and store addresses.

Example A.191 `AddressBook.java`

```
1.    import java.io.IOException;
2.    import java.util.ArrayList;
3.    public interface AddressBook {
4.        public void add(Address address);
5.        public ArrayList getAllAddresses();
6.        public Address getAddress(String description);
7.
8.        public void open();
9.        public void save();
10.   }
```

Retrieving the data for the address book might be very time-consuming, given the incredible popularity of the users. Therefore, the proxy should delay creation of the real address book for as long as possible. The proxy, represented by `AddressBookProxy`, has the responsibility for creating the address book—but only when absolutely necessary.

Example A.192 `AddressBookProxy.java`

```
1.    import java.io.File;
2.    import java.io.IOException;
3.    import java.util.ArrayList;
4.    import java.util.Iterator;
5.    public class AddressBookProxy implements AddressBook{
6.        private File file;
7.        private AddressBookImpl addressBook;
8.        private ArrayList localAddresses = new ArrayList();
9.
10.       public AddressBookProxy(String filename){
11.           file = new File(filename);
12.       }
13.
14.       public void open(){
15.           addressBook = new AddressBookImpl(file);
16.           Iterator addressIterator = localAddresses.iterator();
17.           while (addressIterator.hasNext()){
18.               addressBook.add((Address)addressIterator.next());
```

```
19.             }
20.         }
21.
22.         public void save(){
23.             if (addressBook != null){
24.                 addressBook.save();
25.             } else if (!localAddresses.isEmpty()){
26.                 open();
27.                 addressBook.save();
28.             }
29.         }
30.
31.         public ArrayList getAllAddresses(){
32.             if (addressBook == null) {
33.                 open();
34.             }
35.             return addressBook.getAllAddresses();
36.         }
37.
38.         public Address getAddress(String description){
39.             if (!localAddresses.isEmpty()){
40.                 Iterator addressIterator = localAddresses.iterator();
41.                 while (addressIterator.hasNext()){
42.                     AddressImpl address = (AddressImpl)addressIterator.next();
43.                     if (address.getDescription().equalsIgnoreCase(description)){
44.                         return address;
45.                     }
46.                 }
47.             }
48.             if (addressBook == null){
49.                 open();
50.             }
51.             return addressBook.getAddress(description);
52.         }
53.
54.         public void add(Address address){
55.             if (addressBook != null){
56.                 addressBook.add(address);
57.             } else if (!localAddresses.contains(address)){
58.                 localAddresses.add(address);
59.             }
60.         }
61.     }
```

Note that the `AddressBookProxy` has its own `ArrayList` for addresses. If the user adds an address by calling the add method, the proxy can use its internal address book without using the real address book.

The `AddressBookImpl` class represents the real address book for a user. It is associated with a file that stores an `ArrayList` with all the user's addresses. `AddressBookProxy` would create an `AddressBookImpl` object only when it is needed—when a user called the method `getAllAddresses`, for example.

Example A.193 AddressBookImpl.java

```
1.  import java.io.File;
2.  import java.io.IOException;
3.  import java.util.ArrayList;
4.  import java.util.Iterator;
5.  public class AddressBookImpl implements AddressBook {
6.      private File file;
7.      private ArrayList addresses = new ArrayList();
8.
9.      public AddressBookImpl(File newFile) {
10.         file = newFile;
11.         open();
12.     }
13.
14.     public ArrayList getAllAddresses(){ return addresses; }
15.
16.     public Address getAddress(String description){
17.         Iterator addressIterator = addresses.iterator();
18.         while (addressIterator.hasNext()){
19.             AddressImpl address = (AddressImpl)addressIterator.next();
20.             if (address.getDescription().equalsIgnoreCase(description)){
21.                 return address;
22.             }
23.         }
24.         return null;
25.     }
26.
27.     public void add(Address address) {
28.         if (!addresses.contains(address)){
29.             addresses.add(address);
30.         }
31.     }
32.
33.     public void open(){
34.         addresses = (ArrayList)FileLoader.loadData(file);
35.     }
36.
37.     public void save(){
38.         FileLoader.storeData(file, addresses);
39.     }
40. }
```

AddressBookImpl delegates the task of loading and saving files to a worker class called FileLoader. This class has methods to read and write Serializable objects to a file.

Example A.194 FileLoader.java

```
1.  import java.io.File;
2.  import java.io.FileInputStream;
3.  import java.io.FileOutputStream;
```

```
4.     import java.io.IOException;
5.     import java.io.ObjectInputStream;
6.     import java.io.ObjectOutputStream;
7.     import java.io.Serializable;
8.     public class FileLoader{
9.         public static Object loadData(File inputFile){
10.            Object returnValue = null;
11.            try{
12.                if (inputFile.exists()){
13.                    if (inputFile.isFile()){
14.                     ObjectInputStream readIn = new ObjectInputStream(new FileInput-
       Stream(inputFile));
15.                        returnValue = readIn.readObject();
16.                        readIn.close();
17.                    }else{
18.                        System.err.println(inputFile + " is a directory.");
19.                    }
20.                }else{
21.                    System.err.println("File " + inputFile + " does not exist.");
22.                }
23.            }catch (ClassNotFoundException exc){
24.                exc.printStackTrace();
25.            }catch (IOException exc){
26.                exc.printStackTrace();
27.            }
28.            return returnValue;
29.        }
30.        public static void storeData(File outputFile, Serializable data){
31.            try{
32.                ObjectOutputStream writeOut = new ObjectOutputStream(new FileOutput-
       Stream(outputFile));
33.                writeOut.writeObject(data);
34.                writeOut.close();
35.            }catch (IOException exc){
36.                exc.printStackTrace();
37.            }
38.        }
39.    }
```

The interface `Address` and its implementer `AddressImpl` provide storage for address objects in this example.

Example A.195 `Address.java`

```
1.     import java.io.Serializable;
2.     public interface Address extends Serializable{
3.         public static final String EOL_STRING = System.getProperty("line.separator");
4.         public static final String SPACE = " ";
5.         public static final String COMMA = ",";
6.         public String getAddress();
7.         public String getType();
8.         public String getDescription();
9.         public String getStreet();
```

```
10.        public String getCity();
11.        public String getState();
12.        public String getZipCode();
13.
14.        public void setType(String newType);
15.        public void setDescription(String newDescription);
16.        public void setStreet(String newStreet);
17.        public void setCity(String newCity);
18.        public void setState(String newState);
19.        public void setZipCode(String newZip);
20.    }
```

Example A.196 `AddressImpl.java`

```
1.     public class AddressImpl implements Address{
2.         private String type;
3.         private String description;
4.         private String street;
5.         private String city;
6.         private String state;
7.         private String zipCode;
8.         public static final String HOME = "home";
9.         public static final String WORK = "work";
10.
11.        public AddressImpl(){ }
12.        public AddressImpl(String newDescription, String newStreet,
13.            String newCity, String newState, String newZipCode){
14.            description = newDescription;
15.            street = newStreet;
16.            city = newCity;
17.            state = newState;
18.            zipCode = newZipCode;
19.        }
20.
21.        public String getType(){ return type; }
22.        public String getDescription(){ return description; }
23.        public String getStreet(){ return street; }
24.        public String getCity(){ return city; }
25.        public String getState(){ return state; }
26.        public String getZipCode(){ return zipCode; }
27.
28.        public void setType(String newType){ type = newType; }
29.        public void setDescription(String newDescription){ description = newDescrip-
       tion; }
30.        public void setStreet(String newStreet){ street = newStreet; }
31.        public void setCity(String newCity){ city = newCity; }
32.        public void setState(String newState){ state = newState; }
33.        public void setZipCode(String newZip){ zipCode = newZip; }
34.
35.        public String toString(){
36.            return description;
37.        }
38.        public String getAddress(){
```

```
39.         return description + EOL_STRING + street + EOL_STRING +
40.             city + COMMA + SPACE + state + SPACE + zipCode + EOL_STRING;
41.     }
42. }
```

The DataCreator class creates a test file with a set of sample addresses.

Example A.197 DataCreator.java

```
1.  import java.io.Serializable;
2.  import java.io.ObjectOutputStream;
3.  import java.io.FileOutputStream;
4.  import java.io.IOException;
5.  import java.util.ArrayList;
6.  public class DataCreator{
7.      private static final String DEFAULT_FILE = "data.ser";
8.  
9.      public static void main(String [] args){
10.         String fileName;
11.         if (args.length == 1){
12.             fileName = args[0];
13.         }else{
14.             fileName = DEFAULT_FILE;
15.         }
16.         serialize(fileName);
17.     }
18. 
19.     public static void serialize(String fileName){
20.         try{
21.             serializeToFile(createData(), fileName);
22.         } catch (IOException exc){
23.             exc.printStackTrace();
24.         }
25.     }
26. 
27.     private static Serializable createData(){
28.         ArrayList items = new ArrayList();
29.         items.add(new AddressImpl("Home address", "1418 Appian Way", "Pleas-
    antville", "NH", "27415"));
30.         items.add(new AddressImpl("Resort", "711 Casino Ave.", "Atlantic City",
    "NJ", "91720"));
31.         items.add(new AddressImpl("Vacation spot", "90 Ka'ahanau Cir.", "Haleiwa",
    "HI", "41720"));
32.         return items;
33.     }
34. 
35.     private static void serializeToFile(Serializable data, String fileName) throws
    IOException{
36.         ObjectOutputStream serOut = new ObjectOutputStream(new FileOutput-
    Stream(fileName));
37.         serOut.writeObject(data);
38.         serOut.close();
39.     }
40. }
```

RunPattern demonstrates how the proxy could work in practice. First, it creates an AddressBookProxy and adds several new Address objects to the Proxy. These new addresses will initially be stored locally. It is only when the example calls the method getAllAddresses that the Proxy will create an AddressBookImpl object and retrieve addresses stored in the file.

Example A.198 RunPattern.java

```
1.  import java.io.File;
2.  import java.io.IOException;
3.  import java.util.ArrayList;
4.  public class RunPattern{
5.      public static void main(String [] arguments){
6.          System.out.println("Example for the Proxy pattern");
7.          System.out.println();
8.          System.out.println("This code will demonstrate the use of a Proxy to");
9.          System.out.println(" provide functionality in place of its underlying");
10.         System.out.println(" class.");
11.         System.out.println();
12.
13.         System.out.println(" Initially, an AddressBookProxy object will provide");
14.         System.out.println(" address book support without requiring that the");
15.         System.out.println(" AddressBookImpl be created. This could potentially");
16.         System.out.println(" make the application run much faster, since the");
17.         System.out.println(" AddressBookImpl would need to read in all addresses");
18.         System.out.println(" from a file when it is first created.");
19.         System.out.println();
20.
21.         if (!(new File("data.ser").exists())){
22.             DataCreator.serialize("data.ser");
23.         }
24.         System.out.println("Creating the AddressBookProxy");
25.         AddressBookProxy proxy = new AddressBookProxy("data.ser");
26.         System.out.println("Adding entries to the AddressBookProxy");
27.         System.out.println("(this operation can be done by the Proxy, without");
28.         System.out.println(" creating an AddressBookImpl object)");
29.         proxy.add(new AddressImpl("Sun Education [CO]", "500 El Dorado Blvd.",
    "Broomfield", "CO", "80020"));
30.         proxy.add(new AddressImpl("Apple Inc.", "1 Infinite Loop", "Redwood City",
    "CA", "93741"));
31.         System.out.println("Addresses created. Retrieving an address");
32.         System.out.println("(since the address is stored by the Proxy, there is");
33.         System.out.println(" still no need to create an AddressBookImpl object)");
34.         System.out.println();
35.         System.out.println(proxy.getAddress("Sun Education [CO]").getAddress());
36.         System.out.println();
37.
38.         System.out.println("So far, all operations have been handled by the
    Proxy,");
39.         System.out.println(" without any involvement from the AddressBookImpl.");
40.         System.out.println(" Now, a call to the method getAllAddresses will");
```

```
41.            System.out.println(" force instantiation of AddressBookImpl, and will");
42.            System.out.println(" retrieve ALL addresses that are stored.");
43.            System.out.println();
44.
45.            ArrayList addresses = proxy.getAllAddresses();
46.            System.out.println("Addresses retrieved. Addresses currently stored:");
47.            System.out.println(addresses);
48.        }
49.    }
```

System Pattern Code Examples

Model-View-Controller (MVC)

This code example provides a component-level MVC pattern to manage a contact in the Personal Information Manager. The `ContactModel` class provides the model for this demonstration, in this case storing the contact's first name, last name, title and organization.

Example A.199 `ContactModel.java`

```
1.     import java.util.ArrayList;
2.     import java.util.Iterator;
3.     public class ContactModel{
4.         private String firstName;
5.         private String lastName;
6.         private String title;
7.         private String organization;
8.         private ArrayList contactViews = new ArrayList();
9.
10.        public ContactModel(){
11.            this(null);
12.        }
13.        public ContactModel(ContactView view){
14.            firstName = "";
15.            lastName = "";
16.            title = "";
17.            organization = "";
18.            if (view != null){
19.                contactViews.add(view);
20.            }
21.        }
22.
23.        public void addContactView(ContactView view){
24.            if (!contactViews.contains(view)){
25.                contactViews.add(view);
26.            }
27.        }
28.
29.        public void removeContactView(ContactView view){
30.            contactViews.remove(view);
31.        }
32.
33.        public String getFirstName(){ return firstName; }
34.        public String getLastName(){ return lastName; }
35.        public String getTitle(){ return title; }
36.        public String getOrganization(){ return organization; }
37.
38.        public void setFirstName(String newFirstName){ firstName = newFirstName; }
39.        public void setLastName(String newLastName){ lastName = newLastName; }
40.        public void setTitle(String newTitle){ title = newTitle; }
41.       public void setOrganization(String newOrganization){ organization = newOrgani-
      zation; }
42.
```

```
43.        public void updateModel(String newFirstName, String newLastName,
44.            String newTitle, String newOrganization){
45.            if (!isEmptyString(newFirstName)){
46.                setFirstName(newFirstName);
47.            }
48.            if (!isEmptyString(newLastName)){
49.                setLastName(newLastName);
50.            }
51.            if (!isEmptyString(newTitle)){
52.                setTitle(newTitle);
53.            }
54.            if (!isEmptyString(newOrganization)){
55.                setOrganization(newOrganization);
56.            }
57.            updateView();
58.        }
59.
60.        private boolean isEmptyString(String input){
61.            return ((input == null) || input.equals(""));
62.        }
63.
64.        private void updateView(){
65.            Iterator notifyViews = contactViews.iterator();
66.            while (notifyViews.hasNext()){
67.                ((ContactView)notifyViews.next()).refreshContactView(firstName, last-
       Name, title, organization);
68.            }
69.        }
70.    }
```

The `ContactModel` maintains an `ArrayList` of `ContactView` objects, updating them whenever the model data changes. The standard behavior for all views is defined by the `ContactView` interface method `refreshContactView`.

Example A.200 `ContactView.java`

```
1.    public interface ContactView{
2.        public void refreshContactView(String firstName,
3.            String lastName, String title, String organization);
4.    }
```

Two views are used in this example. The first, `ContactDisplayView`, displays the updated model information but does not support a controller, an example of "view-only" behavior.

Example A.201 `ContactDisplayView.java`

```
1.    import javax.swing.JPanel;
2.    import javax.swing.JScrollPane;
3.    import javax.swing.JTextArea;
4.    import java.awt.BorderLayout;
```

```
5.    public class ContactDisplayView extends JPanel implements ContactView{
6.        private JTextArea display;
7.
8.        public ContactDisplayView(){
9.            createGui();
10.       }
11.
12.       public void createGui(){
13.           setLayout(new BorderLayout());
14.           display = new JTextArea(10, 40);
15.           display.setEditable(false);
16.           JScrollPane scrollDisplay = new JScrollPane(display);
17.           this.add(scrollDisplay, BorderLayout.CENTER);
18.       }
19.
20.       public void refreshContactView(String newFirstName,
21.           String newLastName, String newTitle, String newOrganization){
22.           display.setText("UPDATED CONTACT:\nNEW VALUES:\n" +
23.               "\tName: " + newFirstName + " " + newLastName +
24.                "\n" + "\tTitle: " + newTitle + "\n" +
25.               "\tOrganization: " + newOrganization);
26.       }
27.   }
```

The second view is `ContactEditView`, which allows a user to update the contact defined by the model.

Example A.202 `ContactEditView.java`

```
1.    import javax.swing.BoxLayout;
2.    import javax.swing.JButton;
3.    import javax.swing.JLabel;
4.    import javax.swing.JTextField;
5.    import javax.swing.JPanel;
6.    import java.awt.GridLayout;
7.    import java.awt.BorderLayout;
8.    import java.awt.event.ActionListener;
9.    import java.awt.event.ActionEvent;
10.   public class ContactEditView extends JPanel implements ContactView{
11.       private static final String UPDATE_BUTTON = "Update";
12.       private static final String EXIT_BUTTON = "Exit";
13.       private static final String CONTACT_FIRST_NAME = "First Name  ";
14.       private static final String CONTACT_LAST_NAME = "Last Name  ";
15.       private static final String CONTACT_TITLE = "Title  ";
16.       private static final String CONTACT_ORG = "Organization  ";
17.       private static final int FNAME_COL_WIDTH = 25;
18.       private static final int LNAME_COL_WIDTH = 40;
19.       private static final int TITLE_COL_WIDTH = 25;
20.       private static final int ORG_COL_WIDTH = 40;
21.       private ContactEditController controller;
22.       private JLabel firstNameLabel, lastNameLabel, titleLabel, organizationLabel;
23.       private JTextField firstName, lastName, title, organization;
24.       private JButton update, exit;
```

```
25.
26.       public ContactEditView(ContactModel model){
27.           controller = new ContactEditController(model, this);
28.           createGui();
29.       }
30.       public ContactEditView(ContactModel model, ContactEditController newControl-
      ler){
31.           controller = newController;
32.           createGui();
33.       }
34.
35.       public void createGui(){
36.           update = new JButton(UPDATE_BUTTON);
37.           exit = new JButton(EXIT_BUTTON);
38.
39.           firstNameLabel = new JLabel(CONTACT_FIRST_NAME);
40.           lastNameLabel = new JLabel(CONTACT_LAST_NAME);
41.           titleLabel = new JLabel(CONTACT_TITLE);
42.           organizationLabel = new JLabel(CONTACT_ORG);
43.
44.           firstName = new JTextField(FNAME_COL_WIDTH);
45.           lastName = new JTextField(LNAME_COL_WIDTH);
46.           title = new JTextField(TITLE_COL_WIDTH);
47.           organization = new JTextField(ORG_COL_WIDTH);
48.
49.           JPanel editPanel = new JPanel();
50.           editPanel.setLayout(new BoxLayout(editPanel, BoxLayout.X_AXIS));
51.
52.           JPanel labelPanel = new JPanel();
53.           labelPanel.setLayout(new GridLayout(0, 1));
54.
55.           labelPanel.add(firstNameLabel);
56.           labelPanel.add(lastNameLabel);
57.           labelPanel.add(titleLabel);
58.           labelPanel.add(organizationLabel);
59.
60.           editPanel.add(labelPanel);
61.
62.           JPanel fieldPanel = new JPanel();
63.           fieldPanel.setLayout(new GridLayout(0, 1));
64.
65.           fieldPanel.add(firstName);
66.           fieldPanel.add(lastName);
67.           fieldPanel.add(title);
68.           fieldPanel.add(organization);
69.
70.           editPanel.add(fieldPanel);
71.
72.           JPanel controlPanel = new JPanel();
73.           controlPanel.add(update);
74.           controlPanel.add(exit);
75.           update.addActionListener(controller);
76.           exit.addActionListener(new ExitHandler());
77.
```

```
78.             setLayout(new BorderLayout());
79.             add(editPanel, BorderLayout.CENTER);
80.             add(controlPanel, BorderLayout.SOUTH);
81.         }
82.
83.         public Object getUpdateRef(){ return update; }
84.         public String getFirstName(){ return firstName.getText(); }
85.         public String getLastName(){ return lastName.getText(); }
86.         public String getTitle(){ return title.getText(); }
87.         public String getOrganization(){ return organization.getText(); }
88.
89.         public void refreshContactView(String newFirstName,
90.             String newLastName, String newTitle,
91.             String newOrganization){
92.             firstName.setText(newFirstName);
93.             lastName.setText(newLastName);
94.             title.setText(newTitle);
95.             organization.setText(newOrganization);
96.         }
97.
98.         private class ExitHandler implements ActionListener{
99.             public void actionPerformed(ActionEvent event){
100.                System.exit(0);
101.            }
102.        }
103.    }
```

The updates to the model are possible due to the controller associated with the ContactEditView. In this example, Java event-handling features (and by extension the Observer pattern) manage communication between the ContactEditView and its associated Controller. ContactEditController updates the ContactModel when the update behavior is triggered by the ContactEditView, calling the method updateModel with new data provided by the editable fields of its associated view.

Example A.203 ContactEditController.java

```
1.      import java.awt.event.*;
2.
3.      public class ContactEditController implements ActionListener{
4.          private ContactModel model;
5.          private ContactEditView view;
6.
7.          public ContactEditController(ContactModel m, ContactEditView v){
8.              model = m;
9.              view = v;
10.         }
11.
12.         public void actionPerformed(ActionEvent evt){
13.             Object source = evt.getSource();
14.             if (source == view.getUpdateRef()){
15.                 updateModel();
```

```
16.             }
17.         }
18.
19.         private void updateModel(){
20.             String firstName = null;
21.             String lastName = null;
22.             if (isAlphabetic(view.getFirstName())){
23.                 firstName = view.getFirstName();
24.             }
25.             if (isAlphabetic(view.getLastName())){
26.                 lastName = view.getLastName();
27.             }
28.             model.updateModel( firstName, lastName,
29.                 view.getTitle(), view.getOrganization());
30.         }
31.
32.         private boolean isAlphabetic(String input){
33.             char [] testChars = {'1', '2', '3', '4', '5', '6', '7', '8', '9', '0'};
34.             for (int i = 0; i < testChars.length; i++){
35.                 if (input.indexOf(testChars[i]) != -1){
36.                     return false;
37.                 }
38.             }
39.             return true;
40.         }
41.     }
```

`RunPattern` runs the demonstration for this pattern, creating the model and Swing GUIs for both of the associated views. The update information provided by the `ContactEditView` is reflected in the `ContactDisplayView`, demonstrating the fact that a single model can provide information to multiple view objects.

Example A.204 `RunPattern.java`

```
1.      public interface ContactView{
2.          public void refreshContactView(String firstName,
3.              String lastName, String title, String organization);
4.      }
```

Session

In this example, the client requester uses the server to perform a series of operations for updating contact information in a shared address book. A user can perform four operations:

- Add a contact
- Add an address (associated with the current contact)
- Remove an address (associated with the current contact)
- Save the contact and address changes

These operations are defined in the class `SessionClient`.

Example A.205 `SessionClient.java`

```
1.    import java.net.MalformedURLException;
2.    import java.rmi.Naming;
3.    import java.rmi.NotBoundException;
4.    import java.rmi.RemoteException;
5.    public class SessionClient{
6.        private static final String SESSION_SERVER_SERVICE_NAME = "sessionServer";
7.        private static final String SESSION_SERVER_MACHINE_NAME = "localhost";
8.        private long sessionID;
9.        private SessionServer sessionServer;
10.
11.       public SessionClient(){
12.           try{
13.               String url = "//" + SESSION_SERVER_MACHINE_NAME + "/" +
     SESSION_SERVER_SERVICE_NAME;
14.               sessionServer = (SessionServer)Naming.lookup(url);
15.           }
16.           catch (RemoteException exc){}
17.           catch (NotBoundException exc){}
18.           catch (MalformedURLException exc){}
19.           catch (ClassCastException exc){}
20.       }
21.
22.       public void addContact(Contact contact) throws SessionException{
23.           try{
24.               sessionID = sessionServer.addContact(contact, 0);
25.           }
26.           catch (RemoteException exc){}
27.       }
28.
29.       public void addAddress(Address address) throws SessionException{
30.           try{
31.               sessionServer.addAddress(address, sessionID);
32.           }
33.           catch (RemoteException exc){}
34.       }
35.
```

```
36.        public void removeAddress(Address address) throws SessionException{
37.            try{
38.                sessionServer.removeAddress(address, sessionID);
39.            }
40.            catch (RemoteException exc){}
41.        }
42.
43.        public void commitChanges() throws SessionException{
44.            try{
45.                sessionID = sessionServer.finalizeContact(sessionID);
46.            }
47.            catch (RemoteException exc){}
48.        }
49.    }
```

Each client method calls a corresponding method on the remote server. SessionServer defines the four methods available to the clients through RMI.

Example A.206 SessionServer.java

```
1.    import java.rmi.Remote;
2.    import java.rmi.RemoteException;
3.    public interface SessionServer extends Remote{
4.        public long addContact(Contact contact, long sessionID) throws RemoteExcep-
      tion, SessionException;
5.        public long addAddress(Address address, long sessionID) throws RemoteExcep-
      tion, SessionException;
6.        public long removeAddress(Address address, long sessionID) throws RemoteExcep-
      tion, SessionException;
7.        public long finalizeContact(long sessionID) throws RemoteException, SessionEx-
      ception;
8.    }
```

SessionServerImpl implements the SessionServer interface, providing an RMI server. It delegates business behavior to the class SessionServerDelegate.

Example A.207 SessionServerImpl.java

```
1.    import java.rmi.Naming;
2.    import java.rmi.server.UnicastRemoteObject;
3.    public class SessionServerImpl implements SessionServer{
4.        private static final String SESSION_SERVER_SERVICE_NAME = "sessionServer";
5.        public SessionServerImpl(){
6.            try {
7.                UnicastRemoteObject.exportObject(this);
8.                Naming.rebind(SESSION_SERVER_SERVICE_NAME, this);
9.            }
10.           catch (Exception exc){
11.               System.err.println("Error using RMI to register the SessionServerImpl
      " + exc);
12.           }
```

```
13.         }
14.
15.         public long addContact(Contact contact, long sessionID) throws SessionExcep-
        tion{
16.             return SessionServerDelegate.addContact(contact, sessionID);
17.         }
18.
19.         public long addAddress(Address address, long sessionID) throws SessionExcep-
        tion{
20.             return SessionServerDelegate.addAddress(address, sessionID);
21.         }
22.
23.         public long removeAddress(Address address, long sessionID) throws SessionEx-
        ception{
24.             return SessionServerDelegate.removeAddress(address, sessionID);
25.         }
26.
27.         public long finalizeContact(long sessionID) throws SessionException{
28.             return SessionServerDelegate.finalizeContact(sessionID);
29.         }
30.     }
```

Example A.208 `SessionServerDelegate.java`

```
1.      import java.util.ArrayList;
2.      import java.util.HashMap;
3.      public class SessionServerDelegate{
4.          private static final long NO_SESSION_ID = 0;
5.          private static long nextSessionID = 1;
6.          private static ArrayList contacts = new ArrayList();
7.          private static ArrayList addresses = new ArrayList();
8.          private static HashMap editContacts = new HashMap();
9.
10.         public static long addContact(Contact contact, long sessionID) throws Session-
        Exception{
11.             if (sessionID <= NO_SESSION_ID){
12.                 sessionID = getSessionID();
13.             }
14.             if (contacts.indexOf(contact) != -1){
15.                 if (!editContacts.containsValue(contact)){
16.                     editContacts.put(new Long(sessionID), contact);
17.                 }
18.                 else{
19.                     throw new SessionException("This contact is currently being edited
        by another user.",
20.                         SessionException.CONTACT_BEING_EDITED);
21.                 }
22.             }
23.             else{
24.                 contacts.add(contact);
25.                 editContacts.put(new Long(sessionID), contact);
26.             }
27.             return sessionID;
28.         }
```

```
29.
30.     public static long addAddress(Address address, long sessionID) throws Session-
    Exception{
31.         if (sessionID  <= NO_SESSION_ID){
32.             throw new SessionException("A valid session ID is required to add an
    address",
33.                 SessionException.SESSION_ID_REQUIRED);
34.         }
35.         Contact contact = (Contact)editContacts.get(new Long(sessionID));
36.         if (contact == null){
37.             throw new SessionException("You must select a contact before adding an
    address",
38.                 SessionException.CONTACT_SELECT_REQUIRED);
39.         }
40.         if (addresses.indexOf(address) == -1){
41.             addresses.add(address);
42.         }
43.         contact.addAddress(address);
44.         return sessionID;
45.     }
46.
47.     public static long removeAddress(Address address, long sessionID) throws Ses-
    sionException{
48.         if (sessionID  <= NO_SESSION_ID){
49.             throw new SessionException("A valid session ID is required to remove an
    address",
50.                 SessionException.SESSION_ID_REQUIRED);
51.         }
52.         Contact contact = (Contact)editContacts.get(new Long(sessionID));
53.         if (contact == null){
54.             throw new SessionException("You must select a contact before removing
    an address",
55.                 SessionException.CONTACT_SELECT_REQUIRED);
56.         }
57.         if (addresses.indexOf(address) == -1){
58.             throw new SessionException("There is no record of this address",
59.                 SessionException.ADDRESS_DOES_NOT_EXIST);
60.         }
61.         contact.removeAddress(address);
62.         return sessionID;
63.     }
64.
65.     public static long finalizeContact(long sessionID) throws SessionException{
66.         if (sessionID  <= NO_SESSION_ID){
67.             throw new SessionException("A valid session ID is required to finalize
    a contact",
68.                 SessionException.SESSION_ID_REQUIRED);
69.         }
70.         Contact contact = (Contact)editContacts.get(new Long(sessionID));
71.         if (contact == null){
72.             throw new SessionException("You must select and edit a contact before
    committing changes",
73.                 SessionException.CONTACT_SELECT_REQUIRED);
74.         }
```

```
75.            editContacts.remove(new Long(sessionID));
76.            return NO_SESSION_ID;
77.        }
78.
79.        private static long getSessionID(){
80.            return nextSessionID++;
81.        }
82.
83.        public static ArrayList getContacts(){ return contacts; }
84.        public static ArrayList getAddresses(){ return addresses; }
85.        public static ArrayList getEditContacts(){ return new ArrayList(editCon-
      tacts.values()); }
86.    }
```

SessionServerDelegate generates a session ID for clients when they perform their first operation, adding a Contact. Subsequent operations on the Contact's addresses require the session ID, since the ID is used to associate the addresses with a specific Contact within the SessionServerDelegate.

Any errors produced in the example are represented by using the SessionException class.

Example A.209 SessionException.java

```
1.     public class SessionException extends Exception{
2.         public static final int CONTACT_BEING_EDITED = 1;
3.         public static final int SESSION_ID_REQUIRED = 2;
4.         public static final int CONTACT_SELECT_REQUIRED = 3;
5.         public static final int ADDRESS_DOES_NOT_EXIST = 4;
6.         private int errorCode;
7.
8.         public SessionException(String cause, int newErrorCode){
9.             super(cause);
10.            errorCode = newErrorCode;
11.        }
12.        public SessionException(String cause){ super(cause); }
13.
14.        public int getErrorCode(){ return errorCode; }
15.    }
```

The interfaces Address and Contact, and their implementing classes AddressImpl and ContactImpl, represent the business objects used in this example.

Example A.210 Address.java

```
1.     import java.io.Serializable;
2.     public interface Address extends Serializable{
3.         public static final String EOL_STRING = System.getProperty("line.separator");
4.         public static final String SPACE = " ";
5.         public static final String COMMA = ",";
6.         public String getType();
```

```
7.        public String getDescription();
8.        public String getStreet();
9.        public String getCity();
10.       public String getState();
11.       public String getZipCode();
12.
13.       public void setType(String newType);
14.       public void setDescription(String newDescription);
15.       public void setStreet(String newStreet);
16.       public void setCity(String newCity);
17.       public void setState(String newState);
18.       public void setZipCode(String newZip);
19.   }
```

Example A.211 `AddressImpl.java`

```
1.    public class AddressImpl implements Address{
2.        private String type;
3.        private String description;
4.        private String street;
5.        private String city;
6.        private String state;
7.        private String zipCode;
8.
9.        public AddressImpl(){ }
10.       public AddressImpl(String newDescription, String newStreet,
11.           String newCity, String newState, String newZipCode){
12.           description = newDescription;
13.           street = newStreet;
14.           city = newCity;
15.           state = newState;
16.           zipCode = newZipCode;
17.       }
18.
19.       public String getType(){ return type; }
20.       public String getDescription(){ return description; }
21.       public String getStreet(){ return street; }
22.       public String getCity(){ return city; }
23.       public String getState(){ return state; }
24.       public String getZipCode(){ return zipCode; }
25.
26.       public void setType(String newType){ type = newType; }
27.       public void setDescription(String newDescription){ description = newDescrip-
      tion; }
28.       public void setStreet(String newStreet){ street = newStreet; }
29.       public void setCity(String newCity){ city = newCity; }
30.       public void setState(String newState){ state = newState; }
31.       public void setZipCode(String newZip){ zipCode = newZip; }
32.
33.       public boolean equals(Object o){
34.           if (!(o instanceof AddressImpl)){
35.               return false;
36.           }
```

```
37.            else{
38.                AddressImpl address = (AddressImpl)o;
39.                if (street.equals(address.street) &&
40.                    city.equals(address.city) &&
41.                    state.equals(address.state) &&
42.                    zipCode.equals(address.zipCode)){
43.                    return true;
44.                }
45.                return false;
46.            }
47.        }
48.
49.        public String toString(){
50.            return street + EOL_STRING + city + COMMA + SPACE +
51.                state + SPACE + zipCode + EOL_STRING;
52.        }
53.    }
```

Example A.212 `Contact.java`

```
1.     import java.io.Serializable;
2.     import java.util.ArrayList;
3.     public interface Contact extends Serializable{
4.         public static final String SPACE = " ";
5.         public static final String EOL_STRING = System.getProperty("line.separator");
6.         public String getFirstName();
7.         public String getLastName();
8.         public String getTitle();
9.         public String getOrganization();
10.        public ArrayList getAddresses();
11.
12.        public void setFirstName(String newFirstName);
13.        public void setLastName(String newLastName);
14.        public void setTitle(String newTitle);
15.        public void setOrganization(String newOrganization);
16.        public void addAddress(Address address);
17.        public void removeAddress(Address address);
18.    }
```

Example A.213 `ContactImpl.java`

```
1.     import java.util.ArrayList;
2.     public class ContactImpl implements Contact{
3.         private String firstName;
4.         private String lastName;
5.         private String title;
6.         private String organization;
7.         private ArrayList addresses = new ArrayList();
8.
9.         public ContactImpl(){}
10.        public ContactImpl(String newFirstName, String newLastName,
11.          String newTitle, String newOrganization, ArrayList newAddresses){
12.            firstName = newFirstName;
```

```
13.             lastName = newLastName;
14.             title = newTitle;
15.             organization = newOrganization;
16.             if (newAddresses != null){ addresses = newAddresses; }
17.         }
18.
19.         public String getFirstName(){ return firstName; }
20.         public String getLastName(){ return lastName; }
21.         public String getTitle(){ return title; }
22.         public String getOrganization(){ return organization; }
23.         public ArrayList getAddresses(){ return addresses; }
24.
25.         public void setFirstName(String newFirstName){ firstName = newFirstName; }
26.         public void setLastName(String newLastName){ lastName = newLastName; }
27.         public void setTitle(String newTitle){ title = newTitle; }
28.        public void setOrganization(String newOrganization){ organization = newOrgani-
       zation; }
29.         public void addAddress(Address address){
30.             if(!addresses.contains(address)){
31.                 addresses.add(address);
32.             }
33.         }
34.         public void removeAddress(Address address){
35.             addresses.remove(address);
36.         }
37.
38.         public boolean equals(Object o){
39.             if (!(o instanceof ContactImpl)){
40.                 return false;
41.             }
42.             else{
43.                 ContactImpl contact = (ContactImpl)o;
44.                 if (firstName.equals(contact.firstName) &&
45.                     lastName.equals(contact.lastName) &&
46.                     organization.equals(contact.organization) &&
47.                     title.equals(contact.title)){
48.                     return true;
49.                 }
50.                 return false;
51.             }
52.         }
53.
54.         public String toString(){
55.             return firstName + SPACE + lastName + EOL_STRING + addresses;
56.         }
57.     }
```

RunPattern demonstrates how sessions can be used for communication between clients and servers. The main method creates a server and two clients, and subsequently uses both clients to make edits on Contact objects, adding and removing Address objects.

Example A.214 RunPattern.java

```
1.     import java.io.IOException;
2.     public class RunPattern{
3.         public static void main(String [] arguments){
4.             System.out.println("Example for the Session pattern");
5.             System.out.println("This demonstration will show how a Session can be
       used");
6.             System.out.println(" to organize a series of actions between a client
       and");
7.             System.out.println(" server.");
8.             System.out.println("In this case, clients will use sessions to coordi-
       nate");
9.             System.out.println(" edits of Contact addresses.");
10.            System.out.println();
11.
12.            System.out.println("Running the RMI compiler (rmic)");
13.            System.out.println();
14.            try{
15.                Process p1 = Runtime.getRuntime().exec("rmic SessionServerImpl");
16.                p1.waitFor();
17.            }
18.            catch (IOException exc){
19.              System.err.println("Unable to run rmic utility. Exiting application.");
20.                System.exit(1);
21.            }
22.            catch (InterruptedException exc){
23.             System.err.println("Threading problems encountered while using the rmic
       utility.");
24.            }
25.
26.            System.out.println("Starting the rmiregistry");
27.            System.out.println();
28.            Process rmiProcess = null;
29.            try{
30.                rmiProcess = Runtime.getRuntime().exec("rmiregistry");
31.                Thread.sleep(15000);
32.            }
33.            catch (IOException exc){
34.               System.err.println("Unable to start the rmiregistry. Exiting applica-
       tion.");
35.                System.exit(1);
36.            }
37.            catch (InterruptedException exc){
38.               System.err.println("Threading problems encountered when starting the
       rmiregistry.");
39.            }
40.
41.            System.out.println("Creating the SessionServer and two SessionClient
       objects");
42.            System.out.println();
43.            SessionServer serverObject = new SessionServerImpl();
44.            SessionClient clientOne = new SessionClient();
45.            SessionClient clientTwo = new SessionClient();
46.
```

```
47.            System.out.println("Creating sample Contacts and Addresses");
48.            System.out.println();
49.          Contact firstContact = new ContactImpl("First", "Contact", "primo", "OOI",
        null);
50.            Contact secondContact = new ContactImpl("Second", "Contact", "secondo",
        "OOI", null);
51.            Address workAddress = new AddressImpl("Work address", "5440 Division",
        "Fargo", "ND", "54321");
52.            Address homeAddress = new AddressImpl("Home address", "40 Planar Way",
        "Paris", "TX", "84301");
53.
54.          System.out.println("Adding a contact. Both clients will attempt to edit");
55.           System.out.println(" the same contact at first, which will result in a");
56.            System.out.println(" SessionException.");
57.            try{
58.                clientOne.addContact(firstContact);
59.                clientTwo.addContact(firstContact);
60.            }
61.            catch (SessionException exc){
62.                System.err.println("Exception encountered:");
63.                System.err.println(exc);
64.            }
65.            try{
66.               System.out.println("Adding a different contact to the second client");
67.                clientTwo.addContact(secondContact);
68.              System.out.println("Adding addresses to the first and second clients");
69.                clientTwo.addAddress(workAddress);
70.                clientOne.addAddress(homeAddress);
71.                clientTwo.addAddress(workAddress);
72.                clientTwo.addAddress(homeAddress);
73.                System.out.println("Removing address from a client");
74.                clientTwo.removeAddress(homeAddress);
75.                System.out.println("Finalizing the edits to the contacts");
76.                clientOne.commitChanges();
77.                clientTwo.commitChanges();
78.                System.out.println("Changes finalized");
79.                clientTwo.addContact(firstContact);
80.            }
81.            catch (SessionException exc){
82.                System.err.println("Exception encountered:");
83.                System.err.println(exc);
84.            }
85.            System.out.println("The following lines will show the state");
86.            System.out.println(" of the server-side delegate, which in this");
87.            System.out.println(" example represents a persistent data store.");
88.            System.out.println();
89.            System.out.println("Contact list:");
90.            System.out.println(SessionServerDelegate.getContacts());
91.            System.out.println("Address list:");
92.            System.out.println(SessionServerDelegate.getAddresses());
93.            System.out.println("Edit contacts:");
94.            System.out.println(SessionServerDelegate.getEditContacts());
95.        }
96.    }
```

Worker Thread

In a typical application, certain jobs have to be done. It's not always important that they happen now, just that they do happen. You can compare this to cleaning a house. It's not important that it happen at a particular time, as long as somebody does it sometime this week—or month, or year, depending on your standards.

This example uses a `Queue` to hold tasks. The `Queue` interface defines two basic methods, `put` and `take`. These methods are used to add and remove tasks, represented by the `RunnableTask` interface, on the `Queue`.

Example A.215 `Queue.java`

```
1.     public interface Queue{
2.         void put(RunnableTask r);
3.         RunnableTask take();
4.     }
```

Example A.216 `RunnableTask.java`

```
1.     public interface RunnableTask{
2.         public void execute();
3.     }
```

The `ConcreteQueue` class implements the `Queue` and provides a worker thread to operate on the `RunnableTask` objects. The inner class defined for `ConcreteQueue`, `Worker`, has a `run` method that continually searches the queue for new tasks to perform. When a task becomes available, the worker thread pops the `RunnableTask` off the queue and runs its `execute` method.

Example A.217 `ConcreteQueue.java`

```
1.     import java.util.Vector;
2.     public class ConcreteQueue implements Queue{
3.         private Vector tasks = new Vector();
4.         private boolean waiting;
5.         private boolean shutdown;
6.
7.         public void setShutdown(boolean isShutdown){ shutdown = isShutdown; }
8.
9.         public ConcreteQueue(){
10.            tasks = new Vector();
11.            waiting = false;
12.            new Thread(new Worker()).start();
13.        }
14.
15.        public void put(RunnableTask r){
16.            tasks.add(r);
17.            if (waiting){
```

```
18.             synchronized (this){
19.                 notifyAll();
20.             }
21.         }
22.     }
23.
24.     public RunnableTask take(){
25.         if (tasks.isEmpty()){
26.             synchronized (this){
27.                 waiting = true;
28.                 try{
29.                     wait();
30.                 } catch (InterruptedException ie){
31.                     waiting = false;
32.                 }
33.             }
34.         }
35.         return (RunnableTask)tasks.remove(0);
36.     }
37.
38.     private class Worker implements Runnable{
39.         public void run(){
40.             while (!shutdown){
41.                 RunnableTask r = take();
42.                 r.execute();
43.             }
44.         }
45.     }
46. }
```

Two classes, `AddressRetriever` and `ContactRetriever`, implement the `RunnableTask` interface in this example. The classes are very similar; both use RMI to request that a business object be retrieved from a server. As their names suggest, each class retrieves a specific kind of business object, making `Address` and `Contact` objects from the server available to clients.

Example A.218 `AddressRetriever.java`

```
1.  import java.rmi.Naming;
2.  import java.rmi.RemoteException;
3.  public class AddressRetriever implements RunnableTask{
4.      private Address address;
5.      private long addressID;
6.      private String url;
7.
8.      public AddressRetriever(long newAddressID, String newUrl){
9.          addressID = newAddressID;
10.         url = newUrl;
11.     }
12.
13.     public void execute(){
14.         try{
```

```
15.             ServerDataStore dataStore = (ServerDataStore)Naming.lookup(url);
16.             address = dataStore.retrieveAddress(addressID);
17.         }
18.         catch (Exception exc){
19.         }
20.     }
21.
22.     public Address getAddress(){ return address; }
23.    public boolean isAddressAvailable(){ return (address == null) ? false : true; }
24. }
```

Example A.219 `ContractRetriever.java`

```
1.  import java.rmi.Naming;
2.  import java.rmi.RemoteException;
3.  public class ContactRetriever implements RunnableTask{
4.      private Contact contact;
5.      private long contactID;
6.      private String url;
7.
8.      public ContactRetriever(long newContactID, String newUrl){
9.          contactID = newContactID;
10.         url = newUrl;
11.     }
12.
13.     public void execute(){
14.         try{
15.             ServerDataStore dataStore = (ServerDataStore)Naming.lookup(url);
16.             contact = dataStore.retrieveContact(contactID);
17.         }
18.         catch (Exception exc){
19.         }
20.     }
21.
22.     public Contact getContact(){ return contact; }
23.    public boolean isContactAvailable(){ return (contact == null) ? false : true; }
24. }
```

The RMI server in this example is defined by the `ServerDataStore` interface and its implementer, `ServerDataStoreImpl`.

Example A.220 `ServerDataStore.java`

```
1.  import java.rmi.Remote;
2.  import java.rmi.RemoteException;
3.  public interface ServerDataStore extends Remote{
4.      public Address retrieveAddress(long addressID) throws RemoteException;
5.      public Contact retrieveContact(long contactID) throws RemoteException;
6.  }
```

Example A.221 `ServerDataStoreImpl.java`

```
1.   import java.rmi.Naming;
2.   import java.rmi.server.UnicastRemoteObject;
3.   public class ServerDataStoreImpl implements ServerDataStore{
4.     private static final String WORKER_SERVER_SERVICE_NAME = "workerThreadServer";
5.
6.     public ServerDataStoreImpl(){
7.       try {
8.         UnicastRemoteObject.exportObject(this);
9.         Naming.rebind(WORKER_SERVER_SERVICE_NAME, this);
10.      }
11.      catch (Exception exc){
12.        System.err.println("Error using RMI to register the ServerDataStoreImpl
    " + exc);
13.      }
14.    }
15.
16.    public Address retrieveAddress(long addressID){
17.      if (addressID == 5280L){
18.        return new AddressImpl("Fine Dining", "416 Chartres St.", "New
    Orleans", "LA", "51720");
19.      }
20.      else if (addressID == 2010L){
21.        return new AddressImpl("Mystic Yacht Club", "19 Imaginary Lane", "Mys-
    tic", "CT", "46802");
22.      }
23.      else{
24.        return new AddressImpl();
25.      }
26.    }
27.    public Contact retrieveContact(long contactID){
28.      if (contactID == 5280L){
29.        return new ContactImpl("Dwayne", "Dibley", "Accountant", "Virtucon");
30.      }
31.      else{
32.        return new ContactImpl();
33.      }
34.    }
35.
36.  }
```

The `Address` and `Contact` interfaces define the business objects used in this example, and the implementers `AddressImpl` and `ContactImpl` provide underlying functional behavior.

Example A.222 `Address.java`

```
1.   import java.io.Serializable;
2.   public interface Address extends Serializable{
3.     public static final String EOL_STRING = System.getProperty("line.separator");
4.     public static final String SPACE = " ";
```

```
5.        public static final String COMMA = ",";
6.        public String getType();
7.        public String getDescription();
8.        public String getStreet();
9.        public String getCity();
10.       public String getState();
11.       public String getZipCode();
12.
13.       public void setType(String newType);
14.       public void setDescription(String newDescription);
15.       public void setStreet(String newStreet);
16.       public void setCity(String newCity);
17.       public void setState(String newState);
18.       public void setZipCode(String newZip);
19.   }
```

Example A.223 `AddressImpl.java`

```
1.    public class AddressImpl implements Address{
2.        private String type;
3.        private String description;
4.        private String street;
5.        private String city;
6.        private String state;
7.        private String zipCode;
8.
9.        public AddressImpl(){ }
10.       public AddressImpl(String newDescription, String newStreet,
11.           String newCity, String newState, String newZipCode){
12.           description = newDescription;
13.           street = newStreet;
14.           city = newCity;
15.           state = newState;
16.           zipCode = newZipCode;
17.       }
18.
19.       public String getType(){ return type; }
20.       public String getDescription(){ return description; }
21.       public String getStreet(){ return street; }
22.       public String getCity(){ return city; }
23.       public String getState(){ return state; }
24.       public String getZipCode(){ return zipCode; }
25.
26.       public void setType(String newType){ type = newType; }
27.       public void setDescription(String newDescription){ description = newDescrip-
      tion; }
28.       public void setStreet(String newStreet){ street = newStreet; }
29.       public void setCity(String newCity){ city = newCity; }
30.       public void setState(String newState){ state = newState; }
31.       public void setZipCode(String newZip){ zipCode = newZip; }
32.
33.       public String toString(){
34.           return street + EOL_STRING + city + COMMA + SPACE +
```

```
35.                 state + SPACE + zipCode + EOL_STRING;
36.         }
37.     }
```

Example A.224 Contact.java

```
1.      import java.io.Serializable;
2.      public interface Contact extends Serializable{
3.          public static final String EOL_STRING = System.getProperty("line.separator");
4.          public static final String SPACE = " ";
5.          public String getFirstName();
6.          public String getLastName();
7.          public String getTitle();
8.          public String getOrganization();
9.
10.         public void setFirstName(String newFirstName);
11.         public void setLastName(String newLastName);
12.         public void setTitle(String newTitle);
13.         public void setOrganization(String newOrganization);
14.     }
```

Example A.225 ContactImpl.java

```
1.      public class ContactImpl implements Contact{
2.          private String firstName;
3.          private String lastName;
4.          private String title;
5.          private String organization;
6.
7.          public ContactImpl(){}
8.          public ContactImpl(String newFirstName, String newLastName,
9.              String newTitle, String newOrganization){
10.                 firstName = newFirstName;
11.                 lastName = newLastName;
12.                 title = newTitle;
13.                 organization = newOrganization;
14.         }
15.
16.         public String getFirstName(){ return firstName; }
17.         public String getLastName(){ return lastName; }
18.         public String getTitle(){ return title; }
19.         public String getOrganization(){ return organization; }
20.
21.         public void setFirstName(String newFirstName){ firstName = newFirstName; }
22.         public void setLastName(String newLastName){ lastName = newLastName; }
23.         public void setTitle(String newTitle){ title = newTitle; }
24.         public void setOrganization(String newOrganization){ organization = newOrgani-
        zation; }
25.
26.         public String toString(){
27.             return firstName + SPACE + lastName + EOL_STRING;
28.         }
29.     }
```

RunPattern creates a ConcreteQueue, then uses it to retrieve a sample Contact and two Addresses. The worker thread in the queue processes these requests as they are added to the queue. The ConcreteQueue and its associated worker thread can be used throughout the lifetime of a client application, performing any background task required by the client as RunnableTask objects are added to its queue.

Example A.226 RunPattern.java

```
1.    import java.io.IOException;
2.    public class RunPattern{
3.        private static final String WORKER_SERVER_URL = "//localhost/workerThread-
      Server";
4.        public static void main(String [] arguments){
5.            System.out.println("Example for the WorkerThread pattern");
6.          System.out.println("In this example, a ConcreteQueue object which uses a");
7.            System.out.println(" worker thread, will retrieve a number of objects
      from");
8.            System.out.println(" the server.");
9.            System.out.println();
10.
11.           System.out.println("Running the RMI compiler (rmic)");
12.           System.out.println();
13.           try{
14.               Process p1 = Runtime.getRuntime().exec("rmic ServerDataStoreImpl");
15.               p1.waitFor();
16.           }
17.           catch (IOException exc){
18.             System.err.println("Unable to run rmic utility. Exiting application.");
19.               System.exit(1);
20.           }
21.           catch (InterruptedException exc){
22.             System.err.println("Threading problems encountered while using the rmic
      utility.");
23.           }
24.
25.           System.out.println("Starting the rmiregistry");
26.           System.out.println();
27.           Process rmiProcess = null;
28.           try{
29.               rmiProcess = Runtime.getRuntime().exec("rmiregistry");
30.               Thread.sleep(15000);
31.           }
32.           catch (IOException exc){
33.               System.err.println("Unable to start the rmiregistry. Exiting applica-
      tion.");
34.               System.exit(1);
35.           }
36.           catch (InterruptedException exc){
37.               System.err.println("Threading problems encountered when starting the
      rmiregistry.");
```

```
38.             }
39.
40.         System.out.println("Creating the queue, which will be managed by the worker
        thread");
41.             System.out.println();
42.             ConcreteQueue workQueue = new ConcreteQueue();
43.
44.          System.out.println("Creating the RMI server object, ServerDataStoreImpl");
45.             System.out.println();
46.             ServerDataStore server = new ServerDataStoreImpl();
47.
48.             System.out.println("Creating AddressRetrievers and ContactRetreivers.");
49.             System.out.println(" These will placed in the queue, as tasks to be");
50.             System.out.println(" performed by the worker thread.");
51.             System.out.println();
52.             AddressRetriever firstAddr = new AddressRetriever(5280L,
        WORKER_SERVER_URL);
53.             AddressRetriever secondAddr = new AddressRetriever(2010L,
        WORKER_SERVER_URL);
54.             ContactRetriever firstContact = new ContactRetriever(5280L,
        WORKER_SERVER_URL);
55.
56.             workQueue.put(firstAddr);
57.             workQueue.put(firstContact);
58.             workQueue.put(secondAddr);
59.
60.             while (!secondAddr.isAddressAvailable()){
61.                 try{
62.                     Thread.sleep(1000);
63.                 }
64.                 catch (InterruptedException exc){}
65.             }
66.
67.            System.out.println("WorkerThread completed the processing of its Tasks");
68.             System.out.println("Printing out the retrieved objects now:");
69.             System.out.println();
70.             System.out.println(firstAddr.getAddress());
71.             System.out.println(firstContact.getContact());
72.             System.out.println(secondAddr.getAddress());
73.
74.         }
75.
76.     }
```

Callback

In the Personal Information Manager, one of the items that can vary most in size is a project. A project might consist of only a few tasks, or it could be made up of hundreds or even thousands of individual work steps. This example demonstrates how the Callback pattern could be used to retrieve a project object stored on a server machine.

The interface CallbackServer defines a single server-side method, getProject. Note that the method requires callback information—the client machine name and the name of the RMI client object—in addition to the project ID. The class CallbackServerImpl implements this interface.

Example A.227 CallbackServer.java

```
1.  import java.rmi.Remote;
2.  import java.rmi.RemoteException;
3.  public interface CallbackServer extends Remote{
4.      public void getProject(String projectID, String callbackMachine,
5.        String callbackObjectName) throws RemoteException;
6.  }
```

Example A.228 CallbackServerImpl.java

```
1.  import java.rmi.Naming;
2.  import java.rmi.server.UnicastRemoteObject;
3.  public class CallbackServerImpl implements CallbackServer{
4.      private static final String CALLBACK_SERVER_SERVICE_NAME = "callbackServer";
5.      public CallbackServerImpl(){
6.          try {
7.              UnicastRemoteObject.exportObject(this);
8.              Naming.rebind(CALLBACK_SERVER_SERVICE_NAME, this);
9.          }
10.         catch (Exception exc){
11.           System.err.println("Error using RMI to register the CallbackServerImpl
    " + exc);
12.         }
13.     }
14.
15.     public void getProject(String projectID, String callbackMachine,
16.       String callbackObjectName){
17.         new CallbackServerWorkThread(projectID, callbackMachine, callbackObject-
    Name);
18.     }
19.
20. }
```

In the getProject method, CallbackServerImpl delegates the task of retrieving the project to a worker object, CallbackServerDelegate. This object runs on its own thread and does the work of retrieving a project and sending it to a client.

Example A.229 `CallbackServerDelegate.java`

```
1.  import java.net.MalformedURLException;
2.  import java.rmi.Naming;
3.  import java.rmi.NotBoundException;
4.  import java.rmi.RemoteException;
5.  public class CallbackServerDelegate implements Runnable{
6.      private Thread processingThread;
7.      private String projectID;
8.      private String callbackMachine;
9.      private String callbackObjectName;
10.
11.     public CallbackServerDelegate(String newProjectID, String newCallbackMachine,
12.       String newCallbackObjectName){
13.         projectID = newProjectID;
14.         callbackMachine = newCallbackMachine;
15.         callbackObjectName = newCallbackObjectName;
16.         processingThread = new Thread(this);
17.         processingThread.start();
18.     }
19.
20.     public void run(){
21.         Project result = getProject();
22.         sendProjectToClient(result);
23.     }
24.
25.     private Project getProject(){
26.         return new Project(projectID, "Test project");
27.     }
28.
29.     private void sendProjectToClient(Project project){
30.         try{
31.             String url = "//" + callbackMachine + "/" + callbackObjectName;
32.             Object remoteClient = Naming.lookup(url);
33.             if (remoteClient instanceof CallbackClient){
34.                 ((CallbackClient)remoteClient).receiveProject(project);
35.             }
36.         }
37.         catch (RemoteException exc){}
38.         catch (NotBoundException exc){}
39.         catch (MalformedURLException exc){}
40.     }
41. }
```

In the `CallbackServerDelegate` `run` method, the object retrieves a project by calling the `getProject` method, then sends it to a client with the `sendProjectToClient` method. The latter method represents the callback to the client; the `CallbackServerDelegate` makes a call to an RMI object of type `CallbackClient` on the client machine. The interface `CallbackClient` also defines a single RMI method, `receiveProject`.

Example A.230 `CallbackClient.java`

```
1.    import java.rmi.Remote;
2.    import java.rmi.RemoteException;
3.    public interface CallbackClient extends Remote{
4.        public void receiveProject(Project project) throws RemoteException;
5.    }
```

The implementer of `CallbackClient`, `CallbackClientImpl`, is both a client and a server. Its method `requestProject` looks up the `CallbackServer` and calls the remote method `getProject`. The class also defines the remote method `receiveProject`, which is called by the server work thread when the project is ready for the client. `CallbackClientImpl` has a boolean variable, `projectAvailable`, to allow a client program to determine when the project is ready for display.

Example A.231 `CallbackClientImpl.java`

```
1.    import java.net.InetAddress;
2.    import java.net.MalformedURLException;
3.    import java.net.UnknownHostException;
4.    import java.rmi.Naming;
5.    import java.rmi.server.UnicastRemoteObject;
6.    import java.rmi.NotBoundException;
7.    import java.rmi.RemoteException;
8.    public class CallbackClientImpl implements CallbackClient{
9.        private static final String CALLBACK_CLIENT_SERVICE_NAME = "callbackClient";
10.       private static final String CALLBACK_SERVER_SERVICE_NAME = "callbackServer";
11.       private static final String CALLBACK_SERVER_MACHINE_NAME = "localhost";
12.
13.       private Project requestedProject;
14.       private boolean projectAvailable;
15.
16.       public CallbackClientImpl(){
17.           try {
18.               UnicastRemoteObject.exportObject(this);
19.               Naming.rebind(CALLBACK_CLIENT_SERVICE_NAME, this);
20.           }
21.           catch (Exception exc){
22.             System.err.println("Error using RMI to register the CallbackClientImpl
   " + exc);
23.           }
24.       }
25.
26.       public void receiveProject(Project project){
27.           requestedProject = project;
28.           projectAvailable = true;
29.       }
30.
31.       public void requestProject(String projectName){
32.           try{
```

```
33.             String url = "//" + CALLBACK_SERVER_MACHINE_NAME + "/" +
      CALLBACK_SERVER_SERVICE_NAME;
34.             Object remoteServer = Naming.lookup(url);
35.             if (remoteServer instanceof CallbackServer){
36.                 ((CallbackServer)remoteServer).getProject(projectName,
37.                     InetAddress.getLocalHost().getHostName(),
38.                     CALLBACK_CLIENT_SERVICE_NAME);
39.             }
40.             projectAvailable = false;
41.         }
42.         catch (RemoteException exc){}
43.         catch (NotBoundException exc){}
44.         catch (MalformedURLException exc){}
45.         catch (UnknownHostException exc){}
46.     }
47.
48.     public Project getProject(){ return requestedProject; }
49.     public boolean isProjectAvailable(){ return projectAvailable; }
50. }
```

The basic sequence of action is as follows. When a client requires a project, the `CallbackClientImpl` object calls the method `getProject` on the `CallbackServerImpl` object. The `CallbackServerImpl` creates a `CallbackServerWorkThread` object to retrieve the project. When the `CallbackServerWorkThread` completes its task, it calls the client method `receiveProject`, sending the `Project` instance to the requester, the `CallbackClientImpl` object.

In this example, the interface `ProjectItem` and the classes `Project` and `Task` are used to represent the project resource to be retrieved by the client.

Example A.232 `Project.java`

```
1.  import java.util.ArrayList;
2.  public class Project implements ProjectItem{
3.      private String name;
4.      private String description;
5.      private ArrayList projectItems = new ArrayList();
6.
7.      public Project(){ }
8.      public Project(String newName, String newDescription){
9.          name = newName;
10.         description = newDescription;
11.     }
12.
13.     public String getName(){ return name; }
14.     public String getDescription(){ return description; }
15.     public ArrayList getProjectItems(){ return projectItems; }
16.
17.     public void setName(String newName){ name = newName; }
18.     public void setDescription(String newDescription){ description = newDescrip-
    tion; }
```

```
19.
20.        public void addProjectItem(ProjectItem element){
21.            if (!projectItems.contains(element)){
22.                projectItems.add(element);
23.            }
24.        }
25.
26.        public void removeProjectItem(ProjectItem element){
27.            projectItems.remove(element);
28.        }
29.
30.        public String toString(){ return name + ", " + description; }
31.    }
```

Example A.233 `ProjectItem.java`

```
1.     import java.io.Serializable;
2.     import java.util.ArrayList;
3.     public interface ProjectItem extends Serializable{
4.         public ArrayList getProjectItems();
5.     }
```

Example A.234 `Task.java`

```
1.     import java.util.ArrayList;
2.     public class Task implements ProjectItem{
3.         private String name;
4.         private ArrayList projectItems = new ArrayList();
5.         private double timeRequired;
6.
7.         public Task(){ }
8.         public Task(String newName, double newTimeRequired){
9.             name = newName;
10.            timeRequired = newTimeRequired;
11.        }
12.
13.        public String getName(){ return name; }
14.        public ArrayList getProjectItems(){ return projectItems; }
15.        public double getTimeRequired(){ return timeRequired; }
16.
17.        public void setName(String newName){ name = newName; }
18.        public void setTimeRequired(double newTimeRequired){ timeRequired = newTimeRe-
       quired; }
19.
20.        public void addProjectItem(ProjectItem element){
21.            if (!projectItems.contains(element)){
22.                projectItems.add(element);
23.            }
24.        }
25.
26.        public void removeProjectItem(ProjectItem element){
```

```
27.             projectItems.remove(element);
28.         }
29.
30.     }
```

RunPattern creates a demonstration RMI client and server object. In the example, the main program thread uses the CallbackClientImpl object to request a project from the server, then enters a wait loop until the project is returned.

Example A.235 RunPattern.java

```
1.     import java.io.IOException;
2.     public class RunPattern{
3.         public static void main(String [] arguments){
4.             System.out.println("Example for the Callback pattern");
5.             System.out.println("This code will run two RMI objects to demonstrate");
6.             System.out.println(" callback capability. One will be CallbackClien-
       tImpl,");
7.             System.out.println(" which will request a project from the other remote");
8.             System.out.println(" object, CallbackServerImpl.");
9.             System.out.println("To demonstrate how the Callback pattern allows the");
10.            System.out.println(" client to perform independent processing, the main");
11.            System.out.println(" progam thread will go into a wait loop until the");
12.            System.out.println(" server sends the object to its client.");
13.            System.out.println();
14.
15.            System.out.println("Running the RMI compiler (rmic)");
16.            System.out.println();
17.            try{
18.                Process p1 = Runtime.getRuntime().exec("rmic CallbackServerImpl");
19.                Process p2 = Runtime.getRuntime().exec("rmic CallbackClientImpl");
20.                p1.waitFor();
21.                p2.waitFor();
22.            }
23.            catch (IOException exc){
24.              System.err.println("Unable to run rmic utility. Exiting application.");
25.                System.exit(1);
26.            }
27.            catch (InterruptedException exc){
28.              System.err.println("Threading problems encountered while using the rmic
       utility.");
29.            }
30.
31.            System.out.println("Starting the rmiregistry");
32.            System.out.println();
33.            Process rmiProcess = null;
34.            try{
35.                rmiProcess = Runtime.getRuntime().exec("rmiregistry");
36.                Thread.sleep(15000);
37.            }
38.            catch (IOException exc){
```

```
39.             System.err.println("Unable to start the rmiregistry. Exiting applica-
       tion.");
40.             System.exit(1);
41.         }
42.         catch (InterruptedException exc){
43.             System.err.println("Threading problems encountered when starting the
       rmiregistry.");
44.         }
45.
46.         System.out.println("Creating the client and server objects");
47.         System.out.println();
48.         CallbackServerImpl callbackServer = new CallbackServerImpl();
49.         CallbackClientImpl callbackClient = new CallbackClientImpl();
50.
51.         System.out.println("CallbackClientImpl requesting a project");
52.         callbackClient.requestProject("New Java Project");
53.
54.         try{
55.             while(!callbackClient.isProjectAvailable()){
56.                 System.out.println("Project not available yet; sleeping for 2 sec-
       onds");
57.                 Thread.sleep(2000);
58.             }
59.         }
60.         catch (InterruptedException exc){}
61.         System.out.println("Project retrieved: " + callbackClient.getProject());
62.     }
63. }
```

Successive Update

The example code shows a simple client pull solution for the Personal Information Manager. Clients use the server to centralize information about tasks they are working on. Each client stays up-to-date by periodically requesting updates from the server.

In the sample code, the `PullClient` class retrieves a task for a client. Its responsibility is to locate the RMI server so that it can request tasks on a regular basis.

Example A.236 `PullClient.java`

```
1.   import java.net.MalformedURLException;
2.   import java.rmi.Naming;
3.   import java.rmi.NotBoundException;
4.   import java.rmi.RemoteException;
5.   import java.util.Date;
6.   public class PullClient{
7.       private static final String UPDATE_SERVER_SERVICE_NAME = "updateServer";
8.       private static final String UPDATE_SERVER_MACHINE_NAME = "localhost";
9.       private ClientPullServer updateServer;
10.      private ClientPullRequester requester;
11.      private Task updatedTask;
12.      private String clientName;
13.
14.      public PullClient(String newClientName){
15.          clientName = newClientName;
16.          try{
17.              String url = "//" + UPDATE_SERVER_MACHINE_NAME + "/" +
     UPDATE_SERVER_SERVICE_NAME;
18.              updateServer = (ClientPullServer)Naming.lookup(url);
19.          }
20.          catch (RemoteException exc){}
21.          catch (NotBoundException exc){}
22.          catch (MalformedURLException exc){}
23.          catch (ClassCastException exc){}
24.      }
25.
26.      public void requestTask(String taskID){
27.          requester = new ClientPullRequester(this, updateServer, taskID);
28.      }
29.
30.      public void updateTask(Task task){
31.          requester.updateTask(task);
32.      }
33.
34.      public Task getUpdatedTask(){
35.          return updatedTask;
36.      }
37.
38.      public void setUpdatedTask(Task task){
```

```
39.             updatedTask = task;
40.             System.out.println(clientName + ": received updated task: " + task);
41.         }
42.
43.         public String toString(){
44.             return clientName;
45.         }
46.     }
```

When the client wants to receive updates on a task, it calls the method `requestTask` on the `PullClient`. The `PullClient` object creates a worker thread (see “Worker Thread” on page 517), which is the `ClientPullRequester` object. This object resides on the client, and regularly issues a request to the server for updated task information.

Example A.237 `ClientPullRequester.java`

```
1.     import java.rmi.RemoteException;
2.     public class ClientPullRequester implements Runnable{
3.         private static final int DEFAULT_POLLING_INTERVAL = 10000;
4.         private Thread processingThread;
5.         private PullClient parent;
6.         private ClientPullServer updateServer;
7.         private String taskID;
8.         private boolean shutdown;
9.         private Task currentTask = new TaskImpl();
10.        private int pollingInterval = DEFAULT_POLLING_INTERVAL;
11.
12.        public ClientPullRequester(PullClient newParent, ClientPullServer newUpdate-
       Server,
13.            String newTaskID){
14.            parent = newParent;
15.            taskID = newTaskID;
16.            updateServer = newUpdateServer;
17.            processingThread = new Thread(this);
18.            processingThread.start();
19.        }
20.
21.        public void run(){
22.            while (!isShutdown()){
23.                try{
24.                 currentTask = updateServer.getTask(taskID, currentTask.getLastEdit-
       Date());
25.                    parent.setUpdatedTask(currentTask);
26.                }
27.                catch (RemoteException exc){ }
28.                catch (UpdateException exc){
29.                    System.out.println("  " + parent + ": " + exc.getMessage());
30.                }
31.                try{
32.                    Thread.sleep(pollingInterval);
33.                }
```

```
34.                catch (InterruptedException exc){ }
35.            }
36.        }
37.
38.        public void updateTask(Task changedTask){
39.            try{
40.                updateServer.updateTask(taskID, changedTask);
41.            }
42.            catch (RemoteException exc){ }
43.            catch (UpdateException exc){
44.                System.out.println("    " + parent + ": " + exc.getMessage());
45.            }
46.        }
47.
48.        public int getPollingInterval(){ return pollingInterval; }
49.        public boolean isShutdown(){ return shutdown; }
50.
51.        public void setPollingInterval(int newPollingInterval){ pollingInterval = new-
      PollingInterval; }
52.        public void setShutdown(boolean isShutdown){ shutdown = isShutdown; }
53.    }
```

The RMI server's behavior is defined by the `ClientPullServer` interface and managed by the `ClientPullServerImpl` class. Two methods allow clients to interact with a server, `getTask` and `updateTask`.

Example A.238 `ClientPullServer.java`

```
1.     import java.rmi.Remote;
2.     import java.rmi.RemoteException;
3.     import java.util.Date;
4.     public interface ClientPullServer extends Remote{
5.         public Task getTask(String taskID, Date lastUpdate) throws RemoteException,
      UpdateException;
6.         public void updateTask(String taskID, Task updatedTask) throws RemoteExcep-
      tion, UpdateException;
7.     }
```

Example A.239 `ClientPullServerImpl.java`

```
1.     import java.util.Date;
2.     import java.rmi.Naming;
3.     import java.rmi.server.UnicastRemoteObject;
4.     public class ClientPullServerImpl implements ClientPullServer{
5.         private static final String UPDATE_SERVER_SERVICE_NAME = "updateServer";
6.         public ClientPullServerImpl(){
7.             try {
8.                 UnicastRemoteObject.exportObject(this);
9.                 Naming.rebind(UPDATE_SERVER_SERVICE_NAME, this);
10.            }
11.            catch (Exception exc){
12.                System.err.println("Error using RMI to register the ClientPullServer-
      Impl " + exc);
```

```
13.            }
14.        }
15.
16.        public Task getTask(String taskID, Date lastUpdate) throws UpdateException{
17.            return UpdateServerDelegate.getTask(taskID, lastUpdate);
18.        }
19.
20.        public void updateTask(String taskID, Task updatedTask) throws UpdateExcep-
      tion{
21.            UpdateServerDelegate.updateTask(taskID, updatedTask);
22.        }
23.    }
```

The class UpdateServerDelegate performs the server-side behavior for ClientPullServerImpl. Specifically, it retrieves Task objects, and ensures that up-to-date copies of Tasks are provided to clients by comparing the last update Date.

Example A.240 UpdateServerDelegate.java

```
1.     import java.util.Date;
2.     import java.util.HashMap;
3.     public class UpdateServerDelegate{
4.         private static HashMap tasks = new HashMap();
5.
6.         public static Task getTask(String taskID, Date lastUpdate) throws UpdateExcep-
      tion{
7.             if (tasks.containsKey(taskID)){
8.                 Task storedTask = (Task)tasks.get(taskID);
9.                 if (storedTask.getLastEditDate().after(lastUpdate)){
10.                    return storedTask;
11.                }
12.                else{
13.                  throw new UpdateException("Task " + taskID + " does not need to be
      updated", UpdateException.TASK_UNCHANGED);
14.                }
15.            }
16.            else{
17.                return loadNewTask(taskID);
18.            }
19.        }
20.
21.        public static void updateTask(String taskID, Task task) throws UpdateExcep-
      tion{
22.            if (tasks.containsKey(taskID)){
23.               if (task.getLastEditDate().equals(((Task)tasks.get(taskID)).getLastE-
      ditDate())){
24.                    ((TaskImpl)task).setLastEditDate(new Date());
25.                    tasks.put(taskID, task);
26.                }
27.                else{
28.                    throw new UpdateException("Task " + taskID + " data must be
      refreshed before editing", UpdateException.TASK_OUT_OF_DATE);
```

```
29.                 }
30.             }
31.         }
32.
33.         private static Task loadNewTask(String taskID){
34.             Task newTask = new TaskImpl(taskID, "", new Date(), null);
35.             tasks.put(taskID, newTask);
36.             return newTask;
37.         }
38.     }
```

Any problems encountered during the periodic client pull operations are represented by the `UpdateException` class. The `Task` interface and `TaskImpl` class represent the business elements of the example.

Example A.241 `Task.java`

```
1.  import java.util.Date;
2.  import java.io.Serializable;
3.  import java.util.ArrayList;
4.  public interface Task extends Serializable{
5.      public String getTaskID();
6.      public Date getLastEditDate();
7.      public String getTaskName();
8.      public String getTaskDetails();
9.      public ArrayList getSubTasks();
10.
11.     public void setTaskName(String newName);
12.     public void setTaskDetails(String newDetails);
13.     public void addSubTask(Task task);
14.     public void removeSubTask(Task task);
15. }
```

Example A.242 `TaskImpl.java`

```
1.  import java.util.Date;
2.  import java.io.Serializable;
3.  import java.util.ArrayList;
4.  public class TaskImpl implements Task{
5.      private String taskID;
6.      private Date lastEditDate;
7.      private String taskName;
8.      private String taskDetails;
9.      private ArrayList subTasks = new ArrayList();
10.
11.     public TaskImpl(){
12.         lastEditDate = new Date();
13.         taskName = "";
14.         taskDetails = "";
15.     }
16.     public TaskImpl(String newTaskName, String newTaskDetails,
17.       Date newEditDate, ArrayList newSubTasks){
```

```
18.             lastEditDate = newEditDate;
19.             taskName = newTaskName;
20.             taskDetails = newTaskDetails;
21.             if (newSubTasks != null){ subTasks = newSubTasks; }
22.         }
23.
24.         public String getTaskID(){
25.             return taskID;
26.         }
27.         public Date getLastEditDate(){ return lastEditDate; }
28.         public String getTaskName(){ return taskName; }
29.         public String getTaskDetails(){ return taskDetails; }
30.         public ArrayList getSubTasks(){ return subTasks; }
31.
32.         public void setLastEditDate(Date newDate){
33.             if (newDate.after(lastEditDate)){
34.                 lastEditDate = newDate;
35.             }
36.         }
37.         public void setTaskName(String newName){ taskName = newName; }
38.         public void setTaskDetails(String newDetails){ taskDetails = newDetails; }
39.         public void addSubTask(Task task){
40.             if (!subTasks.contains(task)){
41.                 subTasks.add(task);
42.             }
43.         }
44.         public void removeSubTask(Task task){
45.             subTasks.remove(task);
46.         }
47.
48.         public String toString(){
49.             return taskName + " " + taskDetails;
50.         }
51.     }
```

Example A.243 `UpdateException.java`

```
1.      public class UpdateException extends Exception{
2.          public static final int TASK_UNCHANGED = 1;
3.          public static final int TASK_OUT_OF_DATE = 2;
4.          private int errorCode;
5.
6.          public UpdateException(String cause, int newErrorCode){
7.              super(cause);
8.              errorCode = newErrorCode;
9.          }
10.         public UpdateException(String cause){ super(cause); }
11.
12.         public int getErrorCode(){ return errorCode; }
13.     }
```

RunPattern demonstrates how updates of a Task can be propagated to multiple clients. The main method creates a ClientPullServer and two PullClient objects. Both clients are used to request a common Task, then one of the PullClients makes an update to the Task. The change is reflected in the other client as its worker thread, the ClientPullRequester, polls the server for changes.

Example A.244 RunPattern.java

```
1.  import java.io.IOException;
2.  public class RunPattern{
3.      public static void main(String [] arguments){
4.          System.out.println("Example for the SuccessiveUpdate pattern");
5.          System.out.println("This code provides a basic demonstration");
6.          System.out.println(" of how the client pull form of this pattern");
7.          System.out.println(" could be applied.");
8.          System.out.println("In this case, a change made by a client to a");
9.          System.out.println(" central Task object is subsequently retrieved");
10.         System.out.println(" and displayed by another client.");
11.
12.         System.out.println("Running the RMI compiler (rmic)");
13.         System.out.println();
14.         try{
15.             Process p1 = Runtime.getRuntime().exec("rmic ClientPullServerImpl");
16.             p1.waitFor();
17.         }
18.         catch (IOException exc){
19.           System.err.println("Unable to run rmic utility. Exiting application.");
20.             System.exit(1);
21.         }
22.         catch (InterruptedException exc){
23.           System.err.println("Threading problems encountered while using the rmic
    utility.");
24.         }
25.
26.         System.out.println("Starting the rmiregistry");
27.         System.out.println();
28.         Process rmiProcess = null;
29.         try{
30.             rmiProcess = Runtime.getRuntime().exec("rmiregistry");
31.             Thread.sleep(15000);
32.         }
33.         catch (IOException exc){
34.             System.err.println("Unable to start the rmiregistry. Exiting applica-
    tion.");
35.             System.exit(1);
36.         }
37.         catch (InterruptedException exc){
38.             System.err.println("Threading problems encountered when starting the
    rmiregistry.");
39.         }
40.
```

```
41.         System.out.println("Creating the ClientPullServer and two PullClient
        objects");
42.         ClientPullServer server = new ClientPullServerImpl();
43.         PullClient clientOne = new PullClient("Thing I");
44.         PullClient clientTwo = new PullClient("Thing II");
45.         clientOne.requestTask("First work step");
46.         clientTwo.requestTask("First work step");
47.
48.         try{
49.             Thread.sleep(10000);
50.         }
51.         catch (InterruptedException exc){ }
52.
53.         Task task = clientOne.getUpdatedTask();
54.         task.setTaskDetails("Trial for task update");
55.         clientOne.updateTask(task);
56.
57.         Task newTask = clientTwo.getUpdatedTask();
58.         newTask.setTaskDetails("New details string");
59.         clientTwo.updateTask(newTask);
60.
61.
62.     }
63. }
```

Router

The Router can be useful at various places in the example application. In almost every situation where there is more than one interested party in any event, you can use the Router. The Router is essentially an implementation of a listener structure; you will see some similarities.

The code for the `Message` class is shown here. It is a container for the source (an `InputChannel`) and the actual message—in this case, some `String`.

Example A.245 `Message.java`

```
1.    import java.io.Serializable;
2.    public class Message implements Serializable{
3.        private InputChannel source;
4.        private String message;
5.
6.        public Message(InputChannel source, String message){
7.            this.source = source;
8.            this.message = message;
9.        }
10.
11.       public InputChannel getSource(){ return source; }
12.       public String getMessage(){ return message; }
13.   }
```

Example A.246 `InputChannel.java`

```
1.    import java.io.Serializable;
2.    public interface InputChannel extends Serializable{}
```

The `OutputChannel` is the interface that defines the method for sending the message to the target. Since the `OutputChannel` can be used to communicate between machines, it is defined as a remote interface.

Example A.247 `OutputChannel.java`

```
1.    import java.rmi.Remote;
2.    import java.rmi.RemoteException;
3.    public interface OutputChannel extends Remote{
4.        public void sendMessage(Message message) throws RemoteException;
5.    }
```

The `Router` uses a hash map to store links between the specific `InputChannel` and various `OutputChannels`. When it receives a message, it looks up the destinations in its map.

It loops through the collection and sends the message to each of the destinations. In this example, the `Router` creates a worker thread (see "Worker Thread" on page 517) to send a message to each of its `OutputChannel` objects.

Thread pools are often used to improve performance in applications such as these.

Example A.248 Router.java

```
1.  import java.rmi.Naming;
2.  import java.rmi.RemoteException;
3.  import java.rmi.server.UnicastRemoteObject;
4.  import java.util.HashMap;
5.  public class Router implements OutputChannel{
6.      private static final String ROUTER_SERVICE_NAME = "router";
7.      private HashMap links = new HashMap();
8.  
9.      public Router(){
10.         try {
11.             UnicastRemoteObject.exportObject(this);
12.             Naming.rebind(ROUTER_SERVICE_NAME, this);
13.         }
14.         catch (Exception exc){
15.             System.err.println("Error using RMI to register the Router " + exc);
16.         }
17.     }
18. 
19.     public synchronized void sendMessage(Message message) {
20.         Object key = message.getSource();
21.         OutputChannel[] destinations = (OutputChannel[])links.get(key);
22.         new RouterWorkThread(message, destinations);
23.     }
24. 
25.     public void addRoute(InputChannel source, OutputChannel[] destinations) {
26.         links.put(source, destinations);
27.     }
28. 
29.     private class RouterWorkThread implements Runnable{
30.         private OutputChannel [] destinations;
31.         private Message message;
32.         private Thread runner;
33. 
34.         private RouterWorkThread(Message newMessage, OutputChannel[] newDestina-
    tions){
35.             message = newMessage;
36.             destinations = newDestinations;
37.             runner = new Thread(this);
38.             runner.start();
39.         }
40. 
41.         public void run() {
42.             for (int i = 0; i < destinations.length; i++){
43.                 try{
44.                     destinations[i].sendMessage(message);
45.                 }
46.                 catch(RemoteException exc){
47.                     System.err.println("Unable to send message to " + destina-
    tions[i]);
```

```
48.                     }
49.                 }
50.             }
51.         }
52.     }
```

When using the Router pattern, be careful about the size of message to be delivered. Generally, the message should be as small as possible. It is easy to be fooled by some Java objects, though. An object might have references to other objects, which refer to other objects, and so on—and what seemed like a small object might turn out to be very large indeed. For instance, sending a `java.awt.Button` is not a good idea, because the whole GUI will be serialized and sent.

It's a lot like buying your child a toy in a store. The purchase of a single Outlaw Robot Laser Geek might not seem expensive at first, but by the time you get all the accessories (extra laser pistol, laser-spitting horn-rimmed glasses), you might wonder if it would just be cheaper to buy him or her a sweater.

In this example, the `InputKey` class implements the `InputChannel` interface. It must be sent to the Router using RMI, so this class must redefine the `hashCode` and `equals` methods to make sure objects on different JVMs can be tested for equality.

Example A.249 `InputKey.java`

```
1.    public class InputKey implements InputChannel{
2.        private static int nextValue = 1;
3.        private int hashVal = nextValue++;
4.        public int hashCode(){ return hashVal; }
5.        public boolean equals(Object object){
6.            if (!(object instanceof InputKey)){ return false; }
7.            if (object.hashCode() != hashCode()){ return false; }
8.            return true;
9.        }
10.   }
```

The `RouterClient` class provides a client to the `Router`; this class both sends and receives messages using RMI. The method `sendMessageToRouter` transmits a message to the central router, and the method `sendMessage` (defined by the `OutputChannel` interface) receives messages from the `Router`.

Example A.250 `RouterClient.java`

```
1.    import java.rmi.Naming;
2.    import java.rmi.server.UnicastRemoteObject;
3.    import java.rmi.RemoteException;
4.    public class RouterClient implements OutputChannel{
5.        private static final String ROUTER_CLIENT_SERVICE_PREFIX = "routerClient";
6.        private static final String ROUTER_SERVER_MACHINE_NAME = "localhost";
```

```
7.         private static final String ROUTER_SERVER_SERVICE_NAME = "router";
8.         private static int clientIndex = 1;
9.         private String routerClientServiceName = ROUTER_CLIENT_SERVICE_PREFIX + cli-
       entIndex++;
10.        private OutputChannel router;
11.        private Receiver receiver;
12.
13.        public RouterClient(Receiver newReceiver){
14.            receiver = newReceiver;
15.            try {
16.                UnicastRemoteObject.exportObject(this);
17.                Naming.rebind(routerClientServiceName, this);
18.                String url = "//" + ROUTER_SERVER_MACHINE_NAME + "/" +
       ROUTER_SERVER_SERVICE_NAME;
19.                router = (OutputChannel)Naming.lookup(url);
20.            }
21.            catch (Exception exc){
22.                System.err.println("Error using RMI to register the Router " + exc);
23.            }
24.
25.        }
26.
27.        public void sendMessageToRouter(Message message){
28.            try{
29.                router.sendMessage(message);
30.            }
31.            catch (RemoteException exc){}
32.        }
33.
34.        public void sendMessage(Message message){
35.            receiver.receiveMessage(message);
36.        }
37.
38.        public String toString(){
39.            return routerClientServiceName;
40.        }
41.    }
```

Each RouterClient communicates with a client represented by the RouterGui class. This class provides a simple Swing GUI for sending and receiving messages via the Router. RouterGui implements the Receiver interface, which allows the RouterClient to provide it with real-time updates when it receives a Router message.

Example A.251 Receiver.java

```
1.     public interface Receiver{
2.         public void receiveMessage(Message message);
3.     }
```

Example A.252 RouterGui.java

```
1.    import java.awt.Container;
2.    import java.awt.event.ActionListener;
3.    import java.awt.event.ActionEvent;
4.    import java.awt.event.WindowAdapter;
5.    import java.awt.event.WindowEvent;
6.    import javax.swing.JFrame;
7.    import javax.swing.BoxLayout;
8.    import javax.swing.JButton;
9.    import javax.swing.JTextArea;
10.   import javax.swing.JScrollPane;
11.   import javax.swing.JTextField;
12.   import javax.swing.JLabel;
13.   import javax.swing.JPanel;
14.   import java.io.Serializable;
15.   public class RouterGui implements ActionListener, Receiver{
16.       private static int instanceCount = 1;
17.       private RouterClient routerClient;
18.       private JFrame mainFrame;
19.       private JButton exit, clearDisplay, sendMessage;
20.       private JTextArea display;
21.       private JTextField inputTextField;
22.       private InputChannel inputChannel;
23.
24.       public OutputChannel getOutputChannel(){
25.           return routerClient;
26.       }
27.
28.       public RouterGui(InputChannel newInputChannel){
29.           inputChannel = newInputChannel;
30.           routerClient = new RouterClient(this);
31.       }
32.
33.       public void createGui(){
34.           mainFrame = new JFrame("Demonstration for the Router pattern - GUI #" +
      instanceCount++);
35.           Container content = mainFrame.getContentPane();
36.           content.setLayout(new BoxLayout(content, BoxLayout.Y_AXIS));
37.
38.           JPanel displayPanel = new JPanel();
39.           display = new JTextArea(10, 40);
40.           JScrollPane displayArea = new JScrollPane(display);
41.           display.setEditable(false);
42.           displayPanel.add(displayArea);
43.           content.add(displayPanel);
44.
45.           JPanel dataPanel = new JPanel();
46.           dataPanel.add(new JLabel("Message:"));
47.           inputTextField = new JTextField(30);
48.           dataPanel.add(inputTextField);
49.           content.add(dataPanel);
50.
```

```
51.            JPanel controlPanel = new JPanel();
52.            sendMessage = new JButton("Send Message");
53.            clearDisplay = new JButton("Clear");
54.            exit = new JButton("Exit");
55.            controlPanel.add(sendMessage);
56.            controlPanel.add(clearDisplay);
57.            controlPanel.add(exit);
58.            content.add(controlPanel);
59.
60.            sendMessage.addActionListener(this);
61.            clearDisplay.addActionListener(this);
62.            exit.addActionListener(this);
63.            inputTextField.addActionListener(this);
64.
65.            mainFrame.addWindowListener(new WindowCloseManager());
66.            mainFrame.pack();
67.            mainFrame.setVisible(true);
68.        }
69.
70.        public void actionPerformed(ActionEvent evt){
71.            Object source = evt.getSource();
72.            if (source == sendMessage){ sendMessage(); }
73.            else if (source == inputTextField){ sendMessage(); }
74.            else if (source == clearDisplay){ clearDisplay(); }
75.            else if (source == exit){ exitApplication(); }
76.        }
77.
78.        private class WindowCloseManager extends WindowAdapter{
79.            public void windowClosing(WindowEvent evt){
80.                exitApplication();
81.            }
82.        }
83.
84.        private void exitApplication(){
85.            System.exit(0);
86.        }
87.
88.        private void clearDisplay(){
89.            inputTextField.setText("");
90.            display.setText("");
91.        }
92.
93.        private void sendMessage(){
94.            String data = inputTextField.getText();
95.            routerClient.sendMessageToRouter(new Message(inputChannel, data));
96.            inputTextField.setText("");
97.        }
98.
99.        public void receiveMessage(Message message){
100.           display.append(message.getMessage() + "\n");
101.       }
102.   }
```

RunPattern coordinates a demonstration of the pattern by creating a series of RouterGui objects. In the example, each RouterGui is connected up to some of the others through the Router. This means that a message sent by RouterGui # 4 will be delivered to all of the GUIs, while one sent from RouterGui # 1 will be sent to GUIs # 2 and 3.

Example A.253 RunPattern.java

```
1.   import java.io.IOException;
2.   public class RunPattern{
3.       public static void main(String [] arguments){
4.           System.out.println("Example for the Router pattern");
5.          System.out.println("This code same will create a series of GUIs, and use");
6.           System.out.println(" the Router pattern to map message notifications
     between");
7.          System.out.println(" them. In this code example, the Router will send mes-
     sages");
8.           System.out.println(" between the GUI clients based on the following map-
     ping:");
9.           System.out.println();
10.          System.out.println("\tGUI # 1:\tGUI #2\tGUI #3");
11.          System.out.println("\tGUI # 2:\tGUI #1\tGUI #4");
12.          System.out.println("\tGUI # 3:\tGUI #1\tGUI #4");
13.          System.out.println("\tGUI # 4:\tGUI #1\tGUI #2\tGUI #3\tGUI #4");
14.          System.out.println();
15.
16.          System.out.println("Running the RMI compiler (rmic)");
17.          try{
18.              Process p1 = Runtime.getRuntime().exec("rmic Router");
19.              Process p2 = Runtime.getRuntime().exec("rmic RouterClient");
20.              p1.waitFor();
21.              p2.waitFor();
22.          }
23.          catch (IOException exc){
24.            System.err.println("Unable to run rmic utility. Exiting application.");
25.              System.exit(1);
26.          }
27.          catch (InterruptedException exc){
28.           System.err.println("Threading problems encountered while using the rmic
     utility.");
29.          }
30.
31.
32.          System.out.println("Starting the rmiregistry");
33.          System.out.println();
34.          Process rmiProcess = null;
35.          try{
36.              rmiProcess = Runtime.getRuntime().exec("rmiregistry");
37.              Thread.sleep(15000);
38.          }
39.          catch (IOException exc){
40.             System.err.println("Unable to start the rmiregistry. Exiting applica-
     tion.");
```

```
41.                System.exit(1);
42.            }
43.            catch (InterruptedException exc){
44.               System.err.println("Threading problems encountered when starting the
       rmiregistry.");
45.            }
46.
47.            System.out.println("Creating the Router object");
48.            System.out.println();
49.            Router mainRouter = new Router();
50.
51.            InputKey keyOne = new InputKey();
52.            InputKey keyTwo = new InputKey();
53.            InputKey keyThree = new InputKey();
54.            InputKey keyFour = new InputKey();
55.
56.            System.out.println("Creating the four RouterGui objects");
57.            System.out.println();
58.            RouterGui first = new RouterGui(keyOne);
59.            RouterGui second = new RouterGui(keyTwo);
60.            RouterGui third = new RouterGui(keyThree);
61.            RouterGui fourth = new RouterGui(keyFour);
62.
63.            System.out.println("Creating GUI OutputChannel lists for the Router");
64.            System.out.println();
65.            OutputChannel [] subscriptionListOne = { second.getOutputChannel(),
       third.getOutputChannel() };
66.            OutputChannel [] subscriptionListTwo = { first.getOutputChannel(),
       fourth.getOutputChannel() };
67.           OutputChannel [] subscriptionListThree = { first.getOutputChannel(), sec-
       ond.getOutputChannel(),
68.                                                    third.getOutputChannel(),
       fourth.getOutputChannel() };
69.
70.            mainRouter.addRoute(keyOne, subscriptionListOne);
71.            mainRouter.addRoute(keyTwo, subscriptionListTwo);
72.            mainRouter.addRoute(keyThree, subscriptionListTwo);
73.            mainRouter.addRoute(keyFour, subscriptionListThree);
74.
75.            first.createGui();
76.            second.createGui();
77.            third.createGui();
78.            fourth.createGui();
79.        }
80.    }
```

Transaction

The Personal Information Manager stores appointments based on their date. Naturally, since users lead active lives, appointments change all the time. A user's appointment book is constantly being updated with new or changing appointments.

If a number of users need to agree on a date for an appointment, it would be helpful if their appointment books could coordinate, arriving at a date that would work for everybody. That's what this example demonstrates—how the Transaction pattern can be used to allow address books to reschedule a date for an appointment.

The basic interface that supports transactions is `AppointmentTransactionParticipant`. It defines three methods to manage transactions (`join`, `commit`, and `cancel`) and the business method `changeDate`. This class is a `Remote` class, since it is used to communicate between transaction participants that might reside on different Java Virtual Machines.

Example A.254 `AppointmentTransactionParticipant.java`

```
1.    import java.util.Date;
2.    import java.rmi.Remote;
3.    import java.rmi.RemoteException;
4.    public interface AppointmentTransactionParticipant extends Remote{
5.        public boolean join(long transactionID) throws RemoteException;
6.        public void commit(long transactionID) throws TransactionException, RemoteEx-
      ception;
7.        public void cancel(long transactionID) throws RemoteException;
8.        public boolean changeDate(long transactionID, Appointment appointment,
9.            Date newStartDate) throws TransactionException, RemoteException;
10.   }
```

The class `AppointmentBook` represents a user's calendar, and implements the `AppointmentTransactionParticipant` interface. In addition to providing support to change an `Appointment` date, the `AppointmentBook` can initiate a change of an `Appointment`. Its method `changeAppointment` accepts a transaction ID, an `Appointment` object, an array of other `AppointmentBooks` that should be transaction participants, and an array of possible alternate dates for the appointment. The `changeAppointment` method allows one of the `AppointmentBook` objects to communicate with the others using RMI, calling the `changeDate` method on every one of the participants until all agree on an alternate date for the `Appointment`.

Example A.255 `AppointmentBook.java`

```
1.    import java.util.ArrayList;
2.    import java.util.HashMap;
3.    import java.util.Date;
```

```
4.     import java.rmi.Naming;
5.     import java.rmi.server.UnicastRemoteObject;
6.     import java.rmi.RemoteException;
7.     public class AppointmentBook implements AppointmentTransactionParticipant{
8.         private static final String TRANSACTION_SERVICE_PREFIX = "transactionPartici-
       pant";
9.         private static final String TRANSACTION_HOSTNAME = "localhost";
10.        private static int index = 1;
11.        private String serviceName = TRANSACTION_SERVICE_PREFIX + index++;
12.        private HashMap appointments = new HashMap();
13.        private long currentTransaction;
14.        private Appointment currentAppointment;
15.        private Date updateStartDate;
16.
17.        public AppointmentBook(){
18.            try {
19.                UnicastRemoteObject.exportObject(this);
20.                Naming.rebind(serviceName, this);
21.            }
22.            catch (Exception exc){
23.              System.err.println("Error using RMI to register the AppointmentBook "
       + exc);
24.            }
25.        }
26.
27.        public String getUrl(){
28.            return "//" + TRANSACTION_HOSTNAME + "/" + serviceName;
29.        }
30.
31.        public void addAppointment(Appointment appointment){
32.            if (!appointments.containsValue(appointment)){
33.                if (!appointments.containsKey(appointment.getStartDate())){
34.                    appointments.put(appointment.getStartDate(), appointment);
35.                }
36.            }
37.        }
38.        public void removeAppointment(Appointment appointment){
39.            if (appointments.containsValue(appointment)){
40.                appointments.remove(appointment.getStartDate());
41.            }
42.        }
43.
44.        public boolean join(long transactionID){
45.            if (currentTransaction != 0){
46.                return false;
47.            } else {
48.                currentTransaction = transactionID;
49.                return true;
50.            }
51.        }
52.        public void commit(long transactionID) throws TransactionException{
53.            if (currentTransaction != transactionID){
54.                throw new TransactionException("Invalid TransactionID");
55.            } else {
```

```
56.                 removeAppointment(currentAppointment);
57.                 currentAppointment.setStartDate(updateStartDate);
58.                 appointments.put(updateStartDate, currentAppointment);
59.             }
60.         }
61.         public void cancel(long transactionID){
62.             if (currentTransaction == transactionID){
63.                 currentTransaction = 0;
64.                 appointments.remove(updateStartDate);
65.             }
66.         }
67.         public boolean changeDate(long transactionID, Appointment appointment,
68.           Date newStartDate) throws TransactionException{
69.             if ((appointments.containsValue(appointment)) && (!appointments.contains-
        Key(newStartDate))){
70.                 appointments.put(newStartDate, null);
71.                 updateStartDate = newStartDate;
72.                 currentAppointment = appointment;
73.                 return true;
74.             }
75.             return false;
76.         }
77.
78.         public boolean changeAppointment(Appointment appointment, Date[] possible-
        Dates,
79.           AppointmentTransactionParticipant[] participants, long transactionID){
80.             try{
81.                 for (int i = 0; i < participants.length; i++){
82.                     if (!participants[i].join(transactionID)){
83.                         return false;
84.                     }
85.                 }
86.                 for (int i = 0; i < possibleDates.length; i++){
87.                   if (isDateAvailable(transactionID, appointment, possibleDates[i],
        participants)){
88.                         try{
89.                             commitAll(transactionID, participants);
90.                             return true;
91.                         }
92.                         catch(TransactionException exc){ }
93.                     }
94.                 }
95.             }
96.             catch (RemoteException exc){ }
97.             try{
98.                 cancelAll(transactionID, participants);
99.             }
100.            catch (RemoteException exc){}
101.            return false;
102.        }
103.
104.        private boolean isDateAvailable(long transactionID, Appointment appointment,
105.          Date date, AppointmentTransactionParticipant[] participants){
106.            try{
```

```
107.                for (int i = 0; i < participants.length; i++){
108.                    try{
109.                        if (!participants[i].changeDate(transactionID, appointment,
        date)){
110.                            return false;
111.                        }
112.                    }
113.                    catch (TransactionException exc){
114.                        return false;
115.                    }
116.                }
117.            }
118.            catch (RemoteException exc){
119.                return false;
120.            }
121.            return true;
122.        }
123.        private void commitAll(long transactionID, AppointmentTransactionParticipant[]
        participants)
124.            throws TransactionException, RemoteException{
125.            for (int i = 0; i < participants.length; i++){
126.                participants[i].commit(transactionID);
127.            }
128.        }
129.        private void cancelAll(long transactionID, AppointmentTransactionParticipant[]
        participants)
130.            throws RemoteException{
131.            for (int i = 0; i < participants.length; i++){
132.                participants[i].cancel(transactionID);
133.            }
134.        }
135.        public String toString(){
136.            return serviceName + " " + appointments.values().toString();
137.        }
138.    }
```

The `TransactionException` is a signal exception; it has no special content and gets thrown when an invalid `transactionID` is supplied to some methods. The receiver might report the exception or ignore it, depending on its processing needs.

Example A.256 `TransactionException.java`

```
1.    public class TransactionException extends Exception{
2.        public TransactionException(String msg){
3.            super(msg);
4.        }
5.    }
```

Support classes for this example represent the appointment and its elements, Three interfaces—`Appointment`, `Contact`, and `Location`—define the core business behavior. The classes AppointmentImpl, ContactImpl, and LocationImpl provide implementation for the interface behavior.

Example A.257 Appointment.java

```
1.  import java.util.ArrayList;
2.  import java.util.Date;
3.  import java.io.Serializable;
4.  public interface Appointment extends Serializable{
5.     public static final String EOL_STRING = System.getProperty("line.separator");
6.  
7.      public Date getStartDate();
8.      public String getDescription();
9.      public ArrayList getAttendees();
10.     public Location getLocation();
11. 
12.     public void setDescription(String newDescription);
13.     public void setLocation(Location newLocation);
14.     public void setStartDate(Date newStartDate);
15.     public void setAttendees(ArrayList newAttendees);
16.     public void addAttendee(Contact attendee);
17.     public void removeAttendee(Contact attendee);
18. }
```

Example A.258 AppointmentImpl.java

```
1.  import java.util.ArrayList;
2.  import java.util.Date;
3.  public class AppointmentImpl implements Appointment{
4.      private Date startDate;
5.      private String description;
6.      private ArrayList attendees = new ArrayList();
7.      private Location location;
8.  
9.      public AppointmentImpl(String newDescription, ArrayList newAttendees,
10.       Location newLocation, Date newStartDate){
11.         description = newDescription;
12.         attendees = newAttendees;
13.         location = newLocation;
14.         startDate = newStartDate;
15.     }
16. 
17.     public Date getStartDate(){ return startDate; }
18.     public String getDescription(){ return description; }
19.     public ArrayList getAttendees(){ return attendees; }
20.     public Location getLocation(){ return location; }
21. 
22.     public void setDescription(String newDescription){ description = newDescrip-
    tion; }
23.     public void setLocation(Location newLocation){ location = newLocation; }
24.     public void setStartDate(Date newStartDate){ startDate = newStartDate; }
25.     public void setAttendees(ArrayList newAttendees){
```

```
26.            if (newAttendees != null){
27.                attendees = newAttendees;
28.            }
29.        }
30.
31.        public void addAttendee(Contact attendee){
32.            if (!attendees.contains(attendee)){
33.                attendees.add(attendee);
34.            }
35.        }
36.
37.        public void removeAttendee(Contact attendee){
38.            attendees.remove(attendee);
39.        }
40.
41.        public int hashCode(){
42.            return description.hashCode() ^ startDate.hashCode();
43.        }
44.
45.        public boolean equals(Object object){
46.            if (!(object instanceof AppointmentImpl)){
47.                return false;
48.            }
49.            if (object.hashCode() != hashCode()){
50.                return false;
51.            }
52.            return true;
53.        }
54.
55.        public String toString(){
56.            return "  Description: " + description + EOL_STRING +
57.                   "  Start Date: " + startDate + EOL_STRING +
58.                   "  Location: " + location + EOL_STRING +
59.                   "  Attendees: " + attendees;
60.        }
61.    }
```

Example A.259 `Contact.java`

```
1.     import java.io.Serializable;
2.     public interface Contact extends Serializable{
3.         public static final String SPACE = " ";
4.         public String getFirstName();
5.         public String getLastName();
6.         public String getTitle();
7.         public String getOrganization();
8.
9.         public void setFirstName(String newFirstName);
10.        public void setLastName(String newLastName);
11.        public void setTitle(String newTitle);
12.        public void setOrganization(String newOrganization);
13.    }
```

Example A.260 `ContactImpl.java`

```
1.   public class ContactImpl implements Contact{
2.       private String firstName;
3.       private String lastName;
4.       private String title;
5.       private String organization;
6.
7.       public ContactImpl(){}
8.       public ContactImpl(String newFirstName, String newLastName,
9.           String newTitle, String newOrganization){
10.              firstName = newFirstName;
11.              lastName = newLastName;
12.              title = newTitle;
13.              organization = newOrganization;
14.      }
15.
16.      public String getFirstName(){ return firstName; }
17.      public String getLastName(){ return lastName; }
18.      public String getTitle(){ return title; }
19.      public String getOrganization(){ return organization; }
20.
21.      public void setFirstName(String newFirstName){ firstName = newFirstName; }
22.      public void setLastName(String newLastName){ lastName = newLastName; }
23.      public void setTitle(String newTitle){ title = newTitle; }
24.     public void setOrganization(String newOrganization){ organization = newOrgani-
    zation; }
25.
26.      public String toString(){
27.          return firstName + SPACE + lastName;
28.      }
29.  }
```

Example A.261 `Location.java`

```
1.   import java.io.Serializable;
2.   public interface Location extends Serializable{
3.       public String getLocation();
4.       public void setLocation(String newLocation);
5.   }
```

Example A.262 `LocationImpl.java`

```
1.   public class LocationImpl implements Location{
2.       private String location;
3.
4.       public LocationImpl(){ }
5.       public LocationImpl(String newLocation){
6.           location = newLocation;
7.       }
8.
9.       public String getLocation(){ return location; }
10.
```

```
11.        public void setLocation(String newLocation){ location = newLocation; }
12.
13.        public String toString(){ return location; }
14.    }
```

RunPattern demonstrates coordination among the AddressBook objects to reschedule an appointment. It creates three AddressBooks, setting up conflicting appointments in two of them. Next, it instructs an AddressBook to update the appointment. This results in an appointment in the address books with the first start time available to all three AddressBooks: 12 noon.

Example A.263 RunPattern.java

```
1.    import java.io.IOException;
2.    import java.rmi.Naming;
3.    import java.util.Date;
4.    import java.util.Calendar;
5.    import java.util.ArrayList;
6.    public class RunPattern{
7.        private static Calendar dateCreator = Calendar.getInstance();
8.
9.        public static void main(String [] arguments){
10.           System.out.println("Example for the Transaction pattern");
11.           System.out.println("This code example shows how a Transaction can");
12.          System.out.println(" be applied to support change across a distributed");
13.           System.out.println(" system. In ths case, a distributed transaction");
14.           System.out.println(" is used to coordinate the change of dates in");
15.           System.out.println(" appointment books.");
16.
17.           System.out.println("Running the RMI compiler (rmic)");
18.           System.out.println();
19.           try{
20.               Process p1 = Runtime.getRuntime().exec("rmic AppointmentBook");
21.               p1.waitFor();
22.           }
23.           catch (IOException exc){
24.             System.err.println("Unable to run rmic utility. Exiting application.");
25.               System.exit(1);
26.           }
27.           catch (InterruptedException exc){
28.            System.err.println("Threading problems encountered while using the rmic
      utility.");
29.           }
30.
31.           System.out.println("Starting the rmiregistry");
32.           System.out.println();
33.           try{
34.               Process rmiProcess = Runtime.getRuntime().exec("rmiregistry");
35.               Thread.sleep(15000);
36.           }
37.           catch (IOException exc){
38.              System.err.println("Unable to start the rmiregistry. Exiting applica-
      tion.");
39.               System.exit(1);
40.           }
```

```
41.            catch (InterruptedException exc){
42.                System.err.println("Threading problems encountered when starting the
       rmiregistry.");
43.            }
44.
45.            System.out.println("Creating three appointment books");
46.            System.out.println();
47.            AppointmentBook apptBookOne = new AppointmentBook();
48.            AppointmentBook apptBookTwo = new AppointmentBook();
49.            AppointmentBook apptBookThree = new AppointmentBook();
50.
51.            System.out.println("Creating appointments");
52.            System.out.println();
53.            Appointment apptOne = new AppointmentImpl("Swim relay to Kalimantan (or
       Java)", new ArrayList(),
54.                new LocationImpl("Sidney, Australia"), createDate(2001, 11, 5, 11,
       0));
55.            Appointment apptTwo = new AppointmentImpl("Conference on World Pat-
       ternization", new ArrayList(),
56.                new LocationImpl("London, England"), createDate(2001, 11, 5, 14, 0));
57.            Appointment apptThree = new AppointmentImpl("Society for the Preservation
       of Java - Annual Outing",
58.                new ArrayList(), new LocationImpl("Kyzyl, Tuva"), createDate(2001,
       11, 5, 10, 0));
59.
60.            System.out.println("Adding appointments to the appointment books");
61.            System.out.println();
62.            apptBookOne.addAppointment(apptThree);
63.            apptBookTwo.addAppointment(apptOne);
64.            apptBookOne.addAppointment(apptTwo);
65.            apptBookTwo.addAppointment(apptTwo);
66.            apptBookThree.addAppointment(apptTwo);
67.
68.            System.out.println("AppointmentBook contents:");
69.            System.out.println();
70.            System.out.println(apptBookOne);
71.            System.out.println(apptBookTwo);
72.            System.out.println(apptBookThree);
73.            System.out.println();
74.
75.            System.out.println("Rescheduling an appointment");
76.            System.out.println();
77.            System.out.println();
78.            boolean result = apptBookThree.changeAppointment(apptTwo, getDates(2001,
       11, 5, 10, 3),
79.                lookUpParticipants(new String[] { apptBookOne.getUrl(), apptBook-
       Two.getUrl(), apptBookThree.getUrl() }),
80.                20000L);
81.
82.            System.out.println("Result of rescheduling was " + result);
83.            System.out.println("AppointmentBook contents:");
84.            System.out.println();
85.            System.out.println(apptBookOne);
86.            System.out.println(apptBookTwo);
87.            System.out.println(apptBookThree);
88.        }
89.
90.        private static AppointmentTransactionParticipant[] lookUpPartici-
       pants(String[] remoteUrls){
91.            AppointmentTransactionParticipant[] returnValues =
```

```
92.                 new AppointmentTransactionParticipant[remoteUrls.length];
93.             for (int i = 0; i < remoteUrls.length; i++){
94.                 try{
95.                     returnValues[i] = (AppointmentTransactionParticipant)Nam-
        ing.lookup(remoteUrls[i]);
96.                 }
97.                 catch (Exception exc){
98.                     System.out.println("Error using RMI to look up a transaction par-
        ticipant");
99.                 }
100.            }
101.            return returnValues;
102.        }
103.
104.        private static Date[] getDates(int year, int month, int day, int hour, int
        increment){
105.            Date[] returnDates = new Date[increment];
106.            for (int i = 0; i < increment; i++){
107.                returnDates[i] = createDate(year, month, day, hour + i, 0);
108.            }
109.            return returnDates;
110.        }
111.
112.        public static Date createDate(int year, int month, int day, int hour, int
        minute){
113.            dateCreator.set(year, month, day, hour, minute);
114.            return dateCreator.getTime();
115.        }
116.    }
```

Appendix B

Bibliography

Pattern Origins

This section lists the original source for each pattern.

Creational Patterns

Abstract Factory	GoF
Builder	GoF
Factory Method	GoF
Prototype	GoF
Singleton	GoF

Behavioral Patterns

Chain of Responsibility	GoF
Command	GoF
Interpreter	GoF
Iterator	GoF
Mediator	GoF
Momento	GoF
Observer	GoF
State	GoF
Strategy	GoF
Template Method	GoF
MVC	GoF
Visitor	GoF

Structural Patterns

Adapter	GoF
Bridge	GoF
Composite	GoF
Decorator	GoF
Facade	GoF
Flyweight	GoF
HOPP	Coplien
Proxy	GoF

System Patterns

Session	Lea01
Worker Thread	Lea01
Callback	Lea01
Successive Update	[*None*]
Router (based on Non-Blocking Buffered I/O Pattern)	DPCS
Transaction	Lea01

[CJ2EEP]

Deepak Alur, John Crupi, Dan Malks
Core J2EE Patterns
Prentice Hall, 2001
ISBN 0-13-066586-X

[Bloch01]

Joshua Bloch,
Effective Java, Programming Language Guide
Addison Wesley, 2001
ISBN 0-201-31005-8

[Coplien]

Jim O. Coplien, Douglas C. Schmidt (Editors)
Pattern Languages of Program Design Addison-Wesley, 1995
ISBN 0-201-60734-4

[DPCS]

Design Patterns for Communications Software
Linda Rising (Editor)
Cambridge University Press, 2000
ISBN 0-521-79040-9

[Fowler00]

Martin Fowler
UML Distilled, Second Edition
Addison Wesley, 2000
ISBN 0-201-65783-X

[GoF]

Erich Gamma, Richard Helm, Ralph Johnson, John Vlissides
Design Patterns, Elements of Reusable Object-Oriented Software
Addison Wesley, 1995
ISBN 0-201-63361-2

[Lea00]

Doug Lea
Concurrent Programming in Java, Second Edition
Addison Wesley, 2000
ISBN 0-201-31009-0

[JLS]

Bill Joy (Editor), Guy Steele, James Gosling, Gilad Bracha
The Java Language Specification, Second Edition
Addison Wesley, 2000
ISBN 0-201-31008-2

[JBS]

JavaBeans Specification 1.01
http://java.sun.com/products/javabeans/docs/spec.html

[J2EE00]

Bill Shannon, Mark Hapner, Vlada Matena, James Davidson,
Eduardo Pelegri-Llopart, Larry Cable, Enterprise Team
Java 2 Platform, Enterprise Edition, Platform and Component Specification
Addison Wesley, 2000
ISBN 0-201-70456-0

[Jini01]

Jim Waldo, the Jini Technology Team
The Jini Specifications, Second Edition
Addison Wesley, 2001
ISBN 0-201-72617-3

Index

D

H

I

J

T

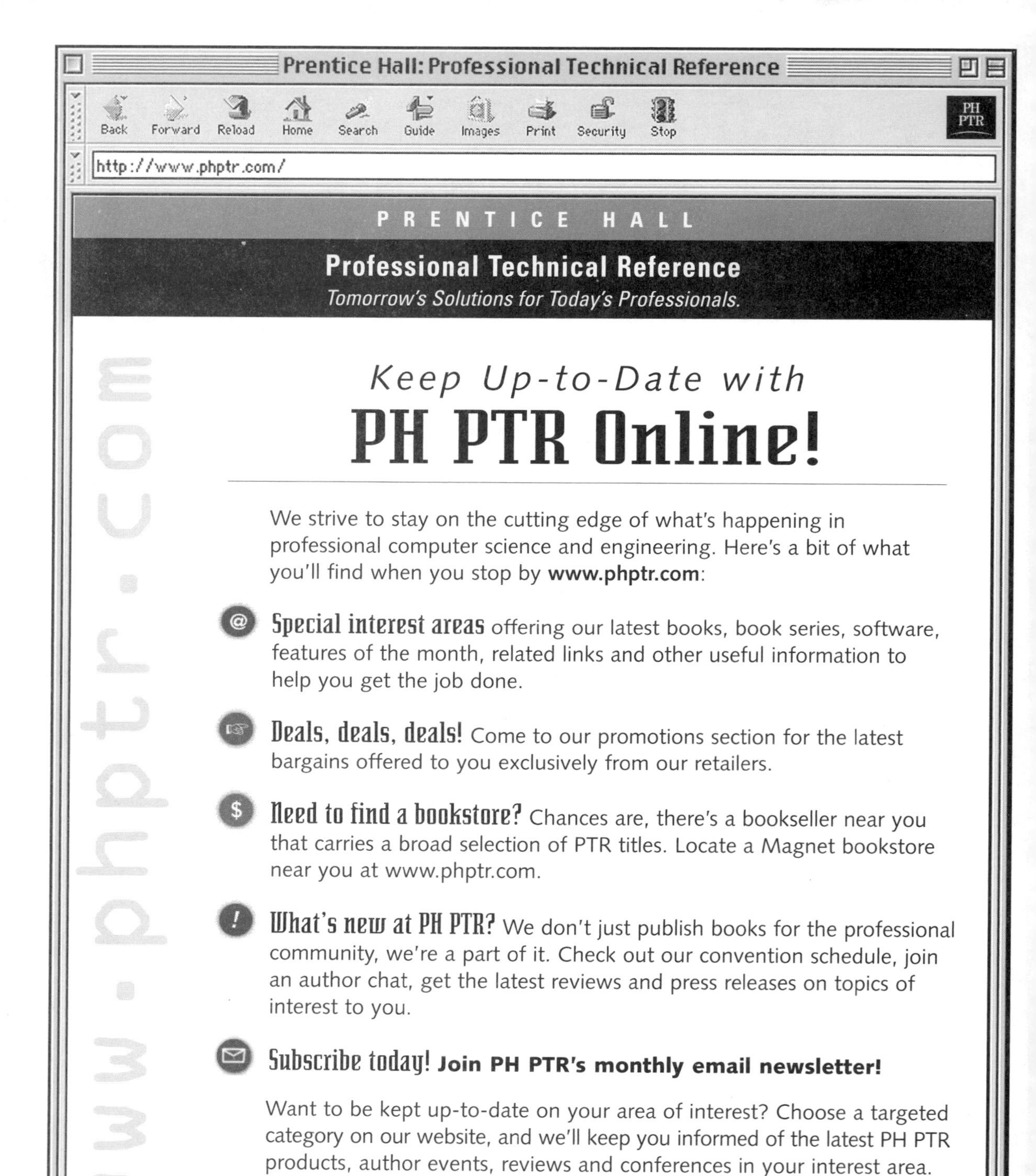
Prentice Hall: Professional Technical Reference
Back
Forward
Reload
Home
Search
Guide
Images
Print
Security
Stop
PH PTR
http://www.phptr.com/
PRENTICE HALL
Professional Technical Reference
Tomorrow's Solutions for Today's Professionals.
www.phptr.com
Keep Up-to-Date with
PH PTR Online!
We strive to stay on the cutting edge of what's happening in professional computer science and engineering. Here's a bit of what you'll find when you stop by www.phptr.com:
Special interest areas offering our latest books, book series, software, features of the month, related links and other useful information to help you get the job done.
Deals, deals, deals! Come to our promotions section for the latest bargains offered to you exclusively from our retailers.
Need to find a bookstore? Chances are, there's a bookseller near you that carries a broad selection of PTR titles. Locate a Magnet bookstore near you at www.phptr.com.
What's new at PH PTR? We don't just publish books for the professional community, we're a part of it. Check out our convention schedule, join an author chat, get the latest reviews and press releases on topics of interest to you.
Subscribe today! Join PH PTR's monthly email newsletter!
Want to be kept up-to-date on your area of interest? Choose a targeted category on our website, and we'll keep you informed of the latest PH PTR products, author events, reviews and conferences in your interest area.
Visit our mailroom to subscribe today! http://www.phptr.com/mail_lists